AMERICAN STUDIES – A MONOGRAPH SERIES
Volume 318

Edited on behalf
of the German Association
for American Studies by
ANKE ORTLEPP
HEIKE PAUL

U.S. American Culture as Popular Culture

Edited by
ASTRID BÖGER
FLORIAN SEDLMEIER

Universitätsverlag
WINTER
Heidelberg

Bibliografische Information der Deutschen Nationalbibliothek
Die Deutsche Nationalbibliothek verzeichnet diese Publikation
in der Deutschen Nationalbibliografie;
detaillierte bibliografische Daten sind im Internet
über *http://dnb.d-nb.de* abrufbar.

UMSCHLAGBILD
Titelbild von beemore via Getty Images

ISBN 978-3-8253-4927-1

Dieses Werk einschließlich aller seiner Teile ist urheberrechtlich geschützt.
Jede Verwertung außerhalb der engen Grenzen des Urheberrechtsgesetzes
ist ohne Zustimmung des Verlages unzulässig und strafbar. Das gilt ins-
besondere für Vervielfältigungen, Übersetzungen, Mikroverfilmungen und
die Einspeicherung und Verarbeitung in elektronischen Systemen.
© 2022 Universitätsverlag Winter GmbH Heidelberg
Imprimé en Allemagne · Printed in Germany
Umschlaggestaltung: Klaus Brecht GmbH, Heidelberg
Druck: Memminger MedienCentrum, 87700 Memmingen

Gedruckt auf umweltfreundlichem, chlorfrei gebleichtem
und alterungsbeständigem Papier

Den Verlag erreichen Sie im Internet unter:
www.winter-verlag.de

Contents

ASTRID BÖGER and FLORIAN SEDLMEIER
Introduction: U.S. Culture as Popular Culture..9

Section I: Film and Television

MAXI ALBRECHT
"A New Beginning": AMC's *The Walking Dead*
and the Serial Post-Western...27

ABIGAIL FAGAN
Jubal Early in Space: The Settler Colonial Hauntings
of Joss Whedon's *Firefly*..45

BRIGITTE GEORGI-FINDLAY
Visions of the Past, Politics of the Present: The Temporalities
of Western Television Series...63

LINDA M. HESS
"What I would have done to have heard a story like mine":
Reading Tig Notaro's and Hannah Gadsby's Stand-up
as Autobiographical Narrative...79

CARSTEN JUNKER
Pernicious Plurability: *Liberty's Kids'* Militainment
and the Lure of Diversity...99

KATJA KANZLER
Conspicuous Contempt: Popular Culture and the Invective
Performativity of Taste...117

MICHAEL LOUIS MOSER
Deviations from Network Late Night and Cable Parody News:
Colbert's *Late Show* and Meyers's *Late Night*......................................135

JOHN STREET
From *The West Wing* to *House of Cards*, from Randy Newman to
Donald Trump: Politics as Popular Culture, Popular Culture
as Politics...153

MARITA STURKEN
Comedy, Genre, and Netflix in Post-Irony American Popular
Culture (or Disruption, Comedy, Humorlessness, and Genre Flail)....175

JENNIFER VOLKMER
Motorcycle Riding in Movies as Modern-Day Pilgrimage
to Masculinity..191

Section II: Literature

LAURA BIEGER
Public Intellectuals, Cultural Fields, and the Predicaments
of Popularity; or, Richard Wright Meets Pierre Bourdieu....................209

RUTH GEHRMANN
"So she would ask me to tell her stories": Indigenous Narratives
of the Apocalypse in Cherie Dimaline's *The Marrow Thieves*............227

ALEXANDRA HARTMANN
"Women's work is never easy, never clean": (Strong) Black
Womanhood and the Carceral State in Tayari Jones's
An American Marriage...247

ZOHRA HASSAN-PIEPER
Muslim Misrepresentation and the Post-Empire Imaginary
in Craig Thompson's *Habibi* (2011)...267

MARIUS HENDERSON
"Matrixial" Dismantlings of Anti-Black Gendered Violence
in Popular Culture..289

MARIAN OFORI-AMOAFO
Different Ways of (Not) Being Black: Blaxploitation Meets
Post-Soul in *I Am Not Sidney Poitier*.......................................309

CLARA PETINO
"Lace Reading" and "Physick Recipes": Wicca and Modern
Witches in Salem Literature..333

HEIKE STEINHOFF
Beyond Hashtags: Popular Feminisms, Body Positivity
and Self-Help Books..351

LISANNA WIELE
Transgression Inscribed: The City Mysteries' Queer Urbanity...........369

HARALD ZAPF
The Long Shadow of Romanticism: (Un-)Popular Theories
of Lyric Poetry and the Popularity of the Lyric...........................387

Section III: Other Media and Art Forms

JULIANE BOROSCH
Changing the Metonymy: Michigan Central Station and the Face
of Detroit..407

DUSTIN BREITENWISCHER
#ART: Westside Gunn's "Aestheticism"......................................429

NAGHMEH ESMAEILPOUR
Transmedial Historiography and the Representation of Iran
and Iranians in Video Games..451

MARLON LIEBER
Money Form and Master Painting, or, When Warhol Wanted
to Paint the Universal Equivalent Form...475

FRANK MEHRING
"You Can't Always Get What You Want!" Sonic State Fantasies
and the Political Use of Popular Music under Barack Obama
and Donald Trump...495

JOHANNES C. P. SCHMID
Internet Memes as Popular Cultural Practices.....................................515

GUNTER SÜß
In Praise of Short Forms: Teaching American Cultural Studies
with Music Videos by African American Artists..................................539

List of Contributors...561

ASTRID BÖGER and FLORIAN SEDLMEIER

Introduction: U.S. Culture as Popular Culture

In the fall of 2001, *Amerikastudien/American Studies* published a special issue titled "Popular Culture." In their introduction, editors Ulla Haselstein, Berndt Ostendorf, and Peter Schneck lucidly discuss how the notion of popular culture, in contradistinction to both folk and mass culture, has gained academic and critical traction since the 1960s. They identify several factors promoting this development. These include, first, shifts in entertainment technologies and media, here measured by "the impact of TV and advertising" as a "culturally hegemonic force."[1] They also encompass, second, a growing sense of cultural relativism that is realized, to different ends, in cultural anthropology and postmodernism. Such relativism destabilizes distinctions between "high" and "low" culture in favor of "a comprehensive set of cultural styles" that rests on practices such as "crossover, creolization and code-switching."[2] And third, scholars of popular culture are concerned with the interplay between "the notion of democratic accessibility and the consumerist appeal of instant gratification,"[3] thus raising important questions of political participation vis-à-vis sheer entertainment value.

Notably, as our colleagues observed, all of these factors coincide with the gradual institutionalization of popular culture as a field of studies, manifest in associations and journals, but also in the inter-disciplinary formation and cross-disciplinary reception of key concepts such as hegemony (as theorized by Antonio Gramsci and Michel

---

[1] Ulla Haselstein, Berndt Ostendorf, and Peter Schneck, "Popular Culture: Introduction," in "Popular Culture," ed. Ulla Haselstein, Berndt Ostendorf, and Peter Schneck, special issue, *Amerikastudien/American Studies* 46, no. 3 (2001): 331.

[2] Ibid., 332; 334

[3] Ibid., 334.

10   Introduction: U.S. Culture as Popular Culture

Foucault, among others), culture industry (Frankfurt School), and subcultural lifestyles (Cultural Studies). Building on this latter aspect, one could make the case that the postwar investment in U.S. popular culture coincides with the consolidation of both para-academic criticism (Clement Greenberg, Susan Sontag) and high theory (Roland Barthes, Jean Baudrillard). At the same time, while the French aristocrat Alexis de Tocqueville began, as early as the 1830s, the inquiry into the culture of an American democratic populace, a striking number of observers since then have been American, including John Dewey, David Riesman, Leslie Fiedler, Daniel Bell, John Fiske, and others, suggesting that the study of popular culture has been embraced in the U.S. more or less from the moment of its inception.

Several contributors to our volume engage these concepts and thinkers by explicitly drawing on the underlying theoretical debates such as hegemonic vs. subcultural practices; the emergence of popular aesthetics as opposed to more traditional or high culture; or the different uses of mass media formations, to name but a few. Others have absorbed the critical language generated by those debates along with its implications. One may take this as a sign that there is now a certain canon of concepts which has become integral to studies of popular culture. This development may indicate the high degree of visibility as well as the institutionalization of these studies and thereby signal that there is no longer a need to legitimize them. With respect to cultural and literary studies at large, the internalization of such key concepts might even dovetail with the recently proclaimed postcritical turn to methods, which challenges the critical authority of theory and proposes a more pragmatic, less ideologically invested approach to the analysis of cultural artefacts.[4] At the same time, several contributors who discuss examples from Black American culture in particular show that "high theory" – the legacy of deconstruction, hermeneutics, and post-structuralism – has not lost its critical steam or conceptual productivity.

Complemented by others, the canonical concepts introduced above also inform the selection and arrangement of texts and thinkers which German studies scholar Thomas Hecken discusses in his account of theories of popular culture. He reminds us that the study of popular

---

[4]   See Rita Felski, *The Limits of Critique* (Chicago: The University of Chicago Press, 2015).

ASTRID BÖGER and FLORIAN SEDLMEIER

culture is inextricable from value judgments which can either discredit the popular as ideologically suspicious or assign it subversive potential for challenging normativity. But before such projected impact can even be addressed, Hecken notes that the success story of popular culture may in fact be contingent on the modern conception of artistic autonomy, which distinguishes aesthetic from moral and educational value. This contextualization, which assumes "die Idee der Regellosigkeit des Schönen,"[5] can partly account for the fact that many twentieth-century students and scholars of popular culture are concerned with its impact in the sense of a *Wirkungsästhetik*.

This critical inclination to account for the aesthetic effects of the popular then prompts questions of cultural value and qualitative difference. On one end of a spectrum of positions, there is the cultural pessimism of the Frankfurt School, where literature and the arts serve the people (conceived as the masses) best when they retain their autonomy and refuse mere profit orientation, and when they avoid both blunt didacticism and amusing distraction to expose the "mass deception," which Max Horkheimer and Theodor Adorno associate with "the culture industry."[6] On the other end of the spectrum, the U.S. pragmatist philosopher John Dewey suggests an integrative conception of aesthetic experience, one that ascribes aesthetic quality to everyday modalities of both living and making art, conceived as a continuity of human experience. In his attempt to restore and defend the common and public good against the alienating forces of modernity, which he considers no less deceptive than Horkheimer and Adorno do,[7] he thus assigns aesthetic experience a comprehensive social function. Literature and the arts, broadly defined, are for Dewey privileged sites for exploring and restoring a sense of democratic community based on "collective individuality" and "collective art."[8]

---

[5] Thomas Hecken, *Theorien der Populärkultur: Dreißig Positionen von Schiller bis zu den Cultural Studies* (Bielefeld: transcript, 2007), 180.

[6] See Max Horkheimer and Theodor W. Adorno, *Dialectic of Enlightenment: Philosophical Fragments*, trans. Edmund Jephcott (Stanford: Stanford University Press, 2012), 94–136.

[7] See John Dewey, *Art as Experience* (New York: Penguin, 2005), esp. 339–363.

[8] Ibid., 334; 359. It may be added, though, that Dewey, at times, also resorts to pejorative vocabulary, which suggests implicit value judgments. In the

12   Introduction: U.S. Culture as Popular Culture

In line with Dewey's open and inclusive definition, the contributions to this volume discuss a wide range of cultural artefacts and their medial manifestations – including memes, hashtags, music, poetry, television formats (reality TV, fictional series, late-night shows, stand-up comedy specials), movies, novels, graphic novels, and video games. In doing so, they largely refrain from value judgments about artistic quality, opting instead for a more nuanced account of aesthetic effects focused on ambiguities. This could be taken as another indicator that the study of artefacts and phenomena of popular culture is no longer in need of legitimation, academic or otherwise, and moreover that many of the forms and genres previously considered trivial or somehow unworthy of academic attention are by now accepted as legitimate objects of study.

From a historical perspective, one may add that the hierarchies of taste were hardly ever stable in American culture, as Lawrence Levine has aptly argued in his study of the Shakespeare reception, even if, by the late nineteenth century, European notions of an elitist culture were shared by many American practitioners and critics of culture.[9] As Berndt Ostendorf puts it, "the American model of legitimation is basically egalitarian, if not populist." This stands in marked contrast to Europe, where "taste and cultural preferences" express social class positions,[10] as amply demonstrated in the works of French sociologist Pierre Bourdieu, among others. Likewise, the formation of American Studies as a field of inquiry rests not only, as is often assumed, on the canonizing efforts of Francis O. Matthiessen.[11] Proponents of what

---

first chapter, he notes that the preservation of the fine arts for "the cultivated" may lead to "esthetic hunger" for "the cheap and the vulgar" among "the mass of people" (ibid., 4). In the last chapter, he maintains that "'art,'" which is "trivial and anecdotal," has been produced "at all times" and may be on display in contemporary exhibitions "*en masse*" (ibid., 354).

[9] See Lawrence W. Levine, *Highbrow/Lowbrow: The Emergence of Cultural Hierarchy in America* (Cambridge: Harvard University Press, 1988).

[10] Berndt Ostendorf, "Why Is American Culture so Popular? A View from Europe," in "Popular Culture," ed. Ulla Haselstein, Berndt Ostendorf, and Peter Schneck, special issue, *Amerikastudien/American Studies* 46, no. 3 (2001): 359.

[11] See F. O. Matthiessen, *American Renaissance. Art and Expression in the Age of Emerson and Whitman* (London: Oxford University Press, 1941).

ASTRID BÖGER and FLORIAN SEDLMEIER

Bruce Kuklick has labeled "the myth-symbol school"[12] have drawn on a wide array of artefacts and materials in their project to consolidate a national cultural imagination. Written against the backdrop of World War II and the emergent bipolar world order, many of these accounts also indicate the colonial and imperial contexts of U.S. popular culture which ensuing generations of critics have first extrapolated and then debunked, the latter interventions having been formulated most forcefully by the loosely-defined group of the New Americanists.[13]

The last aspect points to a crucial insight, namely, that conceptions of popular culture are inextricable from questions of political imagination. The planners of the GAAS Annual Conference 2019 took this into account in their Call for Papers by suggesting an affinity between popular culture and populism. Raymond Williams, in his *Keywords* entry "popular," likewise makes this connection, taking the formation, in 1892, of the People's or Populist Party in the U.S. as a seminal instance.[14] However, the link between the popular and the populist may in fact reach further back than this example, which is a historical exception. Indeed, for Ostendorf, the nexus is rather at the core of the cultural and national self-understanding of America. The success story of U.S. popular culture, he writes, is firmly embedded in "republican *self-government* and *popular sovereignty*."[15] These political imperatives lead to the construction of a "liberal and *popular* New World utopia," whose relentless production of popular culture "may best be explained along the lines of an American exceptionalism buttressed

---

[12] See Bruce Kuklick, "Myth and Symbol in American Studies," *American Quarterly* 24, no. 4 (1972): 435–450.

[13] See Henry Nash Smith, *Virgin Land: The American West as Symbol and Myth* (Cambridge: Harvard University Press, 1950); Leo Marx, *The Machine in the Garden: Technology and the Pastoral Ideal in America* (Oxford: Oxford University Press, 1964). For representative samples of the New Americanist intervention see Donald E. Pease, ed., *New Americanists: Revisionist Interventions into the Americanist Canon* (Durham: Duke University Press, 1994); Donald E. Pease and Robyn Wiegman, eds., *The Futures of American Studies* (Durham: Duke University Press, 2002).

[14] See Raymond Williams, "Popular," in *Keywords: A Vocabulary of Culture and Society* (New York: Oxford University Press, 2015), 181.

[15] Ostendorf, "Why Is American Culture so Popular?," 340.

14 Introduction: U.S. Culture as Popular Culture

by a neo-liberal market economy."[16] Such a view also implies that notions of "the popular as counter-hegemonic," which assume "highly stratified societies with a strong establishment," cannot be easily transferred to the U.S.; "where popular culture rested on the consent of the governed."[17] In consequence, cultural dissent and difference are "a legitimate, even necessary part of a system of checks and balances," resulting in a "dialectical relationship between hegemonic power and popular culture."[18] Some tenets of Ostendorf's analysis, which also views Black American culture, multiculturalism and, more generally, cultural pluralism as constitutive of this dialectic, reverberate in several contributions to this volume. Notably, however, the focus of many of the essays assembled here lies on the contemporary political moment, including the transition from the Obama administration to the Trump presidency, the lingering "war on terror," and the social movements across the political spectrum that occupy streets and hard drives, putting to use in both cases the tools of globally-reaching social media. By implication, the essays in this collection therefore provide critical updates on the continued appreciation of popular culture as an important field of U.S. American as well as global culture. To understand *U.S. Culture as Popular Culture* means to consider both its national and international dimensions.

The nexus between political protest and social media draws attention to another crucial feature of conceptions of popular culture, namely their reliance on ever-evolving media environments. Since the special issue published by *Amerikastudien/American Studies*, which also builds on this insight, those environments have changed significantly. On the one hand, advances in communication technology enhance both global connectivity and transparency. On the other hand, algorithms play a key role in shaping tastes and defining news, in targeting consumers to the point that the mining and control of personal data are a key concern of the information age.[19] The cell phone, as a device and medium that supports all of these developments, may have become the currently

---

[16]   Ibid., 342.
[17]   Ibid., 343.
[18]   Ibid., 344.
[19]   See Shoshana Zuboff, *The Age of Surveillance Capitalism: The Fight for A Human Future at the New Frontier of Power* (London: Profile Books, 2019).

ASTRID BÖGER and FLORIAN SEDLMEIER 15

indispensable and most successful "extension of man."[20] And where human beings cannot succeed in spite of their technological extensions, artificial intelligence is bound to take over. Scholars often resort to a distinction between traditional media and new ones with their respective structures of production and modes of reception. For instance, movie and television critics often address the challenges posed by streaming platforms to network television and Hollywood. Critics of political communication measure the rise of online journalism, with its new, technology-induced formats and genres, against conventional news outlets. The cultural diagnostics offer once again a spectrum of value judgments. Some celebrate the diagnosed fragmentation of the current media environment as a form of participatory democracy, whereas others bemoan the erosion of a cultural consensus once represented by *Leitmedien* and identify a retreat into self-contained bubbles competing for attention that can be monetized by counting "clicks," "hits," and "likes." And yet, there may be an entirely different way of accounting for the contemporary moment. As Henry Jenkins argues, the technological changes to our media environment have a cultural dimension and generate effects of "media convergence." Jenkins understands such convergence as a dynamic process that "alters the relationship between existing technologies, industries, markets, genres, and audiences."[21] His structural analysis is careful not to take sides in the polarized debates on whether technology-induced cultural phenomena can be co-opted or, rather, afford subversion. We find that many contributions to this volume embrace a similarly open spirit of inquiry.

There would have been many different ways of grouping the essays in this volume. We opted to arrange them according to the art forms they discuss. Each section orders the texts alphabetically by the last names of the authors. Film and television as well as literature figure so prominently as to allow for separate sections with ten contributions each. The third cluster of contributions consists of seven essays on architecture, hashtags, memes, music, Pop Art, and video games.

---

[20] See Marshall McLuhan, *Understanding Media: The Extensions of Man* (London: Routledge, 1964).
[21] See Henry Jenkins, "The Cultural Logic of Media Convergence," *International Journal of Cultural Studies* 7, no.1 (2004): 34.

16   Introduction: U.S. Culture as Popular Culture

Film and Television

MAXI ALBRECHT looks at the serial post-Western and, more specifically, AMC's hit TV franchise *The Walking Dead*. This series curiously appears as a revenant of the myth and symbol school's search for a shared national imaginary gone awry. The liminal space, a.k.a. the frontier, returns here as very perilous terrain indeed, leaving viewers with a frighteningly uncertain outlook on humanity's future. ABIGAIL FAGAN's piece echoes the imperial legacy of the Western imaginary, but critically turns it on its head by focusing on the settler colonial hauntings in Joss Whedon's space Western television series *Firefly*. Revisiting core ideologies of Anglo-European settler colonialism through the lens of *terra nullius* or "no one's land," she ties the anxieties of settling back to the historical paradox of inhabiting the uninhabitable, if hardly uninhabited, land. BRIGITTE GEORGI-FINDLAY's contribution also considers the Western, but adds an important temporal dimension by tracing the evolution of the genre from the 1950s onward. She convincingly shows that the Western has always been a revisionist genre, engaged as it is in the cultural politics of its time, but with a few essential constants such as the slipperiness of the masculine prerogative. LINDA HESS adds another perspective to the study of popular culture by looking at women's standup comedy as autobiographical narrative with an unexpected bent, given generic conventions, toward personal suffering. In her analysis, the unfunny inhabits an important political position because it calls into question what is and is not considered funny, and by whom. CARSTEN JUNKER takes a critical look at militainment, a term coined by Roger Stahl to describe media products expressive of state power that are presented as consumable entertainment. Junker applies this critique to the PBS series *Liberty's Kids* on the American Revolutionary War by focusing on its positive depiction of violence on the one hand and its lack of attention to slavery and racism on the other. KATJA KANZLER's contribution looks at the invective mode as an important part of reality television, a genre whose immense popular appeal does not seem to be diminished by the fact that it is often considered of low quality. Kanzler reintroduces the decisive role of taste into the conversation in an attempt to make sense of reality TV's surprisingly lasting success, even among those who claim not to like it. MICHAEL LOUIS MOSER discusses the enduring popularity of U.S.

American late-night talk shows from their inception in the 1950s until today, with a particular focus on their political content. According to his analysis, Stephen Colbert's *Late Show* and Seth Meyers's *Late Night* have diverged from network conventions in the Trump era by taking on partisan politics more directly than the format ordinarily calls for. Drawing on Ankersmit's notion of style, JOHN STREET's contribution frames the chiasmic (and mutually beneficial) relationship between politics and popular culture with a particular focus on the media presence of the Trump presidency, which "has imbued the topic with a renewed relevance and greater urgency," as his piece effectively demonstrates. MARITA STURKEN also takes the norm-defying Trump presidency as a starting point for her analysis of contemporary television comedy but focuses more generally on questions of disruption, humorlessness and genre flail, which she sees as indicative of the broader uncertainties of American life in the early twenty-first century. Turning to the medium of film and the road movie genre in particular, JENNIFER VOLKMER describes motorcycle riding as what she considers a pilgrimage to hegemonic masculinity. She uses the 2007 comedy film *Wild Hogs*, directed by Walt Becker, as a case in point, which makes for interesting comparisons with the TV comedy formats discussed in several other contributions in this volume.

Literature

A number of essays discuss literary subjects, giving readers the opportunity to take stock of this important field of American Studies scholarship when placed in the framework of popular culture. LAURA BIEGER starts the conversation by looking at public intellectuals faced with what she terms "the predicaments of popularity." Against the theoretical backdrop of Bourdieu's work on *The Field of Cultural Production* (1993), among others, she discusses Richard Wright as a Black public intellectual with a critical eye toward the position of the popular within the public sphere more generally. RUTH GEHRMANN discusses Indigenous storytelling in Cherie Dimaline's 2017 young adult novel *The Marrow Thieves*. According to her insightful analysis, the futurist envisioning of the (post-)apocalypse connects with 'old-timey' Native storytelling while also affording an opportunity to negotiate, as

18   Introduction: U.S. Culture as Popular Culture

Gehrmann aptly phrases it, "the relative nature of apocalypse in colonial contexts." The question of female empowerment is at the center of ALEXANDRA HARTMANN's essay. More specifically, her focus lies on popular narratives featuring Black women facing incredible odds while their spouses are incarcerated. Recent novels such as Tayari Jones's *An American Marriage* (2018) popularize the figure of the strong Black woman in order to counter real-life hardship with Black feminist role models. ZOHRA HASSAN-PIEPER looks at Craig Thompson's graphic novel *Habibi* (2011), taking critical issue with what she considers its misrepresentation of Muslims as well as the male gaze's objectification of the female body throughout. Aligning herself with Edward Said's critique of Western projections on the Other within Orientalist discourse, she takes Thompson to task for reiterating anti-Muslim stereotypes. MARIUS HENDERSON explores the presence of anti-Black gendered violence in U.S. popular culture. Inspired by Afropessimist, Afrarealist and Black feminist theorists, his piece aims to dismantle, through careful theoretical explorations, the ontological underpinnings of violence against Blacks on the grounds of both race and gender. MARIAN OFORI-AMOAFO's contribution deals with "Different Ways of (Not) Being Black" across the media of literature and film. She thus reads the British novel *I Am Not Sidney Poitier* by Percival Everett (2009), with its protagonist named Not Sidney Poitier after the famous Black actor, against the backdrop of African American art such as Blaxploitation films fraught with racial stereotypes. A broadly historical approach is employed by CLARA PETINO in her piece on modern witches in Salem literature, which is constituted by a body of around seventy works of fiction that have appeared over the last 200 years, with a marked increase, as Petino notes, since the 1990s. Mostly written by female authors, these works take the empowerment of women through witchcraft and other forces as one of their recurring themes. HEIKE STEINHOFF's piece invites us to consider a best-selling branch of today's literary marketplace, namely self-help books geared primarily toward a female readership in their emphasis on body positivity, among other lifestyle concerns. Informed by a popularized version of academic feminism, these works often display a problematic body politics, as Steinhoff demonstrates. LISANNA WIELE's essay discusses a historical body of fictional works by placing them in a contemporary theoretical frame. The serialized city mystery novels of the antebellum era deserve our renewed attention, as Wiele convincingly shows how their wayward negotiations of the urban grid are expressive of various transgressions, including sexual ones, that ensure their popular appeal. HARALD ZAPF's contribution focuses on lyric poetry, a branch of literature often considered less popular than others, which he situates vis-à-vis theories of lyric poetry since Romanticism. This important context helps explain the growing popularity of Romantic impulses such as intuition, spontaneity, and affect in contemporary lyric poetry, as exemplified by *Instapoetry*, which is widely disseminated via the internet.

Other Media and Art Forms

Through the lens of popular culture studies, a third group of essays engages with a variety of art forms ranging from the built environment to music. JULIANE BOROSCH opens the section with her essay on Detroit architecture and certain landmarks of industrial production in particular, which she understands as expressions of "the visual and verbal language of popular culture." Detroit is an interesting case, both as an urban icon of the past and for its attempts to rebuild itself from its ruins. DUSTIN BREITENWISCHER's contribution focuses on the nexus between hip hop, art and #ART, the latter referring to the ongoing use of a hashtag by Buffalo-based rap artist, gallery owner and fashion label executive Alvin Lamar Worthy, better known as Westside Gunn. Breitenwischer discusses the hashtag project as a strategic use of the new media practice while not losing sight of its larger aesthetic aims. NAGHMEH ESMAEILPOUR looks at video games, likely the most popular (or, in any case, profitable) field of cultural production today. By focusing on the transmedial historiography and using two current mainstream products of U.S. origin as examples, she reveals the limitations, if not strategic misrepresentations, of the depiction of Iranians in these mass-marketed, globalized products. MARLON LIEBER's piece considers Pop Art icon Andy Warhol through the framework of a Marxist analysis of the circulation of money, in this case quite literally via art. Taking as a starting point Warhol's own admission that money was his preferred subject for his paintings, Lieber offers an in-depth meditation on the intricate (as well as near-intrinsic) relationship between money and art. FRANK MEHRING looks at what he calls "Sonic State Fantasies," or

20 Introduction: U.S. Culture as Popular Culture

explicitly political uses of popular music. More specifically, he compares the Obama and Trump presidencies in terms of their different approaches to music, and in so doing adds another important dimension – or rather, medium – to the discussions of contemporary U.S. popular culture assembled in this volume. JOHANNES SCHMID discusses internet memes as a hugely popular form of mass communication and, simultaneously, a still nascent field of digital cultural formation. With its focus on the mediality and usage of memes, his piece traces the phenomenon's development from the relatively obscure origins of internet memes to their global success story, which testifies to an intense need for digital community-building. Finally, GUNTER SÜß's contribution explores the role of music in a rather specific context, namely education. More precisely, Süß discusses the didactic uses of music videos by African American performance artists as a tool for teaching American cultural studies. Several hit releases such as Beyoncé's album *Lemonade* and JAY-Z's *4:44* serve as examples of the changing cultural values (or rather of their rejection, as in the case of racism and misogyny) in hip hop music.

Acknowledgments

This volume would not exist without the conference "U.S.-American Culture as Popular Culture" that preceded it. The Annual Conference of the German Association for American Studies took place from June 13-15, 2019 at the University of Hamburg. It would not have been possible without the support of several institutions and the collective efforts of both colleagues and students. The GAAS and its members generously supported the conference. Special thanks are due to the board of directors for their expert guidance throughout the entire process. Regarding the conference proceedings at hand, we would like to thank the Winter Verlag for their ongoing promotion of the American Studies Monograph Series in which they appear. On the Hamburg side, we were grateful for the kind remarks with which Consul General Richard "Rick" Yoneoka opened the conference. We received generous support from the Hamburgische Wissenschaftliche Stiftung, and we were also lucky to have Wiebold Confiserie Elmshorn as our local sponsor, which added a sweet touch to the entire conference.

With regard to our colleagues, Susanne Rohr and Jan Kucharzewski have to be thanked first and foremost. Both were involved in the planning and organizing from the very beginning. Their expertise and dedication were indispensable in first conceptualizing and then holding the conference. It is also on behalf of them that we would like to give our heartfelt thanks to all the others who worked on the ground and behind the scenes. Christina Meyer, who, like Florian Sedlmeier, joined the organizing committee at a later stage, was no less crucial to the success of the conference. At earlier moments in the planning phase, Julia Lange and Marius Henderson were also involved and helped in preparing the event. A special thank you goes to Jolene Mathieson, who coordinated the planning of the entire conference from start to finish. Her diligence and mindfulness kept the entire committee on track. Nicole Zajac deserves a special mention here, as she was in charge of the finances and of patiently phoning and emailing with the administrative side. Another special thanks goes to Janina Wierzoch for designing a smashing conference program, both in print and online. Without the commitment and work ethic of our student aids who, among many other things, assisted and welcomed the conference participants, we also could not have done it, so thank you once again Katharina Büschler, Nazan Demirci, Elisa Gerlach, Fenja Heisig, Sofia Junghans, Claudius Kesseböhmer, Julia Kisiel, Christina Kutscher, Lynn Mazur, Leonie Milionis, Jonas Paulsen, Marlena Staak, and Dorothee Voss. Last but not least, we would like to thank the technical and administrative staff as well as the cleaning personnel at the University of Hamburg.

Finally, the present collection of essays would not have been possible without the help of Hannah Mück, Nino-Raimondo Torricelli, and Cameron Seglias. We would therefore like to thank Hannah for her diligent language editing. With her precise comments and polite communication, she was a delight to work with. At an early stage, Nino helped in formatting the essays. Cameron took on the massive task of streamlining the citation system and typesetting the final manuscript. His competence and oversight were indispensable. We truly appreciate Hannah's, Nino's, and Cameron's care and patience from beginning to end.

22 Introduction: U.S. Culture as Popular Culture

Works Cited

Dewey, John. *Art as Experience*. New York: Penguin, 2005.

Felski, Rita. *The Limits of Critique*. Chicago: The University of Chicago Press, 2015.

Haselstein, Ulla, Berndt Ostendorf, and Peter Schneck. "Popular Culture: Introduction." In "Popular Culture," edited by Ulla Haselstein, Berndt Ostendorf, and Peter Schneck. Special Issue, *Amerikastudien/American Studies* 46, no. 3 (2001): 331–338.

Hecken, Thomas. *Theorien der Populärkultur: Dreißig Positionen von Schiller bis zu den Cultural Studies*. Bielefeld: transcript, 2007.

Horkheimer, Max, and Theodor W. Adorno. *Dialectic of Enlightenment: Philosophical Fragments*. Translated by Edmund Jephcott. Stanford: Stanford University Press, 2012.

Jenkins, Henry. "The Cultural Logic of Media Convergence." *International Journal of Cultural Studies* 7, no. 1 (2004): 33–43.

Kuklick, Bruce. "Myth and Symbol in American Studies." *American Quarterly* 24, no. 4 (1972): 435–450.

Levine, Lawrence W. *Highbrow/Lowbrow: The Emergence of Cultural Hierarchy in America*. Cambridge: Harvard University Press, 1988.

Marx, Leo. *The Machine in the Garden: Technology and the Pastoral Ideal in America*. Oxford: Oxford University Press, 1964.

Matthiessen, F. O. *American Renaissance: Art and Expression in the Age of Emerson and Whitman*. London: Oxford University Press, 1941.

McLuhan, Marshal. *Understanding Media: The Extensions of Man*. London: Routledge, 1964.

Ostendorf, Berndt. "Why Is American Culture so Popular? A View from Europe." In "Popular Culture," edited by Ulla Haselstein, Berndt Ostendorf, and Peter Schneck. Special Issue, *Amerikastudien/American Studies* 46, no. 3 (2001): 339–366.

Pease, Donald E., ed. *New Americanists: Revisionist Interventions into the Americanist Canon*. Durham: Duke University Press, 1994.

Pease, Donald E., and Robyn Wiegman, eds. *The Futures of American Studies*. Durham: Duke University Press, 2002.

Smith, Henry Nash. *Virgin Land: The American West as Symbol and Myth*. Cambridge: Harvard University Press, 1950.

Williams, Raymond. "Popular." In *Keywords: A Vocabulary of Culture and Society*, 179–181. Oxford: Oxford University Press, 2015.

Zuboff, Shoshana. *The Age of Surveillance Capitalism: The Fight for A Human Future at the New Frontier of Power*. London: Profile Books, 2019.

Section I: Film and Television

MAXI ALBRECHT

"A New Beginning": AMC's *The Walking Dead* and the Serial Post-Western

Cowboy Lore and Zombies: The (Post-)Western and *The Walking Dead*

The first episode of the AMC television series *The Walking Dead* (*TWD*), entitled "Days Gone Bye," featured an iconic shot which arguably may be one of the best-known visuals from the immensely popular show.[1] The long-range shot depicts protagonist Rick Grimes riding into the post-apocalyptic ruins of Atlanta on horseback, a bag of guns slung on his back and his sheriff's hat on his head. The lonesome cowboy bravely ventures into the fallen city on a quest to find his family. It is emblematic of how *TWD* has frequently tapped into the Western genre,[2] which informs much of the show's aesthetics, particularly in the early seasons, and is crucial to the violence and questionable ethics of survival, especially with regard to Rick Grimes as an emerging leader. Jeffrey Sartain describes the corresponding panel from the comic book upon which the series is based as "a modern-day sheriff riding into civilization's figurative sunset," likening Rick Grimes to mythic Western heroes.[3]

---

[1] "Days Gone Bye," *The Walking Dead*, season 1, episode 1. Aired October 31, 2013, on AMC, 00:39:52.

[2] See Jamie Russell, *Book of the Dead: The Complete History of Zombie Cinema* (London: Titan, 2014), 205.

[3] Jeffrey A. Sartain, "Days Gone Bye: Robert Kirkman's Reenvisioned Western *The Walking Dead*," in *Undead in the West II: They Just Keep Coming*, ed. Cynthia J. Miller and A. Bowdoin Van Riper (Lanham: Scarecrow, 2013), 242.

28 AMC's *The Walking Dead* and the Serial Post-Western

That *TWD* draws on the Western genre in its first seasons when depicting the trials of Rick Grimes in the early days of the apocalypse appears self-evident. However, the question of whether *TWD* also engages the Western subversively in genre-blending that is in the spirit of a post-Western appears to be contested. Several studies have come to differing conclusions regarding *TWD*'s ties to the Western genre,[4] while Amanda Keeler firmly argues that Rick Grimes riding into the ruins of a formerly modern city situate *TWD* as a post-Western. I posit here that these different assessments of *TWD's* Westernness or post-Westernness stem from two points of view.

On the one hand, many of the academic studies that emphasize the show's Western qualities were published during earlier seasons, and therefore could not foresee future developments in a narrative so deeply grounded in its own ongoing seriality and eschewal of closure. On the other hand, the term post-Western itself can refer to different kinds of reconfigurations of the Western and has been theorized in various ways. Diane M. Borden and Eric P. Essman argue that, starting in the 1960s, the genre conventions and heroic myths of the Western were challenged and reinvented.[5] They identify two different types of movies that undertook this project in the wake of a period of revisionist history and

---

[4] Cf. P. Ivan Young, "Walking Tall or Walking Dead? The American Cowboy in the Zombie Apocalypse," in *"We're All Infected": Essays on AMC's* The Walking Dead *and the Fate of the Human*, ed. Dawn Keetley (Jefferson: McFarland, 2014), 56–67; Dan Hassler-Forest, "Cowboys and Zombies: Destabilizing Patriarchal Discourse in *The Walking Dead*," *Studies in Comics* 2, no. 2 (2012): 339–355; Sartain, "Days Gone Bye"; Shelley S. Rees, "Frontier Values Meet Big-City Zombies: The Old West in AMC's *The Walking Dead*," in *Undead in the West: Vampires, Zombies, Mummies, and Ghosts on the Cinematic Frontier*, ed. Cynthia J. Miller and A. Bowdoin Van Riper (Lanham: Scarecrow, 2012), 90–102; Amanda Keeler, "A Postapocalyptic Return to the Frontier: *The Walking Dead* as Post-Western," *Critical Studies in Television* 13, no. 4 (2018): 422–437; Dahlia Schweitzer, *Going Viral: Zombies, Viruses, and the End of the World* (New Brunswick: Rutgers University Press, 2018).

[5] Diane M. Borden and Eric P. Essman, "Manifest Landscape/Latent Ideology: Afterimages of Empire in the Western and 'Post-Western' Film," *California History* 79, no. 1 (2000): 30.

post-structuralist theory. A first type of post-Western seeks to challenge and reinvent the classical Western with a clearer understanding of its ideological underpinnings and fault lines.[6] This definition overlaps with another genre designator: the revisionist Western. A second type, according to Borden and Essman, features contemporary settings while "carrying over visual remnants, social and political attitudes and cultural artifacts identified with the 'Old West.'"[7]

With regard to the latter, Keeler's labeling of *TWD* as a post-Western appears logical by virtue of the series being set in a post-apocalyptic near future. But Keeler's argument specifically addresses the show's subversive inversion of Western ideologies associated with "optimism around redemption, renewal, and rebirth."[8] Acknowledging, as most of the other studies mentioned above do, that Rick is cast as a classical Western hero and that the first season's gender politics veer toward the traditional, Keeler also identifies the emergence of post-Western heroines in later seasons.[9] The issue of *TWD*'s identity politics – and, indeed, its politics in general – has been debated even more than its genre allegiances have in both public media and academic analyses. Several studies conclude that *TWD*'s post-apocalyptic world does not result in a *tabula rasa* scenario that eradicates the structural confines of power mechanisms. For instance, Melissa F. Lavin and Brian M. Lowe argue that the first seasons of *TWD* tend to reproduce pre-apocalyptic social roles and hierarchies, but they also acknowledge that the show provides more diverse and non-traditional representations the further it moves into the post-apocalypse.[10]

In the introduction to her volume of essays on *TWD*'s politics of race, gender and sexuality, editor Dawn Keetley also maintains that the

---

[6]   Ibid., 35–36.

[7]   Ibid., 36. For an extensive overview of different theories and conceptualizations of the post-Western, see Neil Campbell, *Post-Westerns: Cinema, Region, West* (Lincoln: University of Nebraska Press, 2013), 1–17.

[8]   Keeler, "A Postapocalyptic Return to the Frontier," 433.

[9]   See ibid., 430.

[10]   See Melissa Lavin and Brian Lowe, "Cops and Zombies: Hierarchy and Social Location in *The Walking Dead*," in *Race, Gender, and Sexuality in Post-Apocalyptic TV and Film*, ed. Barbara Gurr (London: Palgrave Macmillan, 2015), 118–120.

30   AMC's *The Walking Dead* and the Serial Post-Western

show undeniably evolves toward less traditional, complex and mutable identity politics by offering multiple points of identification.[11] Elsewhere, Keetley argues moreover that *TWD*'s ability to accommodate diverging politics is a crucial aspect of its success.[12] Dahlia Schweitzer states that *TWD* is not merely steeped in cowboy lore but actively reinvents and repurposes Western tropes. Naming the show as a prime example, she argues that television narratives which deeply explore the necessities of prolonged survival struggles reflect the reality that one needs a diverse team of survivors in order to make it through. The representation of diverse identities, Schweitzer says, can coexist with the favoring of the rugged individual hero, as such shows tend to replace the individual cowboy with survivor tribes.[13] Conceived as such a series that represents an ongoing survival struggle, *TWD* incorporates aspects other than the diverging politics which Hassler-Forest identifies in the comic books.[14] Consequently, *TWD* may not only reinvent itself periodically; it may also perform a kind of revisionism on itself with regard to both genre and politics.

"A New Beginning" for *The Walking Dead*

In the following analysis, I focus on *TWD*'s season nine premiere, which originally aired on October 7, 2018 on the basic cable network AMC. Its programmatic title, "A New Beginning," is significant not only with regard to the episode's narrative content as well as that of the season overall, but also because it relates to a more encompassing reinvention of the show on the production level. For many years, *TWD* has been a record-breakingly popular show that has dominated the coveted 18 – to

---

[11]   Dawn Keetley, "Introduction: Identity Politics in The Walking Dead," in *The Politics of Race, Gender and Sexuality in* The Walking Dead: *Essays on the Television Series and Comics*, ed. Dawn Keetley and Elizabeth Erwin (Jefferson: McFarland, 2018), 2–3.

[12]   Dawn Keetley, "'The Walking Dead' and the Rise of Donald Trump," *Pop Matters*, March 16, 2016, popmatters.com/the-walking-dead-and-the-rise-of-donald-trump-2495444431.html.

[13]   Cf. Schweitzer, *Going Viral*, 185–188.

[14]   Hassler-Forest, "Cowboys and Zombies," 354.

MAXI ALBRECHT 31

49-year-old viewer demographic on basic cable,[15] frequently even beating out NFL games in its Sunday nighttime slot on AMC.[16] However, both as a singular episode and as a season premiere setting the tone for the episodes to come, "A New Beginning" should be read as an attempt to reinvent the hit show in light of a significant decline in critical ratings and viewer numbers at the time.[17] Following significant discontent over the sixth season's cliffhanger and the subsequent "slaughterfest" that was seasons seven and eight, fans' outrage reached a peak, and a petition called for the removal of Scott Gimple as showrunner after the unexpected death of Carl Grimes.[18]

"A New Beginning," then, was the start of Angela Kang's reign as showrunner – notably as the first woman and first person of color to hold this position on the show. What is more, the departure of Andrew Lincoln as lead protagonist Rick Grimes after only a handful of episodes in the new season was already public knowledge prior to the season airing. While many predicted that his exit would be the final nail in the coffin of a show about things refusing to stay dead,[19] AMC and the

---

[15] Cf. Rick Porter, "Sunday Cable Ratings: 'The Walking Dead' Premiere Kills It with Second-Highest Ratings Ever," *TV by the Numbers*, October 25, 2016, tvbythenumbers.zap2it.com/daily-ratings/sunday-cable-ratings-oct-23-2016-walking-dead-premiere/.

[16] Cf. James Hibberd, "'Walking Dead' Once Again Beats 'Sunday Night Football,'" *Entertainment Weekly*, November 2, 2014, ew.com/article/2014/11/03/walking-dead-ratings-once-again-beat-sunday-night-football/.

[17] Cf. Joe Otterson, "'Walking Dead' Season 8 Finale Ratings Lowest Since Season 1," *Variety*, April 17, 2018, variety.com/2018/tv/news/walking-dead-season-8-finale-ratings-1202754602/.

[18] Cf. Tyler Sigmon, "A Petition for Scott Gimple to Be Removed from *The Walking Dead* Productions and Content," *Change.org*, January 9, 2020, change.org/p/amc-tv-a-petition-for-scott-gimple-to-be-removed-from-the-walking-dead-productions-and-content. While Gimple was perhaps removed as showrunner to appease the fans, he was, in actuality, given the arguably more important, albeit potentially less visible, role of chief content manager for the entire *Walking Dead* franchise at AMC.

[19] Cf. Paul Tassi, "*The Walking Dead*'s Falling Ratings Are about to Get a Whole Lot Worse," *Forbes*, October 14, 2018, forbes.com/sites/insertcoin/2018/10/14/the-walking-deads-falling-ratings-are-about-to-get-a-whole-lot-worse/.

creative team appeared to acknowledge both tacitly and openly that it was time to turn the page. *Talking Dead*, *TWD*'s own live aftershow also offers a preview special during the summer hiatus which teases the new season and clues the audience in on major upcoming developments. The season nine preview special emphasized the changes presented by the new season. Angela Kang's role as the new showrunner took center stage,[20] and she explained that the new season would begin after a significant time jump in the storyworld that would launch a completely "new chapter for the show." She stressed that the show's first eight seasons constituted one chapter, and that season nine would begin a new chapter focused on rebuilding civilization and looking to the past in order to build the present.[21] In an interview, Kang furthermore underlined that, with her new role, female leadership would take center stage both within the story and on the level of production.[22]

These paratextual descriptions[23] indicate that *TWD*'s intra- and extratextual reinvention was to crystallize around two issues: a new era of civilization-building marked by a return to the past in service of the future, as well as more diverse identity politics. These aspects are rife with post-Western tropes and politics, and the setting and plot of "A New Beginning" in particular resonate with the same issues. Armed with a new intro, a new showrunner, and the trumpets of change blowing, this

---

[20] Incidentally, the increased diversity represented by Angela Kang and her vision for the show was apparent in another way during this *Talking Dead* special, as host Chris Hardwick was temporarily replaced by Yvette Nicole Brown after allegations of sexual misconduct caused AMC to reassess his role as host.

[21] "Season 9 Preview Special," *Talking Dead*. Aired August 5, 2018, on AMC, 00:02:45–00:03:50.

[22] Dalton Ross, "'The Walking Dead' EP Says Season 9 Will Focus on Female Leadership," *Entertainment Weekly*, July 17, 2018, ew.com/tv/2018/07/17/walking-dead-season-9-showrunner-female-leadership/.

[23] For an extensive study of *TWD*'s mobilization of paratexts as crucial elements of its "narrative developments, storyworld or character continuity, authorship performances, and the management of viewer responses" (239), see Maria Sulimma, "Serial Gender, Gendered Serialities: Practices of US-American Television Narratives in the 21st Century" (PhD diss., Freie Universität Berlin, 2018).

episode attempts to overtly mark a new beginning for the show both within the storyworld and on the production level.

"A New Beginning" opens with a pre-intro scene sequence that sets the tone not only for this episode but for the half-season story arc to follow.[24] After a bloody war that lasted for two seasons, the season opening emphasizes idyllic, pastoral imagery in the thriving survivors' community of Alexandria, depicting Rick Grimes's happy family unit enjoying a peaceful morning, with few hints at the realities of a violent, post-apocalyptic world. A shift to the defeated community of the former Saviors then introduces continuing tensions in the efforts to rebuild civilization, which simultaneously emphasizes the extreme proficiency all surviving communities have attained in navigating the post-apocalypse at this point. Finally, a major scavenging expedition with members of all the different communities is introduced as the episode's main plot point. After nine years on television, four years of which saw the narrative located on the outskirts of the former U.S. capital, *TWD* goes to Washington on a mission to recover items from the past at a fictional version of the Smithsonian Museum of Natural History. The mission is to recover seeds, an ancient canoe, a plane wagon, and a plow in order to help the newly allied communities grow and to build a new kind of society amid the ruins of the old one. The desired items further mark this episode's (post-)Western ties by evoking the history of Westward expansion, but, crucially, it is now envisioned as a project with a diverse set of characters. While the conquest of the West is of course bound up with the settler-colonial genocide of Indigenous peoples, its rendition in *TWD* features the zombies, which are represented as specifically non-human (see below), as the only 'victims' of the survivors' attempts to (re-)build civilization.

The group's arrival in Washington, D.C. invites comparison with Rick's ride into Atlanta in "Days Gone Bye,"[25] particularly since *TWD* had not featured quests in larger cities since the beginning of the fifth season. While Rick epitomized the singular cowboy hero riding into imminent danger with the sole purpose of finding and saving his

---

[24] "A New Beginning," *The Walking Dead*, season 9, episode 1. Aired October 7, 2018, on AMC, 00:00:00–00:04:50.

[25] "Days Gone Bye," 00:39:52.

34   AMC's *The Walking Dead* and the Serial Post-Western

biological family, the group riding into Washington provides a stark visual contrast. Thus, whereas Rick's entrance scene was a long-range shot that dramatized the singular hero riding into the unknown and amplified both the audience's and the protagonist's ignorance about the post-apocalyptic condition of Atlanta, no such pretense is necessary in Washington because both characters and audience already know what to expect. In Washington, we first see medium-range shots of the destroyed city streets and a few zombies that are agitated by the sounds of approaching horses. Next, Rick and Michonne ride into the scene from off-screen and expertly kill the zombies, making way for the group of riders and a mule-drawn wagon. Instead of focusing on the single white male hero, this sequence highlights the mission's large, diverse group of characters consisting of different ages, genders, sexualities and ethnic groups.[26] The sound of hooves on the pavement and the background music harken back to the frontier and the Old West. At the same time, the zombies' snarling and gurgling tie the conventions of the horror genre to this scene, reminding survivors and audience of the post-apocalyptic reality. With regard to the survivors, the only break from their Western aesthetic and soundscape is Daryl Dixon riding his motorbike,[27] even though the bandana covering his lower face is reminiscent of a Western gunslinger. The imagery and soundscape unmistakably steep the museum mission in references to the past Westward Expansion of the United States.

The visual aesthetic and soundscape of the Western here contrasts with the decaying urban center of Washington, which is represented through overturned cars and the fact that the first zombie in this sequence is wearing a suit that marks him as some type of businessman or politician.[28] Several shots depict glimpses of the Capitol and the Washington Monument in the background, firmly anchoring the pre-intro scenes and the episode as a whole in a space that simultaneously

---

[26]   Ibid., 00:03:40–00:04:50.

[27]   The *Talking Dead* preview special discussed earlier in fact commented on this. Almost the whole main cast learned how to ride horses for this season – except actor Norman Reedus, who plays Daryl Dixon, since he refused to go near the horses.

[28]   Ibid., 00:03:47.

marks the urban past and its post-apocalyptic present. The interplay of these different temporalities and aesthetics is axiomatic for *TWD*'s simultaneous negotiation of the post-Western and post-apocalyptic zombie genres along with their themes and tropes, which mark this specific moment of the show's intra- and extratextual reinvention. This correlates strongly with Neil Campbell's assessment that in the post-Western, "there might live on the haunting presence of the past within the present and future."[29] The past frontier mythology represented here invokes both notions of human progress and violence. The need to survive and build stable and secure communities for the future, which are foundational drivers of human behavior in the present of *TWD*'s storyworld, foreground an absolute need for violence.

"A New Beginning" negotiates these aspects in no uncertain terms. A zombie must first be killed on the steps of the museum in order to gain entrance, while an old banner next to the museum's door reads "looking for fortune in the American West."[30] Surviving the zombie apocalypse always requires violence, embodied in the ever-present threat of the zombies, but this specific moment in the show represents the desire and the rare possibility of thriving – that is, the opportunity to reach a new level of progress. And this is precisely where *TWD*'s moment of reinvention ties in with the (post-)Western on an ideological level rather than merely in terms of temporalities and aesthetics. Optimistic, forward-thinking sentiments mark the progress toward which the group is striving in this episode. As they enter the museum, a smiling Maggie confidently declares: "This is gonna work."[31] Inside the museum's grand entrance hall, a zombie falls from one of the banisters, causing the glass floor to crack. Unperturbed, King Ezekiel proclaims: "Onward, we'll figure it out."[32] Various shots also reveal other banners advertising museum exhibits located under the glass floor, thus framing the group's efforts through the mottos of Manifest Destiny and Westward Expansion.

---

[29] Campbell, *Post-Westerns*, 2.
[30] "A New Beginning," 00:05:36–00:05:51.
[31] Ibid., 00:07:32.
[32] Ibid., 00:08:05–00:08:25.

36   AMC's *The Walking Dead* and the Serial Post-Western

Additionally, the floor below, which contains the exhibit, is filled with zombies. As on Washington's streets and at the museum entrance, the presence of zombies in these scenes marks the post-apocalyptic realities that serve as the main antagonists in this mission. Zombies in this episode are constant reminders that this world is – above all and irredeemably so – about survival. This is blended and entangled with aesthetic and temporal representations of the history of Westward Expansion, the frontier and the Old West. *TWD*'s use of zombies as an antagonistic threat bears a resemblance to Western tropes, as the shambling hordes of the undead are dehumanized objects that need to be evaded, disregarded, removed and eradicated as the survivors progress in this post-apocalyptic storyworld. However, several scholars, such as Schweitzer[33] and Keetley,[34] have pointed out that the show complicates the tradition of othering the zombie. Contrary to other zombie genre fictions, every human in *TWD* carries the disease that causes the dead to rise again regardless of the manner of their death, which severely complicates a clear-cut distinction between zombie and living survivor but also simultaneously acts as a narrative failsafe that enables the endless serial survival of the show itself by ensuring that the antagonistic threat can be infinitely reproduced.

"A New Beginning" inverts the logic of Westward Expansion by sending its characters into the ruins of the metropolis and to a museum to recover the "archived" essence of the Old West as part of their attempt to rebuild civilization. This profound unsettling of direction-alities and tropes drives the simultaneously post-Western and post-apocalyptic underpinnings of *TWD*. The imagination of empty land to be conquered is central to the plot within mythologies of the American frontier that views wilderness as a space for the production of American identity.[35] The spaces of the U.S. American West's wilderness, of course, were never empty but were taken from Indigenous populations

---

[33] Cf. Schweitzer, *Going Viral*, 184.
[34] Cf. Dawn Keetley, "Introduction: 'We're All Infected,'" in *"We're All Infected": Essays on AMC's* The Walking Dead *and the Fate of the Human*, ed. Dawn Keetley (Jefferson: McFarland, 2014), 7.
[35] Cf. Barbara Gurr, "Masculinity, Race, and the (Re?)Imagined American Frontier," in *Race, Gender, and Sexuality in Post-Apocalyptic TV and Film*, ed. Barbara Gurr (London: Palgrave Macmillan, 2015), 35.

in an imperialist, Manifest Destiny-driven conquest. The post-apocalyptic capital, in comparison, cannot lay claim to a false pretense of emptiness as its space is fraught with the fractures of its decaying former civilization. It is in this regard that the zombies take on another function in this specific episode: as the inhabitants of the space, they serve as simultaneous reminders of the past and of previously living humans, and yet they are also the threat that must be eradicated in order for *TWD*'s heroes to prosper and fulfill their own Manifest Destiny of rebuilding civilization.

According to the logic of the show, *TWD*'s characters, by the sole virtue of being alive in "A New Beginning," are undoubtedly the rightful and undisputed masters and conquerors of the post-Western space of the former U.S. capital. A scene in the museum depicts this logic strikingly. Two characters stand off-camera admiring a museum display that shows human evolution from primates to *homo sapiens*, to which a stage represented by a zombie they killed who is now stuck to the board – thus embodying a seemingly final stage – has been added. Chuckling, they remark on this "de-evolution of man" when other members of the survivor group walk past the display in search of their bounty.[36] Their movement – following that of the (de-)evolution of humankind and finally surpassing it, walking out of the frame – clearly marks the survivors as the next stage, moving forward and making progress toward a new and better future.

This new future represented in the hopefulness of the episode's mission and overall goal of the survivor group is also articulated in more inclusive and diverse identity politics. The aforementioned glaring difference between Rick's ride into Atlanta as the lonesome hero cowboy and the entire group's arrival in Washington, D.C. solidifies over the course of this episode into an act of serial self-revision within *TWD*'s overall trajectory. Beyond the diverse composition of the hero survivors in terms of their gender, race, religious affiliation and sexuality, one particular scene stands out. In it, three of the female leads – Michonne, Carol, and Maggie – stroll leisurely down a museum corridor and ponder their new roles as leading figures in their communities. Maggie reports that she was recently officially elected as

---

[36] "A New Beginning," 00:09:46–00:10:17.

38   AMC's *The Walking Dead* and the Serial Post-Western

the Hilltop Colony's leader after the former leader, Gregory, called for a vote. Michonne sardonically remarks on "the rebirth of democracy, by that guy," and both express their happiness that the vote favored Maggie.[37] Carol and Michonne, in turn, are leaders of The Kingdom and Alexandria, respectively, partly because of their relationships but also because of their post-apocalyptic survival skills that have been trained, honed and perfected in the previous seasons.

As the two white women walk on, Michonne stops in front of another history display bearing the headline "A More Perfect Union. The Conflicts that Shaped Our Nation" and studies it.[38] Michonne, the main African American character on the show at this point, appears to be acutely aware of the bloody, imperialist, racist history of the pre-apocalyptic United States symbolized by the bloody handprint that covers the display's section on the Civil War. Towards the end of the episode, in their bed in Alexandria, Michonne tells Rick about her idea for a charter to govern the communities.[39] As in this scene, "A New Beginning" consistently pairs Michonne and Rick as the vanguard of the survivor team: the pre-intro scenes first focused on their domestic bliss in Alexandria; they are the first to kill the zombies in D.C. to ensure the convoy's safe passage; they flank the museum doors upon entrance, and, finally, Michonne kills the zombie barring their way. Through their leadership roles both as individual, proficient survivors and as a couple, Michonne and Rick symbolize "a more perfect union" of their own, and as *TWD*'s major interracial couple they signpost the show's increasingly progressive identity politics, which tie *TWD* to the post-Western in its project of building a future from the past.

---

[37]   Ibid., 00:12:24–00:12:48.

[38]   Ibid., 00:12:47–00:12:58.

[39]   Ibid., 00:41:56–00:43:15. In the same scene, Michonne affirms the term 'charter' in response to Rick's question whether 'constitution' might not be the better term. This insistence on not using the name of a document that condoned and perpetuated the institution of chattel slavery in the U.S. suggests again the episode's insistence on both remembering and perfecting the past in order to build a better future by also pointing to a more inclusive conception of belonging and participation for diverse human characters in this new form of civilization.

MAXI ALBRECHT

Both the election that put Maggie in power and the charter that Michonne would create over the course of season nine pose entirely new developments within *TWD*'s storyworld. They signal the beginning of the show's "new era" both in terms of a hopeful outlook regarding human progress as well as more inclusive identity politics, as women and people of color take on leadership roles and the whole cast becomes increasingly diverse. The new epoch of civilization-building in *TWD*, however, continues to be mired in meritocratic ideals represented and negotiated through the show's championing of the survival of the fittest. In the end, *TWD* appears to continuously fall back on its own ideology that survival is a hard business requiring constant self-discipline – an ideology that is also in line with neoliberal ideals of human subjectivity.[40] In his study of the post-Western, Mark Cronlund Anderson points out that it is "tempting to conclude that frontier westerns promote little more than greater inclusiveness and racial tolerance [...] reflect the central cultural depravity and vacuity of a nation deeply given over to consumerist capitalism."[41] While *TWD* thus performs a kind of revisionism on itself in terms of diversity, I suggest that it demonstrates all the more clearly how mere signposting in terms of more inclusive representation does not necessarily lead to progressiveness.

In the end, due to the conditions of *TWD*'s storyworld but also its serial mode of production, "A New Beginning" and the entire season that follows do not literally constitute a new beginning. Soon after they make it out of Washington, the caravan is attacked by zombies, a minor character dies, the plow is broken, and the survival struggle continues.[42] The remainder of the episode, furthermore, demonstrates that the project of building a new civilization among the different survivor communities is fraught with tension, and the apparent unity represented by the group's arrival in Washington is in fact a tenuous consensus ready to

---

[40] Cf. Maxi Albrecht, "'We Are the Walking Dead,' but 'We Ain't Them': Cognitive Exhaustion and the Figure of the Zombie in AMC's *The Walking Dead*," in *Exhaustion and Regeneration in Post-Millennial North-American Literature and Culture*, ed. Julia Nikiel and Izabella Kimak (Berlin: Peter Lang, 2019), 111; Schweitzer, *Going Viral*, 181.

[41] Mark Cronlund Anderson, *Cowboy Imperialism and Hollywood Film* (Berlin: Peter Lang, 2007), 127.

[42] "A New Beginning," 00:21:19–00:24:23.

40 AMC's *The Walking Dead* and the Serial Post-Western

burst. The episode depicts dissent among the characters over the rules for living together again, over the treatment of their defeated former enemies, and over the distribution of resources among the communities. These instances of dissent subsequently drive the plot of the season and intertwine with Rick Grimes's vision for the new world in light of his imminent departure from the show.

As the group returns from their mission, "A New Beginning" also introduces a broken bridge, which becomes Rick's last project on the show.[43] His plan to rebuild the bridge with the help of all the communities becomes both a material and a metaphoric manifestation of the intersecting and diverging strands of this episode that I have discussed above. Rebuilding the bridge is a communal investment in the future, built from the ruins of what came before and the basis of continued progress for the communities. However, the events leading to Rick's departure from the show result in the apparent sacrifice of both the bridge and Rick's own life in order to prevent a large herd of zombies from endangering the other survivors. The departure of this most prominent character from the ensemble cast is an act of sacrifice which simultaneously exposes the fraught nature of his vision for a peaceful new civilization and paves the way for the other, already fully developed lead characters to represent *TWD*'s increasing post-Western diversity.

"Nothing but a Broke Plow"? – On *The Walking Dead*'s Endless Seriality

Later in the episode, Tammy, the mother of the young man who died on the way back from Washington, D.C., angrily confronts Maggie: "She took our boy out there, and for what? […] Nothing but a broke plow. Isn't that right?" To which Maggie responds, "We found more than just a plow. That run was really important for the future," only to be interrupted by Tammy warning her: "Don't you dare talk to me about no future right now."[44] This argument, which foreshadows several conflicts to follow in the wake of this episode, embodies the central tension of

---

[43] Ibid., 00:20:30–00:20:48.
[44] Ibid., 00:25:19–00:25:58.

TWD's moment of reinvention and of survival in the post-Western post-apocalypse that requires constant struggle. This serial, never-ending survival spirit also enables the show's diverging and evolving politics by reimagining the frontier in a post-apocalyptic setting in which each and every aspect of life is ruled by the need to endure in the environment, against both zombies and human survivors.

As the storyworld necessitates violence, and all settlements are ultimately bound to fail, frontier existence in this show is perennial, both because of the conditions of the storyworld and the mandate of a serial television show to always go on, to progress, and to defer closure, which also ties in with the commercial and economic interests of the production in maintaining AMC's most profitable franchise. These very tensions are at the core of *TWD*'s identity as a serial post-apocalypse that employs Western aesthetics while also performing revisionism on itself, particularly with regard to identity politics and the representation of diverse survivors. *TWD* leaves its characters in a constant struggle to survive and even celebrates that struggle, which is ultimately also what ties it to its neoliberal production context, as the show champions survival and the survivors as bearers of human progress. Frank Kelleter argues that one essential aspect of the cultural work of popular seriality is its embrace of "uncertainty about final outcomes, […] the postponement of a definitive end, [and] the promise of perpetual renewal."[45] *TWD*'s serial mediation of survival and its ability to reinvent itself in terms of genre and in terms of its identity politics drive its evolution from Western to post-Western.

---

[45] Frank Kelleter, "Five Ways of Looking at Popular Seriality," in *Media of Serial Narrative*, ed. Frank Kelleter (Columbus: Ohio State University Press, 2017), 8.

42   AMC's *The Walking Dead* and the Serial Post-Western

Works Cited

"A New Beginning." *The Walking Dead*, season 9, episode 1. Aired October 7, 2018, on AMC.

Albrecht, Maxi. "'We Are the Walking Dead,' but 'We Ain't Them': Cognitive Exhaustion and the Figure of the Zombie in AMC's *The Walking Dead*." In *Exhaustion and Regeneration in Post-Millennial North-American Literature and Culture*, edited by Julia Nikiel and Izabella Kimak, 101–113. Berlin: Peter Lang, 2019.

Anderson, Mark Cronlund. *Cowboy Imperialism and Hollywood Film*. Berlin: Peter Lang, 2007.

Borden, Diane M., and Eric P. Essman. "Manifest Landscape/Latent Ideology: Afterimages of Empire in the Western and 'Post-Western' Film." *California History* 79, no. 1 (2000): 30-41.

Campbell, Neil. *Post-Westerns: Cinema, Region, West*. Lincoln: University of Nebraska Press, 2013.

"Days Gone Bye." *The Walking Dead*, season 1, episode 1. Aired October 31, 2013, on AMC.

Gurr, Barbara. "Masculinity, Race, and the (Re?)Imagined American Frontier." In *Race, Gender, and Sexuality in Post-Apocalyptic TV and Film*, edited by Barbara Gurr, 31–44. London: Palgrave Macmillan, 2015.

Hassler-Forest, Dan. "Cowboys and Zombies: Destabilizing Patriarchal Discourse in *The Walking Dead*." *Studies in Comics* 2, no. 2 (2012): 339–355.

Hibberd, James. "'Walking Dead' Once Again Beats 'Sunday Night Football.'" *Entertainment Weekly*, November 2, 2014. ew.com/article/2014/11/03/walking-dead-ratings-once-again-beat-sunday-night-football/.

Keeler, Amanda. "A Postapocalyptic Return to the Frontier: *The Walking Dead* as Post-Western." *Critical Studies in Television* 13, no. 4 (2018): 422–437.

Keetley, Dawn. "Introduction: Identity Politics in *The Walking Dead*." In *The Politics of Race, Gender and Sexuality in* The Walking Dead: *Essays on the Television Series and Comics*, edited by Dawn Keetley and Elizabeth Erwin, 1–9. Jefferson: McFarland, 2018.

---. "Introduction: 'We're All Infected.'" In *We're All Infected": Essays on AMC's* The Walking Dead *and the Fate of the Human*, edited by Dawn Keetley, 3–25. Jefferson: McFarland, 2014.

---. "'The Walking Dead' and the Rise of Donald Trump." *Pop Matters*, March 16, 2016. popmatters.com/the-walking-dead-and-the-rise-of-donald-trump-2495444431.html.

Kelleter, Frank. "Five Ways of Looking at Popular Seriality." In *Media of Serial Narrative*, edited by Frank Kelleter, 7–34. Columbus: Ohio State University Press, 2017.

Lavin, Melissa, and Brian Lowe. "Cops and Zombies: Hierarchy and Social Location in *The Walking Dead*." In *Race, Gender, and Sexuality in Post-Apocalyptic TV and Film*, edited by Barbara Gurr, 113–124. London: Palgrave Macmillan, 2015.

Otterson, Joe. "'Walking Dead' Season 8 Finale Ratings Lowest Since Season 1." *Variety*, April 17, 2018. variety.com/2018/tv/news/walking-dead-season-8-finale-ratings-1202754602/.

Porter, Rick. "Sunday Cable Ratings: 'The Walking Dead' Premiere Kills It with Second-Highest Ratings Ever." *TV by the Numbers*, October 25, 2016. tvbythenumbers.zap2it.com/daily-ratings/sunday-cable-ratings-oct-23-2016-walking-dead-premiere/.

Rees, Shelley S. "Frontier Values Meet Big-City Zombies: The Old West in AMC's *The Walking Dead*." In *Undead in the West: Vampires, Zombies, Mummies, and Ghosts on the Cinematic Frontier*, edited by Cynthia J. Miller and A. Bowdoin Van Riper, 90–102. Lanham: Scarecrow, 2012.

Ross, Dalton. "'The Walking Dead' EP Says Season 9 Will Focus on Female Leadership." *Entertainment Weekly*, July 17, 2018. ew.com/tv/2018/07/17/walking-dead-season-9-showrunner-female-leadership/.

Russell, Jamie. *Book of the Dead: The Complete History of Zombie Cinema*. London: Titan, 2014.

Sartain, Jeffrey A. "Days Gone Bye: Robert Kirkman's Reenvisioned Western *The Walking Dead*." In *Undead in the West II: They Just Keep Coming*, edited by Cynthia J. Miller and A. Bowdoin Van Riper, 237–254. Lanham: Scarecrow, 2013.

Schweitzer, Dahlia. *Going Viral: Zombies, Viruses, and the End of the World*. New Brunswick: Rutgers University Press, 2018.

44 AMC's *The Walking Dead* and the Serial Post-Western

"Season 9 Preview Special." *Talking Dead*. Aired August 5, 2018, on AMC.

Sigmon, Tyler. "A Petition for Scott Gimple to Be Removed from *The Walking Dead* Productions and Content." *Change.org*, January 9, 2020.change.org/p/amc-tv-a-petition-for-scott-gimple-to-be-removed -from-the-walking-dead-productions-and-content.

Sulimma, Maria. "Serial Gender, Gendered Serialities: Practices of US-American Television Narratives in the 21st Century." PhD diss., Freie Universität Berlin, 2018.

Tassi, Paul. "The Walking Dead's Falling Ratings Are About To Get A Whole Lot Worse." *Forbes*, October 14, 2018. forbes.com/sites/ insertcoin/2018/10/14/the-walking-deads-falling-ratings-are-about-to -get-a-whole-lot-worse/.

Young, P. Ivan. "Walking Tall or Walking Dead? The American Cowboy in the Zombie Apocalypse." In *"We're All Infected": Essays on AMC's* The Walking Dead *and the Fate of the Human*, edited by Dawn Keetley, 56–67. Jefferson: McFarland, 2014.

ABIGAIL FAGAN

Jubal Early in Space: The Settler Colonial Hauntings of Joss Whedon's *Firefly*

Settler colonial ideologies maintain their preeminence through the performative repetition of settler colonial values at all levels of cultural production. Unlike other forms of colonialism, the ultimate goal of settler colonizers is not the exploitation of land and labor from countries considered to be geographically and hierarchically distinct from the metropole. Instead, colonizers in settler colonial contexts aim to erase the existence of the colonized. In order to naturalize their use and ownership of Indigenous nations' land, settler colonizers displace Indigenous nations and erase their cultural legacies. In this paper, I describe how popular culture media participate in this ongoing process of erasure. In television series like *Firefly* (Fox, 2002–2003), Netflix's *The Chilling Adventures of Sabrina* (2018–), and the first season of HBO's *American Gods* (2017), for instance, settler colonial values are reinforced through thematic treatment of the settling of America absent sustained engagement of the Indigenous population who lived on this territory historically and who continues to inhabit it. While *American Gods* ultimately reckoned with this oversight by introducing the Indigenous character Sam Blackcrow (played by Kawennáhere Devery Jacobs, an actress of Kanien'kehá:ka nationality) in its second season, television series like *Firefly* reimagine narratives of Anglo-European settler colonialism through the lens of *terra nullius*. In doing so, popular culture participates in the reification of settler colonial ideologies, which ultimately naturalize a popular understanding of the United States as a nation of immigrants and its original Indigenous inhabitants as physically and culturally erased.

Meaning "no one's land" in Latin, *terra nullius* is central to a number of myths about the national formation of countries like the U.S. that circulate in the media of popular culture. One myth is that there

46 The Settler Colonial Hauntings of Joss Whedon's *Firefly*

were no significant populations present when Europeans arrived on the land that has since become known as the Americas. Because no civilizations were there, this myth suggests, the English, for instance, were justified in claiming this land as their discovery and therefore their property. Any critical consideration of these territories' history reveals this myth to be myth alone, but it operates at numerous levels of settler colonial society, particularly in court cases that debate property rights and in the media of popular culture, such as television series and Blockbuster films. These legal and popular representations of *terra nullius* show us that the concept itself is performative. By repeatedly invoking this myth, artifacts of popular culture like television series participate in the ongoing erasure of Indigenous nations from frontier narratives by depicting the landscapes of American history and imagined American futures as devoid of Indigenous life.

But *terra nullius* also operates in a performative way in critiques of early settlers' world views that recognize Indigenous histories in settler colonial countries. In retellings of first contact between settlers and Indigenous people in legal, historicist, and popular discourse, settlers are often cast as so fundamentally racist that they did not recognize Indigenous people as people. An original and historical racism is blamed for a settler colonial present. This perception of the history of settler colonial countries is particularly attractive to the corporate producers of mass media, because it makes the act of settling appear static, as though it is over and done with. This stasis prevents people today from recognizing themselves as inheritors of settler colonial relationships, particularly in terms of access to wealth. Especially in settler colonial situations such as those in the U.S., Canada, and Australia, moreover, presuming the act of settling to be historically static makes reparations appear impossible or irrelevant. As Lorenzo Veracini has written, settler colonialism functions through a long-term, repetitive, and continuous process of Indigenous nations' material and ideological erasure.[1] In other words, settler colonial nations never stop settling.

Terra nullius serves settler colonial societies today by perpetuating the notion that settling can be a benign act – the mere appropriation of land – and not a violent, dehumanizing ideological and material project

---

[1] Lorenzo Veracini, "Introducing: Settler Colonial Studies," *Settler Colonial Studies* 1, no. 1 (2011): 1–12.

ABIGAIL FAGAN

of physical and cultural genocide. But as scholars such as Michael Connor and Andrew Fitzmaurice have argued, applying the term *terra nullius* to original instances of European settler colonization in the fifteenth through seventeenth centuries is anachronistic: the term itself was not used in popular or legal discourse until the early twentieth century. While Connor ironically uses this fact to performatively delimit Aboriginal claims to land in Australia, thereby creating a kind of *terra nullius* through claims that the concept didn't exist in the eighteenth century,[2] Fitzmaurice proposes that concepts like *terra nullius* were consistently used in international law to argue *against* the settler colonization of the Americas and Australia. Fitzmaurice writes that the term was originally used in 1908 to describe Spitzbergen, an island in the Arctic that was inhabited only in the summer by an ever-changing crew of European fishermen. In fact, the most relevant use of the term in recent international legalese has come from the space race: how do we handle the *terra nullius* of the moon?

While the specific term *terra nullius* was an early twentieth-century invention, scholars and politicians of the sixteenth and seventeenth centuries did adopt Roman laws for their discussions of the colonization of America and Africa, particularly *ferae bestiae* and *res nullius*. Meaning "the law of the wild beasts," *ferae bestiae* can be understood as the "law of the first taker."[3] Fitzmaurice writes, "The theologians of Salamanca, most famously Francesco di Vitoria, used *ferae bestiae* to argue that the Spanish conquests were unjust because the land and property of the vanquished American civilizations clearly had not been

---

[2]   Cf. Michael Connor, *The Invention of Terra Nullius* (Paddington: Macleay, 2005); Lorenzo Veracini, "Terra Nullius and the 'History Wars,'" *On Line Opinion*, February 10, 2006, onlineopinion.com.au/view.asp?article=4141. Aileen Moreton-Robinson describes how English explorers like James Cook misunderstood Aboriginal notions of land ownership and use in order to acquire this land, despite England's official (though disingenuous) stance of respecting Indigenous and Aboriginal land as the opposite of *terra nullius*. See Aileen Moreton-Robinson, *The White Possessive: Property, Power, and Indigenous Sovereignty* (Minneapolis: University of Minnesota Press, 2015), especially 109–122.

[3]   Andrew Fitzmaurice, "The Genealogy of Terra Nullius," *Australian Historical Studies* 38, no. 129 (2008): 6.

48 The Settler Colonial Hauntings of Joss Whedon's *Firefly*

in a state where they could be appropriated by the first taker."[4] This law differs from *terra nullius* in that it places emphasis not on the emptiness of land or object, but on the act of taking and the status of owner. Nevertheless, for the scholars and politicians who employed this Roman law throughout these early centuries of European expansion, *ferae bestiae* was used not to justify colonization but to argue *against* it.

Lauren Benton and Benjamin Straumann add that many Europeans also invoked a conglomerate notion of *res nullius* – which also signifies the lack of ownership rather than the emptiness of land – to navigate relationships with Indigenous people in the Americas in particular. But just as Fitzmaurice argues, Benton and Straumann demonstrate that the vast majority of these theorists, explorers, and conquerors consistently recognized both the occupation of land in the 'New World' and the use to which Indigenous nations put this land, and, therefore, Indigenous ownership of it. Although some English settlers of what would become the U.S. did suggest that the land was rightfully English – rather than Indigenous – according to interpretations of Roman legal concepts like *res nullius* and *ferae bestiae*, these concepts did not become the precedent on which the English acquired land; while members of the Virginia Company espoused *res nullius*, they created (often unfair) trade agreements with Indigenous nations for the land they acquired.[5] I do not make these distinctions in order to justify early settler behavior, but rather to disrupt the notion that early settlers can alone be considered responsible for the violence of settler colonialism; instead, settler colonialism is an ongoing process that obscures its inherently violent operations by allocating this violence to static historical events.

Identifying *terra nullius* as an anachronistic means of critiquing the origins of settler colonial societies points to the performative nature of the term. Myths about the relevance of *terra nullius* are repeated over and over again across numerous levels of society, including law, the media of popular culture, and both scholarly and popular treatments of American history. It is this repetition that allows *terra nullius* to look like an accepted fact even though it never was. Nevertheless, Critical Indigenous scholars such as Aileen Moreton-Robinson, Jodi Byrd, and

---

[4] Ibid., 6–7.
[5] See Lauren Benton and Benjamin Straumann, "Acquiring Empire by Law: From Roman Doctrine to Early Modern European Practice," *Law and History Review* 28, no. 1 (2010): 36.

ABIGAIL FAGAN 49

Roxanne Dunbar-Ortiz have emphasized the point that many settlers behaved as though the *terra* of a wide variety of 'new worlds' was *nullius*. And indeed: without dehumanizing the Indigenous nations of what would become Canada, the U.S., and Australia, these current iterations of white supremacist settler colonial nations could not have developed.[6] But I argue that allowing this early relationship to be understood through *terra nullius* specifically too easily allows legislators, as well as the average consumer of popular culture's products, to accept settler colonialism as a historical event rather than an ongoing process that shaped and continues to shape normative understandings of human relations in these countries. For instance, in the series *The Chilling Adventures of Sabrina*, the settlement narrative of American history is central to the ways that the plot develops, but the Indigenous nations that populated the land on which the fictional setting is based are entirely absent from the story.

Media productions furthermore obscure the historical impact that the existence of Indigenous nations had on European epistemologies. As Sylvia Wynter and Katherine McKittrick have written, this impact did not originate in the shock that the *terra* of the 'New World' was *nullius* – that it was uninhabited – but rather that, to Europeans, the 'New World' was *uninhabitable*.[7] According to Abrahamic worldviews, a continent separate from Europe/Asia/Africa could not exist above the waters of the Atlantic Ocean, which was presumed to seamlessly meet the Pacific. But the discovery that was most antithetical to the Abrahamic world view was that this unexpected continent was in fact inhabited. How were the descendants of Adam and Eve to have populated a continent that was entirely separate from Europe and completely unknown to Europeans? Wynter theorizes Columbus's 'discovery' of the New World as a foundational break that supported the

---

[6] See Moreton-Robinson, *The White Possessive*, 109–122; Jodi Byrd, *The Transit of Empire: Indigenous Critiques of Colonialism* (Minneapolis: University of Minnesota Press, 2011), 22; 63–64; Roxanne Dunbar-Ortiz, *An Indigenous Peoples' History of the United States* (Boston: Beacon Press, 2014), 230–231.

[7] See Katherine McKittrick, *Demonic Grounds: Black Women and the Cartographies of Struggle* (Minneapolis: University of Minnesota Press, 2006), 124–127.

50 The Settler Colonial Hauntings of Joss Whedon's *Firefly*

rise of the scientific, rather than God-governed notion, of "Man."[8] This break arises from the European recognition that the uninhabitable land of the New World was inhabited after all – the shock that this *terra* was by no means *nullius*.

The only real *terra nullius* that earthlings have ever encountered therefore is the *terra nullius* of the moon and the planets beyond it, presuming of course that they are in fact uninhabited. Ironically, very few serial treatments of extraterrestrial travel have conceptualized the solar systems beyond ours as being devoid of life. Series and films like *Star Trek* and *Star Wars* engage the colonization narrative by depicting encounters between the soldiers and citizens that occupy spaceships of discovery and the inhabitants of extraterrestrial planets. And this brings me to *Firefly*, the bizarre, genre-busting series that Joss Whedon created and produced during its very short run on Fox in 2002 and 2003. Drawing on a wide range of familiar genres and narratives, not least Western narratives of benevolent Robin Hood-like vigilantes and explorer-oriented narratives of discovery in space, *Firefly* focuses on the adventures of Captain Malcolm "Mal" Reynolds (Nathan Fillion) and his motley crew, who fly through a solar system of colonized planets, stealing from the rich and selling to the poor. The crew's ironically moralistic modus operandi of kind-hearted crime is complicated by two of its members, Dr. Simon Tam (Sean Maher) and his psychic little sister, River (Summer Glau), who are fugitives from the Alliance, the federal/corporate power of Whedon's futuristic solar system. This paper focuses on the series' final episode, *Objects in Space*, in which the bounty hunter Jubal Early (Richard Brooks) arrives to capture River and return her to the Alliance. Within the strikingly similar narratives of the frontier/space exploration, Mal and his crew can be understood as settler outcasts, quirky figures who are presented as rebelliously occupying the outer borders of the Alliance's territory in order to avoid the duties and restrictions of citizenship under an unjust and normalizing regime.

The insertion of themes from the Western genre into *Firefly*'s plot and setting draws more clearly together the tropes associated with settling a historical American frontier and the plot of space-age

---

[8] See Sylvia Wynter, "Unsettling the Coloniality of Being/Power/Truth/ Freedom: Towards the Human, After Man, Its Overrepresentation – An Argument," *CR: The New Centennial Review* 3, no. 3 (2003): 283–311.

ABIGAIL FAGAN   51

extraterrestrial discovery as inherently evocative of the European colonization of the Americas, Africa, Oceania, and South-East Asia. Mal and his crew are marked by features of both the cowboy and the space explorer. But whereas the cowboy, in particular, is developed in binary relationship to the 'Indian' in the Western genre, character development in *Firefly* proceeds without contrast from indigenous figures like the 'Indian'. Unlike *Star Trek* and *Star Wars*, Whedon made the deliberate decision to imagine his futuristic solar system as populated by the original inhabitants of Earth alone. He said, for instance,

> I wanted to get a show that took the past and the future and put them together by making them feel like the present, by making a show with [...] troubles that people could relate to, as opposed to aliens or bumpy foreheads or ambassadors or things that are not part of everyday life.[9]

Whedon also retained the Western imagery of the American frontier in his reconceptualization of extraterrestrial settler colonialism. Whedon's 'final frontier' is populated by gun-slinging, horse-riding bandits playing out the ur-American struggle between provincial mavericks and the threat of a centralized, totalitarian federal regime or, more fittingly, corporation.

Whedon's adoption of American frontier imagery and development of a space-age provincial slang that emulates the cowboy's twang makes his removal of an indigenous figure from his fictional frontier still more ironic. How does one establish the figure of the cowboy without establishing his constitutive Other, the 'Indian'?

The answer is: through affect. My understanding of affect here draws on the work of Brian Massumi, who argues that affect is a felt perception or sensation that must be differentiated from the linguistic and therefore cognitive articulation of emotions, like sadness or anger.[10] But as in Rachel Greenwald Smith's reading of fiction about traumatic events, I'm less focused on the significance of the distinction between affect and emotion and more interested in the ways that artistic productions evoke a sensation of uncanniness or anxiety in relationship

---

[9] Joss Whedon, "The Making of Firefly," *Firefly: The Complete Series* (Los Angeles: 20th Century Fox, 2005), DVD disc 4.

[10] See Brian Massumi, *Parables for the Virtual. Movement, Affect, Sensation* (Durham: Duke University Press, 2002), 25–27.

52 The Settler Colonial Hauntings of Joss Whedon's *Firefly*

to historical instances of trauma.[11] While I cannot speak to other viewers' felt responses to *Objects in Space*, I do argue that Whedon used cinematic and narrative techniques in order to evoke a sensation of uncanniness or agitation in the episode that recalls a sensation of anxiety that has been historically associated with the process of settling. In other words, while Whedon removes the indigenous figure from his fictional solar system, he retains the tropes and uncanniness of the inhabited uninhabitable that characterizes early America's settler colonial society.

Throughout the series, a group of people called the Reavers are often the source of the characters' terror within the narrative itself, and the Reavers are filmed in ways that exacerbate their uncanniness. Like many racialized figures in narratives of conquest, the Reavers are depicted as abject through their apparent enjoyment of inflicting pain on others, as well as on themselves, especially through bodily modification. The Reavers also appear monstrous because their bodies are confounded visually through camerawork dominated by jump cuts and fast-moving camera panning. The Reavers act, to some extent, like the 'Indians' of the Western genre: they evoke terror because they do not appear to act according to the rational or moral expectations of the series' protagonists, particularly in terms of the way they clothe themselves and surgically manipulate their physical appearances. Nevertheless, I am hesitant to suggest that the Reavers fill the role of indigenous figures in Whedon's Western spacescape. After the series itself was prematurely cancelled in December 2002, Whedon – supported by the series' dedicated fanbase – successfully pitched a film to tie up one of the many storylines towards which the show's fourteen episodes gestured. The film, named *Serenity* (2005) after the somewhat junked spaceship on which Mal and his crew lived, picks up the series' narrative sometime after the final episode, *Objects in Space*. As the film ultimately reveals, the Reavers were originally created by the Alliance's attempts to chemically manipulate human behavior. Because of this origin story, suggesting that the Reavers stand in for the 'Indian' in *Firefly*'s universe also recenters Western epistemology, naturalizing European-centric historical narratives by allowing Europeans to become the alpha and omega of human existence. By rejecting an understanding of the

---

[11] See Rachel Greenwald Smith, "Organic Shrapnel: Affect and Aesthetics in September 11 Fiction," *American Literature* 83, no. 1 (2011): 153–174.

ABIGAIL FAGAN 53

Reavers as 'Indians,' I aim to foreground a decolonial perspective that insists on the existence of other epistemologies and civilizations that preceded Europeans' 'first contact' with, for instance, the Indigenous nations of the territory colonially known as America.[12]

After all, it is not only the Reavers who populate the empty space between worlds that acts as the primary setting for many of *Firefly*'s episodes. By introducing unexpected figures into this space, Whedon performatively employs the uncanniness of the inhabited uninhabitable. *Objects in Space* evokes the uncanniness of Jubal Early's appearance from the start of the episode by introducing the character into the narrative using both dramatic irony and a jump scare. Whedon, who wrote and directed *Objects in Space*, repeatedly plays on the significance of the episode's title by drawing attention to the way that objects and characters occupy their home, the spaceship *Serenity,* as well as the way that *Serenity* itself occupies the emptiness of space. The significance of the *emptiness* of space is emphasized at the beginning of the episode when the image of *Serenity*, a type of spacecraft called "firefly" for its evocation of the insect's body, is suddenly accompanied by the image of another spaceship – Jubal Early's. Immediately after Mal warns his crew, "We are very much alone out here," a sudden clap on the musical track turns Jubal Early's entrance into a jump scare.[13] Early's ship resembles a predatory insect descending on the thick, homey-looking body of Mal's benign 'firefly.'

This jump scare evokes the affective terror of settling the inhabited uninhabitable that is present in much early American literature. The space in which Mal's crew is moving is presumed to be uninhabited

---

[12] During my presentation of an earlier version of this paper, Professor Grace Dillon mentioned a project by Indigenous film students in British Columbia that proclaimed, "We are the Reavers!" This identification is not unfounded: the opposition between the Reavers and Mal's crew certainly recalls the Western genre's binary opposition of 'Indian' and cowboy. But particularly because I am a scholar of Canadian and U.S. settler heritage, I want to hold popular cultural productions of settler-Indigenous relationships accountable to the facts that Indigenous nations continue to exist and that they existed prior to contact with Europeans and beyond European cultural imaginations.

[13] Joss Whedon, "Objects in Space: Commentary by Executive Producer Joss Whedon," *Firefly: The Complete Series* (Los Angeles: 20th Century Fox, 2005), DVD disc 4, 00:05:54.

54   The Settler Colonial Hauntings of Joss Whedon's *Firefly*

because it is uninhabitable: not only is it the deadly vacuum of space, but it is also the space between the impoverished, isolated and primitive outposts of this colonized solar system's "outer rim." The jump scare makes space a science-fiction metaphor for early America's forests. To the settler's eye, these dark, densely packed woods that formed the borders of many settler towns throughout what would become the eastern and midwestern United States were perceived as uncultivated and uninhabitable, largely because the settler was incapable of reading signs of Indigenous civilization and cultivation.[14]

Because the forest was depicted in early American literature as uncultivated and uninhabitable, the original residents of this terrain were cast as monstrous. In early American captivity narratives by women like Mary Rowlandson and Hannah Duston, 'Indian' attacks on settler towns are read not as battles in an ongoing war, but rather as gruesome, monstrous and violent acts that – like the forest – do not signify comfortably in the settlers' symbolic worldview. One salient example of this phenomenon can be found in documents associated with the Salem Witch Trials, in which both the forest and methods of torture undertaken during King Philip's War and King William's War were thematized in narratives of witch afflictions. As Mary Beth Norton has convincingly argued, settlers from Maine fled to Massachusetts during and between these two wars, bringing narratives of dismemberment, murder by mob, and fire-based torture along with them. As these narratives inflected the witch trials, complainants likened Indigenous warriors to witches, reminding settlers that the surrounding forest and the people who inhabited it should be considered satanic. As Cotton Mather wrote in his summary of the witch trials, Puritans were portrayed as being under siege by forest-dwelling witches and Satan because they were God's cultivators in the devil's land.[15] Mather put the forest that housed many Indigenous nations of the eastern seaboard and the Midwest into a binary relationship with the settlers' farmlands. This juxtaposition remains both deeply entrenched and obfuscated in settler popular culture, in which the forest is repeatedly portrayed as dark and scary.[16]

---

[14]   See Dunbar-Ortiz, *An Indigenous Peoples' History*, 27–28.

[15]   Cotton Mather, *Wonders of the Invisible World* (Lincoln: Zea E-Books, 2011), xii.

[16]   This opposition is taken up in Anishinaabe theory and praxis about decolonization or *biskaabiiyang*, as well. See Grace Dillon, *Walking the*

This relationship between the forests cultivated by Indigenous nations and farmlands cultivated by European settlers stands in for an understanding of early America as a battleground. Written records of wars and their aftermath have shown us that the brutality of war is difficult to represent within the symbolic order. This difficulty of making violence signify is exacerbated in a settler colonial system in which families participate directly in the theater of war: families settle land already inhabited by other families. Warriors do not depart for a battleground far away and return physically and psychologically damaged after the war is over. The damage is local. American settlers worked through this damage ideologically by Othering Indigenous warriors and by casting them as irrational yet capable killers who emerged from the uninhabitable to brutally slaughter settler families, who are portrayed as being separate from the war and innocent of the war effort. In this continuous process of Othering the Indigenous inhabitants of the ever-expanding frontier, the American cowboy would later emerge. The cowboy would be typically presented as violent, but ultimately not culpable in genocide – a genocide that is also presented as a static historical event, not an ongoing process. In *Firefly*, this genocide is so complete that the myth of *terra nullius* becomes the underlying assumption of the series' world-building.

And yet, Whedon adopts the uncanny terror of settling in *Firefly* by introducing an inhabitant of the uninhabitable. Jubal Early successfully infiltrates the spaceship-home, *Serenity,* and threatens a variety of the show's main characters in his attempt to kidnap the adolescent fugitive River and return her to the Alliance for a significant bounty. During his search for River, Early uses physical violence and threatens to use sexual violence against members of the ship in a way that is ironically portrayed as both calculating and excessive.

The uncanny terror that Early embodies comes to a head when River accuses him over the ship's communication system of being a sadist. "You like to hurt folk," she says in the cowboy parlance of *Serenity's*

Clouds: An Anthology of Indigenous Science Fiction (Tucson: University of Arizona Press, 2012), 10; and Leanne Betasamosake Simpson, *As We Have Always Done: Indigenous Freedom through Radical Resistance* (Minneapolis: University of Minnesota Press, 2017), 17. As Dillon told me at the 2019 GAAS conference, *biskaabiiyang* can also be translated as "returning to the woods."

56 The Settler Colonial Hauntings of Joss Whedon's *Firefly*

crew.[17] As River continues, narrating her apparently psychic perception that Early tortured a dog as a child, the camera focuses on Early's face. Depicted through a series of jump cuts, Early's response to River's words appears to be a chaotic, extreme, and contradictory variety of emotions: laughter, enjoyment, pride, anger, and confusion. In the director's commentary on the episode, Whedon said that he asked actor Richard Brooks during filming to "Go crazy. React to everything she says as intensely as possible," so that Whedon could ultimately "intercut" these reactions "with the specific purpose of showing a fractured mind."[18] Though Early typically appears calm and cold throughout the episode, Whedon's series of shots here suggests that Early operates beyond the realm of the symbolic in which the other characters function. His ability to coldly and excessively cause pain – and his enjoyment of it – is depicted as uncanny irrationality boiling under his smooth, controlled visage. By emerging from the uninhabitable vacuum of space, Early brings an element of the Other onto the ship *Serenity* itself. In other words, though Whedon does not represent and villainize the Indigenous in his futuristic Western narrative, he does recreate the affective sensation of this villainization, of representing an inhabitant of the uninhabitable as ideologically outside the heroes' symbolic order through the narrative production of an uneasy or anxious affect.

This use of Early as Other is still further complicated in that he is played by the African-American actor, Richard Brooks. Within the narrative itself, Jubal Early's race is irrelevant to the characters. In fact, both the series and the associated film appear to take place in a largely post-racial universe. While characters grapple with hierarchies associated with class and allegiance to the Alliance, characters played by actors of Asian, European, and African descent interact without conflicts associated with race or ethnicity. But as I have been arguing here, the series invokes race-based hierarchies related to the establishment of the United States as a settler colonial and white supremacist nation through its use of generic tropes related to frontier imagery and the processes of settler colonialism. Therefore, while Early's Blackness is irrelevant to the characters, it is significant to the viewers and to the ways in which

---

[17] Whedon, "Objects in Space," 00:36:06.
[18] Ibid.

Blackness is consistently Othered in American media, history, and law. Particularly because *Firefly* does not trouble this alliance of Early's sadism with both his Blackness and his role in the episode as Other, the episode performatively reinforces anti-Black prejudices. In fact, the narrative evokes the stereotype of fatherless Black families that conservative legislators have used to repeal and weaken policies that support African-American communities, in particular, by focusing on Early's childhood relationship with his mother.[19] River tells him that his mother "knew" that he was a sadist, continuing, "Sadness in her when she waved good-bye. She's relieved. Saw a darkness in you."[20] Not only is Early's Otherness underlined by his mother's presumed sense of relief at his departure, this association of the character's psychosis with the narratorial absence of his father invokes anti-Black discourses that compound the racial significance of Early's role as Other. While his capacity to inhabit the uninhabitable unleashes a sensation of uncanniness within the narrative, his Blackness further invokes the cultural narratives that European-Americans used to justify the enslavement of people of African descent. Early's unrelatability in this scene operates on and further underwrites racist tropes associated with both Indigenous and Black Americans.

These layers of racial Othering are made still more ironic by the fact that Whedon got the name for his uncanny villain from American history. The historical Jubal Early was a staunch Confederate during and after the American Civil War who began his military career during the period of Indian Removal in the 1830s and was originally commissioned as a lieutenant to fight the Seminole Nation in Florida. The historical Early's military career throws Whedon's post-racial future into stark relief. Whedon romantically adopts Confederate pathos in his depiction of space-age cowboys at the same time as he erases the foundational role that race played in both settler wars against Indigenous nations and the

---

[19] Hortense Spillers's response to the emphasis on this stereotype in Daniel Patrick Moynihan's 1965 report on Black poverty forms the foundation of significant critical frameworks on global ideologies that operate on and instrumentalize anti-Blackness, particularly Afropessimism. See Hortense Spillers, "Mama's Baby, Papa's Maybe: An American Grammar Book," in *Black, White, and in Color: Essays on American Literature and Culture* (Chicago: University of Chicago Press, 2003), 203–229.

[20] Whedon, "Objects in Space," 00:36:11.

58   The Settler Colonial Hauntings of Joss Whedon's *Firefly*

Civil War itself, i.e., the fact that the Confederates were fighting to uphold the system of race-based slavery. What he retains from these historical events, however, are many of the affective registers. Mal and his crew are steeped in the emotional tensions associated with Confederate sympathizers: they are depicted as heroic losers fighting a lost battle, as heroic losers navigating the inhabited uninhabitable and, by virtue of their wits and the establishment of a settler community, surviving attacks by the uninhabitable's racialized and uncanny Others. The anxiety of navigating the inhabited uninhabitable – the anxiety of settling – is a consistent affective feature of both the series and the film, even though Indigenous figures themselves are not represented.

Even in texts that accept *terra nullius* as an original or simply viable script for narratives of American history and potential American futures, therefore, affective representations of the violence of settling persistently suggest that that *terra* was never *nullius*. While there are no indigenous figures in *Firefly*, the anxiety of settling the inhabited uninhabitable remains a significant narrative tool for developing the familial relationships among the settler protagonists. *Objects in Space* acts as a kind of proxy for the series' unexpected conclusion, because it brings River – who had alienated *Serenity's* crew in an earlier episode – back into the fold as the figure who saved the crew from a violent Other. In contrast, Early and the Others he represents are physically and ideologically excluded in this process. At the end of the episode, he is seen spinning off through space in his thin spacesuit, doomed to die alone and commenting, "Well, here I am."[21]

The narrative production of affect that evokes the anxiety of settling within this episode should not be considered a proximal representation of Indigenous people. In fact, it dangerously removes people from narratives of settling. By retaining the settlers' anxiety, uncanniness, or fear *without* retaining an understanding of this anxiety and fear as being mutually felt between settlers and Indigenous people, artifacts of popular culture like *Firefly* preclude reparations in any form whatsoever. The phobia of xenophobia is affectively confirmed without any risky representation of the Indigenous, representations which could then be actively deconstructed. By removing people from this dynamic, only affect remains. And as Brian Massumi has convincingly demonstrated,

---

[21]   Ibid., 00:43:16.

affect has been employed in the United States' and Australia's xenophobic and violent foreign policy to create a sense of factual threat over the past twenty years.[22] Because *Firefly* melds the genres of the Western and science fiction, it necessarily contends with the narrative of settling – even though it does not contend with narratives of indigeneity. *Firefly* shows us how problematic this oversight is, especially since the narrative of settling and the anxieties of moving through the inhabited uninhabitable are represented in many other artifacts of popular culture as well. Particularly at a time in which xenophobia is a constant companion of political and popular cultural appeals, scholars and consumers of popular culture need to be aware of the way that representations of this kind of anxiety performatively reproduce violent racial hierarchies.

Thank you to René Dietrich and Jens Temmen, whose panel, "The Popular Culture of U.S. Settler Colonialism," was the occasion for this paper. I am also indebted to my co-presenters Ho'esta Mo'e'hahne, Marianne Kongerslev, and Marek Paryż, and the audience of the panel for their challenging feedback. Special thanks to Grace Dillon, who was so generous with her time, experience, and knowledge, and whose feedback has significantly improved the quality of this essay.

---

[22] See Brian Massumi, "The Future Birth of the Affective Fact: The Political Ontology of Threat," in *The Affect Theory Reader*, ed. Melissa Gregg and Gregory J. Seigworth (Durham: Duke University Press, 2010), 52–70.

Works Cited

Benton, Lauren, and Benjamin Straumann. "Acquiring Empire by Law: From Roman Doctrine to Early Modern European Practice." *Law and History Review* 28, no. 1 (2010): 1–38.

Byrd, Jodi. *The Transit of Empire: Indigenous Critiques of Colonialism.* Minneapolis: University of Minnesota Press, 2011.

Connor, Michael. *The Invention of Terra Nullius.* Paddington: Macleay, 2005.

Dillon, Grace, ed. *Walking the Clouds: An Anthology of Indigenous Science Fiction.* Tucson: University of Arizona Press, 2012.

Dunbar-Ortiz, Roxanne. *An Indigenous Peoples' History of the United States.* Boston: Beacon Press, 2014.

Fitzmaurice, Andrew. "The Genealogy of Terra Nullius." *Australian Historical Studies* 38, no. 129 (2008): 1–15.

Massumi, Brian. "The Future Birth of the Affective Fact: The Political Ontology of Threat." In *The Affect Theory Reader*, edited by Melissa Gregg and Gregory J. Seigworth, 52–70. Durham: Duke University Press, 2010.

---. *Parables for the Virtual: Movement, Affect, Sensation.* Durham: Duke University Press, 2002.

Mather, Cotton. *Wonders of the Invisible World.* Lincoln: Zea E-Books, 2011.

McKittrick, Katherine. *Demonic Grounds: Black Women and the Cartographies of Struggle.* Minneapolis: University of Minnesota Press, 2006.

Moreton-Robinson, Aileen. *The White Possessive: Property, Power, and Indigenous Sovereignty.* Minneapolis: University of Minnesota Press, 2015.

Norton, Mary Beth. *In the Devil's Snare: The Witchcraft Crisis of 1692.* New York: Knopf, 2002.

Simpson, Leanne Betasamosake. *As We Have Always Done: Indigenous Freedom through Radical Resistance.* Minneapolis: University of Minnesota Press, 2017.

Smith, Rachel Greenwald. "Organic Shrapnel: Affect and Aesthetics in September 11 Fiction." *American Literature* 83, no. 1 (2011): 153–174.

Spillers, Hortense. "Mama's Baby, Papa's Maybe: An American Grammar Book, 1987." In *Black, White, and in Color: Essays on American Literature and Culture*, 203–229. Chicago: University of Chicago Press, 2003.

Veracini, Lorenzo. "Introducing: Settler Colonial Studies." *Settler Colonial Studies* 1, no. 1 (2011): 1–12.

---. "Terra Nullius and the 'History Wars.'" *On Line Opinion*, February 10, 2006. onlineopinion.com.au/view.asp?article=4141.

Whedon, Joss, director. "The Making of Firefly." *Firefly: The Complete Series*. Los Angeles: 20th Century Fox, 2005. DVD, disc 4.

---. writer and director. "Objects in Space." *Firefly: The Complete Series*. Los Angeles: 20th Century Fox, 2005. DVD, disc 4.

---. "Objects in Space. Commentary by Executive Producer Joss Whedon." *Firefly: The Complete Series*. Los Angeles: 20th Century Fox, 2005. DVD, disc 4.

Wynter, Sylvia. "Unsettling the Coloniality of Being/Power/Truth/ Freedom: Towards the Human, After Man, Its Overrepresentation – An Argument." *CR: The New Centennial Review* 3, no. 3 (2003): 257–337.

BRIGITTE GEORGI-FINDLAY

Visions of the Past, Politics of the Present: The Temporalities of Western Television Series

Western films and television series have performed important 'cultural work' as American origin stories that define and debate core American values and the contradictions of the American historical experience. Many Westerns have imagined the time-space of the 'old West,' mostly understood as the trans-Mississippi West in the decades after the Civil War, as a point of national emergence or social transition. My title addresses the twofold way in which Westerns have used this time-space. On the one hand, they have done so in order to engage with the American past, tell the story of nation-building, and create a fable of national identity by imagining a usable past, society, and hero figure(s). On the other hand (and at the same time), Westerns have used the time-space of the 'old West' to engage with the present moment, transport an agenda of the present, and intervene in contemporary debates and crises. One could argue that the Western, even when it has offered escape and fulfilled nostalgic desires, has always resonated with the cultural moods, fears, and anxieties of its own time. In the following, I will make some observations about how Western television series since the 1950s have vacillated between history, myth and social commentary and have imbued the 'old West' with changing meanings relevant to their particular times. Notably, some of these changes are shown to be related to the shifting mediascapes of the 20th and 21st centuries.

64   Visions of the Past, Politics of the Present

Early Western Television Series of the 1950s and 1960s

From 1949 to the early 1970s, more than 40 prime-time Western television series aired on three networks.[1] My focus will be on four series with a high degree of popularity and relatively long runs: *Gunsmoke* (CBS, 1955–1975), *Rawhide* (CBS, 1959–1966), *Bonanza* (NBC, 1959–1973), and *The Big Valley* (ABC, 1965–1969). All of these shows make claims to being 'truthful' to the spirit of the 'old West' on a paratextual level, i.e., on the level of discourses held by showrunners, critics, and fans of the series. At the same time, all of these series create narratives that strongly resonate with issues of their own time. Thus, one could argue that all of these shows engage with contemporary constructions of the individual, family and community, masculinity (and, implicitly, femininity), fatherhood (and, implicitly, motherhood), and normality and deviance. Constructed as morality tales, they debate ethical and philosophical questions such as ideals of leadership and the nature of good society; the difference between justice, law, and order; and the legitimacy of violence as well. Since all of these programs were supported by commercial sponsors, they also depict contemporary fashion and consumer products. Moreover, in the stories they tell, the shows appeal to anxieties related to the Cold War as well as to suburbia and its particular family and gender dynamics.

One of the shifts that critics have observed within Western series seems to reflect these contemporary concerns. By the late 1950s and early 1960s, the earlier focus on lone hero figures seems to have moved toward a stronger validation of groups, families, and domesticity tied to property.[2] The lone gunslinger, now interpreted as a deviant and dangerous character, is out of place in this serial world. After all, the shows had to appeal to the whole family (parents as well as younger and

[1]   Kathleen L. Spencer, *Art and Politics in* Have Gun – Will Travel*: The 1950s Western as Ethical Drama* (Jefferson: McFarland and Company, 2014), 3.
[2]   Michael T. Marsden and Jack Nachbar, "The Modern Popular Western: Radio, Television, Film and Print," in *A Literary History of the American West*, ed. J. Golden Taylor and Thomas J. Lyon (Fort Worth: Texas Christian University Press, 1987), 1268; Gary A. Yoggy, *Riding the Video Range: The Rise and Fall of the Western on Television* (Jefferson: McFarland and Company, 1995), 77.

older children) at once.[3] All of this tells an interesting story about contemporary shifts from the valuing of individualism toward a validation of family, team-play, and social conformity.[4]

This shift can, for example, be observed within the longest-running of these shows, *Gunsmoke.* In this series, set in the infamous Western town of Dodge City, the protagonist Marshal Matt Dillon is initially represented as a brooding, introspective, vulnerable and troubled man suffering in a harsh world. In the course of the series, however, his detached stance softens and shifts toward identification with a small community of friends that functions as an extended family.

Gunsmoke's Kansas could also be interpreted as a reflection of a Cold War-era world that places specific demands on its protagonists. In this dangerous world, people do not show much restraint or sympathy for each other. They are prone to mass hysteria, mob violence, intolerance and unruly behavior that transgresses moral boundaries (including shooting people out of spite or bullying the weak and helpless). In this anarchic environment, the Marshal needs to function as a force for order. While he achieves a modicum of (temporary) order through gun violence in the earlier seasons, he later uses emotional sensibility, psychology, detective work, dialogue, diplomacy and tactical negotiation. One could argue that this says something about visions of a Cold War global order and the role of military power in such a world. Richard Slotkin has read this Western figure in another context as a reflection of a contradictory American self-image: "at once supremely powerful and utterly vulnerable, politically dominant yet helpless to shape the course of critical events."[5] If Dodge City is made to stand in for America, it is an America constantly in danger, vulnerable and under threat, both from the outside and from within. It functions as an allegory of a 1950s Cold War America that, in this case, has the right kind of lawman to resolve conflicts and deescalate violence, a man who works in the service of that America but at the same time questions whether he should really belong to it.

The program also can be read as reflecting contemporary anxieties about individualism and manhood. This is especially visible in the

---

[3] Richard Schickel, *Clint Eastwood* (London: Arrow Books, 1996), 110.

[4] Marsden and Nachbar, "The Modern Popular Western," 1268–1269.

[5] Richard Slotkin qtd. in Schickel, *Clint Eastwood*, 111.

66   Visions of the Past, Politics of the Present

contradictions represented by the figure of the Marshal. He combines both a strong personal moral compass and a strong sense of social responsibility. He is both an individualist and a selfless man, without material self-interest and without a home. He does not distinguish between the private and the professional. In the context of the 1950s' debates around the family, the corporate workplace, and consumerism, he may be seen as providing an alternative model of masculinity for the family man of that era. At the same time, he embodies the professionalism of the corporate man.

The shift from valuing the lone gunslinger toward validating communities is also reflected in *Rawhide.* In this Western cattle-drive series, the cowboy is "no longer a free atomic individual, but the member of a group."[6] This is "not an ideal democratic community" since it "has a rigid chain-of-command headed by a trail boss" and is organized almost like an army with only one man in charge.[7] But it becomes a team when crisis arrives. The series thus can be understood as engaging with issues of leadership in a democratic society that is constantly under threat. The leader, represented by the trail boss Gil Favor, has to make difficult decisions (almost) by himself. He has to lead and yet be like the other guys, and he is the last one to take his boots off. While he is no authoritarian, he expects discipline and is able to delegate authority to a certain degree. He is a man of organization and a team player. The show thus can be seen as engaging with contemporary concepts and contradictions tied to masculinity, leadership and corporate work.

One of the most popular of these early shows, *Bonanza,* puts a particular focus on family, fatherhood, male domesticity, and property. Here we even have an all-male family comprised of men who are allowed to show love for each other and who at the same time represent a 'Western' standard of masculinity. In this universe, women may play important roles now and then, but they invariably have to disappear again. This expulsion of women may say something about contemporary anxieties concerning women's shift from the home to the workplace,

[6]   Ralph Brauer and Donna Brauer, *The Horse, the Gun and the Piece of Property: Changing Images of the TV Western* (Bowling Green: Bowling Green University Popular Press, 1975), 91.
[7]   Ibid., 85–86.

men's role in society, and family dynamics.[8] The Cartwrights can also be said to represent ambivalent masculinities: strong, sensitive men of action and men interested in education who are able to show emotions and exert violence. While the show moves its men into the realm of the domestic, it leaves them free of the constraints of a (corporate) work-place and gendered domesticity. The Cartwright family of men thus fulfills gendered escapist fantasies, embodying male characters that can now and then enjoy the rewards provided by the Western landscape, the saloon, play, or life in a simplified natural and social environment. Like the Western hero, they hover between a strong sense of individualism and a strong sense of social responsibility.

There is also a shift to be observed within the series that seems to address changes in conceptions of fatherhood at the time. Ben Cartwright, the father of three adult sons, goes from being a strict patri-archal figure to a warmer, more sensitive mentor. He seems to reflect the ambivalence of a time when men were urged to form emotional bonds with their children but were supposed to be strong family patriarchs at the same time.[9]

Moreover, the initially rather hostile relations between the Cartwrights and the residents of Virginia City become more cooperative over the course of the series. The Cartwrights evolve from aristocratic owners of a baronial estate into middle class entrepreneurs and respected members of the town. The showrunners seem to have updated the traditional family along lines more acceptable for the time. In addition, the Cartwrights reference the Cold War context and the new inter-national role of the U.S. The show suggests that, in a world where the reach of the law still does not extend far, this family of men functions as a private force for order, as citizen-soldiers prepared to fight with military force if necessary. They are depicted as men who are able to fight both in self-defense and for the freedom of others beyond the borders of their home. *Bonanza* thus seems to address the fear that postwar ideals of American manhood (those represented in family sitcoms of the time, for instance) might be deficient within a Cold War context.

---

[8] Spencer, *Art and Politics in* Have Gun – Will Travel, 12.

[9] Ibid., 16.

68   Visions of the Past, Politics of the Present

The Big Valley then tries to heal the disappearance of women in *Bonanza* by putting a woman at its center. Barbara Stanwyck plays a tough mother figure, a widowed matriarch who, though capable of fending for herself outside the home, nevertheless leaves the management of the ranch to her sons. This show tries to complicate the earlier series' male escapist fantasies while at the same time reestablishing visions of a male-dominated economic order.

All of the protagonists in these aforementioned series are presented as idealists defending an American system based on freedom, democracy and (over the course of time) tolerance. They are always ready to sacrifice themselves for each other or for others in need of help. They thus stand for a pioneer past that viewers can look up to and build on, a past that is not always perfect (especially with regard to the treatment of Native Americans and ethnic minorities), but redeemable. The shows thus fashion an American past with shortcomings. And even if they did not really address the origins of these shortcomings, the series still spoke to compelling anxieties about America's ability to live up to its founding ideals. Viewers could see themselves, or images of themselves, in these characters, and could measure themselves against these pioneers. Thus, these programs seem to have been able to voice concerns about contested issues of their time "within the constraints of mass market episodic television."[10]

Some scholars have argued that these series, by fashioning American men as reluctant warriors in noble defense of a free world, also prepared Americans for their new role on the world stage. However, by constructing contradictory models of heroism, the series also addressed and negotiated changes in the contemporary American social and cultural landscape by engaging with new gender roles and controversial themes of their time: racial discrimination and civil rights, war and violence, environmentalism, youth rebellion and the counterculture, religious diversity, addiction, disability. *Gunsmoke*'s Marshal Dillon meditated on the personal cost of violence, while *Bonanza*'s family constellation showed how pliant the 1950s idea of the nuclear family actually was.[11]

[10]   Ibid., 44.
[11]   Andrew Ross, "Families, Film Genres, and Technological Environments," *East-West Film Journal* 4, no. 1 (1989): 9–10.

BRIGITTE GEORGI-FINDLAY

Concerning the cultural politics of the series, one could argue that they played both sides of the political field – liberal and conservative – and were, within the constraints of network television, priming their audience for change without creating too much controversy. For example, until the early 1960s, the serial universe was mostly white (with the exception of some Native American and Hispanic characters). By the mid-1960s, the series increasingly addressed racial relations by including storylines that featured African American characters. In 1964, *Bonanza* aired an episode, "Enter Thomas Bowers," based on a historical African American singer suspected of being a runaway slave. By presenting the racial drama surrounding an African American opera singer performing in Virginia City who is shunned by the town's good society, the show referenced racial issues of its own time. As Spencer points out, this episode was almost not aired due to concerns by General Motors, the show's sponsor, that Southern viewers would boycott their car dealerships. However, the company's threat to withdraw as the show's sponsor was met with considerable negative publicity, "coupled with resistance from NBC and the NAACP, and capped by the promised resignation of all four stars," which subsequently caused GM to abandon its decision.[12] Moreover, in 1965, *Rawhide* introduced the African American actor Raymond St. Jacques as Simon Blake, making him "the first black man to have a regular role on a television western."[13] By the late 1960s and early 1970s, *Bonanza* also included more stories that can be read as a reference to the counterculture and antiwar protests.

Western Series in Transition: From the 1970s to the 1990s

Most Western series, sharing the fate of the movie Western, were canceled by the mid-1970s. Arguably, in the wake of Vietnam and Watergate, civil rights protests, and countercultural sensibilities (particularly with regard to representations of violence as well as racial and sexist stereotyping), Westerns no longer resonated with viewers'

---

[12]   Spencer, *Art and Politics in* Have Gun – Will Travel, 176.
[13]   Schickel, *Clint Eastwood*, 164.

70 Visions of the Past, Politics of the Present

pre-vailing cultural moods.[14] The only successful Western series of the 1970s and 1980s seems to have been *Little House on the Prairie* (NBC, 1974–1984). Overtly targeting a family audience of both children and adults, the series addressed issues related to family life (the problems of growing up, raising children, jealousy, school, peer pressure, taking risks, dealing with the death of a loved one and the desire for independence). Yet the series also touched on concerns that contemporary society tackled more reluctantly: child abuse, premarital sex, aging, addiction, disability, economic crisis, materialism, prejudice, and racial relations. The series raised the question of whether these issues were relevant not only for nineteenth-century rural Americans, but for late-twentieth-century suburban and urban Americans as well. All of them were going through comparable economic and cultural crises, whether in the 1870s or in the 1970s.

Engagement with American history in *Little House on the Prairie* is visible at times in references to contemporary America. For example, the episode "Centennial," which aired in July 1976, deals with events of Independence Day in July 1876, when the farmers are as sick and tired of government taxes as their 1970s suburbanite counterparts are and there is not much patriotic feeling left. More than in the earlier Western series, tolerance for cultural difference and the integration of marginalized others are important messages in *Little House*, reflecting 1970s debates around affirmative action and diversity. The series also makes subtle references to the Vietnam war.

Perhaps one could even read *Little House on the Prairie* as a manual for the young families of the 1970s. The series appeals to counter-cultural sensibilities, building on viewers' potential dreams of a simpler life within a small community. There is more critical engagement with consumer culture and materialism than in earlier series. Thus, the pioneer family seems to serve as a model for "the countercultural family bent on some degree of agrarian self-sufficiency."[15] The 'look' of the series has a 1970s aesthetic when it comes to the males' hairstyles, for instance.

---

[14] J. Fred MacDonald, *Who Shot the Sheriff? The Rise and Fall of Television Westerns* (Westport: Praeger, 1987), 87–89.

[15] Ross, "Families, Film Genres, and Technological Environments," 10.

As Ella Taylor has argued, *Little House on the Prairie* "painlessly reconciled traditional values of simplicity, decency, and community with visions of progress and modernity."[16] Among those older values foregrounded are: hard work, frugality, the value of community, discipline, heeding parental authority, and keeping promises. Yet they are also given a modern spin and updated for a 1970s audience. This is especially articulated in the concepts of masculinity and fatherhood (less so in terms of motherhood). Men like Charles Ingalls seem to represent a new kind of fatherhood ideal, able to be both mentor and authority figure while also expressing emotion and displaying physical power.

In the end, this series raises questions that may resonate with audiences no matter what time they live in: To what extent is the individual autonomous and free to aspire to something? How much does one have to subject oneself to community expectations? And how can family and community help in a crisis?

This perspective on a pioneer past that illustrates individual and national responsibilities still holds true for a 1990s show which is in some ways revisionist but which upholds a vision of pioneer America that was not always perfect yet still redeemable: *Dr. Quinn, Medicine Woman* (CBS, 1992–1998). This program updates the Western series for the 1990s by writing women and minorities into the frontier narrative. The stories resonate with 1990s debates by integrating a mixture of feminist, conservative and postfeminist ideologies into the female protagonist's worldview. More so than the earlier series, *Dr. Quinn* acknowledged the multicultural nature of the Western frontier (and was accused of being overly politically correct). This locates the series not only within contemporary battles over multiculturalism but also within historical revisionism with regard to the 'old West' that had taken hold in academia and popular culture by the late 1980s.[17]

---

[16] Ella Taylor, *Prime-Time Families: Television Culture in Postwar America* (Berkeley: University of California Press, 1989), 37.

[17] See, e.g., Patricia Nelson Limerick, *The Legacy of Conquest: The Unbroken Past of the American West* (New York: W. W. Norton, 1987); Richard White, *'It's Your Misfortune and None of My Own': A New History of the American West* (Norman: University of Oklahoma Press, 1991).

72 Visions of the Past, Politics of the Present

The 'New' Western Series

Engagement with historical revisionism became particularly strong and obvious in two series of the early twenty-first century, when a new televisual landscape enabled the revival of the Western series in new contexts such as the aftermath of 9/11, an economic crisis and a crisis of masculinity.

Deadwood (HBO, 2004–2006) uses the same time-space as most Westerns on the big and small screen, imagining the frontier as the cradle of modern America. In *Deadwood*, and also in *Hell on Wheels* (AMC, 2011–2016), the past is reimagined as one that burdens future Americans with a heavy load to carry. Critics have remarked on *Deadwood*'s "greater faithfulness to an actual past, one that implicitly had been masked, ignored, or suppressed in previous iterations of the genre on television." The show is perceived as reflecting critically on the "Western's hybridity as history and myth [...] or its traditional phallocentrism and emphasis on male homosociality."[18] The idea that *Deadwood* is a revisionist historical project is supported by showrunner David Milch in several paratextual formats (documentaries on the DVD, an accompanying book), in which he and the cast of the show are granted authority as popular historians writing a more 'accurate' history of the 'old West' and taking a more "honest look at the American past" than earlier historians, Western films and series.[19] They are providing a "historical corrective."[20] As the last words spoken in the series – uttered in resignation by main character Al Swearengen while cleaning up blood after one of many brutal (but seemingly necessary) killings – suggest, *Deadwood* will not tell its viewers "something pretty."

If the story of *Deadwood* is an allegory of American nation-building, that nation is shown to have been built on muddy ground, on sexism and racism, violence, corruption, and the quest for power and profit. That nation, the series tells its viewers, is not built on idealism and democracy but on materialism and individual self-interest. In the story told by *Deadwood* about the emergence of a social order, there are no

[18] Allison Perlman, "*Deadwood*, Generic Transformation, and Televisual History," *Journal of Popular Film & Television* 39, no. 2 (2011): 104.
[19] Ibid., 105.
[20] Ibid., 111.

BRIGITTE GEORGI-FINDLAY

hero figures, only people able to manipulate and network, negotiate and compromise in a social context that functions in perpetual crisis mode. And yet, even in gritty Deadwood, a sense of family and community emerges. Although for most characters, family is a site of past abuse and trauma, they nevertheless create temporary alliances and relationships out of need. Also, the nostalgic, romanticizing, softening use of the camera as well as the music suggest hope and salvation. The credit sequence even uses the liberatory promises of the Western.

All of these claims made about the American past resonate with the show's own present moment. As Perlman has noted, the series' revival of the TV Western has raised the question "whether and how the Western can matter to our contemporary moment." She points out that "much of the critical scholarship on *Deadwood* has interpreted the series' depiction of the past as an allegory or comment on the issues and conflicts of our present." This scholarship has interpreted the series as an engagement with neoliberalism, post-9/11 anxieties, the nature of communication in an information society, and the crises of the present moment.[21]

A similar historical process is dramatized in *Hell on Wheels*. The series provides a history lesson about the discrimination of women and minorities as well as the role of social and racial hierarchies. It portrays railroad building not so much as a result of pioneering idealism and genius but as a site of collusion between politics and capital, of corruption and speculation that victimizes ethnically and racially minoritized laborers and that functions as site of labor conflicts. In this world, there is no hope of support from the government or the democratic system. The railroad camp is represented as a site of violence and trauma and thus reflects the open wound left by the Civil War. At the same time, the stories told around the camp point to the emergence of a new transitional social order in which emotional bonds, family and community relations as well as pragmatic alliances between underdogs and power brokers can help to heal these wounds and provide emotional support and forces for resistance. Although the series revolves around a complex male hero figure and masculinity issues related to him, it is the community that seems to be the center of interest.

[21] Ibid., 104.

74 Visions of the Past, Politics of the Present

Like *Deadwood, Hell on Wheels* says something critical about American nation-building and the character of the nation that has emerged from this process. The series resonates with issues such as the crisis of masculinity and fraught racial relations, sexual abuse of women, the moral costs of war, the lack of a sense of home in America, the end of the American dream, and general cultural/political polarization. However, even if both shows lay claim to a critical project of historical revision and showing the 'authentic' West, the 'old West' is still imbued with a nostalgic haze, which may say something about the continuing attraction of a romanticized West.

Hell on Wheels is unique among the series I have discussed so far in that it experiments with narrative time by using flashbacks, complex intertexts and musical counterpoints. An even more radical experiment with narrative time can be observed in *Westworld* (HBO, 2016, 2018, 2020), which also continues *Deadwood*'s attempt at demythologizing the American West. *Westworld* mixes the Western genre with science fiction, exposing the Western as a flawed origin story. The games played by the guests of Westworld, a Western-themed adventure park, allow them to live out their darkest fantasies and serve to illuminate the dark impulses underlying American nation-building. The robot "hosts" function as "vulnerable citizens forced to repress atrocities so that their nation can drape a patriotic story over its ugly history."[22] The series raises contemporary questions related to artificial intelligence, post-humanism, and the borders between the human and the robot. Critics have emphasized a feminist approach in *Westworld* that thematizes sexual assault in the time of #MeToo. Yet one could argue that the series sensationalizes what it condemns, satisfying the taboo desires of a (formerly) niche consumer base by testing the boundaries of representing sex, violence, and nudity. Thus, the series arguably profits from the same cultural needs it seeks to expose critically while refusing a clear moral point of view.

The same applies to *Westworld*'s project of demythologizing the Western. The series references 'old' and revisionist Westerns by copy-

[22] Emily Nussbaum, "The Meta-Politics of 'Westworld,'" *The New Yorker*, October 17, 2016, newyorker.com/magazine/2016/10/24/the-meta-politics-of-westworld.

ing, re-enacting, and quoting iconic scenes, camera shots, plots, characters and themes from films such as *Stagecoach, My Darling Clementine, The Searchers, The Wild Bunch* as well as *The Good, the Bad, and the Ugly.* It features a multiplicity of competing Western scripts and Western conventions, illuminating the scripted quality of the Western. It seeks to revise the Western by flipping the iconography of the American West. *Westworld* asks viewers to rethink the violent impulses underlying American national mythology, suggesting that the Western setting brings out a problematic 'core program' in its visitors which is shown to be defined by anarchic impulses, a quest for power, violence, and abuse against women and minorities. As the series suggests, one part of this cultural attitude can also be located in a deep-seated habit of forgetting these dark sides and creating a clean slate again and again (in the same way a host's hard drive is cleared – though not always successfully – of any memory). Moreover, the Western setting of the theme park serves to expose the West(ern) as a commodity, an artistically manufactured myth perpetuated by the entertainment industry. And still, the series reiterates the utopian potential of the frontier myth in its focus on the emergence of the human potential of androids. While critiquing the Western myth, *Westworld* uses West(ern) iconography for its own marketing purposes, thus boosting the success of the series.

Concluding Remarks

Since the 1950s, Western television series have engaged with the American past to create a narrative of a national American identity. Although the early shows made certain claims to respecting historical truth (on both the textual and paratextual level), by the 1990s Western films and series had embarked on a project of historical revisionism, demythologizing the 'old West' by aiming for a historically correct rendition of frontier life. This is reflected in both the budget invested in period detail and in the way the showrunners and cast now self-style themselves as popular historians with regard to the social and cultural hierarchies of the frontier. Although truth claims had been part of earlier programs' rhetoric of distinction, historical revisionism became an intrinsic part of quality branding in an early twenty-first-century

American mediascape where narrowcasting strategies seem to have won out (at least for a while) over broadcasting. However, more recent Western series also walk a fine line between claims of historical 'authenticity' and the cultural politics of the present moment. In their search for niche audiences, showrunners have sought to bring the 'old West' in sync with both their own and their intended audiences' contemporary agendas. In this, they are not much different from their predecessors. Where they may differ to a certain degree is in the way they represent a dark, dirty, unheroic 'old West' as the cradle of America, and also in the ways they comment on the present moment. Due to industry constraints, earlier Western series had to play to all sides of the political spectrum and thus seem to have reflected the mainstream cultural consensus of their time. And yet, in order to keep in sync with their audiences (and attract new ones), they also may have tested the boundaries of what could be represented and said in their own time, functioning as social analysts and reflecting on cultural change. Social analysis then seems to have become one of the trademarks of the more recent series discussed above, which appear to take the task of critical intervention into contemporary cultural and political debates very seriously. As in earlier series, the 'old West' is made to stand for America, for better or worse (with greater emphasis recently on the latter). As a final note, however, I would argue that when it comes to engaging with the history of Native-white relations, none of the series shows much interest in critically coming to terms with white settler colonialism.

BRIGITTE GEORGI-FINDLAY

Works Cited

Bonanza. Produced by D. Dortort. NBC, 1959–1973.

Brauer, Ralph, and Donna Brauer. *The Horse, the Gun and the Piece of Property: Changing Images of the TV Western.* Bowling Green: Bowling Green University Popular Press, 1975.

Deadwood. Produced by D. Milch. HBO, 2004–2006.

Dr. Quinn, Medicine Woman. Produced by B. Sullivan. CBS, 1992–1998.

Gunsmoke. Produced by N. MacDonnell and J. Meston. CBS, 1955–1975.

Hell on Wheels. Produced by J. Gayton and T. Gayton. AMC, 2011–2016.

Limerick, Patricia Nelson. *The Legacy of Conquest: The Unbroken Past of the American West.* New York: W. W. Norton, 1987.

Little House on the Prairie. Produced by M. Landon and E. Friendly. NBC, 1974–1982.

MacDonald, J. Fred. *Who Shot the Sheriff? The Rise and Fall of Television Westerns.* Westport: Praeger, 1987.

Marsden, Michael T., and Jack Nachbar. "The Modern Popular Western: Radio, Television, Film and Print." In *A Literary History of the American West,* edited by J. Golden Taylor and Thomas J. Lyon, 1263–1282. Fort Worth: Texas Christian University Press, 1987.

Nussbaum, Emily. "The Meta-Politics of 'Westworld'." *The New Yorker,* October 17, 2016. newyorker.com/magazine/2016/10/24/the-meta-politics-of-westworld.

Perlman, Allison. "*Deadwood,* Generic Transformation, and Televisual History." *Journal of Popular Film & Television* 39, no. 2 (2011): 102–112.

Rawhide. Produced by B. Brady. CBS, 1959–1966.

Ross, Andrew. "Families, Film Genres, and Technological Environments." *East-West Film Journal* 4, no. 1 (1989): 6–26.

Schickel, Richard. *Clint Eastwood.* London: Arrow Books, 1996.

Spencer, Kathleen L. *Art and Politics in* Have Gun – Will Travel*: The 1950s Western as Ethical Drama.* Jefferson: McFarland and Company, 2014.

Taylor, Ella. *Prime-Time Families: Television Culture in Postwar America.* Berkeley: University of California Press, 1989.

The Big Valley. Produced by A. Bezzerides and L. Edelman. ABC, 1965–1969.

Westworld. Produced by J. Nolan and L. Joy. HBO, 2016, 2018.

White, Richard. *'It's Your Misfortune and None of My Own': A New History of the American West*. Norman: University of Oklahoma Press, 1991.

Yoggy, Gary A. *Riding the Video Range: The Rise and Fall of the Western on Television*. Jefferson: McFarland and Company, 1995.

LINDA M. HESS

"What I would have done to have heard a story like mine": Reading Tig Notaro's and Hannah Gadsby's Stand-up as Autobiographical Narratives

Three Scenes of Suffering in Stand-up Comedy[1]

In 1985, Lawrence E. Mintz argued in *American Quarterly* that "humor is a vitally important social and cultural phenomenon" and that "stand-up comedy [...] is the most interesting of all the manifestations of humor in the popular culture,"[2] at the same time lamenting that the genre was undervalued and under-researched. Since then, stand-up comedy and its scholarship have proliferated in various ways. In this article, I will consider two contemporary stand-up comedians, Tig Notaro and Hannah Gadsby, whose shows provide excellent case studies for recent developments in stand-up as a social and (pop-)cultural phenomenon. In the 2010s, Notaro and Gadsby each made headlines with stand-up routines in which they told their audiences deeply personal stories of suffering. They had each been working fairly successfully in stand-up for several years and had appeared in various roles on television shows, but neither was particularly widely known yet. This changed abruptly when their sets centered on autobiographical narratives of suffering became breakout shows. The overnight media attention pivoted on three central moments in their respective performances:

Moment 1) In August 2012, Tig Notaro stepped onto the stage of the Largo nightclub in Los Angeles to perform her show *Tig Has Friends*,

---

[1] CW: The section "Timing the Unfunny" of this article contains quotations from Hannah Gadsby's *Nanette* that describe violent sexual assault.

[2] Lawrence E. Mintz, "Standup Comedy as Social and Cultural Mediation," *American Quarterly* 37, no. 1 (1985): 71.

as she had done on previous dates. But just four days earlier, she had been diagnosed with breast cancer, and so, instead of proceeding with her prepared set, she greeted the audience with the following words: "Hello. I have cancer. How are you? Is everybody having a good time? I have cancer"[3] Listening to the audio recording of that evening's show,[4] one can hear that the reaction of the audience is varied. Some laugh out loud. Some laugh nervously. Others remain quiet. Notaro acknowledges her deviation from regular stand-up comedy, stating, "It's weird because with humor, the equation is tragedy plus time equals comedy. I am just at tragedy right now."[5] Then she continues, elaborating on her mother's unexpected death shortly before her own cancer diagnosis, and joking about her cumulative tragedy. Throughout the set, some audience members make sounds of empathy rather than amusement; but the audience does not get angry or impatient about Notaro's deviation from the program. They cheer loudly at the end of the show.

Moment 2) In 2014, Notaro took the performance of her autobiographical illness narrative even further. During her show *Boyish Girl Interrupted*, Notaro exposed the scars from her double mastectomy, performing the rest of the show topless. The audience's reaction is a full minute of not laughter, but cheering. Nor could the desired reaction have been laughter. Had the audience laughed at Notaro for taking her shirt off, had they jeered at it as a sexual gesture, or had they been repulsed, the moment would have been embarrassing, not empowering for her. A review in *Bustle* captured the reaction from audience and critics alike: "As a woman who already faced judgment from others due to her androgyny and the removal of her breasts, Notaro's statement was one unapologetically fueled by her desire to combat normative gender aesthetics and roles, as well as her own fear of cancer. And that is 100 percent pure courage."[6]

---

[3] Tig Notaro, *Live* (Bloomington: Secretly Canadian, 2013), 00:00:38–00:00:52.

[4] The owner of the Largo recorded Notaro's set, and it became widely available as the album *Live* (Heritage).

[5] Notaro, *Live*, 00:01:13–00:01:35.

[6] Gina Vaynshteyn, "Tig Notaro Does Half Her Stand-Up Set Topless After Being Heckled and Anyone Who Wasn't Already in Love with Her Is Falling Hard," *Bustle*, November 9, 2014, bustle.com/articles/48238-tig-

LINDA M. HESS

Moment 3) In 2017, Australian stand-up comedian Hannah Gadsby debuted her show *Nanette* in Australia; the show reached much larger audiences in June 2018 when it became available on Netflix. Approximately a month after its Netflix release, *Nanette* was named "the Most Discussed Comedy Special in Ages" by the *New York Times*.[7] After a fairly conventional opening, Gadsby declares about seventeen minutes into the show that she will have to "quit comedy" because the very framework of stand-up comedy forces her to turn hurtful experiences into jokes. Her performance then reaches an abrupt turning point when she reveals that an encounter with an aggressive, hetero-sexist[8] man, which she had earlier related as a joke, actually ended with that man violently assaulting Gadsby. The audience becomes quiet. However, despite the sudden shift to absolute seriousness, they cheer and applaud Gadsby at the end of the show.[9]

Despite their various differences, the two comedians' stand-up routines share two significant aspects: they both perform stand-up as autobiographical narrative, and the success of both performances revolves around the unfunny. Gadsby's set even garnered claims of "breaking" or "destroying" comedy.[10] I argue that Notaro's and Gadsby's fusion of (unfunny) autobiographical narrative and stand-up comedy highlights comedy's significance as a participant in public

notaro-does-half-her-stand-up-set-topless-after-being-heckled-and-anyone-who-wasnt-already.

[7] Judy Berman, "'Nanette' Is the Most Discussed Comedy Special in Ages: Here's What to Read About It," *The New York Times*, July 13, 2018, nytimes.com/2018/07/13/arts/television/nanette-hannah-gadsby-netflix-roundup.html.

[8] I use the term 'heterosexist' rather than 'homophobic' here to indicate that hostility towards LGBTQ* persons is the result of societal and individual prejudice rather than an anxiety disorder.

[9] See Rebecca Krefting's article, "Hannah Gadsby Stands Down," *Journal of Cinema and Media Studies* 58, no. 3 (2019): 165–170 for an insightful discussion of the differences between the live performances of *Nanette* and the recorded Netflix special.

[10] See, for example, the headline "The Comedy-Destroying, Soul-Affirming Art of Hannah Gadsby," *The New York Times*, July 24, 2018, or "Hannah Gadsby Broke Comedy: So What's She Building Now?," *The Washington Post*, July 12, 2019.

82   Stand-up as Autobiographical Narrative

discourse. Their performances resonate with contemporaneous discussions about political correctness, call-out/cancel culture, and the #MeToo movement. Moreover, as two lesbian comics who do not conform to societal norms of femininity and gender, and who address this fact on stage, Gadsby and Notaro serve as noteworthy examples within ongoing debates about who finds representation within comedy.

Stand-up as Autobiography

While many stand-up comedians include (presumably) personal anecdotes in their acts, Notaro's and Gadsby's use of autobiographical narrative breaks the divide between on-stage and off-stage personae. It is vital to their narratives that their on-stage personae are framed as identical to their off-stage personalities and that their performed narratives are understood as *true* stories. In this way, Gadsby and Notaro fulfill what Philippe Lejeune designates as the *autobiographical pact*,[11] which "determines the attitude of the reader" towards the work, meaning that readers (or, in this case, the audience) will expect that the author, narrator, and protagonist of the autobiographical work are one and the same person. If the audience found out at any point that either Notaro's or Gadsby's stories were invented, or even if they were a friend's true story instead, the comedians likely would not have met with similar success. Moreover, the autobiographical nature of their stand-up comedy provides the performances with a crucial political component, because their performances do the work of reclaiming personal stories and also of reclaiming agency. Both comedians address their need to prioritize narrative over comedic entertainment. Gadsby emphasizes that continually freezing "an experience at its trauma point and [...] seal[ing] it off into jokes" traumatized her further, and that she now "need[s] to tell [her] story properly" in order to be able to overcome her trauma.[12] Notaro explains to her audience that really did not feel she "could just

---

[11] Philippe Lejeune, "The Autobiographical Pact," in *On Autobiography* (Minneapolis: University of Minnesota Press, 1989), 14.

[12] Hannah Gadsby, *Nanette*. Aired June 19, 2018, on Netflix, 00:40:29–00:41:13.

tell normal jokes"[13] when she stepped out onto the stage after her diagnosis. In an interview, she elaborated, "It felt so silly and irrelevant to think about [...] observational jokes [...] in light of what was going on with me."[14]

The performances are thus framed as variations of what Sidonie Smith and Julia Watson, in their work *Reading Autobiography,* call "scriptotherapy." While Gadsby's and Notaro's narratives are performed on stage, they still carry the term's denotation as narratives that function as "a mode of self-healing" and as a process of working through trauma.[15] Scholars of autobiographical narratives, specifically of those describing severe illness and traumatic experiences, have observed the significance of agency in such works. Both comedians exemplify the need to reclaim their story by telling it. The positive audience reaction also attests to the ongoing popularity of the "confessional" genre. In their 2006 article "Talking Alone: Reality TV, Emotions, and Authenticity," Minna Aslama and Mervi Pantti attest to the prominence of "confessional and therapeutic strategies" in popular media culture, specifically in reality television.[16] While stand-up comedy is not reality television, the same combination of confession, emotion, and authenticity nevertheless seems to be highly successful, as audiences celebrated Notaro's and Gadsby's shows despite the breaches of expectations in terms of comedy.

While Notaro's cancer narrative focuses on physical illness, Gadsby's story addresses the traumatic impact of heterosexist violence and internalized stigma on her mental health. Gadsby in particular also highlights the need for her story to be *heard*, emphasizing the significance of finding one's own experiences represented. Arthur W. Franck explains that "[p]art of what turns stories into testimony is the call made

---

[13] Notaro, *Live*, 00:27:05.

[14] Andrew Marantz, "Good Evening. Hello. I Have Cancer," *The New Yorker*, October 5, 2012, newyorker.com/culture/culture-desk/good-evening-hello-i-have-cancer.

[15] Sidonie Smith and Julia Watson, *Reading Autobiography: A Guide for Interpreting Life Narratives* (Minneapolis: University of Minnesota Press, 2001), 202; 23.

[16] Minna Aslama and Mervi Pantti, "Talking Alone: Reality TV, Emotions, and Authenticity," *European Journal of Cultural Studies* 9, no. 2 (2006): 167–168.

upon another person to receive that testimony."[17] When Gadsby relates how, in her early twenties, two men raped her, she voices the grievous lack of public discourse at the time, stating, "What I would have done to have heard a story like mine. Not for blame, [...] but to feel less alone."[18] Her tone thus becomes not only serious but also deeply political when she ties her critique of self-deprecatory humor to the public conversation about sexual harassment and rape, which gained wider traction when the #MeToo hashtag proliferated on social media in 2017.[19] In this way, Gadsby's performance also establishes a connection between the urgency of a highly current political debate and the popular modes of confessional and therapeutic language that brought the debate wider attention. The MeToo hashtag thus enabled confessions – ways of speaking up about intimate and hidden details, especially those previously kept silent by shame. The proliferation of such confessions then also allowed for recognition and community building.

By contrast, Notaro's narrative appears much less political, especially since breast cancer has received an increasing amount of attention since the late 1980s, and positive "survivor" narratives are largely uncritically embraced in public discourse. One outspoken critic, Barbara Ehrenreich, laments this survivor discourse in her 2010 article *Smile! You've Got Cancer*, stating that "staying/thinking positive" has seemingly become the only acceptable response, whereas expressions of anger, despair, or numbness are strongly discouraged within the community. Notaro's decisions, first to include her announcement "I have cancer" in her comedy set, and, later, to expose her mastectomy scars to the audience, seem at first glance seem to fit in with the positive survivor attitudes that dominate the breast cancer movement, particularly if one regards how media headlines (and sometimes also

---

[17] Arthur W. Franck, *The Wounded Storyteller: Body, Illness, and Ethics* (Chicago: The University of Chicago Press, 1995), 143.

[18] Gadsby, *Nanette*, 01:03:38.

[19] The #MeToo movement was founded in 2006 to help survivors of sexual violence. It was founded by Tarana Burke and focused particularly on young black women and girls who had become victims of sexual violence (MeToomvmt.org/about). #MeToo became visible in mainstream media after several women spoke out about having been sexually harassed by film producer Harvey Weinstein.

Notaro herself) framed the humor as part of the healing process.[20] However, Notaro also defies the positive survivor discourse in important ways. Her decision to talk about her diagnosis during her stand-up set meant bringing painful topics to comedy in order to process confusion, shock, and pain, not bringing comedy to a painful topic in order to deny those emotions. Moreover, her decision to take her shirt off on stage during *Boyish Girl Interrupted* harks back to Audre Lorde's writing in her *Cancer Journals* (1982), in which she problematizes the critique she faced from medical personnel for refusing to wear a prosthetic breast after her left breast had to be removed.[21] In taking off her shirt, Notaro tackles two social taboos: the taboo against women being topless in public (and the impossibility of reading the occurrence as not sexual), and the taboo against deviating from the approved breast cancer discourses, which still embrace normative femininity (*pink* ribbon culture) as one of the core scripts for how one becomes a competent "survivor." Through this act, her stand-up comedy gains a political dimension, and the audience, applauding, clearly reads Notaro's narrative and embodied testimony to her experience of breast cancer as an act of empowerment.

Both comedians have since expanded the autobiographical stories they told on stage. Gadsby's *Ten Steps to Nanette* was published in 2022 by the Australian imprint Allen & Unwin. Notaro's *I'm Just a Person* was published by Harper Collins in 2017.[22] While Anne-Marie Evans

---

[20] Mahita Gajanan, "Tig Notaro on Why Humor Was Instrumental to Healing After Her Cancer Diagnosis: 'Something Has to Break the Tension,'" *Time*, October 17, 2019,
time.com/5699703/tig-notaro-on-why-humor-was-instrumental-to-healing-after-her-cancer-diagnosis-something-has-to-break-the-tension/.

[21] Lorde's *Cancer Journals* also voice a crucial critique of racism as it intersects with sexism (and classism) with regard to healthcare. For example, none of the breast prostheses available would have matched her actual skin color (46), and Black women are frequently exposed to more harmful environments than white women (82).

[22] In fact, the success of Notaro's and Gadsby's shows led to a variety of what one might call 'spinoffs.' Notaro retold the story of her mother's death and her own subsequent cancer diagnosis in a semi-autobiographical/ fictionalized version in the Amazon Prime production *One Mississippi*, which ran for two seasons (2015–2017). In 2015, Netflix released the

86 Stand-up as Autobiographical Narrative

argues that writing memoirs, or "femoirs," as she calls them, has become a trend among female comedians,[23] Gadsby's and Notaro's specific use of the autobiographical (also on stage) enables what Beck Krefting has identified as critical "metacommentary on comedy,"[24] which pays attention to how comedy works within an industry of comedy and within larger societal structures. In this context, instances of the unfunny and of uncomfortable humor gain particular significance.

Timing the Unfunny

As stand-up comedy formats have proliferated in the last two decades, a number of female comedians, such as Tina Fey, Sarah Silverman, and Ali Wong, have gained visibility. This development is mirrored in scholarship, where, next to articles such as Gayle Salamon's "What Do We Learn About Rape Jokes from Rape Jokes About Rape Jokes?" (2017), two notable book-length studies, Rebecca Krefting's *All Joking Aside* (2014) and Sabrina Fuchs Abrams's edited collection *Transgressive Humor of American Women Writers* (2017), attest to the currency of examining the role of gender in comedy. While some argue that the advent of streaming services has democratized access to comedy platforms, effectively helping more woman comedians to succeed, Rebecca Krefting cautions against believing the meritocracy myth that

---

documentary *Tig*, which chronicles the year following her breast cancer diagnosis alongside the unexpected success of her viral performance at the Largo in 2012. Gadsby followed up her Netflix success by giving a nineteen-minute *TED Talk*, in which she provided background on writing *Nanette* and addressed being diagnosed with autism and struggling with mental illness. She has also since addressed her autism diagnosis more thoroughly in her show *Douglas* (2019), released as a Netflix comedy special in May 2020.

[23] Anne-Marie Evans, "Funny Women: Political Transgressions and Celebrity Autobiography," in *Transgressive Humor of American Women Writers*, ed. Sabrina Fuchs Abrams (Cham: Palgrave, 2017), 156.

[24] Rebecca Krefting, "Hannah Gadsby Stands Down: Feminist Comedy Studies," *Journal of Cinema and Media Studies* 58, no. 3 (2019): 165. Krefting uses the term specifically with regard to Hannah Gadsby, but I argue that it fits Notaro's comedy as well.

new media platforms (like YouTube, Netflix, Amazon) afford success based solely on comedic content.[25] While social media can transform what would otherwise have been largely individual responses into *viral* reactions, and while Krefting points out that "the Internet has proven quite helpful in dispelling the belief that women are not funny," she also echoes Micia Mosely's call to "interrogate which women get to be visible and the kind of women's humor the public consumes."[26] Notaro's and Gadsby's comedy participates in debates about gender and women in comedy, but their sets are of particular interest because of the ways in which they create an economy of laughter that pivots on moments of non-laughter and that also critiques attitudes towards femininity in society at large.

The unfunny has long carved out its niche in comedy. Nicholas Holm dedicates a whole chapter of *Humour as Politics* to comedy that lives off "scenarios not typically regarded as humorous" but that rather "would be [...] understood as horrifying, or, in more theoretically laden terms, abject."[27] What is often called "cringe humor," exemplified in various shows such as *Jackass*, *The Office*, or the movie *Borat* (2006), Holm identifies as "uncomfortable" or "disquieting humour," which "lingers on quietly terrible moments that are not allowed to pass quickly, but are instead studied and meditated on in ways that reconfigure not just the affective valence of humour, but the very bounds of what can be interpreted as comic."[28] Notaro's and particularly Gadsby's stand-up performances differ from Holm's examples, but they both qualify as variations of "uncomfortable humor" nevertheless. When Notaro recounts addressing her five-year-old self in a photograph with the line "You are gonna get cancer!" and then walking away while the girl in the photograph continues to stand immobile with a big smile on her face and "no idea what cancer [is],"[29] it draws a big laugh from the audience, but it also captures perfectly the pain and disbelieving shock of such a

---

[25] Rebecca Krefting, "Dueling Discourses: The Female Comic's Double Bind in the New Media Age," in *Transgressive Humor of American Women Writers*, ed. Sabrina Fuchs Abrams (Cham: Palgrave, 2017), 233.

[26] Ibid., 239.

[27] Nicholas Holm, *Humor as Politics: The Political Aesthetics of Contemporary Poetry* (New York: Palgrave, 2017), 89.

[28] Ibid., 91.

[29] Notaro, *Live*, 00:04:05–00:04:26.

88 Stand-up as Autobiographical Narrative

diagnosis. Notaro lingers on the horrible moment as she expands the backstory and informs her audience that, on top of her cancer diagnosis, her mother had just died tragically: "She tripped, hit her head, and died."[30] Throughout her set, people laugh, but Notaro also comments on frequent sighs and moans of sympathy from the audience ("Who is taking this so hard?"). At one point, she protests that she cannot understand why people in the audience are so affected by the death of her mother, saying, "You didn't know her."[31] Notaro's objection only highlights the relatability of her situation. Painful news of an unexpected death or severe illness are familiar to almost anyone.

While Notaro time and again returns to jokes, Gadsby does not. Instead, she emphasizes that the very framework of stand-up comedy encourages jokes about violent, painful, and shameful memories:

> Do you remember that story about that young man who almost beat me up? It was a very funny story. [...] I couldn't tell that story as it actually happened. [...] [T]hat man realized his mistake. And he came back. And he said, "Oh, no, I get it. You're a lady faggot. I'm allowed to beat the shit out of you," and he did! He beat the shit out of me and nobody stopped him. And I didn't... report that to the police, and I did not take myself to hospital, and I should have. And you know why I didn't? It's because I thought that was all I was worth. [...] And that was not homophobia, pure and simple, people. That was gendered. If I'd been feminine, that would not have happened. I am incorrectly female. I am incorrect, and that is a punishable offense. And this tension, it's yours. I am not helping you anymore.[32]

Gadsby here exemplifies Sarah Ahmed's figure of the "feminist killjoy," who "spoils the happiness of others" and "ruins the atmosphere" by refusing to accommodate prejudice and violence.[33] The moment in Gadsby's set is built to make the audience cringe as the mood shifts, and two things happen simultaneously: Gadsby's despair comes to the forefront, and audience members realize that they are implicated in the

---

[30] Ibid., 00:12:56.
[31] Ibid., 00:13:08.
[32] Gadsby, *Nanette*, 00:58:56–01:00:22.
[33] Sarah Ahmed, "Killing Joy: Feminism and the History of Happiness," *Signs* 35, no. 3 (2010): 581–582.

situation because they are the ones who laughed at that story earlier. While one could argue that here Gadsby leaves humor behind altogether, this moment brings out two significant features that Holm highlights in his definition of uncomfortable humor. Number one, Gadsby's shift transgresses boundaries of "proper behavior" and instead "offer[s] up the potential of anxiety, awkwardness, and empathetic suffering." Additionally, here, the audience is not just presented with "instances of suffering existing alongside humor, but suffering utterly entangled with it."[34] Granted, this conflation of suffering and humor is not the same as laughing at physical stunts producing predicable pain, which is a staple of shows such as *Jackass*.[35] However, Gadsby likewise illustrates a deep entanglement of suffering and humor because she reveals how much the audience's enjoyment is based on her repeated self-infliction of pain as she crafts her jokes.

One may also see Notaro's and Gadsby's performances as variants of what Krefting calls *charged humor* in her 2014 book *All Joking Aside*. Charged humor "seeks to represent the underrepresented, to empower and affirm marginalized communities and identities," and it frequently covers "social inequalities, national contradictions, and negative representations" and calls "attention to hateful language, power relations, and cultural grievances."[36] Notaro and Gadsby expose their own vulnerability and represent the underrepresented through their very stage presence. Notaro openly represents androgynous bodies and bodies that have *not* been surgically reconstructed to look feminine after a mastectomy. Gadsby represents what she calls "being incorrectly female"; she speaks out about being stigmatized, and she addresses her ongoing struggle to cope with experiences of rape and harassment. Moreover, Notaro's and Gadsby's performances point to the discrepancy between wielding power on stage as a female comic and but not having that same power offstage, and they remind us that "rhetorical gestures of empowerment" can easily "ring hollow when compared to women's or any marginalized person's experiences."[37]

---

[34] Holm, *Humor as Politics*, 91.

[35] Ibid., 94.

[36] Rebecca Krefting, *All Joking Aside* (Baltimore: Johns Hopkins University Press, 2014), 21.

[37] Krefting, "Hannah Gadsby Stands Down," 168.

90 Stand-up as Autobiographical Narrative

The decision to incorporate the unfunny therefore appears particularly politically charged when one considers that the questions "Can't you take a joke?" and "Can women be funny?" still appear as two sides of a coin that has not lost its currency in the twenty-first century. In fact, both Gadsby and Notaro not only skillfully time moments of the unfunny – of non-laughter – but they also self-reflexively comment on their craft to their audience. Notaro's comedy frequently draws "attention to its form."[38] Thus, she follows up her announcement of her cancer diagnosis by laying out the comic formula that tragedy plus time equals comedy, adding, "I am just at tragedy right now." In effect, by pointing out to the audience how her "cancer declaration" upends expectations of a stand-up's first line on stage, she essentially explains how her breaking the convention qualifies as the incongruity that creates a joke.[39] In *Boyish Girl Interrupted* and in her new Netflix special *Happy to Be Here*, Notaro also repeatedly deconstructs her own jokes, letting the audience witness the craft as craft. She has commented that, while she is "in some way breaking a major rule of comedy" by "walking through [the joke] with the audience," this meta-approach gives her a sense of authenticity on stage.[40]

Gadsby likewise comments on the inner workings of humor. Right before she tells the full story of being assaulted, she reminds the audience of her skill as a comedian: "Do you remember that story about that young man who almost beat me up? It was a very funny story. It was very funny, I made a lot of people laugh about his ignorance, and the reason I could do that is because I'm very good at this job."[41]

---

[38] Jason Zinoman, "Repeating a Repetition Repeatedly Once Again," *The New York Times*, June 24, 2012, nytimes.com/2012/06/25/arts/tig-notaro-meets-taylor-dayne-again-and-again.html3.

[39] In *Humor as Politics*, Holm sums up the incongruity theory of humor as follows: "Incongruity theory proposes that humour arises when a particular interpretation or understanding of a statement or situation is suddenly disproved and another substituted instead" (11).

[40] Steve Greene, "Tig Notaro on *Star Trek*, Moving on from *One Mississippi*, and Breaking One of the Biggest Rules of Comedy," *IndieWire*, May 22, 2018, indiewire.com/2018/05/tig-notaro-netflix-happy-to-be-here-star-trek-interview-1201967394/.

[41] Gadsby, *Nanette*, 00:58:56.

Gadsby's and Notaro's very skills as comedians rely on timing moments of the unfunny. When Notaro reveals her mastectomy scars to her audience, they cheer, but they do not laugh: there is no joke. Instead, the cheers serve at once as applause for her courage and as affirmation that the topic needs to become more public. When Gadsby tells the audience that she was raped in her early twenties, no one laughs: there is no joke. If either one of them did not "master" those situations or their timing – if members of the audience laughed during those moments – their performances would fail spectacularly.

These moments of the unfunny express a political dimension of humor because they both call into question what a joke is and can be read as commentary on the stereotype that women are not funny. Krefting points out that "performed comedy has a long history of pushing the boundaries of social acceptability, of toying with the taboo."[42] Notaro pushes the limit of what can be the subject of laughter (cancer). Gadsby pushes the limit from the other direction: she questions whether some subjects that we have laughed at in the history of comedy are simply not funny. Gadsby risks alienating her audience because, only a little while ago, they were laughing about what is now revealed to have been a traumatizing situation. They have been duped. At the same time, the opposition between her and her audience is not complete because Gadsby includes herself in the group of those who have been duped or coerced into laughing at the unfunny. This realization is part of her confession. Seeing the unfunny as the moments that give those comedy sets their political edge and considering these instances of the unfunny not as incidental, but as integral to these stand-up performances, raises new questions about the current function of the political in comedy.

But Is It Comedy?

Various reviews celebrated Notaro's and Gadsby's shows as "radical" and "transformative" when they came out. Holm cautions that it "is somewhat counterintuitive to assume that texts that are not only produced and distributed by major media companies, but also celebrated

---

[42] Krefting, *All Joking Aside*, 61.

92   Stand-up as Autobiographical Narrative

by institutionally powerful taste-makers and gatekeepers are somehow representative of an authentic and profound opposition to the status quo in any straightforward way."[43] In Peter Moskowitz's opinion, *Nanette* embodies precisely this problem. In his review of the show, he states, "Comedy can be radical; it's just that when it is, it's not typically on Netflix." In fact, he sees *Nanette* as part of the "Wokeness Industrial Complex,"[44] arguing that Gadsby makes straight cis people feel good about themselves rather than challenging her audience to act. In a similar vein, Gwen Snyder entitled her review "The Neoliberal Letdown of *Nanette*."[45]

That *Nanette* has received a much more controversial reception than Notaro's *Live* or *Boyish Girl Interrupted* is likely the result of Gadsby's "killjoy" turn to humorlessness, whereas Notaro returns to jokes. Harvey Mindess has observed that humorlessness is generally associated with "the religious zealot, the righteous patriot, the racial bigot, and the black power militant [who] are all, it is said, incapable of laughter at the particular topic about which they feel so intensely."[46] Over the last six years, various news articles have debated the question of whether political correctness was or was not "killing comedy." The question of where the borders of comedy lie and whether or not there are certain topics – for example, rape jokes[47] – that are simply never funny is probably as old as comedy itself. Rebecca Krefting argues that there is only "one categorically unfunny thing about Gadsby's remonstrations against sexism, gender violence, and homophobia in *Nanette*. That she

---

[43] Nicholas Holm, "'Against the Assault of Laughter:' Differentiating Critical and Resistant Humor," in *Comedy and Critical Thought: Laughter As Resistance*, eds. Krista Bonello Rutter Giappone, Fred Francis, and Ian MacKenzie (New York: Rowman and Littlefield, 2018), 39.

[44] Peter Moskowitz, "The Nanette Problem," *The Outline*, August 20, 2018, theoutline.com/post/5962/the-nanette-problem-hannah-gadsby-netflix-review.

[45] Gwen Snyder, "The Neoliberal Letdown of Nanette," *The Medium*, July 16, 2018, medium.com/@gwensnyder/the-neoliberal-letdown-of-nanette-2ffff40f41724.

[46] Harvey Mindess qtd. in Holm, *Humor as Politics*, 43.

[47] Gilbert, *Performing Marginality*, 12.

had to say it at all."[48] In 2017, in the midst of the #MeToo movement, stand-up comedian Louis C.K. was accused by female co-workers of masturbating in front of them, and he admitted the allegations were true.[49] In 2018, he included a rape joke in his comeback set.[50] After 2020, when Donald Trump, of "grab-'em-by-the-pussy" fame, ran for re-election as president of the United States, it seemed not very surprising that questions of comedy and politics appear critically intertwined, that the borders of comedy would be newly and hotly debated, and that "comedy is freshly dangerous."[51]

While Lauren Berlant and Sianne Ngai, among others, point out that comedy is "[a]lways crossing lines,"[52] they simultaneously emphasize that for many people, "comedy without pleasure or laughter violates itself more extremely than, say, porn that does not produce a desired arousal or a weepie that doesn't make you cry."[53] People's response to *Nanette* in particular expressed doubt as to whether Gadsby's show counted as comedy,[54] while online discussion forums similarly categorized Notaro as an "inspirational speaker" rather than a comedian, and one response even called her show a "cancer scam."[55] Krefting

---

[48] Rebecca Krefting, "Hannah Gadsby: On the Limits of Satire," *Studies in American Humor* 5, no. 1 (2019): 102.

[49] Melena Ryzik et al., "Louis C.K. Is Accused by 5 Women of Sexual Misconduct," *The New York Times*, November 9, 2017, nytimes.com/2017/11/09/arts/television/louis-ck-sexual-misconduct.html. In the wake of these allegations, in Season Two of her show *One Mississippi*, Tig Notaro focused an entire episode on sexual harassment (the example is also masturbation), which can easily be read as a comment on Louis C.K.

[50] Clarisse Loughrey, "Louis C. K. Tells 'Rape Whistle' Joke in First Stand-Up Set Since Sexual Misconduct Admission," *The Independent*, August 30, 2018, independent.co.uk/arts-entertainment/comedy/news/louis-ck-rape-whistle-joke-new-york-comedy-cellar-set-sexual-misconduct-a8514031.html.

[51] Lauren Berlant and Sianne Ngai, "Comedy Has Issues," *Critical Inquiry* 43, no. 2 (2017): 234–235.

[52] Ibid., 235.

[53] Ibid., 239.

[54] Krefting, "Hannah Gadsby," 99.

[55] Matt Hayden, "Tig Notaro Was Not Funny on Conan," *Comedy and Satire*, March 15, 2013, comedysatire.com/blog/tig-notaro-was-not-funny-on-conan.

94 Stand-up as Autobiographical Narrative

quotes Gadsby's response to allegations that *Nanette* may simply not be comedy: "Nobody would ever say that to a man doing a subversive comedy show or showing his vulnerability on stage. He'd be called a genius pushing the genre."[56] Tig Notaro's and Hannah Gadsby's performances, including their comments on the inner workings of comedy, highlight the fact that women are still simultaneously called upon to "prove" their funniness and are rebuked for being humorless. Gadsby moreover expresses larger concerns about oppressive structures in "comedy as performance practice."[57] For many who saw *Nanette*, Gadsby's "calling out" of double standards and expression of anger clearly hit a (positive) nerve. In the last few years, discussions about who is allowed to express anger and under which circumstances has been at the core of social media exchanges and debates about practices of "cancelling." As Meredith D. Clark points out, the term and act of "canceling" has its "origins in queer communities of color."[58] It indicates resistance and an "accountability practice of otherwise disempowered peoples" who do not have the clout and gatekeeping powers of, for example, producers, casting directors, or journalists. In this way, canceling actually "compel[s] us to identify who or what defines the disputed concept of the public sphere, who sets the rules of engagement, and thus what is considered "talking back" to dominant discourses."[59] Once again, it is specifically Gadsby's performance that engages these practices, but her success with her audiences and the prominence of those debates since then illustrates that those modes of speaking up and speaking out are part of larger societal negotiations about whose viewpoint and experience counts as important and noteworthy.

The debates around Notaro's and Gadsby's shows illustrate that Mintz's observation from 1985 still holds true in 2020: "[H]umor [and specifically stand-up comedy] is a vitally important social and cultural phenomenon."[60] But humor does not simply equal jokes and throw-away punchlines. We can certainly debate whether we find any given

[56] Gadsby qtd. in Krefting, "Hannah Gadsby," 99.
[57] Krefting, "Hannah Gadsby Stands Down," 166.
[58] Meredith D. Clark, "Drag Them: A Brief Etymology of So-called 'Cancel Culture,'" *Community and the Public* 5, nos. 3–4 (2020): 89.
[59] Ibid., 90.
[60] Mintz, "Standup Comedy as Social and Cultural Mediation," 71.

comedian funny, radical, or transformative; Notaro's and Gadsby's performances caution against automatically locating the unfunny "outside" of comedy. They use the stand-up stage to reclaim personal stories, but their orchestrations of the unfunny quite possibly also illustrate a skillful gauging of the current demand for such a move. That simply means that they are good at their job. These two comedians take on the unfunny in different ways, but both push the boundaries of humor, and both use the unfunny, of all things, to showcase their comedic skill.

Works Cited

Ahmed, Sarah. "Killing Joy: Feminism and the History of Happiness." *Signs* 35, no. 3 (2010): 571–594.

Aslama, Minna, and Mervi Pantti. "Talking Alone: Reality TV, Emotions, and Authenticity." *European Journal of Cultural Studies* 9, no. 2 (2006): 167–184.

Berlant, Lauren, and Sianne Ngai. "Comedy Has Issues." *Critical Inquiry* 43, no. 2 (2017): 234–235.

Berman, Judy. "'Nanette' Is the Most Discussed Comedy Special in Ages: Here's What to Read About It." *The New York Times*, July 13, 2018. nytimes.com/2018/07/13/arts/television/nanette-hannah-gadsby-netflix-roundup.html.

Clark, Meredith D. "Drag Them: A Brief Etymology of So-called 'Cancel Culture.'" *Community and the Public* 5, nos. 3–4 (2020): 88–92.

Evans, Anne-Marie. "Funny Women: Political Transgressions and Celebrity Autobiography." In *Transgressive Humor of American Women Writers*, edited by Sabrina Fuchs Abrams, 155–173. Cham: Palgrave, 2017.

Franck, Arthur W. *The Wounded Storyteller: Body, Illness, and Ethics*. Chicago: The University of Chicago Press, 1995.

Gadsby, Hannah. *Nanette*. Aired June 19, 2018, on Netflix.

Gajanan, Mahita. "Tig Notaro on Why Humor Was Instrumental to Healing After Her Cancer Diagnosis: 'Something Has to Break the Tension.'" *Time*, October 17, 2019. time.com/5699703/tig-notaro-on-why-humor-was-instrumental-to-healing-after-her-cancer-diagnosis-something-has-to-break-the-tension/.

Gilbert, Joanne. *Performing Marginality: Humor, Gender, and Cultural Critique.* Detroit: Wayne State University, 2004.

Greene, Steve. "Tig Notaro on Star Trek, Moving on from One Mississippi, and Breaking One of the Biggest Rules of Comedy." *IndieWire*, May 22, 2018. indiewire.com/2018/05/tig-notaro-netflix-happy-to-be-here-star-trek-interview-1201967394/.

Hayden, Matt. "Tig Notaro Was Not Funny on Conan." *Comedy and Satire*, March 15, 2013. comedysatire.com/blog/tig-notaro-was-not-funny-on-conan.

Holm, Nicholas. "'Against the Assault of Laughter:' Differentiating Critical and Resistant Humor." In *Comedy and Critical Thought: Laughter As Resistance*, edited by Krista Bonello Rutter Giappone, Fred Francis, and Ian MacKenzie, 31–44. New York: Rowman and Littlefield, 2018.

---. *Humor as Politics: The Political Aesthetics of Contemporary Poetry*. New York: Palgrave, 2017.

Krefting, Rebecca. *All Joking Aside*. Baltimore: Johns Hopkins University Press, 2014.

---. "Dueling Discourses. The Female Comic's Double Bind in the New Media Age." In *Transgressive Humor of American Women Writers*, edited by Sabrina Fuchs Abrams, 231–250. Cham: Palgrave, 2017.

---. "Hannah Gadsby: On the Limits of Satire." *Studies in American Humor* 5, no. 1 (2019): 93–102.

---. "Hannah Gadsby Stands Down: Feminist Comedy Studies." *Journal of Cinema and Media Studies* 58, no. 3 (2019): 165–170.

Lejeune, Philippe. "The Autobiographical Pact." In *On Autobiography*, 3–30. Minneapolis: University of Minnesota Press, 1989.

Loughrey, Clarisse. "Louis C.K. Tells 'Rape Whistle' Joke in First Stand-Up Set Since Sexual Misconduct Admission." *The Independent*, August 30, 2018. independent.co.uk/arts-entertainment/comedy/news/louis-ck-rape-whistle-joke-new-york-comedy-cellarset -sexual-misconduct-a8514031.html.

Marantz, Andrew. "Good Evening. Hello. I Have Cancer." *The New Yorker*, October 5, 2012. newyorker.com/culture/culture-desk/good-evening-hello-i-have-cancer.

Mintz, Lawrence E. "Standup Comedy as Social and Cultural Mediation." *American Quarterly* 37, no. 1 (1985): 71–80.

Moskowitz, Peter. "The Nanette Problem." *The Outline*, August 20, 2018. theoutline.com/post/5962/the-nanette-problem-hannah-gadsby -netflix-review.

Notaro, Tig. *Live*. Bloomington: Secretly Canadian, 2013.

Ryzik, Melena, et al. "Louis C.K. Is Accused by 5 Women of Sexual Misconduct." *The New York Times*, November 9, 2017. nytimes.com/2017/11/09/arts/television/louis-ck-sexual-misconduct. html.

Smith, Sidonie, and Julia Watson. *Reading Autobiography: A Guide for Interpreting Life Narratives*. Minneapolis: University of Minnesota Press, 2001.

Snyder, Gwen. "The Neoliberal Letdown of Nanette." *The Medium*, July 16, 2018. medium.com/@gwensnyder/the-neoliberal-letdown-of-nanette-2ffff40f41724.

Vaynshteyn, Gina. "Tig Notaro Does Half Her Stand-Up Set Topless After Being Heckled and Anyone Who Wasn't Already in Love with Her Is Falling Hard." *Bustle*, November 9, 2014. bustle.com/articles/48238-tig-notaro-does-half-her-stand-up-set-topless-after-being-heckled-and-anyone-who-wasnt-already.

Zinoman, Jason. "Repeating a Repetition Repeatedly Once Again." *The New York Times*, June 24, 2012. nytimes.com/2012/06/25/arts/tig-notaro-meets-taylor-dayne-again-and-again.html3.

CARSTEN JUNKER

Pernicious Plurability: *Liberty's Kids*' Militainment and the Lure of Diversity

Militainment is a portmanteau word coined, evidently, by combining the words military and entertainment. In *Militainment, Inc.: War, Media, and Popular Culture* (2010), Roger Stahl defines the term as "state violence translated into an object of pleasurable consumption."[1] This paper brings *Liberty's Kids*, an American animated children's TV program, within the purview of the conceptual concerns delineated by militainment, a framing for which the show seems an implausible candidate. There are two apparent reasons for this counterintuitive confrontation; the first concerns the target audience of the show. A forty-part series that first aired on the Public Broadcasting Service (PBS) in 2002–2003, *Liberty's Kids* was originally commissioned by PBS to educate six- to eleven-year-olds about the founding years of the United States.[2] Its protagonists are children – among them Sarah Philips, a fifteen-year-old investigative journalist from England who reports for Benjamin Franklin's newspaper from the perspective of a British loyalist and is an antagonist to James Hiller, Franklin's apprentice and a young, stern American patriot. As a program that uses entertaining means to meet educational ends, the show may more likely fall under the rubric designated by another portmanteau word: *edutainment*. So, what does an educational vehicle about early U.S. American history have to do with militainment?

---

[1] Roger Stahl, *Militainment, Inc.: War, Media, and Popular Culture* (London: Routledge, 2010), 6.

[2] Andrew M. Schocket, *Fighting over the Founders: How We Remember the American Revolution* (New York: New York University Press, 2015), 143–144.

100 Pernicious Plurability

A simple answer would be that it prominently features a war: the American Revolutionary War. But the American Revolution presents yet another reason why *Liberty's Kids* hardly seems to qualify as a candidate for militainment. *Liberty's Kids* does not easily tie in with discussions about militainment, as these discussions have sought to interrogate the nexus between U.S. popular culture and the recent wars in Afghanistan, Iraq, and elsewhere. So far, the term has shaped debates over questions of how the entertainment industry has enlisted viewers on the so-called home front into contemporary warfare abroad and made them affirm the legitimacy of U.S. military deployment. As Stahl suggests, militainment is about "state violence [...] not of the abstract, distant, or historical variety but rather [of] an impending or current use of force, one directly relevant to the citizen's current political life."[3]

I object to what I call the *recency bias* of Stahl's important considerations to argue instead that militainment, as an analytical concept, can also usefully be applied in order to grasp the extent to which depictions of *prior* wars in history can impact viewers' attitudes toward past and present wars. Why should *Liberty's Kids* not make the Revolutionary War immediately relevant to its target audience, shape its young viewers' outlook on wars in general and teach them a powerful history lesson that impacts their present attitudes toward state violence (the first airing of the last four episodes of *Liberty's Kids* coincided with the 2003 invasion of Iraq)? *Liberty's Kids* occupies a special role in the annals of U.S. popular culture, notably because it features the Revolutionary War in the first place, but also because it provides "the most sustained filmic treatment ever made on the American Revolution."[4] The show has shaped the way numerous cohorts of viewers perceive this war – it remains freely available on the internet today. *Liberty's Kids* thus deserves to be analyzed as militainment and can, in turn, expand the scope of the concept's analytical reach.

While the show might be expected to encourage children to take a critical stance toward wars, the following reading highlights that, indeed, it cannot only frame a war that dates back almost two and a half centuries in entertaining ways, it also trains its viewers to adopt an affirmative attitude toward the use of military force. The show is marked

---

[3] Stahl, *Militainment, Inc.*, 6.
[4] Schocket, *Fighting over the Founders*, 143.

by a tension between the desire to depict violence as reprehensible and the undeniable entertainment value of violent conflict, making the idea of violence as a last resort a supposedly acceptable but, in fact, insidious compromise. As I argue further, it exerts a specific kind of violence: an epistemic violence that derives its force, paradoxically, from reiterating a romanticizing narrative of the early years of American nation-building.[5] In lieu of a focus on the hegemony of white elder statesmen – whose interest in securing their freedom from Britain and their freedom to own other human beings was more important than securing freedom for all – the show's narrative essentially excuses the violence enacted then and now on people of color as a result of the structural racism that pervades America. It does so by projecting backward the sentimental image of a luring, carefree diversity, an image of what I suggest to call *plurability*: a desirable but unattained pluralization at the structural and symbolic level of this wished-for diverse national community.

Tantalizing Violence

Liberty's Kids runs over fifteen hours and covers the military action of numerous battles fought over a time period of more than one and a half decades, from the Boston Tea Party (1773) in its first episode to the inauguration of George Washington as the first president of the United States (1789) in its last. Not counting the recurring outbursts of violence that preceded its outbreak – which the series also shows – the Revolutionary War spanned more than seven years, from the battles of Lexington and Concord (1775) that mark the beginnings of the war to the American victory and British surrender at Yorktown, VA (1781) that ended hostilities, to the signing of the Preliminary Treaty of Paris (1782), which formally concluded the war.

---

[5] Even where to begin and locate the multi-sited primal scenes of what would become the United States, including an emphasis on enslaved Africans and Indigenous Americans, and how to weave these scenes into a non-exclusionary genealogical narrative of foundational moments that overcomes a focus on 1776 are crucial questions in cultural-historiographic and public debates. For one recent contribution to these debates, see Michelle M. Wright, "1619: The Danger of a Single Origin Story," *American Literary History* 32, no. 4 (2020): 1–12.

102 Pernicious Plurability

In other words, there are numerous battles to cover, and *Liberty's Kids* does not shy away from doing so. No fewer than thirteen episodes feature battles.[6] Still, as an educational program for children, the producers of *Liberty's Kids* sought to create a show that was dedicated to non-violence. They sought to create a program that depicted the Revolutionary War by showing as little violence as possible. They were "very concerned about guns" because they were "mindful of the industry maxim that kids 'watch up'"[7] – in other words, that children younger than those at whom the show is targeted might also watch it – and the producers' concern begs the question of whether there is ever an appropriate age at which to see guns being fired on television, to be numbed, as it were, and – to reframe Neil Postman[8] – amused to death. But while those responsible for the show aimed to minimize on-screen violence, they realized they could not do without guns entirely, not least for reasons of plot development. According to one programmer, the director, screenwriters, and producers of the show stressed that "the audience would be clear *why* there was conflict, not distracted by the conflict."[9]

The issue of showing *why* there is conflict has a lot to do with *how* the series shows the shooting of a gun. The sixth episode is instructive in this respect. Titled "The Shot Heard 'Round the World," it depicts how one shot initiated the Battles of Concord and Lexington. At first, the episode shows how both sides, Revolutionaries and Loyalists, are reluctant, if not outright unwilling, to initiate military action: "Neither side wishes to fight," stresses Sarah's cousin Tom, a British Loyalist soldier.[10] On the other side of the divide, Captain John Parker, commanding the colonial militia at the battle of Lexington, admonishes

---

[6] These include the Battles of Lexington and Concord, Bunker Hill, Long Island, Fort Washington, Trenton, Ridgefield, Brandywine, Saratoga, Monmouth, Flamborough Head, Fort Charlotte, Rhode Island, and Yorktown.

[7] Schocket, *Fighting over the Founders*, 147.

[8] Neil Postman, *Amusing Ourselves to Death: Public Discourse in the Age of Show Business* (New York: Penguin, 2006).

[9] Qtd. in Schocket, *Fighting over the Founders*, 147. My emphasis.

[10] "The Shot Heard Round the World," *Liberty's Kids*, episode 6, created by Kevin O'Donnell and Michael Maliani, directed by Judy Reilly. Aired September 9, 2002, on PBS, 00:08:08.

his men: "Don't fire unless fired upon."[11] But when the minutemen refuse to surrender their arms to the British, a shot is fired – it remains unclear by whom – and this triggers both sides to open fire. The sequence that follows is a collage of various grim images of war action, during which we hear and see a fusillade of gunshots underlaid by a similarly grim soundtrack. This sequence spans more than one and a half minutes of the episode.[12] To James's later question: "Who fired first?" Capt. Parker responds, "It doesn't matter. It has brought us to war."[13] A similar scene is repeated in Concord, when the colonists say: "We'll not fire on the King's troops unless we're fired upon first."[14] And indeed, the British are the ones who open fire and the shooting on both sides begins again. This time, the shooting sequence spans more than thirty seconds.[15] During the battle, Sarah's cousin Tom is killed. Although the commanders of the British troops had wanted to avoid this violent conflict, the British soldiers play it out vehemently; they use military force to exercise what the young American journalist James calls British "tyranny."[16]

In spite of the show's attempts to reduce on-screen violence, then, there is a good portion of it in this episode. Quantitatively speaking, violent scenes take up almost a tenth of the episode's time. But what is even more noteworthy is the quality of the violence depicted. Violence is not shown in order to glorify Americans as potential heroes – a role that the show could also have them play at the outbreak of the Revolution. At the same time, violence is not trivialized; rather, its use is depicted as illegitimate aggression on the British side and as legitimate self-defense on the American side of the conflict. Americans are depicted as victims of British violence, despite the fact that the episode leaves the question of who fired the first shot unanswered. In this way, the show puts its young viewers in a mindset of legitimate American patriotism. It makes them see, literally, that it is necessary for the American militiamen to defend themselves against an overpowering enemy for a good cause. Even the loyal British subject Sarah, who

---

[11] Ibid., 00:09:02.
[12] Ibid., 00:10:25–00:12:05.
[13] Ibid., 00:12:23–00:12:29.
[14] Ibid., 00:17:19.
[15] Ibid., 00:18:00–00:18:33.
[16] Ibid., 00:04:10.

104   Pernicious Plurability

mourns her British cousin's death by an American bullet, decides to move on to report on the outbreak of the war with her American friend James (and becomes increasingly convinced of the cause of American nation-building throughout the series), making her mentor Benjamin Franklin proud of her.

Revolutionary Enslavism

Liberty's Kids' coverage of the Revolutionary War is noteworthy not only for its extensive depiction of violence, but also when we consider that this war has received relatively little attention from creators of popular culture, as Andrew Schocket observes in *Fighting over the Founders: How We Remember the American Revolution* (2015).[17] One explanation for the relatively meager treatment of the Revolutionary War as an "object of pleasurable consumption"[18] is the fact that many of its protagonists, as owners of enslaved people, were beneficiaries of the regime of enslavement and therefore do not easily qualify as admirable heroes, let alone role models in war films and other forms of popular entertainment.

And indeed, *Liberty's Kids* covers the issue of enslavement in part underhandedly when it reproduces an idealizing narrative of U.S. American nation-building, according to which an emerging nation has to inevitably and legitimately defend its freedom and fight against British "tyranny." By having James refer to British "tyranny," as he does in episode six,[19] the show takes up and reproduces a topos of American Revolutionary rhetoric common during the war itself. American patriots used the topos of British tyranny to argue that the decision to take up arms was legitimate because the British were violating Americans' right to trade freely and imposing stifling taxation without giving them

---

[17] Schocket's list includes the movies *The Declaration of Independence* (1911); *The Howards of Virginia* (1940); *Revolution* (1985); *Sweet Liberty* (1986); *The Patriot* (2000); *National Treasure* (2004); the Disney television series *Swamp Fox* (1959-1961); the musical *1976* (1969). Schocket, *Fighting over the Founders*, 128–34. The successful *Hamilton: An American Musical* (2015) should be added here.

[18] Stahl, *Militainment, Inc.*, 6.

[19] "Shot," 00:04:10.

representation in British Parliament. They found they could increase the effectiveness of this topos – and here we arrive at the issue of slavery in the colonies and how it is addressed in *Liberty's Kids* – by comparing the assumed victimization of American colonists with the victimization of Africans enslaved by them. This comparison culminated in patriots calling themselves slaves to the British, a metaphorization of the term slavery that ultimately detached it from its reference to the literal apparatus of enslavement in North America.

As a backdrop to the show, let us consider how the historical figure of Thomas Jefferson, also featured in the series, used the term "slavery" in a rhetorical maneuver to substantiate a critique of the relationship between Britain and the North American colonies. An illustrative instance of this can be found in Jefferson's "Summary View of the Rights of British America" (1774): "Single acts of tyranny may be ascribed to the accidental opinion of a day; but a series of oppressions, begun at a distinguished period, and pursued unalterably through every change of ministers, too plainly prove a deliberate and systematical plan of reducing us to slavery."[20] The way Jefferson mobilizes the topos of British tyranny allows him to decry unjust economic exploitation and political domination over the colonists. However, he was able to describe the colonists' situation in terms of slavery only because he could count on his contemporaries' awareness of the atrocities to which the enslaved were subjected.

It is for this reason that *Liberty's Kids* confronts head-on the fact that Jefferson owned people himself. It shows Sarah's consternation over Jefferson's proprietorship of "other human beings,"[21] "his awful hypocrisy on the issue of slavery."[22] When Sarah confronts him, Jefferson responds defensively: "Yes, but I have proclaimed slavery an abomination that must be brought to an end,"[23] declaring it, however,

---

[20] Thomas Jefferson, "A Summary View of the Rights of British America," in *Thomas Jefferson: Writings*, ed. Merrill D. Peterson (New York: Library of America, 1984), 110.

[21] "Conflict in the South," *Liberty's Kids*, episode 33, created by Kevin O'Donnell and Michael Maliani, directed by Judy Reilly. Aired January 21, 2003, on PBS, 00:08:04–00:08:09.

[22] Ibid., 00:15:35–00:15:38.

[23] Ibid., 00:20:05–00:20:11.

106   Pernicious Plurability

one among "countless issues to be addressed," [24] and adding patronizingly, "we are great [men], great with human flaws as well as human hopes. [...] If we cannot correct this abomination, then those who follow us shall"[25] – words which ultimately appease Sarah.

While I have argued elsewhere[26] that evoking and appropriating the term "slavery" for discursive and political gain could put the brutality of the de facto enslavement regime into perspective and downplay it, a different aspect of this rhetorical operation is relevant in my reading of the children's show: the paradox of recognizing the obvious illegitimacy of the literal practice *and* still actively striving to create political circumstances under which its continuation would be possible. Numerous American slaveholding patriots used the topos of British tyranny to argue that they were fighting legitimately for their freedom from the Crown so that they could retain their freedom to continue trading in and owning enslaved Africans. This was a time when the abolitionist movement that sought to end the triangular trade in enslaved Africans was in full swing in the English-speaking transatlantic sphere, posing a threat to the beneficiaries of the trade.

The show's depiction of Jefferson's half-hearted stance toward gradual abolition corroborates – if in subtle ways – historian Gerald Horne's observation that, contrary to the assumption that the American Revolution inaugurated gradual abolition, "1776 led to the ossification of slavery,"[27] and that numerous revolutionaries fought for freedom from Britain *because of* their aim to protect their rights to trade in Africans for immense profits and to hold on to the apparatus of enslavement. This historiographical position on the Revolution indeed departs from a contrasting paradigm which holds that freedom from Britain was achieved *despite* the enslavement regime being upheld. In contrast to the *despite* paradigm, according to which the celebratory insistence on freedom and the simultaneous practice of enslavement

---

[24] Ibid., 00:20:22–00:20:24.

[25] Ibid., 00:20:39–00:20:59.

[26] Carsten Junker, *Patterns of Positioning: On the Poetics of Early Abolition* (Heidelberg: Universitätsverlag Winter, 2016), 144–151.

[27] Gerald Horne, *The Counter-Revolution of 1776: Slave Resistance and the Origins of the United States of America* (New York: New York University Press, 2014), 7.

generate a "supreme paradox,"[28] the *because-of* paradigm highlights the image of the United States as the modern cradle of freedom and its factual practices of human and social degradation and exclusion as two constitutive flipsides of one coin – it points to an "antagonism"[29] between civil society and slavery that, for the sake of civic advance, could not be resolved.

Where to locate *Liberty's Kids* on this spectrum, reaching from the *despite* paradigm to the *because-of* paradigm, cannot be answered unequivocally. The last episode of the show is instructive in terms of its ambiguous stance toward enslavement, depicting it largely as a technical problem to be handled by white statesmen. It covers the 1787 Constitutional Convention, assembled to establish an inner-American political order following the Revolutionary War by balancing states' rights and federal powers in light of factions divided over matters of the slave trade and slavery, and by reaching a compromise that "allowed not only for the continuation of slavery in the South [...] but also for the granting of disproportionate political power to slave states."[30] Upon learning that the elder statesmen have ultimately decided to prioritize the political stability of not just any nation-state, but one that allows enslavement over abolition, Moses, a free man, is patronized by Franklin:

> FRANKLIN. The delegates have reached an odious compromise between the North and the South. It was the only way to save the union.
>
> MOSES. How long will this union last? A country that keeps so many of its people in bondage. I'm a peace-loving man, Ben, and I'm afraid of the price we might have to pay to win freedom for everyone.

---

[28] David Brion Davis, "Re-Examining the Problem of Slavery in Western Culture," *Proceedings of the American Antiquarian Society* 118 (2009): 254.

[29] Frank B. Wilderson III, *Red, White & Black: Cinema and the Structure of U.S. Antagonisms* (Durham: Duke University Press, 2010), 149.

[30] Jill Lepore, *This America: The Case for the Nation* (New York: Liveright, 2019), 31.

108 Pernicious Plurability

> FRANKLIN. I am, too, my friend. We have fought one war for liberty; I hope we won't have to fight another.[31]

For Franklin, the Revolutionary War is the price to pay for his liberty as a citizen. And while he would not want to pay another price – a future civil war – to abolish slavery, Moses certainly sees enslaved people paying a daily price on the way to *their* freedom, if it is ever to be reached. This price includes the incessant struggle against their horrific exposure to what Orlando Patterson calls "naked force," "natal alienation," and "dishonor [as] a generalized condition."[32] The sentimental framing of Franklin's attitude in this dialogue of the concluding, fortieth episode of *Liberty's Kids* suggests that the series opts for the *despite* paradigm: the struggle for freedom from Britain allows a freedom for some that could eventually lead to the freedom of others. Ultimately, however, the show depicts Franklin as content with establishing a unified nation that maintains slavery by necessity, hence stressing that this freedom for some is facilitated by others' unfreedom. Overall, *Liberty's Kids* does not show the Revolutionary War as a pivotal inaugural point for the abolition of slavery. In that sense, it offers militainment that leans toward the *because-of* paradigm side. Freedom comes at a high price – *Liberty's Kids*' "Price of Freedom"[33] is a freedom that white men enjoy from Britain, and it is a freedom that accepts the continuation of enslavement, affirming what Sabine Broeck, with reference to Saidiya Hartmann, has called "enslavism," or "the ongoing afterlife of social, cultural and political anti-Blackness in the future that

---

[31] "We the People," *Liberty's Kids*, episode 40, created by Kevin O'Donnell and Michael Maliani, directed by Judy Reilly. Aired April 4, 2003, on PBS, 00:18:32–00:19:08.

[32] Orlando Patterson, *Slavery and Social Death: A Comparative Study* (Cambridge: Harvard University Press, 1982), 3; 7; 11.

[33] The phrase is taken from an exhibition titled *The Price of Freedom: Americans at War*, on display at the time of writing this article (August 2019), at the Smithsonian's *National Museum of American History* on the National Mall in Washington, D.C. The exhibit "surveys the history of America's military from the French and Indian Wars to the present conflict in Iraq, exploring ways in which wars have been defining episodes in American history."

transatlantic enslavement has made."[34] Notably, *Liberty's Kids* does not present anti-Black violence overtly, thereby exploiting it as a spectacle for pleasurable consumption. Rather, it engages with the violence of structural racism implicitly, alluding to the wrongness of slavery in a sentimental mode ("I'm a peace-loving man, Ben").

Pernicious Plurability

How to weigh the problem of enslavement posed a challenge for the creators of *Liberty's Kids* at PBS, not least because it is a network which caters to a demographically diverse audience and, according to its mission statement, "empowers individuals to achieve their potential and strengthen the social, democratic, and cultural health of the U.S."[35] Indeed, a war fought in the interest of white colonial settlers cannot easily be reconciled with PBS's mission to "educate, inspire, entertain and express a diversity of perspectives."[36] And while *Liberty's Kids* presents a diversified set of characters and thus seeks to reach a demographically diverse audience for whom the American Revolution could be an empowering reference point, it is not educational in the sense it purports to be, and, in fact, its intentions backfire. The show's explicit educational intention of overcoming the origins and persistence of an image of the future U.S. nation-state as a largely white male project cannot necessarily be aligned with its effect: the retrojection of an all-too-easygoing image of demographic plurality. The show narrates history by placing a broad range of different characters at the root of U.S. nation building, among them the impressive young, white, female aspiring investigative journalist Sarah. Another central character is a sympathetic employee at Franklin's printing shop named Moses, a Black, self-made man who was born in West Africa and, because of his ingenuity, was able to buy his freedom. Moses now keeps an eye on the minors in Franklin's care during his absence, one of whom is Henri, an

[34] Sabine Broeck, "'It is always now' (Beloved): Notes on the Urgency of Enslavism Theory, and Studies," *Zeitschrift für Anglistik und Amerikanistik: A Quarterly of Language, Literature and Culture* 65, no. 2 (2017): 137.

[35] "Mission," PBS, accessed August 22, 2019, pbs.org/about/about-pbs/mission-statement/.

[36] Ibid.

110   Pernicious Plurability

orphaned eight-year-old French boy. To present a demographically diverse cast, the show also includes such characters as the Jewish merchant and Masonic leader Moses Michael Hays, the colonial governor of Spanish Louisiana and viceroy of New Spain Bernardo de Gálvez, and, among the few Native American characters, the Mohawk leader Joseph Brant.

The show reframes rules of overwhelming social deagentization – rules which divest characters of agency if they do not occupy the position of white, male, property-owning adult citizens – by presenting exceptional characters like Sarah and Moses who defy these rules. But by depicting these anachronistic figures, the show paints a luring picture of diversity rather than opting for a critical assessment of the structural inequalities of the early U.S. nation-state. Precisely because Sarah and Moses are not representative of the respective demographics they represent, the show reproduces a mythical image of American self-fashioning. In this way, it creates an impression that everyone can be free, enjoy equal rights and overcome race- and gender-based inequalities. Declaring diversity and showing its lure forfeits, in effect, a chance to depict the political struggles actually involved in granting citizenship rights to a broader, more demographically inclusive future nation. The show thus misses out on an opportunity to portray *plurability*, a desirable yet unachieved and seemingly unachievable institutional and symbolic diversification that requires an incessant struggle for the recognition of rights and a more equitable distribution of resources. Had the show depicted its characters in less anachronistic ways, it could have elaborated on a narrative of the obstructive mechanisms of exclusion that Moses and Sarah's peers faced.

As edutainment, *Liberty's Kids* cannot resolve the friction between its educative purpose of empowering today's diversified audience and the fact that its entertainment factor resides with its structures of identification, affording uplifting stories only of exceptional individuals. *Liberty's Kids'* projection of a racially, culturally, and socially diverse young republic and its accompanying trivialization of internal conflicts among different demographics constitute a subtle act of epistemic violence exerted on those who watch and learn from it. The pernicious aspect of this act lies in preventing its viewers from learning about unequal distributions of power. *Liberty's Kids'* price of freedom – the price the show and its viewers pay for an empowering depiction of

CARSTEN JUNKER   111

characters like Sarah or Moses – is thus willful ignorance of the structural inequalities that pervade so many different subjects and of the freedom denied to all those whom the show does not depict.

Coda

This exercise of epistemic violence brings us back to the concept of militainment. As Stahl has suggested, the concept of militainment refers to the phenomenon of current wars being medially framed as entertaining; it points to specific ways of narrativizing and aestheticizing war. Moreover, it points to the fact that different branches of popular culture take up military themes, one effect of which can be the promotion or propagation of war. Undermining the recency bias of militainment, *Liberty's Kids* calls for including shows like itself that narrativize wars other than the recent ones. If we construe militainment in a broader sense, we can ask about the repercussions of past wars for popular entertainment and the potential effects of consuming, and being consumed and entertained by, narrativizations of various historical wars – effects which can, ultimately, also create young citizen-soldiers who may become complicit in the military apparatus of the United States. The sporadic presence of the American Revolution in the world of popular culture notwithstanding, *Liberty's Kids* raises questions that have general relevance, such as how popular culture can reduce the complexity of *any* military event so that those fighting can be turned into heroes by whom audiences can be entertained and with whom they may identify.

And there is yet another facet of militainment that deserves close attention, one which has to do with drawing out the implications of not only of how and to what effect war is medially framed in popular culture, but of how popular culture itself can be understood and analyzed as a weapon as well. The point of this metaphor is that popular culture in its various forms of expression, including *Liberty's Kids*, can be considered aggressive – that there is something intrinsically violent in popular culture. Consider the extremely confrontational practices and invasive methods with which different media target their audiences. The semantic framing of media in a terminology of war highlights this potential aggressiveness of media. As an example, Stahl points to the

112   Pernicious Plurability

term "blockbuster" which "originally referred to a large aerial bomb."[37] Here, military jargon serves to illustrate the great, commercially successful impact of a Hollywood movie. Figuratively, the movie drops on the entertainment market like a bomb would. This imagery of popular culture as a weapon is also reminiscent of the Frankfurt School and its legacy of critiquing mass media and the products of a repressive culture industry capable of making consumers receptive to fascist propaganda and capitalist ideology. *Liberty's Kids* is part of a contemporary body of successful militainment that gives critical theory renewed urgency, and not only because of its long grim and numbing sequences of war action.[38]

While *Liberty's Kids* cannot be categorized as militainment in the simple sense of legitimizing war in order to glorify it, the show contributes in meaningful ways to the concept of militainment. Its potential danger to its young viewers lies where popular culture becomes a weapon that exerts *epistemic* violence, causing damage among its consumers along the way. *Liberty's Kids* vindicates violence in subtle ways, enlisting its youngster audience to indulge in an idealizing and entertaining narrative of American exceptionalism that downplays structural inequalities in the service of celebrating the founding of a nation-state that exerted political power to realize its goal of freedom. But this was a freedom only for some, leaving out many along the way. Rather than making the American Revolution a reference point that could empower a wide range of young viewers, *Liberty's Kids*, in effect, undermines this purpose of empowerment by clothing a white male project of nation-building in the alluring garb of easygoing diversity. Pointing out the potential for harm that the show allows and even promotes, and keeping an eye on who has what price to pay for freedom during and in the wake of the Revolutionary War, we can expand the scope of inquiry that the concept of militainment facilitates in the study of American popular culture. Directing our attention to *plurability* in the process, we can gain a better sense of how popular

---

[37] Stahl, *Militainment, Inc.*, 4.

[38] For recent work that highlights and critiques ways in which critical theory is implicated in structures of coloniality, see Amy Allen, *The End of Progress: Decolonizing the Normative Foundations of Critical Theory* (New York: Columbia University Press, 2017); Sabine Broeck, *Gender and the Abjection of Blackness* (Albany: SUNY Press, 2018).

forms of cultural expression disengage from the unremitting struggles of the many who fight for their rights in a war-torn world.[39]

---

[39] Initial ideas for this article were presented at the workshop "Images of War: U.S. Popular Culture as Militainment" during the 66th Annual Conference on *U.S. American Culture as Popular Culture* of the German Association for American Studies, held at Universität Hamburg in June 2019. Thank you to the workshop organizers, Katharina Gerund and Mareike Spychala. I also extend my thanks to the editors of the present volume, Astrid Böger and Florian Sedlmeier, for their useful comments.

Works Cited

Allen, Amy. *The End of Progress: Decolonizing the Normative Foundations of Critical Theory*. New York: Columbia University Press, 2017.

Broeck, Sabine. *Gender and the Abjection of Blackness*. Albany: SUNY Press, 2018.

---. "'It is always now' (Beloved): Notes on the Urgency of Enslavism Theory, and Studies." *Zeitschrift für Anglistik und Amerikanistik: A Quarterly of Language, Literature and Culture* 65, no. 2 (2017): 137–143.

"Conflict in the South." *Liberty's Kids*, episode 33, created by Kevin O'Donnell and Michael Maliani, directed by Judy Reilly. Aired January 21, 2003, on PBS.

Davis, David Brion. "Re-Examining the Problem of Slavery in Western Culture." *Proceedings of the American Antiquarian Society* 118 (2009): 247–266.

Horkheimer, Max, and Theodor Adorno. "The Culture Industry: Enlightenment as Mass Deception." In *Dialectic of Enlightenment*, translated by John Cumming, 120–167. New York: Continuum, 1999.

Horne, Gerald. *The Counter-Revolution of 1776: Slave Resistance and the Origins of the United States of America*. New York: New York University Press, 2014.

Jefferson, Thomas. "A Summary View of the Rights of British America." In *Thomas Jefferson: Writings*, edited by Merrill D. Peterson, 103–122. New York: Library of America, 1984.

Junker, Carsten. *Patterns of Positioning: On the Poetics of Early Abolition*. Heidelberg: Universitätsverlag Winter, 2016.

Lepore, Jill. *This America: The Case for the Nation*. New York: Liveright, 2019.

"Mission." PBS, Accessed 22 Aug. 2019. pbs.org/about/about-pbs/mission-statement/.

Patterson, Orlando. *Slavery and Social Death: A Comparative Study*. Cambridge, MA: Harvard University Press, 1982.

Postman, Neil. *Amusing Ourselves to Death: Public Discourse in the Age of Show Business*. New York: Penguin, 2006.

Schocket, Andrew M. *Fighting over the Founders: How We Remember the American Revolution.* New York: New York University Press, 2015.

Stahl, Roger. *Militainment, Inc.: War, Media, and Popular Culture.* London: Routledge, 2010.

The Price of Freedom: Americans at War. National Museum of American History, Washington, D.C, accessed August 22, 2019. americanhistory.si.edu/exhibitions/price-of-freedom.

"The Shot Heard Round the World" *Liberty's Kids*, episode 6, created by Kevin O'Donnell and Michael Maliani, directed by Judy Reilly. Aired September 9, 2002, on PBS.

"We the People." *Liberty's Kids*, episode 40, created by Kevin O'Donnell and Michael Maliani, directed by Judy Reilly. Aired April 4, 2003, on PBS, 2003.

Wilderson III, Frank B. *Red, White & Black: Cinema and the Structure of U.S. Antagonisms.* Durham: Duke University Press, 2010.

Wright, Michelle M. "1619: The Danger of a Single Origin Story." *American Literary History* 32, no. 4 (2020): 1–12.

KATJA KANZLER

Conspicuous Contempt: Popular Culture and the Invective Performativity of Taste

For more than two decades, there has been a remarkable, and remarkably conspicuous, discourse around the branch of television culture know as reality TV. Sometimes, this discourse has appeared in extraordinary contexts, such as a 2001 episode of the ABC talk show *Nightline* in which host Ted Koppel engages his guest Kurt Vonnegut in a discussion of reality TV, using some of the face time he has with the renowned writer to ponder whether reality TV is "the end of civilization" and to publicly agree that its creators are "scumbags."[1] At other times, it is the sheer extent and intensity of this discourse that is noteworthy: Journalistic outlets regularly run sensationalized exposés by insiders of the reality TV industry which reveal and continually re-reveal the 'fakery' behind reality TV.[2] Public figures and commentators of all stripes regularly spice up their commentary with put-downs of reality TV and often make headlines for doing so.[3] Celebrities from the

---

[1] "Is Reality TV the End of Civilization?" *ABC News*, January 7, 2006, abcnews.go.com/US/story?id=93079&page=1.

[2] For a few arbitrary examples – some of which tackle the reality TV industry as a whole while others address individual formats – see Christian Guiltenane, "The Shocking Moments When We Realised that Reality Shows Are Faked," *Digital Spy*, April 19, 2019, digitalspy.com/TV/a862034/reality-TV-staged-fake/; Lauren Piester, "Real or Fake? The Truth about Some of Your Favorite Reality TV Shows," *E News*, November 9, 2018, eonline.com/news/985791/real-or-fake-the-truth-about-some-of-your-favorite-reality-TV-shows; Todd Van Luling, "Here's What Really Happened to the Cars from 'Pimp My Ride,'" *HuffPost*, February 25, 2015, huffpost.com/entry/pimp-my-ride-cars_n_666384 0.

[3] For an (again largely arbitrary) example, see Gill Pringle, "Robocop's Gary Oldman: 'My Dog Has More Dignity than the Kardashians,'" *The*

118   Popular Culture and the Invective Performativity of Taste

more legitimate branches of culture regularly get air time for bad-mouthing reality TV and its celebrities; the phenomenon is widespread enough that hit lists of the 'best insults' against reality TV have become a thing.[4] And a rapidly growing number of books – from the journalistic to the scholarly – have invested in unfolding the ills of reality TV, often in language that stands out for its passion and polemical tone.[5]

Evidently, we love to talk about how bad reality TV is – and my choice of pronoun here is meant to highlight how our own scholarship can be part of this discourse. It is this appeal of reality TV as an object of contempt, and the cultural work that attendant practices of contempt do, that I am interested in. I proceed from the observation that there is a performative surplus to such practices of contempt, which suggests that there is more at stake here than a critique of reality TV; that, indeed, all the censorious talk might have little to do with reality TV itself. I want to use the concept of taste to tackle this performative surplus and to argue that performances of contempt for reality TV are tied to a larger invective practice that has been fundamental to the field of popular culture.

In the following, I want to re-frame practices of taste by focusing on this performative dimension, which I describe as revolving around conspicuous contempt. In looking at a few select formations of conspicuous contempt of the popular, I will outline how these practices draw on a remarkably durable repertoire of invective narratives. My excursions into these formations will eventually bring me to the

Independent, February 10, 2014, independent.co.uk/arts-entertainment/films/features/robocops-gary-oldman-on-the-kardashians-and-being-the-highest-grossing-actor-in-film-history9120010.html. The article is a feature on actor Gary Oldman and his new film, but it headlines him for insulting Kim Kardashian.

[4]   For a good illustration of this phenomenon, see Danielle Tullo, "The 24 Meanest Things Celebrities Have Said about the Kardashians," *Cosmopolitan*, April 4, 2016, cosmopolitan.com/entertainment/celebs/news/a44747/mean-things-celebrities-have-said-about-the-kardashians/.

[5]   One example is media scholar Jennifer Pozner who writes: "Follow me into the rabbit hole of Reality TV, and let's take a look at how television's Svengalis want us to see ourselves." Jennifer L. Pozner, *Reality Bites Back: The Troubling Truth about Guilty Pleasure TV* (New York: Seal Press, 2010), 8.

KATJA KANZLER

phenomenon of reality TV, and I will end by proposing a set of questions that emerge when approaching (self-)descriptions of reality TV against the backdrop of this legacy of conspicuous contempt that pervades delineations of the popular.

My point of departure is the observation – not entirely new – that taste is a key factor in the constitution of the popular as a cultural field.[6] If we conceive of popular culture not as a clearly delineable set of texts and artifacts but as a discursive practice that produces and performs a category we call popular culture, then practices of taste play a significant role. Popular culture has, to a significant extent, been interpellated through taste-driven practices of disparagement. The particulars of these practices may have varied across historical and medial contexts, but they share an invective logic that draws on an authority of taste. Examples range from the tirades against slowly proliferating forms of theatrical entertainment in eighteenth- and nineteenth-century North America; to Nathaniel Hawthorne's famous diatribe against the "damned mob of scribbling women" and their bestselling novels, which he calls "trash" he would be ashamed of; to the contempt for the dime novels favored by working-class readers in the nineteenth century; to the dismissals of jazz as either 'barbaric' or 'commercial' music in the early twentieth century; to the manifold rants against electronic game culture in more recent decades. Across a variety of historical constellations, arbiters of taste have interpellated popular culture as inferior, debased, illegitimate, ridiculous, dangerous. The contempt they so conspicuously perform proceeds from a notion 'good culture' that is often so self-confidently yielded that it remains implicit, demarcated and valorized only through the deprecation of the allegedly

---

[6] The idea that popular culture is a social formation that is shaped by structures of inequality is, of course, fundamental to the discipline of Cultural Studies, as is the observation that the category of the popular emerged in tandem with and in contradistinction to the category of high culture. Lawrence Levine's classic *Highbrow/Lowbrow: The Emergence of Cultural Hierarchy in America* (Cambridge: Harvard University Press, 1988) probes the historical processes by which the notion of a popular culture established itself in the United States. Another classic study that needs to be mentioned in this context is Herbert Gans's *Popular Culture and High Culture: An Analysis and Evaluation of Taste* (New York: Basic Books, 1999), which I discuss in greater detail later in this essay.

120   Popular Culture and the Invective Performativity of Taste

'bad.' Taste, of course, is also performed through explicit praise for the allegedly valuable and sophisticated, yet the field of popular culture highlights how pervasively taste relies on performances of contempt for the antithesis of legitimate culture.

Such invective performances of taste have marked the popular as a cultural field throughout its history. They have been operative in popular culture's perpetual definition as Other, the counterpart to legitimate, 'highbrow' culture. They have been equally operative in popular culture's responses to this Othering – responses that range from affirmations of its 'non-elite' difference to denials of this difference in efforts of self-legitimization. The extent to which invective performances of taste have shaped the popular also becomes visible in the waves of gentrification that regularly cut through the field of popular culture, and in the dynamics by which some of its forms are elevated into newly legitimate art by claiming distinction from other, 'regular' instances of the popular. And, finally, it has manifested itself in the currents of resignification that have marked popular culture practices of the last half-century especially – currents of resignification in which subcultures valorize as 'camp' or 'cult' the popular formations deprecated by mainstream arbiters of taste.

Approaching taste as a performative practice that runs to a large extent on invective brings several things into focus. Most notably, it directs attention to the role of performance in contexts of social distinction, or, more precisely, to the role that performative affect and emotion play there. The significance of feeling in contexts of taste is already implied in its very terminology. As Raymond Williams notes in his classic *Keywords*, the meaning of the word 'taste' was originally closely related to that of the modern words 'touch' and 'feel'[7] – that is, to a form of sensory, somatic experience. While this original meaning of 'taste' was subsequently overwritten by a meaning synonymous with 'discrimination' and, still later, by connotations of judgment,[8] the embodied dimension has continued to resonate in the concept and social practice of taste. It has continued to resonate in the authority on which performances of taste tend to draw – an authority of embodied

---

[7] Raymond Williams, *Keywords: A Vocabulary of Culture and Society* (Oxford: Oxford University Press, 1983), 313.

[8] Ibid.

'knowing' that distinguishes what is good from what is bad. It further resonates in how performances of taste draw on emotional registers that can be productively described as those of contempt. William Ian Miller has discussed contempt as an emotion that is particularly rich and flexible in terms of its performative repertoire: "We recognize contempt as a complex which can be made of various admixtures of affect and social style. [...] most of us will have no trouble imagining contempt colluding with pity as well as scorn and derision, bemusement as well as smugness; with haughtiness, disgust, revulsion, and horror; with love as well as hatred, indifference, disdain, snubbing, ignoring, sneering."[9] Approaching taste as a performative practice that feeds on invective highlights the fact that conspicuous contempt – in all its performative range and various shades of intensity – plays a key role in negotiations of social distinction, providing the emotive fuel on which these negotiations run.

These social stakes in performances of taste have, of course, been most influentially theorized by Pierre Bourdieu, who conceptualized taste as a social practice through which social distinctions are articulated.[10] In his view, taste performs the cultural capital on which distinction builds: cashing in on it, keeping it in circulation and thus securing its value. Bourdieu most strongly makes the case for how practices of taste articulate class positions, but a mere glance at the invective making of the popular in a U.S.-American context shows that more – and more intricately intertwined – vectors of inequality need to be considered. The invective performativity of taste negotiates webs of classed, gendered, and racialized distinction that are highly complex and, historically, highly dynamic.

Bourdieu's notion of taste has played a considerable role in Popular Culture Studies, most classically perhaps in Herbert Gans's *Popular Culture and High Culture: An Analysis and Evaluation of Taste* (1974). Gans's book aims to vindicate popular culture by diagnosing hierarchies of taste in United States culture. These hierarchies are closely tied to inequalities in US society that fuel pervasive attacks on the cultural

---

[9] William Ian Miller, *The Anatomy of Disgust* (Cambridge: Harvard University Press, 1997), 214.

[10] Pierre Bourdieu, *Distinction: A Social Critique of the Judgment of Taste* (Cambridge: Harvard University Press, 1984).

122   Popular Culture and the Invective Performativity of Taste

practices of taste publics dominated by marginalized groups. And while the particular taste publics he identifies, and the language he uses to talk about them, might be debatable, Gans's point about how and to what effect taste hierarchies operate very much continues to carry weight.

What also remains compelling is Gans's analysis of the narratives that underwrite performances of contempt for popular culture.[11] I want to suggest that the four narrative dynamics he identifies in discursive practices of the 1970s reach far beyond their historical moment and continue to structure the invective making of the popular. First, he calls attention to the narrative which alleges that popular culture is unsophisticated and of low quality because it is commercially produced. This narrative relies – as do all the discursive dynamics Gans discusses – on a dichotomous juxtaposition of the popular and legitimate culture, the latter of which is constructed, through this juxtaposition, as valuable because it is supposedly not commercial. Non-commerciality is thus conflated with artistic quality, and commerciality with a lack of such quality. Second, Gans points to the narrative that popular culture threatens high culture. In this narrative, popular culture takes away high culture's space, luring both artists and audiences away from more valuable forms of expression; or, popular culture co-opts the styles and techniques of legitimate culture, thereby debasing them and making them useless for artistic expression. Third, there is the narrative that popular culture harms the people who consume it – that it provides escapist fantasies which distract them from what they should care about instead, giving them wrong and dangerous ideas about life or causing them serious emotional harm. And the fourth narrative that Gans identifies revolves around the claim that popular culture ruins society. Gans paraphrases this narrative: "The wide distribution of popular culture not only reduces the level of cultural quality – or civilization – of the society, but also encourages totalitarianism by creating a passive audience peculiarly responsive to the techniques of mass persuasion used by demagogues bent on dictatorship."[12]

Since the middle of the twentieth century, the anti-popular discourse that organizes around these narratives has focused on one medium in particular: television. By mid-century, television had become a primary

---

[11]   Gans, *Popular Culture*, 29.
[12]   Ibid.

KATJA KANZLER 123

object in this invective making of the popular – a primary site where taste has been performed through practices of disparagement. The homing in on television becomes apparent in numerous discursive contexts.

One notable context can be found in academia, or more precisely in the branch of scholarship known as cultural critique.[13] Since the 1960s, cultural critique has focused much of its critical energy on the medium of television, from Daniel Boorstin's *The Image*,[14] which casts television as a threat to American democracy because it socializes the public into expecting mindless spectacle rather than sober and serious news coverage; to Neil Postman's *Amusing Ourselves to Death*,[15] whose polemical contempt for television is already signaled by the book's title; to, maybe least overtly, Robert Putnam's *Bowling Alone*,[16] which argues that civic engagement in the United States is on a dangerous path of decline and points to the mass media, and most prominently to television, as the culprit of this development.

Yet this invective homing in on television is not limited to academia by far. It can also be observed in more widely circulating discourses such as the one around TV Turnoff Week, a campaign that started in the 1990s and continues to this day, having undergone several name changes in the meantime that include Digital Detox Week and, currently, Screen-Free Week.[17] This name change indicates not only

[13] My suggestion here that certain formations of humanities scholarship can be productively interrogated through the lens of conspicuous contempt resonates with some of the points made by Rita Felski, who scaffolds her "critique of critique," among other things, by pointing to the affective dimension of critical practice and to the social context in which this affectivity accrues meaning: "Rather than an ascetic exercise in demystification, suspicious reading turns out to be a style of thought infused with a range of passions and pleasures, intense engagements and commitments." Rita Felski, *The Limits of Critique* (Chicago: University of Chicago Press, 2015), 10.

[14] Daniel J. Boorstin, *The Image: A Guide to Pseudo-Events in America* (New York: Harper and Row, 1961).

[15] Neil Postman, *Amusing Ourselves to Death: Public Discourse in the Age of Show Business* (New York: Penguin, 1985).

[16] Robert D. Putnam, *Bowling Alone: The Collapse and Revival of American Community* (New York: Simon and Schuster, 2000).

[17] "Campaign for a Commercial-Free Childhood," *Screen-Free Week*, accessed

124   Popular Culture and the Invective Performativity of Taste

that, thanks to changes in the media ecosystem, television might be in the process of losing its singular position as an invective target; it also highlights what Jason Mittell identified in an analysis of the earlier TV Turnoff Week, namely a pervasive use of affectively charged drug- and addiction-related metaphors in the campaign's invective construction of television.[18] Throughout these and so many other discursive practices, it has been television that is singled out as the most detrimental and dangerous incarnation of 'bad' popular culture. In ways that resonate with the anti-pop narratives identified by Herbert Gans, television is presented as circulating low-quality content because the TV industry just wants to make money, or as disseminating materials that are described as emphatically lacking in substance or merit but excelling in sensationalist appeal.[19]

Television is also regularly described as being harmful to the more valuable and important forms of culture, especially literature and cinema.[20] There is a similarly pervasive narrative that television harms the people who watch it. At times, actualizations of this narrative point to children as being particularly likely to be harmed by television, but they also often construct other audiences as child-like because of their inability to handle television. Notably, the audiences who issue such warnings are usually framed as different from the audiences who receive them: the allegedly less-educated poor, the allegedly less-refined rural, or the amorphous 'masses,' for that matter.[21] And, finally, television is

---

February 1, 2020, screenfree.org/.

[18] Jason Mittell, "The Cultural Power of an Anti-Television Metaphor: Questioning the 'Plug-In Drug' and a TV-Free America," *Television & New Media* 1, no. 2 (2000): 217.

[19] For example, Boorstin's notion of "pseudo events" illustrates this line of argument, as does his conceptualization of celebrities as personas "distinguished by their well-knownness more than by any other quality." Boorstin, *The Image*, 154.

[20] Among the publications I just mentioned, this point is made with particular fervor by Postman who "lament[s]" that the "ascendancy of the Age of Television" contributes to a "decline of the Age of Topography." Postman, *Amusing Ourselves to Death*, 8.

[21] Again, Postman's book is a venue where this line of argument surfaces in exemplary fashion. In a passage dedicated to lamenting the state of public education, his book moves from castigating *Sesame Street* as an "expensive

regularly cast as a threat to American society, putting it on a path of civilizational decline and making its citizens unfit for democracy by socializing them to be passive and easily manipulated consumers.

Most of the contempt for television that is performed in these discourses directs itself at the medium as a more abstract whole rather than at individual programs or genres. Yet as the medium matures, it begins to diversify and becomes a playground for waves of gentrification which frame some television as 'better' than the rest. In other words, television begins to host the dialectic of disparagement and praise that is fundamental to practices of taste in its intramedial discourses. This is what Michael Z. Newman and Elana Levine extensively discuss in their book *Legitimating Television*.[22] They outline how, almost from the beginning of the medium, some television sought distinction by claiming to be better than the medium's 'regular' programming – genres like live anthology dramas or TV documentaries in the 50s and 60s, for example. Later programs like *M.A.S.H.* or *Hill Street Blues* were also positioned as creatively going beyond the formulas that allegedly mark 'regular' TV, and as telling stories that were relevant to contemporary society (unlike the allegedly trivial content that pervades the rest of the medium). Discourses that seek to gentrify some television – both back then as well as in the more recent era of 'quality TV' – tend to originate within the TV industry and its efforts to target more upscale audience demographics by offering them a platform for performances of taste-based distinction. Choosing 'quality' material always affords an opportunity to perform contempt for the 'non-quality.' Then as now, the praise showered on some television always rides a wave of contempt for other television.

For much of the medium's history, the daytime soap opera served as the primary discursive punching-bag in this regard. Robert C. Allen, in his study *Speaking of Soap Operas*, traces back this tradition of conspicuous disdain for soaps all the way to the 1940s, when it was directed at the TV genre's precursor: radio. Looking at numerous

---

illustration of the idea that education is indistinguishable from entertainment" to speculating that the audience of a televised rape trial "could barely tell the difference between the trial and their favorite mid-day soap opera." Ibid., 94.

[22] Michael Z. Newman and Elana Levine, *Legitimating Television: Media Convergence and Cultural Status* (London: Routledge, 2011).

126   Popular Culture and the Invective Performativity of Taste

examples of anti-soap invective, he finds that such practices place soap operas in "a discursive space so far outside the boundaries of normative aesthetics that they could be used as the *sine qua non* of anti art."[23] Tania Modleski's equally classic study *Loving With a Vengeance* highlights how this recurrent use of the soap as a point of reference in discourses of cultural value is tied to a distinctly gendered hierarchy of taste:

> If television is considered by some to be a vast wasteland, soap operas are thought to be the least fertile spot in the desert. The surest way to damn a film, a television program, or even a situation in real life is to invoke an analogy to soap operas. In the same way that men are often concerned to show that what they are, above all, is not women, not 'feminine,' so television programs and movies will, surprisingly often, tell us that they are not soap operas.[24]

The pervasive framing of soaps as "the *sine qua non* of anti art" performs a distinction in which gender is the dominant, if not the only, vector of inequality; and Modleski, along with several other feminist critics, points to the long tradition this gendered discourse has in constructions of art and the artistic.

Newman and Levine argue that this dynamic is still at work in the 'quality TV' discourse of the early 2000s. The 'quality' discourse in and around TV programs of the recent 'golden age' still seeks to generate legitimacy and value by depreciating the soap opera. Newman and Levine, as well as other scholars, note that this is all the more remarkable given that this 'quality TV' actually has a good deal in common with soaps, most notably their serialized form of storytelling. Yet golden age programs routinely disavow this connection and work to make the point that they are not soaps. They do this through their own narrative and stylistic choices, and in the way these choices are semanticized through extra-textual discourse (e.g., their investment in formal aesthetics, their focus on male anti-heroes, their reliance on spectacles of violence, their nods to genres that are connoted as

---

[23]   Robert C. Allen, *Speaking of Soap Operas* (Chapel Hill: University of North Carolina Press, 1985), 12.

[24]   Tania Modleski, *Loving with a Vengeance: Mass-Produced Fantasies for Women* (Hamden: Shoestring Press, 1982), 78.

masculine, and the framing of all this as 'cinematic' and 'transgressive'). The distinction that 'quality TV' claims is still performed through gender tropes, Newman and Levine argue: "much of what gets praised about prime-time seriality is framed in masculinist terms that work to distance such programming from its feminized other."[25]

I want to suggest that the dynamic Newman and Levine describe in the 'quality' discourse of the early 2000s is now in the process of changing. It is no longer the soap opera that stands as the epitome of 'trash TV,' but reality TV. Contempt for reality TV has become the key site for both the construction of televisual quality and for performances of taste. The replacement of the soap opera as the discursive punching bag in negotiations of prestige and legitimacy is, of course, tied to the diminishing role of daytime soap operas in (post-)television programming – a decline that has been long in the making and that accelerated when the multiplication of TV content in the age of 'peak TV' challenged the soap's pole position in the field of daytime entertainment.[26] Also, the process in which reality TV has overtaken the soap opera as the icon of 'trash TV' has been a gradual one. Reality TV has been around since the beginning of the recent 'quality' era, and the two are deeply entangled as elements of the medium's diversification. In fact, Jane Feuer observed as early as 2007 that "[r]eality TV is the great other to quality drama."[27]

I would argue that what is new, however, is the pervasiveness with which this othering is performed through conspicuous practices of contempt. Once again, the discourse tends to organize around the narratives Herbert Gans identified in much older performances of taste. The narrative pattern that deprecates popular culture for being

---

[25] Newman and Levine, *Legitimating Television*, 82.

[26] As, e.g., Ford, de Kosnik, and Harrington outline, reality TV was a significant part of the new competition in (post-) TV culture that, arguably, elbowed out the daytime soap. Sam Ford et al., "Introduction: The Crisis of Daytime Drama and What It Means for the Future of Television," in *The Survival of Soap Opera: Transformations for a New Media Era*, ed. Sam Ford et al. (Oxford: University of Mississippi Press, 2011), 3–21.

[27] Jane Feuer, "HBO and the Concept of Quality TV," in *Quality TV: Contemporary American Television and Beyond*, ed. Janet McCabe and Kim Akass (London: I.B. Tauris, 2007), 156.

128   Popular Culture and the Invective Performativity of Taste

commercially produced is actualized in the motif of reality TV's cheapness in particular: Again and again, critics have pointed out that reality TV is cheap to make, framing this cheapness as being metonymic of low quality.[28] Additionally, the narrative that deprecates popular culture for allegedly causing social harm permeates the construction of reality TV as 'trash TV.' A Google search of the phrase "reality TV dumbing down society" on a day selected at random generated more than 300,000 hits linking to all kinds of sources. The taste public constituted by humanities scholarship has also contributed to this narrative. Scholarship in the broader context of American Studies has almost consistently approached reality TV through a hermeneutics of suspicion, proceeding from the assumption that its social effects could only be measured in terms of harm. This is remarkable, given that – at the exact same time – scholarship on other segments of television culture, such as so-called 'quality TV,' has gravitated toward a hermeneutics of trust. In addition, research in non-Western countries on the social effects of reality TV tends to be much more varied than the 'suspicious' research conducted in a US context.[29]

A third pattern identified by Herbert Gans that is quite prominent in the trashing of reality TV is the narrative that it is harming the people who watch it, as 'these people' are unable to see through the machinations of reality TV and because, above all, they buy into its claim of representing reality. And, again, scholarship has contributed to this narrative through the numerous studies that demystify the reality claims of reality TV. Such lines of scholarship operate on the more or less explicitly articulated assumption that reality TV's original audience does not comprehend the genre's central illusion, and that they are therefore vulnerable to the programs' detrimental content.[30] In addition,

---

[28]   Annette Hill, in her study of reality TV, points to cheapness as a regularly recurring trope in public discourse on this segment of television culture. Annette Hill, *Reality TV: Audiences and Popular Factual Television* (London: Routledge, 2005), 7.

[29]   The contributions in, e.g., Marwan M. Kraidy and Katherine Sender, eds., *The Politics of Reality Television: Global Perspectives* (London: Routledge, 2010) bear ample testimony to this diversity in international scholarship.

[30]   Such lines of scholarship often operate under the assumptions of mass culture theory that cultural studies scholars have criticized for framing popular audiences as passive and at the mercy of a powerful culture industry.

members of upscale taste publics also advance this narrative when they talk about their own consumption of reality TV in terms of a 'guilty pleasure.'[31] Such talk fashions their consumption of reality TV into a form of 'slumming,' of taking time off from one's usual, elevated standards of taste for an excursion into the substandard. By framing their own pleasure in reality TV as 'guilty,' speakers distinguish themselves from an assumed regular audience of the genre, an audience that allegedly does not feel guilty about enjoying such material. While the 'guiltily pleased' emphasize that they watch reality TV with a degree of distance and reflexivity, the 'regular' viewer is concurrently cast as lacking these aspects, as naively and passively absorbing reality TV's content. Like all performances of taste that work as practices of distinction, invectives against reality TV are ultimately invectives against its presumed audience. They construct this audience as a group that is simultaneously othered and deprecated: judged for its alleged cultural preferences and media practices, blamed for its receptivity to allegedly inferior cultural materials and responsible, therefore, for these materials' ongoing circulation, if not their existence. This audience is also blamed for being a weak link in the social fabric, a risk group for anything from civilizational decline to the demise of democracy.

In many ways, then, descriptions of reality TV as 'trash TV' are part of the legacy of the invective making of the popular and its contouring

For two exemplary studies that specifically grapple with the question of how much reality TV does or does not manipulate audiences with its reality claims, see Anita Biressi and Heather Nunn, *Reality TV: Realism and Revelation* (New York: Columbia University Press, 2005); and David S. Escoffery, ed., *How Real Is Reality TV? Essays on Representation and Truth* (Jefferson: McFarland, 2014).

[31] The sociologists Charles McCoy and Roscoe Scarborough conducted an empirical study of how people who identify as 'cultured' watch TV content that they themselves label as 'bad.' Discourses of 'guilty pleasure' are one of the media practices they diagnosed; others are practices of ironic consumption and invocations of a camp sensibility. While McCoy and Scarborough interpret these practices as coping mechanisms by which people deal with their transgression of their own aesthetic norms, I would add that there is a performative, other-directed dimension to these practices. Charles Allan McCoy and Roscoe C. Scarborough, "Watching 'Bad' Television: Ironic Consumption, Camp, and Guilty Pleasure," *Poetics* 47 (2014): 41–59.

130   Popular Culture and the Invective Performativity of Taste

through practices of conspicuous contempt. Approaching reality TV culture through the lens of this legacy brings into focus a set of questions that promise to shed further light on the distinction work that can contaminate engagement with this branch of television culture, and I want to conclude by pointing to three such areas of inquiry. For one, such an approach encourages closer attention to the performative dynamics in depreciations and criticisms of reality TV. It is not just the content of censorious discourse that is meaningful – the very act of articulating censure also signifies, in ways that highlight how practices of depreciative judgment are always socially embedded. If, as I have been arguing, affectivity plays a central role in the performative work of such practices, it seems worthwhile to ask how put-downs of reality TV express ways of feeling – ones tied to contempt, for example – and to which things, practices, and people such discursive practices attach these feelings.[32]

Second, looking at reality TV through the lens of the legacy I sketched out above encourages us to ask what social position(s) are being vilified as the presumed audience of this iteration of 'trash TV.' In older articulations of the soap opera as 'trash TV,' the presumed audience was women – or, more narrowly, women without careers outside the home. Anti-soap invectives thus negotiated an intersectional web of distinction in which gender was quite dominant. In put-downs of reality TV, class seems to play a more central role, but it requires closer scrutiny to disentangle the ways in which particular instances of depreciation interlace negotiations of class with other markers of distinction. For example, who, socially speaking, is the presumed audience of *Keeping Up with the Kardashians* in the numerous invectives directed at the show during its fourteen-year run? What audience is imagined as being behind *The Bachelor* and its many spin-offs, or behind *Duck Dynasty*, and how does censure of these shows construct and judge these implied audiences?

---

[32]   The direction in which I take this question owes to Sara Ahmed's conceptual figure of 'sticky feelings' – her approach to the "cultural politics of emotion" as processes of circulation, in which feelings "circulate between bodies [and objects]," "sticking" to some while "sliding" over others. Sara Ahmed, *The Cultural Politics of Emotion* (Edinburgh: Edinburgh University Press, 2014), 4–16.

Finally, approaching reality TV against the backdrop of the invective making of the popular invites us to be on the lookout for processes of gentrification. Indeed, recent years seem to bear witness to tendencies of diversification within the field of reality TV with the emergence of a sector that is described, and describes itself, as 'Quality Reality TV.' Much of this development is tied to the entry of new players into the reality TV market, especially Netflix, whose 'original productions' *Tidying Up with Marie Kondo* and *Queer Eye* are prime examples of formats that are regularly praised for being 'better' reality TV – better because they are allegedly so different from 'regular' reality TV.[33] It is worthwhile to look more closely at the conditions that enable the rise of such (self-)descriptions, and to ask whether or not articulations of gentrified reality TV recalibrate the distinction work that is performed in discursive practices around this branch of television culture.

[33] E.g. Sarah Archer, "Tidying Up with Marie Kondo Isn't Really a Makeover Show," *The Atlantic*, January 4, 2019, theatlantic.com/entertainment/archive/2019/01/tidying-up-with-marie-kondo-netflix-show-kon-mari-review/579400; Tyler Coates, "Tidying Up with Marie Kondo Is the Reason All Your Friends Are Suddenly Into Folding," *Esquire*, January 8, 2019, esquire.com/entertainment/TV/a25780969/tidying-up-with-marie-kondo-netflix-review/; Lucas Mann, "A Gentler Reality Television," *The Paris Review*, May 8, 2018, theparisreview.org/blog/2018/05/08/a-gentler-reality-television/.

132   Popular Culture and the Invective Performativity of Taste

Works Cited

Ahmed, Sara. *The Cultural Politics of Emotion*. Edinburgh: Edinburgh University Press, 2014.

Allen, Robert C. *Speaking of Soap Operas*. Chapel Hill: University of North Carolina Press, 1985.

Archer, Sarah. "Tidying Up with Marie Kondo Isn't Really a Makeover Show." *The Atlantic*, January 4, 2019. theatlantic.com/entertainment/archive/2019/01/tidying-up-with-marie-kondo-netflix-show-kon-mari-review/579400/.

Biressi, Anita, and Heather Nunn. *Reality TV: Realism and Revelation*. New York: Columbia University Press, 2005.

Boorstin, Daniel J. *The Image: A Guide to Pseudo-Events in America*. New York: Harper and Row, 1961.

Bourdieu, Pierre. *Distinction: A Social Critique of the Judgment of Taste*. Translated by Richard Nice. Cambridge: Harvard University Press, 1984.

"Campaign for a Commercial-Free Childhood." *Screen-Free Week*, accessed February 1, 2020. screenfree.org/.

Coates, Tyler. "Tidying Up with Marie Kondo Is the Reason All Your Friends Are Suddenly Into Folding." *Esquire*, January 8, 2019. esquire.com/entertainment/TV/a25780969/tidying-up-with-marie-kondo-netflix-review/.

Escoffery, David S., ed. *How Real Is Reality TV? Essays on Representation and Truth*. Jefferson: McFarland, 2014.

Felski, Rita. *The Limits of Critique*. Chicago: University of Chicago Press, 2015.

Feuer, Jane. "HBO and the Concept of Quality TV." In *Quality TV: Contemporary American Television and Beyond*, edited by Janet McCabe and Kim Akass, 145–157. London: I.B. Tauris, 2007.

Ford, Sam, et al. "Introduction: The Crisis of Daytime Drama and What It Means for the Future of Television." In *The Survival of Soap Opera: Transformations for a New Media Era*, edited by Sam Ford et al., 3–21. Oxford: University of Mississippi Press, 2011.

Gans, Herbert J. *Popular Culture and High Culture: An Analysis and Evaluation of Taste*. New York: Basic Books, 1999.

Guiltenane, Christian. "The Shocking Moments When We Realised that Reality Shows Are Faked." *Digital Spy*, April 19, 2019. digitalspy.com/TV/a862034/reality-TV-staged-fake/.

Hill, Annette. *Reality TV: Audiences and Popular Factual Television*. London: Routledge, 2005.

"Is Reality TV the End of Civilization?" *ABC News*, January 7, 2006. abcnews.go.com/US/story?id=93079&page=1.

Kraidy, Marwan M., and Katherine Sender, eds. *The Politics of Reality Television: Global Perspectives*. London: Routledge, 2010.

Levine, Lawrence W. *Highbrow/Lowbrow: The Emergence of Cultural Hierarchy in America*. Cambridge: Harvard University Press, 1988.

Mann, Lucas. "A Gentler Reality Television." *The Paris Review*, May 8, 2018.
theparisreview.org/blog/2018/05/08/a-gentler-reality-television/.

McCoy, Charles Allan, and Roscoe C. Scarborough. "Watching 'Bad' Television: Ironic Consumption, Camp, and Guilty Pleasure." *Poetics* 47 (2014): 41–59.

Miller, William Ian. *The Anatomy of Disgust*. Cambridge: Harvard University Press, 1997.

Mittell, Jason. "The Cultural Power of an Anti-Television Metaphor: Questioning the 'Plug-In Drug' and a TV-Free America." *Television & New Media* 1, no. 2 (2000): 215–238.

Modleski, Tania. *Loving with a Vengeance: Mass-Produced Fantasies for Women*. Hamden: Shoestring Press, 1982.

Newman, Michael Z., and Elana Levine. *Legitimating Television: Media Convergence and Cultural Status*. London: Routledge, 2011.

Piester, Lauren. "Real or Fake? The Truth about Some of Your Favorite Reality TV Shows." *E News*, November 9, 2018. eonline.com/news/985791/real-or-fake-the-truth-about-some-of-your-favorite-reality-TV-shows.

Postman, Neil. *Amusing Ourselves to Death: Public Discourse in the Age of Show Business*. New York: Penguin, 1985.

Pozner, Jennifer L. *Reality Bites Back: The Troubling Truth about Guilty Pleasure TV*. New York: Seal Press, 2010.

Pringle, Gill. "Robocop's Gary Oldman: 'My Dog Has More Dignity than the Kardashians.'" *The Independent*, February 10, 2014. independent.co.uk/arts-entertainment/films/features/robocops-gary-oldman-on-the-kardashians-and-being-the-highest-grossing-actor-in-film-history-9120010.html.

Putnam, Robert D. *Bowling Alone: The Collapse and Revival of American Community*. New York: Simon and Schuster, 2000.

Tullo, Danielle. "The 24 Meanest Things Celebrities Have Said about the Kardashians." *Cosmopolitan*, April 4, 2016. cosmopolitan.com/entertainment/celebs/news/a44747/mean-things-celebrities-have-said-about-the-kardashians/.

Van Luling, Todd. "Here's What Really Happened to the Cars from 'Pimp My Ride.'" *HuffPost*, February 25, 2015. huffpost.com/entry/pimp-my-ride-cars_n_6663840.

Williams, Raymond. *Keywords: A Vocabulary of Culture and Society*. Oxford: Oxford University Press, 1983.

MICHAEL LOUIS MOSER

Deviations from Network Late Night and Cable Parody News: Colbert's *Late Show* and Meyers's *Late Night*

Since its debut in 1954, the late night talk show television genre has regularly relied on "political moments," which I define as political humor, conversations, confessionals, and/or other modes of presentation that incorporate the topic of politics in a broad sense. Late night talk shows from Steve Allen's *Tonight!* (NBC: 1954–1957) to Stephen Colbert's *Late Show* (CBS: 2015–) have featured political jokes, hosted political guests, and aired politically themed sketches. For generations now, Americans have tuned in to watch their favorite late-night host lampoon politicians with comedic jabs or listen to a political guest be interviewed from the guest couch. At the height of network dominance in the late 1970s a single program, *The Tonight Show Starring Johnny Carson* (NBC: 1962–1992), averaged over seventeen million American viewers a night.[1] Although the current fragmented marketplace divides the viewership of these programs, their original television broadcasts still attract an average of over twelve and a half million viewers overall per night and millions more in online views in the days following.[2] In this fragmented marketplace, cable parody news programs like *The Daily Show with Jon Stewart* (Comedy Central: 1999–2015) disseminated more forceful and potentially divisive political moments to narrowcast audiences. However, the late night talk shows on network

---

[1] Bernard Timberg and Bob Erler, *Television Talk: A History of the TV Talk Show* (Austin: University of Texas Press, 2004), 106.

[2] Alex Welch, "Late-Night Ratings, May 13–17, 2019: 'Colbert' Rises to the Top," *TV by the Numbers*, May 21, 2019.

136   Deviations from Network Late Night and Cable Parody News

largely continued to produce mass-appeal content to ever smaller audiences. Toward the end of David Letterman's run as host of *The Late Show* (CBS: 1993–2015), the program did start to occasionally break from network conventions with its political moments, but it would not be until the transition to new hosts in the mid-2010s that significant changes in political moments would occur on network television. Two of the current programs that have disrupted network late-night conventions are *The Late Show with Stephen Colbert* and *Late Night with Seth Meyers* (NBC: 2014–) which have handled their programs' political moments differently than their comedic predecessors on network television did over the previous fifty years. Some of the styles and techniques of today's *Late Show* and *Late Night* have similarities to cable parody news programs of the past twenty years, while other elements are completely new. In this essay, I will show that the two subgenres I call "network late night" and "cable parody news" have historically handled political moments in two distinct traditions. Furthermore, I will introduce three ways in which Colbert's *Late Show* and Meyers's *Late Night* deviate from both the traditions of network late night and cable parody news by producing programs that utilize new constructs of partisan politics, political forums, and political sensationalism and amplification. By focusing on these deviations, this essay will expand on how political moments and narrowcasted content have disrupted the genre conventions that had remained relatively stable from 1962 to 2015. A genre long recognized for its even-handed political moments featuring hosts such as Johnny Carson and Jay Leno is now virtually unrecognizable with its newfound devotion to critically engaging with current events and its abandonment of big-tent content.

Network Late Night vs. Cable Parody News

In the mid-2010s, some twenty-five years after the networks' dominance in U.S. television began to wane, the late night talk shows that appeared on network and cable channel programming continued to handle their political content and formats in two distinct ways. The main distinctions are often determined by how much political humor the show disseminates, whether the humor is satirical or non-satirical, whether the show is parodic or non-parodic, and how the show is distributed and ultimately received. In this section, I will outline the two templates: one being that of network late night and the other being cable parody news, both of which had unique trajectories up until 2015.

Network late night describes content that is historically broadcast for mass audiences on network channels, offers political humor but rarely political satire, and is non-parodic. The television network NBC was the first channel to broadcast what is now known as a late night talk show with *Tonight!* (now *The Tonight Show*) in 1954. This program laid the foundation for what the subgenre of network late night would become. As Timberg suggests, the early network late night talk shows were "designed to air topics appealing to the widest possible audience"; this approach can also be referred to with terms such as broadcasting, mass-market appeal, or big-tent.[3] These network late night programs typically displayed segments such as a comedic monologue, sketch comedy, celebrity interviews, and musical performances. From the Carson-era *Tonight Show* (1962–1992) until the retirement of David Letterman and Jay Leno in the mid-2010s, network late night sought to target a mass-market audience by airing content that would not alienate any specific American demographic. This ambition determined how they conducted their political moments and illustrates their unwillingness to use political satire.

Cable parody news refers to programming that is historically narrowcasted for niche audiences on cable channels, focuses on the political sphere, offers political humor (or more biting political satire) and is parodic. What this essay calls cable parody news, scholars reference with various terms such as Gray et al.'s "satirical television,"[4] "satire news,"[5] "parodic news shows,"[6] "alternative journalism"[7] and

---

[3]   Timberg and Erler, *Television Talk*, 5–6.

[4]   Jonathan Gray et al., *Satire TV: Politics and Comedy in the Post-Network Era* (New York: New York University Press, 2009).

[5]   Sophia A. McClennen and Remy M. Maisel, *Is Satire Saving Our Nation? Mockery and American Politics* (New York: Palgrave Macmillan, 2014).

[6]   Amber Day, *Satire and Dissent: Interventions in Contemporary Political Debate* (Bloomington: Indiana University Press, 2011).

[7]   Geoffrey Baym, *From Cronkite to Colbert: The Evolution of Broadcast News* (Boulder: Paradigm, 2010).

138   Deviations from Network Late Night and Cable Parody News

"political entertainment television."[8] Some network programs, such as NBC's *That Was The Week That Was* (NBC: 1964–1965) or *Saturday Night Live*'s (NBC: 1975–) with its recurring "Weekend Update" sketch, played with the idea of parody news before the cable boom. However, these early parodies still represent what Gray et al. call the "older network model," which, again, was distributed on network television, offered little political satire and was generally suited for mass-market appeal.[9]

By 1989, there were already seventy-nine channels offered on cable and fifty-three million households that had subscriptions. Following this proliferation of channels, programmers shifted away from the "older network model" and started to create narrowcasted and genre-blurring entertainment.[10] In the 1990s, a new model for the late night talk show emerged: the subgenre of cable parody news which centered on mimicking television news and often exhibited riskier interactions with political moments than what had previously been seen on the networks. Some of the early programs that broadly fit into this subgenre are Bill Maher's *Politically Incorrect* (Comedy Central/ABC: 1993–1996/1997–2002), *Dennis Miller Live* (HBO: 1994–2002), Michael Moore's *TV Nation* (NBC/Fox: 1994/1995), and *The Daily Show with Craig Kilborn* (Comedy Central: 1996–1998). However, it is *The Daily Show with Jon Stewart* that constitutes an ideal rubric for calibrating whether a program is a cable parody news program or not. Stewart's *Daily Show* used the parody of the news not as a joke in itself, but as a vehicle to produce a program rooted in political satire and political dialogue.[11] *The Daily Show* provided not just the tame political one-liners displayed on Letterman's *Late Show* or Leno's *Tonight Show*, but also enacted more biting, thesis-driven, and possibly audience-alienating political satire, which would become the main hallmark of the subgenre.

---

[8]   Jeffrey P. Jones, *Entertaining Politics: Satire Television and Political Engagement* (Plymouth: Rowman & Littlefield, 2010).

[9]   Gray et al., *Satire TV*, 48.

[10]   "History of Cable," *California Cable & Telecommunications Association*, accessed December 3, 2019, calcable.org/learn/history-of-cable/.

[11]   Day, *Satire and Dissent*, 58.

MICHAEL LOUIS MOSER
139

Deviation One: Partisan Politics

For most of the broadcast history of network late night, hosts such as Johnny Carson, David Letterman, and Jay Leno refrained from partisan politics that had the potential to offend audiences. In this essay, the term partisan politics refers to a situation when a program displays support for, commitment to and/or outspoken favoritism of one political ideology, a party, or its politicians. Lichter et al. states that Johnny Carson's jokes "were never risky or cutting-edge. Instead, they were more a reflection or barometer of the public mood."[12] Carson-style political one-liners targeted politicians' foibles, gaffes and tropes rather than policy, and the punchline was typically rooted in a clearly ridiculous and fictitious premise. Carson established a genre convention which stipulated that when network late night dealt with politics, it should do so in a non-partisan way and with a mass-market approach. Letterman and Leno, I suggest, largely followed Carson's tame approach to political humor. Jay Leno, host of *The Tonight Show* from 1993 to 2014, was asked in a 1992 *60 Minutes* (CBS: 1968) interview whether he was a Republican or Democrat and responded,

> Uh, I'm neither actually. I'm neither, I try to remain a staunch independent. Cause every time I think I'm a Republican they do something greedy and every time I think I'm a Democrat they do something stupid.[13]

Hosts of network late night programs made a conscious effort to take humorous jabs at both political parties so as to not be seen as being in any one political corner. However, it is important to note that David Letterman's *Late Show* became slightly more politically partisan in its final ten years on the air. In a 2017 *Vulture* interview, Letterman stated that *The Daily Show* "made it so that not doing political stuff got to be the elephant in the room."[14] From the mid-2000s to 2015, Letterman

---

[12] S. Robert Lichter et al., *Politics is a Joke! How TV Comedians Are Remarking Political Life* (Boulder: Westview Press, 2015), 21.

[13] Jay Leno, *60 Minutes*, by Steve Kroft, 1992.

[14] Qtd. in David Marchese, "In Conversation: David Letterman," *Vulture*, March 5, 2017, vulture.com/2017/03/david-letterman-in-conversation.html.

140   Deviations from Network Late Night and Cable Parody News

occasionally ridiculed President George W. Bush's administration and the National Rifle Association (NRA), but these few partisan outbursts were unusual occurrences for network late night.

In contrast, beginning in the 1990s, the hosts of cable parody news programs were more willing than their network counterparts to interweave entertainment and politics, and this more direct integration led to moments that were more politically charged.[15] As Day mentions, these new narrowcast programs offered content "aimed specifically at an audience that [would] appreciate it and [was] unlikely to be viewed by those outside the taste culture who might find it offensive."[16] The cable parody news hosts of the 1990s and 2000s except for Dennis Miller all skewed left of center, but these hosts still did not want to be seen as favoring the Democrats. Bill Maher's opinions, for instance, often fell along liberal ideological lines, yet he still regularly attacked the Democratic Party for being too elitist, too cowardly, too disunited in their messaging and too moderate. *The Colbert Report*, for its part, was a deadpan spoof of a right-wing style pundit program like *The O'Reilly Factor* (Fox News Channel: 1996–2017) and can be read as largely anti-Republican. Any time Colbert's character celebrated conservative ideology, for instance, he was actually attacking it. Still, Colbert argued off-camera that his program was, as Jones states, "no warrior in anybody's army."[17] And like Leno in the 1990s, Jon Stewart was not willing to be placed on either side of the political spectrum in the 2000s and is quoted as saying that "the point of view of the show is we're passionately opposed to bullshit. Is that liberal or conservative?"[18]

Since the 2016 presidential election, Colbert's and Meyers's programs have attached themselves to the Democratic Party and its ideology, a new phenomenon for network late night programs. Stephen Colbert is quoted in 2019 as stating that

> it was a different time when [Leno] was hosting. Now there's one subject [President Trump and his administration], so people can see your

---

[15]   Timberg and Erler, *Television Talk*, 189.

[16]   Day, *Satire and Dissent*, 53.

[17]   Jones, *Entertaining Politics*, 203.

[18]   Jon Stewart qtd. in ibid, 55.

politics more, but I'm fine with that. I don't think there's anything wrong with it [...].[19]

Colbert's *Late Show* has no problem with wearing its political beliefs on its sleeve. After Colbert conducted an interview with Hillary Rodham Clinton two weeks before the 2018 midterm elections, *The Late Show with Stephen Colbert*'s official Facebook page posted a message titled "A message from Hillary Clinton [American flag emoji]," followed by a meme of Clinton with text that read: "Regardless of party or no party, people who are worried about the lack of accountability, trying to exercise checks and balances with this president, have got to turn out and vote."[20] Clinton's quote was taken directly from the show's interview segment that aired the day before, and it is difficult to interpret the post as anything other than a display by *The Late Show* of its opposition to the Trump administration and of its favoritism toward the Democrats. Meyers's *Late Night* has also allied itself with the Democratic Party with the recurring segment called "A Closer Look". The "Closer Look" segment focuses on a given political topic or target for between seven and eighteen minutes and has continuously attacked the Trump administration and/or expressed support for the Democratic Party. *Late Night* displays partisanship for the Democratic Party and even regularly promotes democratic socialist values in the program. In a February 2019 segment, "The Real National Emergency Is Climate Change,"[21] Meyers spends eight minutes defending the Green New Deal, Congresswoman Alexandria Ocasio-Cortez and Senator Bernie Sanders while attacking Fox News Channel coverage, President Trump and Republican representatives. Colbert's *Late Show* and Seth Meyers's *Late Night* are willing to anchor themselves to partisan politics on

---

[19] Will Thorne, "Stephen Colbert on His 'Terrible' First Six Months at 'The Late Show,'" *Variety*, March 17, 2019, variety.com/2019/tv/news/stephen-colbert-late-show-trump-1203165111/.

[20] "A Message from Hillary Clinton," The Late Show with Stephen Colbert, Facebook, September 21, 2018, facebook.com/colbertlateshow/photos/a.706301389514615/1558438070967605/?type=3&theater.

[21] Late Night with Seth Meyers, "The Real National Emergency Is Climate Change: A Closer Look," YouTube, February 20, 2019, www.youtube.com/watch?v=mC4bYqbQihI.

142   Deviations from Network Late Night and Cable Parody News

network television, whereas previous narrowcast cable parody news programs tried to maintain at least the illusion of neutrality by simply being "passionately opposed to bullshit."[22]

Deviation Two: Political Forum

Political guests such as politicians, journalists, pundits, and military generals have appeared on network late night programs since they first aired in the 1950s. However, the political conversations offered throughout most of network late night's history were generally not interested in pursuing dialogue on political policy, governance, or complex societal issues. Still, the first two hosts of *The Tonight Show*, Steve Allen and Jack Paar (from 1954–1957 and 1957–1962, respectively), did veer their programs toward discussions with their guests on political and social issues. Allen's *Tonight Show* hosted guests like Eleanor Roosevelt and General Omar Bradley, and Allen addressed topics like blacklisting, civil rights, and drug abuse on-air.[23] Paar, too, featured political guests and conversations during his tenure and, in the run-up to the 1960 presidential election, hosted both John F. Kennedy and Richard Nixon on his program. However, these politically-infused conversations lasted for only the first eight years on network late night before taking a fifty-year hiatus. The subsequent host of *The Tonight Show*, Johnny Carson, was reluctant to book political guests during the show's thirty-year run. In a 1978 *60 Minutes* interview, Carson stated that dealing with serious issues was "a real danger" and that he would not use his "show as a forum" because he did not think he "should do that as an entertainer."[24] David Letterman, Jay Leno and Conan O'Brien hosted an increased number of political guests throughout their respective runs from the 1990s to the 2010s, but they often did so while not engaging directly with politics or policy. The conversations typically involved personal and family stories rather than governance; Gray et al.

---

[22] Stewart qtd. in Jones, *Entertaining Politics*, 55.

[23] Ben Alba, *Inventing Late Night: Steve Allen and the Original Tonight Show* (Amherst: Prometheus Books, 2005), 146.

[24] Johnny Carson, *60 Minutes*, by Mike Wallace, 1979.

mentions that these three hosts would "rarely challenge their [political] guests with more than a playful joke here or there."[25] Again, Letterman was more politically outspoken during his last ten years as host and clashed with Senator Rand Paul, Bill O'Reilly and Scott McClellan (press secretary under President George W. Bush) in guest interviews. But these interactions were the exception, not the norm. Hence, I argue that network late night usually remained impartial and uncritical in political moments during guest interviews from 1962 to 2015.

Programs such as Stewart's *Daily Show*, *Dennis Miller Live*, *The Colbert Report*, and Maher's two shows *Politically Incorrect* and *Real Time* (HBO: 2003–) have showcased Democratic, Republican and Independent politicians, authors, journalists, and pundits in their guest interviews. Here, I propose that these cable parody news programs created a political forum on television by producing a public meeting space in which the host and/or panel would discuss political and social issues with their guests. In interviews with politicians or journalists, these five programs steer the conversations away from the guests' personal lives and toward political conversations on policy. McClennen and Maisel state that hosts Miller and Maher "really grilled their guests while making the interview fun and funny. Viewers were educated and entertained."[26] Smith asserts that Stewart's *Daily Show* started to book fewer Hollywood celebrities as guests and started to book more "experts" who could discuss and analyze topics like the Iraq War and civil rights.[27] Furthermore, these shows created a platform that was inclusive toward both of the major U.S. political parties, as members of both political parties regularly appeared on Stewart's *Daily Show* and *The Colbert Report* during their runs.[28] Today, Maher's *Real Time* still hosts panels of celebrities, politicians and journalists who offer a diverse array of lived experiences and political stances from which to engage with political and social issues. Hosts like Jon Stewart and Bill Maher are not interested in hearing a candidate's political talking points or

---

[25] Gray et al., *Satire TV*, 153.

[26] McClennen and Maisel, *Is Satire Saving*, 63–64.

[27] Chris Smith, *The Daily Show (the Book): An Oral History as Told by Jon Stewart, Correspondents, Staff and Guests* (New York: Grand Central Publishing, 2016), 80.

[28] Gray et al., *Satire TV*, 91; 132.

144   Deviations from Network Late Night and Cable Parody News

family anecdotes; they wanted to engage their guests in a politically oriented conversation and/or debate.

Like cable parody news, Colbert's *Late Show* and Meyers's *Late Night* regularly function as political forums, featuring conversations with celebrities, news personalities and politicians on political and social issues. But these conversations are becoming more partisan than what has previously been seen. Both Colbert and Meyers regularly host news personalities such as pundits and journalists on their programs. In 2018, for instance, Colbert hosted forty-three interviews with thirty-six different news personality guests and Meyers hosted twenty-five interviews with twenty-two different guests. However, these new political forums are now constructed along partisan lines. The conversations in interviews with these news personalities normally revolve around topical political events and regularly involve some Trump administration-bashing, as many of the guests come from central- and/or liberal-oriented news media outlets like NBC, CBS, CNN, MSNBC, *The New York Times* and *The Washington Post*. Only two out of thirty-six Colbert guests were conservative-leaning journalists (Chris Wallace of Fox News Channel and Margaret Hoover of PBS), and Meyers had no conservative-leaning journalists on *Late Night* in 2018.[29] Furthermore, unlike cable parody news, which has generally hosted politicians from a wide political spectrum, Colbert's and Meyers's political forum provides a platform for almost exclusively Democratic guests. In 2018, only four of Colbert's twenty-seven politician guests were Republicans: Senator Rand Paul, Omarosa Manigault Newman, Senator Ben Sasse and Senator Jake Flake, all of whom have been outspoken critics of President Trump.[30] Only one of Meyers's twelve politician guests in 2018 was a Republican: Governor John Kasich, also a critic of President Trump.[31] Hence, the political forums on *The Late Show* and *Late Night* function along partisan lines, too.

---

[29]   "Episode List: *The Late Show with Stephen Colbert*," *IMDb*; "Episode List: *Late Night with Seth Meyers*," *IMDb*.

[30]   "Episode List: The Late Show."

[31]   "Episode List: Late Night."

As mentioned previously, network late night rarely provided in-depth political conversations before 2015, and cable parody news programs curbed guests from delivering political talking points. I argue that Colbert and Meyers, by contrast, offer their political guests a forum and place to deliver stump speeches. In an April 2016 interview with Senator Bernie Sanders, Seth Meyers twice afforded Sanders the opportunity to expound on healthcare, family and medical leave, income and wealth inequality, large corporations not paying their fair share of taxes, and failing infrastructure.[32] Colbert, too, indulges politicians by providing them with a platform for similar stump speeches, during which he normally nods his head in agreement and the audience occasionally even applauds. In 2019 alone, twelve Democratic presidential candidates appeared on Colbert's *Late Show*. Furthermore, Stephen Colbert encourages political conversations with A-list celebrities (not including high-profile political celebrities). His conversations with these celebrities typically revolve around three themes: promoting liberal values, slamming the Trump administration, and allowing celebrities to talk about their political activism, which often serves from liberal-leaning causes. For instance, Colbert prompted Julianne Moore to talk about her activism for "commonsense gun safety," and after Colbert got Jeff Daniels fired up in a political conversation, Daniels stated that the Democrats needed a 2020 candidate "that can punch him [President Trump] in the face."[33] Colbert's and Meyers's network programs are shifting away from the celebrity promos and chit-chat that have largely driven guest interview segments for fifty years, replacing them instead with a political forum. But this forum in one with a disproportionately low number of conservative voices.

---

[32] Late Night with Seth Meyers, "Sen. Bernie Sanders on His 2016 Presidential Campaign and Young Voters," YouTube, June 22, 2019, www.youtube.com/watch?v=JXe-03TLdkU.

[33] The Late Show with Stephen Colbert, "Julianne Moore: It's Important to Embarrass Your Kids," YouTube, March 5, 2019, www.youtube.com/watch?v=KxArofErmzk; The Late Show with Stephen Colbert, "Jeff Daniels Says To Kill A Mockingbird Is A 'Right Hook' To White Liberals," YouTube, July 31, 2019, www.youtube.com/watch?v=pg2ZbALKRxI.

146   Deviations from Network Late Night and Cable Parody News

Deviation Three: Political Sensationalism and Amplification

By deriding politicians in nightly joke monologues and offering politicians a platform to discuss their personal lives, network late night programs are partly responsible for the sensationalism and amplification of American politics. Therefore, I would argue that these hosts perhaps naïvely at times contributed to the "celebrification" and sensationalism of politics. In this essay, I define political sensationalism as language, style and/or subject matter that is embellished or used to excite audiences, and political amplification as the way these programs set agendas and propagate discourses. Prior to the 2016 presidential election, the political interviews and political humor traditionally featured by hosts like Carson, Leno, Letterman, Conan, Kilborn, Ferguson, and Kimmel were generally neither satirical nor policy-driven. This disengaged political stance can still be seen in *The Tonight Show Starring Jimmy Fallon* (NBC: 2014–), in which Fallon presents his political moments in a less partisan and biting fashion than his contemporaries do. In a September 2016 interview, Fallon hosted Republican presidential nominee Donald Trump, throwing him softball questions about his childhood home, why a child would want to be president and if he still wanted to continue to run for president. In both in the interview and a sketch piece, Fallon never challenges Trump with more than a light comedic jab, which, in turn, led critics and fans to criticize *The Tonight Show* and Fallon for normalizing Trump and his candidacy.[34] Fallon's unwillingness to engage in a political forum and challenge Trump follows the "older network model" of playing to the middle and trying not to alienate viewers. However, even though Fallon might be pushing laughs over political ideology, in contemporary America, this safe or disinterested engagement with the political sphere can also turn away viewers. Fallon, like his network predecessors, acts with the instincts of a comedian and rarely as a journalist.

Cable parody news programs have also sensationalized and amplified politics with their entertainment-based talk shows. Nevertheless, programs like *The Daily Show with Jon Stewart* and *The Colbert*

---

[34]   Dave Itzkoff, "Jimmy Fallon Was on Top of the World. Then Came Trump," *The New York Times*, May 17, 2017.

Report used their exaggerated parodies to deconstruct the sensationalism of twenty-first century politics and its coverage by the television news media, and to amplify underreported stories. Amarasingam argues that *The Daily Show* and *The Colbert Report* took on a task that was "largely abandoned – holding politicians and the media accountable for what they say and do (and don't say and do)."[35] McClennen and Maisel claim that *The Daily Show*'s and *The Colbert Report*'s satire "works as a fact-checker for the mainstream news" and catches "the mainstream news making mistakes, misrepresenting facts, and distracting the public."[36] Satirists like Stewart and Colbert were contributing not only comedic jabs but were actively deconstructing the shortcomings of the media and its journalists or the government and its politicians. While the political and media landscapes were both becoming more entertainment-oriented and sensational, Baym explains, these satirical cable parody news programs functioned as "the flip side of infotainment, the politicization of the aesthetic-expressive sphere."[37] In an era that can place ratings, spectacle, spin and ideology over factual reporting or accurate answers, Stewart and Colbert (as host of *The Colbert Report*) function not only as comedians, but as government and media watchdogs as well.

In contrast, Colbert and Meyers operate without the naïveté of their network predecessors by both sensationalizing and amplifying their political moments. Whereas a Carson, Leno, or Letterman monologue once used a handful of politically-based one-liners as part of larger topical monologue, Colbert's monologues and Meyers's desk pieces relentlessly focus on political topics for between eight and thirteen minutes. However, unlike Stewart's *Daily Show* or *The Colbert Report*, Colbert's *Late Show* and Meyers's *Late Night* rarely deconstruct the lapses of the media or act as a watchdog. These programs amplify political stories that are already circulating in the print and television news media. In a typical cycle, CNN or *The New York Times* reports the facts, and Colbert's and Meyers's programs then add a satirical twist and present their redacted interpretations of the topical political event, thus

---

[35] Amarnath Amarasingam, ed., *The Stewart/Colbert Effect: Essays on the Real Impacts of Fake News* (Jefferson: McFarland, 2011), 129.

[36] McClennen and Maisel, *Is Satire Saving*, 64.

[37] Baym, *From Cronkite to Colbert*, 17.

148   Deviations from Network Late Night and Cable Parody News

amplifying the original reporting. Whereas Stewart's *Daily Show* once used his extended desk pieces to point out biased or spectacle-driven reporting by news channels like MSNBC or ABC News, *The Late Show* and *Late Night* closely align their interpretations of the news with preexisting narratives that have been constructed and disseminated by the media. When Stephen Colbert was asked by *The New York Times Magazine* columnist David Marchese if his show feeds the "political punditsphere we seem to be mired in, where it feels as if we're all mad at one another all the time," Colbert answered, "It might. The behavior I'm exhibiting fits my genre, which is not supposed to have respectability." Colbert later continued, "So am I part of the problem? That is not for me to say. I just think I'm doing my job."[38] Satirizing the "political punditsphere" was the central premise of *The Colbert Report*, and Colbert would not now be able to definitively claim that his current *Late Show* is not an example of what he once mocked. Colbert's and Meyers's programs steer their content toward political moments in monologues, desk pieces and interviews, but they lack the distance of previous cable parody news programs. For instance, Day states that Stewart's *Daily Show* functioned as a "journalistic outsider throwing stones rather than seeming like a part of the political establishment they critique."[39] *The Late Show* and *Late Night* function less as investigative journalism or watchdog formats. Rather, they resemble tabloid journalism or op-eds.

Conclusion

Based on their political moments alone, I argue that it is hard to confuse Colbert's *Late Show* and Meyers's *Late Night* with network late night or cable parody news programs that aired before 2015. What I hope to have demonstrated is how these new satirical network late night programs have routinely displayed partisan politics in favor of liberal values and the Democratic Party; how they furthermore provide a political forum

[38]   David Marchese, "Stephen Colbert on the Political Targets of Satire," *The New York Times Magazine*, May 31, 2019.

[39]   Day, *Satire and Dissent*, 85.

for politicians, news personalities, and celebrities to voice their opinions and ideologies; and finally, how they sensationalize and amplify politics differently than their predecessors. In an era of online streaming and an already-fragmented marketplace, it is no longer the norm for network late night programs to disseminate content for mass audiences. Of today's five main network late night programs *Jimmy Kimmel Live!*, *The Tonight Show with Jimmy Fallon*, *Late Night with Seth Meyers*, *The Late Late with James Corden*, and *The Late Show with Stephen Colbert*, only Fallon's and Corden's resembles the older network model of mass appeal that disseminates little satire or dissent. Political moments will continue to be a part of late night talk shows, but the genre's ability or willingness to speak to large swaths of the American public is swiftly diminishing.

150   Deviations from Network Late Night and Cable Parody News

Works Cited

Alba, Ben. *Inventing Late Night: Steve Allen and the Original Tonight Show*. Amherst: Prometheus Books, 2005.

Amarasingam, Amarnath, ed. *The Stewart/Colbert Effect: Essays on the Real Impacts of Fake News*. Jefferson: McFarland, 2011.

Baym, Geoffrey. *From Cronkite to Colbert: The Evolution of Broadcast News*. Boulder: Paradigm Publishers, 2010.

Carson, Johnny. *60 Minutes*, by Mike Wallace, 1979.

Day, Amber. *Satire and Dissent: Interventions in Contemporary Political Debate*. Bloomington: Indiana University Press, 2011.

"Episode List: *Late Night with Seth Meyers*." *IMDb*, accessed December 12, 2019. imdb.com/title/tt3513388/episodes?year=2018&ref_=tt_eps_yr_2018.

"Episode List: *The Late Show with Stephen Colbert*." *IMDb*, accessed December 12, 2019. imdb.com/title/tt3697842/episodes?year=2018.

Gray, Jonathan, et al. *Satire TV: Politics and Comedy in the Post-Network Era*. New York: New York University Press, 2009.

"History of Cable." *California Cable & Telecommunications Association*, accessed December 3, 2019. calcable.org/learn/history-of-cable/.

Itzkoff, Dave. "Jimmy Fallon Was on Top of the World. Then Came Trump." *The New York Times*, May 17, 2017.

Jones, Jeffrey P. *Entertaining Politics: Satire Television and Political Engagement*. Plymouth: Rowman & Littlefield Publishers, 2010.

Late Night with Seth Meyers. "Sen. Bernie Sanders on His 2016 Presidential Campaign and Young Voters." YouTube, June 22, 2019. www.youtube.com/watch?v=JXe-03TLdkU.

---. "The Real National Emergency Is Climate Change: A Closer Look." YouTube, February 20, 2019. www.youtube.com/watch?v=mC4bYqbQihI.

Leno, Jay. *60 Minutes*, by Steve Kroft, 1992.

Lichter, S. Robert, et al. *Politics is a Joke! How TV Comedians Are Remarking Political Life*. Boulder: Westview Press, 2015.

Marchese, David. "In Conversation: David Letterman." *Vulture*, March 5, 2017. vulture.com/2017/03/david-letterman-in-conversation.html.

---. "Stephen Colbert on the Political Targets of Satire." *The New York Times Magazine*, May 31, 2019.

McClennen, Sophia A., and Remy M. Maisel. *Is Satire Saving Our Nation? Mockery and American Politics*. New York: Palgrave Macmillan, 2014.

Otterson, Joe. "'Late Show with Stephen Colbert' Narrowly Tops Late-Night Ratings for 2018-2019 Season." *Variety*, May 22, 2019. variety.com/2019/tv/news/late-show-with-stephen-colbert-ratings-2018-2019-1203223520/.

Smith, Chris. *The Daily Show (the Book): An Oral History as Told by Jon Stewart, Correspondents, Staff and Guests*. New York: Grand Central Publishing, 2016.

Timberg, Bernard, and Bob Erler. Television Talk: *A History of the TV Talk Show*. Austin: University of Texas Press, 2004.

The Late Show with Stephen Colbert. "A Message from Hillary Clinton." Facebook, September 21, 2018. facebook.com/colbertlateshow/photos/a.706301389514615/1558438070967605/?type=3&theater.

---. "Jeff Daniels Says To Kill A Mockingbird Is A 'Right Hook' To White Liberals." YouTube, July 31, 2019. www.youtube.com/watch?v=pg2ZbALKRxI.

---. "Julianne Moore: It's Important to Embarrass Your Kids." YouTube, March, 5, 2019. www.youtube.com/watch?v= KxArofErmzk.

Thorne, Will. "Stephen Colbert on His 'Terrible' First Six Months at 'The Late Show.'" *Variety*, March 17, 2019, variety.com/2019/tv/news/stephen-colbert-late-show-trump-1203165111/.

Welch, Alex. "Late-Night Ratings, May 13–17, 2019: 'Colbert' Rises to the Top." *TV by the Numbers*, May 21, 2019. tvbythenumbers.zap2it.com/weekly-ratings/late-night-ratings-may-13-17-2019-colbert-rises-to-the-top/.

JOHN STREET

From *The West Wing* to *House of Cards*, from Randy Newman to Donald Trump: Politics as Popular Culture, Popular Culture as Politics

Introduction

It is said that "all political careers end in failure." The same is probably true of academic careers. We do not suffer the peculiar punishment of electoral defeat, but my suspicion is that we rarely answer satisfactorily the questions we set ourselves. That certainly is true for me. I have spent much time and energy in an attempt to understand how exactly politics and popular culture are related. In one sense, then, this chapter is another of those attempts. What gives it some merit, I hope, is that the case of former President Donald Trump has imbued the topic with a renewed relevance and greater urgency.

The relationship between politics and popular culture has, I think, been identified in at least four different ways. The first, and perhaps most familiar, is the view of popular culture as a form of political communication. Popular culture is understood, by this account, to articulate and convey political ideas, values and sentiments, and to mark social and political change through them. We need only to recall how the Woodstock festival came to embody the spirit of the 1960s, or how hip hop has given voice to the African American experience in the late twentieth century. This leads to a second aspect of the relationship, in which popular culture acts to engage audiences in politics and to mobilise them to act politically. The example of soul music and the civil rights movement is an illustration of this. The second element helps to establish the third, in which popular culture gives rise to a distinct kind of politics, most obviously that of the celebrity politician. Here we need only to think of how the movie actor Ronald Reagan became president.

154   Politics as Popular Culture, Popular Culture as Politics

There is a fourth version, too, of the relationship between politics and popular culture. This occurs when politics acts on popular culture, most blatantly in the guise of censorship but also in the form propaganda, and, less obviously but perhaps more significantly, in the policies that determine the character of, and access to, popular culture (through copyright policy, for example). My focus, in what follows, is on the first three of these links.

Politics and popular culture: A multi-dimensional relationship

In a 2018 article for the *New Yorker*, the US political scientist Yasha Mounk reported this anecdote:

> When Donald Trump first announced that he would seek the Republican nomination, many journalists dismissed his Presidential bid as a publicity stunt. The Huffington Post said it had planned to cover the candidate in its entertainment section. "Our reason is simple: Trump's campaign is a sideshow," readers were told. "We won't take the bait. If you are interested in what The Donald has to say, you'll find it next to our stories on the Kardashians and The Bachelorette."[1]

While this may say something about the limits to the *Huffington Post*'s powers of political prediction, it is more interesting for what it has to say about the link between politics and entertainment. The assumption is, it seems, that the two do not belong together. Politics is serious; entertainment is not. A similar distinction is implied in a newspaper report about the British politician Boris Johnson, in which he was described as "[a] celebrity, not a leader."[2] You cannot be both. Distinctions of this kind feed into the view that politics risks being 'infected' by popular culture. Something of this attitude can be detected in the journalist Simon Kuper's understanding of how populist skills derive from popular culture skills:

---

[1] Yasha Mounk, "Too Much Democracy," *The New Yorker*, November 12, 2018, 48.
[2] Headline in *The Guardian*, July 18, 2019.

Populists separate campaigning from governance. Their leaders are selected not for any governing skills but strictly for their ability to drive engagement. That's why many of them – Beppe Grillo, Boris Johnson, Trump – come from entertainment industries.[3]

Such thoughts are extended to account for how citizens themselves engage with politics, which, it is argued, is being 'Netflixised' or 'Spotifised.' The talk is of a "pick 'n' mix culture" defining the conduct of, and attitudes to, politics.[4]

Underlying these observations is the idea that politics, or more particularly political campaigning, is increasingly conducted according to roles and rules that derive from popular culture. This is evident in even the most minor of ways – in the use of images and typography from *Game of Thrones* to convey President Trump's messages ("Winter is Coming"/ "Sanctions are Coming"), or in the choice of songs used to open political rallies. The novelist Dave Eggers, reporting on a Trump event, observed:

> This day in El Paso, as the attendees filed into the Coliseum, a 30-minute mix of songs, instructions and archival recordings played in a loop [...] There was a lot of Queen and [...] Elton John. 'Free Bird' was followed closely by the Village People's 'Macho Man'. [...] [and then] the Rolling Stones' 'Sympathy for the Devil'.[5]

The use of popular culture by campaigning politicians is itself premised on the idea that popular culture conveys political meaning and generates political insights. Such claims are endorsed by recent work in international relations. Daniel Furman and Paul Musgrave, for example, argue that the novels of Tom Clancy inform readers about international politics: "People learn about world politics from fictional narrative

---

[3] Simon Kuper, "Secrets of the Populist Playbook," *Financial Times*, March 14, 2019.

[4] Gillian Tett, "Trump, Oprah and the era of pick 'n' mix politics," *Financial Times*, June 13, 2018.

[5] Dave Eggers, "Sympathy for the Devil," *The Guardian Review*, March 2, 2019, 9.

156   Politics as Popular Culture, Popular Culture as Politics

sources."[6] William Clapton and Laura Shepherd contend that *Game of Thrones* provides viewers with an appreciation of gendered power in a way that standard international relations texts do not. Works of fiction, they say, enable us to "learn about global politics" because "they (re)present ideas about power, legitimacy, authority, gender, race and belonging in sophisticated, varied ways."[7] Popular culture as a source of political information almost has the status of conventional wisdom.

Scholars such as Liesbet van Zoonen have further refined our appreciation of the knowledge that popular culture conveys.[8] She has identified the different narratives deployed in fictional accounts of politics: the quest, bureaucracy, conspiracy and soap opera. And together with Dominic Wring, van Zoonen has demonstrated – as Steve Fielding has done with film and James Brassett and Alex Sutton have done with political satire – that these narratives dominate UK television's fictional portrayal of politics.[9] A similar account can be given of how U.S. television has portrayed politics, from the idealism of the *West Wing* to the cynicism of *House of Cards* and the satire of *Veep*.

This research tends to focus on the content of popular culture, and to leave readers to speculate on its impact. There are exceptions to this rule, however.[10] And in one very obvious respect, popular culture has been implicated directly in the rise of the political phenomenon of the celebrity politician. Popular culture personas and platforms have come

---

[6]   Daniel Furman and Paul Musgrave, "Synthetic Experiences: How Popular Culture Matters for Images of International Relations," *International Studies Quarterly* 61, no. 3 (2017): 503.

[7]   William Clapton and Laura Shepherd, "Lessons from Westeros: Gender and power in Game of Thrones," *Politics* 37, no. 1 (2017): 9.

[8]   Liesbet van Zoonen, *Entertaining the Citizen: When Politics and Popular Culture Converge* (New York: Rowman & Littlefield), 2005.

[9]   Liesbet van Zoonen and Dominic Wring, "Trends in Political Television Fiction in the UK: Themes, Characters and Narratives, 1965–2009," *Media, Culture and Society* 34, no. 3 (2012): 263–279; Steve Fielding, "A Mirror for England? Cinematic Representations of Politicians and Party Politics, ca. 1944–64," *Journal of British Studies* 47, no. 1 (2008): 107–128; James Brassett and Alex Sutton, "British Satire, Everyday Politics: Chris Morris, Armando Iannucci and Charlie Brooker," *British Journal of Politics and International Relations* 19, no. 2 (2017): 245–262.

[10] Ruben Durante et al., "The Political Legacy of Entertainment TV," *American Economic Review* 109, no. 7 (2019): 2497–2530.

to be seen as the mechanisms by which politicians secure electoral success and power. A typical argument is the one offered by television critic Emily Nussbaum:

> [I]f *The Apprentice* didn't get Trump elected, it is surely what made him electable. Over fourteen seasons, the television producer Mark Burnett helped turn the Donald Trump of the late nineties [...] into a titan of industry, nationally admired for being, in his own words, "the highest-quality brand."[11]

The political scientist David Runciman offers a similar analysis of the Trump Presidency:

> The template for this presidency is reality television. The lead character is playing a part that depends on his own words and actions and yet is entirely contrived. The drama is organised around a series of showdowns and confrontations when everything seems to be on the line and yet nothing is at stake.[12]

These accounts view popular culture as producing politics.

If such insights are valid, popular culture produces the 'popularity' of politicians, but it also produces the language in which they speak. This latter idea is vividly illustrated by Fintan O'Toole in his book *Heroic Failure*, in which he traces the specifically English support for Brexit in the culture of novels, films and music. He argues that the vote to leave the EU was a by-product of punk rock:

> Had it not had the genius of Take Back Control, a perfect slogan for the Leave campaign would have been Never Mind the Bollocks, Here's Brexit! For it is in punk that we find [...] the nihilistic energy that helped to drive the Brexit impulse.[13]

---

[11] Emily Nussbaum, "The TV That Created Donald Trump," *The New Yorker*, July 24, 2017.

[12] David Runciman, "I Didn't Do Anything Wrong in the First Place," *London Review of Books*, October 11, 2018.

[13] Fintan O'Toole, *Heroic Failure: Brexit and the Politics of Pain* (London: Head of Zeus, 2018), 128.

158   Politics as Popular Culture, Popular Culture as Politics

O'Toole's analysis is persuasive, or at least seductive, for those who want to place popular culture near the center of politics. But such speculation, however insightful or resonant, is no substitute for more careful analysis and theorization. For this reason, I want to turn now to a fundamental element of the attempt to link politics to popular culture. This is the question of what we mean when we speak of 'politics.'

Speaking of Politics

There are many different, and competing, definitions of politics. And the claim that popular culture has any significant political role draws on some definitions and not others. For those who see politics simply as the operation of formally constituted governments, and of the policies that emanate from such governments, there is little room for popular culture in their accounts. But for those who, like Colin Hay, see politics as a constructivist exercise, the cultural realm assumes greater importance. Hay writes that "politics is concerned [...] with the construction and, ideally, the realization of a sense of the collective good."[14] Such a definition does not necessarily imply a role for popular culture. The process of construction might be determined by the design of the electoral system as much as by cultural factors. But it certainly allows for the possibility that culture will be important.

The question then becomes: important in what way? This leads us into debates about how political processes of construction themselves are to be understood. In his *The Philosophy of Social Science*, Martin Hollis suggests that these debates can be understood to fall within the quadrants of a matrix in which the choice is between "explanation" and "understanding" on the one hand, and "holism" and "individualism" on the other.[15] Whereas explanations of the world seek out the causes of actions, understandings are more interested in the reasons for those actions. And whereas holism looks at society as a whole entity, individualism concentrates on the individuals who are deemed part of that society. For Hollis, these competing perspectives yield a matrix in

[14]   Colin Hay, *Why We Hate Politics* (Cambridge: Polity Press, 2007), 2.
[15]   Martin Hollis, *The Philosophy of Social Science* (Cambridge: Cambridge University Press, 1994).

JOHN STREET 159

which each quadrant (Figure 1) tells a different story about why things are as they are.

	Explanation	Understanding
Holism	Systems	'Games'
Individualism	Agents	Actors

Fig. 1

While it might be assumed that these are discrete positions and perspectives, Hollis contends that they are all inadequate, and that there is a constant cycle at play. To illustrate this with reference to culture, a systems approach would focus on the idea of culture as a *system* of beliefs that informs all social behavior. It gives rise to the arguments found, for example, in Samuel Huntingdon's "clash of civilizations."[16] But critics of such an account might wish to contend that it neglects the process by which individuals act as *agents* of the supposed system of beliefs. This takes us into the realm of Gabriel Almond and Sidney Verba's notion of individually acquired "political culture," of which critics then ask: so how is it that individuals come to act on their beliefs?[17] To which the answer is: they interpret these beliefs in the way that *actors* interpret a script.[18] And this, in turn, leads to the question of how the script was written. To which the answer is: by the rules that govern how scripts are written. Think here of Mary Douglas and Aaron

---

[16] Samuel Huntington, *The Clash of Civilizations and the Remaking of World Order* (New York: Simon & Schuster, 2002).

[17] Gabriel Almond and Sidney Verba, *The Civic Culture: Political Attitudes and Democracy in Five Nations* (Princeton: SAGE, 1963).

[18] Bruno Latour, *Reassembling the Social: An Introduction to Actor-Network-Theory* (Oxford: Oxford University Press, 2007).

160   Politics as Popular Culture, Popular Culture as Politics

Wildavky's understanding of why actors differ in their views of risk.[19] Douglas and Wildavky argue that risk is a product of the structure of the *game* actors inhabit. And this, in turn, takes us back to the beginning, to the question of how these games themselves are created, and to the idea of a "system."

This endless cycle is not a counsel of despair. Rather, it suggests that in invoking culture (or any other factor) in accounting for social life, we take a position on what best accounts for the actions or behavior we observe. The position we take will profoundly affect the importance we attribute to (popular) culture in making sense of politics.

In what follows, I adopt the position taken by a writer who, I want to suggest, has much to offer those who see an intimate link between popular culture and politics: Frank R. Ankersmit. In his book *Political Representation*, Ankersmit echoes Hollis's divide between explanatory and interpretative perspectives.[20] He identifies two paradigms for accounting for the political world. In the first (and most common) paradigm the focus is on *agents* (politicians, voters, bureaucrats, etc.), who are seen as the "causal agents in sociopolitical reality." This approach is characteristic of the writings of both Marx and Hegel, in which class or reason serve to motivate those agents.[21] Ankersmit contrasts this approach with a second paradigm in which the "focus [is] on the *interaction* between [...] political agents," on the "empty space between agents."[22] He attributes this view to Tocqueville and Machiavelli.

For Ankersmit, this second paradigm is much more powerful in its ability to make sense of political life in that it captures the realities of political representation and political power. It achieves this by viewing politics "as if from the moon" and as an "aesthetic" activity.[23] This is most vividly illustrated in his understanding of the idea of political representation. Ankersmit argues that representation is not simply a matter of presenting political reality to those whose votes are being

---

[19] Mary Douglas and Aaron Wildavsky, *Risk and Culture: An Essay on the Selection of Technological and Environmental Dangers* (London: University of California Press, 1983).

[20] F. R. Ankersmit, *Political Representation* (Stanford: Stanford University Press, 2002).

[21] Ibid., 133–134.

[22] Ibid., 133.

[23] Ibid., 134.

JOHN STREET   161

sought, but rather a matter of *creating* that reality aesthetically. As he writes, "in a representative democracy all legitimate political power is essentially aesthetic."[24] It depends on the *representation* of reality. "Political reality," he suggests in an earlier book, "does not exist *before* political representation but only exists *through* it."[25] Ankersmit's approach to political power and political representation has a further key implication, which is that in understanding political life, we need to focus "not on *content*, but on the *style(s)* of interaction."[26] He rejects the criticism leveled at a politician (or artist) who is accused of being, as the saying goes, "all style and no content." The style *is* the content. "[S]tyle," he contends, "does not tell us *why*, but *how* individuals think or act."[27] And he continues: "What we see as the person's style will be *what he is like to us*."[28]

In appealing to the idea of style, Ankersmit is drawing upon an understanding of art and music. He discusses, for example, a piano piece by Robert Schumann in which the melody that is heard cannot, he argues, be found in the score. It exists in the space between notes (in the interaction of them). In the same way, he argues:

> A painter's or sculptor's style is to a large extent independent of content: one recognises a painter by style and not by the subjects chosen for his or her paintings. Similarly, we can speak meaningfully about political style without involving ideological or party-programmatic consider-ations.[29]

By way of illustration, think of how different artists depict bowls of fruit or chairs. The objects – the content – is the same throughout, but the impression created is different in each instance because of the painter's style. Ankersmit writes:

---

[24] Ibid., 118.
[25] F. R. Ankersmit, *Aesthetic Politics* (Stanford: Stanford University Press, 1996), 48; his emphasis.
[26] Ankersmit, *Political Representation*, 135; his emphasis.
[27] Ibid., 150.
[28] Ibid., 151; his emphasis.
[29] Ankersmit, *Aesthetic Politics*, 157.

162   Politics as Popular Culture, Popular Culture as Politics

> [W]hen asking himself or herself how best to represent the represented, the representative should ask what political style would best suit the electorate. And this question really requires an essentially *creative* answer [...] there exists no style in the electorate itself that is quietly waiting to be copied [...][30]

Ankersmit's view of politics as an aesthetic enterprise opens up the possibility that popular culture plays a central role. This is not an original claim, but I do not think enough has been made of its importance to the issue of how politics and popular culture might be linked.[31]

Political Style and Popular Culture

There are two ways in which style matters to politics. First, political style is increasingly borrowed from popular cultural style. And second, contemporary populist politics itself is seen as a defining case of politics as style.

Arnold Schwarzenegger's election as governor of California can be seen as an example of the first. He incorporated popular culture into his political communication and campaigning. As Steven Ross observes:

> During his gubernatorial run, he [Schwarzenegger] shunned traditional news outlets and placed entertainment shows at the centre of his campaign. He announced his candidacy on *The Tonight Show*, publicized it on *Oprah*, and made speeches that used lines from his movies – like promising voters that politicians who were not doing their job would be told *"Hasta la vista*, baby."[32]

Similar stories are told of Ronald Reagan's election to the presidency, and, as we shall see, of Donald Trump's. Suffice it to say, at this point, popular cultural style is understood to enable aspiring politicians to project a political image and claim the right to speak for the people.

---

[30] Ankersmit, *Political Representation*, 54.

[31] See, for example, John Corner and Dick Pels, eds., *Media and the Restyling of Politics* (London: SAGE, 2003).

[32] Steven Ross, *Hollywood Left and Right: How Movie Stars Shaped American Politics* (Oxford: Oxford University Press, 2011), 364.

Closely associated with the use of popular culture in politics is the concept of populism. The primary claim of populism that the populist represents the people against "them" – the elite or the establishment – fits neatly with the common understanding of popular culture as the culture of the people. It is not the high culture of the privileged; it requires no special skills of interpretation nor does it set barriers to entry and access. What is more, it can be argued that populism is to be understood *as a political style*.

This is the suggestion made by Benjamin Moffitt and Simon Tormey. They, like Ankersmit, see politics in aesthetic terms. Political style, they write, is "the repertoires of performance that are used to create political relations."[33] And again, as with Ankersmit, this puts "the issue of how representation operates to the forefront of any discussion of populism [...]."[34] The politician is to be understood as an artist and a performer, such that "the performance can actually change or create the audience's subjectivity."[35]

Moffitt and Tormey, together with Ankersmit, lay the foundations for a more robust account, or at least a more theoretically grounded one, of how politics and popular culture are related. But in stressing the political aspects of the role of style and aesthetics, they say relatively little about the cultural dimension. How, and in what ways, does cultural style speak to, and about, politics? Why do some styles resonate while others don't? And indeed, what does it mean to 'resonate'?

In asking such questions, we are not short on answers. There are many writers who describe the political significance of popular culture, with Greil Marcus being one of the best known. In his much-admired *Mystery Train*, Marcus traces the links between the American Dream, the U.S. Constitution and popular music.[36] Here is a typical sentence: "Elvis Presley's career defines success in a democracy that can perhaps recognize itself best in its popular culture."[37] Marcus's book invests popular culture with the capacity to express political ideas and ideals. A

---

[33] Benjamin Moffitt and Simon Tormey, "Rethinking Populism: Politics, Mediatisation and Political Style," *Political Studies* 62, no. 2 (2014): 387.

[34] Ibid., 393.

[35] Ibid., 389.

[36] Greil Marcus, *Mystery Train: Images of America in Rock and Roll Music* (New York: E. P. Dutton, 1975).

[37] Ibid., 205.

164 Politics as Popular Culture, Popular Culture as Politics

more recent example is Joshua Clover's *1989: Bob Dylan Didn't Have This to Sing About*. "Popular culture," Clover says, is "where market and imagination struggle over consciousness, over what's thought and what's thinkable."[38]

As a fan, I want such claims to be true. I want to believe that music or films make a real difference in the way we live and act politically. One of the objects of my fandom is Randy Newman, an artist who features prominently in Marcus's *Mystery Train*. And certainly, it is possible to hear, in a song like "Rednecks" from Newman's 1974 album *Good Old Boys*, what seems like the authentic voice of the 'left behind,' of Republican voters through the ages:

> Last night I saw Lester Maddox on a TV show
> With some smart-ass New York Jew
> And the Jew laughed at Lester Maddox
> And the audience laughed at Lester Maddox too
> Well, he may be a fool but he's our fool
> If they think they're better than him they're wrong
> So I went to the park and I took some paper along
> And that's where I made up this song [...].[39]

The words, and Newman's gruff voice, evoke the sense of resentment felt by the white working class of the American South (and might seem as apposite now as it did when it was written). But the song can't be considered only in these terms. Newman's fanbase was not, after all, comprised of those about whom he sang. Apart from his songs for Hollywood movies, he has had few 'hits' (apart from "Short People"). And the song "Rednecks" subverts its own opening theme when, in the closing verse, the singer recounts the 'ghettos' of the North that, it is suggested, are no better than those of the South. The ostensible subject of the song, Newman himself acknowledges, wouldn't know the names of these places.[40] Whatever "Rednecks" is saying about America cannot

---

[38] Joshua Clover, *1989: Bob Dylan Didn't Have This to Sing About* (Berkeley: University of California Press, 2009), 2.

[39] Randy Newman, "Rednecks," YouTube, May 24, 2015, www.youtube.com/watch?v=o80BB0qZoVM.

[40] Keith Negus, "Authorship and the Popular Song," *Music and Letters* 92, no. 4 (2012): 607–629.

be easily read or assumed. Who hears it and what they hear cannot be easily discerned. The same might be said of a later Newman song, "A Word in Defense of Our Country" (2006), in which he appears to defend George W. Bush against the mockery Bush was then receiving ("Now, the leaders we have / While they're the worst that we've had / Are hardly the worst / This poor world has seen").[41] It might be a patriotic song of praise; or it might be an ironic put down. And how should Newman's niche readings of the American experience be set against the sentiments evoked by the country star Garth Brooks, the biggest-selling male artist in the U.S.? Brooks is far more popular than Newman, but his success rarely if ever attracts the attention of cultural critics like Marcus or Clover.[42]

These ambiguities and questions are characteristic of all forms of popular culture. Childish Gambino's music video for "This is America" (2018) has been viewed many millions of times.[43] It has been understood as giving voice to the Black Lives Matter movement and speaking to the contemporary African American experience. But what the song and its visual accompaniment are saying, how Gambino (the actor Donald Glover) understands 'America,' or, more importantly, what its audience sees and hears, is less clear.

This is not to suggest that we should dismiss all claims that argue for viewing popular culture politically. Far from it. Rather, I would suggest that we need to take the politics *more seriously*. We should apply the ideas of political style to how we understand popular culture. In the case of music, this has at least two implications. The first involves the notion of persona. The second involves how we read and understand the lyrics.

Performers, particularly of popular music, create and adopt personas in order to communicate with their audience. When we are listening to a song, the musicologist Allan Moore argues, "we are listening to a persona, projected by a singer, in other words to an artificial construct-

---

[41] Randy Newman, "A Few Words in Defense of Our Country (Official Video)," YouTube, September 1, 2016,
www.youtube.com/watch?v=E0EAwSpTcM4.

[42] Although *Time* described Brooks as 'America's unlikeliest of political counselors' after he performed at President Biden's inauguration. Philip Elliott, "The Healing Power of Garth Brooks," *Time*, January 26, 2021. My thanks to Astrid Böger for this.

[43] Available at https://www.youtube.com/watch?v=VYOjWnS4cMY.

166   Politics as Popular Culture, Popular Culture as Politics

ion that may, or may not, be identical with the person(ality) of the singer."[44] The artifice of the persona – the style – is key to how the song is heard and what meaning it conveys. Randy Newman, Childish Gambino or Garth Brooks are creating a voice with which to speak, and people to whom they speak. This is what happens in popular culture and, in Ankersmit's view, in politics. Understanding the persona is key to understanding what is being communicated. But more than this, the process of communication entails a form of representation, of speaking for or from the experiences of a people or an identity.

The persona, though, is only part of the communicative process. Lyrics are also involved. There has been much debate within popular music studies as to how the words are to be understood.[45] This debate was made very public when Bob Dylan received the Nobel Prize for Literature in 2016. Implicit in the decision was the idea that Dylan's lyrics were poems, were literature. But such a view is disputed, most notably by Simon Frith, who treats poetry and song lyrics as entirely different forms of communication and expression. Indeed, he contends, lyrics need to be understood more as drama or speech-making. "Lyrics are a form of rhetoric or oratory," he writes, "we have to treat them in terms of the persuasive relationship set up between singer and listener. From this perspective, a song doesn't exist to convey the meaning of the words; rather, the words exist to convey the meaning of the song."[46]

Frith develops this argument to make a further point about how songs, especially those with political intent, work. He is skeptical that songs mobilize people, as some social movement theorists claim.[47] Rather, he argues that songs affect how we express ourselves, how we acquire a voice: "The most significant political effect of a pop song is not on how people vote or organize, but on how they speak."[48] An

---

[44] Allan Moore, *Song Means: Analysing and Interpreting Recorded Popular Song* (Farnham: Routledge, 2012), 179.

[45] Simon Frith, "Why Do Songs Have Words?," in *Music for Pleasure* (Cambridge: Polity Press, 1988), 105–128.

[46] Simon Frith, *Performing Rites* (Oxford: Oxford University Press, 1996), 166.

[47] For example, Ronald Eyerman and Andrew Jamison, *Music and Social Movements* (Cambridge: Cambridge University Press, 1998).

[48] Frith, *Performing Rites*, 169.

example of this is Lesley Gore's 1963 hit "You Don't Own Me."[49] In 2012, the song was revived in a video in support of the Obama re-election campaign. The original song provided the soundtrack, but the accompanying visual imagery was of multiple women and girls singing along to the song. The song gave them a voice, a means of expressing their thoughts and feelings. Another example is the use of music by the U.S. State Department during the Cold War as a form of propaganda, and more. Danielle Fosler-Lussier writes of how "[t]he practice of musical diplomacy, at once fabricated and genuine, helped to create the personal experiences and global sensibilities of the Cold War era."[50]

What I have suggested in this section (and it is no more than a suggestion) is that popular cultural style connects to politics through, in the case of music, the persona and the lyrics. These co-exist as a performance, in which the persona represents and the lyrics persuade. If there is any validity in this understanding of the link between style and politics, it may help us to better understand the phenomenon of the celebrity politician in general, and Donald Trump in particular.

Style, Persona, Representation and Donald Trump

Earlier, I quoted Ankersmit as arguing that every political representative has to ask themselves "how best to represent the represented," and that "this question really requires an essentially *creative* answer [...] in the sense that there exists no style in the electorate itself that is quietly waiting to be copied [...]."[51] I want to return to this issue by considering

---

[49] "'You Don't Own Me' PSA," YouTube, October 22, 2012, www.youtube.com/ watch?v=XMxtbAP2cyU. Here is a sample of the lyrics, "You don't own me / I'm not just one of your many toys / You don't own me / Don't say I can't go with other boys / And don't tell me what to do / Don't tell me what to say / And please, when I go out with you / Don't put me on display 'cause / You don't own me / Don't try to change me in any way / You don't own me / Don't tie me down 'cause I'd never stay."

[50] Danielle Fosler-Lussier, *Music in America's Cold War Diplomacy* (Berkeley: University of California Press, 2015), 225.

[51] Ankersmit, *Aesthetic Politics*, 54.

168   Politics as Popular Culture, Popular Culture as Politics

how Donald Trump responded to this challenge.[52] My approach involves looking at how journalists and political commentators have described Trump's campaigning and governing style, and how they use the tropes and forms of popular culture to capture its distinctive character.

David Runciman, for example, compares the former President to the television character played by Ricky Gervais and Steve Carell: "The person Trump most resembles is David Brent from *The Office*. He has the grating inadequacy, knee-jerk nastiness, the comical self-delusion."[53] And Trump himself, according to the author Mark Singer, "[d]eep down [...] wants to be Madonna."[54] The music industry blogger Bob Lefsetz chose a different musical analogy: "Trump is a Heavy Metal Band [...] Donald Trump is a rock star, if you go back to what that once upon a time meant, someone who adhered to his own vision living a rich and famous lifestyle who cared not a whit what others said."[55] The TV critic Emily Nussbaum preferred to see Trump as a comedian. Where Barack Obama's "sophisticated small-club act [...] was dry and urbane," Trump "was a hot comic, a classic Howard Stern guest." Nussbaum continues: "[Trump] was the insult comic, the stadium act, the ratings obsessed headliner who shouted down hecklers."[56] These accounts of who or what Trump is, and what form of popular culture captures his persona and style are linked to explanations of his success.

In accounting for Trump's rise, the U.S.-based political commentator Andrew Sullivan points to Trump's involvement in "the populist circuses of pro wrestling and New York City tabloids, via reality television and Twitter."[57] This is similar to the way that Emily

---

[52]   This section draws upon a previously published article by John Street, "What is Donald Trump? Forms of 'Celebrity' in Celebrity Politics," *Political Studies Review* 17, no. 1 (2019): 3–13.

[53]   Runciman, "I Didn't Do Anything."

[54]   Mark Singer, *Trump and Me* (London: Tim Duggan, 2016), 22; 36.

[55]   Bob Lefsetz, "Trump is a Metal Band," *The Lefsetz Letter*, May 2016, lefsetz.com/wordpress/2016/05/09/trump-metal-band/.

[56]   Emily Nussbaum, "Tragedy Plus Time," *The New Yorker*, January 23, 2017.

[57]   Andrew Sullivan, "America Has Never Been So Ripe for Tyranny," *The New York Times Magazine*, May 1, 2016.

Nussbaum saw, as was noted earlier, *The Apprentice* as making Trump "electable," if not getting him elected.[58]

Trump's claim of representing the people is realized through a relationship to his supporters that bears a close, or direct, resemblance to the dynamic between audiences and popular culture. In drawing on the analogy to popular culture, the commentators evoke not only Trump's style, but how that style works to engage his audience, to give them an identity and language. Ankersmit notes that a politics of style necessarily gives the audience a decisive role: "[T]he notion of political style [...] gives the citizen the same authority of judgment as the connoisseur possesses with relation to the works he or she examines."[59] For some writers, this translates into a view of the relationship as that of star and fan, as opposed to representative and citizen.[60] Certainly, it suggests that the link between politics and popular culture exists at a more than superficial level. Rather, it forms a constitutive part of representative democracy in the twenty-first century.

Conclusion

My claim about the importance of popular culture to our understanding of Donald Trump and of politics more generally is, of course, subject to any number of challenges. What I have tried to outline here is the kind of framework needed to make the claim plausible at the very least. This framework is drawn, first, from an account of how politics is to be defined and understood, and, second, by making use of Ankersmit's notion of style as the key term in establishing the potential importance of popular culture. The final step was to indicate how popular culture itself might be understood to work politically. At each level of this argument, there are serious questions to be asked and alternative answers to be considered. What I offer here, therefore, is one way of

---

[58] Nussbaum, "The TV That Created Donald Trump," *The New Yorker*, July 24, 2017.

[59] Ankersmit, *Political Representation*, 157.

[60] van Zoonen, *Entertaining Politics*; Jonathan Dean, "Politicising Fandom," *British Journal of Politics and International Relations* 19, no. 2 (2017): 408–424.

endorsing positively the suggestion that politics and popular culture are intimately linked, and that understanding U.S. politics also involves studying U.S. popular culture.

Acknowledgements

Many debts have been incurred in the course of writing this piece. In particular, I owe thanks to Professor Astrid Böger, Professor Philipp Gassert and other members of the German Association for American Studies and the University of Hamburg, who invited me to give a keynote and who proved to be the most helpful and welcoming of hosts. I am also very grateful to Professor Christian Lammert, who kindly introduced and chaired my talk, and to the GAAS audience who raised questions that I have tried (and no doubt failed) to address here.

Works Cited

Almond, Gabriel, and Sidney Verba. *The Civic Culture: Political Attitudes and Democracy in Five Nations*. Princeton: SAGE, 1963.

Ankersmit, F.R. *Aesthetic Politics*. Stanford: Stanford University Press, 1996.

---. *Political Representation*. Stanford: Stanford University Press, 2002.

Brassett, James, and Alex Sutton. "British Satire, Everyday Politics: Chris Morris, Armando Iannucci and Charlie Brooker." *British Journal of Politics and International Relations* 19, no. 2 (2017): 245–262.

Clapton, William, and Laura Shepherd. "Lessons from Westeros: Gender and Power in Game of Thrones." *Politics* 37, no. 1 (2017): 9.

Clover, Joshua. *1989: Bob Dylan Didn't Have This To Sing About*. Berkeley: University of California Press, 2009.

Corner, John, and Dick Pels, eds. *Media and the Restyling of Politics*. London: SAGE, 2003.

Dean, Jonathan. "Politicising fandom." *British Journal of Politics and International Relations* 19, no. 2 (2017): 408–424.

Douglas, Mary, and Aaron Wildavsky. *Risk and Culture: An Essay on the Selection of Technological and Environmental Dangers*. London: University of California Press, 1983.

Durante, Ruben, et al. "The Political Legacy of Entertainment TV." *American Economic Review* 109, no. 7 (2019): 2497–2530.

Eggers, Dave. "Sympathy for the Devil." *The Guardian Review*, March 2, 2019.

Elliott, Philip. "The Healing Power of Garth Brooks." *Time*, January 26, 2021.

Eyerman, Ronald, and Andrew Jamison. *Music and Social Movements*. Cambridge: Cambridge University Press, 1998.

Fielding, Steve. "A mirror for England? Cinematic Representations of Politicians and Party Politics, ca. 1944–64." *Journal of British Studies* 47, no. 1 (2008): 107–128.

Fosler-Lussier, Danielle. *Music in America's Cold War Diplomacy*. Berkeley: University of California Press, 2015.

Frith, Simon. *Performing Rites*. Oxford: Oxford University Press, 1996.

172   Politics as Popular Culture, Popular Culture as Politics

---. "Why Do Songs Have Words?" In *Music for Pleasure*, 105–128. Cambridge: Polity Press, 1988.

Furman, Daniel, and Paul Musgrave. "Synthetic Experiences: How Popular Culture Matters for Images of International Relations." *International Studies Quarterly* 61, no. 3 (2017): 503–516.

Gambino, Childish [Donald Glover]. "This is America." YouTube, accessed January 2, 2022. https://www.youtube.com/watch?v=VYOjWnS4cMY.

Hay, Colin. *Why We Hate Politics*. Cambridge: Polity Press, 2007.

Hollis, Martin. *The Philosophy of Social Science*. Cambridge: Cambridge University Press, 1994.

Huntington, Samuel. *The Clash of Civilizations and the Remaking of World Order*. New York: Simon & Schuster, 2002.

Kuper, Simon. "Secrets of the Populist Playbook." *Financial Times*, March 14, 2019.

Latour, Bruno. *Reassembling the Social: An Introduction to Actor-Network-Theory*. Oxford: Oxford University Press, 2007.

Lefsetz, Bob. "Trump is a Metal Band." *The Lefsetz Letter*, May 9, 2016. lefsetz.com/wordpress/2016/05/09/trump-metal-band/.

Marcus, Greil. *Mystery Train: Images of America in Rock and Roll Music*. New York: E. P. Dutton, 1975.

Moffitt, Benjamin, and Simon Tormey. "Rethinking Populism: Politics, Mediatisation and Political Style." *Political Studies* 62, no. 2 (2014): 381–397.

Moore, Allan. *Song Means: Analysing and Interpreting Recorded Popular Song*. Farnham: Routledge, 2012.

Mounk, Yascha. "Too Much Democracy." *The New Yorker*, November 12, 2018.

Negus, Keith. "Authorship and the Popular Song." *Music and Letters* 92, no. 4 (2012): 607–629.

Newman, Randy. "A Few Words in Defense of Our Country (Official Video)." YouTube, September 1, 2016. www.youtube.com/watch?v=E0EAwSpTcM4.

---. "Rednecks." YouTube, May 24, 2015. www.youtube.com/watch?v=o80BB0qZoVM.

Nussbaum, Emily. "The TV That Created Donald Trump." *The New Yorker*, July 24, 2017.

---. "Tragedy Plus Time." *The New Yorker*, January 23, 2017.

O'Toole, Fintan. *Heroic Failure: Brexit and the Politics of Pain.* London: Head of Zeus, 2018.

Ross, Steven. *Hollywood Left and Right: How Movie Stars Shaped American Politics.* Oxford: Oxford University Press, 2011.

Runciman, David. "I Didn't Do Anything Wrong in the First Place." *London Review of Books*, October 11, 2018.

Singer, Mark. *Trump and Me.* London: Tim Duggan, 2016.

Street, John. "What is Donald Trump? Forms of 'Celebrity' in Celebrity Politics." *Political Studies Review* 17, no. 1 (2019): 3–13.

Sullivan, Andrew. "America Has Never Been So Ripe for Tyranny." *The New York Times Magazine*, May 1, 2016.

Tett, Gillian. "Trump, Oprah and the Era of Pick 'n' Mix Politics." *Financial Times*, June 13, 2018.

van Zoonen, Liesbet. *Entertaining the Citizen: When Politics and Popular Culture Converge.* New York: Rowman & Littlefield, 2005.

van Zoonen, Liesbet, and Dominic Wring. "Trends in Political Television Fiction in the UK: Themes, Characters and Narratives, 1965–2009." *Media, Culture and Society* 34, no. 3 (2012): 263–279.

"'You Don't Own Me' PSA." YouTube, October 22, 2012. www.youtube.com/watch?v=XMxtbAP2cyU.

MARITA STURKEN

Comedy, Genre, and Netflix in Post-Irony American Popular Culture (or Disruption, Comedy, Humorlessness, and Genre Flail)

In the summer of 2018, President Trump threw what was then commonly referred to by his political opponents as a "temper tantrum," storming out of a meeting with Congressional leaders on infrastructure and holding a supposedly impromptu press conference (albeit with pre-prepared signs) in the White House Rose Garden that verged on a crazed rant. Stunned reporters attempted to cover the rant within the norms of political reporting, but the next day most major newspapers did what they had increasingly resorted to in the Trump era, which was to run a story about how late-night political comedy shows had made fun of the president's performance, replete with tweets and clips. That this was the strategy for political coverage in the Trump era is perhaps not surprising, because this norm-defying president made traditional modes of political performance obsolete, providing instead deranged and unpredictable soundbites to feed Twitter's and cable news' appetite for drama and unscripted content. In the Trump era, the norms of American political and public life were disrupted beyond recognition.

As the United States emerges from the Trump era and into a still uncertain future, it is worth situating the disruption of the Trump presidency within the broader disruptions of American life in the early twenty-first century. In this paper, I am interested in looking at the intersections of the disruption of political and presidential norms, the disruption of media consumption, the disruption of television viewership and the disruption of genre. In her epic survey of American history, *These Truths*, Jill Lepore defines the last two decades specifically as an era of disruption in American history, one that includes not only Y2K at the turn of the millennium; the attacks of 9/11; the rise of the tech

176   Comedy, Genre, and Netflix in Post-Irony American Popular Culture

industry; the disruption of the media through deregulation and consolidation; the rise of social media; and the demise of traditional journalism; but also the 2008 election of Barack Obama; the rise of social movements such as the Tea Party, Occupy Wall Street, and Black Lives Matter; the Patriot Act; the Wars in Afghanistan and Iraq; and the election of Donald Trump in 2016.[1] Undergirding these political disruptions are disruptions of entire industries, continued job loss in the manufacturing sector, the financial crisis of 2008, and the class divisions arising from economic hardship in large parts of the country. Disruption can act as a force that demands more of norms, narratives, and industries. Disruption can also bring about divides and divisions, scapegoating, and othering because of the fear, insecurity, and desperation it can sow.

What does this disruption mean for American popular culture? And, moreover, what *is* popular culture in this norm-defying era? Is it YouTube? Twitter? Amazon? Netflix? And what genres, if any, could respond to and make sense of the United States in the era of Trump, a man who honed his image through the genre of reality television? I aim here to grapple with these issues, particularly in relation to the role of comedy in mediating disruption, using Lauren Berlant's work on comedy and humorlessness as a guide.

In attempting to make sense of these issues, I am an academic who teaches and studies popular culture, but I have also been – as were many of my fellow citizens during the Trump era and in its aftermath – a traumatized citizen existing in a space of constant anxiety with regard to the state of the nation. And we are still anxious. I was, like many others, unprepared for the surge of anger, xenophobic rage, cruelty to desperate refugees, rising white nationalism, and the continued support in the heartland and among Republicans for the Trump cult of personality. It has been hard to accept the enduring appeal of Trump's politics of grievance and anger. Our democracy continues to be endangered. We hope the rule of law will survive. In the meantime, we watch Netflix.

---

[1]   Jill Lepore, *These Truths: A History of the United States* (New York: Norton, 2018), chapter 16.

Netflix and Genre

In order to consider the disruptions taking place in American popular culture, in genre, and in American political culture, we need to start with the disruptions taking place in media consumption. I take the example of Netflix as my point of departure. A game changer in the economic terrain of entertainment media, Netflix is now in the unenviable position of being the target of competing imitators. Disney and other studios are now expanding their own online streaming services, so the 'Netflix factor' may be diminished in future years. At this moment, however, its power to shape entertainment media on a global scale is unparalleled. We are only just beginning to understand how dramatically the rise of broadband online streaming has changed media consumption world-wide, and how it is now changing entertainment media production as well. While the demise of the collective movie theater experience has long been mourned (especially in the wake of the pandemic), it is now the collective (family) experience of television that is being rendered obsolete. Now, each member of the family watches their own screen (phone, iPad, laptop) with headphones on, and the fractured viewing experience has been normalized.

Netflix has established a new frontier for television through on-demand viewing, as well as new modes of genre, taste, and viewing practices. Netflix's business model is central to its disruption of genre and audiences. In the world of Netflix, data is the key factor in not only determining taste and reinventing genre, but in greenlighting production. As Michael D. Smith and Rahul Telang explain in their book, *Streaming, Sharing, Stealing*, Netflix has disrupted traditional pro-duction gatekeeping by using data, rather than the creation and reception of a pilot episode, to make decisions about production.[2] They describe a meeting in 2011 with the creative team of *House of Cards*, who, despite the high-profile talent lined up behind their production, had trouble getting a studio to greenlight a pilot because conventional wisdom dictated that no political drama since *The West Wing* had sold. Netflix,

---

[2] Michael D. Smith and Raul Telang, *Streaming, Sharing, Stealing: Big Data in the Future of Entertainment* (Cambridge: The MIT Press, 2016), chapter 1.

by contrast, came to the meeting armed with aggregated data and greenlighted two seasons worth of episodes based on data indicating that fans of director David Fincher and actor Kevin Spacey as well as Netflix subscribers who had previously watched the British *House of Cards* would constitute a guaranteed audience. In addition, Netflix planned to release each full season in one 'drop,' so that subscribers could binge-watch all they wanted without commercial interruptions. At the time, the greenlight without a pilot, the two-season deal, and the all-at-once release were scorned by the industry, but these practices are now the norm at Amazon, Netflix, and other streaming services. As the producers noted at the time, the two-season commitment also changed the show's writing and structure, as each episode was able to spend less time recapping content. All of this also points to the ways that pilots have historically been gatekeeping mechanisms that have stifled production.

It is perhaps surprising that the vast economic power Netflix enjoys on a global scale is due to its subscription business model. Originally launched as a DVD rental subscription service, it began offering streaming in 2007. In April 2019, Netflix had over 148 million subscribers worldwide, which meant it increasingly had funds available for content production, which it had begun in 2012. Subscription business models have not only been thriving in comparison with advertising business models in television; they are also increasingly on the rise in newspaper subscriptions (often attributed to a 'Trump Bump'), music streaming services such as Spotify and Pandora, and subscription websites such as *Medium*. This is having an ongoing impact on advertising revenues, which have already been deeply impacted by the dominance of Google and Facebook. Ten years ago, the rise of the subscription model was not yet clearly on the horizon, and there was little understanding of the potential disruptive aspects of such a basic model.

A key outcome of the subscription model is the availability of data, which allows Netflix algorithms to customize recommendations from its vast content offerings for specific viewers. Customization starts at the moment of login by asking, "Who is watching?" (and thus discouraging family viewing). Algorithms gauge future behavior on the basis of past behavior, defying the long convention of using demographics (age, gender, race, economic status, etc.) to predict viewer interest. Early research at Netflix found that past viewing experiences were far more predictive than demographics. Viewers today might fall into one of Netflix's more than 2,000 'microclusters,' or taste communities, rather than demographic segments. "Nowadays, in our modern world, hit play once and it tells us volumes more than knowing you're a 31-year-old woman or a 72-year-old man or a 19-year-old guy," Netflix Vice President Todd Yellin told *New York Magazine*.[3] Netflix can make increasingly tailored recommendations to viewers that defy conventional notions of audience.

One of the effects of this is a complete disruption of genre – Netflix does not trade in genre, so to speak. Its genre categories are increasingly microgenres, divided into taste categories (if you liked that, you will like this…) rather than the traditional categories of comedy, drama, science fiction, etc. According to *New York Magazine*, Netflix calls these groupings of similar programs "verticals" – highly specific film and television genres such as young-adult comedies, period romances, or sci-fi adventures.

Algorithms have gotten a lot of bad press lately, and arguably deservedly so, because of the ways that social media algorithms augment engagement and thus amplify content that engages a range of negative affective responses, such as anger, outrage, and hate. It could certainly be argued that social media algorithms helped elect Trump and have exacerbated political divisions in the U.S. But with its genre-defying model, Netflix demonstrates an algorithmic model that is about creating connectedness across traditional cultural boundaries rather than sowing negative engagement. Netflix is phenomenally global. Having begun international streaming in 2010, it is now streaming in over 190 countries and has more subscribers outside the United States than in it; it has programs subtitled in twenty-six languages and has increased the amount of dubbed content it offers. Importantly, it also has a vast amount of non-U.S. content and is producing original content outside the U.S., funding productions in France, Spain, Brazil, India, South Korea, and the Middle East.

---

[3] Josef Adalian, "Inside the Binge Factory," *New York Magazine*, June 11, 2018.

180   Comedy, Genre, and Netflix in Post-Irony American Popular Culture

This means that Netflix might actually be a model for a more cosmopolitan effect of algorithms. *New York Times* technology columnist Farhad Manjoo writes that:

> Despite a supposed surge in nationalism across the globe, many people like to watch movies and TV shows from other countries... Instead of trying to sell American ideas to a foreign audience, Netflix is aiming to sell international ideas to a global audience. A list of Netflix's most watched and most culturally significant recent productions looks like a Model United Nations: Besides Marie Kondo's show, there's the comedian Hannah Gadsby's "Nanette" from Australia; from Britain, "Sex Education"; "Elite" from Spain; "The Protector" from Turkey; and "Baby" from Italy."[4]

Manjoo argues that norm-changing programs like these have become popular and influential in markets they otherwise would not have reached, with *Sex Education* sparking debate about sex education in Thailand, for instance. The globalization of Netflix has not been without its roadblocks and stumbles, however. As Ramon Lobato notes in his recent book *Netflix Nations*, Netflix has come up against regulatory barriers in many countries and was unable to enter the vast Chinese market – it partnered with a Chinese streaming service to carry its content instead.[5]

This brings us to the phenomenon of *Nanette*. Netflix has been a huge platform for stand-up and political comedy. The site offers a vast array of edgy stand-up routines from Dave Chappelle, Kevin Hart, Tig Notaro, Trevor Noah, and others. This means that it streams numerous uncensored, boundary-pushing, stand-up routines for global audiences. After it was released by Netflix in 2018, *Nanette* received an enormous amount of attention and critical acclaim. This quirky rumination on comedy and sexual identity by the previously unknown Hannah Gadsby became a huge global hit despite the fact that, as many commentators have noted, queer feminist comedians normally play to much smaller crowds. One could therefore argue that the algorithmic structure of

---

[4]   Farhad Manjoo, "Netflix is the Most Intoxicating Portal to Planet Earth," *The New York Times*, February 22, 2019.

[5]   Ramon Lobato, *Netflix Nation: The Geography of Digital Distribution* (New York: New York University Press, 2019), chapter 4.

Netflix, in its global promotion of *Nanette*, allows for niche cultural products to travel in ways that can open up space for new voices.

Much credit can be given to the complexity of Gadsby's performance, but for the purposes of my argument I would also like to note here that the performance is a genre-defying one, so much so that it generated considerable debate about whether it was a comedy. This, in fact, was Gadsby's intent. She asks: What is it not okay to laugh about in this moment (for her, that moment is about identity, sexual violence, and tensions around gender fluidity)? Is the comedy genre a way of avoiding addressing pain and difficult issues? Yet it may be that her work demonstrates precisely how comedy as a genre has the flexibility to engage disruption, morph into new subgenres, and make connections across traditional cultural divides.

Gadsby's performance aims to deconstruct comedy in relation to how it creates and dispels tension. Lauren Berlant and Sianne Ngai have written that "Comedy's pleasure comes in part from its ability to dispel anxiety…but it doesn't simply do that. As both an aesthetic mode and a form of life, its action just as likely produces anxiety: risking transgression, flirting with displeasure, or just confusing things in a way that both intensifies and impedes the pleasure."[6]

As Gadsby gets further into her performance, her tone continues to shift, becoming darker as she narrates her experiences of homophobia, misogyny and sexual violence, and the cruelties she has experienced because of others' perception of her as being different and what she terms her "gender not normal" status. She argues that her comedy, which had been done in the very common mode of self-deprecation, was ultimately a detriment to her own self; her performance in *Nanette* is a demand that we rethink our laughter at these comedic modes. Gadsby's refusal to continue to engage in comedy at her own expense resonates with audiences, as it allows her to turn comedic laughter around and expose its potential cruelty. Gadsby may move from comedy toward dark truths, but comedy is what provides the means to test and gauge where the audience will go with her. Her performance thus disrupts the genre of comedy in order to reinvent rather than reject it.

---

[6] Lauren Berlant and Sianne Ngai, "Comedy Has Issues," *Critical Inquiry* 43, no. 2 (2017): 233.

182   Comedy, Genre, and Netflix in Post-Irony American Popular Culture

Comedy Disrupted/Post-Irony and Post-Genre

This brings us back to the question of disruption and genre. U.S. popular culture in the 1990s was replete with irony, so much so that after 9/11, irony and ironic humor came under attack for their tonal dissonance with the consequences of actual violence. Ironic humor was the norm in the era of Jon Stewart's *Daily Show*, a show that had a deeply formative influence on today's political comedic landscape. Irony is about the construction of the knowing viewer who understands the sources and references and rejects sentiment. In this context, genres become genre parodies, at once following the formula and commenting upon it. This "waning of genre," according to Berlant, creates openings.[7] In other words, as genres fracture and fade, we lose the comfort of their familiar conventions. But a post-genre context might be one in which we acquire new skills that enable us to understand the crises of our time.

In the era of Netflix and Trump, irony is less dominant and genre has been micro-clustered, hybridized, and effectively mashed up. Let's take, for example, 2018's *Vice*, a film about former vice president Dick Cheney and the ways he, as the architect of the response to 9/11 and the wars in Afghanistan and Iraq, effectively ran a shadow government during the Bush Administration. The film was directed by Adam McKay, who had made a career out of irreverent Will Ferrell comedies like *Talladega Nights* and *Anchorman* and talky films like *The Big Short*. McKay stated at the time, "I think we're just barreling toward a post-genre world [...] Something can be horribly tragic, tear inducing tragic, and something can be funny, or it can split the structure, and audiences can handle it [...] the saturation of media we have now with streaming and YouTube and all of that, audiences have gotten really sharp."[8]

Tonally, *Vice* careens through a range of modes to explore the scheming, the brutality, and the power-grabbing antidemocratic machinations of the Bush-Cheney administration, but, importantly, it is rarely ironic. The film jumps instead from straight dramatic depiction to

---

[7]   Lauren Berlant, *Cruel Optimism* (Durham: Duke University Press, 2011), 6.

[8]   Scott Myers, "Interview: Adam McKay," *Go Into the Story*, December 30, 2018, gointothestory.blcklst.com/interview-adam-mckay-5a7912ab8387.

satire to dark comedy to the absurd (such as a scene in which Dick and Lynn Cheney recite lines from *Macbeth* while contemplating whether Dick should become Vice President). *Vice* plays with viewer's expectations at every turn, by, for example, presenting an alternative outcome and then running fake credits in the middle of the film, or by having Dick Cheney's heart transplant donor, an Iraq War veteran, narrate the film. In one scene, a menu of torture practices is offered up to Cheney and his cronies in a high-end restaurant.

How does the comedic aspect of *Vice* serve as political critique? Does it encourage us to laugh at Bush and Cheney's war crimes and the damage they inflict on US democracy? *Vice* is a political critique of American empire as comedy. Yet in a certain sense, the film's tonal post-genre shifts perform the labor of making the Cheney story watchable rather than so distressing that it cannot be stomached. The film is a kind of instructional farce, a comedic docudrama that swerves through a range of modes while explicating complex aspects of Cheney's shadow executive status. I would argue that dark comedy veering in and out of straight drama, farce, and pedagogy provides the appropriate mix of emotional registers for the film's deconstruction of the undermining – if not the destruction – of U.S. democracy in the post-9/11 era. Finally, the film even critiques itself in a post-credits sequence featuring a mock focus group session that devolves into a screaming match, effectively telling viewers: we can't use jokes to bridge the political divide.

Comedy and Trump

What, then, of the state of comedy in popular culture in the Trump era? Many commentators felt that satire was the first mode to fail under Trump. Trump frequently appeared to be performing a satire of himself by slurring, cajoling, and performing exaggerated gestures. It was commonly noted that Trump "does a better Trump" than his imitators. This was a problem for comedy. As PJ O'Rourke states, "Trump is a joke, but you can't make a joke about a joke or you quit being the

184   Comedy, Genre, and Netflix in Post-Irony American Popular Culture

comedian on the stage and start being the heckler in the crowd because you're angry. Comedy, of course, has a lot to do with anger."[9]

Berlant argues that the opposite of comedy is not tragedy but humorlessness, and the strange combination of comedic and humorless behavior in the former president prompted many debates about whether Trump was good or bad for comedy. Numerous commentaries have suggested that Trump destroyed not only satire, but even fiction and other genres. For instance, the White House Correspondents' Association dinner, an annual affair that has historically been an occasion for politicians and journalists to comedically "roast" each other, has not had a comedian as its host since Michelle Wolf made fun of White House press secretary Sarah Sanders, and the Trump crew (Trump himself had refused to attend) left in a wounded huff. It's now an apocryphal story that Trump decided to run for president after sitting in fuming silence as Barack Obama (whose comedic timing is extraordinary) ribbed him at the 2011 Correspondents' Dinner, saying, "Obviously we all know about your credentials and breadth of experience. You fired Gary Busey [on *Celebrity Apprentice*]. And these are the kind of decisions that would keep me up at night." In this story, it was the cruelty of comedic roasting that sent the country down the intensely destructive path of the cult of aggrieved masculinity.

The inability of the press and comedians to participate in a shared comedy roast would appear to be evidence that comedy was in serious trouble during the Trump era. But humorlessness is also potentially fertile ground for comedy. Trump can be very entertainingly funny, but, as Kurt Anderson noted in the Intelligence Squared debate "Is Trump Bad for Comedy?", Trump is good for comedy because "He gives comedy the power to unsettle him. And comedy at his expense really does upset him, which strikes me is good for comedy and America."[10] Anderson and his fellow comedians at *Spy Magazine* had a history of targeting Trump (in one prank, they sent checks for miniscule, gradually diminishing amounts of money to wealthy people, and Trump was one of a handful who cashed the final check for 13 cents). Trump was an easy target for the irreverent *Spy* because he was so thin-skinned.

---

[9]   "Trump is Bad for Comedy," *Intelligence² Debates*, November 1, 2018, www.intelligencesquaredus.org/debates/trump-bad-comedy.

[10]   Ibid.

Humorlessness in the powerful, however, can be insidious. Berlant notes that "If you already have structural power your humorlessness increases your value and your power... Meanwhile, the privileged demand that the less privileged not be humorless... the person who names the problem becomes the problem. And if the person who names the problem is a kind of subject like a feminist, a person of color, a politicized queer, or/and a trans person, the privileged devalue them [...]." Gadsby performs this dynamic many times, in particular in her riff about being called "too sensitive" to homophobic and racist jokes. Humorlessness has been a hugely powerful force in Trump's popularity, as the hurt feelings and the sense of woundedness shifted via Trump from the margins to the mainstream. The aggrieved victim status of the most powerful person in the nation was a toxic mix of affect and power, one that continues to feed his supporters' anger at cultural elites (such as comedians).

It is thus no surprise that political comedy has been criticized for its degradation of those who live in the "flyover zones" of the country and whose sense of being looked down upon by coastal elites made Trump's particular combination of aggrieved hostility appealing. In other words, political comedy has been accused of helping to increase support for Trump because of its exacerbation of the political divide. As Caitlin Flanagan wrote in *The Atlantic*,

> The late-night political-comedy shows – principally Trevor Noah's *Daily Show*, Samantha Bee's *Full Frontal*, and John Oliver's *Last Week Tonight* – staked their territory during the heat of the general election: unwavering, bombastic, belittling, humiliating screeds against Donald Trump. Fair enough..... But somewhere along the way, the hosts of the late-night shows decided that they had carte blanche to insult not just the people within this administration, but also the ordinary citizens who support Trump, and even those who merely identify as conservatives.[11]

The genre of political comedy can be destructive when it seeps into cruelty.

---

[11] Caitlin Flanagan, "How Late-Night Comedy Fueled the Rise of Trump," *The Atlantic*, May 2017.

186   Comedy, Genre, and Netflix in Post-Irony American Popular Culture

Political Comedy Disrupted

So where has disrupted political comedy gone in order to reinvent itself? Late night political comedians like Stephen Colbert, John Oliver, Trevor Noah, Samantha Bee, Seth Myers, Jimmy Fallon, Jimmy Kimmel, and others have been working overtime to wrestle with comedy's challenges and have, as I noted at the outset, regularly filtered into mainstream media as a means of navigating the satire of Trump's presidency. These shows are increasingly edgy (Bee), they offer increasingly instructive forms of comedic news (a genre established by Jon Stewart with *The Daily Show* and continued by Oliver), and they are increasingly cosmopolitan (Noah). It's worth noting that Colbert, who built his career deploying ironic humor while in character as a right-wing TV host, now plays it straight by deconstructing the news as himself. He told the *New York Times* that the intention of *The Late Show*'s nightly monologue is not to jump from punchline to punchline but to "tell you what happened today." He stated, "It's almost as if the president is trying to cast a spell to confuse people so they cannot know the true nature of reality, and what we do is pick apart the way in which the [expletive] was sold to you. I think that's why it's going well. Our job is to identify the [expletive], and there's never been more."[12] Similarly, John Oliver's show is a deeply researched analysis of contemporary issues that is sophisticated enough to fit neatly into a college classroom.

This would seem to take political comedy down the road of instruction. One example of this genre comes to us, not surprisingly, from Netflix: Hasan Minhaj's appropriately and ironically titled show, *Patriot Act*. Minhaj, a Muslim Indian-American who began his comedy career on the *Daily Show*, describes the show's format as an "investigative visual comedic podcast" in which he stands on a stage surrounded by large screens that regularly display graphs and statistics. The show is a kind of pedagogical comedy, a hybrid of stand-up and a TED talk. A list of the show's topics illustrates its instructive range: Affirmative Action, Drug Pricing, Student Loans, Civil Rights Under Trump, Indian Elections, Oil, Amazon, and so on. Minhaj regularly deploys his status as a Muslim-American and a member of an immigrant

[12] David Marchese, "Stephen Colbert on the Political Targets of Satire," *The New York Times Magazine*, May 31, 2019.

family in order to intervene in discussions about ethnicity and race and examine the particular demands on and of immigrant families.

Minhaj begins his show with an intro in which he depicts himself as a traumatized citizen, both surrounded by and peering anxiously at the theater of the political divide. In *Patriot Act*, comedy has to be in service of pedagogy. Minaj performs with a kind of earnestness, interpellating his audience as those who want to know more in order to understand the state of things at the present moment. The show has a global reach, which produced a mini-crisis that exposed the limits of Netflix's global ambitions. In an episode on Saudi Arabia, Minhaj's discussed the history of the U.S.-Saudi relationship and the murder of journalist Jamal Khashoggi, and he criticized Prince Mohammed bin Salman from a Muslim's perspective. The episode was banned in Saudi Arabia because it violated laws governing criticism of the royal family, but Netflix made the decision to keep the rest of its shows – and the other episodes of Patriot Act – streaming in the country. It's hard to argue with that decision in retrospect when one imagines young Saudi women watching *Nanette* or *Queer Eye for the Straight Guy* behind closed doors.

In *Patriot Act*, Minhaj bounds around the stage, pointing to his surrounding screens in a geeky way for the infographics they deliver; his explication of an issue is punctuated by jokes. The appeal of a show like *Patriot Act* is that, at its core, it believes we as citizens can resist the destructive forces of our government by exposing their schemes and being better-informed citizens. However, this relies on the idea that being uninformed due to a constant diet of Fox News is what is making Trump supporters follow him despite his cons and lies. That, of course, is an illusion. The bitter truth is that politics is much more about affect than facts, and Trump's capacity to sell himself as the aggrieved victim is far more powerful than Minhaj's PowerPoint-style takedowns. The show raises interesting questions about where the genre of comedy takes us in moments of crisis and the flexibility of the comedy genre. Yet despite critical acclaim, *Patriot Act* was cancelled by Netflix in August 2020.

188   Comedy, Genre, and Netflix in Post-Irony American Popular Culture

Genre Flail

I am aware that this essay is a bit of a post-genre mix, symptomatic of our contemporary crisis of interpretation. Have I achieved the proper genre balance, have I connected Netflix to comedy to genre to Trump? Like Gadsby, I want to get off the hook here by telling you I know I have a genre problem. Berlant uses the term "genre flail" to describe those moments of disruption in our chosen "objects," be they modes of analysis, political identities, institutional frameworks, etc. She writes, "Genre flailing is a mode of crisis management that arises after an object, or object world, becomes disturbed in a way that intrudes on one's confidence about how to move in it. We genre flail so that we don't fall through the cracks of heightened affective noise into despair, suicide, or psychosis." [13]

While I understand the post-genre mode of popular culture in terms of possibilities of intervention, Berlant's concept of genre flail is an appropriate descriptor of the state of the traumatized citizen, with whom I identified at the beginning of this essay. How to resist, how to survive, how to retain hope in this moment of flailing, when institutions, foundations, the nation, democracy, and the planet are at risk. Is this the end of American dominance as a global superpower? What is the genre of this crisis? We ask these questions in a certain way every day. Berlant continues:

> Countless encounters since the Trump election hiccup into the genre flail in the riff on *what's happening*? Anything anyone writes in the ongoing [...] eddy of his world-shaking thud [...] is a genre flail. Protest is a genre flail; riot, sometimes too, and so is whatever we do off the cuff or in a last minute insert when we're giving a conference talk and cannot not comment on the present moment, in which the speaker presumes that we're all disoriented or in crisis and wanting to fix the world.

We cannot *not* comment on the present moment. In that sense, we certainly need comedy, and we need to be attentive to those modes of popular culture that enable us to listen, analyze, connect, and watch across digital platforms. This brings me back to Gadsby:

[13]   Lauren Berlant, "Genre Flailing," *Capacious: Journal for Emerging Affect Inquiry* 1, no. 2 (2018): 157.

I wrote a comedy show that did not respect the punchline – that line where comedians are expected and trusted to pull their punches and turn them into tickles. I did not stop, I punched through that line into the metaphorical gaps of my audience. I did not want to make them laugh, I wanted to take their breath away, to shock them, so that they could listen to my story and hold my pain, as individuals, not as a mindless laughing mob [...] the point was to break comedy so that I could rebuild it and reshape and re-form it so that it could hold what I needed to share, and that is what I meant when I said I quit comedy.[14]

Perhaps, within these strategies of post-genre popular culture, these forms of newly reshaped comedy can bring us hope.

---

[14] Hannah Gadsby, *Three Ideas. Three Contradictions. Or not*, TED, April 2019.

Works Cited

Adalian, Josef. "Inside the Binge Factory." *New York Magazine*, June 11, 2018.

Berlant, Lauren. *Cruel Optimism*. Durham: Duke University Press, 2011.

---. "Genre Flailing." *Capacious: Journal for Emerging Affect Inquiry* 1, no. 2 (2018): 156–162.

Berlant, Lauren, and Sianne Ngai. "Comedy Has Issues." *Critical Inquiry* 43, no. 2 (2017): 233–249.

Flanagan, Caitlin. "How Late-Night Comedy Fueled the Rise of Trump." *The Atlantic*, May 2017.

Gadsby, Hannah. "Three Ideas. Three Contradictions. Or not." TED, April 2019.

Lepore, Jill. *These Truths: A History of the United States*. New York: Norton, 2018.

Lobato, Ramon. *Netflix Nations: The Geography of Digital Distribution*. New York: New York University Press, 2019.

Manjoo, Farhad. "Netflix is the Most Intoxicating Portal to Planet Earth." *The New York Times*, February 22, 2019.

Marchese, David. "Stephen Colbert on the Political Targets of Satire." *The New York Times Magazine*, May 31, 2019.

Myers, Scott. "Interview: Adam McKay." *Go Into the Story*, December 30, 2018. gointothestory.blcklst.com/interview-adam-mckay-5a7912ab8387.

Smith, Michael D., and Raul Telang. *Streaming, Sharing, Stealing: Big Data in the Future of Entertainment*. Cambridge: The MIT Press, 2016.

"Trump Is Bad for Comedy." *Intelligence[2] Debates*, November 1, 2018. www.intelligencesquaredus.org/debates/trump-bad-comedy.

JENNIFER VOLKMER

Motorcycle Riding in Movies as Modern-Day Pilgrimage to Masculinity

Introduction

Popular culture is a crucial element in the formation and consolidation of national myths.[1] In the United States, road movies and Westerns in particular contribute to national myths that were established before the modern feature movie but are still perpetuated in contemporary popular products. These are the myths of Westward Movement, the frontier, and self-reliance. These myths and national myth-making are closely entwined with popular culture and are, moreover, heavily gendered. They are associated with men, excluding women and other genders as well as types of masculinities that are incompatible with these national myths. Through popular culture and protagonists' journeys it becomes clear who is and who is not able to reconcile their identity with the national myth; grounds for this are, among others, race, class, gender, and sexual orientation.

To illustrate this point, I will look at the 2007 comedy film *Wild Hogs*, starring Tim Allen (Doug), John Travolta (Woody), Martin Lawrence (Bobby), and William H. Macy (Dudley) as four middle-aged men who embark on a road trip from Connecticut to Los Angeles to escape their stifling suburban lives and do something meaningful that reminds them of their youth. Along the way, they have to face several obstacles such as disapproving families, sleeping outside, and, most importantly, angering a biker gang. The latter leads to a showdown fight at the end of the movie between the gang on the one side and, on the

---

[1] See Tim Edensor, "Automobility and National Identity: Representation, Geography and Driving Practice," *Theory, Culture & Society* 21, nos. 4–5 (2004): 102.

192 Modern-Day Pilgrimage to Masculinity

other side, the four protagonists who, together with a group of small-town inhabitants, defend the town against the destructive biker gang.

The trip resembles a pilgrimage, and it is an example of the depiction of middle-aged men who use motorcycle riding as proof of their masculinity. I thus argue that motorcycle riding in *Wild Hogs* becomes a pilgrimage the characters undertake in order to prove their masculinity. This means the men have an implicitly idealized image of what traits a man should have/exhibit. At the beginning of the movie, they realize that they fall short of this image, either because they have lost some of these traits or because they never had them. These traits are: independence/freedom to make their own decisions (Doug, Bobby), facing danger/going into the wild (all four), proving their physical strength/superiority over other men (all four), and dominance over women (all four, but mostly Doug, Bobby, Dudley). Despite the men having individual characteristics that make up their individual masculinities, by the end of the film they all are 'corrected' to the point where they all exhibit the same major traits. The motorcycle road trip thus became a pilgrimage to their masculinity, and the film constructs a hegemonic masculinity within its confines instead of celebrating the men's different masculinities. As a side effect, this renders women and other masculinities that deviate from this hegemonic masculinity as inferior.

I use the concept of hegemonic masculinity defined by Connell as: "It is, rather, the masculinity that occupies the hegemonic position in a given pattern of gender relations, a position always contestable."[2] In 2019, Messerschmidt clarified this with: "I define hegemonic masculinities as those masculinities constructed locally, regionally, and globally that legitimate an unequal relationship between men and women, masculinity and femininity, and among masculinities." Messerschmidt goes on to explain that "Hegemonic masculinities acquire their legitimacy by embodying materially and/or discursively culturally supported 'superior' gender qualities in relation to the embodiment or symbolization of 'inferior' gender qualities."[3]

[2] R. W. Connell, *Masculinities* (Berkeley: University of California Press, 2005), 76.

[3] James W. Messerschmidt, "Hidden in Plain Sight: On the Omnipresence of Hegemonic Masculinity," *A Journal of Culture and Society* 12 (2019): 17.

In this case the 'location' will be the film. I look at the way the main characters interact with each other, the female characters, and the other male characters who ride motorcycles to approve or disapprove of certain behaviors. All these relationships then construct the hegemonic masculinity within the film. The recurring themes where the superior/inferior dichotomy is clearly shown are: heterosexuality vs. (perceived) homosexuality; pater familias vs. mater familias; physical violence vs. non-violent conflict resolution; vigilante justice vs. legal action. These conflicting themes are very much imbedded within motorcycle riding in the film, since the question is raised as to who a real rider is, i.e., who is allowed to ride and keep riding.

Pilgrimage

Pilgrimages are usually undertaken to either prove one's faith or to strengthen and regain it, or some combination of these. Either way, it presupposes a belief system, whether religious or secular. By going on the pilgrimage, the pilgrim accepts that belief system, and if the pilgrim is successful they will strengthen this system for themselves, and possibly others. Translating this to my case study means that the protagonists believe in a certain idea of masculinity: heterosexual, assertive over women and other men, physically strong and able to fight and win, self-sufficient/no reliance on the state for physical protection (of property). They want to represent this idealized masculinity/this belief system (i.e., this way of being/acting as a man is desirable over other ways of being/acting as a man, especially in relation to women). By striving for it they validate these traits as desirable and thus construct the hegemonic masculinity in the film. This contributes to maintaining the hierarchy of men over women, and it invalidates the personal brands of masculinity the characters started out with as insufficient because each character, in his own way, fails to live up to the ideals presented in the hegemonic masculinity the film constructs.

Hegemonic masculinities are not static but "[...] can be contested and undermined through alternative practices that do not support gender hegemony [...]."[4] Some of the traits the main characters start out with,

---

[4]   Ibid., 26.

194 Modern-Day Pilgrimage to Masculinity

e.g., not engaging in physical violence with other motorcycle riders, could present such an undermining if these traits were maintained. But the characters paint these potentially subversive traits as 'inferior,' and thus the film contributes to reaffirming the aforementioned traits as part of dominant masculinity while confirming the gender hierarchy as well. Therefore, in terms of the pilgrimage, the protagonists not only fail to subvert the gender hegemony, they also strengthen the belief in it for others, especially the audience. Particularly because the protagonists' former traits of being rather 'soft'[5] both physically as well as figuratively, and thus coded as 'weak' in comparison to the biker gang, and are considered problems to be overcome. A pilgrimage means transformation, and the pilgrimage west is deemed the right method to transform these men's masculinities.

Kruse Knight identifies three stages a pilgrim will go through: "journey away from their homes and daily routines, experience transition at a pilgrimage site, and later reincorporate into society."[6] The movie thus not only provides the audience with the details of the protagonists' lives before pilgrimage as a point of comparison, it also establishes what qualities necessitate a pilgrimage in the first place, coding their masculinities as negative and undesirable. We are immediately introduced to the daily routines and living situations of the four protagonists, being presented with the aspects of their lives they are unhappy with.

Doug's life has simply become restrained and boring. He has a good home life with a wife (Jill Hennessy) and a son (Dominic Janes), and an apparently successful dental practice. But he addresses his wife during a family dinner, saying "I think, you think I am a boring guy. I am old, and boring now. I've become lame. I think everybody thinks that at this table."[7] This mostly reflects his own thoughts since his wife never said this, and he includes himself by saying "everybody at this table." In the

---

[5] The TV show *Good Omens* (2019) impressively shows through Aziraphale that a masculine-presenting character considered rather soft, even calling himself so, and who is physically not close to the muscle-packed 'lean mean fighting machine,' can be strong and save the world.

[6] Cher Krause Knight, *Power and Paradise in Walt Disney's World* (Gainesville: University of Florida Press, 2014), 27.

[7] *Wild Hogs*, directed by Walt Becker, USA 2007, 00:14:00.

same scene Doug goes on to say "I am wild and free [...] and a man!"[8] Therefore, he himself points out what is going wrong in his life and connects the remedy to it to his masculinity.

Dudley is shown to be unable to dominate women's perception of him. In his introductory scene, he pretends to read a paper while ogling a woman who is working on her laptop, and tries to get her attention. He impresses the woman by demonstrating that his computer can be voice controlled. While this is now a common and widely used technology in multiple kinds of devices, this was not the case in 2007 when this type of technology did not yet work reliably, was only in developing stages and was not available to the public. Thus, possessing such technology conveys that the owner has a lot of money to be able to afford such an exclusive technology, and/or works in developing these technologies, which is a high-profile profession. In short, this demonstration suggests Dudley has status. Initially, this works because the woman does look up and smiles at him throughout a short exchange (although she never gets to speak).[9] However, when Dudley tries to build on his initial success by using the computer-specific lingo "alternative specs," the machine shows its faultiness by taking the term as an internet search command for "alternative sex." Immediately the entire café hears and is repulsed by the search results being loudly proclaimed over the computer's speakers. All of Dudley's attempts to shut it off fail until he accidentally spills coffee over the computer. Meanwhile the woman has left the café.[10] Since she knew that the search was an accident, I draw the conclusion that Dudley was only attractive to her because of his status with regard to computers. But the faulty technology destroyed that high status and thus ended the attractiveness. The faulty technology exposes the faults in Dudley's masculinity. To be successful with women, Dudley is thus portrayed as needing to be in control of himself, of his surroundings, and of the women he is interested in.

Bobby, similarly, is not assertive enough to control the perception the women in his life have of him. His wife (Tichina Arnold), the family's breadwinner, commands him to "stay" as she leaves for her high-paying job. His daughters don't listen to him. Neither does his

---

[8] Ibid., 00:15:00.
[9] This also means that his looks aren't the obstacle to his dating success.
[10] Ibid., 00:05:00.

196 Modern-Day Pilgrimage to Masculinity

younger child (Cymfenee) adhere to his calmly delivered "inside voice" when she tells him to listen to her screaming. Nor does his teenaged daughter (Drew Sidora) take any of his criticism regarding her clothing into account. Watching the scene, his mother-in-law (Bebe Drake) explains to him, "It is hard for kids to respect the man that don't do none of the providing'" and calls him "the lazy man" on top of it.[11]

Many things have gone wrong in Woody's life, which is why he just wants to leave town and initiates the road trip. His wife, a swimsuit model that made him the envy of the men surrounding him,[12] has left him. He seems to have lost his money as well,[13] but he keeps all these things hidden from his friends. In a way, Woody's journey could be considered subversive of the hegemonic masculinity constructed through the changes the other characters undergo, because by the end he opens up about his problems to his friends. However, none of his problems are actually addressed; the moment remains a mere moment of confession, but there is no reward for the vulnerability, no further sharing of emotions or problems. Rather, it is a small acknowledgement to the instance that sparked the journey before Woody's storyline is dropped completely. Instead, I argue that his journey is connected more to physicality. His status in the beginning was dependent on having a wife and money. Losing them – and I intentionally treat his wife as a possession here through word choice because this is how she is presented in the film – damages his masculinity and thus his position in the gender hierarchy. However, by the end of the movie he is confident again, even without regaining his lost possessions. What did change, though, is his approach to problem solving. Woody goes from running away from debtors to physically fighting a threat.

Therefore, we come to the first step: all four protagonists must leave home to travel in order to transform. The site initially presented as the pilgrimage site is Los Angeles. However, their transformation, and thus masculinities, are tied to their motorcycles, meaning their transformation to/restoration of accepted masculinity ('real men') will be completed

---

[11] Ibid., 00:03:00. Bobby is also essentially not working, neither in his profession as a plumber nor on the book for which he took a year off work to write. But because of space constraints and the fact that the job aspect is not addressed at the end of the film, I leave it out here.

[12] Ibid., 00:11:00.

[13] Ibid., 00:06:00.

when they have proven to be 'real bikers.' In the film this is shown by the four protagonists being accepted as 'real bikers' by men that are already established as such by the narrative. Consequently, the true site of transformation, and thus the second stage of the pilgrimage, is the site where they meet and defeat the 'real bikers' they encounter in the desert. Los Angeles can still be seen as the pilgrimage site, though, since the pilgrimage is also about finishing the trip. The third step of reintegration into society happens right after the fight. This is not explicitly shown as the protagonists returning to their geographical home, but rather a return to their homes represented by the arrival of Bobby's wife, Doug's wife and child, and Dudley's new girlfriend (Marisa Tomei).[14] While everyone is still happy about the end of the fighting, and celebrating, the camera shows Dudley kissing his girlfriend in the crowd and then shows the wives arriving. Bobby's wife immediately confronts him yelling "what is going on" since he lied to her about going to a plumbing conference. Here the relationship pattern from the beginning is repeated, she talks without caring what he has to say and commands: "I want you to get your ass in that van because we are going home."[15] This time, however, he does not acquiesce, but talks over her. To be clear, Bobby doesn't yell or get mean, all he does is make himself heard and calmly explain that he is "tired of being talked at." When she starts to contest that claim she actually illustrates his point and agrees with this herself when he points it out. Following Bobby's demonstration of assertiveness, she immediately becomes complacent and agrees with everything, and they make up with a kiss. Her rightfully raised point of him deceiving her about his whereabouts is simply dropped. Doug's wife is just glad that he is still alive, but he has finally earned the respect of his son. No longer is he "old, boring and lame"[16] as per his own assessment from his introductory scene; what Doug did is "awesome" in the eyes of his son, who wants to tell his friends about it immediately.[17] This moment of reunification after the protagonists' transformation is a

---

[14] As already mentioned above, John Travolta's story line is dropped for the most part and doesn't constitute a real solution. Technically, he does not have a home to return to since his wife has left him and he is heavily in debt and cannot afford his house anymore.

[15] Ibid., 01:26:00.

[16] Ibid., 00:14:00.

[17] Ibid., 01:27:00.

Modern-Day Pilgrimage to Masculinity

means of showing us how they have changed, thus contrasting their interactions to with those from the beginning of the film. Therefore, it can be said that the movie *Wild Hogs* represents a pilgrimage for the four protagonists since they are shown leaving their homes and daily routines, going to a pilgrimage site and undergoing change there, and are then also shown re-integrating into the society they left at the beginning.

Road Movie Genre

David Laderman describes the road movie's connection to freedom through mobility,[18] which is exactly what the Wild Hogs strive for; they want to break out of their lives, and from the conventions built around them.[19] In essence, they feel oppressed by their lives, which appear boring to them, and a society which perceives them as boring and laughable, and they seek the glory of their younger years when they were supposedly more independent and adventurous. These latter qualities are more in line with masculinity, since femininity is associated with the (stable) home. Here we can see how the hegemonic masculinity is constructed in the film and affirms gender stereotypes. The men need to leave the house and home to feel masculine, while the women remain stationary and presumably care for the children without support from the fathers. While the men are able and even encouraged to leave, the women then have no choice but to stay unless they are willing to abandon their children and homes. Women are then denied the chance to experience the same degree of freedom through travel or experience independence from the responsibility of daily life, from the reproductive work (cooking, cleaning, childcare) that enables the men's freedom. Since the women's wishes and needs in this movie are never communicated, we can conclude that they are subordinated to those of the men.

However, it is never a question if the Wild Hogs will return to their former lives. For them, it was always about proving that they could

---

[18] David Laderman, *Driving Visions: Exploring the Road Movie* (Austin: University of Texas Press, 2002), 49.

[19] I am aware that *Wild Hogs* does not meet the definition for road movies by most academics, including Laderman, but to the general public it still appears to be one.

reach the pilgrimage site of Los Angeles, proving that they are 'real men' in the sense of the self-imposed ideals of the hegemonic masculinity constructed in the film, and then returning as these 'real men' to their old lives, reintegrating into the same society they found so oppressive at the beginning. Permanent change is not desired; the oppression is not located in society or lifestyle. Rather, the oppression is self-contained in the aging bodies of these men. The personal pilgrimage of the protagonists is framed as successful when they are depicted at the beach in Los Angeles after their transformation. However, it is never established that this change is a lasting or sustainable one. What does remain the same, or is even strengthened, though, is the bond between the four men – but given the homophobia present throughout the movie, this bond is portrayed in a strictly non-sexual way.

Homophobia

As Guerrero states, the "male buddy films [...] were most obviously a reaction [...] to the then emergent Women's Movement"[20]; he places their start in the late 1960s/early 1970s and includes *Easy Rider* (1969) as one of the first ones, a film which also happens to be the progenitor (along with *Bonnie and Clyde* [1967]) of the road movie as a genre. When a female character – otherwise unimportant to the story – is inserted into the story merely as a means to make a statement about the sexuality of the protagonists – also unimportant to the story – this per-petuates homophobia because the only function of her presence is to assure the viewers that the male protagonists are interested in women and not in each other; ambiguity is not allowed. When homosexuality or queerness is addressed at various points throughout the movie *Wild Hogs*, it is either ridiculed as a joke or directly seen as a threat to the men's aspired masculinity/the hegemonic masculinity constructed in the movie. When homosexuality is seen as a threat, it is almost always em-bodied by William H. Macy's character, Dudley. Later on, the audience is assured that Dudley is heterosexual because he 'gets the girl' at the end of the movie. Since bisexuality is such a rare occurrence in films –

---

[20] Ed Guerrero, "The Black Image in Protective Custody," in *Black American Cinema*, ed. Manthia Diawara (New York: Routledge, 1993), 239.

to the point that it practically does not exist in mainstream movies as a viable interpretation[21] – Dudley must, therefore, be straight, which assuages all fears regarding his sexuality. However, at the beginning of the film, Dudley's friends constantly ridicule him for his 'unmanly' behavior such as hugging, wearing a helmet, and enjoying the smell of Woody's cologne; they are afraid he might be queer and how that would then reflect on them.[22] When Dudley crashes his motorcycle on their weekly ride to the pub, he is shown to be the least capable rider of the four and needs to ride with one of the others to get to the pub. This latter aspect sparks off quite the queerphobic scene. It is absolutely common for motorcycle riders to ride as a passenger on another person's motorcycle. Despite this, in comedies where the male protagonist's masculinity is being questioned as part of the story line, sharing space on a motorcycle is too intimate and sexualized, implying that both of the riders could be queer if they do not fight tooth and nail against this arrangement.[23] In *Wild Hogs,* Woody immediately gets angry at Dudley for being too close while on the bike with him, threatening, "if you ever lay your head on my back again when you are riding bitch, I'll throw you in the traffic."[24] Here, anger and the threat of physical violence are used to demark the lines of acceptable male behavior. In this interaction, Dudley's masculinity is marked as inferior and unacceptable. Because the other men confirm Woody's opinion (albeit in a less extreme way) and Dudley stops arguing his point, their interaction has constructed a hegemonic masculinity that does not accept physical closeness between men, let alone homosexuality. The easiest way to dispel suspicions of

---

[21] Looking, for example, at popular lists about the best bisexual movies on various internet sites, it stands out that they all mention how difficult it is to find films that feature bisexuality, but even more so that the films they do feature are mainly films that were released after *Wild Hogs* or are European films from before 1990. See, e.g., The British Film Institute or Men's Health Magazine.

[22] *Wild Hogs*, 00:10:00.

[23] Sexualizing the simple act of two people riding on a motorcycle also completely ignores the fact that parents often take their children on bikes as well, and it also implies that the only person on the back of a motorcycle is a woman the rider is sexually interested in, perpetuating queerphobia yet again.

[24] Ibid.

homosexuality, however, is to have female partners for male characters, a concept which was discussed in the section about pilgrimage.

Violence

Another important aspect in establishing superiority over women and other men is violence. The violence portrayed in *Wild Hogs* is directed at the clearly identifiable 'bad guys,' as is common in Hollywood movies. Here, good and bad people are neatly separated, and the idea of the 'right' kind of violence by the 'right people' is thus reinforced. However, violence and vigilantism tend to go hand in hand and become inseparable in genre movies. Violence is not condoned in American culture on the surface, but once it comes to 'standing one's ground' (the maxim of being strong and defending one's own property), life and values easily surpasses the dictum of 'violence is bad.' Robert Maxwell Brown has detailed the connection between the two in his book *No Duty to Retreat*, in which he also explains that property, life, and values, coupled with the disappearing of the "duty to retreat" from American law when it comes to self-defense, essentially erodes the notion of self-defense and becomes a justification of (arbitrary) violence. David Laderman ascribes to the road movie genre both a "focus on masculinity" and a tendency to treat "violence as a progressive gesture, an instrument of liberation,"[25] making violence seem inevitable in this story. The travel alone was not enough to prove anything beyond a doubt. The men, who are usually placid and non-confrontational and concede to their wives on everything, need to prove that they can stand their ground. The threat of real bodily harm being their last test, or, as Laderman says, the "instrument of their liberation."[26]

If violence is so easily justifiable by law by evoking the notion of self-defense, then violence in almost any circumstance can be justified, leading, in turn, to the use of violence in the pursuit of securing or gaining status. In the movie, the biker gang uses violence to gain status by causing the townspeople to fear for their property, sources of income, and physical well-being. This violence is deemed bad by the pro-

---

[25] Laderman, *Driving Visions*, 21–22.
[26] Ibid., 22.

202 Modern-Day Pilgrimage to Masculinity

tagonists and townspeople, and subsequently by the movie. This value judgement is facilitated by the biker gang being coded as the villains of the movie when they are introduced. They terrorize the small town, and it is clear that the gang started the violence against the townspeople, who are innocent. At no point does the film discuss systemic issues that might lead to crime and violence, such as people being denied jobs because they ride motorcycles. Neither are social class or mental health considered, despite the conflict also obviously being a class conflict, because the members of the biker gang are working class while the middle-class townspeople who own property are being aided by the upper- middle class protagonists. Since police are not in control of the situation, the only way to protect the townspeople's property is through more violence in the name of self-defense. The violence used to fight off the biker gang is condoned and justified in American culture, and possibly even by law. But this becomes vigilante justice, because the biker gang commits a crime, or crimes, by destroying property. There-fore, in a functioning society, the gang could – and should – be reported to the police, who would then turn them over to the justice system which would punish them accordingly.[27] In Western political thought, the state has the monopoly on violence in a working society. Grossly simplified, this means that as soon as the state cannot guarantee the safety of its citizens other forces of order-making move in to fill the vacuum of establishing order.[28] No state wants to lose policing power in this way, because it means the sole authority of the state is being questioned and contested, leading, in the worst-case scenario, to the overthrow of the (legitimate) government, a coup d'état.

The state authorities that are supposed to have the monopoly on violence are repeatedly shown as weak and not capable of the job, not ubiquitous enough, or too easily overpowered by the villain(s) of the piece. Thus, this movie not only provides another stepping stone for the belief that state authorities are weak, but also connects the concept to hegemonic masculinity. It perpetuates the idea that citizens cannot rely on the state for help, while also suggesting that only someone who can

---

[27] Or alternatively, in a police-less society, any other regulative body that would restore justice.

[28] Thus breeching the social contract that makes society and government possible in the first place, as proposed e.g. by Hobbes.

physically defend themselves against any perceived threat is a 'real man.' This further implies that women also need to rely on a 'real man' for protection which would influence their choice of partner. This then again also excludes queerness because a female partner would not be able to provide adequate protection. This connection between hetero-sexuality and violence then helps construct the hegemonic masculinity in this film. To drive the point home even further, the movie does show law enforcement officers: the ones working in the town, and one who also rides a motorcycle and is also the only clearly queer character in the movie. This motorcycle cop (John C. McGinley) is portrayed as in-competent due to his sexuality, as failing to do his job because he rather pursues men that do not want to be pursued. Thus, this character simul-taneously consolidates the point: queerness is not desirable, and law enforcement officers are not doing their job or are weak and unhelpful to law-abiding citizens. It also turns queerness not only into a joke but into a direct threat to masculinity.

Conclusion

I set out to show that *Wild Hogs* is essentially a pilgrimage undertaken by the protagonists to transform their masculinities into a version that they idealize. Therefore, I looked at how national myths are made and maintained in popular culture and how intricately this is tied to ideas about gender. Because all these characters eventually end up with the same key traits, and their interactions with women and other men eventually show the protagonists to be superior in relation to them, and they are admired by them by the end, a hegemonic masculinity is con-structed within the film. Through the four protagonists Doug, Woody, Bobby and Dudley, the audience is shown which traits in men are considered undesirable, or desirable and granting them the respect of others. Connecting this to a pilgrimage guarantees reintegration into society. Suddenly the protagonists of this movie are not transgressors, but part of society. They partake in punishing the actual transgressors: the biker gang. *Wild Hogs* thus appropriates the transgressive elements of motorcycle riding for the conformist man and further renders the transgressors as undesirable instead of showing solidarity. This results in the reaffirming of heterosexuality, dominance over women, self-reliance and violence as important traits for men in America – and for the United States itself as a society – in a movie that is otherwise seemingly harmless, humorous fun.

Works Cited

Brown, Richard Maxwell. *No Duty to Retreat: Violence and Values in American History and Society*. New York: Oxford University Press, 1991.

Connell, R. W. *Masculinities*. Berkeley: University of California Press, 2005.

Diawara, Manthia, ed. *Black American Cinema*. New York: Routledge, 1993.

Edensor, Tim. "Automobility and National Identity: Representation, Geography and Driving Practice." *Theory, Culture & Society* 21, nos. 4–5 (2004): 101–120.

Gatling, Margaret, et al. "Representations of Middle Age in Comedy Film: A Critical Discourse Analysis." *The Qualitative Report* 19, no. 12 (2014): 1–15.

Guerrero, Ed. "The Black Image in Protective Custody." In *Black American Cinema*, edited by Manthia Diawara, 237–246. New York: Routledge, 1993.

Knight, Cher Krause. *Power and Paradise in Walt Disney's World*. Gainesville: University Press of Florida, 2014.

Laderman, David. *Driving Visions: Exploring the Road Movie*. Austin: University of Texas Press, 2002.

Messerschmidt, James W. "Hidden in Plain Sight: On the Omnipresence of Hegemonic Masculinity." *A Journal of Culture and Society* 12 (2019): 14–29.

Schatz, Thomas. "The Western." In *Handbook of American Film Genres*, edited by Wes D. Gehring, 25–46. Santa Barbara: Greenwood, 1988.

Wild Hogs. Directed by Walt Becker. USA, 2007.

Section II: Literature

LAURA BIEGER

Public Intellectuals, Cultural Fields, and the Predicaments of Popularity; or, Richard Wright Meets Pierre Bourdieu

The most popular issue of the political magazine *Foreign Policy* is its annual publication of "The Top 100 Global Thinkers."[1] Founded by Harvard professor Samuel P. Huntington and his banker, editor, publisher, and diplomat friend Warren Demian Manshel during the Vietnam War in the spirit of bringing alternative, jargon-free views on U.S. foreign politics to a general audience, the magazine has been publishing these lists since 2005. Selection is based on the originality and impact of a thinker's ideas, with past nominees including Angela Merkel, Pope Francis, Ayaan Hirsi Ali, Martha Nussbaum, Bill Gates, and Mark Zuckerberg. One of the things that makes these lists popular is that readers get to determine the top 20 candidates in an online poll (2009 was a record year, with over 500,000 participants). This 'popular vote' on the world's intellectual leaders, which permeates public discourse through a sizable amount of coverage in mainstream media, is not the only listing and ranking of thinkers engaged in the common good. From *Prospect* (with which *Foreign Policy* initially cooperated on its top 100 list) to *The Guardian* and *Current Affairs* to *The Washington Post*, newspapers evaluate the public relevance and the impact of intellectual work by publishing, assessing, and reporting on lists on a regular basis.

---

[1] This essay began to take shape during my stay as a Feodor Lynen Fellow at Harvard University in 2019, and was completed during my fellowship in 2021. Special thanks go to the Alexander von Humboldt Foundation for supporting my work, and to Werner Sollors and Glenda Carpio, my generous hosts.

210 Richard Wright Meets Pierre Bourdieu

I mention this phenomenon for two reasons. First, the urge to validate intellectuals in the form of ranking and measuring exposes a structural tension between publicness and popularity that both enables and constrains their work. *Prospect* editor Tom Clark described this urge as "anti-intellectual, more Top Trump than top scholarship" in the very issue that revived this tradition, and his self-conscious remark is a reminder of the slippery slope between the popular and the populist that is endemic to all forms of anti-intellectualism.[2] But whether popular in the sense of speaking to the people or populist in the sense of speaking on their behalf, the work of the intellectual is not untouched by the issue of popularity. And the reason for this is that the authority of the intellectual depends on a publicness that is popular in the sense of being affirmed by a substantial number of people. Indeed, what counts as substance here is contingent upon the kind of people affirming a public figure. In my attempt to understand how this dependency shapes the role of the intellectual in American culture, I draw on Bruce Robbins's account of the intellectual as a "figure of the political imagination, a character who cannot be separated from the various political narratives in which he or she appears, grounded in the emergences and declines of successive oppositional forces and institutions."[3] And if the urge to rank and measure the work of this figure is a driving force in this narrative production today, the anti-intellectualism engrained in it points toward a desire for tangible results that even the best kind of thinking does not always yield, and at times even has to reject.

Moreover, and crucially, the popular appeal of ranking and measuring intellectual work that manifests itself in the public discourse on intellectuals today indicates a specifically American disposition – an uneasiness about "the viability of what is still sometimes called 'the profession of thought,'" which Helen Small has aptly described as "a new and predominantly American anxiety." In her introduction to the volume *The Public Intellectual*, Small departs from the observation that the term "public intellectual" is an addition to the vocabulary of a cultural debate that is both recent and problematic. "What kind of

---

[2] Tom Clark, "The World's Top 50 Thinkers 2019," *Prospect*, July 16, 2019, prospectmagazine.co.uk/magazine/prospect-worlds-top-50-thinkers-2019.

[3] Bruce Robbins, "Introduction: The Grounding of Intellectuals," in *Intellectuals: Aesthetics. Politics, Academics*, ed. Bruce Robbins (Minneapolis: The University of Minnesota Press, 1990), xxiv.

intellectual," she rightly asks, "would not merit the adjective 'public' – even if only by dint of being published, or of speaking to others?"[4] For her, the near-pleonasm of the term is linked to a self-consciousness surrounding the work of the intellectual in the United States, where "[speaking] of oneself as 'intellectual' is equivalent to arrogance and egotism, for it suggests that there is a category of persons who are 'not-intellectual.'"[5] In other words, intellectualism is suspect to Americans because it strains deep-seated ideas about egalitarianism (Richard Hofstadter's *Anti-Intellectualism in American Culture* is still the authoritative book on this issue). With this disposition in mind, the need to emphasize the publicness of the intellectual that animates the coinage of the new term becomes tangible as "a defensive mechanism" of the self-consciousness surrounding the intellectual's work: "a deliberate decision to assert, in the face of perceived opposition, not just the continuing serviceability of the word 'intellectual,' but protest (too much?) that those to whom it is applicable, including perhaps oneself, have a role to play in public life."[6]

So, with Small as our guide, the figure of the public intellectual comes into view as "the product of a specifically American cultural and historical context" – even though she is quick to add that "the concerns it formalizes are in no way confined to the United States."[7] Based on this lucid observation, I want to think about the structural tensions between publicness and popularity that manifest themselves in the self-consciousness surrounding the work of the intellectual as a special feature of American culture as popular culture (and reaching beyond the U.S. due to its globality). In doing so, I want to consider the effects – or predicaments – that these tensions have on the intellectual situated within this culture. And while most work on public intellectuals is concerned with the question of whether or not the history of this figure is a history of decline, I am interested in the social and cultural (dis)position of the intellectual undergirding this narrative. Based on my conviction that space and place are not a stage on which history plays out but rather are active participants in shaping its course, I argue that the position of the

---

[4]   Helen Small, "Introduction," in *The Public Intellectual*, ed. Helen Small (Oxford: Blackwell Publishing, 2002), 1.
[5]   Joyce Carol Oates qtd. in ibid.
[6]   Ibid., 1–2.
[7]   Ibid., 2.

intellectual in American culture, marked as it is by the tension between the public and the popular described above, is endowed with an authority that is grounded in a vexed autonomy. An autonomy that is not owned but given, and which depends on an affirmation that the intellectual must court without binding herself to it. I thus agree with Bruce Robbins that "we must not call for a return of intellectuals to an illusory state of prior autonomy, but must reconsider the political narratives whose peripeteias and dénouements have left the intellectual hanging or unraveling." And since this also means that "we must consider the intellectual as a character in search of a narrative,"[8] this essay seeks to explore the setting from which such a narrative unfolds.

One may think of this setting in terms of the public sphere, defined by Jürgen Habermas as "the realm of our social life in which something approaching public opinion can be formed."[9] The figure of the intellectual exists as a player with heightened stakes in the formation of public opinion that takes place in this realm. For Habermas, publicness in the public sphere is primarily a function of rational deliberation. Indeed, the public sphere is a realm in which the discursive publicness of deliberation and debate replaces the representational (and primarily ocular) publicness of the court in medieval, feudalistic societies, with the effect of establishing a new (primarily auditive) social sphere grounded in the authority of private persons using their reason in public.[10] The result is a profound shift in the organization of power. Through the emergence of a "public authority" grounded in discourse, the new sphere can position itself against the elected officials and formal representatives of the governing body. In principle, every citizen should have access to the public sphere and the authority that it affords; this is the democratic promise of popular sovereignty, even though it is not democracy's reality. For Habermas, "a portion of it comes into being in every conversation in which private individuals assemble to form a public body. They then behave neither as business or professional people transacting private affairs, nor like members of a constitutional

---

[8] Robbins, "Introduction," xxiv–v.

[9] Jürgen Habermas, "The Public Sphere: An Encyclopedia Article," *New German Critique* 3 (1974): 49.

[10] See also my essay "Learning from Hannah Arendt," in *American Counter/Publics*, ed. Ulla Haselstein et al. (Heidelberg: Universitätsverlag Winter, 2019), 37–52.

order subject to the legal constraints of a state bureaucracy" but as a "public body" conferring "in an unrestricted fashion – that is with the guarantee of freedom of assembly and association and the freedom to express and publish their opinions – about matters of general interest."[11] And if the authority of the public and the power that can be mobilized through it resides in positioning the public sphere against both the state and the market, intellectuals are, perforce their ties to this sphere, privileged shareholders of this authority.

Before taking a closer look at this position and the authority that it affords, I want to turn to yet another aspect of public sphere publicness, namely its ties to being published. The publicness that gave rise to the public sphere as a discursive sphere of deliberation and debate is firmly rooted in the medium of print.[12] It was indeed the new type of print-based publicness that turned the public sphere into a political institution in its own right. Printing technology brought into the world new possibilities of doing and making things public, which turned the discursive publicness of rational deliberation into "the organizational principle for the procedures of the organs of the state themselves."[13] Habermas exemplifies this claim with the rule of law, a founding principle of democratic governance emerging from a public discourse which endorsed an abstract and universally binding understanding of the law as a result of the mass circulation of printed texts. These texts were not only available on an unprecedented scale, but read with the understanding that an indeterminate number of unknown *others* were reading them, too.[14]

What does the discursive publicness of print and its importance for the emergence of the public sphere as a democratic institution mean for the figure of the intellectual acting within this sphere and on behalf of this institution? It means, first and foremost, that the intellectual's

[11] Habermas, "The Public Sphere," 49.

[12] See also my essay "Reading for Democracy," in "Democratic Cultures and Populist Imaginaries," ed. Donald E. Pease, *REAL Yearbook of Research in English and American Literature* 34 (2018): 203–219.

[13] Jürgen Habermas, *Structural Transformations of the Public Sphere: An Inquiry into a Category of Bourgeois Society*, trans. Thomas Burger and Frederick Lawrence (Cambridge: MIT Press, 1989), 83.

[14] Cf. Michael Warner, *Publics and Counterpublics* (Cambridge: Zone Books, 2002), 55–65.

position and act of positioning *in and as public* is historically tied to *being published*. It is indeed no coincidence that public figures are often published authors; a published author is always already a public figure. With Pierre Bourdieu, we might say that a position in the literary field comes with a privilege (or burden) in tow: that of taking a position in the public sphere. The intellectual, with her aspiration of having an impact on the discourse that is the life-blood of this social realm, epitomizes a logic in which being published is key to gaining access to that sphere and a voice in the discourse sustaining it. For Bourdieu, Émile Zola's use of his reputation as a writer to speak out against the Dreyfus affair is exemplary in this regard: "According to the model invented by Zola, we can and must intervene in the world of politics, but with our own means and ends. Paradoxically, it is in the name of everything that assures the autonomy of their universe that artists, writers or scholars can intervene in today's struggles."[15] I will turn to the Black American writer and intellectual Richard Wright to further explore and complicate this assumption. But first, I want to ask: What makes Wright and Zola intellectuals? Who qualifies as an intellectual? Similar to the question of what literature or art is, this question is categorically unsettled because, just like literature and art, the figure of the intellectual has no intrinsic meaning or value. Rather, its meaning and value are under constant negotiation in the social field in which this question occurs, and the occurrence of the question somewhere in the social world is key to the constitution of the field in which it is negotiated. From this Bourdieusian point of view, the question of what or who an intellectual is generates activities in and across the social and cultural fields in which the intellectual is situated; these fields historically include the literary field and the public sphere. Typically, these activities link social commentary to acts of self-positioning – not out of vanity but because there is no other way of speaking in public. Indeed, self-positioning is a necessity because the public sphere is a force field that thrives on taking positions. And the staggering inequality, even in the most democratic societies, of access to this sphere and of taking positions in it is a painful reminder that it has never been a level playing field. So yes, publicness is a privilege.

---

[15]   Pierre Bourdieu, *Free Exchange* (Cambridge: Polity Press, 1994), 38.

The acts of positioning necessary for becoming a public figure are public to the minimal degree that they involve publication – and to the maximal degree of invoking change (of address, opinion, outlook, or behavior) in the public sphere, and possibly also in the world beyond. For Bourdieu, positioning acts are conducted in relation to all other positions available and all other positions already taken in the field: one belongs to a field when one is able to have an impact on it. And this brings me to the position of the intellectual, about which Bourdieu writes that

> artists and writers, and more generally intellectuals, are a dominated fraction within the dominant class. They are dominant in so far as they hold the power and privileges conferred by the possession of cultural capital and even, at least as far as certain of them are concerned, the possession of a volume of cultural capital great enough to exercise power over cultural capital; but writers and artists are dominated in their relations with those who hold political and economic power.[16]

Elsewhere he states that "the cultural producers are able to use the power conferred to them [in this way], especially in moments of crisis, by their capacity to put forward a critical definition of the social world, to mobilize the potential strength of the dominated classes and subvert the [prevailing social] order."[17] Moreover, and crucially, Bourdieu stresses that, unlike in earlier times, domination does not reside in personal relations; it is structural in the sense of being embedded in the market mechanisms that regulate the field of cultural production. Similar to the inversion of the economic logic that grants the literary field a relative autonomy from other social field, the intellectual's position of domination within the dominant class allows her to assert "the role, won and defended against the dominant, of the free, critical thinker, the intellectual who uses his or her specific capital, won by virtue of

[16] Pierre Bourdieu, "The Intellectual Field: A World Apart," in *In Other Words: Essays towards a Reflexive Sociology* (Stanford: Stanford University Press, 1990), 145.

[17] Pierre Bourdieu, *The Field of Cultural Production: Essays on Art and Literature* (New York: Columbia University Press, 1993), 44.

216   Richard Wright Meets Pierre Bourdieu

autonomy and guaranteed by the very autonomy of the field, to intervene in the field of politics."[18]

I now want to explore and complicate this claim by turning to Richard Wright. The publication of his first novel *Native Son* (1940) had such profound impact on the perception of racial injustice in the U.S. that it prompted Irving Howe to write: "The day *Native Son* appeared, American culture was changed forever."[19] It was in part through reviews by renowned intellectuals such as Howe that *Native Son* carved out a position that transformed the literary field in ways that enabled its writer to become an authoritative public figure. Indeed, from Bourdieu's practice theoretical view, the novel and its reviews come into view as actors on a public stage, where they are interacting with other co-actors (authors and publishers, buyers and readers, the novel's iconic protagonist) with the result of gathering and exchanging symbolic and cultural capital for literary fame and public authority. Entering the literary field when modernism, even in the socially engaged variety that was the hallmark of the depression era, had exhausted itself, *Native Son* captured its readers with its blunt style (it opens with the ring of an alarm clock) and its boldly unsympathetic protagonist (Bigger Thomas is a rapist and murderer). In a forthcoming essay, I consider the novel's maverick brand of modernism – which has been viewed as naturalism, psychological realism, African American Modernism, gothic and detective fiction – as the product of a literary system deeply pervaded by modern mass media. It needs to be stressed, however, that the issue is about more than style or form in a narrow, apolitical sense: Wright could only absorb these traditions once he had managed to become a member of the reading public, which in the Jim Crow South of his upbringing was as much a closed system as it was a cultural field principally open only to anyone making the right moves.

Wright exploits this contradiction in *Black Boy* (1945). Indeed, his autobiography (and second bestseller) features the intricate scheme through which he gained access to a racist and segregated reading public as a formative act of self-authorization. One may even think of the feedback loop set in motion by this well-known episode in *Black Boy* as a retroactive authorization of *Native Son*, both in terms of its style and

---

[18]   Bourdieu, "The Intellectual Field," 145.
[19]   Irving Howe, "Black Boys and Native Sons," *Dissent* (1963): 354.

its subject matter. The books that Wright reports to have read perfectly match the catalogue of traditions mentioned above, while the account of his upbringing lends authority to Wright as the creator of the shocking protagonist that was key to his instantaneous fame. In his authoritative account of Wright as a public intellectual, Robert Reid-Pharr mentions in passing Wright's "well-honed strategies to narrate his celebrity, his status as public intellectual." To which he is quick to add: "What gets in the way, of course, is the fact that the categories of celebrity and intellectual are difficult to maintain one with the other." And if "the danger that the so-called public intellectual most often faces is that he will inadvertently find himself becoming a sort of publicity intellectual," defined by Reid-Pharr as an intellectual stifled by commercial success and tradition, it is all the more striking that, at least in his early career, Wright's celebrity and his status as a public intellectual sustained one another.[20] Responsible for this was what may very well have been his narrative superpower: moving back and forth between fictional and non-fictional writing. Like no one before him (except for maybe Zora Neale Hurston) and many after him (from James Baldwin and to Jesmyn Ward), Wright used the authority of his personal life to add weight to his fictional work while using his success in the literary world to raise his voice in the public sphere and make audible the voices of other Black writers. *Native Son* demanded this strategy; 'going autobiographical' was essential to authorizing a creation so controversial that it could not be authorized in one single act. Indeed, authorizing *Native Son* was both a consecutive effort and a lucrative enterprise which involved lecturing and writing about "How 'Bigger' Was Born," working with *Life* magazine on a photo tribute to *Native Son's* setting, and adapting the novel for stage and screen with such renowned collaborators as Paul Green, Orson Welles, Canada Lee, and Pierre Chenal.

Note how the dynamics that sustain Wright's interlocking positions in the literary/cultural field and the public sphere gravitate toward the visual (photography, theatre, film, public lectures). Wright had his portraits featured in popular magazines such as *Life* and *Ebony* while

---

[20] Robert Reid Pharr, *Once You Go Black: Choice, Desire, and the Black Intellectual* (New York: New York University Press, 2007), 41. My reading of Wright as a modernist celebrity author draws on Loren Glass, *Authors Inc.* (New York: New York University Press, 2004).

218   Richard Wright Meets Pierre Bourdieu

writing political essays for the *Atlantic Monthly* and *New Masses*. This is not the place for an in-depth exploration of the shared labor between text and image that becomes tangible here, but I want to at least point toward it. The combined use of text and image became a driving force in the self-positioning acts of public intellectuals with the rise of photography, yes. But it has been instrumental in building a robust public sphere all along. Newspapers and magazines are such powerful public media because pages (and especially front pages) are designed with the sensibility of making images, often including images. Speaking in images is another common strategy of engaging the public. Its mobilizing force is captured in the editorial "To the Public," written by William Lloyd Garrison to launch his abolitionist newspaper, the *Liberator*. After several paragraphs of rational argumentation, Garrison shifts gears:

> I am aware, that many object to the severity of my language; but is there not cause for severity? I will be as harsh as truth, and as un-compromising as justice. On this subject, I do not wish to think, or speak, or write, with moderation. No! no! Tell a man whose house is on fire, to give a moderate alarm; tell him to moderately rescue his wife from the hands of the ravisher; tell the mother to gradually extricate her babe from the fire into which it has fallen; – but urge me not to use moderation in a cause like the present. I am in earnest – I will not equivocate – I will not excuse – I will not retreat a single inch – AND I WILL BE HEARD.[21]

Note the armada of violent, sentimental images put to work in this passage, and note further how they are flanked by visual markers (from exclamation marks to hyphens to capitals), which increase impact by amplifying volume. So yes, Garrison's editorial enlists the power of the visual, the imagistic, for public engagement. And if exploiting this power was merely rhetorical at first, the *Liberator* soon began using engravings to illustrate the injustices of slavery in its banner and on its front page. At around the same time, another famous abolitionist and writer, Frederick Douglass, became the most photographed American of the nineteenth century and an early theoretician of the new medium – because he recognized photography's power for self-positioning in ways

---

[21]   William Lloyd Garrison, "To the Public," *The Liberator*, January 1, 1831.

that enhanced his capacity to affect public discourse and promote social change while publicly reclaiming the Black body.[22]

The topic obviously deserves further scrutiny, but I hope the brevity with which I have addressed it suffices to show how shortsighted it is to dismiss the presence of images in the public sphere as a sign of decline brought about by modern mass media. And if the shared labor of text and image has been vital to creating a robust public sphere all along, the pull toward the visual that becomes tangible here is indicative of a transformation in which the photographic image – through the ease of its technological reproducibility and its mass-mediated capacity to attract attention – is a main player rather than a fraud subsidy in public discourse. Moreover, it is no coincidence that Wright's endorsement of photography takes place as the public sphere is on the brink of being revamped by another powerful transformation brought about by a new visual/popular medium: television. Indeed, a new alliance between intellectuals and popular magazines takes shape at precisely this time. From *Life* and *Ebony*, to *Time* and *Harper*, to *Esquire* and *Playboy*, the combination of cutting-edge journalism with gorgeous photographs is a driving force behind this transformation. It will come into full bloom in the guise of New Journalism, which also gave rise to a new type of intellectual: the *photogenic intellectual*, embodied by Hannah Arendt, Susan Sontag, James Baldwin, Joan Didion, Norman Mailer, and Tom Wolfe, of which Wright was an early prototype.

Tying this back to Habermas's emphasis on rational deliberation, what I have argued so far complicates this model in suggesting that "thinking," and especially "thinking in print," is insufficient when trying to make sense of the figure of the intellectual and its role and place in the public sphere. And if our present social/digital media age has heightened the demand that public discourse attract attention, Wright's use of photography is indicative of that same demand. But Wright's case also shows that attracting attention is not enough. To establish a position

---

[22] For a remarkable collection of these photographs and a thoughtful introduction to them, see John Stauffer et al., *Picturing Frederick Douglass* (New York: Norton & Company, 2015). The volume also contains Douglass's previously unpublished theorizations of the new medium, its visual aesthetics, and its potential to promote social change. On the significance of photography for reclaiming the Black body, see Sara Blair, *Harlem Crossroads* (Princeton: Princeton University Press, 2007).

from which he could speak with sustained authority, he had to bind and secure attention. Wright's will to claim such a position takes the reins when the Book of the Month Club, a mail-order business with close to half a million subscribers and perhaps the most powerful marketing engine of literature at the time, approaches him with the offer (the first for a Black American writer) to publish and promote *Native Son*. The Book of the Month Club's selection not only afforded Wright an immediate exposure to a mass audience. It also made the publication of his first novel a media event. Wright seized the opportunity, which involved severe changes to the manuscript (cutting a masturbation scene at the movies, or editing out the white millionaire philanthropist's daughter's desire for the Black servant) that remained in place until the Library of America published a restored version of the text more than fifty year later. These changes have often been viewed as market forces impinging on an original artwork.[23] Yet if we are willing to bracket this logic of damage and repair, we can see another reality emerge: one in which Wright, in playing along with the Book of the Month Club's requests, displays a "feel for a game,"[24] in which success in the literary field directly translates into public authority. And we see how public figures like Wright gain latitude in intervening in public discourse due to the authority that interlocking their positions in the literary field and the public sphere through an increased publicity affords.

Even so, the main beneficiaries of the shift of power brought about by the rise of the public sphere were not intellectuals like Wright and the people for whom he spoke, but the new ruling class, the bourgeoisie. For Jean-Paul Sartre, intellectuals hold their social and cultural position qua appointment by the bourgeoisie. And while "false intellectuals" perpetuate the hegemonic power of the class that appointed them, true ones bend this power in the interest of the people. The true intellectual "must make use of the capital of knowledge [she] has acquired from the dominant class in order to help raise popular culture – that is to say, to

---

[23] See for instance Kenneth Kinnamon, "Introduction," in *New Essays on Native Son*, ed. Kenneth Kinnamon (Cambridge: Cambridge University Press, 1990), 1–34; Laurence Cossu-Beaumont, "Richard Wright and his Editors," in *Richard Wright in a Post-Racial Imaginary*, ed. Alice Mikal Craven and William E. Dow (New York: Bloomsbury, 2014), 83–98.

[24] Bourdieu, *Cultural Production*, 47.

lay the foundations of a universal culture."[25] With Bourdieu, we can understand the essay, "A Plea for Intellectuals," in which Sartre makes these claims, as both an intervention into the debate about what kind of society France should become in the post-war years and a deliberate act of the author's positioning himself as someone with stakes in the outcome of that debate. Moreover, and crucially, Sartre's "Plea" articulates these stakes through an explicit commitment to popular culture – a commitment that both reinforces and refracts the print-based, highbrow publicness of the intellectual as a player in the literary field. The utopian world, in which the intellectual succeeds in using her insights about the dominant class to help build a culture that is popular in the sense of being fully egalitarian and inclusive, is indeed a world without intellectuals – not least because no one could appoint them anymore. But the only figure with the power to bring about this new world inhabits a position that cannot be subsumed in it.

In this view, the intellectual is a tragic hero endowed with an authority that can translate itself into world-changing impact because her position is that of an outsider, "outlawed by the privileged classes, suspect to the under-privileged classes."[26] Publicness as radical independence from institutions secures this position. For Howe, the public intellectual "writes about subjects outside of his field."[27] For Russell Jacobi, public intellectuals ceased to exist when the outsider position of Howe and his kind was abandoned by a generation of intellectuals that came of age in the universities and stayed there, writing in specialized jargon, publishing in specialized venues for their specialized peers, leaving the larger culture impoverished by turning inward. But there are also voices that encourage "a rethinking of the nature of professionalism, redefining the intellectual and the public sphere so as to allow for a responsiveness to new, as well as older forms of culture, and for the intellectual as an active, rather than a remotely adjudicatory, presence in political and cultural life."[28] For those who can no longer lay claim to an outsider position because they belong to an institution, the

---

[25] Jean-Paul Sartre, "A Plea for Intellectuals," in *Between Existentialism and Marxism* (New York: William Morrow, 1976), 262.

[26] Ibid.

[27] Howe qtd. in George Sciaballa, *What are Intellectuals Good For?* (Boston: Pressed Wafer, 2009), 5.

[28] Small, "Introduction," 4.

222   Richard Wright Meets Pierre Bourdieu

neuralgic point of this exercise is envisioning ways of achieving a certain degree of emancipation from the pressures of professionalization from within that institution. Edward Said, writing in the early 1990s, believed that the pressures of expertise could be countered by "amateurism, the desire to be moved not by profit or reward but by love for and unquenchable interest in the larger picture, in making connections across lines and barriers, in refusing to be tied down to a specialty, in caring for ideas and values despite the restrictions of a profession."[29] Note how Said's endorsement of the amateur allows him to square the intellectual's need to be an outsider with the demand to be popular: the figure of the amateur marks a radically egalitarian and inclusive position, everyone can claim it. But in 2020, with an amateur in the White House, with self-appointed social media pundits dissecting public discourse, with mobilization against the professional class (journalists, politicians, scientists) at a historical high, and with self-publishing services available to non-professional writers of all walks of life, the position of the amateur has lost its emancipatory allure.

So, where does this leave us? The specialty (and special authority) of intellectuals of the Irving Howe type, writes George Sciaballa in response to Jacobi's lament of their demise, "lay not in unearthing generally unavailable facts but in penetrating especially deep into the shared culture, in grasping and articulating its contemporary moral/political relevance with special originality and force."[30] But what if the connective tissue of a shared culture never existed, or existed only to the degree that the conditions under which this culture was shared were dismissed as irrelevant? What special authority would be demanded of intellectuals then? Sensibility now matters less than facts, writes Sciaballa in 2009, and his proposition reads like a prediction in a world of "alternative facts." That Ta-Nehisi Coates has become one of the most authoritative public intellectuals in the U.S. today with an article that reopened the case for reparations for the descendants of slaves by meticulously exposing the facts of racist real estate sales practices supports this point. But Coates's subsequent involvement in reviving the *Black Panther* comic series, writing for Netflix, and publishing a novel

---

[29] Edward Said, "Professionals and Amateurs," in *Representations of the Intellectual* (New York: Vintage Books, 1996), 74.
[30] Sciaballa, *What Are Intellectuals Good For?*, 5.

on the Underground Railroad featuring a protagonist equipped with the superpowers of a Marvel hero also exposes a persistent need of the public intellectual to popularize social critique. And perhaps it is also indicative of a utopian desire to lay the foundations for a more broadly shared culture to serve as the connective tissue for a reckoning with matters of common concern. Of these, the interlocking histories of slavery and structural racism are among the most pressing, and only an authority that is ruthlessly popular can lead the way.

Works Cited

Bieger, Laura. "Committed Writing as Common Ground: Jesmyn Ward's Poetics of Breathing While Black." *Amerikastudien/ American Studies* 66, no. 1 (2021): 73–79.

---. "Learning from Hannah Arendt; or, the Public Sphere as a Space of Appearance and the Fundamental Opacity of the Face-to-Face." In *American Counter/Publics*, edited by Ulla Haselstein et al., 37–52. Heidelberg: Universitätsverlag Winter, 2019.

---. "Reading for Democracy." In "Democratic Cultures and Populist Imaginaries," edited by Donald E. Pease. *REAL Yearbook of Research in English and American Literature* 34 (2018): 203–219.

Blair, Sara. *Harlem Crossroads: Black Writers and the Photograph in the Twentieth Century*. Princeton: Princeton University Press, 2007.

Bourdieu, Pierre. *The Field of Cultural Production: Essays on Art and Literature*. New York: Columbia University Press, 1993.

---. "The Intellectual Field: A World Apart." In *In Other Words: Essays towards a Reflexive Sociology*, translated by Matthew Adamson, 140–149. Stanford: Stanford University Press, 1990.

---. *Free Exchange*. Cambridge: Polity Press, 1994.

Clark, Tom. "The World's Top 50 Thinkers 2019." *Prospect*, July 16, 2019. prospectmagazine.co.uk/magazine/prospect-worlds-top-50-thinkers-2019.

Cossu-Beaumont, Laurence. "Richard Wright and his Editors: A Work Under the Influence? From the Signifyin(g) Rebel to the Exiled Intellectual." In *Richard Wright in a Post-Racial Imaginary*, edited by Alice Mikal Craven and William E. Dow, 83–98. New York: Bloomsbury, 2014.

Garrison, William Lloyd. "To the Public." *The Liberator*, January 1, 1831.

Glass, Loren. *Authors Inc.: Literary Celebrity in Modern United States, 1880-1980*. New York: New York University Press, 2004.

Habermas, Jürgen. *Structural Transformations of the Public Sphere: An Inquiry into a Category of Bourgeois Society*. Translated by Thomas Burger and Frederick Lawrence. Cambridge: MIT Press, 1989.

---. "The Public Sphere: An Encyclopedia Article." *New German Critique* 3 (1974): 49–55.

Hofstadter, Richard. *Anti-Intellectualism in American Life.* New York: Alfred Knopf, 1963.

Howe, Irving. "Black Boys and Native Sons." *Dissent* (1963): 353–368.

Kinnamon, Kenneth. "Introduction." In *New Essays on Native Son*, edited by Kenneth Kinnamon, 1–34. Cambridge: Cambridge University Press, 1990.

Reid Pharr, Robert. *Once You Go Black: Choice, Desire, and the Black Intellectual.* New York: New York University Press, 2007.

Robbins, Bruce. "Introduction: The Grounding of Intellectuals." In *Intellectuals: Aesthetics. Politics, Academics*, edited by Bruce Robbins, ix–xxvii. Minneapolis: The University of Minnesota Press, 1990.

Said, Edward. "Professionals and Amateurs." In *Representations of the Intellectual*, 73–83. New York: Vintage Books, 1996.

Sartre, Jean-Paul. "A Plea for Intellectuals." In *Between Existentialism and Marxism*, 228–285. New York: William Morrow, 1976.

Sciaballa, George. *What are Intellectuals Good For?* Boston: Pressed Wafer, 2009.

Small, Helen. "Introduction." In *The Public Intellectual*, edited by Helen Small, 1–18. Oxford: Blackwell Publishing, 2002.

Stauffer, John, et al. *Picturing Frederick Douglass: An Illustrated Bibliography of the Nineteenth Century's Most Photographed American*. New York: Norton & Company, 2015.

Warner, Michael. *Publics and Counterpublics*. Cambridge: Zone Books, 2002.

Wright, Richard. *Native Son.* In *Richard Wright: Early Works*, 444–850. New York: Library of America, 1991.

Wright, Richard. *Black Boy (American Hunger).* In *Richard Wright: Later Works*, annotated by Arnold Rampersad, 1–366. New York: Library of America, 1991.

RUTH GEHRMANN

"So she would ask me to tell her stories": Indigenous Narratives of the Apocalypse in Cherie Dimaline's *The Marrow Thieves*

Storytelling, Indigenous Futurisms for Adolescents, and Popular Culture

When Thomas King explains: "The truth about stories is that that's all we are," he presents storytelling as an identity-defining trait.[1] Stories, and the act of storytelling, become a tool to create meaning and consequently define both peoples and their communities. This central capacity of storytelling holds true even though postmodernism has been defined by its "incredulity towards metanarratives,"[2] as narrative functions as an elemental part of collective memory, prominently featured in reiterations of myths or religious texts. As bases for community formation, stories appear as value systems in metaphorical form. In their ability to make the abstract concrete, stories gain particular relevance for disenfranchised groups and enable the juxtaposition of subversive ideas and dominant worldviews.

This political potential of storytelling is also revealed in oral traditions of Indigenous communities. The Métis author Cherie Dimaline perceives storytelling as a vital part of her Indigenous identity and asserts: "We are the people of story."[3] Here, storytelling is presented as a distinct feature of Indigenous peoples and as one that pertains to communal self-actualization. The subversive potential of Indigenous

---

[1] Thomas King, *The Truth About Stories: A Native Narrative* (Minneapolis: University of Minnesota Press, 2008), 2.

[2] Jean-François Lyotard, *The Postmodern Condition: A Report on Knowledge* (Norfolk: Manchester University Press, 1984), xxiv.

[3] The Agenda with Stephen Paikin, *Reclaiming Lost Dreams*, YouTube, August, 2018, youtube.com/watch?v=n746oUqBc_k, 00:07:18.

storytelling is underlined by Aman Sium and Eric Ritskes, who explain: "Stories in Indigenous epistemologies are disruptive, sustaining, knowledge producing, and theory-in-action. Stories are decolonization theory in its most natural form."[4] The pluripotent significance of stories comes to the fore: They are framed as a subversive force that appears as decolonization in and of itself. The differentiation between oral tradition and "literature" further illustrates the significance of form in colonial contexts. Daniel Heath Justice emphasizes the decisive quality of this differentiation, given that "a social evolutionary bias presumes that the oral is a less developed version of the written."[5] An emphasis on the political significance of oral storytelling thus also subverts this bias and advocates for the resilience of oral storytelling.

Given the vital role of storytelling in Indigenous traditions, it seems unsurprising that Indigenous futurisms have also navigated its significance in their visions of the future. 'Indigenous futurisms' emerged as a term when Grace L. Dillon explained in 2012: "Writers of Indigenous futurisms sometimes intentionally experiment with, sometimes intentionally dislodge, sometimes merely accompany, but invariably *change* the perimeters of sf [science fiction]."[6] Concepts of science fiction, a field that has been criticized for its employment of colonial tropes,[7] are brought under scrutiny and enriched to include multifaceted Indigenous contexts. Rather than viewing Indigenous perspectives as an addition to "factual" western understandings of science, Indigenous futurisms emphasize the permeability of such understandings and their necessary limitedness.

Indigenous futurisms also contribute to the pop cultural field of young adult fiction (YA). YA is closely related to its market: It is named after its target audience, young adults, and has become a major force in

---

[4]   Aman Sium and Eric Ritskes, "Speaking Truth to Power: Indigenous Storytelling as an Act of Living Resistance," *Decolonization: Indigeneity, Education & Society* 2, no. 1 (2013): ii.

[5]   Daniel Heath Justice, *Why Indigenous Literatures Matter* (Waterloo: Wilfrid Laurier University Press, 2018), 20.

[6]   Grace L. Dillon, "Introduction," in *Walking the Clouds: An Anthology of Indigenous Science Fiction*, ed. Grace L. Dillon (Tucson: University of Arizona Press, 2012), 3; emphasis in original.

[7]   John Rieder, *Colonialism and the Emergence of Science Fiction* (Middletown: Wesleyan University Press, 2008), 2.

the literary market.[8] This orientation also positions YA within the sphere of popular culture, a field which has attracted a vast array of theoretical engagement yet remains difficult to define.[9] Dick Hebdige offers a broad definition by positioning popular culture in the post-war period and connecting the term to "a set of generally available artefacts: films, records, clothes, TV programmes, modes of transport, etc."[10] This suggested availability interrelates popular culture with the market, and John Storey explains that, given the term's emphasis on popularity, "any definition of popular culture must include a quantitative dimension."[11] YA fiction, with its emphasis on a target audience and bestselling franchises, offers itself as a fitting case study in popular culture.

As YA continues to develop, Indigenous futurisms have also contributed to its diversification. Lynette James explains with reference to this intersection: "Emerging primarily from authors of color who identify as First Nations, Native or Indigenous peoples, these works offer fertile ground for conversations about, and the development of, more diverse perspectives in YA sf."[12] A major contribution to the study of Indigenous YA is Mandy Suhr-Sytsma's *Self-Determined Stories* (2018), in which she explains that Indigenous contributions interrelate questions of communal sovereignty and individual identity formation.[13] The presence of writers of color is especially relevant for speculative YA fiction, as the field has been criticized for a lack of diverse

---

[8]   Balaka Basu et al., "Introduction," in *Contemporary Dystopian Fiction for Young Adults: Brave New Teenagers*, ed. Balaka Basu et al. (New York: Routledge, 2013), 1.

[9]   For further reference on theoretical approaches to popular culture see Dominic Strinati, *An Introduction to Theories of Popular Culture* (London: Routledge 2004).

[10] Dick Hebdige, *Hiding in the Light: On Images and Things* (London: Routledge, 1988), 47.

[11] John Storey, *Cultural Theory and Popular Culture: An Introduction* (Edinburgh: Pearson, 2006), 4.

[12] Lynette James, "Children of Change, Not Doom: Indigenous Futurist Heroines in YA," *Extrapolation* 57, no. 2 (2016): 152.

[13] Mandy Suhr-Sytsma, *Self-Determined Stories: The Indigenous Reinvention of Young Adult Literature* (Ann Arbor: Michigan University Press, 2019), xx.

230 Indigenous Narratives of the Apocalypse

characters.[14] Representation is of particular importance because YA has been known to educate its readers and showcase protagonists developing political agency.[15] While Kenneth L. Donelson speaks of "saccharine didacticism" in YA from the 1940s and 1950s,[16] Basu et al. detect similar tendencies in 2014.[17] Fittingly, readers of YA have become deeply invested in the politics of representation; and comments posted on popular sites such as Twitter and Goodreads influence publishing strategies.[18]

Within the field of Indigenous-authored speculative fiction for adolescents, Cherie Dimaline's *The Marrow Thieves* (2017) constitutes a compelling addition. Following YA conventions, Dimaline herself underlines that *The Marrow Thieves* is supposed to educate its audience: "There's been some very troubled history in Canada, I want them [young people] to not shy away from that and I want them to know that they are absolutely empowered to make changes."[19] Dimaline presents her novel as both a reminder of Canada's colonial past and a call to action for her young audience to develop an active stance with regard to the future of the country. The author's interpretation of her own work clearly emphasizes the political dimension that is expressed in the novel's story.

---

[14] Mary J. Couzelis, "The Future is Pale: Race in Contemporary Young Adult Dystopian Novels," in *Contemporary Dystopian Fiction for Young Adults: Brave New Teenagers*, ed. Balaka Basu et al. (New York: Routledge, 2013), 131–144.

[15] For further reference on YA's depiction of political agency see Lindsay Morton and Lynette Lounsbury, "Inertia to Action: From Narrative Empathy to Political Agency in Young Adult Fiction," *Papers: Explorations into Children's Literature* 23, no. 2 (2015): 53–70.

[16] Kenneth L. Donelson, "Growing Up Real: YA Literature Comes of Age," in *Young Adult Literature: Background and Criticism*, ed. Millicent Lenz and Ramona M. Mahood (Chicago: American Library Association, 1980), 60.

[17] Basu et al., "Introduction," 5.

[18] For an overview of controversial discussions about YA titles, see Katy Waldman, "In Y.A. Where Is the Line Between Criticism and Cancel Culture?" *The New Yorker*, March 21, 2019, newyorker.com/books/under-review/in-ya-where-is-the-line-between-criticism-and-cancel-culture.

[19] The Agenda with Stephen Paikin, 00:01:39.

The Marrow Thieves was a major success: It was a finalist for the Canada Reads competition and won the prestigious Kirkus Prize in 2017. The novel conjures a post-apocalyptic future: Climate change has transformed the world, and a group of traumatized protagonists is on the run in the rough wilderness of what was once Canada. The Indigenous group from North America represents different age groups and diverse backgrounds. The characters French and RiRi are Métis, for example, while their father figure Miig is Anishinaabe, and Isaac and Chi-Boy are Cree. The shared experience of their journey, however, seems to eclipse these differences and emphasizes a communal sense of trauma, the need for familial ties, and a desire for shared traditions and stories. In Dimaline's future Canada, non-Indigenous parts of society have lost the ability to dream, a phenomenon that leads to widespread mental health issues. The discovery that Indigenous peoples are not afflicted by the plague leads to the ruthless exploitation of Indigenous groups, whose extracted bone marrow restores the ability to dream. The extraction of bone marrow is linked to the atrocities of Canada's residential school system, which was "[d]esigned to strip Indigenous people of their languages and cultures [...]."[20] In the narrator's future, the protagonists are hunted by ruthless Recruiters working at so-called "schools," to which Indigenous peoples are taken and from which they seldom return. As Diana Brydon explains, "this new colonial system literally crushes people to death, distilling their bone marrow to steal their ability to dream."[21] Narrated by the Métis adolescent Francis, nicknamed French, the novel follows his group on their way north as they search for refuge; it traces their trauma but also their stories and budding relationships.

As Henrietta Lidchi and Suzanne Newman Fricke suggest, "Indigenous Futurisms are part of a larger trend to disrupt and diversify the frames of reference of speculative fiction [...]"[22] and the post-

---

[20] Jeff Corntassel and Chaw-win-is T'lakwadzi, "Indigenous Storytelling, Truth-telling, and Community Approaches to Reconciliation," *English Studies in Canada* 35, no. 1 (2009): 138.

[21] Diana Brydon, "Risk, Mortality, and Memory: The Global Imaginaries of Cherie Dimaline's *The Marrow Thieves*, M. G. Vassanji's *Nostalgia*, and André Alexis's *Fifteen Dogs*," *Revista Canaria de Estudios Ingleses* 78 (2019): 100.

[22] Henrietta Lidchi and Suzanne Newman Fricke, Future History: Indigenous Futurisms in North American Visual Arts," *World Art* 9, no. 2 (2019): 100.

232 Indigenous Narratives of the Apocalypse

apocalypse offers ample ground for Indigenous engagements. Building upon the interrelations of post-apocalyptic fiction and Indigenous storytelling, the following discussion focuses on three key aspects of *The Marrow Thieves*: stories as a means of recreating the past, the role of Indigenous languages as a subversive and powerful tool, and, lastly, the significance of storytelling in relation to the speaker and their audience. The analysis of these aspects emphasizes that *The Marrow Thieves* navigates the post-apocalypse by using storytelling as a means of creating a connection with an ultimately unreachable "before" and thereby imagines the individual experience of the Indigenous apocalypse.

Old-Timey Storytelling

French and his companions have experienced a personal apocalypse: For years, they have been running through a landscape shaped by ecological fallout. All of them have lost their families and have experienced other traumatic events. Despite their differences, however, the group's youth share a fascination with "old-timey" ways: acts and behavior they perceive as traditional and which they attempt to reach via stories or reenactments. French explains:

> Us kids, we longed for the old-timey. We wore our hair in braids to show it. We made sweat lodges out of broken branches dug back into the earth, covered over with our shirts tied together at the buttonholes. Those lodges weren't very hot, but we sat in them for hours and willed the sweat to pop over our willowy arms and hairless cheeks.[23]

"Old-timey" refers to Indigenous traditions that are no longer part of the new generation's lived experience and that can only be encountered in reminiscence. French and his companions imitate these traditions, yet they do not fully understand their purpose. Even though the characters are depicted as being driven by a genuine desire, their building of sweat lodges is presented as a game. The quote especially emphasizes their youth ("hairless cheeks") and the desperation of their attempt ("willed the sweat"). Yet although their sweat lodge does not function properly,

[23] Cherie Dimaline, *The Marrow Thieves* (Toronto: DCB, 2017), 21–22.

they visit it together as a community; their infatuation with the past leads to shared experiences. Their communal longing for the past does not teach them how to properly build a sweat lodge, yet it creates a new sense of community built on their shared desire and the games it inspires.

The creation of new artistic approaches based on what is believed to be tradition is further exemplified when the young generation inserts its own experiences into what it perceives as traditional frames:

> We were singing a song we'd made up to an old-timey round dance double beat [...]
> *Way ya, hey ya, hey ya, way ha*
> *I don't know where we're going*
> *Don't know where we've been*
> *Way hey ya*
> *All I know is I'll keep walking*
> *Can't get taken in*
> *Way hey ya.*[24]

As French explains, the song is supposed to be reminiscent of a traditional form, yet its content is clearly inspired by the adolescents' experience. This intersection ties into Matthew Krystal's understanding that "dance is about two basic human tensions: between cultural continuity and cultural change at the collective level and between individual expression and group conformity at the personal level."[25] At the same time, the young group's song expresses their uncertainty about their destination as they "don't know where [they]'re going," and simultaneously shows their state of separation from tradition because they "[d]on't know where [they]'ve been". On the one hand, it thereby illustrates their lack of direction with regard to both their loss of geographical certainty and the disruption of their traditions. On the other hand, the song presents a warning and a mode of action: The need to continue walking is directly linked to the dangers that otherwise await the singers. Their journey is inseparably tied to the brutality of

---

[24] Ibid., 36.
[25] Matthew Krystal, *Indigenous Dance and Dancing Indian: Contested Representation in the Global Era* (Boulder: University Press of Colorado, 2012), 6.

234   Indigenous Narratives of the Apocalypse

abduction and the exploitation that awaits them in the schools. While they allude to the group's situation, the lyrics nevertheless appear as a playful example of the characters writing themselves into traditional patterns and establish that current experiences are turned into narrative in order to be remembered and shared.

The group's adult members, Miig and Minerva, serve as the main point of reference to a time before the apocalypse. Miig, who is a father figure to French, not only tells what is referred to as "Story" – the tale of how their world came to be, which will be discussed later on – but also teaches them survival skills. Even though he is close to French and the younger generation, they do not always fully understand him. When Miig teaches them how to hunt, French comments:

> Miig said it was Apocalyptic Boy Scouts. We didn't know what in the hell he was talking about, but we liked fashioning bows and arrows and whooping to each other through the bush and feeling all Chiefy.[26]

The fact that Miig's reference is lost on French highlights the gap between the generations. The comment is a humorous reference to the Boy Scouts organization, which is assumed to be familiar to the reader. The remark also appears to be an allusion to the controversial roots of boy scouting in Canada: At the beginning of the twentieth century, members of the "Woodcraft Indians" were taught survival skills believed to have been inspired by an Indigenous lifestyle.[27] Miig's banter about the "Apocalyptic Boy Scouts" gains further depth in the context of colonial tropes, which are utterly lost on French and his generation. Rather than presenting an artificial, possibly exploitative and colonialist approach to Indigenous knowledge, the Boy Scouts reference appears as a validating allusion to the old-timey. The fact that they feel "all Chiefy" indicates that they place their skills with bows and arrows – which might also appear to be a child's game – in relation to their Indigenous heritage. The contact with the previous generation thus underlines the youths' eagerness to learn about a time before, yet it also establishes a knowledge gap between the generations in which signifiers – and the ability to understand them – are necessarily lost.

---

[26] Dimaline, *The Marrow Thieves*, 34.
[27] Brian Morris, "Ernest Thompson Seton and the Origins of the Woodcraft Movement," *Journal of Contemporary History* 5, no. 2 (1970): 185.

These examples emphasize that the young generation has disconnected from Indigenous tradition and assigned the term "old-timey" to what they interpret as Indigenous knowledge of a time before. Their attempts are thus presented as playful approaches to a lost past. At the same time, however, they are driven by a deep desire to reconnect with traditions prior to the rupture. The sense of disconnection calls for a continuous translation in which remnants of the past are reinterpreted and reinscribed with new meanings shaped by the post-apocalypse. Fittingly, Dimaline's text deliberately relates itself to the genre of post-apocalyptic fiction and its interest in reconstructing the past by quoting Cormac McCarthy's *The Road* (2006): "Where you've nothing else, construct ceremonies out of the air and breathe upon them."[28] The young generation's ceremonies are new, but they are constructed based on the stories they are told and shaped by the stories they tell themselves.

Language and Storytelling

Obviously, storytelling and language are closely connected and intricately linked to community and identity formation. This role is made clear by the banning of Indigenous languages in colonial contexts such as Canada's residential school system. In an interview, Dimaline herself speaks about her grandmother's use of Michif and argues that the language "holds understandings that English just can't."[29] To Judy Iseke-Barnes, "learning the language is part of healing the wounds of the colonial past and reconnecting to an Indigenous past and future."[30] Iseke-Barnes's statement positions language at the intersection of past and future, a notion that is also of vital interest to *The Marrow Thieves*.

In the novel, the young generation speaks English and communicates with the previous generation in this language. It is primarily through Minerva, the group's elder, that French encounters Anishinaabe-

---

[28] Dimaline, *The Marrow Thieves*, n.p.

[29] The Agenda with Stephen Paikin, 00:03:44.

[30] Judy Iseke-Barnes, "Politics and Power of Languages: Indigenous Resistance to Colonizing Experiences of Language Dominance," *Journal of Thought* 39, no. 1 (2004): 53.

236 Indigenous Narratives of the Apocalypse

mowin.[31] To him, knowing the language is a desirable privilege, and he is shocked to hear that Rose, and not he, has learned some words:

> "How do you have language?" My voice broke on the last syllable. My chest tightened. How could she have the language? She was the same age as me, and I deserved it more. I don't know why, but I felt certain that I did. I yanked my braid out of the back of my shirt and let it fall over my shoulder. Some kind of proof, I suppose.[32]

The emphasis on "having" language, on owning it, introduces knowledge of the language as a highly valued personal possession. The varying use of the definite article and the shift between "language" and "the language" illustrates the specific value of Indigenous languages while presenting it as the sole language of importance to the narrator. Speaking the language becomes more than a mere means of communication; rather, its words are meaningful in and of themselves. Here, learning the language is portrayed as a prize that needs to be earned. Fittingly, French asserts his right to the language by establishing his authority through his age and the fact that he wears a braid, which is a clear signifier of his traditional appearance and his connection to the old-timey. "Having language," then, constitutes a privilege and is part of highly prestigious knowledge.

Language is granted magical appeal in the novel, giving it even greater significance. The most powerful example of the potential of language is Minerva's destruction of a school. When the Recruiters and Cardinals apply their tubes to remove her bone marrow, Minerva sings in her language and wreaks destruction:

> She sang. She sang with volume and pitch and a heartbreaking wail that echoed through her relatives' bones, rattling them in the ground under the school itself. Wave after wave, changing her heartbeat to drum, morphing her singular voice to many, pulling every dream from her own marrow and into her song. And there were words: words in the language

---

[31] For further reference on the Indigenous languages spoken in the novel, see Patrizia Zanella, "Witnessing Story and Creating Kinship in a New Era of Residential Schools: Cherie Dimaline's *The Marrow Thieves*," *Studies in American Indian Literatures* 32, nos. 3–4 (2020): 189.

[32] Dimaline, *The Marrow Thieves*, 38.

that the conductor couldn't process, words the Cardinals couldn't bear, words the wires couldn't transfer.

As it turns out, every dream Minerva had ever dreamed was in the language. It was her gift, her secret, her plan.[33]

Minerva's destruction of the school is tied into the place's colonial past, to the land her relatives were buried in. Here, language becomes an active part of resistance and is directly related to the voices that precede Minerva's. Minerva herself is well aware of her power – it is "her gift, her secret, her plan" – while the Recruiters are bound to underestimate the elderly lady and the power of her heritage. The destruction of the school presents a metaphorical rendering of the eroding force of Indigenous knowledge on colonial world-building. As Sean Teuton explains, almost all Indigenous songs "recognize the power of language to address and even alter the universe."[34] This notion is literalized in Minerva's song, through which subversive potential becomes physical reality. Language thereby also reveals its political power within oppressive systems.

The use of language in *The Marrow Thieves* is related to power, and it offers individual meaning to its protagonists. To French, language is portrayed as a unique privilege and a means of forming a connection to Indigenous tradition. In Minerva's song, language becomes a physical force and a means of rebellion whose power is known only to the speaker herself. In a post-apocalyptic world, the spoken word, as Brydon argues, is thus granted specific relevance, as the young generation perceives older characters "as holding the key to their survival – and their return to home – through their fluency in Cree."[35] Similar to Iseke-Barnes's understanding of Cree as a contribution to "healing the wounds of the colonial past,"[36] Dimaline's novel portrays linguistic knowledge as forging new bonds to a lost past and as defying processes of objectification and exploitation.

---

[33] Ibid., 172.

[34] Sean Kicummah Teuton, *Native American Literature: A Very Short Introduction* (Oxford: Oxford University Press, 2018), 103.

[35] Brydon, "Risk, Mortality, and Memory," 110.

[36] Iseke-Barnes, "Politics and Power of Languages," 53.

238 Indigenous Narratives of the Apocalypse

Who Tells Stories – and Who Listens?

At first glance, it might appear as if Miig was the only member of the group allowed to tell stories. Gathering the group on specific evenings, he presents them with "Story," in which he creates a narrative of the apocalypse and educates the young generation. In doing so, Miig uses Story to construct the country's past and intersect oral tradition with history, thus correlating with LeAnne Howe's concept of "tribalography."[37] Miig's story is part of a specific performance:

> Miig stood, pacing his Story pace, waving his arms like a slow-motion conductor to place emphasis and tone over us all. We needed to remember Story. It was his job to set the memory in perpetuity. He spoke to us every week. Sometimes Story was focused on one area [...] But every week we spoke, because it was imperative that we know. He said it was the only way to make the kinds of changes that were necessary to really survive.[38]

Miig's story of the apocalypse also depicts how the group came to be and appears reminiscent of Howe's understanding of creation stories, which, "as numerous as Indian tribes, gave birth to our people."[39] The importance of Story for community formation is underlined by the shared experience Miig creates.[40] He appears as the conductor of not only the story he tells but the audience he tells it to. As he paces in "his Story pace," Miig's body becomes an integral part of the narrative and aligns itself with the story. The depiction of Miig resonates with Scott Momaday's understanding of the role of the storyteller:

> The storyteller is the one who tells the story. To say this is to say that the storyteller is preeminently entitled to tell the story. He is original and

---

[37] LeAnne Howe, "Tribalography: The Power of Native Stories," *Journal of Dramatic Theory and Criticism* 14, no. 1 (1999): 118.

[38] Dimaline, *The Marrow Thieves*, 25.

[39] Howe, "Tribalography," 118.

[40] For further reference on the correlation between storytelling and kinship in the novel, see Zanella, "Witnessing Story and Creating Kinship."

creative. He creates the storytelling experience and himself and his audience in the process.[41]

In French's account, the notion of creating both storyteller and audience is underlined when Miig places "emphasis and tone" on them. The repetition of "create" appears particularly noteworthy with regard to Miig, who attempts to create a past unknown to his listeners. Story is therefore a form of education which cultivates knowledge and passes on information. Miig's understanding that Story is needed to "really survive" relates to the perseverance of traditions and knowledge as forms of meaning-making in the apocalypse the group is facing. The practice of passing on stories as narratively coded knowledge systems presents those stories as instructive tools. Fittingly, Teuton concludes that "[n]arrative serves to explain the world, especially when that world faces crisis."[42] The crisis the community faces, their structural exploitation and accompanying displacement, thereby stands in opposition to the coherency established by storytelling.

While French listens excitedly to Story, RiRi is not allowed to hear it yet – at the age of seven, she is deemed too young. However, French soon begins to tell her his own version of Story:

> I heard Story, she did not. So she would ask me to tell her stories, innocently enough, but desperate for some understanding, the understanding that was withheld from her youth so that she could form into a real human before she understood that some saw her as little more than a crop.[43]

RiRi's desire to hear Story clearly emphasizes its significance in meaning-making and its role in her personal development. Here, storytelling is tied to the transition to adulthood, a relationship that is further emphasized when French passes on Story and inscribes himself into a lineage of storytellers. By adjusting Story to cater to RiRi, French highlights, as Teuton explains, that "the oral tradition's ever-changing body of communally derived philosophy, in fact, challenges the very notion of

---

[41] N. Scott Momaday, *The Man Made of Words* (New York: St. Martin's Press, 1997), 3.

[42] Teuton, *Native American Literature*, 5.

[43] Dimaline, *The Marrow Thieves*, 27.

240 Indigenous Narratives of the Apocalypse

stasis."[44] Miig's Story is thereby translated into the stories told by French, who in turn adjusts his narration for his audience, RiRi. Miig's "Story," which remains capitalized and in the singular throughout the novel, is portrayed as the authoritative version that is adjusted and subsequently disseminated in French's non-capitalized and plural "stories." The act of storytelling is thus presented as highly context-sensitive and as a continuous, ever-changing process.

In addition to Story, the group also cultivates the telling of their own background stories. These "coming-to stories" reveal the protagonists' past experiences and give form to the trauma they have encountered. Even though Miig is the group's storyteller, he does not narrate these experiences. Instead, he explains: "That's the rule. Everyone's creation story is their own."[45] Miig's comment emphasizes the personal quality of specific stories and underlines a possessive relationship between story and storyteller. To Dimaline, this relationship is significant. She frames her characters' coming-to stories according to Indigenous tradition and what she calls "Indian geography."[46] The author also explains:

> Indigenous stories are different. We're generally raised in story. We have traditional stories that hold our teachings. A lot of our culture is held within our stories. And there's different protocols and permissions that come with Indigenous stories.[47]

Here, Dimaline underlines that stories pertain to specific realms and cannot be simply told at will. Miig's insistence on who gets to tell which stories mirrors this framing of stories as being deeply entangled with individual responsibility. The acceptance of this responsibility, however, pertains to the group as a whole and positions the role of storyteller as one that is shifting, yet central to communal proceedings. Moreover, Dimaline's statement underlines that Miig, as the storyteller, follows specific protocols that are upheld in regard to both Story and each individual's narrative.

---

[44] Teuton, *Native American Literature*, 22.

[45] Dimaline, *The Marrow Thieves*, 79.

[46] The Agenda with Stephen Paikin, 00:07:45.

[47] Deborah Dundas, "Cherie Dimaline: Hopes and Dreams in the Apocalypse," *Toronto Star*, November 6, 2017, thestar.com/entertainment/books/2017/11/06/cherie-dimaline-hopes-and-dreams-in-the-apocalypse.html.

Exploring the question of who tells stories and who listens thus sheds light on the performative act of storytelling and the responsibility of the storyteller. Even though Miig is the group's distinguished storyteller, he does not tell each individual's story – that task remains the group's responsibility. As French translates Story to RiRi, the ever-changing relationships forged by stories come to the fore: Telling a story to a specific audience shapes group dynamics and constitutes a significant part of French's development into an adult.

Conclusion

This article has presented three aspects – storytelling as a means to create coherence, the significance of language, and the responsibility of storytelling – to underline Dimaline's complex engagement with Indigenous storytelling in a post-apocalyptic world. Stories serve as a means to establish coherence with a time before the protagonists' apocalypse and are closely tied to Indigenous language and tradition. The novel thereby negotiates post-apocalyptic motifs, such as changing group dynamics and a journey with an unknown destination, and explores them in an Indigenous framework.

In *The Marrow Thieves'* future, French and his companions are presented as opposites of the "vanishing Indian" trope: They form a community of stories even if their surroundings imagine their non-existence. The novel thus also endorses Gerald Vizenor's concept of survivance: "Native survivance is an active sense of presence over absence, deracination, and oblivion; survivance is the continuance of stories, not a mere reaction, however pertinent."[48] Rather than framing agency in terms of physical prowess, knowledge is the decisive factor in Dimaline's future. The ability to tell stories is thereby directly linked to growing up and gaining control: Miig leads the group and is its storyteller: Minerva is the group elder and destroys a school with her song. Fittingly, French's transition into adulthood is not only accompanied by his budding relationship to Rose but by his role as RiRi's storyteller as well.

---

[48] Gerald Vizenor, *Survivance: Narratives of Native Presence* (Lincoln: University of Nebraska Press, 2008), 1.

242   Indigenous Narratives of the Apocalypse

The post-apocalypse is closely interrelated with this negotiation of storytelling. Firstly, the post-apocalypse reveals the fleetingness of objects: In a group which must carry its supplies, oral tradition excels as a method for storing and passing on information. Secondly, the novel also portrays a world in which borders have eroded, thereby emphasizing their constructed nature. Katja Sarkowsky has argued for the simultaneous significance and artificiality of national borders in Indigenous contexts, a notion that the neglect of city names and geographical mapping in post-apocalyptic fiction also invokes.[49] Lastly, Dimaline's work emphasizes the relative nature of apocalypse in colonial contexts. As Dillon notes, "it is almost commonplace to think that the Native Apocalypse, if contemplated seriously, has already taken place."[50] She thereby forces the reader to consider the apocalyptic quality of colonial encounters for Indigenous communities. As Miig explains, "We've survived this before. We will survive it again."[51] Rather than give up hope, Dimaline's characters form a community – one that might just be built upon the stories they tell.

On an extradiegetic level, Dimaline's novel counters the absence of Indigenous authors in the field of popular culture. Lipan Apache YA author Darcie Little Badger asserts: "It almost feels like in fiction, people think we didn't survive, but we did, and we're still flourishing."[52] The relevance of this presence appears obvious, as the "control of media representation and of cultural self-definition asserts and signifies cultural and political sovereignty itself."[53] By opting to write YA fiction, Indigenous authors oppose clichéd representations in the popular realm and reinscribe Indigenous presence in post-apocalyptic landscapes and

---

[49] Katja Sarkowsky, "Comparing Indigenous Literatures in Canada and the United States," in *The Palgrave Handbook of Comparative North American Literature*, ed. Reingard M. Nischik (New York: Palgrave, 2014), 85.

[50] Dillon, "Introduction," 8.

[51] Dimaline, *The Marrow Thieves*, 33.

[52] Badger qtd. in Alexandra Alter, "'We've Already Survived an Apocalypse'. Indigenous Writers Are Changing Sci-Fi," *The New York Times,* August 14, 2020.

[53] Pamela Wilson and Michelle Stewart, "Introduction," in *Global Indigenous Media: Cultures, Poetics and Politics*, ed. Pamela Wilson and Michelle Stewart (Durham: Duke University Press, 2008), 5.

in the minds of young readers. Like their storytelling protagonists, then, these YA authors use their stories to educate younger generations.

244   Indigenous Narratives of the Apocalypse

Works Cited

Brydon, Diana. "Risk, Mortality, and Memory: The Global Imaginaries of Cherie Dimaline's *The Marrow Thieves*, M. G. Vassanji's *Nostalgia*, and André Alexis's *Fifteen Dogs*." *Revista Canaria de Estudios Ingleses* 78 (2019): 97–112.

Basu, Balaka, et al. "Introduction." In *Contemporary Dystopian Fiction for Young Adults: Brave New Teenagers*, edited by Balaka Basu et al., 1–15. New York: Routledge, 2013.

Corntassel, Jeff, and Chaw-win-is T'lakwadzi. "Indigenous Storytelling, Truth-telling, and Community Approaches to Reconciliation." *English Studies in Canada* 35, no. 1 (2009): 137–159.

Couzelis, Mary J. "The Future Is Pale: Race in Contemporary Young Adult Dystopian Novels." In *Contemporary Dystopian Fiction for Young Adults: Brave New Teenagers*, edited by Balaka Basu et al., 131–144. New York: Routledge, 2013.

Dillon, Grace L. "Introduction." In *Walking the Clouds: An Anthology of Indigenous Science Fiction*, edited by Grace L. Dillon, 1–12. Tucson: University of Arizona Press, 2012.

Dimaline, Cherie. *The Marrow Thieves.* Toronto: DCB, 2017.

Donelson, Kenneth L. "Growing Up Real: YA Literature Comes of Age." In *Young Adult Literature: Background and Criticism*, edited by Millicent Lenz and Ramona M. Mahood, 58–67. Chicago: American Library Association, 1980.

Dundas, Deborah. "Cherie Dimaline: Hopes and Dreams in the Apocalypse." *Toronto Star*, November 6, 2017, thestar.com/entertainment/books/2017/11/06/cherie-dimaline-hopes-and-dreams-in-the-apocalypse.html.

Hebdige, Dick. *Hiding in the Light: On Images and Things*. London: Routledge, 1988.

Howe, LeAnne. "Tribalography: The Power of Native Stories." *Journal of Dramatic Theory and Criticism* 14, no. 1 (1999): 117–125.

Iseke-Barnes, Judy. "Politics and Power of Languages: Indigenous Resistance to Colonizing Experiences of Language Dominance." *Journal of Thought* 39, no. 1 (2004): 45–81.

Justice, Daniel Heath. Why Indigenous Literatures Matter. Waterloo: Wilfrid Laurier University Press, 2018.

King, Thomas. *The Truth About Stories: A Native Narrative*. Minneapolis: University of Minnesota Press, 2008.

Krystal, Matthew. *Indigenous Dance and Dancing Indian: Contested Representation in the Global Era*. Boulder: University Press of Colorado, 2012.

Lidchi, Henrietta, and Suzanne Newman Fricke. "Future History: Indigenous Futurisms in North American Visual Arts." *World Art* 9, no. 2 (2019): 99–102.

Lyotard, Jean-François. *The Postmodern Condition: A Report on Knowledge*. Norfolk: Manchester University Press, 1984.

Momaday, N. Scott. *Man Made of Words*. New York: St. Martin's Press, 1997.

Morris, Brian. "Ernest Thompson Seton and the Origins of the Woodcraft Movement." *Journal of Contemporary History* 5, no. 2 (1970): 183–194.

Morton, Lindsay, and Lynette Lounsbury. "Inertia to Action: From Narrative Empathy to Political Agency in Young Adult Fiction." *Papers: Explorations into Children's Literature* 23, no. 2 (2015): 53–70.

Rieder, John. *Colonialism and the Emergence of Science Fiction*. Middletown: Wesleyan University Press, 2008.

Sarkowsky, Katja. "Comparing Indigenous Literatures in Canada and the United States." In *The Palgrave Handbook of Comparative North American Literature*, edited by Reingard M. Nischik, 85–102. New York: Palgrave, 2014.

Sium, Aman, and Eric Ritskes. "Speaking Truth to Power: Indigenous Storytelling as an Act of Living Resistance." *Decolonization: Indigeneity, Education & Society* 2, no. 1 (2013): i–x.

Storey, John. *Cultural Theory and Popular Culture: An Introduction*. Edinburgh: Pearson, 2006.

Strinati, Dominic. *An Introduction to Theories of Popular Culture*. London: Routledge, 2004.

Suhr-Sytsma, Mandy. *Self-Determined Stories: The Indigenous Reinvention of Young Adult Literature*. Ann Arbor: Michigan University Press, 2019.

Teuton, Sean Kicummah. *Native American Literature: A Very Short Introduction*. Oxford: Oxford University Press, 2018.

246 Indigenous Narratives of the Apocalypse

The Agenda with Stephen Paikin. "Reclaiming Lost Dreams," YouTube August 22, 2018. youtube.com/watch?v=n746oUqBc_k.

Vizenor, Gerald. *Survivance: Narratives of Native Presence*. Lincoln: University of Nebraska Press, 2008.

Waldman, Katy. "In Y.A. Where Is the Line Between Criticism and Cancel Culture?" *The New Yorker*, March 21, 2019. newyorker.com/books/under-review/in-ya-where-is-the-line-between-criticism-and-cancel-culture.

Wilson, Pamela, and Michelle Stewart. "Introduction." In *Global Indigenous Media: Cultures, Poetics and Politics*, edited by Pamela Wilson and Michelle Stewart. Durham: Duke University Press, 2008.

Zanella, Patrizia. "Witnessing Story and Creating Kinship in a New Era of Residential Schools: Cherie Dimaline's *The Marrow Thieves*." *Studies in American Indian Literatures* 32, no. 3–4 (2020): 176–200.

ALEXANDRA HARTMANN

"Women's work is never easy, never clean": (Strong) Black Womanhood and the Carceral State in Tayari Jones's *An American Marriage*

African Americans are incarcerated at a rate five times higher than white Americans, and with 2.2 million[1] Black men currently under correctional supervision, there are a lot of Black women – partners, mothers and daughters – either waiting for "their" men to get out or dealing with the repercussions of incarceration, parole and probation. A 2015 study shows that almost half of African American women have a family member in prison and suggests that the "spillover effects of mass imprisonment on American families and communities may be even larger than the direct effects on [incarcerated] adult men."[2] After all, these women bear the stigma of incarceration alongside the people incarcerated and face economic hardships as well as an increased risk of abuse and illness, among many other consequences.[3]

---

[1] Imprisonment rates have decreased in recent years, but Black men are still disproportionately affected by mass incarceration, cf. "U.S. Incarceration Rates by Race, 2010," Prison Policy Initiative, accessed March 12, 2022, prisonpolicy.org/graphs/raceinc.html.

[2] Hedwig Lee et al., "Racial Inequalities in Connectedness to Imprisoned Individuals in the United States," *Du Bois Review: Social Science Research on Race* 12, no. 2 (2015): 277.

[3] Michelle Alexander's *The New Jim Crow: Mass Incarceration in the Age of Colorblindness* (New York: The New Press, 2010) reignited scholarly interest in mass incarceration; cf. also Loïc Wacquant, *Punishing the Poor: The Neoliberal Government of Social Insecurity* (Durham: Duke University Press, 2009). For works with an explicit focus on the impact on women, see, for example, Beth Richie, *Arrested Justice: Black Women, Violence, and*

248 Black Womanhood and the Carceral State

In the arts, these women's experiences have emerged as a popular topic in filmic as well as literary narratives. Examples that come to mind that make "Black women on the outside" a crucial part of the narrative of *male* incarceration are Barry Jenkins's film *If Beale Street Could Talk*, Patrisse Khan-Cullors's memoir *When They Call You a Terrorist*, and Tayari Jones's novel *An American Marriage* (all from 2018). These texts chronicle the emotional and economic distress of women whose loved ones are in prison alongside the gendered role expectations they are met with. While the focus on "women on the outside" might be less spectacular than a focus on the incarcerated, it is fundamentally important because it is these women who often serve as the backbone of many African American communities. While their distress might not be the immediate result of the carceral state, it shapes the (public) feelings of a large section of the population. Just as these women are often rendered invisible in real life, so too has the trope of Black women "on the outside" received little scholarly attention thus far.

Their many differences notwithstanding, these narratives share a feminist interest in depictions of Black women as they engage with the stereotype of the strong Black woman (SBW) – a role expectation and gender ideal that remains popular in Black life and continues to dominate cultural representations of Black womanhood. Often, the woman on the outside becomes the strong Black woman, and she is always already policed by that very image. In fact, the image may have experienced a revival in the carceral state that has made so many women the primary caretakers of their families. Ultimately, the SBW stereotype celebrates Black women's strength and support but, at the same time, treats these attributes as a given. The SBW stereotype creates an expectation that others (husbands, fathers, brothers) have of Black women *and* one they have of themselves, as is often the case with social roles.

However, rather than simply perpetuating or plainly rejecting the stereotype, many of these narratives critically reflect on it. Using *An*

America's Prison Nation (New York: New York University Press, 2012); and Angela Bruns and Lee Hedwig's sociological study "Partner Incarceration and Women's Substance Use," *Journal of Marriage and the Family* 82 (2020): 1178–1196.

American Marriage as a case study, I argue that the novel wrestles with the SBW stereotype by painting a more nuanced picture of Black womanhood that neither rejects Black women's strength outright nor simply embraces it. Rather, it shows how this perceived strength often takes on oppressive forms of its own as it limits Black women's self-agentic choices. At the same time, it is attuned to the fact that Black gender exists in a structurally anti- Black world that often targets Black life regardless gender identity. *An American Marriage* demonstrates the SBW image's pervasive grasp on the cultural perception of Black women but productively complicates it through a discourse of shared vulnerability.[4]

Strength Meets Respectability: The Strong Black Woman

The SBW stereotype determines what is considered appropriate Black female behavior. Cheryl Woods-Giscombé argues that it "is a multi-dimensional phenomenon encompassing characteristics such as obligation to manifest strength, emotional suppression, resistance to vulnerability and dependence, determination to succeed, and obligation to help others."[5] As Cailyn Petrona Stewart notes, the SBW "is by default a natural endurer of stress and pain" who "carries on the onerous weights and trickle down effects of society's oppressive systems." She "learns that her needs always come behind the needs of others."[6] The historical roots of this stereotype lie in the exploitation and destruction of Black (family) life that occurred during slavery and that has continued well into the twenty first century through over-policing and incarceration. Many Black women have had to play their part in order to secure their families' survival in the face of anti- Black terror. At the

---

[4] This is not to deny the direct harm that Black women face by law enforcement; in fact, Black women are the fastest growing group in the prison population.

[5] Cheryl Woods-Giscombé, "Superwoman Schema: African American Women's Views on Stress, Strength, and Health," *Qualitative Health Research* 20, no. 5 (2010): 678–679.

[6] Cailyn Petrona Stewart, "The Mule of the World: The Strong Black Woman and The Woes of Being 'Independent,'" *Knots* 3 (2017): 32–33.

250 Black Womanhood and the Carceral State

same time, the racialized gender ideal has long expected Black women to combine strength with respectability[7] and thus to embody two seemingly contradictory traits: whereas the former requires self-reliance and courage, the latter necessitates obedience and care for others.

Black respectability first emerged in the late nineteenth century as a primarily middle-class ideology that employed traces of the image of the SBW throughout. Evelyn Brooks Higginbotham locates respectability politics' origins in the Black Baptist church, where women "felt certain that 'respectable' behavior in public would earn their people a measure of esteem from white America."[8] With racial uplift as one of its main goals, the politics of respectability often encouraged and monitored socially compatible and compliant behavior and ethics in African Americans so that they would find acceptance in hegemonic white American society.[9] These politics inform Black middle-class life to this day and continue to shape a SBW stereotype that remains pervasive and is widely recognized. Michelle Obama and Oprah Winfrey are but two of the SBW's most famous and successful representatives. This

---

[7] Cf. Maria S. Johnson, "Strength and Respectability: Black Women's Negotiation of Racialized Gender Ideals and the Role of Daughter-Father Relationships," *Gender and Society* 27, no. 6 (2013): 889–890.

[8] Evelyn Brooks Higginbotham, *Righteous Discontent: The Women's Movement in the Black Baptist Church, 1880–1920* (Cambridge: Harvard University Press, 1993), 14.

[9] Higginbotham emphasizes that the movement was complex though. Many measures were simultaneously progressive and conservative, such as demanding the right to vote for every Black person "who is an intelligent and industrious citizen" (ibid., 222). Here conservatism and progressivism collide. Today, respectability is a highly contested framework, often criticized as confining and elitist. Brittney Cooper pushes back against the dominance of respectability and shows how, historically, many Black women were too rebellious to "be housed in an intellectual history of respectability." Brittney Cooper, *Beyond Respectability: The Intellectual Thought of Race Women* (Champaign: University of Illinois Press, 2017), 13. Despite such attempts to recuperate these women's achievements, a conservative strand of respectability politics still dominates much of Black (middle-class) life.

visibility makes it easy, in turn, to identify the SBW's (modern) others: the angry Black woman and the welfare queen.[10]

The SBW stereotype works so well because it often simultaneously relies on the *weak Black man* who is irresponsible and/or incapable of caring for his kin as its counterpart. Patricia Hill Collins observes that the SBW image calls for "a strength that is placed in service to White power and authority" because it "helps justify racial inequality to White Americans and suppress resistance among African Americans."[11] This is due in no small part to the fact that the stereotype serves Black patriarchal structures to just as great an extent. This "trap of loyalty" Beth Richie notes, causes many Black women to "go to great lengths to show solidarity with men, even when it means denying their pain and compromising their safety."[12]

Consequently, the stereotype's effects are grave, both for the individual as well as the community. Woods-Giscombé shows how the SBW (self-) image is at the root of many mental as well as physical and chronic health issues, ranging from depression to diabetes and hypertension. Even though the role has some perceived benefits, its limitations are severe because these women's health and safety are directly impacted by the stereotype.[13] Moreover, this stereotype ultimately undermines the concept of community by emphasizing individuality and reassuring women that they can and should deal with problems privately; it disallows vulnerability by encouraging Black women to deny their emotions and fears. Self-reliance is the ultimate goal, but only as long as it conforms to accepted gender roles. As such, despite having class-specific versions, the SBW stereotype crosses class

---

[10] As with all stereotypes, these controlling images are fluid and overlap. Michelle Obama, for instance, has been stereotyped as an angry Black woman more than once. Reflecting on media representations of herself in *Becoming* (New York: Crown, 2018), Obama notes, "I was female, black, and strong, which to certain people [...] translated only to 'angry'" (ibid., 265).

[11] Patricia Hill Collins, *Black Sexual Politics: African Americans, Gender, and the New Racism* (London: Routledge, 2004), 179–180.

[12] Beth E. Richie, *Arrested Justice: Black Women, Violence, and America's Prison Nation* (New York: New York University Press, 2012), 37.

[13] Woods-Giscombé, "Superwoman Schema," 677–678.

252   Black Womanhood and the Carceral State

boundaries while often accounting for and reiterating power imbalances between Black men and women within a white supremacist environment. The gender ideal of the SBW resonates throughout Jones's *An American Marriage* and finds both its implementation and subversion within.

Democracy, Popular Culture and Oprah's Book Club

An American Marriage has been widely read and well-received in the United States and abroad. While it won the Women's Prize for Fiction in 2019, it arguably received its greatest boost from being an Oprah's Book Club pick in 2018. Jamilah King insists that "Oprah's stamp of approval on your book can make your career, massively boost your book sales, and get your book into the mainstream like really nothing else can, even a Nobel Prize."[14] Indeed, Oprah Winfrey's influence on the making and shaping of American tastes and opinions – the "Oprahification" of America[15] – can hardly be overemphasized. Oprah makes *culture popular*.

The way I use *popular culture*, however, relates not just to statistics alone. In contrast to definitions of popular culture as, for instance, a mass phenomenon produced for and consumed by many, I want to recuperate a more basic definition that is primarily concerned not with sales or the number of consumers, but with its democratic potential instead. I take my cue from Jenn Brandt and Callie Clare, who propose considering "popular culture as a site of struggle and an instrument of democracy."[16] "Products of popular culture, whether mediated or not," they insist, "can be strong motivators in helping individuals question

---

[14] Jamilah King, "Oprah's Book Club Changed the Game – and Created a New World for Black Readers Like Me," *MotherJones*, November 1, 2019, motherjones.com/media/2019/11/oprah-book-club-apple-tv-plus-relaunch-legacy-black-writers/.

[15] Cf. Jaap Kooijman, *Fabricating the Absolute Fake: America in Contemporary Pop Culture* (Amsterdam: Amsterdam University Press, 2008), 47.

[16] Jenn Brandt and Callie Clare, *An Introduction to Popular Culture in the US: People, Politics, and Power* (London: Bloomsbury, 2018), 16.

power structures and implement desired change."[17] It is important to note, though, that this is merely a possibility – there is no certainty in this process.

In light of this approach to popular culture, it is easy to see why selection by Oprah's Book Club is important not only in monetary terms, but in terms of how it has directed attention to topics that reside at the center of society but that many are oblivious to. Between 1996 and 2010, more than a third of the books selected by the book club were written by people of color, including many African American women. Since taking the book club online, this trend has continued with selections such as Ta-Nehisi Coates's *The Water Dancer* (2019) and Michelle Obama's *Becoming* (2018). An entire field of study has evolved around Oprah since the early 2000s and I take seriously the potential impact the book club has had in making visible those experiences which are essential to social life and yet have remained invisible for too long. Simon Stow considers Oprah's Book Club to be just the right vehicle to advance (liberal) democratic values.[18] *An American Marriage* advances some of these values by interweaving the politics and institutional injustices of the American landscape with the intimacy of family life, friendship and marriage.

Unwinding Strong Black Womanhood in *An American Marriage*

Life as a Black American and the arbitrary injustices this entails is central to *An American Marriage*, and yet it is not simply a tale about wrongful and racist incarceration practices. As Carrie O'Grady writes, Jones's work "is as much an exploration of modern gender roles as it is an inquiry into social justice, particularly the male burden."[19] In this

---

[17] Ibid.
[18] Cf. Simon Stow, "The Way We Read Now: Oprah Winfrey, Intellectuals, and Democracy," in *The Oprah Affect: Critical Essays on Oprah's Book Club*, ed. by Jaime Harker and Cecilia Konchar Farr (New York: State University of New York Press, 2008), 291–292.
[19] Carrie O'Grady, "*An American Marriage* by Tayari Jones Review – A Marvellous Feat of Storytelling," *The Guardian*, May 15, 2019,

254 Black Womanhood and the Carceral State

essay, rather than exploring the representation of the "male burden" as an isolated phenomenon, I want to analyze the ways in which the novel ponders the consequences of injustice and their echoes into the world beyond the prison walls. It is clear right from the start that unfreedom does not apply only to those incarcerated but also extends to those on the outside.

The novel begins by introducing readers to Celestial and Roy, a young and successful middle-class couple. While on a trip to his childhood home, Roy is falsely accused of having raped a woman and is subsequently sentenced to serve twelve years in prison. Three years into his sentence, Celestial ends their marriage while promising to offer her support as a friend. She has fallen in love with her childhood friend, Andre, and begins a new relationship with him. After a total of five years in prison, Roy is released early and wants to return to his old life that no longer exists. Jones examines how Roy, Celestial and their families deal with the changes. Without a doubt, Roy is the novel's primary victim – the victim of a white supremacist system that locks up Black people for being in the wrong place at the wrong time. But the novel insists that this fact does not render his wife's pain any less meaningful. She, too, is a victim, not only of white supremacy but, on another level, of the expectation that a Black woman ought to combine strength and respectability.

The novel's emphasis on Roy's innocence is particularly striking. Rather than offering an easy way out or a justification for moving on and leaving her suffering husband, the novel paints Celestial's decision as a decision she has reached on her own and based on her personal needs – it is a decision that puts her own happiness before his. Reviving the epistolary genre, Jones uses letter exchanges between Roy and Celestial to trace their relationship while Roy is incarcerated. Their letters offer the reader intimate insights into their increasingly deteriorating marriage. They begin to fall apart: promises of faithfulness for the next twelve years end with a Dear John letter Celestial sends Roy, ending their romantic relationship. One of the most poignant exchanges consists of letters, each a mere one sentence in length, that

theguardian.com/books/2019/may/15/an-american-marriage-by-tayari-jones-review.

ALEXANDRA HARTMANN

unmistakably demonstrate the complexity of vulnerability and injustice. Having learned that Celestial is divorcing him, Roy writes, "I'm innocent," to which Celestial replies, "I'm innocent, too."[20] This exchange introduces central questions about responsibility and loyalty and confronts readers with two seemingly competing views: Roy has been falsely convicted of rape and rightly insists that he is not responsible for his imprisonment; Celestial, however, insists that she has not brought on the situation either but is suffering the consequences nonetheless. In addition, the novel has three different narrators: Celestial, Roy and Andre. Jones gives all three of them a space to voice their thoughts and feelings. This allows readers to experience the characters' varying perspectives on the same events.

The letters and the, at times, competing narrative voices indirectly explore Celestial's responsibility towards both herself and others. The question is not so much under what circumstances she is permitted to leave Roy, but whether it is permitted at all. How much do her life and happiness matter, even or especially while her husband is incarcerated? Can she be self-agentic, or is that degree of independence and "positive" selfishness misplaced because it decenters him? Celestial's decision to divorce Roy and start a new relationship already signals resistance to the image of the respectable SBW who is expected to put others first and willingly accept her responsibility for her husband's fate.

At the same time, Celestial's decision triggers harsh but predictable responses. The world around her reacts in ways that punish and/or reject her behavior as inappropriate. She is held responsible for Roy's happiness or unhappiness; in a sense, she receives more blame for his situation than the prison system does. Here, we see institutional guilt transformed into personal guilt – as inhabited by a Black woman. It is the older male generation that stands out as strongly judgmental. Celestial's father, painted as loving and caring in so many ways throughout the novel, shuns her behavior and tellingly chooses to address her new fiancé Andre before her, by saying:

---

[20] Tayari Jones, *An American Marriage* (Chapel Hill: Algonquin Books of Chapel Hill, 2018), 84.

256 Black Womanhood and the Carceral State

> I have one thing to say to you, as a black man: Roy is a hostage of the state. He is a victim of America. The least you could do is unhand his wife when he gets back. […] This ain't complicated. You want this man to come home after five years in the state penitentiary for some bullshit he didn't even do, and you want him to come back and see his wife with your little ring on her finger and you talking about you love her? I'll tell you what Roy is going to see: he is going to see a wife who wouldn't keep her legs closed and a so-called friend who doesn't know what it is to be a man, let alone a black man.[21]

Several aspects can be noted here: Celestial's father accuses his daughter of sexual promiscuity and disloyalty. Moreover, he condemns the criminal justice system as steeped in systemic racism; he knows that Roy's Blackness was the key factor in the accusation, trial and sentence. Both of these culminate in his appeal to Andre's masculinity and empathy for a fellow Black man who has been wronged by the state. Finally, by talking to André first, he denies Celestial the agency to make her own decision.

It is only afterwards that Celestial's father turns to her, now chastising her for wrongfully putting her own needs above Roy's: "What is all this stuff about love and her own mind. I don't mean to be harsh, but this is bigger than any little romance. […] What did Roy do to deserve any of this. He didn't do anything but be a black man in the wrong place at the wrong time. This is basic."[22] For Celestial's father, the question becomes one of race loyalty in the face of white supremacy, and she is expected to be a SBW who can downplay emotions and accept the cards she has been dealt, all the while considering those close to her instead of herself. Celestial's independence and bravery as a self-reliant businesswoman is only permissible if she is still submissive to her husband. Her father is wedded to the ideology of respectability. Celestial fails to meet the expectations with which a Black woman is confronted by refusing to "provide any type of support which is never too small nor too big."[23] Instead, she demonstrates an independence that puts herself before Roy.

---

[21] Ibid., 121.
[22] Ibid., 122.
[23] Stewart, "The Mule of the World," 33.

The father's repeated emphasis on the fact that Roy is a Black man is meaningful for his interpretation of the situation; Celestial's actions (as well as Andre's) are not simply consequential for the marriage but, rather, take on a greater meaning. In leaving Roy, Celestial has not only let Roy down; she has failed to perform the role of the ideal woman as the stronghold of Black life, both willing and able to bear the brunt of white supremacy for everyone else. Roy expresses similar expectations: "How hard could it be to stay off your back for five years? How hard could it be to make a tired man feel welcome? I picked soybeans when I was in prison. I have a degree from Morehouse College and I'm working the land like my great-great-granddaddy."[24] Roy's trauma is also clearly racialized. When Celestial asks if he would "have waited on [her] for five years," Roy draws attention to the distinct nature of his social position as a Black man: "'Celestial,' he said, like he was talking to someone very young, 'this shit wouldn't have happened to you in the first place.'"[25] Implying that she is simply too naïve to understand what it means to be a Black man in America, Roy can only conceive of himself as the situation's greatest and possibly sole victim.

In addressing these gendered role expectations, *An American Marriage* echoes a 1984 conversation between Audre Lorde and James Baldwin in which the two debate the effects of anti- Black violence related to gender. As their conversation shows, a shared racial history of oppression cannot overshadow the differently lived and gendered experiences of Black women and men. The tension remains ultimately unresolved in their discussion; even after conceding Lorde's justified remarks that Black women are often the target of racist violence and patriarchy, Baldwin insists that Black men face greater danger: "But you don't realize that in this republic the only real crime is to be a Black man?"[26]

Both the novel and the Baldwin-Lorde conversation resonate indirectly with an ongoing debate around and within Afropessimism, namely the role of gender or, more precisely, the place of Black women

---

[24] Jones, *An American Marriage*, 268.

[25] Ibid., 283.

[26] James Baldwin and Audre Lorde, "Revolutionary Hope: A Conversation Between James Baldwin and Audre Lorde," *Essence Magazine*, 1984, n.p.

and their experiences within the discourse. In its broadest sense, Afropessimism asserts that there is a fundamentally antagonistic relationship between Blackness and the human species – it conceives of Black life as social death.[27] Here, Blackness is defined first and foremost by anti- Blackness. While Afropessimist observations regarding the pervasive nature of anti-Blackness are important, several problems arise from and within this school of thought. In the context of this essay, it is at least necessary to question how an Afropessimist approach can translate into praxis and embrace the complexity of and differences in experiences. Jennifer Nash, for example, worries that "the dead are always figured as black men, and black women are those who mourn, who grieve, and who make visible black male suffering," thus rendering Black female suffering invisible.[28] Similarly, Patrice D. Douglass wonders: "How is a story told such that the grandiosity of Black death is held at the forefront of concern while respecting that Black death arises in many forms?"[29] Asked differently: what happens to intersectional approaches when gender and class concerns are either ignored or downplayed because of the dominant Black/Human non-relationship in Afropessimism?

It is questions like these that Afropessimism – as a theoretical field with practical implications – needs to consider.[30] In fiction, we already see a possible unfolding. *An American Marriage* carefully balances the structural disregard and gratuitous violence that Blackness is subjected to by paying attention to the different forms these injustices take, including their varied consequences. Black men are, of course, very often the target of direct violence by the state. At the same time, however, the novel meaningfully provides room for resulting problems

---

[27] Frank B. Wilderson III, *Afropessimism* (New York: Liveright, 2020), 245. For a detailed discussion of social death see Jared Sexton, "The Social Life of Social Death: On Afro-Pessimism and Black Optimism," *InTensions* 5 (2011).

[28] Jennifer C. Nash, *Black Feminism Reimagined: After Intersectionality* (Durham: Duke University Press, 2019), 22.

[29] Patrice D. Douglass, "Black Feminist Theory for the Dead and Dying," *Theory & Event* 21, no. 1 (2018): 107.

[30] For other problems in Afropessimist thought cf. Lewis R. Gordon, "Afro Pessimism," *Contemporary Political Theory* 17, no. 1 (2017): 105–137.

of those left behind (e.g., in this case, the disruption of a shared life). Without disregarding Nash's and Douglass's urgent concerns about Black women as immediate victims of the state, it is important to note how *An American Marriage* re-centers the attention on Black women "on the outside" and thus begins to blur the lines between immediate and mediated victimhood. By taking "spillover effects" into account, it allows the reader to see them as being equally pressing as the initial violence. The novel portrays the complexity and multidimensionality of suffering. It is through the recognition of a shared, if not identical, *vulnerability* that the characters can begin to undo the harm. This does not make the reasons for their respective situations disappear because anti- Blackness remains pervasive. But it does indeed provide a way to stop "killing each other off"[31] and stop hurting and harming each other.

Through its discourse of vulnerability, *An American Marriage* finds a way to voice suffering as a direct consequence of anti- Black racism without muting related forms of pain. At first, however, the dictates of respectability and loyalty briefly appear to triumph as Celestial succumbs to the expectations of the SBW role. She knows that "[a]ll around Roy were the shards of a broken life, not merely a broken heart. Yet who could deny that I was the only one who could mend him, if he could be healed at all? Women's work is never easy, never clean."[32] Celestial has decided to grant Roy's happiness greater importance than her own; she settles into the idea of breaking up with Andre to alleviate Roy's pain and try once more to have a relationship with him. This much, she is certain, she owes him, a Black man so horrifically wronged by the system. For a moment, she falls back into the behavior expected of her.

Interestingly, the very moment in which Celestial tries to downplay her own vulnerability in comparison to Roy's is also the moment in which his "awakening" takes place, allowing him to see that she is suffering from the long-term effects of incarceration, too. Just as they are about to have sex after reconciling, Roy finally recognizes Celestial's own pain. It is a difficult awakening for him: her vulnerability might be different from his own, yet he understands it as

---

[31] Lorde in Baldwin and Lorde, "A Revolutionary Hope," n.p.
[32] Jones, *An American Marriage*, 285.

260   Black Womanhood and the Carceral State

being equally unsettling. He tells her, "I know who I married, too. You're *in* me. When I touch you, your flesh communicates with my bones. You think I can't feel how sad you are?" "'I'm scared,' she said, her fingers transmitting a miserable willingness. 'It's hard to start over.'"[33] The "miserable willingness" her body communicates signals that she cannot use reason to override her personal needs. Similarly, Roy's realization of Celestial's vulnerability is not a mere act of cognition and reason; rather, it is one of affect, and he allows himself to be moved by her bodily response. If Judith Butler is right that "vulnerability [i]s a precondition of the 'human,'"[34] then Roy recognizes his and Celestial's shared humanity in the shared vulnerability that both are (finally) able and allowed to express. They grant room for and pay attention to each other's pain.

By locating the moment of healing on the affective level, the novel circumvents the problem of casting Celestial in the script of the controlling image. Through the affective recognition of her vulnerability, Roy experiences his ethical responsibility for her well-being. This mutual recognition does not override Roy's suffering and the terrible wrong he has been subjected to. Nor does it undo the pervasive and violent logic of anti- Blackness. But the very recognition of shared vulnerability that the racist logic denies them also marks the *beginning* of the undoing of that world. The protagonists refuse to perpetuate the violence, and recognition prevents the violence from seeping further into the relationship. Her agony is just as visible and valid as his – and this opens the possibility for a different future for both.

Black Feminism's Popular Dimension?

An American Marriage takes up important theoretical questions and offers possible, if imperfect, solutions. While the novel rejects Afro-pessimism's basis and conclusions even as it partially affirms its analysis, it is firmly rooted in Black feminism and takes seriously the

---

[33]   Ibid., 299.
[34]   Judith Butler, *Precarious Life: The Power of Mourning and Violence* (New York: Verso Books, 2004), 43.

1977 Combahee River Collective's intersectional analysis of oppression.[35] Black women's social positioning forces them to constantly wrestle with their personal and institutional life circumstances. This becomes especially pressing when their loved ones are forced out of their lives. Black women are often represented as strong and enduring and are expected to be so because of the wrongs their loved ones have experienced. But these expectations are tremendously harmful, too. Consequently, it is no surprise that we find the SBW stereotype being challenged in narratives about male incarceration. Even as these narratives center on the plight of Black men, they do so in a way that allows the reader to see its intricate connection to the plight of Black women.

Consequently, in *An American Marriage*, Black women's lives revolve around a triad of love, resistance to structural injustices, and a particularly profound need for self-love. *An American Marriage* is an indictment of the prison-industrial complex and structural oppression writ large, but it accomplishes this without disallowing the richness or the vulnerability of Black women's existence. While Black men are often deemed the greatest victims of the carceral state, it is important to consider their fates and mourn their deaths without neglecting others. Greater attention is being paid to the plight of Black women in the wake of the Black Lives Matter movement, but this intersectional movement – founded by three Black feminists – still has to contend with gendered differences that too often grant greater visibility to the suffering of Black men.[36]

Popular culture can help undo that dynamic by offering and promoting alternative perspectives on mass incarceration and state-sanctioned anti- Black violence. If, as Stuart Hall insists, popular culture is a site where "collective social understandings are created,"[37] then it is also site where they are *re*created. In selecting *An American Marriage*,

---

[35] Cf. Keeanga-Yamahtta Taylor, *How We Get Free: Black Feminism and the Combahee River Collective* (Chicago: Haymarket Books, 2017), 15–27.

[36] Cf. Barbara Ransby, *Making All Black Lives Matter: Reimagining Freedom in the Twenty-First Century* (Berkeley: University of California Press, 2018), 109.

[37] Stuart Hall, "The Rediscovery of 'Ideology': The Return of the Repressed in Media Studies," in *Cultural Theory and Popular Culture: A Reader*, ed. John Storey (London: Routledge, 2019), 106.

Oprah's Book Club draws attention to a novel that takes up and refocuses a familiar narrative of mass incarceration by highlighting the (inner) social life of a "Black woman on the outside." Insisting that the consequences incarceration has on those left behind are highly relevant, the novel simultaneously rejects the controlling image of the SBW as ultimately harmful, not just to the women themselves but also their intimate and social lives. Ending on acceptance for Celestial's wish to put herself first, the novel invites readers to reconsider common notions of justice and injustice. It calls on them to recognize the need to see each other beyond gendered and racialized scripts. Thus, Oprah's Book Club indirectly advocates mutual recognition as a prerequisite for democratic practice.

Works Cited

Alexander, Michelle. *The New Jim Crow: Mass Incarceration in the Age of Colorblindness*. New York: The New Press, 2010.

Baldwin, James, and Audre Lorde. "Revolutionary Hope: A Conversation Between James Baldwin and Audre Lorde." *Essence Magazine*, 1984.

Brandt, Jenn, and Callie Clare. *An Introduction to Popular Culture in the US: People, Politics, and Power*. London: Bloomsbury, 2018.

Bruns, Angela and Hedwig Lee. "Partner Incarceration and Women's Substance Use." *Journal of Marriage and the Family* 82 (2020): 1178–1196.

Butler, Judith. *Precarious Life: The Power of Mourning and Violence*. New York: Verso Books, 2004.

Collins, Patricia Hill. *Black Sexual Politics: African Americans, Gender, and the New Racism*. London: Routledge, 2004.

Cooper, Brittney C. *Beyond Respectability: The Intellectual Thought of Race Women*. Champaign: University of Illinois Press, 2017.

Douglass, Patrice D. "Black Feminist Theory for the Dead and Dying." *Theory & Event* 21, no. 1 (2018): 106–123.

Gordon, Lewis R. "Afro Pessimism." *Contemporary Political Theory* 17, no. 1 (2017): 105–137.

Hall, Stuart. "The Rediscovery of 'Ideology': The Return of the Repressed in Media Studies." In *Cultural Theory and Popular Culture: A Reader*, edited by John Storey, 94–123. London: Routledge, 2019.

Higginbotham, Evelyn Brooks. *Righteous Discontent: The Women's Movement in the Black Baptist Church, 1880-1920*. Cambridge: Harvard University Press, 1993.

Johnson, Maria S. "Strength and Respectability: Black Women's Negotiation of Racialized Gender Ideals and the Role of Daughter-Father Relationships." *Gender and Society* 27, no. 6 (2013): 889–912.

Jones, Tayari. *An American Marriage*. Chapel Hill: Algonquin Books of Chapel Hill, 2018.

King, Jamilah. "Oprah's Book Club Changed the Game – and Created a New World for Black Readers Like Me." *MotherJones*, November 1, 2019. motherjones.com/media/2019/11/oprah-book-club-apple-tv-plus-relaunch-legacy-black-writers/.

Kooijman, Jaap. *Fabricating the Absolute Fake: America in Contemporary Pop Culture*. Amsterdam: Amsterdam University Press, 2008.

Lee, Hedwig, et al. "Racial Inequalities in Connectedness to Imprisoned Individuals in the United States." *Du Bois Review: Social Science Research on Race* 12, no. 2 (2015): 269–282.

Nash, Jennifer C. *Black Feminism Reimagined: After Intersectionality*. Durham: Duke University Press, 2019.

Obama, Michelle. *Becoming*. New York: Crown, 2018.

O'Grady, Carrie. "*An American Marriage* by Tayari Jones Review – A Marvellous Feat of Storytelling." *The Guardian*, May 15, 2019. theguardian.com/books/2019/may/15/an-american-marriage-by-tayari-jones-review.

Ransby, Barbara. *Making All Black Lives Matter: Reimagining Freedom in the Twenty-First Century*. Berkeley: University of California Press, 2018.

Richie, Beth E. *Arrested Justice: Black Women, Violence, and America's Prison Nation*. New York: New York University Press, 2012.

Sexton, Jared. "The Social Life of Social Death: On Afro-Pessimism and Black Optimism." *InTensions* 5 (2011): 1–47.

Stewart, Cailyn Petrona. "The Mule of the World: The Strong Black Woman and The Woes of Being 'Independent.'" *Knots* 3 (2017): 31–39.

Stow, Simon. "The Way We Read Now: Oprah Winfrey, Intellectuals, and Democracy." In *The Oprah Affect: Critical Essays on Oprah's Book Club*, edited by Jaime Harker and Cecilia Konchar Farr, 277–293. New York: State University of New York Press, 2008.

Taylor, Keeanga-Yamahtta. *How We Get Free: Black Feminism and the Combahee River Collective*. Chicago: Haymarket Books, 2017.

"U.S. Incarceration Rates by Race, 2010." Prison Policy Initiative, accessed March 22, 2022. prisonpolicy.org/graphs/raceinc.html.

Wacquant, Loïc. *Punishing the Poor: The Neoliberal Government of Social Insecurity.* Durham: Duke University Press, 2009.

Wilderson, Frank B., III. *Afropessimism.* New York: Liveright, 2020.

Willingham, Breea C. "Black Women's Prison Narratives and the Intersection of Race, Gender, and Sexuality in US Prison." *Critical Survey* 23, no. 3 (2011): 55–66.

Woods-Giscombé, Cheryl. "Superwoman Schema: African American Women's Views on Stress, Strength, and Health." *Qualitative Health Research* 20, no. 5 (2010): 668–683.

ZOHRA HASSAN-PIEPER

Muslim Misrepresentation and the Post-Empire Imaginary in Craig Thompson's *Habibi*

The graphic novel has a long history of tackling thorny political issues – Art Spiegelman's *Maus* (1992) being a prominent example. The most recent example of a controversy within this genre that electrified readership is that of the conflicted Muslim superhero. A growing number of female Muslim superheroes indicates a shift in the visual storytelling of Muslim characters to boot, and this shift is a disturbing one. Examples of this can be found in the following Muslim graphic narratives: G. Willow Wilson's *Ms. Marvel* and *Magnus Chase and the Gods of Asgard's* Muslim character Samirah al-Abbas, and Craig Thompson's *Habibi* (2011).[1] These female characters are often in conflict with their religious loyalties to Islam, and their representations are tied to violence and oppression metonymically enhanced by dress and costume. Possible readings are of course always in tension with preferred readings, turning graphic narratives into complex fields of

---

[1] In addition to using the terms "graphic novel" and "comic," I work with the definition of "graphic narrative." I follow Daniel Stein's and Jan-Noël Thon's suggestion to "[…] retain the historically resonant and culturally specific terms 'comic strip' and 'graphic novel' while also subscribing to the more general notion of 'graphic narrative,' signaling both the aim of developing a comics narratology (or graphic narrative theory) and an awareness of the transcultural and transnational varieties of graphic storytelling […]." Daniel Stein and Jan-Noël Thon, "Introduction: From Comic Strips to Graphic Novels," in *From Comic Strips to Graphic Novels: Contributions to the Theory and History of Graphic Narrative*, ed. Daniel Stein and Jan-Noël Thon (Berlin: De Gruyter, 2015), 7.

268 Muslim Misrepresentation and the Post-Empire Imaginary

multiple struggles and into a medium of cultural diagnosis.[2] The polysemy of textual agencies inhibits a coherent ideological position, as do constitutive narrative elements such as visual imagery, words, panel structure, and the employment of characters. As a result, these texts reveal the necessity of being critically examined within the "triad of popular culture, populism and politics."[3]

Muslim misrepresentation in the public sphere is now more widespread and detailed. Geopolitical events such as the 9/11 attacks and the global war on terror which was responsible for the occupation of Iraq and Afghanistan were crucial in the shaping of the Muslim Other in the public discourse. North America's and Europe's decision to make drastic cuts to refugee admissions with the aim of restricting or closing paths to legal immigration has exacerbated anti-immigrant and anti-Muslim discourse. Additionally, transnational, anti-globalist discourse and the fearmongering rhetoric of right-wing, populist movements repeatedly frame the Muslim diaspora as evil and backwards. These narratives convey an unambiguous and emotionally compelling narrative to the public, suggesting that Muslims are a threat to Christian culture as well as a threat to Western security. Moreover, the continuous development of anti-terror infrastructure and policies further cultivates an imminent, pervasive fear of Muslims and translates into different states of emergency in the public sphere.[4] Every instance of emergency can be connected to an archive of media images, suggesting that these images are self-explanatory instead of requiring explanation, and that they are self-serving. Therefore, building visual imagery requires close introspection with regard to the performative and theatrical nature of the public sphere, and to the relationship between spectator and image. Laura Bieger argues:

---

[2] For a detailed analysis of comics and readers in this field of cultural diagnosis, see Daniel Stein's *Authorizing Superhero Comics: On the Evolution of a Serial Genre* (Columbus: Ohio State University Press, 2021).

[3] Conference description of the 66th Annual Meeting of the German Association for American Studies, U.S.-American Culture as Popular Culture, June 13–15 Hamburg, 7.

[4] Cf. Russ Castronovo and Susan Gillman, *States of Emergency: The Object of American Studies* (Chapel Hill: The University of North Carolina Press, 2009).

ZOHRA HASSAN-PIEPER

> [...] the public sphere is a spatial form that does not depend on people assembling at a particular place. Its primary mode of spatial production – (mass) mediated discourse – reaches across space and time, connecting people at different locations (writing desks, reading chairs, newsrooms, living rooms, coffee shops, public parks), thus generating not only a complex net of social relations but an equally complex net of spaces and places, some of which are more public than others.[5]

Bieger emphasizes that the theatricality of public space is constrained to time and place. Therefore, building visual imagery requires an investigation of the performative and theatrical nature of the public sphere, and the relationship between spectator and image. For example, Craig Thompson's American graphic novel *Habibi*, and its multimodal storytelling mode, reproduces Orientalist stereotypes, exploits a repertoire of media images that were used in the emergency narrative on the war on terror, and engages in hegemonic schemes of anti-Muslim representation. Credited with being riveting art, it is actually anti-Muslim propaganda.

Set in a fictional country called Wanatolia, Thompson's *Habibi* covers 672 pages. The protagonists are orphaned runaway child slaves: a light-skinned ten-year-old-girl, Dodola, and the even younger, very dark-skinned African boy, Zam, who is also called Habibi (Arabic for 'darling').[6] As the narratives begins, the two have been living in a shipwrecked boat in the desert – effectively on their own island, isolated from the rest of the world. Dodola starts off as a mother-like figure to Zam, even providing food by prostituting herself until she is abducted by the Sultan of Wanatolia and forced to live in a harem. Zam, meanwhile, wants nothing more than to protect and provide for Dodola, even becoming a eunuch in order to gain access to ways of finding and reuniting with her. He unwillingly ends up in the same harem as Dodola. It's only when the Sultan of Wanatolia gives the order to drown Dodola

---

[5] Laura Bieger, "Learning from Hannah Arendt; or the Public Sphere as a Space of Appearance and the Fundamental Opacity of the Face-to-Face," in *American Counter/Publics*, ed. Ulla Haselstein et al. (Heidelberg: Universitätsverlag Winter, 2019), 45.

[6] The graphic novel is drawn in black and white, but the way in which Dodola is rendered makes clear that, compared to Zam, she is lighter-skinned but non-Caucasian.

270 Muslim Misrepresentation and the Post-Empire Imaginary

in the sea that Zam is able to rescue her. In the end, they both leave Wanatolia because of the country's rapid modernization, which they are not comfortable with. The novel ends with the two adopting a child slave.

Habibi's mixed reviews, and the somewhat excessive magnitude of their claims, both positive and negative, illustrate how individuals might grapple with the author's aesthetic choices, allowing for potent opposition between characters and ideas. Praise for Craig Thompson's graphic novel *Habibi* in contemporaneous reviews is extremely strong.[7] Zadie Smith highlights the work as a "remarkable feat of research, care, and black ink, and a reminder that all 'People of the book,' despite the division of their individual traditions share a mosaic of stories."[8] Smith acknowledges that Muslim representation is the core of Thompson's graphic narratives but fails to comment on its stereotypical depiction. Thierry Groensteen refers to Habibi as "sensual, erudite, committed, feisty, cruel, and both contemporary and timeless."[9] Lisa Shea from *Elle* magazine elevates Thompson to the "Charles Dickens of the genre, able to capture all the scary, heartbreaking, brave, uplifting details of his characters' fates while orchestrating the big-picture machinations that connect them to the lives and times of his readers."[10]

These critics herald this particular American graphic novel for its richness and boldness of vision while ignoring the political and moral message *Habibi* sends. In her review, Zadie Smith criticizes the male gaze "lingering on Dodola's body [frame after frame]: she spends two thirds of this book naked."[11] What Smith does not mention is how Thompson is all too ready to engage in female – but not male – sexual exploitation by depicting numerous rape scenes. The *Guardian*'s Michel

---

[7] Craig Thompson, *Habibi* (London: Faber & Faber, 2011).

[8] Zadie Smith, "Reviews: New Books by Zadie Smith," *Harper's Magazine*, September 2011, harpers.org/archive/2011/09/new-books-29/.

[9] Thierry Groensteen, "Craig Thompson, *Habibi*," in *The Expanding Art of Comics: Ten Modern Masterpieces*, ed. Thierry Groensteen (Jackson: University Press of Mississippi, 2017), 146.

[10] Lisa Shea, "A Magic Carpet Ride – An Epic Sage Spanning Arab and Christian Traditions and Modernity Dazzles the Imagination," *Elle*, September 19, 2011, www.elle.com/culture/books/ reviews/a11768/habibi-review/.

[11] Smith, "Reviews: New Books," 76.

Faber refers to *Habibi* as "an orgy of art for its own sake."[12] Faber does not address the seriousness with which Thompson engages in Muslim misrepresentation and the subsequent effects it might have on the population's perception. The *New York Times*' Robyn Creswell argues that "Thompson makes no pretension to realism. But the originals were fantasies too, and it's often hard to tell whether Thompson is making fun of Orientalism or indulging in it."[13] Creswell omits the scale of representational issues which stem from a history of Muslim experiences being filtered through white lenses and the fact that they are not refracted through the consciousness of the author. The most pointed examination of *Habibi* comes from Nadim Damluji. He comments on the fact that "[t]he artistic playground that he chose of barbaric Arabs devoid of history but not savagery is a well-trod environment in Western literature, and one, that is consistently reinforced in the pages of *Habibi*. In too many panels, Thompson conjures up familiar and lazy stereotypes of Arabs."[14] The aforementioned exaggerations and drastic contrasts employed in *Habibi* typify both superficial commonalities of Muslim majority countries as well as sexuality that evokes an intense, specific set of visual associations.

Habibi is built on intermedial and intertextual condensations and reductions. It evokes notions of Richard Burton's *Arabian Nights*,[15] early nineteenth-century Orientalist paintings, and Hollywood cinematographic representations of Arabs. In fact, the graphic novel helps to revive the popularization of a mysterious Other, therefore aiding a resurgence of Orientalism in American popular culture through the additional usage of emergency narratives. In an interview with the *New Statesman*, Thompson explains:

[12] Michel Faber, "Habibi by Craig Thompson – Review," *The Guardian*, September 16, 2011, www.theguardian.com/books/2011/sep/16/habibi-craig-thompson-review.

[13] Robyn Creswell, "The Graphic Novel as Orientalist Mash-Up," *The New York Times*, October 14, 2011, www.nytimes.com/ 2011/10/16/books/ review/habibi-written-and-illustrated-by-craig-thompson-book-review.html.

[14] Nadim Damluji, "The Spectre of Orientalism in Craig Thompson's Habibi," *Medium*, February 20, 2017, medium.com/@ndamluji/the-spectre-of-orientalism-in-craig-thompsons-habibi-dde9d499f403

[15] Sir Richard Francis Burton, *The Arabian Nights: Tales From a Thousand and One Nights* (New York: Modern Library, 2004).

272   Muslim Misrepresentation and the Post-Empire Imaginary

> Edward Saïd talks about Orientalism in very negative terms because it reflects the prejudices of the west towards the exotic east. But I was also having fun thinking of Orientalism as a genre like Cowboys and Indians is a genre – they're not an accurate representation of the American west, they're like a fairy tale genre. The main influences and inspirations though were Arabic calligraphy, geometric patterns, and ornamentation though.[16]

Saïd's Orientalism primarily concerns itself with a mutual and interdependent binary opposition of the Western Self and Eastern Other. He writes that the "analysis of the Orientalist text places emphasis on the evidence, which is by no means invisible, for such representations as *representations*, not as 'natural' descriptions for the Orient."[17] Orientalist discourse is full of ambivalence rather than any reality underlying its depictions. Still, it is an integral part of Western mindset. The idea of "playing cowboys and Indians" has long been fraught with ambivalence, too. Philip Deloria states that the "practice of playing Indian has clustered around two paradigmatic moments – the Revolution, which rested on the creation of a national identity, and modernity, which has used Indian play to encounter the authentic amidst the anxiety of urban industrial and postindustrial life." Deloria's praxeological understanding of the "axis of distance" and the "axis of value" argues that Native Americans always oscillate between the positive and negative Native American Other, between identification and distance.[18] When Thompson considers Orientalism as a special form of "playing Indian" and especially as a fairy-tale genre, he normalizes a process of Othering. His discursive maintenance of cultural myths helps to shape a discourse that excludes his characters from the circulation of knowledge created about them. In my analysis, I will argue that *Habibi* bears the weight of cumulative repetitions that resuscitate and reactivate the image of orientalist framework. By focusing on cruelty; the dehumanization of characters; and the hypersexualized, subjugated female Muslim located in an

---

[16] Liam McLaughlin, "Comic Book Creators Are Really Trying to Create a Visual Music," *The New Statesman*, September 1, 2011.

[17] Edward W. Saïd, *Orientalism* (London: Vintage Books, 1979), 22.

[18] Philip Joseph Deloria, *Playing Indian* (New Haven: Yale University Press, 1998), 175.

unknown imperial topography; *Habibi* essentializes Muslim represent-ation. This graphic narrative novel is a classic example of what Barbara Buchenau and Virginia Richter define as the post-empire imaginary, which is rooted in changes of repertoire.[19] According to Buchenau and Richter:

> In our definition, the post-empire imaginary is conceived spatially, rooted in actual imperial topographies, as well as temporally, connected to the historical past on the one hand and an uncertain, frightening or comforting future on the other. Despite its rootedness in real space and history, the post-empire imaginary is also deeply invested in arbit-rariness and in transparency.[20]

The authors highlight that, on the one hand, post-empire negotiates and engenders meaning through time and space; on the other hand, it morphs into an unstable framework that thrives on tension and unpredictability of representation. Buchenau and Richter conclude: "Empires are thus constituted interrelationally (…) when they draw on but modify previous sets of rules and regulations."[21] They point out how concurrent imag-

---

[19] For the notion of the repertoire see Diana Taylor, *The Archive and the Repertoire: Performing Cultural Memomry in the Americas* (Durham: Duke University Press, 2003), 19–20. Taylor postulates that the transmitting and storing of cultural knowledge is based on "supposedly enduring material (i.e., texts, documents, buildings, bones)." That is to say, on the archive, and on "the so-called ephemeral repertoire of embodied practice/knowledge (i.e., spoken language, dance, sports, ritual)." Taylor's approach constitutes a deliberate investment in performance studies in order to initiate an epistemic change that no longer privileges writing but instead centers on nonverbal practices. Taylor explains the ways in which repertoire makes influences and traditions visible, ultimately fostering varied practices but requiring presence – in other words, people's participation – in order to produce knowledge.

[20] The post-empire imaginary consists of "a repertoire of rules, gestures, and styles, and an archive of images, narratives, and affects derived from historical empires." Barbara Buchenau and Virginia Richter, "Introduction: How to Do Things with Empires," in *Postempire Imaginaries? Anglophone Literature, History and the Demise of Empire*, ed. Barbara Buchenau and Virginia Richter (Leiden: Brill, 2015), xxiii.

[21] Ibid., xxii.

274 Muslim Misrepresentation and the Post-Empire Imaginary

inaries intersect effectively because they originate in pre-existing views and values. And as Alfred Hiatt notes:

> Histories – and images – of empires have a way of recurring, less in the sense of possession or haunting than in the mode of Ortelius's *Romani Imperii Imago*, as the mask of the ancestor accompanying, informing the contemporary interpreters of power.[22]

The post-empire imaginary and the changes of repertoire help, accordingly, to reinstate racist views of the Other – but what if arbitrariness presides over transparency?

Repertoire in Craig Thompson's *Habibi:* Imperial Topographies, Characters and Calligraphy

The visual language of *Habibi* suggests the conflation of the Ottoman Empire with a mashup of various Muslim-majority countries. A closer look at the panels (figures 1–3) highlights that Wanatolia's most prevalent spatial landmarks are desert, sands, palm trees and the Palace of Tears. These images evoke "pictures in our head" that Jack G. Shaheen describes as a "'seen one, seen 'em all' setting, which I call 'Arabland'. […] The desert locale consists of an oasis, oil wells, palm trees, tents, fantastically ornate palaces, sleek limousines, and of course, camels."[23] Yet calling this geographical topography Wanatolia both causes and obscures the change of repertoire. Choosing the name Wanatolia has implications for how a reader might approach the task of interpreting the graphic novel.

---

[22] Alfred Hiatt, "Maps of Empires Past," in *Postempire Imaginaries? Anglophone Literature, History and the Demise of Empire*, ed. Barbara Buchenau and Virginia Richter (Leiden: Brill, 2015), 19.

[23] Jack G. Shaheen, *Reel Bad Arabs*: *How Hollywood Vilifies a People* (Northampton: Olive Branch Press, 2009), 14. Shaheen establishes a catalogue of Arab and Muslim stereotypes that are used in Hollywood media films, and he also points out the misconceptions these stereotypes create. His survey consists of 1,100 films.

Fig. 1: "Arabland" – The Desert Locale and Camels, *Habibi*, 80.

Fig. 2: "Arabland" – Palm Trees, *Habibi*, 258.

276   Muslim Misrepresentation and the Post-Empire Imaginary

Fig. 3: "Arabland" – The Palace of Tears, *Habibi*, 208.

The complex processes which attach meaning to places – inscribing the texts of our everyday lives with ideological messages about the past – make versions of history appear to be the natural order of things. Making reference to Anatolia in the name Wanatolia offers open-ended possibilities for reading and comprehension. Such a history cannot be found in the graphic novel, but is rather contextual information that the reader must locate herself. One way of reading Wanatolia is to consider it as a new way of centralizing the East over the West. Alluding to the Ottoman empire might conjure up images of Ottoman policies toward non-Muslims, thereby priming the reader to accept Islam as monolithic and intolerant. Or, what if Wanatolia functions as a homopheme, leaving one with the impression that there is one Anatolia and conflating the Ottoman Empire with various Muslim-majority countries? This way of reading would negate the geopolitical differences and histories of these countries. Another possible reading could suggest that the story takes place in "Wan[na]tolia" – perhaps emphasizing the desire of wanting it to be Anatolia because it is a place that actually existed?

Characters also play a pivotal role with regard to the notion of repertoire. *Habibi* employs another change of repertoire in choosing to depict as its protagonists two former child slaves, whose function would typically be limited to that of minor characters.[24] Alex Woloch's seminal work *The One vs. The Many* examines the role of minor characters, their relation to other characters, and their position within the narrative as a whole. For Woloch, the tension between story and discourse makes for an uneven balance between characters. He defines character-space as "[...] that particular and changed encounter between an individual human personality and a determined space and position within the narrative as a whole." [25] Applying Woloch's framework to Habibi would too readily assign Dodola to a position of fully developed individuality. The reader sees her as fighting her aggressors and using her sexuality to provide for Zam/Habibi. But this is false. Actually, *Habibi* rejects the 'one vs. many' character-system, destabilizes the process of character-ization, and engages in the depiction of female sexploitation. For ex-ample, the second time Dodola prostitutes herself to two male leaders of a passing caravan, the panels, which are far more numerous, are also far more explicit. The sexual intercourse with the older man takes up three panels and employs standard sex moans ("Uhh," "Ahh," "Ihh"). The sex scene with the younger man is more graphic and extensive. This one contains 37 panels, two of which are full-page.[26] The following panels (Fig. 4) detail the beginning of the sexual encounter with the younger man. Every panel features Dodola's nudity and focuses on either Dodola's full body or parts of her body such as her hands, her back and her face.

---

[24] In the graphic novel, we are presented with a typology of alternating, flat characters used not only for alleged comic relief, for example, lazy palace personnel and a farting dwarf. They reinstate the typology of the vilification of Muslim men. These Muslim men are predominantly depicted as misogynistic, violent and exploitative characters who use trite phrases ("Women's pleasure just makes 'em emotional," 157) and engage in cliché dialogue ("The palace of Tears ain't a bad set-up for us eunuchs, though, 'cuz these girls are REAL LONELY and thirsty for whatever sensual attention they get. You hear what I'm saying," 385).

[25] Alex Woloch, *The One vs. the Many*: *Minor Character and the Space of the Protagonist in the Novel:* (Princeton: Princeton University Press, 2003), 14.

[26] Thompson, *Habibi,* 150–157.

Fig. 4a: Sexploitation in *Habibi*, 149.

Fig. 4b: Sexploitation in *Habibi*, 150.

Fig. 4c: Sexploitation in *Habibi*, 151.

Fig. 4d: Sexploitation in *Habibi*, 152.

280   Muslim Misrepresentation and the Post-Empire Imaginary

It is precisely the spreading of her legs, the zooming in on her buttocks and her face, that both evokes the male gaze and reminds readers of porn. The French *bande dessinée* style distracts the reader from the reality that Dodola is being exploited. Thompson seems to wish to present her as a strong woman choosing to sell her body in order to feed and protect her friend; since she has no other possibility to help him, she is being exploited. *Habibi* never departs from portraying Dodola as the victimized Muslim woman. Thematically, *Habibi* takes up the issue of arranged marriages, too, which is inextricably linked to the stereotypical depiction of Muslim females.[27] Dodola's arranged marriage at the beginning of the graphic narrative is reminiscent of Stephanie Sinclair's UNICEF Photo of 2007, which depicts an eleven-year-old girl sitting on the floor next to her soon-to-be 40-year-old husband in her family's home somewhere in Afghanistan.[28] In *Habibi*, media imagery based on the emergency narrative based, in turn, on the war on terror implies that Thompson is manipulating his readers: the master narrative of the oppressed female Muslim presides over notions of agency and subjectivity. Again, it becomes evident that Dodola's character is reduced to an essentialist stereotype.

With regard to the other minor male characters, one finds example of what Shaheen refers to the Ali Baba Kit:

> To complement Arabland's desert landscapes, producers provide performers with 'Instant Ali Baba Kits.' Property masters stock the kits with curved daggers, scimitars, magic lamps, giant feather fans, and nargelihs. [...] Robed actors are presented with dark glasses, fake black beards, exaggerated noses, worry beads, and checkered bornooses.[29]

In Thompson's graphic narrative, every violent interaction includes a dagger and men wearing robes, beards and/or mustaches, turbans and glasses. Upon closer inspection, the diversity of headwear might suggest

---

[27] According to UNICEF's program on "Child Marriage," "[c]hild marriage refers to any formal marriage or informal union between a child under the age of 18 and an adult or another child."

[28] UNICEF, "UNICEF Photo of the Year 2007," December 24, 2007, www.unicef.de/informieren/aktuelles/photo-of-the-year/contest-2007.

[29] Shaheen, *Reel Bad Arabs*, 14.

a broader sense of representation, therefore changing the repertoire of homogenous attire that is attributed to Arab men.

Fig. 5: Headwear and Dress, *Habibi*, 319.

For example, instances in which the marketplace is depicted show men wearing thobes, which are associated with Kuwait or the United Arab Emirates. In the same scene, some men wear a ghutra – a rectangular headscarf with a robe. Still others wear Shalwar kameez (a tunic robe), and a few of them wear the izar, which can be found in the UAE, the Indian subcontinent and South Asia. A closer look at the headwear reveals turbans that can be associated with countries such as Iran and Afghanistan. Other head coverings such as the fez are usually worn in Morocco, Lebanon and Syria. These representations should be regarded as a strategy that obfuscates the fact that certain types of Islamic headwear and clothing can be attributed to regional and local identity. By conflating topo-geographical identities, Arabs and Muslims become indistinguishable from one another. In terms of the aesthetic rendering of the male characters' physiognomy, they are drawn as hook-nosed,

282   Muslim Misrepresentation and the Post-Empire Imaginary

bald and fat individuals.[30] Problematic, too, is the simianizatâon of the black eunuch.[31] The men are predominantly portrayed as misogynistic abusers whose actions and behavior are based on ignorance and violence. Thus, in *Habibi*, one is left with the motif of the brutal, hook-nosed, intransigent male Arab Muslim who inflicts sexual violence on the hypersexualized female Muslim.

Equally problematic is Thompson's use of Thuluth and Naskh forms of Arab calligraphy. The change of repertoire occurs through the usage of an actual Arabic word and Arabic calligraphy instead of foreign writing – or undecipherable writing appearing on, for example, tanks used in Hollywood movies that create suspicion of a dangerous Other. In the opening scene of *The English Patient* (1996), Arabic scripture is written from left to right. Among observant Muslims, Arab calligraphy never illustrates an image or appears near one (unlike the initial letter in the medieval Christian *Book of Hours*).[32] For Muslims, calligraphy is meant to allow scripture to speak for itself; what renders the words holy is their separation from images, which are seen as adulterating it.

In *Habibi*, the beautiful renderings practically force the reader to stop and appreciate them. Yet, it was not Thompson who produced all of the calligraphy appearing in the graphic novel. According to Thompson's notes, some of the calligraphy depicts Qur'an verses produced by various artists.[33] Since he credits only some pages that employ calligraphy, it is impossible to pinpoint provenance and authorship throughout the graphic narrative. Thompson asked Tunisian calligraphy artist Lassaâd Metoui to produce the following image for him (figure 6).[34]

---

[30] Historically, the hook-nosed stereotype is rooted in antisemitic and Nazi propaganda from the 1930s.

[31] See Wulf D. Hund et al., *Simianization: Apes, Gender, Class, and Race* (Münster: LIT Verlag, 2015).

[32] Cf. Catholic Church, *Book of Hours* [1524], Washington D.C., Library of Congress, accessed June 10, 2021, www.loc.gov/resource/rbc0001.2003 rosen 0014/?sp=1.

[33] Thompson, *Habibi*, 568–569.

[34] See Thompson's note on page 569, in which he credits Lassaâd Metoui calligraphy.

Fig. 6: Calligraphy by Lassaâd Metoui, *Habibi*, 405.

Metoui has also contributed calligraphy to, for example, Khalil Gibran's poetry collection *Love Letters in the Sand* (2016). Metoui and Thompson must have had some awareness of the fact that this image would be understood differently by non-Muslims than by Muslims. We can assume that any observant Muslim would find calligraphy embedded in the profile of a naked woman disrespectful: the effect of combining these two aspects would be to secularize a religious idea and break a taboo. But in a post-9/11 world, in which anti-Muslim racism is omnipresent, Muslims seek solace and inspiration in the Qur'an especially. This is not to say that artistic freedom is impermissible. Rather, Thompson should be aware that his work is not only provocative, but that the inner processing of such images requires emotional labor. Thompson creates the impression that he wants to promote interfaith dialogue. When looking at the cover, one cannot deny its startling resemblance to the Qur'an. Because Arabic scripture is written from right to left, the ostensible cover of the graphic novel would have to be located at the back. Additionally, no images are used on the cover of the Qur'an or throughout. By imprinting ornaments and the image of Dodola and Zam on a spine on the left-hand side (Japanese and Arabic books both tend to have the spine on the right), Thompson disregards the fact that a Qur'an is meant to placed upright but not with the spine facing outward.

Habibi highlights the flaws of the post-empire imaginary. Thompson's changes of repertoire underpin paradox and provisionality in the text. The graphic narrative demonstrates that empire proliferates in the present, and it possibly helps to exacerbate perennial themes in anti-Muslim discourse. The enthralled reviews of *Habibi* are not only a successful marketing scheme, they also contribute to the formation of the graphic narrative as a highly crafted theatrical peritext. The graphic narrative is in many ways akin to various interpretations of Islamo-phobia, "the new progeny of Orientalism."[35] Misrepresentations of Muslims by non-Muslim authors raise the question of those authors' need to fictionalize Muslim experience. This does not mean that non-Muslim authors should not depict Muslim experience. But doing so without any sense of writing about "the Orient," about stereotypes, or about their own misunderstanding of religious concepts within Islam is unfortunate. Appreciation and validation of Muslim representation can only occur when non-Muslim authors listen, engage meaningfully with insiders, and create responsibly.

---

[35] Khalid A. Beydoun defines Islamophobia as "[...] the new progeny of Orientalism, a worldview that casts Islam as the civilizational antithesis of the West and that is built upon the core stereotypes and baseline distortions of Islam and Muslims embedded in American institutions and the popular imagination by Orientalist theory, narratives, and law." *American Islamophobia: Understanding the Roots and Rise of Fear* (Oakland: University of California Press, 2018), 28.

Works Cited

Beydoun, Khalid A. *American Islamophobia. Understanding the Roots and Rise of Fear*. Oakland: University of California Press, 2018.

Buchenau, Barbara, and Virginia Richter. "Introduction: How to Do Things with Empires." In *Post-Empire Imaginaries? Anglophone Literature, History, and the Demise of Empires*, edited by Barbara Buchenau, Virginia Richter, and Marijke Denger. Leiden: Brill, 2015.

Bieger, Laura. "Learning from Hannah Arendt; or the Public Sphere as a Space of Appearance and the Fundamental Opacity of the Face-to-Face." In *American Counter/Publics*, edited by Ulla Haselstein et al., 37–52. Heidelberg: Universitätsverlag Winter, 2019.

Burton, Richard, Francis, Sir. *The Arabian Nights:Tales From One Thousand and One Nights*. New York: Modern Library, 2004.

Castronovo, Russ, and Susan Gillman. *States of Emergency: The Object of American Studies*. Chapel Hill: The University of North Carolina Press, 2009.

Catholic Church. *Book of Hours* [1524]. Washington D.C.: Library of Congress, accessed June 10, 2021.
www.loc.gov/resource/rbc0001.2003rosen0014/?sp=1.

"Conference Description." 66th Annual Meeting of the German Association for American Studies. U.S.-American Culture as Popular Culture. Hamburg 2019.

Creswell, Robyn. "The Graphic Novel as Orientalist Mash-Up." The New York Times, October 14, 2011. www.nytimes.com/2011/10/16/books/review/habibi-written-and-illustrated-by-craig-thompson-book-review.html.

Damluji, Nadim. "The Spectre of Orientalism in Craig Thompson's *Habibi*." *Medium*, February 20, 2017. medium.com/@ndamluji/the-spectre-of-orientalism-in-craig-thompsons-habibi-dde9d499f403.

Deloria, Philip Joseph. *Playing Indian*. New Haven: Yale University Press, 1999.

Emig, Rainer. "The Hermeneutics of Empire. Imperialism as an Interpretation Strategy." In *Post-Empire Imaginaries? Anglophone Literature, History, and the Demise of Empires*, edited by Barbara Buchenau, Virginia Richter, and Marijke Denger, 51–67. Leiden: Brill, 2015.

286   Muslim Misrepresentation and the Post-Empire Imaginary

Faber, Michel. "*Habibi* by Craig Thompson – Review." *The Guardian*, September 16, 2011. www.theguardian.com/books/2011/sep/16/habibi-craig-thompson-review.

Gibran, Khalil. *Love Letters in the Sand. The Love Poems of Khalil Gibran*. London: Souvenir Press, 2016.

Groensteen, Thierry. *The Expanding Art of Comics. Ten Modern Masterpieces*. Trans. Ann Miller. Jackson: University of Mississippi Press, 2017, 145–162.

Hiatt, Alfred. "Maps of Empires Past." In *Post-Empire Imaginaries? Anglophone Literature, History, and the Demise of Empires*, edited by Barbara Buchenau, Virginia Richter, and Marijke Denger, 1–23. Leiden: Brill, 2015.

Hund, Wulf D., Charles W. Mills, and Silvia Sebastiani. *Simianization: Apes, Gender, Class, and Race*. Münster: LIT Verlag, 2015.

Saïd, Edward W. *Orientalism*. London: Vintage Books, 1979.

Shaheen, Jack G. *Reel Bad Arabs: How Hollywood Vilifies a People*. Northampton: Olive Branch Press, 2009.

Shea, Lisa. "A Magic Carpet Ride – An Epic Sage Spanning Arab and Christian traditions and Modernitzy Dazzles the Imagination." Elle.com, September 19, 2011. www.elle.com/culture/books/reviews/a11768/habibi-review/.

Smith, Zadie. "New Books by Zadie Smith." *Harper's Magazine*, September 2011. harpers.org/archive/2011/09/new-books-29/.

Stein, Daniel. *Authorizing Superhero Comics: On the Evolution of a Serial Genre*. Columbus: The Ohio State University Press, 2021.

Stein, Daniel, and Jan-Nöel Thon. "Introduction: From Comic Strips to Graphic Novels." In *From Comic Strips to Graphic Novel: Contributions to the Theory and History of Graphic Narrative*, edited by Daniel Stein and Jan-Nöel Thon, 1–26. Berlin: de Gruyter, 2015.

Taylor, Diana. *The Archive and the Repertoire: Performing Cultural Memory in the Americas*. Durham: Duke University Press, 2003.

Thompson, Craig. *Habibi*. London: Faber & Faber, 2011.

Woloch, Alex. *The One vs. The Many: Minor Characters and the Space of the Protagonist in the Novel*. Princeton: Princeton University Press, 2003.

UNICEF. "Child Marriage," June 2021. www.unicef.org/protection/child-marriage.

---. "UNICEF Photo of the Year 2007," December 24, 2007. www.unicef.de/informieren/aktuelles/photo-of-the-year/contest-2007.

MARIUS HENDERSON

"Matrixial" Dismantlings of Anti-Black Gendered Violence in Popular Culture

In her text "Extended Notes on the Riot," Saidiya Hartman references roughly fifty artists, activists and theorists, most of whom are associated with the Black radical tradition, in one long sentence.[1] In this sentence, Hartman alludes to key concepts attributed to each person referenced and situates the referenced positions in an ongoing history of fugitivity and refusal. Hartman ends the sentence with the following phrase: "and Moor Mother making dissident music of all of this."[2] What is it about Moor Mother's music that might have inspired this phrase? What constitutes the capacity of Moor Mother's music to cause the referenced critical positions to resonate with each other, even if some of these positions diverge from each other in significant ways? I argue that the more than solely artistic, pop cultural work of Moor Mother and her collective, the Black Quantum Futurism Collective, encompasses modes of aesthetic-political practice which foster pertinent contributions to the foundational critique of structural anti-Black gendered violence and which I conceptualize as "matrixial dismantlings."

Methodologically, my text is committed to a practice of – in Fred Moten's terms – "thinking along with"[3] recent critical approaches toward formations of anti-Black gendered violence under the prevailing conditions of structural anti-Blackness. My chapter is indebted to the work of critics situated in the context of contemporary Black feminist and Afropessimist theory. I am trying to sit, think, and write *with* these

---

[1] Saidiya Hartman, "Extended Notes on the Riot," *e-flux* 105, December 2019, www.e-flux.com/journal/105/302565/extended-notes-on-the-riot/.

[2] Ibid.

[3] Fred Moten, *Black and Blur* (Durham: Duke University Press, 2017), xi.

290 Anti-Black Gendered Violence in Popular Culture

approaches as well as with the (pop) cultural productions being addressed in my writing.

I argue that the work of Moor Mother and the Black Quantum Futurism Collective seeks to dismantle the paradigmatic logic of anti-Black gendered violence and its ontological as well as political and libidinal underpinnings. Following the work of contemporary Afro-pessimist and Black feminist theorists, structural anti-Blackness can be conceptualized as being engrained in metaphysical and gratuitous, un-gendering violence as well as in intimate violence against implicitly gendered reproductivity. And the artistic works I address conceptually and critically respond to the interlacings of these manifestations of anti-Blackness.

The Black Quantum Futurism Collective was founded in Philadelphia by Camae Ayewa, aka Moor Mother, and Rasheedah Phillips. The work of the collective can be situated in the context of popular culture, though not based on grounds of quantifiable "popularity" and not only because it intersects with fields of popular music. I would situate the collective's work in popular culture due to the fact that it is "popular" in the sense of being "for the people" and generative toward the enablement of cultural productions "by the people," with respect to Black diasporic communities in particular. This notion of the "popular" can also be related to Raymond Williams's elaborations on the popular and popular culture, beginning with the derivation of the term "popular" from Latin *popularis*, "belonging to the people."[4] I argue that the Black Quantum Futurism Collective's work operates on this level of the popular. In the context of the concept-ualization of U.S. American culture as popular culture, the collective's work contests paradigmatic racialized conditions of these cultural form-ations. The collective's practices that I conceive of as "matrixial dismantlings" touch upon the ancillary function which the violent ex-clusion of "a people," enfleshed Black being, fulfills for popular cultural formations grounded in an exclusionary, racialized conceptualization of "We the People."

The Black Quantum Futurism Collective has taken to heart Audre Lorde's famous dictum that "*the master's tools will never dismantle the*

---

[4] Raymond Williams, *Keywords: A Vocabulary of Culture and Society* (London: Fontana Press, 1983), 236.

master's house [italics in original]"[5] and produces conceptual tools targeted at the dismantling of structural conditions of anti-Blackness. The collective also embodies Lorde's dictum quite literally as it responds to the ongoing history of anti-Black housing policies, especially in marginalized Philadelphian communities where the collective is situated, via not only artistic practices but also community work such as the fostering of legal support networks.[6] When read rather literally, Lorde's dictum has a hands-on dimension in the call for a practical, embodied undoing of the "master's house," as well as more figurative connotations insofar as the dismantling of the "master's house" also pertains to the undoing of the epistemic bases of anti-Blackness. In Black Quantum Futurism's practice, these spheres are enfleshed and inseparably interlaced.

Thinking with and through the "Black Matrix"

This article's conceptual angle is crucially indebted to Joy James's theorization of what she terms "the black matrix," which generates a critical practice she calls "Afrarealism."[7] James proposes that "Afrarealism sees through the lens of a black matrix."[8] She conceptualizes the Black *matrix* – from the Latin term for "womb" (and/or "breeding female"), which is derived from *mater*/"mother" – as an originary formation entangled with the emergence of structural anti-Blackness and its constitutive role in the development of modern Western political ontology, epistemology and "intimate state violence," in which

---

[5] Audre Lorde, "The Master's Tools Will Never Dismantle the Master's House," in *Sister Outsider: Essays & Speeches* (Berkeley: Crossing Press, 1984), 112.

[6] The collective also published three edited collections of experimental and theoretical writing which present Afrofuturist or Black Quantum Futurist reconceptualizations of space-time and housing justice activism, among other issues, and which are entitled: *Black Quantum Futurism: Theory & Practice, Vol. I* (2015), *Space-Time Collapse I: From the Congo to the Carolinas* (2016), and *Space-Time Collapse II: Community Futurisms* (2020).

[7] Cf. Joy James, "Afrarealism and the Black Matrix: Maroon Philosophy at Democracy's Border," *The Black Scholar* 43, no. 4 (2013): 124–131.

[8] Ibid., 124.

292   Anti-Black Gendered Violence in Popular Culture

"[v]iolations of black productivity coexist with terror against black reproductivity."[9] She elaborates further: "The official chronology of and narratives about violence and terror that constitute U.S. democracy's borders" – from enslavement to mass incarceration – "crowd out the black matrix, displacing it from philosophical inquiries into subjugation."[10]

However, James's aim is not to position more public incidents of anti-Black violence against male-gendered persons against anti-Black intimate violence that targets female-gendered reproductivity. She points out that her invocation of Afrarealism and the black matrix "is not [concerned] about which (trans)gendered being suffers most under racial subjugation."[11]

Joy James's genealogy of the Black matrix resonates with Hartman's meditations on the marginalization of Black women's reproductive labor in "narratives of black insurgency, resistance, and refusal."[12] Hartman also invokes a matrixial vocabulary in her delineation of racial slavery and its afterlife: "The modern world follows the belly. Gestational language has been key to describing the world-making and world-breaking capacities of racial slavery."[13] Moreover, Hartman also comments on the relative lack of visibility granted to Black feminized reproductive labor in accounts of resistance against anti-Blackness:

> Where does the *impossible domestic* fit into the general strike? What is the text of her insurgency and the genre of her refusal? What visions of the future world encourage her to run, or propel her flight? [...] Strategies of endurance and subsistence do not yield easily to the grand narrative of revolution, nor has a space been cleared for the sex worker, welfare mother, and domestic laborer in the annals of the black radical tradition.[14]

This matrixial notion of insurgent Black un/feminized reproductive labor reverberates in the work of the Black Quantum Futurism

9   Ibid., 125.
10   Ibid., 126.
11   Ibid.
12   Saidiya Hartman, "The Belly of the World: A Note on Black Women's Labors," *Souls* 18, no. 1 (2016): 171.
13   Ibid., 166.
14   Ibid., 171.

Collective, perhaps most explicitly in the work of Camae Ayewa, whose stage name, Moor Mother, already embodies the matrixial. Moor Mother amplifies perspectives of Black reproductive laborers and draws attention to the formative function of their "people rearing" (un/popular) work which forms the basis for cultural work more generally, while being structurally exposed to assaults. The matrixial is invoked in Ayewa's work via a commitment to concomitant interlacing and laceration, to "separation-in-jointness,"[15] and thus to the notion of the "matrixial," as Bracha L. Ettinger has theorized it and from whom I am drawing this term. According to Ettinger, the matrixial, an enfleshed metaphor, constitutes a mode of trans-subjective relationality that is conceptually modeled after a matrix, that is, after a form which becomes materialized as an outside which is also an inside, and which mediates the meeting and thriving of two or more bodies. Ettinger defines the matrixial as being enfolded in an "affective economy" in "which the feminine (neither male nor female) is fully active and informing knowledge and the ethical realm."[16] For Ettinger, a matrixial form carries the potential for "differentiation in co-emergence." She attributes this matrixial potentiality to bodies of all genders while simultaneously defining the matrixial as "feminine" and "neither male nor female."[17] Her matrixial theory thus resignifies heteronormative, binary conceptualizations of maternity and implicitly denaturalizes the equation of matrixiality with cis-femininity.

Sounding/Thinking Matrixially

The Black Quantum Futurism Collective does not enact pop cultural, politico-aesthetic practices that perpetuate narratives of progressively linear, vertical rising-above or uplifting "respectability politics." Rather, Black Quantum Futurism's practices are committed to practices of layering, surrounding, enveloping and enfleshment, that is, practices to which I would refer as matrixial. I will turn now to the musical output of

---

[15] Bracha L. Ettinger, *The Matrixial Borderspace* (Minneapolis: University of Minnesota Press, 2006), 140.

[16] Bracha L. Ettinger, "Matrixial Trans-Subjectivity," *Theory, Culture & Society* 23, nos. 2–3 (2006): 218.

[17] Ibid., 218–219.

294   Anti-Black Gendered Violence in Popular Culture

the Black Quantum Futurism Collective and Moor Mother, which diverges from hegemonic modes of contemporary popular as well as avant-garde music.

Robin James concedes that, in terms of their dramaturgic structure, recent mainstream pop songs no longer simply proceed in a linear progressive manner and no longer propose an outlook toward redemptive futurity.[18] Noisy dissonances and disruptive intensities, which may even be linked to traumatic shocks, have been incorporated into contemporary pop songs lyrically as well as in terms of musical form. However, the incorporation of these elements, which might once have been regarded as avant-garde and transgressive, ultimately serves to maintain the preservation of the socio-economic status quo.[19] Robin James defines this status quo as neoliberal and links the increased incorporation of disruptive intensities to particular resilience discourses. In a neoliberal context, resilience amounts to the individualized ability to continuously endure and quickly recover from instances of distress. Instances of severe distress even become desirable to individuals if they are able to supersede these experiences and generate surplus value from them, according to Robin James.[20]

The sonic and verbicovisual intensities the Black Quantum Futurism Collective disseminates, however, neither serve antiquated avant-garde aesthetics of transgression, nor do they perpetuate the neoliberal paradigm of individualized resilience. The intensities which permeate Moor Mother's musical output include reverberations of collectively experienced instances of anti-Black un/gendered violence in conjunction with resonant re-soundings of enfleshed acts of survival, refusal, and care in the face of said violence – not geared toward individual gain, but devoted to an ante- or sub-subjective "we" beyond merely representational modes of resistance and beyond individualistic "rags to riches" narratives, or, in terms of affective politics, narratives of the successful supersession of individualized trauma.

[18] Cf. Robin James, *Resilience & Melancholy: Pop Music, Feminism, Neoliberalism* (Winchester: Zero Books, 2015), 60–61.

[19] Cf. Robin James, *The Sonic Episteme: Acoustic Resonance, Neoliberalism, and Biopolitics* (Durham: Duke University Press, 2019), 40–53.

[20] Cf. ibid., 8–12; 43–48.

Sound, and thinking both through and with sound,[21] is essential to the Black Quantum Futurism Collective's matrixial dismantlings of anti-Black gendered violence. The coupling of thinking and sounding disentangles thinking from its predominant association with vision, which it has carried throughout Western modernity. Hegel-inspired self/other dialectics and similar renditions of subjectivation as well as representational politics of recognition appear to rely upon ocular-centric paradigms. The Black Quantum Futurism Collective does not reproduce spectacular re-presentations of Black death, whether in visual or another form, but generates conceptual fields where modes of critically thinking through repercussions of anti-Black gendered violence can reverberate and matrixially unfold.

Reverberation subdues representation in the work of Black Quantum Futurism. The layered soundscapes of Black Quantum Futurism and Moor Mother can be envisioned as fugitive "e/scapes" – for instance, in two tracks from the project *The Afterlife of Events*,[22] which is dedicated to Sandra Bland[23] and whose sonic layers consist of an audio recording of Bland's brutal arrest, samples of a 1940s gospel choir recording and analog synthesizer sounds. In these sounding escapes, an ethereal

---

[21] I am drawing on the interwoven notions of "thinking sound/sound thinking" from the work of Weheliye. Cf. Alexander G. Weheliye, *Phonographies: Grooves in Sonic Afro-Modernity* (Durham: Duke University Press, 2005), 8–12; 199 ff.

[22] Cf. Black Quantum Futurism, *The Afterlife of Events*, December 2015, www.blackwomxntemporal.net/the-afterlife-of-events.

[23] Cf. African American Policy Forum, *Say Her Name: Resisting Brutality against Black Women*, last modified July 2015, static1.squarespace.com/static/53f20d90e4b0b80451158d8c/t/560c068ee4b0af26f72741df/14436286 86535/AAPF_SMN_Brief_Full_singles-min.pdf: "On July 10, 28-year-old Sandra Bland was pulled over for failing to signal a lane change, and, as a video of her arrest shows, was pinned to the ground and surrounded by police officers. Bland was heard questioning the officers about why they had slammed her head to the ground, and complaining that she could not hear. Officers charged her with assault and held her in the Waller County Jail. Bland was found dead in her cell three days later. Bland had recently driven from suburban Chicago to Texas to begin a new job at her alma mater, Texas Prairie View A & M. Officials maintain that her death was a suicide, but Bland's friends and family members adamantly reject this explanation and suspect foul play."

296 Anti-Black Gendered Violence in Popular Culture

communal enfleshedness, becomes palpable but not palatable. These soundscapes evoke refusals of capture. The layered voices of an emergent ensemble touch one another under conditions of impossibility, resounding from within a "matrix of (im)possibility,"[24] from within the structural conditions of gratuitous anti-Black violence.

Again, Black Quantum Futurism's work does not focus on the representation of exceptional individuals and their spectacular overcoming of adversity but rather confronts the pervasiveness of anti-Black gendered violence in the everyday. This becomes especially pertinent in the work of Moor Mother, whose genre-defying music draws on a broad range of generic influences, from free jazz and rap to afro-punk traditions, and ambient soundscapes, as well as on the aesthetics of genres such as black metal, industrial and noise. The latter are genres of un/popular music notorious for certain white supremacist and misogynist tendencies, to say the least, and which are subversively resignified in Moor Mother's musical work.

Moor Mother undermines conventional conceptualizations of noise, as standing in binary opposition to "silence," "signal," or "music." Inspired by the work of Marie Thompson, I would describe Moor Mother's take on noise as "object-oriented." Whereas subject-oriented approaches toward noise are embedded in liberal humanist conceptualizations of individual taste[25] an object-oriented approach towards noise focuses on what sound is capable of doing, whether it is invested in the "power-over" or the "power-to," and not primarily in what it means.[26] This perspective renders noise more ambiguous, open-ended, or *matrixial*, and likewise "popular," in the original sense of the term, as horizontally belonging to the people.

Moreover, what also links the occurrence of noise in Moor Mother's music to the popular, as a form of originary commonness, is that noise emerges as a quotidian phenomenon. Noise in its violent form appears

---

[24] Frank B. Wilderson III, *Red, White & Black: Cinema and the Structure of U.S. Antagonisms* (Durham: Duke University Press, 2010), 84.

[25] Cf. Marie Thompson, *Beyond Unwanted Sound: Noise, Affect and Aesthetic Moralism* (New York: Bloomsbury Academic, 2017), 17–23.

[26] Cf. guestlistener, "Beyond the Grandiose and the Seductive: Marie Thompson on Noise," *Sounding Out!*, April 10, 2017, soundstudies blog.com/2017/04/10/noise-beyond-the-grandiose-and-the-seductive-an-interview-with-marie-thompson/.

or, rather, occurs, and *is* there in Moor Mother's music. I would also regard the noise that pervades Moor Mother's music as a manifestation of what Christina Sharpe has termed "the weather," the "total climate" of anti-Blackness.[27] And this repetitive, non-linear "total climate" of anti-Blackness is evoked throughout Moor Mother's song lyrics and poetry, as the quote from the song "Deadbeat Protest" illustrates, for instance:

> [...] Trying to save my black life by fetishizing my dead life
> No, get away from me
>
> You can see my dead body at the protest
> You can see my dead body at the protest [...][28]

The lyrics, which are shouted in a hardcore punk manner, comment quite explicitly on the prevalent fetishistic aestheticization of Black death, in which Blackness is denied life and treated as disposable, even in certain seemingly "progressive," predominantly white liberal humanist artistic and activist practices. The phrase "You can see my dead body at the protest" is repeated four times in the chorus and thus draws attention to the historical and contemporary repetitions of police killings of Black persons as well as the violent injuries and killings by executive forces which have repeatedly occurred at protests against anti-Black violence. Concomitantly, the phrase "you can *see* my dead body" critically alludes to the spectacularizing circulation of images of Black death, which fulfills an animating aesthetic function in structurally anti-Black, (popular) cultural settings.

Without resorting to abstract metaphoricity, Moor Mother/Camea Aywe expresses a refusal to be fetishistically encased in social and/or biological death. And in many of Ayewa's lyrics, the repetitive violation of Black life is linked to assaults on Black female-gendered reproductivity. This can be seen in the following quotes from Ayewa's poetry

---

[27] Christina Sharpe, *In the Wake: On Blackness and Being* (Durham: Duke University Press, 2016), 21.

[28] Moor Mother, "Deadbeat Protest," track 3 on *Fetish Bones*, compact disc (Don Giovanni Records, 2016).

298   Anti-Black Gendered Violence in Popular Culture

collection *Fetish Bones*, which also partially appear in song lyrics on the
Moor Mother record of the same name[29]:

> [...] / that you must be both / dead and alive / want us to be / dead when
> a man wants to beat us / when they wanna rape us / dead when the police
> kill me / alive when the police kill you / alive when it's time to be in
> they kitchens / when it's time to push out they babies [...] [30]

> [...] the continual humiliation / of a black women's body / remember? /
> it happen again/ two days ago / right here in Philadelphia // [...] at this
> point we are under siege / [...][31]

Moor Mother's approach toward anti-Black gendered violence is
invested in practices of caring sustenance, materialized in sonic
strategies of recurrence, such as delay, reverb and looping: "i am
looking after us / alla us / those hiding inside hiding."[32] Sampling, as a
practice popularized by hip-hop, is used to interlace various
temporalities and historical events, "hiding inside hiding." These
matrixial strategies branch out into reruns and remixes, and into gestures
of caring for and carrying on *with* another. Hence, these are conceptual
and embodied practices of improvised relationality in the face of the
perpetual onslaught against relationality, which, as Patrice D. Douglass
and Frank B. Wilderson III argue, is inherent to structural anti-
Blackness.[33]

Moreover, Moor Mother's practice of sampling strays from merely
"digging in the crates," as the practice of finding samples is referred to
in hip-hop contexts. Moor Mother's sampling supplements and overdubs
digging with practices of layering, enfolding and enfleshment. Digging
may appear to carry phallogocentric overtones, especially if rendered as

---

[29] Spelling and syntax in all quoted material has been reproduced exactly.

[30] Camae Ayewa, "Battlefield Replica Symmetry Retrospectra," in *Fetish
Bones* (Philadelphia: House of Future Sciences Books, 2016), 13–14.

[31] Camae Ayewa, "Sleep Study," in *Fetish Bones* (Philadelphia: House of
Future Sciences Books, 2016), 37.

[32] Camae Ayewa, *Analog Fluids* (Philadelphia: House of Future Sciences
Books, 2019), 66.

[33] Cf. Patrice Douglass and Frank Wilderson, "The Violence of Presence:
Metaphysics in a Blackened World," *The Black Scholar* 43, no. 4 (2013):
117.

a practice which reaches toward some kind of originary presence.[34] Layering and enfolding are more horizontally-oriented motions. Once again, these practices are not only evoked on a metaphorical level but also "literally" and materially enacted via the implementation of audio-visual techniques of super(im)position and matrixial constellation. And in a self-reflexive poetological move, a speaker in one of Ayewa's poems explicitly conjoins epistemological digging with the multi-vectorial, matrixial act of tangling: "we out here anti god be no more wires / digging in tangling our thoughts."[35]

Anti-Black Un/Gendered Violence – Enfleshment – Ethereal Departures

Many Black feminist critics state that the call for paying more public attention to lethal state violence directed at Black cis and trans women, trans men, femmes, and gender non-conforming, intersex, and non-binary people ought not to be pitted against the higher attention around killings of Black cis men. Patrice D. Douglass, for instance, emphasizes that "the issue of Black gender is more complex than the dichoto-mization of death."[36] What renders Black gender somewhat paradoxical and difficult to grasp, according to Douglass and other Afropessimist theorists, is that gender is grounded in the category of the "human," from whose ontological and epistemological realm Black positionalities are constitutively excluded by being subjected to "the openness and gratuity of (un)gendering violence."[37] Therefore, the thinking of Black gender undermines and "dismantles" the paradigmatic assumptions of (humanist) gender, as Douglass states: "Black gender as a theorem, not a thing, dismantles the predicate of gender. [...]. The core of Black feminist concerns is how to account for the gravity of gender violences that lack a proper name."[38] And this dismantling capacity of Black

---

[34] Cf. Simone White, *Dear Angel of Death* (Brooklyn: Ugly Duckling Presse, 2018), 76–86.

[35] Camae Ayewa, "Circuity City," in *Analog Fluids* (Philadelphia: House of Future Sciences Books, 2019), 27.

[36] Patrice D. Douglass, "Black Feminist Theory for the Dead and Dying," *Theory & Event* 2, no. 1 (2018): 108.

[37] Ibid., 109.

[38] Ibid. 116.

300 Anti-Black Gendered Violence in Popular Culture

gender echoes in the matrixial practices of the Black Quantum Futurism Collective.

The notion of the "ether," both as the medium for sonic radio waves and, in its archaic sense, as a "rarefied and elastic substance formerly thought to permeate all space, including the interstices between the particles of ordinary matter,"[39] becomes a helpful notion to invoke when thinking about sound and un/gendered violence alongside Black Quantum Futurism's aesthetic-political practices. A constellation of these practices, with notions of matrixial dismantling and the ether, palpably enables further critical resonances. Black Quantum Futurism matrixially dis/mantles and permeates the ether precisely because it sifts through and peels the layers of the epistemic, ontological and experiential conditions of possibility in world-making anti-Black un/gendered violence; for instance, by listening to and touching upon the "After Images"[40] of the "reproductive afterlife of slavery."[41] Black Quantum Futurism thus utilizes sound to un/think to what extent "the world" is held together by anti-Blackness, by the ontologized reduction of Black bodies to "flesh." Hortense J. Spillers's theorization of the flesh has recently been evoked in conjunction with the notion of the ether, leading to a conceptualization of Black flesh, as also being somewhat interlaced with the ether in the sense of forming the abjected pillars of "the world of Man"[42] qua their constitutive relegation to a sphere of social death. Alexander G. Weheliye elaborates on the connection between flesh, as created by anti-Black dispossession, and the ether:

> In the absence of kin, family, gender, belonging, language, personhood, property, and official records, among many other factors, what remains is the flesh, the living speaking, thinking, feeling, and imagining flesh: the ether that holds together the world of Man while at the same time forming

[39] "ether, n." *OED Online*, December 2021, www.oed.com/view/Entry/64728.

[40] This is the title of a song on Moor Mother's second LP, *Analog Fluids of Sonic Black Holes*, vinyl LP (Don Giovanni Records, 2019).

[41] Cf. Alys Eve Weinbaum, *The Afterlife of Reproductive Slavery: Biocapitalism and Black Feminism's Philosophy of History* (Durham: Duke University Press, 2019), 1–6.

[42] Alexander G. Weheliye, *Habeas Viscus: Racializing Assemblages, Biopolitics, and Black Feminist Theories of the Human* (Durham: Duke University Press, 2014), 40.

the condition of possibility for this world's demise. It's the end of the world – don't you know that yet?[43]

Due to its constitutive function, albeit by negating erasure, flesh, which in/forms "ether," also holds the potential to end this world – meaning the epistemic, political ontological and metaphysical basis of the world, as Weheliye and other critics, such as J. Kameron Carter and Sarah Jane Cervenak, claim. Carter and Cervenak argue accordingly: "The ether of blackness is, indeed, the condition of possibility of this world, the mythic ground that intoxicates and fortifies whiteness, that which is held and expelled."[44] In addition to its (meta-)physical connotations, the notion of the ether encapsulates aspects of (sonic) artistic practice for Weheliye, Carter and Cervenak, as exemplified in the allusion to Sun Ra's Afrofuturist jazz in the Weheliye quote above.

As intimated, the concepts of Weheliye, Carter, and Cervenak are fundamentally inspired by Spillers's theorization of Black bodies' violent reduction to "ungendered" flesh under enslavement. Bodies with wombs were denied the hegemonically humanizing feature of gender, reduced to commodified and thus accumulable nonhuman objects, while simultaneously being exploited for their reproductive capacities, which are gendered "female" within the normative heterosexual matrix, and subjected to sexualized violence.[45]

Black Quantum Futurism's and Moor Mother's dismantling practices of sound-thinking evoke Black un/gendered flesh as a matrixial, ether-like, mantling structure, which, qua being constitutively excluded and exposed to gratuitous violence, [46] has been relegated to fulfilling a para-digmatic function in the development of "the human" and "human culture" for centuries and up until today – e.g., as condensed in the image of a dead Black body which can be used by the entire non-Black

---

[43] Ibid.

[44] J. Kameron Carter and Sarah Jane Cervenak, "Black Ether," *CR: The New Centennial Review* 16, no. 2 (2016): 205.

[45] Cf. Hortense J. Spillers, "Mama's Baby, Papa's Maybe: An American Grammar Book," in *Black, White, and in Color: Essays on American Literature and Culture* (Chicago: Chicago University Press, 2003), 204–208.

[46] See Wilderson's seminal claim that Black "grammars of suffering" have been constituted by the exposure to gratuitous violence since the transatlantic enslavement trade. Cf. Wilderson, *Red, White & Black*, 11–16.

302   Anti-Black Gendered Violence in Popular Culture

world as a raft to survive a flooding, which appears in Moor Mother's song "Time Float."[47]

Concomitantly, the matrixial evocation of flesh in Moor Mother's work holds a certain potential that hints at the undoing of a world whose entire "semantic field" "is sutured by anti-Black solidarity," to use Wilderson's terms.[48] Moor Mother tunes into the enfleshed ether which surrounds and permeates a (popular) culture that is structurally entrenched in white supremacy and anti-Blackness. Two of Moor Mother's full-length LPs lyrically end in renditions of ongoingness as well as in visions of potential endings of a world that is grounded in anti-Black un/gendered violence. The lyrics to the final track, titled "Passing of Time," on her 2019 album, *Analog Fluids of Sonic Black Holes*, encompass the lines: "it's so soft to the skin / when you land on the cotton fields of democracy / it's so soft / and my momma, my grand-momma, my great-great-grandmother they picked so much cotton they saved the world / […] all by themselves / and it's so soft."[49] I read the quoted lyrics as instances of what I would term metonymic sarcasm. I read the reference to the soft enwrapping of skin by cotton picked by the speaker's enslaved ancestors who "saved the world" – "the human world," constituted by anti-Blackness – as a sarcastic recitation and reminder that, in the words of Alexis Pauline Gumbs, "it is slaveship womb work to make sure every time humans be what they be."[50] Moor Mother's song lyrics and Ayewa's poetry are filled with instances of sarcasm, which I would read as a further emanation of the enfleshed matrixial dismantling of anti-Black un/gendered violence. Interestingly, the term "sarcasm" is etymologically related to the flesh, as it is derived from Greek *sarkazein* "tear flesh" and "speak bitterly."[51] Ayewa's lyrics "speak bitterly" through the flesh. Moreover, Ayewa's sarcasm undermines pathologizing renditions of Black motherhood and matrixiality,

---

[47]   Moor Mother, "Time Float," track 13 on *Fetish Bones*, compact disc (Don Giovanni Records, 2016).

[48]   Wilderson, *Red, White & Black*, 58.

[49]   Moor Mother, "Passing of Time," track 13 on *Analog Fluids of Sonic Black Holes*, vinyl LP (Don Giovanni Records, 2019).

[50]   Alexis Pauline Gumbs, *Spill: Scenes of Black Feminist Fugitivity* (Durham: Duke University Press, 2016), 129.

[51]   "sarcasm, n." *OED Online*, December 2021, www.oed.com/view/Entry/170938.

and thus partakes in a practice which, in the words of Jared Sexton, could be depicted as "a transvaluation of pathology itself, something like an embrace of pathology without pathos."[52] Moor Mother's matrixial embrace of "pathology without pathos," which un/folds qua sarcasm, critically intervenes into re-soundings of what Spillers has theorized as the cultural "vestibular"[53] function that Black flesh has fulfilled for the emergence of hegemonic U.S. American culture, including popular culture. Traversing the "cultural vestibularity"[54] of the flesh, Moor Mother's sarcasm manifests as counter-fetishistic, sarcolemmal[55] matrixiality. It lays bare the *Fetish Bones* of anti-Black un/gendered violence while simultaneously proliferating layers of communal en-fleshment in waves of visions of possible endings of an anti-Black world: "its over / endings / retrocausality / aint no more / [...] / for you to feed on and / fetishize;"[56] "if you kill us all / we hold so much gravity / yall gon float away."[57]

This is what constitutes matrixial dismantlings of anti-Black un/gendered violence as the laying bare of constitutive epistemic layers and a concurrent spreading out and layering anew, in folds and un-foldings, in loops of trauma and "loopholes of retreat," in popular culture, by and for the people, and beyond. Moor Mother's and Black Quantum Futurism's aesthetic-political practices affirm un/gendered reproductivity, sustenance and endurance by sounding out and thinking through sound without spilling over into fantasies of teleological re-demption. Their matrixial dismantlings seek to maximize critical and

---

[52] Jared Sexton, "The Social Life of Social Death: On Afro-Pessimism and Black Optimism," *InTensions* 5 (2011): 28.

[53] Spillers, 207.

[54] Ibid.

[55] Alluding to the sarcolemma, i.e., the "fine transparent tubular sheath investing muscular fibre." "sarcolemma, n." *OED Online*, December 2021, www.oed.com/view/Entry/170977. Based on its etymology, "sarcolemma" literally means "fleshy husk," and I am invoking it as an allusion to the constitutive, enveloping function which violated and accumulated Black flesh has fulfilled for the "functioning" of Western modernity.

[56] Camae Ayewa, "Full Culture," in *Fetish Bones* (Philadelphia: House of Future Sciences Books, 2016), 115.

[57] Camae Ayewa, "Haiku Moor Gravity," in *Fetish Bones* (Philadelphia: House of Future Sciences Books, 2016), 93.

possibly fugitive potential from within a position of being exposed to the ostensible permanence of structural anti-Blackness, which holds potentiality in a permanent state of crisis.

Works Cited

African American Policy Forum. *Say Her Name: Resisting Brutality against Black Women*, last modified July 2015.
static1.squarespace.com/static/53f20d90e4b0b80451158d8c/t/560c0
68ee4b0af26f72741df/1443628686535/AAPF_SMN_Brief_Full_sin
gles-min.pdf.

Ayewa, Camae. *Fetish Bones*. Philadelphia: House of Future Sciences Books, 2016.

---. *Analog Fluids*. Philadelphia: House of Future Sciences Books, 2019.

Black Quantum Futurism. *The Afterlife of Events*, December 2015. blackwomxntemporal.net/the-afterlife-of-events.

Carter, J. Kameron, and Sarah Jane Cervenak. "Black Ether." *CR: The New Centennial Review* 16, no. 2 (2016): 203–224.

Douglass, Patrice D. "Black Feminist Theory for the Dead and Dying." *Theory & Event* 21, no. 1 (2018): 106–123.

Douglass, Patrice, and Frank Wilderson. "The Violence of Presence: Metaphysics in a Blackened World." *The Black Scholar* 43.4 (2013): 117–123.

"ether, n." *OED Online*, December 2021.
www.oed.com/view/Entry/64728.

Ettinger, Bracha L. *The Matrixial Borderspace*. Minneapolis: University of Minnesota Press, 2006.

---. "Matrixial Trans-Subjectivity." *Theory, Culture & Society* 23, nos. 2-3 (2006): 218–222.

guestlistener. "Beyond the Grandiose and the Seductive: Marie Thompson on Noise." *Sounding Out!*, April 10, 2017. soundstudiesblog.com/2017/04/10/noise-beyond-the-grandiose-and-the-seductive-an-interview-with-marie-thompson/.

Gumbs, Alexis Pauline. *Spill: Scenes of Black Feminist Fugitivity*. Durham: Duke University Press, 2016.

Hartman, Saidiya. "The Belly of the World: A Note on Black Women's Labors." *Souls* 18, no. 1 (2016): 166–173.

---. "Extended Notes on the Riot." *e-flux* 105, December 2019. e-flux.com/journal/105/302565/extended-notes-on-the-riot/.

James, Joy. "Afrarealism and the Black Matrix: Maroon Philosophy at Democracy's Border." *The Black Scholar* 43, no. 4 (2013): 124–131.

James, Robin. *Resilience & Melancholy: Pop Music, Feminism, Neoliberalism*. Winchester: Zero Books, 2015.

---. *The Sonic Episteme: Acoustic Resonance, Neoliberalism, and Biopolitics*. Durham: Duke University Press, 2019.

Lorde, Audre. "The Master's Tools Will Never Dismantle the Master's House." In *Sister Outsider: Essays and Speeches*, 110–113. Berkeley: Crossing Press, 1984.

Moor Mother. *Fetish Bones*. Compact disc. Don Giovanni Records, 2016.

---. *Analog Fluids of Sonic Black Holes*. Vinyl LP. Don Giovanni Records, 2019.

Moten, Fred. *Black and Blur*. Durham: Duke University Press, 2017.

"sarcasm, n." *OED Online*, December 2021. www.oed.com/view/Entry/170938.

"sarcolemma, n." *OED Online*, December 2021. www.oed.com/view/Entry/170977.

Sexton, Jared. "The Social Life of Social Death: On Afro-Pessimism and Black Optimism." *InTensions* 5 (2011): 1–47.

Sharpe, Christina. *In the Wake: On Blackness and Being*. Durham: Duke University Press, 2016.

Spillers, Hortense J. "Mama's Baby, Papa's Maybe: An American Grammar Book." In *Black, White, and in Color: Essays on American Literature and Culture*, 203–229. Chicago: University of Chicago Press, 2003.

Thompson, Marie. *Beyond Unwanted Sound: Noise, Affect and Aesthetic Moralism*. New York: Bloomsbury Academic, 2017.

Weheliye, Alexander G. *Phonographies: Grooves in Sonic Afro-Modernity*. Durham: Duke University Press, 2005.

---. *Habeas Viscus: Racializing Assemblages, Biopolitics, and Black Feminist Theories of the Human*. Durham: Duke University Press, 2014.

Weinbaum, Alys Eve. *The Afterlife of Reproductive Slavery: Biocapitalism and Black Feminism's Philosophy of History*. Durham: Duke University Press, 2019.

White, Simone. *Dear Angel of Death*. Brooklyn: Ugly Duckling Presse, 2018.

Wilderson, Frank B., III. *Red, White & Black: Cinema and the Structure of U.S. Antagonisms*. Durham: Duke University Press, 2010.

Williams, Raymond. *Keywords: A Vocabulary of Culture and Society.* London: Fontana Press, 1983.

MARIAN OFORI-AMOAFO

Different Ways of (Not) Being Black: Blaxploitation Meets Post-Soul in *I Am Not Sidney Poitier*

Introduction

> I'll take their stale old crappy shows and air them again and again until they sit in people's heads like jingles [...] Society, some like to call it the culture these days, shouldn't be subjected to that kind of pernicious and deleterious rubbish [...] That's why I'm going to take over television and air that trash every day several times a day instead of only once a week. That way we'll all become desensitized to its harmful and consumptive effects by sheer overexposure. That's what I mean by jingles. They'll become meaningless and innocuous little ditties.[1]

In the above quotation, the character Ted Turner – a business mogul and guardian to the eponymous protagonist of the novel *I Am Not Sidney Poitier*, and an allusion to the real-life founder of CNN and president of Turner Broadcasting – announces the critique of mass media entertainment that is central to the novel during a conversation with the character Not Sidney Poitier. The subsequent abrupt transition from Turner's critique to a talk about recreational sailing, which follows the quoted lines, exemplifies the novel's fast-moving collage of information, which seems to imitate the practice of zapping through TV channels in its formal transition.

Since Keith B. Mitchell and Robin G. Vander, editors of *Perspectives on Percival Everett,* brought attention to the inadequate scholarship on *I Am Not Sidney Poitier* author Everett, his writing has

---

[1] Percival Everett, *I Am Not Sidney Poitier* (Minneapolis: Graywolf Press, 2009), 12–13.

310 Different Ways of (Not) Being Black

garnered more critical examination. Criticism and categorization of Everett and his contemporaries' work as "experimental," and therefore inaccessible and foreign to the African American experience, stems from the belief that these authors' inventive styles do not convey "authentic" Black experiences.[2] Everett's rich array of novels, short stories, and poetry show that this claim is inaccurate. Vander and Mitchell argue that post-1960s African American writers like Everett engage in rewritings and the pluralization of blackness, representing a broad spectrum rather than a single view of African American lifeworld and culture.[3] Despite these inaccessibility claims, Everett successfully narrates the futility and pitfalls of essentializing Black identity in this entertaining novel.

I Am Not Sidney Poitier follows Not Sidney's episodic movements, which are modelled on the *bildungsroman*, as he attempts to redefine himself against mainstream hyper-visual and stereotypical depictions. I argue that Not Sidney's performances interrogate the typecast roles of Sidney Poitier through parodical and ironical allusions. Everett positions his novel as a highly entertaining antidote to various film and television history trends, entertainment, and popular culture. For African Americans, the "all-Black" film portrayed an "Other lifestyle rather than the normal one."[4] This alternate depiction, I contend, symbolizes African Americans' othered position in US cultural history. The protagonist's identity performance thus subverts socially sanctioned otherness and stereotypical characterization through his newfound agency as a financially independent young man in the aesthetically liberated space of the novel. Hence, Not Sidney 'sticks it' to socially instituted racism, stereotypical representation fueled by constrained Hollywood financing, and the entertainment media.

The intersections between African American culture, intellectual work, politics, cultural advancement, and social protest defined African American arts for the better part of the 19th and 20th centuries. Therefore,

---

[2]   Keith B. Mitchell and Robin G. Vander, "Introduction: Changing the Frame, Framing the Change: The Art of Percival Everett," in *Perspectives on Percival Everett*, eds. Keith B. Mitchell and Robin G. Vander (Oxford: University Press of Mississippi, 2013), xi.

[3]   Ibid.

[4]   Novotny Lawrence, *Blaxploitation Films of the 1970s: Blackness and Genre* (London: Routledge, 2008), 8.

culture and identity are entangled, especially for African Americans, because society perceives their identity through race constructs. According to Paul C. Taylor, "race-talk" is a complex, interpretive, and expressive language that produces "race-thinking" – the sorting of people based on appearance and ancestry.[5] Race-talk allows individuals to make sense of the unfamiliar by projecting the familiar,[6] making race-talk and race-thinking subjective and arbitrary. The language of race mediates our experiences and allows for the negative manipulation of race, leading to "overly rigid generalizations about the behavior of racially defined groups" and produces racial stereotyping.[7]

Identity discourses – closely connected to race and ethnicity – have shifted from that of a stable marker to a complex signifier that is always in flux. Judith Butler, for instance, argues that gender is a societal construct and that "performativity," repetitive acts of doing gender, consolidates gender binaries.[8] Butler contends that "[t]he iterability of performativity is a theory of agency,"[9] meaning that agency is neither apolitical nor free from power. Agency, then, depends on power to be realized.[10] Concerning racial identity, Casey Hayman reiterates Fred Moten's argument that "black subjectivity is essentially performative."[11] Hayman advocates for a "performative paradigm" in rethinking Black agency and expression beyond "attempts to correct the negative, hyper-visible stereotypes perpetuated within the dominant white gaze."[12] Everett's titular character signals the problem of identity formation vis-à-vis stereotypical ascriptions and racialism. The perpetuation of stereotypes in the "all-Black" film shows Hollywood's insufficient grasp of

---

[5]   Paul C. Taylor, *Race: A Philosophical Introduction* (Cambridge: Polity, 2004), 24.

[6]   Ibid., 5.

[7]   Ibid., 5–7.

[8]   Judith Butler, *Gender Trouble: Feminism and the Subversion of Identity* (New York: Routledge Classics, 2007), xv.

[9]   Ibid., xxv.

[10] Ibid.

[11] Casey Hayman, "Hypervisible Man: Techno-Performativity and Televisual Blackness in Percival Everett's *I Am Not Sidney Poitier*," *MELUS* 39, no. 3 (2014): 137.

[12] Ibid.

312   Different Ways of (Not) Being Black

Black culture[13] and helps explain Not Sidney's predicament. The iconography of Sidney Poitier's work in the 1960s and 1970s greatly influenced representations of the Black male body on the silver screen. Blaxploitation films critiqued Poitier's "wholesome" performances of acceptable Hollywood blackness.[14] Everett's novel cites yet denies both Hollywood and blaxploitation representations through the protagonist's resistance to stereotypical typecasting and to homogenizing representations of Black identity.

This article argues that the novel employs intertextual and intermedial strategies that dovetail with Mark Anthony Neal and Bertram D. Ashe's African American "post-soul aesthetics" to interrogate problematic representations of Black identity. First, I interpret the parodical and ironical re-enactments of Sidney Poitier films, which serve as intertextual and intermedial points of reference in the novel, not only as a corrective strategy to re-script Black identity away from the often-one-dimensional characterizations portrayed in blaxploitation films, but as a critique of the consumerism of pop culture and entertainment industry symbolized by Hollywood. Second, I analyze these literary enactments as a strategy "to trouble blackness"[15] from within the African American community by highlighting the repressive colorcoding which perpetuates stereotypes. Third, I argue that the intertextual and intermedial references function as subversive strategies against the deployment of blaxploitation tropes for identification and to restore agency to Black identity performance.

Black Representation and the Ambivalence of the Blaxploitation Turn

In *I Am Not Sidney Poitier* Everett presents a dynamic interplay between postmodernism, intermediality, and blaxploitation. I observe that the

---

[13] See Lawrence, *Blaxploitation Films*, 7.

[14] See John Semley, "Who's Bleeding Whom? Analyzing the Cultural Flows of Blaxploitation Cinema, Then and Now," *Cineaction* 80 (2010): 25; Mark Anthony Neal, *Soul Babies: Black Popular Culture and the Post Soul Aesthetics* (London: Routledge, 2002), 28.

[15] Bertram D. Ashe, "Theorizing the Post-Soul Aesthetic: An Introduction," in "Post-Soul Aesthetic," special issue, *African American Review* 41, no. 4 (2007): 614.

making of intermedial references to blaxploitation tropes while simultaneously rejecting them through re-readings of Black representations is central to the Black Vernacular trope of Signifyin(g).[16] The novel signals older genres (slave narratives, neo-slave narratives, blaxploitation films) and reworks them to critique the media and movie industries for their stereotypical representations of African Americans. Everett's novel further plays with parody, irony, duplication, mirroring, and the text's status as metafiction to defer and destabilize notions of identity.

Despite the critiques of blaxploitation, the genre attempts, albeit in a flawed way, to answer the "marginalization and tokenization of Black representation of the American experience."[17] For John Semley, the recent return to blaxploitation concerns "aesthetics of exploitation" and is "motivated by a contemporary ironic fetish for all things kitsch and camp,"[18] a knack for ironic reversal, and resistance. Hence, Semley asserts that "Blaxploitation carries both *restorative and counteractive properties*—able to reinvigorate communities of American Blacks by way of *self-styled on-screen representation*, while also overwriting the hitherto existing assumptions of American blackness that marked everything from Sambo to Sidney Poitier."[19] Blaxploitation's ambivalence reflects the divided stance in scholarship and Black culture about the genre's usefulness in thinking about identity representations. Phillip Lamar Cunningham uses *neo-blaxploitation* to show how "contemporary texts that feature Black protagonists negotiate with archetypes, iconography, and themes of blaxploitation."[20] Everett's use of Poitier filmic texts as vignettes and ironic signaling allows for a reading of the novel as neo-blaxploitation.

---

[16] See Henry Louis Gates, Jr., *The Signifying Monkey: A Theory of African American Literary Criticism* (Oxford: Oxford University Press, 1988).

[17] Semley, "Who's Bleeding Whom?, 23.

[18] Ibid., 22.

[19] Ibid., 23; emphasis added.

[20] Phillip Lamarr Cunningham, "The Limits of Neo-Blaxploitation: Considering David F. Walker's *Nighthawk* and *Power Man and Iron Fist*," *Fire!!!* 4, no. 2 (2018): 98.

314 Different Ways of (Not) Being Black

Post-Soul Aesthetics Meets Blaxploitation: The Beginnings of Blaxploration?

'Postblack'[21] is a term deployed to describe African Americans' artistic production in the post-civil rights era; its ethos is found in the word "Freestyle."[22] A move to free both artists and their works from normative societal scripting of blackness. Postblack and post-soul, terms often used interchangeably, employ non-traditional representations via humor, irony, and the reappropriation of established stereotypes. Postblack artists demand and establish artistic individuality free from socio-cultural constraints.[23] I prefer the term "post-soul aesthetics" as employed by Neal and Ashe because it scrutinizes and decenters the concept of "Black" along with any idea of an "authentic" identity. Soul, as evoked in African American culture, signals an "authentic," often singular spirit and identity that is traditionally expressed with regard to "music, food," and people.[24] Soul becomes problematic, I believe, when deployed simplistically to represent the Black lifeworld, ultimately leading to stereotypes. Post-soul usefully centers diversity and hybridity and resists such homogenization of Black identity.

Post-Soul Matrix

Ashe provides a descriptive and analytical framework for examining post-soul texts, a "triangular post-soul matrix" which consists of "the cultural mulatto archetype; the execution of an exploration of blackness

---

[21] Here, I follow Christian Schmidt's deployment of postblack not to signal that race is passé nor an adamant refusal of race but rather a way of signaling the freedom of 'Black artists' to interrogate race without undue expectations, Cf. Christian Schmidt, *Postblack Aesthetics: The Freedom To be Black in Contemporary African American Literature* (Heidelberg: Universitätsverlag Winter, 2017), 2.

[22] Thelma Golden, introduction to *Freestyle: The Studio Museum in Harlem*, ed. Christine Y. Kim and Franklin Sirmans (New York: Studio Museum in Harlem, 2001), 14.

[23] Ibid., 14–15.

[24] Ashe, "Theorizing the Post-Soul Aesthetic," 617.

[or blaxploration]; and, lastly, the signal, allusion-disruption gestures."[25] My emphasis in this paper will be on the last two elements of Ashe's matrix. First, the "cultural mulatto" is an intermixture of cultural experiences and shifts from the "tragic mulatto" trope,[26] and it eschews reiterating an aesthetics of victimization and despair. Instead, it represents artists and texts that deliberately traverse "the traditionally separated racial lines in US Popular culture" and display "[a] hybrid, fluid, elastic...sense of black identity."[27] Second, blaxploration is a "propensity to trouble blackness...[which] is constantly in flux."[28] Ashe deliberately signifies the blaxploitation films, but, in contrast to that genre's 'stick it to the Man' form, post-soul's "artistic freedom" allows, through blaxploration, for a commitment to explorations of blackness that go beyond communal loyalty.[29] Blaxploration then expands blackness through the parodies of the Sidney Poitier films and "Signifyin(g) [as]...repetition with a signal difference"[30] through "*allusion-disruption* strategy."[31] The allusion-disruption strategy involves references to Black Vernacular tropes, literary traditions, artistic movements, and cultural histories in a discursive practice, and, in this case, it offers jumping-off points for rethinking black represent-ation.

(Not) Resisting Sidney Poitier: Name-Calling and Mass Media (Ted) Representations

This section focuses on the role of signifying practices and (mis)-representations that impose restrictions on the protagonist's identity

---

[25] Ibid., 613.

[26] Ibid., 613–614.

[27] Ibid., 614.

[28] Ibid., 614–615.

[29] Ibid., 614.

[30] Gates, *The Signifying Monkey*, xxiv.

[31] Ashe, "Theorizing the Post-Soul Aesthetic," 615; emphasis in original. Although Ashe does not explicitly reference Henry Louis Gates Jr. nor his book *The Signifying Monkey*, his use and delineation of "signal" and "signifyin(g)" suggests the influence of Gate's signifyin(g) theory on his work.

316   Different Ways of (Not) Being Black

performance through preconceived notions of blackness and identity. Not Sidney relies on his identity performance to resist and subvert societal and mass media representations of blackness. Lâle Demirtürk has suggested that equating the body with the self becomes experiential, thus necessitating that racialized bodies challenge their ascribed selves through "race performativity."[32] Not Sidney's character challenges demeaning stereotypical descriptions of blackness by signal-mocking entertainment media, blaxploitation, and early blackface minstrelsy.[33] Instead, Not Sidney's identity performance ennobles Black representation.

> I never knew the story of my name. One might have thought that my mother imagined that our last name, rare as it was, was enough to confuse with Sidney Poitier, the actor, and so I was to be *Not* Sidney Poitier. However, her puzzled expression led me to believe that my name had nothing to do with the actor at all, that *Not Sidney* was simply a name that she had created, with no consideration of the outside world. She liked it, and that was enough.[34]

As the quotation indicates, Not Sidney's existence challenges traditional wisdom. His mother delivers him after "twenty-four months" (instead of nine) in a "forty-hour" labor and gives him an "odd" name,[35] Not Sidney Poitier, which is not only unexpected but is in defiance of normative naming, a "negation."[36] His birth attracts "voyeurs,"[37] and he is thus a spectacle from birth, one who would make sensational news in con-

---

[32] Emine Lâle Demirtürk, *How Black Writers Deal with Whiteness: Characterization Through Deconstructing Color* (New York: Edwin Mellen Press, 2008), 8–9.

[33] For a detailed analysis of mass media entertainment, minstrelsy and Black identity, see Ronald Jackson's *Scripting the Black Masculine Body: Identity, Discourse, and Racial Politics in Popular Media* (Albany: State University of New York Press, 2006), 20–25.

[34] Everett, *I Am Not Sidney Poitier*, 7; emphasis in original.

[35] Ibid., 4.

[36] Sarah Griffin, "This Strange Juggler's Game: Forclusion in Percival Everett's *I Am Not Sidney Poitier*," in *Perspectives on Percival Everett*, eds. Keith B. Mitchell and Robin G. Vander (Oxford: University Press of Mississippi, 2013), 20.

[37] Everett, *I Am Not Sidney Poitier*, 4.

temporary times. His rebellious name, a symbol of his mother's attitude, exemplifies the rebellious exploration and "'troubling' of blackness" and identity that Ashe calls blaxploration.[38] From the onset, Not Sidney is shaped by societal norms and mass media consumerism, even though he insists that his unconventional name was an invention of his mother's created against the norms of naming and against the media represent-ation of the leading Black actor Sidney Poitier in the diegesis. I contend that this conscious disregard for both pop culture consumerism and representation makes them relevant for the titular character. Not Sidney Poitier's foremost, daunting task is to define himself against his double – the famous actor Sidney Poitier, who serves as the measure of Black male identity and a lens through which to view all blackness. Mis-recognition and prejudiced hyper-recognition through not seeing, gazing, norms, and politics of recognition, and (in)visibility besiege the protagonist in his identity performance. Much like the stereotypical images reproduced through mass media entertainment and which often leave other characters humorously confused, "Everett's parodic mirrors yield nothing but distortions and inversions," Christian Schmidt observes.[39]

Not Sidney inherits a fortune as a result of his mother's proactive investments, ultimately leading him to a poignant moment where he buys the fictional NET "Nigger Entertainment Television" company.[40] Not Sidney's tutor Betty hints at how his affluence and closeness to the entertainment industry are vital in shaping events in his life. Acutely aware of the overdramatized white paternalism in American culture, the novel ensures Turner employs an army of Black women to nurture Not Sidney when he relocates to his house after his mother's death.[41] Betty is one of the women hired from Spelman College, a fictional version of the real-world historically Black liberal arts college for women. She teaches Not Sidney that "[t]he mass media and the oil, they're the movers, the facilitators"; and that politicians were just pawns;[42] and that

---

[38] Ashe, "Theorizing the Post-Soul Aesthetic," 614.
[39] Christian Schmidt, "The Parody of Postblackness in *I Am Not Sidney Poitier* and the End(s) of African American Literature," *Black Studies Papers* 2, no. 1 (2016): 116.
[40] Ibid., 144.
[41] Everett, *I Am Not Sidney Poitier*, 8.
[42] Ibid., 10.

318   Different Ways of (Not) Being Black

Ted Turner, a symbol of media entertainment, is a "parasite."[43] However, the lesson is wasted on the 11-year-old, Not Sidney, because he likes his guardian, Turner. Not Sidney's fondness for Ted changes throughout the narrative as he matures and experiences the realities of living in the shadow of a Hollywood icon. For Not Sidney, however, this parasitic relationship attached to his name and the personal nature of his attachment to his name makes it impossible for him to shed it, draining him of his own identity. His name becomes a burden because it determines his relationships with other characters in the novel.

Later in the novel, for instance, when Ruby Larkin tells her husband that the name of their daughter Maggie's boyfriend is Not Sidney, her husband, Ward Larkin, retorts, "Hmmph. Some kind of ghetto nonsense, no doubt."[44] He assumes that Not Sidney is poor and low-class based on his unusual name. Similarly, when Not Sidney introduces himself to his Morehouse college roommate Morris Chesney, Morris assumes because of Not Sidney's name that he is stupid.[45] Naming and the false assumptions made because of names are essential features of the novel. As Claudine Raynaud asserts, Everett's novel "stages a cynical and hilarious twist on African American nomination and its troubled history."[46] The novel uses naming as a mode of signification through various techniques – *mise en abyme*, text as metafiction, and wordplay – which culminate in irony typical of, but not exclusive to, the postmodernist critique. Morris' insult and attempt to belittle Not Sidney for his unconventional name instead solidifies and recognizes by accident that "not only was [he] *Not* Sidney Poitier, but also that [he] was *not* Sidney Poitier."[47] Morris' statement indicates the game the novel plays on the literary character, referentiality, and signification. More importantly, it shows how society repeatedly reduces Not Sidney to his name's signifier but does not or refuses to recognize the person.

Furthermore, race-thinking is helpful in explaining Not Sidney's over-generalization in the novel via paternalistic and often-racist name-calling such as 'the N-word,' "boy," and "slave," and it explains the

---

[43] Ibid.

[44] Ibid., 131.

[45] Ibid., 92.

[46] Claudine Raynaud, "Naming, Not Naming and Nonsense in *I Am Not Sidney Poitier*," *Lectures du Monde Anglophone/LMA* 1 (2015): 1.

[47] Everett, *I Am Not Sidney Poitier*, 92; emphasis added.

prejudiced origins of his mistreatment. Not Sidney finds this racial categorization insane and unfamiliar despite its seemingly structured nature. He, therefore, questions and subverts the validity of such categorization and name-calling through his identity performance. The running gag of the novel is the irony and pun of the protagonist's name, Not Sidney Poitier. Irony works through duplication of actual people and "unnatural" or "antimimetic" logic.[48] Both the fictional doubles and the ridiculous name-calling culminate in the cameos of Percival Everett as a professor of Nonsense and of the now infamous Bill Cosby as a keynote speaker during Not Sidney's matriculation at Morehouse College, another fictional version of a real-world, historically Black college.[49] Duplicity and mirroring destabilize perceptions and limits of acceptable Black nomenclature. Moreover, the doubling of other fictional characters, including Scrunchy, Feet, Maurice/Morris, and George, reflects the insufficiency of hinging identities on names. In the next section, I build on this claim to show how blaxploration is useful to circumvent the limits imposed on Black identity expressions by society.

The novel crucially triples our protagonist's identity as Not Sidney Poitier, Sidney Poitier, not Not Sidney Poitier. Nominally, three characters exist in the diegetic world: the protagonist Not Sidney Poitier, his actor-double Sidney Poitier, and a boy called Sidney.[50] In the narrative, Not Sidney's fully developed three-dimensional identity – one with a playful, literal three-sidedness – is comprised of Not Sidney Poitier (his given name), the actor Sidney Poitier's double (established through several situations of mistaken and misrecognized identity), and not Not Sidney Poitier, an identity that arises from the insistence of other characters and culminates in his unlawful arrest for killing the man for whom he is a dead ringer in Smuteye. Once vindicated, Not Sidney calculates "that if that body in the chest was Not Sidney Poitier, then [he] was not Not Sidney Poitier and that by all [he] knew of logic and double negatives, [he] was therefore Sidney Poitier."[51] However, until

---

[48]   Christian Schmidt, "Postblack Unnatural Narrative – Or, is the Implied Author of Percival Everett's *I Am Not Sidney Poitier* Black?" in *Narrative, Race, and Ethnicity in the United States*, eds. James J. Donahue et al. (Columbus: Ohio State University Press, 2017), 86.

[49]   For the respective scenes see Everett, *I Am Not Sidney Poitier*, 82–97.

[50]   Ibid., 18.

[51]   Ibid., 212.

320   Different Ways of (Not) Being Black

now, his seemingly illogical characterization has only pointed to a parody of logic. One such reference is to Black Vernacular English, "in which double negatives do not amount to affirmation."[52] The character intervenes in name-calling and problematizes readings of Black grammar and naming traditions by other characters as illogical. Thus, all efforts to make sense of Not Sidney's identity and determine who he "really" is only results in comical confusions and stereotyping. By making it impossible to constrain his identity (already signaled by his name), the novel critiques mimetic mirroring and allows Not Sidney's identity performance to escape stereotyping.

Blaxploration and (Not) Being Black

My goal in this section is to analyze how blaxploration in the novel becomes a means of stretching the tropes of blackness to escape the confines of reductive and confining blackness. Blaxploration enables Not Sidney to expand his identity beyond socio-cultural conscriptions. *I Am Not Sidney Poitier* complicates blaxploitation's accurate yet one-directional critique of Hollywood stereotyping – the stereotyping of the Black community by the "white" establishment – by emphasizing the complex mechanisms of identity formation. The novel comments on the community's internal diversities by alluding to historical racism, classism, and slavery. The pun on Not Sidney's name, the continual deferral and the constant conflation of his identity with the diegetic actor – coupled with the trap of nominal homonymy to the name of real-life Sidney Poitier – mock the idea of a single Black "soul." The novel paradoxically presents the seemingly unpresentable and unrepresentative aspects of racial and cultural identities in order to assert the multiplicity of blackness and Black culture. It shows how these aspects of African American racial and cultural identities result from historical racist discourses.

Not Sidney questions normative notions of blackness and resists representations of ethnic homogeneity. In Everett's novel, the diversity of the African American community is prominently on display in Not Sidney's encounter with his girlfriend Maggie Larkins' family in

---

[52]   Raynaud, "Naming, Not Naming," 7.

chapter four, which features an intermedial reference to the 1967 film *Guess Who's Coming to Dinner*. Everett defamiliarizes the film's classic narrative to paradoxically make it more recognizable to the African American community. In the original film, Sidney Poitier's character John Prentice, a widowed doctor, meets Joanna Drayton (Katharine Houghton), an open-minded young white woman who brings him home to introduce him to her parents over Thanksgiving dinner. Various characters' opinions about the couple's compatibility drive the plot. However, the novel departs significantly from the film in order to emphasize and "trouble blackness"[53] from within the African American community. Not Sidney's unusually calm, stunned, and sometimes seemingly indifferent reaction to racism and racialism in his encounter with the Larkins reflects the goal of postblack and post-soul writers to decenter race while simultaneously unpacking race as a perennial concern of the African American community and of literary explorations.

The description of Maggie's neighborhood and house foregrounds her class identity and indicates potential problems for Not Sidney. The drive from the airport to Maggie's house is close to the Washington, DC Potomac River, and her house is a big "midsixties' split-level with a three-car garage and an expanse of lawn."[54] It has a "holly-hedge-lined driveway," a packed "Cadillac to a side porch... an anteroom [and a] breakfast room."[55] Readers then encounter the housemaid and nanny, an older woman called Violet. Maggie's proximity to power, as indicated by the Potomac, her family's affluence, and the color code of the housemaid's name, set the stage for the Larkin household's initial misconceptions about Not Sidney. Violet ignores him when he tries to greet her.[56] The family's unfriendliness only worsens with each member he meets, and Not Sidney feels unwelcome.

While Not Sidney fails to recognize the difference in skin tones between the Larkins and himself at first because it does not make any difference to him, Ruby Larkin, Maggie's mother, a conservative enthusiast who is anti-gay, anti-welfare, and anti-affirmative action,[57]

---

[53] Ashe, "Theorizing the Post-Soul Aesthetic," 614.

[54] Everett, *I Am Not Sidney Poitier*, 126.

[55] Ibid.

[56] Ibid.

[57] Ibid., 128.

322 Different Ways of (Not) Being Black

contrarily describes him as being "just so dark."[58] Here, Not Sidney refuses to partake in the "color caste politics": the internal race prejudice against darker-skinned African American community members.[59] Violet, the housemaid, also participates in this politics of color, explicitly alluding to the history of slavery by using derogatory words against Not Sidney and by deploying racist stereotypes. Not Sidney, sensing her animosity towards him during his visit, asks the inevitable question, "[d]o you have a problem with my skin color?"[60] Her response to him replays the infamous "white angel versus black devil" stereotype when she asserts that "*Mister* and *Missus* have worked too hard...[t]o have a *black boy* like you come around *Miss* Maggie."[61] Not Sidney immediately recognizes the pattern of stereotypes and retorts, "[t]his is not the antebellum south and you're not a house slave."[62] Moreover, when he insists that both he and Violet are of the same complexion, she snaps and insists that she sees herself as "milk chocolate" and Not Sidney as "dark cocoa, dark as Satan."[63] By stylistically making the Larkins light-skinned (their skin, along with their name, signals a combination of light and dark and is a signal to the traditional "mulatto" trope), the novel represents the complexity of issues of identity and race through the different hues of the characters' skin, thereby highlighting the problem of colorism within the African American community. On the surface, it problematizes the assumption of a single African American identity and shows how racism and colorism work within the community. However, it also critiques the baggage of historical racist discourse by reflecting oppressive racial stereotypes on a deeper level. After his confrontation with Violet, Not Sidney becomes horrifyingly observant of "skin tones."[64]

Fresh off this miseducation and hostile encounter with Nanny Violet, Not Sidney goes to dinner. When he meets the Reverend Golightly and his family at the dinner table, he places them on a color chart. The Reverend, for example, "was the color of coffee with a generous helping

---

[58] Ibid., 131.
[59] Neal, *Soul Babies*, 47.
[60] Everett, *I Am Not Sidney Poitier*, 154.
[61] Ibid.; emphasis added.
[62] Ibid., 155.
[63] Ibid.
[64] Ibid.

of cream"; his wife had a little "more cream"; and, finally, their "[t]hirty-year-old [son] Jeffrey was an albino."[65] Jeffrey is the only person who is "completely lacking pigment and outside of the bizarre game" of skin coding.[66] Thus, Jeffrey is essentially free of both pigment and prejudice in his interactions with Not Sidney. By depicting in-group differences and prejudices, the novel challenges homogenization and stereotypical representations of African Americans through race politics. Thus, the systematic treatment of Not Sidney as an *Other* in Maggie's home further questions how notions of racism and racialism may erroneously be represented mainly as "white" acts directed toward Blacks. Finally, at dinner, the Reverend says grace in a hilariously long prayer in which he not only itemizes each dish but also offers thanks for their possessions, their "good blood," and their "distance from the thickening center."[67] By showing the friendship between the Larkins and the Golightlys, and by showing the Reverend as being representative of religious institutions, the novel shows how community cornerstones such as religion and family institutions sometimes consolidate the deep-seated nature of classicism, racism, and colorism within the Black community.

"Allusion-Disruption" and Parody as Subversive Strategies

In what remains, I will analyze how the novel employs the "allusion-disruption gesture" to interrogate the old modes of conceiving Black identity performance through irony and parody. Simon Dentith defines *parody* as "any cultural practice which provides a relatively polemical allusive imitation of another cultural production or practice."[68] His definition signals "allusion-disruption gestures" and "signifyin(g)." Parodical allusions are employed variously in the novel, but I focus on those allusions to movie plots that are utilized in the novel to disrupt and subvert the mimetic mirroring of the diegetic actor Sidney Poitier onto the independent identity performance of the protagonist Not Sidney Poitier. Demirtürk argues that Everett's narrative "exposes the dis-

---

[65] Ibid.
[66] Ibid., 156.
[67] Ibid., 159.
[68] Simon Dentith, *Parody* (London: Routledge, 2005), 9.

324 Different Ways of (Not) Being Black

junction between essentialized black bodies... produced by the disembodied white gaze in popular culture and the individuated black selves... who depart from the accepted norms of recognition."[69] The novel alludes, through the intermedial repurposing of Sidney Poitier film plots, to the extratextual misrepresentation of Black identity in Hollywood films. Not Sidney's three-sidedness constitutes an exploration of blackness and his established negation of visual culture's identity status quo. This way, he rejects diegetic actor Sidney Poitier's performance, the racialized representation of Black identity in films, and slavery's historical stereotyping. The novel employs the symbol of mirrors (through character duplication and actual mirror scenes)[70] to indicate the process of failed identification and to critique Hollywood's reproduction of stereotypes as well as and its failure to represent Black identity objectively. More importantly, the mirror signifies the futility of representing identity mimetically, which is part of the argument I have tried to convey thus far about how prejudiced representations of blackness delimit the full expression of Black identities.

Not Sidney enters a second dream world in which he "encounter[s] various other worlds wherein the filmic or televisual and the 'real' blur."[71] The additional conflation of filmic parodies with the narrative permits another blurring layer through narrative doubles in the diegetic world. The diegetic movie star is *not* Sidney Poitier, the real-world actor. Such doubling generates confusion and offers commentary on the problematics of mimetic mirroring of identity. However, Not Sidney finds agency in historical distance through the dream space, which allows him to shed each of the characters the actor Sidney Poitier portrays through re-enactments. In doing so, he maps an independent identity for himself. He embraces various identities (as Raz-ru, a nineteenth-century slave overseer; a Maroon; a falsely convicted man; a physician; a vagabond) while typifying a limitless potential for

---

[69] Emine Lâle Demirtürk, "Rescripted Performances of Blackness as 'Parodies of Whiteness': Discursive Frames of Recognition in Percival Everett's *I Am Not Sidney Poitier*," in *The Contemporary African American Novel: Multiple Cities, Multiple Subjectivities, and Discursive Practices of Whiteness in Everyday Urban Encounters* (Teaneck: Fairleigh Dickinson University Press, 2012), 87–88.

[70] Everett, *I Am Not Sidney Poitier*, 142; 191.

[71] Hayman, "Hypervisible Man," 143; emphasis in original.

blackness – blaxploration – that allows him the freedom to remake and decipher a distinct identity for himself.

Harvey Young maintains that misrecognition through 'racial profiling' contributes to Othering by reducing identity to visible markers such as skin color and overlooking unmarked aspects such as sexuality, religion, and class.[72] The Black body thus becomes hyper-visualized.[73] This negative perception through racial profiling, I believe, becomes ingrained in others' consciousness, consequently informing the Othering of Black bodies. In the second chapter, two Sidney Poitier films, *The Defiant Ones* and *A Patch of Blue,* blend seamlessly and are parodied. In a re-enactment of the former movie's opening scene, Everett pens a backstory for the random arrest of Noah Cullen – now Not Sidney Poitier. When Not Sidney leaves his Atlanta home and travels South, he is arrested in "Peckerwood County" on suspicion of criminality because he drives an expensive car, and for being "uppity" with a police officer, George.[74] Not Sidney is racially profiled and incarcerated without a fair trial[75] and, in keeping with the film, is forced by the justice system into a modern-day chain gang as punishment for "vagrancy."[76] Everett alludes to the unjust criminal justice system in the US, to slavery, and to the vagrancy laws of the postbellum South[77] that criminalized Black (male) bodies.

The subsequent events are eerily like enslavement. A judge sentences Not Sidney Poitier to "the work farm,"[78] the symbolic equivalent of a slave plantation, and then forced into a chain gang. He escapes from this 'gang' with his white prison mate Patrice after their prison transport vehicle is in an accident while Not Sidney and Patrice

---

[72] Harvey Young, *Embodying Black Experience: Stillness, Critical Memory, and the Black Body* (Ann Arbor: University of Michigan Press, 2010), 10–11.

[73] Ibid., 12.

[74] Everett, *I Am Not Sidney Poitier*, 47–48.

[75] Ibid. 48.

[76] Ibid., 49.

[77] See Douglas A. Blackmon, *Slavery by Another Name: The Re-enslavement of Black Americans from the Civil War to World War II* (New York: Doubleday, 2008), 1–2.

[78] Everett, *I Am Not Sidney Poitier*, 48.

326 Different Ways of (Not) Being Black

are shackled together.[79] The police pursue them with hounds[80] as they wade through the water,[81] evoking images of runaway slaves.[82] Their mutual bond is significant in unpacking how Black identity formation is constrained under the shadow of historical slavery and slavery's after-lives. Nevertheless, by severing the two men's chains, Not Sidney symbolically frees himself of the historical chain of slave identity stereotyping, which established many Black stereotypes. Through the dream space, Everett allows for a much-needed distance in which Not Sidney's character can develop his identity in the knowledge of, but away from, the shadow of slavery.

(Not) Becoming Sidney Poitier

As the novel comes to a close, (Not) Sidney Poitier impersonates his actor double and receives the award for the "Most Dignified Figure in American Culture"[83] – though it is ultimately ambiguous who the recipient is.[84] The ambiguity persists because, after Not Sidney's assist-ant, Podgy, reserves a car to take Not Sidney from LAX to his hotel. He is once again misrecognized and mistaken for the actor by a British driver who asks the forbidden question,

> "Are you *not* Sidney Poitier?"
> "I *am*, I said."[85]

[79] Ibid., 49.
[80] Ibid., 54.
[81] Ibid., 56.
[82] Ibid., 53.
[83] Everett, 234.
[84] Casey Hayman, for example, reads the novel as a *bildungsroman* in which Not Sidney "becomes" Sidney Poitier at the end (Hayman, "Hypervisible Man," 135–154). Lâle Demirtürk has a similar reading, cf. "Rescripted Performances of Blackness as 'Parodies of Whiteness': Discursive Frames of Recognition in Percival Everett's *I Am Not Sidney Poitier*," in *The Contemporary African American Novel: Multiple Cities, Multiple Subjectivities, and Discursive Practices of Whiteness in Everyday Urban Encounters* (Teaneck: Fairleigh Dickinson University Press, 2012), 85–109.
[85] Everett, *I Am Not Sidney Poitier*, 231; emphasis added.

Claudine Raynaud, for example, focuses on homophony to explore the protagonist's name puns. However, I observe that Not Sidney's name offers a disjuncture between homonyms – Not and not – which allows for a small chance that, occasionally and fleetingly, he is indeed Not Sidney Poitier, even if his interlocutors are ignorant of this fact. The misrecognition continues with the bellhop and desk clerk at his hotel, who both greet him before a film award ceremony as "Mr. Poitier" but observe that he is "looking younger."[86] After he dines with doubles of Elizabeth Taylor and Harry Belafonte at the award ceremony, Not Sidney remains unfamiliar with the awards and categories (something the actor Sidney Poitier would likely recognize).[87] Our protagonist is sure that someone has mistaken him for the actor yet again (the airport taxi driver). In his acceptance speech for the award, Not Sidney references his battle against his double: "I have learned that my name is not my name. It seems you all know me and nothing could be further from the truth and yet you know me better than I know myself, perhaps better than I can know myself."[88] Here, Not Sidney bemoans the hyper-visibility of his famous namesake against whom he is misidentified and for whom the (re)produced image of his Black identity is earmarked and measured. His speech recognizes a structural problem of misrecognition, which plagues the justice system and often victimizes African Americans, leading to false arrests and convictions based on blind faith in "eyewitness accounts" without proper scrutiny. In the novel, the protagonist suffers this fate at the hands of the police both in Peckerwood County and Smuteye.

Another turn in this misrecognition scheme, which follows a similar logic than that of the "color caste,"[89] has its roots in slave history. From the beginning of the novel, the first-person narrative – "I was born"[90] – references slave narratives, whose formulaic structure James Olney has usefully examined.[91] The early suspicions about Not Sidney's parentage reflect the suspicion that shadowed mixed-race children during slavery.

---

[86] Ibid., 231.
[87] Ibid., 232.
[88] Ibid., 234.
[89] Neal, *Soul Babies*, 47.
[90] Everett, *I Am Not Sidney Poitier*, 3.
[91] James Olney, "'I Was Born': Slave Narratives, Their Status as Autobiography and as Literature," *Callaloo* 20 (1984): 46–73.

328 Different Ways of (Not) Being Black

Even though children often bear a physical resemblance to their fathers, mixed-race children were largely denied and ignored by their fathers and society. Thus, their presence remained hypervisible yet invisible. Likewise, although Not Sidney resembles the diegetic actor Sidney Poitier, the only link to the actor is the rumor of a possible relationship between Not Sidney's mother and the actor. The only clue readers have is that his mother had a brief affair with a man "who may or may not have been Sidney Poitier," the man he suspects to be his father[92] but also who may or may not be Sidney Poitier, the actor receiving the award. This gap in full knowledge of his parentage leaves his connection or non-connection to the diegetic actor largely unresolved. Nevertheless, just as stereotypes persist because others blindly believe in them, society believes in the possibility of a relationship to the diegetic actor. It thus confines Not Sidney to this role, which shapes his identity and relationships in the novel.

Conclusion

The awardee concludes that neither the prying eyes of society nor representation by Hollywood can objectively or thoroughly represent him. When he suggests that his mother's and his tombstone read "**I AM NOT MYSELF TODAY**,"[93] readers confront a disjunction of signifier and the signified. Here, however, Not Sidney's words are all capitalized, and so there is no way of knowing if he is asserting that he is *not* Sidney Poitier or that he is Not Sidney Poitier and having a terrible day with misrecognition. Readers wonder whether the recipient is Not Sidney Poitier, the protagonist; Sidney Poitier, the diegetic actor; or not Not Sidney Poitier, other people's imagination of what Not Sidney Poitier should or should not be. The references to Sidney Poitier movies with their own diegetic worlds further complicate the identification of the protagonist. Yet, it is instructive to remember that the story of "Sidney Poitier," which the novel playfully performs, is not unique but rather represents a prevalent problem of Black representation, symbolized in the award recipient and his recognition of the futility of the search for

[92] Everett, *I Am Not Sidney Poitier*, 5.
[93] Ibid., 234.

identity. This futility is partly due to the elusiveness of identity, and partly due to racialized and homogenizing notions of Black identity as they are projected through popular visual culture and media-circulated (mis)representations.

330 Different Ways of (Not) Being Black

Works Cited

A Patch of Blue. Directed by Guy Green. Metro-Goldwin-Mayer, 1965.

Ashe, Bertram D. "Theorizing the Post-Soul Aesthetic: An Introduction." In "Post-Soul Aesthetic," special issue, *African American Review* 41, no. 4 (2007): 609–623.

Blackmon, A., Douglas. *Slavery by Another Name: The Re-enslavement of Black Americans from the Civil War to World War II.* New York: Doubleday, 2008.

Butler, Judith. *Gender Trouble: Feminism and the Subversion of Identity.* New York: Routledge Classics, 2007.

Cunningham, Phillip Lamarr. "The Limits of Neo-Blaxploitation: Considering David F. Walker's *Nighthawk* and *Power Man and Iron Fist.*" *Fire!!!* 4, no. 2 (2018): 94–112.

Demirtürk, Emine Lâle. *How Black Writers Deal with Whiteness: Characterization Through Deconstructing Color.* New York: Edwin Mellen Press, 2008.

---. "Rescripted Performances of Blackness as 'Parodies of Whiteness': Discursive Frames of Recognition in Percival Everett's *I Am Not Sidney Poitier.*" In *The Contemporary African American Novel: Multiple Cities, Multiple Subjectivities, and Discursive Practices of Whiteness in Everyday Urban Encounters*, 85–109. Teaneck: Fairleigh Dickinson University Press, 2012.

Dentith, Simon. *Parody.* London: Routledge, 2005.

Everett, Percival. *I Am Not Sidney Poitier.* Minneapolis: Graywolf Press, 2009.

Gates, Henry Louis, Jr. *The Signifying Monkey: A Theory of African American Literary Criticism.* Oxford: Oxford University Press, 1988.

Golden, Thelma. Introduction. In *Freestyle: The Studio Museum in Harlem*, edited by Christine Y. Kim and Franklin Sirmans, 14–15. New York: Studio Museum in Harlem, 2001.

Griffin, Sarah. "This Strange Juggler's Game: Forclusion in Percival Everett's *I Am Not Sidney Poitier.*" In *Perspectives on Percival Everett*, edited by Keith B. Mitchell and Robin G. Vander, 19–34. Oxford: University Press of Mississippi, 2013.

Guess Who's Coming to Dinner? Directed by Stanley Kramer. Columbia Pictures, 1967.

Hayman, Casey. "Hypervisible Man: Techno-Performativity and Televisual Blackness in Percival Everett's *I Am Not Sidney Poitier*." *MELUS* 39, no. 3 (2014): 135–154.

Jackson, L. Ronald. *Scripting the Black Masculine Body: Identity, Discourse, and Racial Politics in Popular Media*. Albany: State University of New York Press, 2006.

Lawrence, Novotny. *Blaxploitation Films of the 1970s: Blackness and Genre*. London: Routledge, 2008.

Mitchell, Keith B., and Robin G. Vander. "Introduction: Changing the Frame, Framing the Change: The Art of Percival Everett." In *Perspectives on Percival Everett*, edited by Keith B. Mitchell and Robin G. Vander, ix–xvii. Oxford: University Press of Mississippi, 2013.

Neal, Mark Anthony. *Soul Babies: Black Popular Culture and the Post Soul Aesthetics*. London: Routledge, 2002.

Olney, James. "'I Was Born': Slave Narratives, Their Status as Autobiography and as Literature." *Callaloo* 20 (1984): 46–73.

Raynaud, Claudine. "Naming, Not Naming and Nonsense in *I Am Not Sidney Poitier*." *Lectures du Monde Anglophone/LMA* 1 (2015): 1–15.

Schmidt, Christian. *Postblack Aesthetics: The Freedom To Be Black in Contemporary African American Literature*. Heidelberg: Universitätsverlag Winter, 2017.

---. "Postblack Unnatural Narrative – Or, is the Implied Author of Percival Everett's *I Am Not Sidney Poitier* Black?" In *Narrative, Race, and Ethnicity in the United States*, edited by James J. Donahue et al., 82–94. Columbus: Ohio State University Press, 2017.

---. "The Parody of Postblackness in *I Am Not Sidney Poitier* and the End(s) of African American Literature." *Black Studies Papers* 2, no. 1 (2016): 113–132.

Semley, John. "Who's Bleeding Whom? Analyzing the Cultural Flows of Blaxploitation Cinema, Then and Now." *Cineaction* 80 (2010): 22–29.

Taylor, Paul C. *Race: A Philosophical Introduction*. Cambridge: Polity, 2004.

The Defiant Ones. Directed by Stanley Kramer. United Artists, 1958.

Young, Harvey. *Embodying Black Experience: Stillness, Critical Memory, and the Black Body*. Ann Arbor: University of Michigan Press, 2010.

CLARA PETINO

"Lace Reading" and "Physick Recipes": Wicca and Modern Witches in Salem Literature

To this day, Salem, Massachusetts remains inseparable from its religious history and the Puritan theocracy of the Colonial era that led to the infamous witch trials of 1692. But while the witch was once seen as the town's biggest threat, she has made contemporary Salem the United States' number-one Halloween destination: witch-related tourism attracts several hundred thousand tourists per year. Moreover, while negotiating the tension between exploring and exploiting its history, Salem has ironically become an "epicenter of the millennial witchcraft community;"[1] modern pagans (especially Wiccans) and self-proclaimed witches pride themselves on Salem's newfound (religious) tolerance and diversity. Erica Feldman, "the unofficial face of the town's con-temporary magic scene," explains that, whether despite or because of its history, "[t]here are a lot of us [witches] here [in Salem] because it's the one place in the world that really embraces the figure of the witch."[2]

In recent years and decades, this reappropriation of the witch as a figure of (female) empowerment has occurred in all fields of popular culture, from the *Harry Potter* books and films, to the Netflix series *Chilling Adventures of Sabrina*, and even to online activism against the Donald Trump presidency (#BindTrump, #MagicResistance). And it is significantly discernible in what I call Salem literature, a corpus of well

---

[1] Jessica Bateman, "Why Salem's Modern-Day Witchcraft Scene is Giving Rise to 'Magic Tourism,'" *The Independent*, August 7, 2017, independent. co.uk/travel/americas/salem-witchcraft-scene-magic-tourism-feminism-hipster-modern-day-massachusetts-new-england-donald-trump-spells a7877521.html.

[2] Ibid.

334   Wicca and Modern Witches in Salem Literature

over 70 works of fiction of the past 200 years[3] (with a distinct increase since the 1990s) that are set in historical or contemporary Salem and which tell, retell and set the story and/or its legacy in the present. In works of the past two decades in particular, this growing corpus is represented by a decidedly female authorship and strong female protagonists whose ancestral psychic powers and supernatural healing abilities make them all the more fitting in modern-day Salem. Focusing on bestselling works by Brunonia Barry and Katherine Howe, this paper explores witchcraft and religion as well as witchcraft *as* religion in (literary) Salem.

A Brief History of the Witch

While the term *witch* is derived from the Old English *wicca/wicce* (a male/female magician), it is inextricably associated with the female sex, and the concept of the witch is much older than the word itself. Witchlike figures can be found in ancient cultures from around the world[4] and have often been associated with fertility goddesses, i.e., with positive connotations of sexuality and power. This is not the case in Christian texts. While I do not want to oversimplify the link between monotheism and witchcraft persecution (which was carried out by more secular than religious leaders), the Bible attributes susceptibility to the devil's seductions to the female sex: Eve causes the fall of man by giving in to the temptation of the snake. Moreover, it contains the dire imperative later used to justify executions of accused witches – the vast majority of whom were women – in Europe and America:[5] "thou shalt

---

[3]   2020 marks the bicentennial of the first fictionalization of the Salem witch trials, the anonymously published *Salem, an Eastern Tale.*

[4]   Kristen J. Sollée, *Witches, Sluts, Feminists: Conjuring the Sex Positive* (Berkeley: ThreeL Media, 2017). Sollée enumerates exemplarily the "Sumerian tales of Inanna", the "Egyptian legends of Isis" and the "Hindu myths of Kali" (ibid., 21).

[5]   The exact number of victims is debated by historians to this day. Figures differ from source to source, ranging from 50,000 to 200,000. However, scholars largely agree on what percentage of those executed were women: this is usually estimated to have been between 75 and 85 percent. The claim

CLARA PETINO 335

not suffer a witch to live" (Exodus 22:18). The 1486 *Malleus Maleficarum* or 'Witch Hammer,' which legalized organized persecution, is also particularly outspoken on the mental and physical relationship between female witches and the devil. The authors warn of incubi and succubi (demons who force themselves on women and men, respectively); witches were believed to have sex with the devil and his demons (preferably at a 'witches' sabbath') and to let their animal familiars suck on their 'witch's teat'. Although this "teat" – for which the accused were searched during interrogations – could be any kind of skin irregularity, some historians suggest that it was often the clitoris,[6] reinforcing the sexual association and the perceived threat the witches' seductive power posed to men. Of course, the image of a witch riding a broomstick has sexual undertones, too: this phallic household object is (ab)used to literally escape the domestic space, repudiating a woman's role as housewife and mother. The *Malleus Maleficarum* authors' misogynistic sentiments are eventually summed up in the statement that all witchcraft "is governed by carnal lusting, which is insatiable in [women]."[7] The image of the witch as both luring vixen and old hag has thus been shaped predominantly by men. Sollée states in *Witches, Sluts, Feminists*: "Women are frightening for being unattractive, sexually unappealing, and past their prime" just as they are "frightening when young and attractive because the witch is also charming, bewitching, beguiling, and sexually irresistible [...]."[8]

Reasons given for the European persecutions range from sectarian and political conflicts, to epidemic plagues and economic crises, to clashes between Christian believers and nature-worshipping pagans. Some sources also claim that (female) folk healers and midwives were

made by some feminist authors (e.g., Gage; Ehrenreich and English) that 9 million women were executed has been historically refuted.

[6] Cp. Jia Tolentino, "The Truth about Witches: An Interview with Katherine Howe," *Jezebel*, October 29, 2014, jezebel.com/the-truth-about-witches-an-interview-with-katherine-ho-1649987737. Katherine Howe is a historian as well as a writer of historical fiction. She also teaches in the American Studies Program at Cornell University.

[7] Henricus Institoris and Jacobus Sprenger, *Malleus Maleficarum,* trans. and ed. Christopher S. Mackay (Cambridge: Cambridge University Press, 2006), 122.

[8] Sollée, *Witches, Sluts, Feminists*, 18.

especially vulnerable to persecution because they helped with births, contraception and abortions, and because, by using more effective and less painful medical methods, they "circumvent[ed] the male-dominated medico-religious system."[9] But while no interpretation accounts for all cases, these examples show that the witch generally represents the *Other,* whether as a result of her profession or intellect, her unorthodox (love) life or her exceptionally high or low economic and social position.[10] Of course, mentally ill women (and men) were also easy targets of witchcraft accusations.

The only organized witch trials in the United States were entirely different in method and scope from the European ones – especially regarding their Protestant background and the possibility of being spared from prison and execution through confession. Yet many of the misogynistic views evident in the persecutions in Europe reverberated in Salem: "Of the 20 people executed at Salem, 14 were women. Twenty-five of the 31 people tried and convicted were women. 104 of the 141 people arrested were women."[11] And although it is often the fate of male victims that has made its way into the cultural memory, such as the case of Giles Corey, tragic hero of plays by Mary Eleanor Wilkins Freeman and Henry Wadsworth Longfellow,[12] or Arthur Miller's protagonist John Proctor, most of these men were only arrested and tried after their wives had already been accused of witchcraft.

It was the women who deviated most from societal norms who were likely to be accused: Bridget Bishop, the first person to be executed, had been previously accused of witchcraft for murdering her husband and

---

[9] Ibid., 41.

[10] This association has survived to this day. Powerful women are frequently called witches: Margaret Thatcher and, more recently, Hillary Clinton both received the tag several times – in Clinton's case, "a witch with a capital 'B.'" Cf. Stacy Schiff, "Witchcraft on the Campaign Trail," *The New York Times*, October 30, 2016, nytimes.com/2016/10/31/opinion/witchcraft-on-the-campaign -trail.html.

[11] Lori Lee Wilson, *The Salem Witch Trials: How History is Invented* (Minneapolis: Lerner Publications Company, 1997), 75.

[12] Mary Eleanor Wilkins Freeman, *Giles Corey, Yeoman: A Play* (New York: Harper, 1893); Henry Wadsworth Longfellow, *Giles Corey of the Salem Farms*, in *The New England Tragedies* (Boston: Ticknor and Fields, 1868), 103–179.

was furthermore involved in real estate disputes. In the cultural memory, she is also remembered for opposing Puritan clothing standards, wearing a red dress instead of the standard muted colors which symbolized decency.[13] One noteworthy accusation also involved her spectrally entering the bedchamber of Marshal Herrick, "the account of [which]," as Katherine Howe points out, "illustrates the sexual threat embodied by witches, particularly the threat that they posed to male authority."[14] The first three accused were equally deviant: Tituba, the minister's slave from Barbados; Sarah Good, an unpopular, impoverished woman; and Sarah Osborne, a widow of dubious reputation who had recently married her formerly indentured servant. However, while these 'witches' were also subject to the laws of men, the accusations were started and fueled by the 'afflicted girls' and supported by many adult women (and men). Carol F. Karlsen thus rightly points out in her seminal study *The Devil in the Shape of a Woman* that the (Salem) witchcraft persecutions were "a deeply ambivalent but violent struggle *within* women as well as an equally ambivalent and violent struggle *against* them."[15]

Women – Witches – (Literary) Salem

Women and witches have therefore been traditionally associated with each other, as have Salem and witches, and, consequently, Salem and women. This triangle is also reflected in contemporary Salem literature: since the 1990s, only two novels out of more than 20 have been written

---

[13] Historians, however, believe that the association is incorrect and that Bridget Bishop was confused with tavern keeper Sarah Bishop. Cp. Sollée, *Witches, Sluts, Feminists*, 104.

[14] Katherine Howe, ed., *The Penguin Book of Witches* (New York: Penguin, 2014), 166.

[15] Carol F. Karlsen, *The Devil in the Shape of a Woman: Witchcraft in Colonial New England* (New York: Norton & Company, 1987), xv.

338   Wicca and Modern Witches in Salem Literature

by male authors.[16] In a post on "Salem as Character," Brunonia Barry even finds that, in her novels, Salem itself is "definitely female."[17]

Ann Chase is a recurring character in Barry's three Salem novels, *The Lace Reader* (2006), *The Map of True Places* (2010) and *The Fifth Petal* (2017), all of which tell the story of a young female protagonist who has or had serious psychological problems due to a traumatic childhood in Salem, but who is also gifted with precognition and second sight. Eventually, each of them finds a home in Salem, as it is the one place where their gifts can help them and others to better understand both the past and the future. Although these women would be worth discussing in more detail, the limited scope of this paper allows for a focus on only one character. I have chosen Ann Chase because she serves as a uniting element in Barry's Salem universe, which is set between roughly the 1980s and 2015.

In an allusion to Salem's real-life witchcraft scene, *The Lace Reader*'s protagonist Towner Whitney introduces Ann by stating that "with the exception of Laurie Cabot,[18] Ann Chase is the most famous witch in Salem […]."[19] Back in the late 1970s, Ann, who started out as a hippie, "had found her home port" in Salem,[20] where she began "honing her skills" as a "seer."[21] She practices and teaches herbalism, meditation, phrenology, as well as (love) spells and conducts readings of tarot cards and lace in her Shop of Shadows on Pickering Wharf.[22] The shop's name, as explained in *The Map of True Places*, "was a reference to the *Book of Shadows*, a well-known journal used by real witches to record spells, rituals and philosophy, as well as recipes for herbal potions and teas."[23] Ann is also leading a coven, a group of witches (often

[16]   Robin Cook's 1995 *Acceptable Risk* and Richard Francis's 2016 *Crane Pond.*

[17]   Brunonia Barry, "Happy Halloween! Love, Salem," *Writer Unboxed*, October 31, 2014, writerunboxed.com/2014/10/31/happy-halloween-love-salem/.

[18]   I will discuss Laurie Cabot at the end of this paper.

[19]   Brunonia Barry, *The Lace Reader* (New York: Harper, 2010), 59.

[20]   Ibid., 60.

[21]   Ibid., 153.

[22]   Lace reading is a fictional tradition presented as real in the world of the novel.

[23]   Brunonia Barry, *The Map of True Places* (New York: Harper, 2011), 160.

exclusively female) that is used for discussion, study, support and consciousness-raising. Indeed, her circle intends to positively influence not only their own lives, but larger energetic processes as well: In *The Fifth Petal*, they are performing a "*cure* for climate change."[24] Over the years and decades, Ann has thus become not only a tourist attraction but a leading figure among self-proclaimed New Age witches. In fact, like the archetypal witch who is said to "mark the movement of the sun, moon, and stars and relate that movement to life and events on earth,"[25] Ann, too, structures her life according to a lunar calendar and can anticipate the weather and read astrological charts. By integrating strong notions of popular belief, Barry thus creates a twenty-first-century version of the witch whose nature-based medicinal knowledge and psychic gifts help with things deemed out of human control. As a town celebrity as well as a prospective "Wiccan high priestess,"[26] Ann also demonstrates that touristy, witchy fun and serious religious practice do not have to be mutually exclusive.

Although, by her own account, Ann identifies as a "grey witch" – referring to a combination of helpful white and harmful black magic – she refuses to "share any information that could potentially hurt anyone."[27] Ann has even "started a foundation: an antidefamation league that helped educate the public about the witches' harmless religious practices."[28] Nevertheless, Ann combines her positive reinterpretation of the witch with stereotypical attributes: she wears "full witch regalia"[29] in all-black and has several cats. Her outward appearance, her lifestyle and her behavior also allude to a sexual nature often attributed to witches. She is "six feet tall with thick red hair free-falling halfway down her back" and is said to have "a magnetic charge that defied normal boundaries."[30] She is known for recipes for potency and fertility potions, her reading room is "more brothel than witch's lair"[31] and she is un-married, has no children and practices free love. And although religious

---

[24] Brunonia Barry, *The Fifth Petal* (New York: Crown, 2017), 224.
[25] Wilson, *The Salem Witch Trials*, 9.
[26] Barry, *The Map of True Places*, 165.
[27] Ibid.
[28] Barry, *The Fifth Petal*, 203.
[29] Barry, *The Lace Reader*, 302.
[30] Barry, *The Fifth Petal*, 16.
[31] Barry, *The Map of True Places*, 238.

340   Wicca and Modern Witches in Salem Literature

hardliners repeatedly show ill will toward Ann, Barry emphasizes in all three novels that Ann's unorthodox lifestyle could not find a better home than contemporary Salem, demonstrating the stark contrast to the town's Colonial past. Her novels thus celebrate a progressive development of the place and its (religious) connotation – as Ann Chase herself remarks in *The Lace Reader*: "look how far we've come."[32]

The most interesting aspect about Ann Chase, however, is what inspired her lifestyle: she is "a direct descendant of Giles and Martha Corey,"[33] both of whom were executed as witches in 1692. This (apparent) puzzle appears repeatedly in Salem literature: Brunonia Barry and Katherine Howe are themselves descendants of women executed in 1692 and so are many of their characters,[34] and while it is emphasized that their ancestors were victims of a dangerous brew of superstition, bigotry and misogyny, their fictional descendants have inherited actual witch character traits, albeit positive ones. Though it was published long before the aforementioned novels, Bernard Rosenthal's *Salem Story* rightly states: "a problem endemic to stories about Salem" is "that of proclaiming the injustice of what happened, rejecting the idea of witchcraft, while at the same time keeping the titillation of witchcraft as a central motif."[35] This curious synergy also appears in *The Physick Book of Deliverance Dane* (2009).

Howe's debut novel tells the story of Constance "Connie" Goodwin, a Ph.D. candidate in American Colonial history at Harvard who rediscovers the accused witch Deliverance Dane's "Physick Book," a collection of herbal remedies and spells for all purposes.[36] The "shadow

---

[32] Barry, *The Lace Reader*, 61.

[33] Ibid., 59.

[34] Brunonia Barry is descended from Rebecca Nurse; Katherine Howe's ancestor is Elizabeth Howe. Both were hanged on July 19, 1692. In fact, "in a moment of surreal spookiness," Howe discovered – like Connie in the novel – "that Deliverance Dane was her eighth great grandmother *after* the publication of *The Physick Book of Deliverance Dane*." Cp. Helen Peppe, "Thou Shalt Not Suffer a Witch to Live," *The American Interest*, December 1, 2017.

[35] Bernard Rosenthal, *Salem Story: Reading the Witch Trials of 1692* (Cambridge: Cambridge University Press, 1993), 165.

[36] Howe takes some liberties with her biography: While the historical Deliverance Dane, although she and her husband Nathaniel were "respected

book" inspires Connie to study the practice of actual witchcraft in Colonial New England as her dissertation topic. Despite being strictly rooted in academic thinking, Connie herself soon experiences inexplicable physical sensations, visions, and the ability to ease physical harm. Like the archetypal witch who is "believed to have inherited her magic powers,"[37] she eventually finds out that Deliverance Dane was her own ancestor, and that Connie comes from a long tradition of female healers, "a genealogy that was undeniable."[38]

The relation between women and witchcraft in the novel is established from the very first scene in which Connie is introduced to the reader. Her doctoral exam closes with the task: "provide the committee with a succinct and considered history of witchcraft in North America."[39] Pulling out her "mental drawers," Connie wonders: "Was it under *W*, for 'Witchcraft'? No. Or was it listed under *G*, for 'Gender Issues'?" Eventually, she finds it under "*F*, for 'Folk Religion, Colonial Era'"[40] – the three terms are inseparable. Indeed, many historians agree that, due to the almost universal belief in witchcraft in Colonial America, many people did share and use magic recipes and cures. Elizabeth Reis writes in *Damned Women*: "No doubt some of the accused practiced various forms of magic, but magical practice was not uncommon; it was not what the confessors admitted to; and it certainly was not what these trials were about."[41] In her *Day-to-Day Chronicle* of the Salem trials, Marilynne K. Roach further elaborates:

members of the community", was indeed arrested and imprisoned and Nathaniel consequently "became an active member of the Andover resistance," she was eventually released on bail. Cp. Enders A. Robinson, *Salem Witchcraft and Hawthorne's* House of the Seven Gables (Bowie: Heritage Books, 1992), 299. There is also no proof of her work as a 'cunning woman' and, unlike in Howe's novel, she was not a widow and single mother.

[37] Wilson, *The Salem Witch Trials*, 9.
[38] Katherine Howe, *The Physick Book of Deliverance Dane* (New York: Hachette, 2009), 292.
[39] Ibid., 11.
[40] Ibid., 14.
[41] Elizabeth Reis, *Damned Women: Sinners and Witches in Puritan New England* (Ithaca: Cornell University Press, 1997), 9.

342   Wicca and Modern Witches in Salem Literature

The closest New England *may* have had to magic professionals were the cunning folk, village specialists who revealed unknown and future events, offered healing, or identified evil witches. They were sometimes called 'good witches' or 'healing witches,' but considered their results due to natural magic, the work of holy angels, or a gift from God. Such practitioners – though not the ministers – considered this consistent with Christianity.[42]

Deliverance Dane, whose story runs parallel to Connie's in the novel, also regards her abilities as "God's healing power on earth."[43] A widow and single mother who helps numerous villagers with their ailments, Dane is generally popular in the community. However, her work and social status also make her easily assailable; she is eventually accused of witchcraft by a man whose daughter Dane was unsuccessful in treating. The novel thus puts forth that women who were "trying to take too much power into their own hands"[44] were likely to become victims of patriarchal Puritan society. The compatibility, or rather inseparability, of Dane's positive interpretation of witchcraft and her belief in God is also demonstrated by Connie's New Age mother Grace, herself a widow and single mother in New Mexico who, in many respects, parallels the character of Ann Chase in Barry's novels.[45] For as long as Connie can remember, her mother has been known for her healing abilities, reading and cleansing people's "auras"[46] and "energy fields."[47] She regards life on earth as the creation of an "intelligent Goddess"[48] – a gynocentric genesis that again invokes the origin of the figure of the witch – and she believes in the impact of weather patterns and "the rhythms of the world around us"[49] on human consciousness. Grace's well-intentioned powers are strikingly demonstrated when, from thousands of miles away, she

---

[42] Marilynne K. Roach, *The Salem Witch Trials: A Day-to-Day Chronicle of a Community Under Siege* (Lanham: Taylor Trade Publishing, 2004), xxv.

[43] Howe, *The Physick Book*, 360.

[44] Ibid., 84.

[45] However, neither Grace, nor Connie, nor any of the other characters in Barry's novels who are gifted with extrasensory perception dress 'witchy' like Ann Chase.

[46] Ibid., 114.

[47] Ibid., 28.

[48] Ibid., 236.

[49] Ibid., 235.

CLARA PETINO   343

magically burns a sign on Connie's door to protect her from an anticipated evil (of which Connie is unaware at the time). The description of this circle reads as follows:

> It held a smaller circle inside it, like a target, bisected along both axes by lines. In the top half sat the word *Alpha*, written in an uneven, almost archaic, hand, with two crosses or hatch marks above it. In the upper-left quadrant, on the outer rim, was the word *Meus* with crossed hatch marks on either end. In the same position on the upper-right quadrant of the circle appeared the word *Adjutor*, also framed by crossed hatch marks. Echoing the pattern, in the lower half of the circle, were the words *Omega* in the center, *Agla* in the lower-left quadrant, and *Dominus* in the lower right, each bracketed by crossed hatch marks.[50]

Both Connie and her friends initially mistake the sign for a satanic threat, but, upon further investigation of its parts, they realize that "[t]he circle's meant to be *protective*, rather than hostile."[51] Dissecting the components, they find out that the combined words "*Dominus adjutor meus*" are Latin for "God my helper;"[52] *alpha* and *omega* refer in this context to "the divine that is both the beginning and the end,"[53] and *Agla* is a kabbalist notarikon for "*Atah Gbor Leolam Adonai*, an unspeakable name for God sometimes translated as 'Lord God is eternally powerful.'"[54] The inscriptions are thus "names of God in Latin, Hebrew and Greek, all written around a request for God's help" and, fittingly, surrounded by crosses.[55] The correct interpretation of this sign reflects the need for a positive view of modern witchcraft and paganism, often misinterpreted as Satanism by the public.

Through her academic research of Deliverance Dane's life, work and legacy, Connie is not only able to come up with a "feminist reconception of vernacular magic"[56] that enables her to rewrite the history of witches in a positive way, she also rewrites her own identity as a part of that history. She improves her relationship with her mother by realizing their

---

[50] Ibid., 174.
[51] Ibid., 242.
[52] Ibid., 175.
[53] Ibid., 191.
[54] Ibid., 193.
[55] Ibid., 242.
[56] Ibid., 356.

344   Wicca and Modern Witches in Salem Literature

shared gifts, she has the first happy relationship of her life, and – quite unlike in traditional quests – she even manages to use her newfound powers to save her boyfriend's life.[57] Professionally as well as in private, Connie becomes a strong, happy, independent woman and scholar.

Beyond Literature

This paper initially broached the question of how the witch has become a figure of female empowerment in real life, too, especially since the feminist movement of the 1960s. The political W.I.T.C.H. groups are exemplary: founded on Halloween 1968, they were active in the women's liberation movement in the United States and, "dressed in Halloween-chic shifts and pointy black hats," they targeted "capitalism and corporations as the engines driving sexism of the day."[58] This re-appropriation of the witch notably coincided with a rising interest in popular beliefs such as pagan practice in the United States as well as with the rise of tourism in Salem.

Wicca, derived from the origin of the word *witch*, is usually defined as an Occultist, neo-Pagan or New Age belief, or as a nature-worshipping religion and practice, the followers of which often identify as witches. Made famous by the British author Gerald Gardner and, in particular, his 1954 book *Witchcraft Today*, Wicca promoted the revival of ancient paganism. Wiccan teaching and practice in the U.S. was subsequently driven mainly by Zsuzsanna Budapest, founder of the first feminist witches' coven, and Miriam Simos, alias Starhawk, whose 1979 book on Wiccan belief, *The Spiral Dance,* became a classic. "To reclaim the word *Witch* is to reclaim our right, as women, to be powerful," she

---

[57] Connie realizes over the course of the novel that a curse on her family is the reason her female ancestors were all widows and single mothers; they lost the loves of their lives far too early under inexplicable circumstances. Connie, in danger of experiencing the same fate, nonetheless manages to overcome the curse and rescue her boyfriend Sam.

[58] Sollée, *Witches, Sluts, Feminists*, 53. Originally abbreviating Women's International Terrorist Conspiracy from Hell, they later used other words to suit the initials depending on the current cause, cp. ibid., 52–53.

writes.[59] Though subdivided into many different traditions, Wiccans, as reflected in the character of Ann Chase, praise Celtic and Roman gods and goddesses, practice tarot and herbalism and use spiritual powers to effect positive change in the world. Statistics show that the number of followers in the United States continues to rise: around 340,000 Americans identify as Wiccan and/or Pagan.[60] And while both men and women practice Wicca, it is particularly women of all professions and denominations for whom "witchcraft practices that might once have spelled death for women are now life-affirming."[61] For while they are opposed to restrictive church doctrine, many Wiccans have been brought up as Christians, and, as reflected in the character of Grace Goodwin in *The Physick Book of Deliverance Dane*, are therefore inclusive of Christian beliefs and values. Sollée writes that "witches can follow any religion and still practice witchcraft."[62] However, they strongly distance themselves from Satanism, and raising public awareness of Wiccans' harmless nature is not an idea that exists only in fiction. Ann Chase's antidefamation league has many real-life equivalents, the most prominent of which are the Witches Education League and the Witches League of Public Awareness, "an international organization [...] which works to end prejudice and bigotry against witches and witchcraft."[63] It is not surprising that both are headquartered in Salem.

Following the collapse of industry dominance of the 1950s, the town of Salem began to market its contested past in the wake of the witches' comeback. The opening of the Salem Witch Museum in 1972 and the 1970 on-site filming of episodes of the TV series *Bewitched* (1964–1972) – itself notable as an important step in witches' development in popular culture – and, most importantly, the appearance of Laurie Cabot

---

[59]   Starhawk, *The Spiral Dance: A Rebirth of the Ancient Religion of the Goddess* (San Francisco: Harper & Row, 1989), 22.

[60]   Cp. Sangeeta Singh-Kurtz and Dan Kopf, "The US Witch Population has Seen an Astronomic Rise," *Quartz*, October 4, 2018, qz.com/quartzy/ 1411909/the-explosive-growth-of-witches-wiccans-and-pagans-in-the-us/.

[61]   Sollée, *Witches, Sluts, Feminists*, 14.

[62]   Ibid., 144.

[63]   Rosemary Ellen Guiley, *The Encyclopedia of Witches and Witchcraft* (New York: Facts on File, 1989), 385.

346 Wicca and Modern Witches in Salem Literature

(*1933) significantly contributed to Salem's unique contemporary renown.[64]

A high priestess of modern witchcraft, Cabot has not only been awarded the title "Official Witch of Salem"[65] but was recently described as "the most famous practicing witch in the country."[66] Like Barry's Ann Chase, Cabot plays with the stereotypical image of the witch by wearing black clothes and a pentagram necklace. She opened the first of the now-numerous witch shops in Salem and has written books such as *The Witch in Every Woman* (1997). Moreover, she founded the afore-mentioned Witches League for Public Awareness in 1986 to educate the public and has taught "Witchcraft as a Science" classes at a high school and at Salem State College.[67] And while many younger self-proclaimed witches view her appropriation of those executed in 1692 critically – Cabot believes that they were practicing witches who died for modern witches' freedom[68] – she is widely credited with making Salem "a safe space for practicing witches."[69] Because of Cabot's work, "Salem's Witch Community was soon represented on both the Salem Chamber of Commerce *and* the Council of Churches"[70] – a big step, for when Wicca first was introduced, "the idea of witchcraft as a religion was a new concept for 99.9 per cent of the population [of the U.S.]."[71]

While Cabot has receded from the public in her old age, her legacy of reclaiming the place whose name is synonymous with witchcraft

[64] "Around the same time, several respectable Salem institutions, such as the local paper, the Chamber of Commerce, and the Police Department, adopted *Witch City* logos," depicting a witch flying on a broomstick. Cp. Frances Hill, "Salem as Witch City," in *Salem: Place, Myth, and Memory*, eds. Dane Anthony Morrison and Nancy Lusignan Schultz (Boston: Northeastern University Press, 2004), 285.

[65] Honoring Cabot's work with dyslexic children, Governor Michael Dukakis gave her this title.

[66] Billy Baker, "She Brought Magic to Salem. She has Mixed Feelings about it," *The Boston Globe*, October 26, 2017, bostonglobe.com/metro/2017/10/26/witch/gIeQ13bUSWp03K0RmC9UgL/story.html.

[67] Guiley, *The Encyclopedia of Witches*, 48.

[68] Cp. Hill, "Salem as Witch City," 286.

[69] Baker, "She Brought Magic."

[70] Roach, *The Salem Witch Trials*, 585.

[71] Owen Davies, *America Bewitched: The Story of Witchcraft After Salem* (Oxford: Oxford University Press, 2013), 208.

persecutions is carried on by modern self-proclaimed witches in both fiction and real life. Their interconnections are manifold: as tourist shops and museums display works of 'Salem literature,' the fictional depiction of the 'witch city' continues to promote Salem's image as a hotspot for all things supernatural, making readers all over the world want to experience the unique spatiality and spirituality for themselves.

Tim Delaney writes in "Popular Culture: An Overview" that "[p]opular culture allows large heterogeneous masses of people to identify collectively" and that it "serves an inclusionary role in society as it unites the masses" while at the same time "provid[ing] individuals with a chance to change the prevailing sentiments and norms of behavior [...]."[72] As such, contemporary Salem literature, which has both a mass and a niche appeal, proves to be, as a part of popular culture, a vehicle for and a reflection of social change in one of the United States' most contested places.

In conclusion, I return to Erica Feldman, who is not only the leader of a coven but also the owner of HausWitch Home & Healing, "a modern metaphysical lifestyle brand and shop" combining, as she declares on her website, "the principles of earth magic, meditation, herbalism, and interior decorating *to bring magic and healing into everyday spaces*."[73] This statement says, in a nutshell, what this paper has shown: in the wake of the reappropriated witch becoming a cultural figure of power, Salem has gone from being a place where unruly women were put on trial for their lives to a place whose very spatiality has *become* female. The real-life witches of Salem, as well as a vibrant collection of female authors and their strong female characters, carry their message of healing magic far beyond the city limits and shores of Salem.

---

[72] Tim Delaney, "Popular Culture: An Overview," *Philosophy Now* 64 (2007): 6–7.

[73] "Our Shop," About HausWitch, HausWitch, accessed January 10, 2020, hauswitchstore.com/pages/about; emphasis mine.

348 Wicca and Modern Witches in Salem Literature

Works Cited

Baker, Billy. "She Brought Magic to Salem. She Has Mixed Feelings about it." The Boston Globe, October 26, 2017. bostonglobe.com/metro/2017/10/26/witch/gIeQ13bUSWp03K0RmC 9UgL/story.html.

Barry, Brunonia. The Lace Reader. New York: Harper, 2010.

---. The Map of True Places. New York: Harper, 2011.

---. The Fifth Petal. New York: Crown, 2017.

---. "Happy Halloween! Love, Salem." Writer Unboxed, October 31, 2014. writerunboxed.com/2014/10/31/happy-halloween-love-salem/.

Bateman, Jessica. "Why Salem's Modern-Day Feminist Witchcraft Scene is Giving Rise to 'Magic Tourism.'" The Independent, August 7, 2017. independent.co.uk/travel/americas/salem-witchcraft-scene-magic-tourism-feminism-hipster-modern-day-massachusetts-new-england-donald-trump-spells-a7877521.html.

Davies, Owen. America Bewitched. The Story of Witchcraft After Salem. Oxford: Oxford University Press, 2013.

Delaney, Tim. "Popular Culture: An Overview." Philosophy Now 64 (2007): 6–7.

Guiley, Rosemary Ellen. The Encyclopedia of Witches and Witchcraft. New York: Facts on File, 1989.

Henricus Institoris and Jacobus Sprenger. Malleus Maleficarum. Volume II, The English Translation. Translated and edited by Christopher S. Mackay. Cambridge: Cambridge University Press, 2006.

Hill, Frances. "Salem as Witch City." In Salem: Place, Myth, and Memory. Edited by Dane Anthony Morrison and Nancy Lusignan Schultz, 283–296. Boston: Northeastern University Press, 2004.

Holy Bible. King James Version. Philadelphia: National Publishing Company, 1978.

Howe, Katherine. The Physick Book of Deliverance Dane. New York: Hachette, 2009.

---, ed. The Penguin Book of Witches. New York: Penguin, 2014.

Karlsen, Carol F. The Devil in the Shape of a Woman. Witchcraft in Colonial New England. New York: Norton & Company, 1987.

Longfellow, Henry Wadsworth. Giles Corey of the Salem Farms. In The New England Tragedies, 103–179. Boston: Ticknor and Fields, 1868.

Peppe, Helen. "Thou Shalt not Suffer a Witch to Live." *The American Interest*, December 1, 2017.

Reis, Elizabeth. *Damned Women. Sinners and Witches in Puritan New England*. Ithaca: Cornell University Press, 1997.

Roach, Marilynne K. *The Salem Witch Trials. A Day-by-Day Chronicle of a Community Under Siege*. Lanham: Taylor Trade Publishing, 2004.

Robinson, Enders A. *Salem Witchcraft and Hawthorne's* House of the Seven Gables. Bowie: Heritage Books, 1992.

Rosenthal, Bernard. *Salem Story: Reading the Witch Trials of 1692*. Cambridge: Cambridge University Press, 1993.

Schiff, Stacy. "Witchcraft on the Campaign Trail." *The New York Times*, October 30, 2016. nytimes.com/2016/10/31/opinion/witchcraft-on-the-campaign-trail.html.

Singh-Kurtz, Sangeeta, and Dan Kopf. "The US Witch Population has Seen an Astronomic Rise." *Quartz*, October 4, 2018. qz.com/quartzy/1411909/the-explosive-growth-of-witches-wiccans-and-pagans-in-the-us/.

Sollée, Kristen J. *Witches, Sluts, Feminists: Conjuring the Sex Positive*. Berkeley: ThreeL Media, 2017.

Starhawk. *The Spiral Dance. A Rebirth of the Ancient Religion of the Goddess*. San Francisco: Harper & Row, 1989.

Tolentino, Jia. "The Truth about Witches: An Interview with Katherine Howe." *Jezebel*, October 29, 2014. jezebel.com/the-truth-about-witches-an-interview-with-katherine-ho-1649987737.

Wilkins Freeman, Mary Eleanor. *Giles Corey, Yeoman: A Play*. New York: Harper, 1893.

Wilson, Lori Lee. *The Salem Witch Trials. How History is Invented*. Minneapolis: Lerner Publications Company, 1997.

HEIKE STEINHOFF

Beyond Hashtags: Popular Feminisms, Body Positivity and Self-Help Books

In 2018, Rachel Hollis, founder of a lifestyle website and CEO of her own multi-million-dollar media company, published her best-selling self-help book *Girl, Wash Your Face*. A *New York Times* #1 bestseller, the book sets out to dismantle twenty lies that, according to Hollis, have been "perpetuated by society, the media, our family,"[1] and that she and the 'girls' addressed have told themselves and that have held them back from "becom[ing] who [...] [they] were meant to be."[2] Tapping into the feminist notion of consciousness-raising, Hollis addresses such aspects as female sexuality, motherhood, co-dependency and body weight. Hollis had already gained wide visibility in American popular culture in 2015, when she shared a photo of herself on her Facebook page that presented her, then 32 and a mother of three, in a bikini, showing signs of stretch marks and slightly flabby skin on her stomach. Soon, the picture went viral and was heralded as an example of what has come to be referred to as body positivity. Originating in the fat acceptance movement of the late 1960s and sharing concerns of the women's liberation movement of roughly the same time, body positivity has recently been popularized as a movement that promotes acceptance and love of all bodies hegemonically coded as deviant, ugly or unruly.

However, Hollis personifies that which is ironic with regard to many of the popular examples and increasingly commodified discourses of body positivity: She is white, (now) middle- or even upper-class, cis-gendered, heterosexual, slender and – apart from her stretch marks and sagging belly button – perfectly in line with hegemonic ideals of con-ventional female beauty. While co-opting a strongly feminist-inflected

[1]   Rachel Hollis, *Girl, Wash Your Face* (Nashville: Thomas Nelson, 2018), xii.
[2]   Ibid., cover.

352   Popular Feminisms, Body Positivity and Self-Help Books

rhetoric of self-love, female empowerment, and body positivity in her lifestyle advice, Hollis simultaneously reiterates a makeover discourse of self-optimization that asks women to discipline themselves in quite normative ways. Conceiving of her body as testimony to her tenacity, endurance and reproductive power, Hollis reproduces notions of female bodies as being in need of discipline through weight-loss practices and evaluation by the male gaze, while, at the same time, she promotes confidence and female agency. Female empowerment, in Hollis's transmedia self-help business, is often linked to processes of consumption: Besides the purchase of her books, Hollis offers various forms of consumer advice on her website, e.g., buying the right outfit to help you work out harder, and she sells her own coaching sessions and personal growth conferences called RISE.[3] Like many contemporary self-help books, *Girl, Wash Your Face* uses a rhetoric of positive psychology, which "proposes that happiness, resilience and 'positive' emotions can be consciously worked on and increased."[4] The book constructs an ideal of a self-governing female subject whose goal is not so much social change but entrepreneurship, both in the sense of business and in the sense of becoming the manager of her own life. Hollis's message is blatant: "if you're unhappy – *that's on you!*"[5]

Taking Hollis's example as its cue, this chapter will explore the body and identity politics of contemporary body positive self-help books, reading them as manifestations of popular feminism and its slippages.[6] Advice literature – be it in the form of books, blogs or vlogs – offers us valuable insights into contemporary imaginations of the 'ideal' self. Advice constitutes a technology of governmentality in the Foucauldian

---

[3]   Rachel Hollis, accessed March 28, 2020, https://msrachelhollis.com/.

[4]   Sarah Riley et al., "The Gendered Nature of Self-Help," *Feminism and Psychology* 29, no. 1 (2019): 5.

[5]   Hollis, *Girl, Wash Your Face*, 5.

[6]   I borrow from Sarah Banet-Weiser's conceptualization of popular feminism as referring to a feminism that has indeed become popular, that circulates in popular media, and – in line with Stuart Hall's definition of popular culture – presents a site of cultural contestation and power struggle. Cf. Sarah Banet-Weiser, *Empowered: Popular Feminism and Popular Misogyny* (Durham: Duke University Press, 2018). As employed in this essay, popular feminisms – in the plural – is used as an umbrella term that comprises different (including both postfeminist and fourth wave) tendencies.

sense, i.e. a technique of power, a form of governing the conduct of individuals and populations.[7] Self-help books, in particular, function as scripts for self-government. They present a technology of domination and a technology of the self, defined by Foucault as techniques that

> permit individuals to effect by their own means or with the help of others a certain number of operations on their own bodies and souls, thoughts, conduct, and way of being, so as to transform themselves in order to attain a certain state of happiness, purity, wisdom, perfection, or immortality.[8]

In a convergent media environment, where online media have often been at the forefront of circulating popular feminist and body positive messages and agendas, self-help books have come to be embraced as a central means of transmitting them offline and in a condensed version. Studying these books from a discourse analytical perspective allows us to shed light on the 'regimes of truth' and ideals of selfhood that they (re)produce.

Going beyond hashtags, I will analyze in this chapter three body positive self-help books in order to elucidate the blurry lines that frame contemporary feminisms and their body politics, and to extend the insights of the few existent studies on body positivity, which have primarily focused on its manifestations online. Whereas Hollis's self-help publications capitalize on neoliberal notions of female empowerment and gesture towards body positive attitudes while not subscribing to any feminist or body positive agenda, Jes Baker's *Things No One Will Tell Fat Girls: A Handbook for Unapologetic Living* (2015) and Sonya Renee Taylor's *The Body is Not an Apology: The Power of Radical Self-Love* (2018) present outspokenly feminist and explicitly body positive self-help books authored by self-identified activists who can be aligned with what has been referred to as 'fourth wave feminism.' Both authors, like Hollis, promote their messages online through blogs and other forms of social media activism but have also turned to offering advice

---

[7] Cf. e.g. Heidi Marie Rimke, "Governing Citizens Through Self-Help Literature," *Cultural Studies* 14, no. 1 (2000): 61–78.

[8] Michel Foucault, "Technologies of the Self," in *The Essential Foucault: Selections from Essential Works of Foucault, 1954–1984*, eds. Paul Rabinow and Nikolas S. Rose (New York: The New Press, 2003), 146.

354   Popular Feminisms, Body Positivity and Self-Help Books

offline through 'inspirational talks' and self-help books. Reading these books against the foil of *Girl, Wash Your Face* shows how Baker and Taylor seek to dispel the culturally dominant discourse of neoliberal self-optimization and yet ultimately remain invested in it. Both publications cast bodily self-love not so much as neoliberal self-improvement, but reframe it as a resource for a feminist revolution. Consciously embracing an intersectional-feminist approach, these publications mobilize a feminist rhetoric of patriarchal oppression and call for the re-discovery of some form of 'authentic' and naturalized form of embodiment. Their publications seek to disrupt the individualist narratives of resilience that are typically identified with contemporary self-help literature and realign self-help with an impetus for collective action. At the same time, an analysis of the two texts reveals how body positive self-help produces cultural discourses of recognition, authenticity, hygiene and (mental) self-transformation that link it to the very same cultural discourses, economies, media markets and modes of subjectification that it seeks to resist. The aim of this essay is to elucidate the nuances and overlaps of these different yet converging cultural logics.

Postfeminism and the Fourth Wave: From Makeover to Love Your Body

Postfeminism as well as fourth wave feminism are contested and quite nebulous terms that have been defined in different ways. Both have been closely linked to popular culture and media. Yet it is difficult to neatly distinguish one from the other or to establish clear boundaries that separate both from the feminisms that they supposedly replace, continue or challenge.[9] Postfeminism has become widely used at least since the

---

[9]   The notion of feminist 'waves' has always been problematic, since it tends to divide feminist movements along generational lines and suggests that there are moments of feminist inactivity in-between, while at the same time occluding overlaps and continuities between the discerned waves as well as internal divisions within. Cf., e.g. Jennifer Baumgardner, *F'em! Goo Goo, Gaga, and Some Thoughts on Balls* (New York: Seal Press, 2011); Nicola Rivers, *Postfeminism(s) and the Arrival of the Fourth Wave: Turning Tides* (Cham: Palgrave, 2017). With regards to the present moment, a variety of

HEIKE STEINHOFF 355

1990s and has variously been defined as a backlash against feminism, a historical shift in feminism, or an alignment with other post-movements such as post-modernism or post-structuralism. Particularly in the work of Rosalind Gill, postfeminism has been defined as a "sensibility" that entangles both feminist and anti-feminist ideas[10] and is "deeply enmeshed with neoliberalism."[11] Postfeminist media discourses link the responsibilization of the self, associated with neoliberalism as a mode of governmentality and political rationality,[12] to notions of female agency. In terms of its body politics, postfeminism has been linked to makeover discourses that ask women to modify their bodies, often in line with normative notions of femininity.[13] A feminist and neoliberal rhetoric of choice and empowerment has been attached to practices of self-surveillance and to practices of bodily modification like dieting, cosmetic surgery, or fashion, all of which have been framed as technologies of self-care rather than as ways of disciplining female bodies. Bodily transformations are coded as revelations of one's authentic self and as paths towards health and happiness. As various scholars have noted,[14] makeover discourses are highly gendered, classed and raced: The ideal neoliberal and postfeminist subject in American mainstream popular

different, though related, terms and concepts besides those discussed in this essay have been introduced in an attempt to describe contemporary feminisms, including neoliberal feminism, digital feminism or pop feminism (cf. Sarah Banet-Weiser et al., "Postfeminism, Popular Feminism and Neoliberal Feminism? Sarah Banet-Weiser, Rosalind Gill and Catherine Rottenberg in Conversation," *Feminist Theory* (2019): 1–22; and Carrie Smith-Prei and Maria Stehle, *Awkward Politics: Technologies of Popfeminist Activism* (Montreal: McGill-Queen's University Press, 2016).

[10] Cf. Rosalind Gill, "Postfeminist Media Culture: Elements of a Sensibility," *European Journal of Cultural Studies* 10, no. 2 (2007): 147–166.

[11] Rosalind Gill, "Post-Postfeminism? New Feminist Visibilities in Postfeminist Times," *Feminist Media Studies* 16, no. 4 (2016): 613.

[12] Cf. Thomas Lemke, "'The Birth of Bio-Politics' – Michel Foucault's Lecture at the Collège de France on Neo-Liberal Governmentality," *Economy and Society* 30, no. 2 (2001): 203.

[13] Cf. e.g. Gill, "Post-Postfeminism"; Heike Steinhoff, *Transforming Bodies: Makeovers and Monstrosities in American Culture* (Basingstoke: Palgrave, 2015); Brenda Weber, *Makeover TV: Selfhood, Citizenship, and Celebrity* (Durham: Duke University Press, 2009).

[14] Cf. e.g. ibid.

356 Popular Feminisms, Body Positivity and Self-Help Books

culture is predominantly imagined as white, cis-gendered, heterosexual, able-bodied and middle-class.[15] Postfeminist and neoliberal logics have recently intensified with the introduction of new technologies and have spread to include more and more new areas and states of the female body.[16]

However, they have also been met with resistance: The increasingly widespread influence of discourses of body positivity seems to replace or at least challenge the dominant makeover narrative, and various visible popular feminist discourses contest the body and identity politics aligned with postfeminist neoliberal notions of the self. Often, these developments have been associated with the emergence of so-called fourth wave feminism, understood as a 'resurgence' of the visibility of feminist activism in popular media and of its popularity among young women at the beginning of the second decade of the new millennium.[17] Most prominently, fourth wave feminism has been linked to social media, celebrity feminism, a 'call out culture' that challenges sexism, and an awareness of intersectionality. Like other previous and contemporary feminisms, much of what has been labeled the fourth wave centers on the female body[18] – a key political strategy being the re-signification of 'transgressive' or 'deviant' bodies as signifiers of resistance, examples of which include the 'pussy hats' worn by protestors at the Women's March on Washington in 2017, menstruation activism, or breastfeeding protests and other forms of collective and individual body positive protest. Body positive activism is a claim to

---

[15] Postfeminism, however, has been identified as a sensibility that also shapes the lives of non-white, lesbian or older women and needs to be studied as an intersectional and transnational concept (cf. the studies mentioned in Gill, "Post-Postfeminist," 619–620).

[16] Ana Sofia Elias et al., "Aesthetic Labour: Beauty Politics in Neoliberalism," in *Rethinking Beauty Politics in Neoliberalism*, eds. Ana Sofia Elias et al. (London: Palgrave, 2017), 26–30.

[17] Whereas Cochrane dates the beginning of Fourth Wave Feminism in 2013, Baumgardner argues that it already began in 2008 (cf. Cochrane, *All the Rebel Women*; and Baumgardner, *F'em!*).

[18] This includes the ontological question of what constitutes the category of woman, of who is included and who is excluded by the various body and identity politics. Generally, the fourth wave has been characterized as intersectional and trans-inclusive.

recognition in a mainstream culture that has excluded particular bodies or subjected them to a stigmatizing stare.[19] Particularly on social media platforms, body positivity has been associated with sharing images or texts that seek to challenge normative notions of what constitutes beautiful bodies by promoting self-love and bodily acceptance no matter one's size, race, ethnicity, age, ability, gender or sexual self-identification. It relies on a politics of visibility that has, however, become increasingly commodified in an economy of visibility, where, as Sarah Banet-Weiser puts it, "the *spotlight* on their bodies, their visibility, the number of views, is in fact its politics."[20]

In mainstream media and lifestyle advice such as Hollis's self-help book, body positive messages have been co-opted in postfeminist rhetoric and perpetuate the neoliberal and beauty discourses that they purport to disrupt. An emphasis on choice disguises structural inequalities, a focus on diversity conceals that the 'new' models often only present a tiny shift from the ideal of female attractiveness, and companies that have been invested in producing women's dissatisfaction with their own bodies are now promising a revolution of body positivity while apparently still clinging to the notion that the female body is hard to love.[21] Commercial "love your body discourses" especially, as Elias and Gill have argued, have simply turned the bodily makeover into a psychic one:[22] Confidence becomes the new technology of sexiness, which has replaced beauty as the key feature of normative femininity in contemporary media culture.[23] In response to this increasing commodification and postfeminist or neoliberal appropriation of body

[19] Cf. the theory on staring developed by Rosemarie Garland-Thomson, *Staring: How We Look* (Oxford: Oxford University Press, 2009).

[20] Sarah Banet-Weiser, *Empowered: Popular Feminism and Popular Misogyny* (Durham: Duke University Press, 2018), 27.

[21] Cf. Ana Sofia Elias and Rosalind Gill, "'Awaken your incredible': Love Your Body Discourses and Postfeminist Contradictions," *International Journal of Media and Cultural Politics* 10, no. 2 (2014): 179–188.

[22] Ibid., 185.

[23] As this book goes to print, Shani Orgad and Rosalind Gill publish their study *Confidence Culture* in which they read Hollis's second self-help book *Girl, Stop Apologizing* as one prime manifestation of this cult(ure). Many of their observations resonate wih my reading of Hollis's first book in this chapter. Cf. Shani Orgad and Rosalind Gill, *Confidence Culture* (Durham: Duke University Press, 2022).

358   Popular Feminisms, Body Positivity and Self-Help Books

positivity, some activists have turned to terms like body neutrality or body liberation to shift the focus from an always positive attitude towards one's own body and what has come to be perceived as an obligation to love oneself, to a message of neutrality and acceptance, and, moreover, a call to not only identify oneself through one's body. As these debates, shifts, overlaps and entanglements indicate, the distinctions between different forms of contemporary feminisms and their body politics are never clear-cut.[24]

Body Positive Self-Help Books: From Radical Self-Love to Feminist Activism

As my introductory analysis reveals, Rachel Hollis's *Girl, Wash Your Face* provides a textbook illustration of neoliberal and postfeminist biopedagogical discourses that teach people, and women especially, how to live. *Girl, Wash Your Face* is a best-selling example taken from a plethora of similar books that focus on bodily self-love and self-care, and that "marr[y] seemingly pro-feminist sentiments of body positivity and self-acceptance with appearance concerns (that tie women's value back to their bodies), the consumption of products, and a blurring of economic and psychological language."[25] While deeply rooted in historical notions of self-invention and the myth of the American Dream, contemporary self-help literature has particularly been linked to the construction of the neoliberal ideal of the 'enterprising self' who treats her body and life as a project.[26] As it addresses its readers as 'lacking,' 'suffering' subjects, who are in need of help and fixing, self-help literature pathologizes certain forms of being and offers tools,

---

[24]   As Nicolas Rivers also argues, "postfeminism is not a static term – or indeed phenomena – and as such, the arrival of fourth-wave feminism may signal the transformation of postfeminism(s) and the need for continued interrogation, rather than its demise." Cf. Rivers, *Postfeminism(s)*, 4.

[25]   Riley et al., "The Gendered Nature of Self-Help," 9.

[26]   Ulrich Bröckling, *Das Unternehmerische Selbst: Soziologie einer Subjektivierungsform* (Frankfurt am Main: Suhrkamp, 2007); Heidi Marie Rimke, "Governing Citizens Through Self-Help Literature," 61–78; Micki McGee, *Self-Help, Inc.: Makeover Culture in American Life* (Oxford: Oxford University Press, 2005).

including the purchase of these books, for self-improvement. Expressive of contemporary therapeutic culture, self-help

> interpellate[s] human beings as 'psychological beings', to interrogate and narrate themselves in terms of a psychological 'inner life' that holds the secrets of their identity, which they are to discover and fulfil, which is the standard against which the living of an 'authentic' life is to be judged.[27]

The necessity of realizing one's full potential becomes a naturalized technology of neoliberal governmentality, embedded in a discourse of happiness in which "to seek after happiness is [represented as a means] to empower oneself."[28] Exemplifying a general shift in lifestyle expertise, in *Girl, Wash Your Face*, authority is no longer dependent on formal education or professional status but is rather gained through personal experience and a notion of 'authenticity' constructed through the author's personal narratives of vulnerability, trauma, body shame, failure and resilience.[29] Hollis's confessional, but often also quite humorous, 'girl talk' allows her to create an affective relation to her female readers and establish her role as experienced life coach who speaks as the implied reader's best friend. At the same time, repeatedly showcasing her own bodily and personal vulnerability, e.g. "I peed my pants," helps to conceal Hollis's privileged position as a white, heterosexual, cis-gendered, able-bodied and rich young woman.[30]

Whereas many self-help books align with the neoliberal and postfeminist discourses exemplified by Hollis's lifestyle advice, self-

---

[27] Nikolas Rose, *Inventing Our Selves: Psychology, Power and Personhood* (Cambridge: Cambridge University Press, 2001), 22.

[28] Sam Brinkley, *Happiness as Enterprise: An Essay on Neoliberal Life* (Albany: SUNY Press, 2014), 18.

[29] For studies of lifestyle expertise, cf. also Tania Lewis, "Branding, Celebretization, and the Lifestyle Expert," *Cultural Studies* 24 (2010): 580–598; Stephanie A. Baker and Chris Rojek, *Lifestyle Gurus: Constructing Authority and Influence Online* (New York: Polity Press, 2020).

[30] Cf. Negra's similar argument about Sherryl Sandberg's *Lean In* (2013). Since the completion of this essay in early 2020, Hollis has faced increasing public criticism for remarks perceived as racist and classist, as well as for acts of plagiarism. Moreover, she disappointed some of her conservative Christian followers by announcing her divorce.

360 Popular Feminisms, Body Positivity and Self-Help Books

identified activists like Jes Baker and Sonya Renee Taylor seek, to different degrees, to counter this impetus with calls for explicitly feminist, intersectional and collective action in the mode of fourth wave activism. Like Hollis, whose follow-up to *Girl, Wash Your Face* is entitled *Girl, Stop Apologizing* (2019), Baker and Taylor subscribe to a notion of (female) empowerment that is linked to notions of "living unapologetically"[31] and to stop acting as if the body was an apology.[32] In contrast to Hollis, though, both link this call for empowerment to a rhetoric of political activism already evident on the book covers in Baker's pen name, The Militant Baker, and Taylor's use of the word "radical." Again, like Hollis, Baker and Taylor rely on their own confessional stories of suffering, body shaming and transformation, significantly coding acts of visibility in which they inscribe their marginalized bodies into visual conventions of female (self-) sexualization as a starting point for their path towards self-love. Yet they also seek to construct a notion of collectivity and polyvocality by including the stories of others in their books. Baker does so through the integration of nine guest essays to add to or counterbalance her own voice as a white fat woman, while Taylor embraces an explicitly intersectional queer-feminist approach not only through the integration of stories or by referring to her own black, queer, fat body, but also by referencing academic sources like the work of Kimberlé Crenshaw. Similar to Naomi Wolf's 1990 feminist bestseller *The Beauty Myth*, which argued that beauty functions as a form of patriarchal backlash against female empowerment – a theory that is frequently referenced in body positive self-help books – Taylor's and Baker's texts operate according to a logic of oppression. Female bodies especially but, in *The Body is Not an Apology*, also bodies that are 'Othered' in terms of race, ethnicity, class, sexuality or ability are thus understood to be oppressed, disciplined and regulated by a patriarchal media and medical complex. Taylor calls this "body terrorism," a provocative and loaded political metaphor that aligns with the radical political goals of her project.

---

[31] Jes Baker, *Things No One Will Tell Fat Girls: A Handbook for Unapologetic Living* (New York: Seal Press, 2015).

[32] Sonya Renee Taylor, *The Body is Not an Apology* (Oakland: Berrett-Koehler Publishers, 2018).

The remedy that the books promise resides in providing their implied readers with alternative knowledge and truths about their bodies, beauty, health and behavior. In this context, body positive self-help revives tactics of second wave feminist consciousness-raising groups like the Boston Women's Health Collective, which sought to reclaim authority over women's bodies from the hands of male medical professionals. Knowledge, activities and guidelines offered in contemporary body positive self-help books resonate with such second wave efforts and a time when self-help "referred not to individual self-improvement but to cooperative efforts for mutually improved conditions on the part of a community of peers."[33] *Things No One Will Tell Fat Girls* and *The Body is Not an Apology* aim to replace the dominant regimes of truths about beauty and health with experiential, academic and 'alternative' medical truths, such as feminist scholarship, the medical approach of Health at Every Size or exercises to touch and get to know one's body. Observing one's own thoughts, body and actions and internalizing or rather embodying the knowledge offered by these self-help books becomes part of body positivity's bio-pedagogical call for self-love, liberation and social change.

Whereas Baker still partakes in the neoliberal individualistic narrative of a progression 'from vulnerability to resilience' also propagated by Hollis's book, Taylor encodes vulnerability as the route towards oneself *and* to a collective bond with others. Hers is a rhetoric that invokes (religious) notions of compassion and at the same time is reminiscent of recent academic discussions of vulnerability as a potential resource for resistance.[34] Vulnerability and failure are embraced as chances to address asymmetries of power and disrupt conventional logics of success, a tactic that is, however, haunted by its appropriation into a consumer cultural market where "[v]ulnerability becomes a kind of capital, a resource, or an asset, making its way into public discourse."[35] According to a cultural system in which the

---

[33] McGee, *Self-Help, Inc.*, 18.

[34] Cf. e.g. Judith Butler et al., *Rethinking Vulnerability and Resistance* (Durham: Duke University Press, 2016).

[35] Anu Koivunen et al., *The Power of Vulnerability: Mobilising Affect in Feminist, Queer and Anti-Racist Media Cultures* (Manchester: Manchester University Press, 2018), 6.

362   Popular Feminisms, Body Positivity and Self-Help Books

individual body is read as a symbol of the social body and vice versa,[36] both books suggest that the social body is toxic and that this manifests itself in individual suffering (e.g. self-hatred, eating disorders, etc.). In turn, becoming aware of both their oppression and inherent beauty and healing the relationship to their bodies are coded as the implied readers' routes towards self-love and cultural change.

As Baker herself recently stated, her self-help advice as promoted in *Things No One Will Tell Fat Girls* has reproduced many of the neoliberal aspects of the body positivity movement, including an emphasis on individual self-improvement, self-love, and happiness.[37] Reiterating postfeminist notions of empowerment, *Things No One Will Tell Fat Girls* ultimately asks its readers, who are predominantly coded as young women, to gain back control over their own bodies. In contrast, Taylor places her spiritual concept of 'radical self-love' in opposition to notions of self-confidence and self-acceptance. "Radical self-love," she argues, is a "deeper, wider, more original" and interdependent concept, one aware of the fact that "our society requires a drastic political, economic, and social reformation in the ways in which we deal with bodies and body difference."[38] Her book is about more than beauty; it is about embodiment. Assessing one's own complicity in what bell hooks has called the "white supremacist, capitalist, patriarchy"[39] is at the core of many of the reflection exercises. This emphasis on awareness reproduces the culturally widespread therapeutic ethos while also pre-senting part of an increasingly popularized 'woke culture.' Challenging normative notions of beauty, physical health, and aesthetic labor, and asking her readers to examine their own implicit biases, *The Body is Not an Apology* relies on psychotherapeutic discourses and a spiritual rhetoric of authentic selfhood that counters and yet resonates with contemporary makeover culture. Radical self-love, as Taylor suggests, "is not a destination you are trying to get to; it is who you already are,"[40]

---

[36] Mary Douglas, *Purity and Danger: An Analysis of Concepts of Pollution and Taboo* (New York: Routledge, 2002).

[37] Cf. Jes Baker, *Landwhale* (New York: Polity Press, 2018), 243–245.

[38] Taylor, *The Body is Not an Apology*, 7.

[39] bell hooks, *Feminism is For Everybody: Passionate Politics* (Cambridge: South End Press, 2000), 4.

[40] Taylor, *The Body is Not an Apology*, xiii.

HEIKE STEINHOFF 363

it is "our inherent natural state"[41] that has, however, been occluded from us due to the "social, political and economic systems of oppression."[42] Thus, *The Body is Not an Apology* subscribes to a naturalized notion of a pre-discursive authentic body and bodily love, located in childhood or even right after birth. In a similar vein, Baker locates an inherent potential of resistance in the physical body when she argues that "95 percent of women's bodies will naturally refuse to become that which we see portrayed in the media as desirable, no matter what they do."[43] To recover one's access to this natural state of embodiment means purifying the body from the toxicity of body shame. As Taylor writes:

> In the study of infectious diseases, epidemiologists use what is called the 'epidemiological triad' to explain how pathogens spread from person to person. This triad consists of an agent, a host, and an environment. [...] In the work of radical self-love, body shame is the dis-ease, we are the host, and body terrorism is the environment.[44]

Employing a discourse of toxicity and bodily hygiene is typical of body positive self-help books.[45] They re-signify the culturally prevalent rhetoric of conventional diet talk, in which detox is linked to reducing weight, while mobilizing the term's origin in medical discourses and 'alternative' (i.e., non-official) medical discourses in particular. Ultimately, however, such rhetoric also helps to uphold a notion of mental if not bodily purity and health, of hygiene, order and control.

Things No One Will Tell Fat Girls and *The Body is Not an Apology* reproduce self-help culture's tendency to construct a flawed self that is "'ontologically separate from itself'"[46] and in need of greater self-mastery over her thoughts, behavior, and the affective relationship to her own body and those of others in order to travel the road towards a better life. They emphasize patience and self-care and allow for failure, yet both books ultimately remain caught up in the narrative framework of

---

[41] Ibid., 10.
[42] Ibid.
[43] Baker, *Things No One Will Tell Fat Girls*, 10.
[44] Taylor, *The Body is Not an Apology*, 112.
[45] Cf., for example, Megan Jayne Crabbe, *Body Positive Power* (London: Vermilion, 2017).
[46] Hazleden qtd. in Riley et al., "The Gendered Nature of Self-Help," 5.

364   Popular Feminisms, Body Positivity and Self-Help Books

the genre and the neoliberal notion of self-improvement, in particular through mental, but also bodily, 'labor.' The way "back to ourselves"[47] is coded as a courageous journey that requires hard work and tiny steps, and also often a re-direction of consumption patterns, including abstinence from 'toxic' media content and replacing it with 'better' content. Baker in particular provides detailed information on what kind of body positive media or products to consume. Eventually, Taylor, too, interpellates her readers as self-governing citizens who turn into motors for social change. "Our contemporary regime of the self", as Nikolas Rose puts it, "is not 'antisocial'. [...] Yet, however 'social' this field may be, it can be turned to the account of the enterprising self: for in recognizing the dynamic nexus of interpersonal relations that it inhabits, selves can place these under conscious control and the self can learn the skills to shape its relations with others so that it will best fulfill its own destiny."[48] *The Body is Not an Apology* asks readers to disengage from false beliefs because "[l]iberation is the opportunity for every human, no matter their body, to have unobstructed access to their highest self; for every human to live in radical self-love."[49]

Conclusion

Body positive self-help books make use of discourses of self-love, happiness and empowerment that are deeply entangled with neoliberal citizenship and different formations of popular feminist politics. In mainstream texts such as Hollis's and in advice from self-identified activists like Baker and Taylor, self-mastery and self-care – two of the central technologies of the self that are promoted by these texts – are employed in significantly different and yet similar ways. As authors and activists, women like Baker and Taylor partake in the dominant cultural narratives, seeking to shift the rules of the game while at the same time profiting off the very consumer cultural system that hitherto excluded them. They practice what Carrie Smith-Prei and Maria Stehle have termed "awkward politics": "They do not or cannot detach from the

---

[47]   Taylor, *The Body is Not an Apology*, 58.
[48]   Rose, *Inventing Our Selves*, 159.
[49]   Taylor, *The Body is Not an Apology*, 116.

economy that enables them; rather they stick to that economy in an uncomfortable awkwardness."[50]

Despite their emphasis on failure, vulnerability, patience and social change, these books already introduce the reader in their cover images to the happy, individual, 'after' bodies/selves that these books promise through the author's own narrative of (mental) transformation. Whereas *Things No One Will Tell Fat Girls* features an hourglass silhouette that Baker self-critically describes in the book as a marketing tool, the cover of her second book *Landwhale* (2018) shows Baker herself happily smiling into the camera, sporting a swimsuit. The cover image of *The Body is Not an Apology* displays Taylor's naked black, fat, queer body surrounded by an aureole. The cover is emblematic of the book's radical and spiritual approach, as it inserts her body into white heteronormative religious iconography while already pointing towards the author's function as an inspirational figure. Recently, Taylor began offering "radical self-love life lift retreats" in New Zealand. Similar programs are offered by other body positive celebrity activists. Tapping into the language and structures of the wellness industry on the one hand while resonating with long-standing feminist ideas about creating spaces of mutual care on the other hand, such offers reproduce the consumer cultural logic in which well-being is, at least partly, sold as achievable through a never-ending process of consumption, including all of the social exclusions and inequalities that this entails. Body positive self-help books are a heterogenous genre that blurs the lines of popular feminisms, shifting between postfeminist and 'fourth wave' politics, or rather illustrating the impossibility of drawing any clear-cut line between them.

---

[50] Smith-Prei and Stehle, *Awkward Politics*, 11.

Works Cited

Baker, Jes. *Things No One Will Tell Fat Girls: A Handbook for Unapologetic Living*. New York: Seal Press, 2015.

---. *Landwhale*. New York: Seal Press, 2018.

Baker, Stephanie A., and Chris Rojek. *Lifestyle Gurus: Constructing Authority and Influence Online*. New York: Polity Press, 2020.

Banet-Weiser, Sarah, et al. "Postfeminism, Popular Feminism and Neoliberal Feminism? Sarah Banet-Weiser, Rosalind Gill and Catherine Rottenberg in Conversation." *Feminist Theory* (2019): 1–22.

Banet-Weiser, Sarah. *Empowered: Popular Feminism and Popular Misogyny*. Durham: Duke University Press, 2018.

Baumgardner, Jennifer. *F'em! Goo Goo, Gaga, and Some Thoughts on Balls*. New York: Seal Press, 2011.

Boston Women's Health Collective. *Our Bodies, Ourselves: A Book by and for Women*. New York: Simon & Schuster, 1973.

Brinkley, Sam. *Happiness as Enterprise: An Essay on Neoliberal Life*. Albany: SUNY Press, 2014.

Bröckling, Ulrich. *Das Unternehmerische Selbst: Soziologie einer Subjektivierungsform*. Frankfurt am Main: Suhrkamp, 2007.

Butler, Judith, et al. *Rethinking Vulnerability and Resistance*. Durham: Duke University Press, 2016.

Cochrane, Kira. *All the Rebel Women: The Rise of the Fourth Wave of Feminism*. London: Guardian Books, 2013.

Crabbe, Megan Jayne. *Body Positive Power*. London: Vermilion, 2017.

Douglas, Mary. *Purity and Danger: An Analysis of Concepts of Pollution and Taboo*. New York: Routledge, 2002.

Elias, Ana Sofia, et al. "Aesthetic Labour: Beauty Politics in Neoliberalism." In *Rethinking Beauty Politics in Neoliberalism*, edited by Ana Sofia Elias et al., 3–50. London: Palgrave, 2017.

Elias, Ana Sofia, and Rosalind Gill. "'Awaken your incredible': Love Your Body Discourses and Postfeminist Contradictions." *International Journal of Media and Cultural Politics* 10, no. 2 (2014): 179–188.

Foucault, Michel. "Technologies of the Self." In *The Essential Foucault: Selections from Essential Works of Foucault, 1954–1984*, edited by Paul Rabinow and Nikolas S. Rose, 145–169. New York: The New Press, 2003.

---. "The Subject and Power." In *The Essential Foucault: Selections from Essential Works of Foucault, 1954–1984*, edited by Paul Rabinow and Nikolas S. Rose, 126–144. New York: The New Press, 2003.

Garland-Thomson, Rosemarie. *Staring: How We Look*. Oxford: Oxford University Press, 2009.

Gill, Rosalind. "Postfeminist Media Culture: Elements of a Sensibility." *European Journal of Cultural Studies* 10, no. 2 (2007): 147–166.

---. "Post-Postfeminism: New Feminist Visibilities in Postfeminist Times." *Feminist Media Studies* 16, no. 4 (2016): 610–630.

Hollis, Rachel. *Girl, Wash Your Face*. Nashville: Thomas Nelson, 2018.

---. *Girl, Stop Apologizing*. New York: HarperCollins, 2019.

hooks, bell. *Feminism Is for Everybody: Passionate Politics*. Cambridge: South End Press, 2000.

Johnston, José, and Judith Taylor. "Feminist Consumerism and Fat Activists: A Comparative Study of Grassroots Activism and the Dove Real Beauty Campaign." *Signs Journal of Women in Culture and Society* 33, no. 4 (2008): 941–966.

Koivunen, Anu. *The Power of Vulnerability: Mobilising Affect in Feminist, Queer and Anti-Racist Media Cultures*. Manchester: Manchester University Press, 2018.

Lemke, Thomas. "'The Birth of Bio-Politics' – Michel Foucault's Lecture at the Collège de France on Neo-Liberal Governmentality." *Economy and Society* 30, no. 2 (2001): 190–207.

Lewis, Tania. "Branding, Celebretization, and the Lifestyle Expert." *Cultural Studies* 24 (2010): 580–598.

McGee, Micki. *Self-Help, Inc.: Makeover Culture in American Life*. Oxford: Oxford University Press, 2005.

Negra, Diane. "Claiming Feminism: Commentary, Autobiography and Advice Literature For Women in the Recession." *Journal of Gender Studies* 23, no. 3 (2014): 275–286.

Orgad, Shani, and Rosalind Gill, *Confidence Culture*. Durham: Duke University Press, 2022.

Riley, Sarah, et al. "The Gendered Nature of Self-Help." *Feminism and Psychology* 29, no. 1 (2019): 3–18.

Rimke, Heidi Marie. "Governing Citizens Through Self-Help Literature." *Cultural Studies* 14, no. 1 (2000): 61–78.

Rivers, Nicola. *Postfeminism(s) and the Arrival of the Fourth Wave: Turning Tides*. Cham: Palgrave, 2017.

Rose, Nikolas. *Inventing Our Selves: Psychology, Power and Personhood*. Cambridge: Cambridge University Press, 2001.

Sastre, Alexandra. "Towards a Radical Body Positive: Reading the Online 'Body Positive Movement.'" *Feminist Media Studies* 14, no. 6 (2014): 929–943.

Smith-Prei, Carrie, and Maria Stehle. *Awkward Politics: Technologies of Popfeminist Activism*. Montreal: McGill-Queen's University Press, 2016.

Steinhoff, Heike. *Transforming Bodies: Makeovers and Monstrosities in American Culture*. Basingstoke: Palgrave, 2015.

Taylor, Sonya Renee. *The Body is Not an Apology*. Oakland: Berrett-Koehler Publishers, 2018.

Weber, Brenda. *Makeover TV: Selfhood, Citizenship, and Celebrity*. Durham: Duke University Press, 2009.

Wolf, Naomi. *The Beauty Myth: How Images of Beauty Are Used Against Women*. London: Chatto and Windus, 1990.

LISANNA WIELE

Transgression Inscribed: The City Mysteries' Queer Urbanity

"You see, the entire arrangements of this place may be explained in one word – it is easy enough for a stranger – that's you, my boy – to find his way *in*, but it would puzzle him like the devil to find his way *out*."[1]

The serialized antebellum city mystery novels penned by George Lippard, George Thompson, and Ned Buntline not only referenced real cityscapes to appeal to their readership, they also rewrote the growing American metropolis into a topsy-turvy space of social transgressions beyond the urban grid. They dramatized the city as a space that was intensely disorienting to those who only perceived it from the outside and could only be entered with the help of those who claimed access through insider knowledge, namely, the narrators and focalizers of these novels. Mary Unger refers to George Lippard's fictionalized departure from the regulating urban grid of Philadelphia in *The Quaker City* as the construction of "queer space,"[2] adopting the term to mean not only 'peculiar' or 'strange,' but also as signifying "marginalization, non-normativity, and counterhegemony" suggesting "a degree of antagonism with dominant power structures."[3] This reading is a departure from the terminology of a 'queer space' as it is generally understood in the field of Queer Theory – a non-normative space of liberation and a cultural

[1] George Lippard, *The Quaker City or, the Monks of Monk Hall: A Romance of Philadelphia Life, Mystery, and Crime*, ed. David S. Reynolds (Amherst: University of Massachusetts Press, 1995), 53.
[2] Mary Unger, "'Dens of Iniquity and Holes of Wickedness': George Lippard and the Queer City," *Journal of American Studies* 43, no. 2 (2009): 320.
[3] Ibid.

370   The City Mysteries' Queer Urbanity

counterpoint to a hegemonic, heterosexual social order. Rather, it specifically considers queer spaces in antebellum city mysteries as locations for transgressions across the borders of social classes. No matter their original purpose, these locations exude a sense of danger and immortality, and the transgressions they enable emerge from the existence of anomalous – queer – spaces in the texts.

In this essay, I therefore aim to illustrate how this queering of the city takes place in select works of Lippard and Thompson, and how it enables transgressive narratives within an expanding, serialized popular culture. The following three case studies, on George Lippard's *The Quaker City; or, The Monks of Monk Hall*; George Thompson's *City Crimes – Or Life in New York and Boston*; and Thompson's lesser-known work *The Locket*, examine the ways in which the texts introduce aberrant 'queer' spaces in the cities and the functions those spaces have in the texts. I suggest that these functions are twofold. They provide shock value essential to maintain reader engagement in serial sensationalist literature, but they also enable narrative transgressions that would otherwise have no space in the antebellum urban grid yet are crucial to the social critique the city mysteries present.

Firmly embedded in an evolving tradition of serial storytelling within the antebellum press circuit, the city mysteries represent "one paradigmatic example of a new nexus of mass newspapers, serial narration, and popular genre formation."[4] The works publicly called out corrupt urban elites, from bankers and judges to politicians and clergymen, voicing the grievances of the 'lower millions' who increasingly populated urban centers. They performed the cultural labor of not only providing literary entertainment but of shaping a particular public and popular discourse about the antebellum city. I argue that the era's larger "shift towards the sensational" that David S. Reynolds detects in the newspaper culture of the era but that also impacted the development of

---

[4]   Daniel Stein and Lisanna Wiele, "Introducing Popular Culture – Serial Culture: Serial Narrative in Transnational Perspective, 1830s–1860s," in *Popular Culture – Serial Culture: Serial Narrative in Transnational Perspective, 1830s–1860s*, eds. Daniel Stein and Lisanna Wiele (London: Palgrave Macmillan, 2019), 2.

literary fiction[5] was part of a movement towards the transgressive. All of the "crudities and energies"[6] of the antebellum city mystery generate unique narrative spaces within this cultural imagination. The genre in fact provides space to reflect American culture *in* and *as* popular culture – its authors' social and political concerns about a young nation divided are spread via the popular print medium and negotiate social issues within popular, sensationalist narrative tropes.

Based on the historical 1843 Mercer-Heberton case involving sexual assault, stolen honor, and consequential murder, Lippard's *The Quaker City* spins a sensationalist, urban gothic yarn which evolved throughout ten installments published between 1844 and 1845 and were later compiled into one volume that is said to have sold over 100,000 copies. The novel was adapted as a stage play that was never performed, however, due to public threats received prior to its premiere at Philadelphia's Chestnut Street theatre.[7] Lippard's *The Quaker City* is in many ways, not least due to its seemingly erratic serialization,[8] a fragmented text, and, at the same time, it is dense in its language and spatial imagination, perverting sentimentalist narratives by sensationalizing the aberrant spaces of the city. The genre fits firmly into Reynold's assertions on subversive literature that allowed the ambiguities arising in

---

[5] David Reynolds, *Beneath the American Renaissance: The Subversive Imagination in the Age of Emerson and Melville* (Cambridge: Harvard University Press, 1988), 169.

[6] Ibid., 206.

[7] David Reynolds, "Introduction," in *The Quaker City; or, The Monks of Monk Hall: A Romance of Philadelphia Life, Mystery, and Crime, by George Lippard*, ed. David S. Reynolds (Amherst: University of Massachusetts Press, 1995), xiii. For a comprehensive discussion and analysis of *The Quaker City*'s theatrical adaptations, see Sari Altschuler, "'Picture it all, Darley': Race Politics and the Media History of George Lippard's *The Quaker City*," *Nineteenth-Century Literature* 70 (2015): 65–101; Sari Altschuler and Aaron M. Tobiason, "Playbill for George Lippard's *The Quaker City*," *PMLA* 129 (2014): 267–273.

[8] The installments of the text were not published as complete episodes but rather ended with arbitrary interruptions of the text, at times coinciding with a sentence or paragraph ending, at other times interrupting a sentence. For a detailed analysis of the publication history of *The Quaker City*, see Christopher Looby, "Lippard in Part(s): Secrecy and Seriality in *The Quaker City*," *Nineteenth-Century Literature* 70 (2015): 1–35.

372 The City Mysteries' Queer Urbanity

an environment of social and moral upheaval to "erupt volcanically, in often chaotic, fragmented fashion."[9]

Alois Hahn has stated that transgression exposes and stabilizes the norm,[10] and I would argue that the 'provocative vigor' of transgression is sustained in return by serialization, as each installment revisits and expands transgression once more. The newspaper, as part of everyday life and discourse for all classes, invades the intimate home sphere of the readers; its serial narratives trigger speculation and concern about the continuation of the plot(s) whose closure is continuously delayed. The city mysteries' readership is agitated once more with each installment of the serial, which may ultimately amass hundreds of pages, maintaining a level of provocation and repeatedly facilitating what Durkheim calls the effervescence of indignation, or outrage.[11] Through this continued reader engagement, the effect of the serial transgresses the boundaries of, say, a complete, bound novel. Beyond this effect and its potential for political agitation when embedded in a real-world setting, the queer city of the mysteries invites its readers to at least imaginatively commit the acts of transgression the novels describe by consuming them as sensational entertainment and by 'lusting' for the next installment which promises more horrific and revolting content. The voyeuristic practice of enjoying these novels is, according to Mike Presdee, "transgressing in itself, and produces both pleasure and guilt."[12] As Surkis writes, the sensation of transgression is "conditioned by a cognizance of the taboo"[13] and "*heightens* or creates an awareness of the law."[14] This heightened awareness is undoubtedly the basis for any type of agitation *against* the law or the norm. But how does the fictional 'non-norm-conforming' cityscape foster narrative transgression, both on a formal as well as a content level? Each installment of the serial is made possible by utilizing a

---

[9] Ibid., 9.

[10] Alois Hahn, "Transgression und Innovation," in *Poetologische Umbrüche*, eds. Werner Helmich et al. (Paderborn: Fink, 2002), 454.

[11] Ibid., 455.

[12] Mike Presdee, *Cultural Criminology and the Carnival of Crime* (London: Routledge, 2001), 84.

[13] Judith Surkis, "No Fun and Games Until Someone Loses an Eye: Transgression and Masculinity in Bataille and Foucault," *Diacritics* 26, no. 2 (1996): 19.

[14] Ibid., 20.

previously undefined number of queer locations and plot elements, driving the sensationalist narrative further and further forward into a disfigured version of urban society known to its readers. This space, including its characters, is defined by a questioning and upending of not only the city grid, but authority figures – a disruption which, as Presdee writes, is intimately connected with acts of transgression.[15]

In Lippard's *Quaker City*, it is the text's "spatial deviance"[16] which generates its reformative potential. Lippard "portrays an urban landscape that resists the colonizing impulses of a grid system tied to Neoplatonic ideals of egalitarian 'space,' a system embraced by William Penn, Thomas Jefferson [and] cartographers of the nineteenth century [...]."[17] The text's initial protagonist, Arlington Byrnewood, is introduced by the rake Gus Lorrimer to a "queer old house [...] where the very devil is played under a cloak, and sin grows fat within the shelter of quiet rooms and impenetrable walls"[18] and in which the 'secret life' of Philadelphia materializes. Chapter 6, titled "Monk Hall," begins with a footnote alerting the reader that no one "who wishes to understand this story in all its details will fail to peruse this chapter."[19] Indeed, understanding the layout of "Monk Hall" is essential to also understanding not only the geographical but also the political implications of Lippard's text. It is here that the reader is intimately introduced to the space that every plot and character of the narrative is somehow connected to (and if every character is, then so is every reader); and it is here that the core of Lippard's social critique becomes dramatically apparent. Entering the queer spaces of the city mysteries always involves an uneasy descent; in the case of the *Quaker City*, the reader is taken down a "subterranean stairway, surrounded by the darkness of midnight," where it is difficult to subdue "a feeling of awe" that spreads "like a shadow"[20] over one's soul. Monk Hall itself is described as a series of subterranean chambers below the pre-revolutionary mansion that was once distinctive but is now surrounded by uniform brick dwellings. The queer old mansion, a remnant of an America long past, seems to disappear, suppressed

---

[15]   Presdee, *Cultural Criminology*, 38.
[16]   Unger, "Dens of Iniquity," 320.
[17]   Ibid, 319.
[18]   Lippard, *The Quaker City*, 23.
[19]   Ibid., 46.
[20]   Ibid., 53.

374   The City Mysteries' Queer Urbanity

between "a mass of miserable frame houses" flinging themselves "madly into the gutter" and a "long line of dwellings, offices, and factories, looming in broken perspective."[21] Meanwhile, residents of the surrounding city possess only "remarkable ignorance"[22] regarding the building's existence and history. The mansion, and Monk Hall below, escape Philadelphia's rigid urban grid – its location is notoriously difficult to find and "proves to be a geographical loophole,"[23] as Unger puts it. This cavity of an unaccounted for and neglected space allows for the transgressive behaviors that expose the shortcomings of the city beyond. The space, described as though it truly existed, hidden away somewhere in Philadelphia, may shock the reader into recognizing, on one hand, those transgressive behaviors that occur past their own doorstep, and on the other hand, the amorality within, leading to ideas of reform. The locale is as elusive and seductive as Lippard's narrative is to its readers. It challenges Philadelphia's "geography of authority,"[24] suggesting an alternative hermeneutic of the city and, on a larger scale, the nation. If, as scholars have pointed out,[25] antebellum readerships took to literature about the city in order to make sense of it, Lippard offered a rewriting of the city that could alter this understanding.

Monk Hall resists a "national ideology invested in regulatory institutions such as patrilineage"[26] and perverts not only space, but genealogy – the Quaker City's characters are conceived from twisted heritages minted in dishonesty, violence, and incest. Corrupt urban spaces in Lippard are tied to this "degenerative genealogy,"[27] which brings forth mostly immoral citizens. One such citizen is Devil Bug, the guardian of Monk Hall. Devil Bug was born in a brothel and grew up orphaned in squalor and wretchedness; he is described as standing "apart

---

[21] Ibid., 48.
[22] Ibid., 49.
[23] Unger, "Dens of Iniquity," 321.
[24] Ibid., 331.
[25] See, for example, Daniel Stein, "Serial Politics in Antebellum America: On the Cultural Work of the City-Mystery Genre," in *Media of Serial Narrative*, ed. Frank Kelleter (Columbus: Ohio State University Press, 2017), 53–73; and David M. Stewart, *Reading and Disorder in Antebellum America* (Columbus: Ohio State University Press, 2011).
[26] Unger, "Dens of Iniquity," 320.
[27] Ibid., 334.

from the human race" and being hideously disfigured and unimaginably cruel, a "moral monstrosity."[28] He is one of the "uncanny bodies," according to Shelley Streeby, who points out that not only is their existence marked by their gender, class, and race, but it also "signals the return of what was repressed or abjected by republican constructions of personhood and citizenship."[29] Devil Bug is "portrayed in such a way that we are forced to sympathize" with him, despite "his unprecedented devilishness."[30] His catchphrase "I wonder how *that'll work*" echoes the reader's thoughts at pivotal moments in the narrative and accompanies Devil Bug's gradual evolution throughout the story from callous doorkeeper to compassionate father upon finding out that one innocent girl, Mabel, is in fact his daughter. While in Monk Hall, Devil Bug diligently and cruelly fulfills his role as groundskeeper, scheming, torturing, and killing, and sharing his ongoing musings about the events of the novel with the reader. His "disturbingly sarcastic, darkly humorous" way of speaking, as well as his "gleeful" reactions at the "social horrors" that he witnesses, serve as a startling "unmasking device"[31] for the reader. His malice not only transgresses conventions of morality and good taste, but his position – or, rather, non-position – in society enables him to serve as a vehicle for queering space by virtue of his entirely non-conforming existence. Unlike other characters, Devil Bug does not "wear a false face,"[32] and throughout the narrative, it becomes apparent that his straightforward cruelty is preferable to the fake morality enacted by the upper class. Devil Bug continuously tries to make sense of city society and the other characters' relationships to one another, and he does so from the unique perspective of the painfully honest outcast. Like the space of Monk Hall itself, he is an anomaly, which makes him perhaps the most complex character in the text.

Accordingly, Devil Bug serves as a receptacle of another 'queer' vision of the city. In a dream, he receives a dystopian vision of the last day of Quaker City in the year 1950. On this last day, liberty is no more,

---

[28] Lippard, *The Quaker City*, 107.
[29] Shelley Streeby, "Haunted Houses: George Lippard, Nathaniel Hawthorne, and Middle-Class America," *Criticism* 38, no. 3 (1996): 450.
[30] Reynolds, *Beneath the American Renaissance*, 201.
[31] Reynolds, "Introduction," xl.
[32] Ibid.

376   The City Mysteries' Queer Urbanity

and a new monarchy has been instated. Patriots are imprisoned and the dead are rising in anticipation of final judgement. The chapter serves as a harsh critique of those betraying what Lippard considered American ideals of equality and liberty from unjust rulers. It provides dramatic visualization of a nation in which his warnings about the growing exploitation of the working class and the danger of moneyed elites being instituted as American royalty have not been heeded. Transatlantic dependence has proven fatal, and the city has been turned into a barely recognizable nightmare. A gray-haired antiquary in possession of an old American flag serves as a reminder of the failed American experiment, of a country which "was born, grew to vigorous youth" only to be "massacred by her pretend friends. Priest-craft, and Slave-craft, and Traitor-craft […]."[33] As scholars have pointed out, the scene is a most apt working-class critique of the dangers Lippard believed America was facing, but it is also a spatial and temporal transgression of geographical and social bounds.[34] In his dream, Devil Bug travels to the future, entering 'The Theatre of Hell' in a grotesquely distorted version of Philadelphia. If Monk Hall was previously staged as the worst imaginable place in the city, its violence and immorality has now taken over all of Philadelphia. Once more, Lippard's perversion of urban space serves to accuse the new social elites of violating ideals of American republican order and equality.

George Thompson's 1849 novel *City Crimes* utilizes the transgressive potential of queer space and uncanny bodies to a degree that can only be described as repulsive (and therefore effective in garnering an attentive readership). According to Looby, Thompson regularly presented "enchanting visions of erotic and criminal excess," arousing not only resentment or envy, but a "proto-typical understanding of structured social inequity, public moral hypocrisy, and legal corruption."[35] Correspondingly, Thompson is most effective in utilizing

---

[33] Lippard, *The Quaker City*, 388.

[34] For an in-depth analysis of Lippard's dystopian vision of Philadelphia, see Nathaniel Williams, "George Lippard's Fragile Utopian Future and 1840s American Economic Turmoil," *Utopian Studies* 24 (2013): 166–183.

[35] Christopher Looby, "George Thompson's 'Romance of the Real': Transgression and Taboo in American Sensation Fiction," *American Literature* 65, no. 4 (1993): 654.

the sensationalist genre in favor of audience uproar. In *City Crimes*, the novel's introductory underground locale is, similar to Monk Hall, a den of evil which upends the social conventions of the aboveground. The 'Dark Vaults' are a cavernous system of chambers that extend "far into the bowels of the earth" and into the sewers below Manhattan's notorious Five Points district. Like Monk Hall, the Dark Vaults require an eerie descent: "Down, down, they went, far into the bowels of the earth; groping their way in darkness, and often hazarding their necks by stumbling upon the steep and slippery steps."[36] The mysterious labyrinth runs far and wide; its origins remain unclear. The pseudo-anarchist commune of criminals within is ruled by a faux-king and deity of villainy – the Dead Man. Once more, it is a corrupt king whose existence proves a threat to the republic. The Dead Man, a cadaverous being of "frightful appearance,"[37] inhabits and exposes those pockets of perverted urban space where transgression reigns. He also is a most stark reminder that such an entity may not be constrained within rigid systems of society, or (during his stint at Sing Sing) even prison. The antebellum belief in the dual purpose of prison – the rehabilitation of inmates on one hand and modeling order in a disorderly society on the other[38] – fails entirely, and *City Crimes* demonstrates that, within a corrupt and divided society, the only order successfully established is that of the twisted moral subversion of the Dark Vaults and its inhabitants.[39] If Lippard's Devil Bug transgresses the line between human and animal, the Dead Man treads the line between life and death, between being invisible and being seen, between existing in society and existing only as a violent reminder of the wrongs society has committed.

---

[36] George Thompson, *City Crimes; or, Life in New York and Boston* (Boston: Berry & Co, 1849), 30.

[37] Ibid., 32.

[38] David J. Bodenhamer, "Criminal Punishment in Antebellum Indiana: The Limits of Reform," *Indiana Magazine of History* 82, no. 4 (1986): 358.

[39] For a detailed analysis of this subject, see Lisanna Wiele, "Dead Man Walking: On the Physical and Geographical Manifestations of Sociopolitical Narratives in George Thompson's City Crimes – or Life in New York and Boston," in *Popular Culture – Serial Culture: Serial Narrative in Transnational Perspective, 1830s–1860s*, eds. Daniel Stein and Lisanna Wiele (London: Palgrave Macmillan), 247–271.

378   The City Mysteries' Queer Urbanity

If death in itself is a transgression of being, as Foucault argues,[40] the Dead Man has succeeded in placing his effect in a space beyond the 'text' of the city.

Born into squalor and orphanhood in Boston, the Dead Man is immediately disenfranchised by a society that holds no place for him; consequently, he creates space for himself in an effort to "plunder the world."[41] A prison sentence only encourages him to commit more severe crimes upon his release, and he first poses as a doctor who facilitates abortions before taking up the priesthood and becoming a local leader in the temperance movement. A necessary precursor to his continued criminal career is the Dead Man's disfiguration, through which he manages to escape the world he inhabits once more. By means of a chemical procedure, the villain permanently alters his appearance in order to inspire "universal terror" at first sight.[42] At this critical point of his genesis as the harbinger of not death, but reform appeals, one might consider Foucault's "A Preface to Transgression" in which he questions the nature of transgression and its dialectic potential. If one assumes that, as Foucault states, transgression must be "detached from its questionable association to ethics" and "liberated from the scandalous and subversive,"[43] what remains of its impact? The moral questions posed by the city mysteries are manifold, ranging from the exploitation of the lower classes to the plight of the working poor, complex racial politics, and critical reflections on the role of women. These questions are firmly grounded in the everyday lives of urban citizens in a still-evolving republic, and, although often idealistic, they are far from pondering higher ethical concerns. The scandalous, the subversive and the transgressive are necessary and productive in maintaining an interested readership, triggering public discourse, and remaining relevant in the popular literary circuit.

George Thompson's 1855 novel *The Locket: A Romance of New York* queers city space in yet another way, not with a den of evil but

---

[40] Qtd. in Surkis, "No Fun and Games," 19.

[41] Thompson, *City Crimes*, 135.

[42] Ibid., 138.

[43] Michel Foucault, "A Preface to Transgression," in *Language, Counter-Memory, Practice: Selected Essays and Interviews*, trans. and ed. Donald F. Bouchard (Ithaca: Cornell University Press, 1977), 35.

with a hidden passageway that connects the upper ten thousand and the lower millions, eventually enabling fraternization between the two groups. The story begins with two houses in lower Manhattan, one an "aristocratic" new home and the other its neighbor, an ancient wooden tenement described as "for those low and vulgar people [...] the poor."[44] A child chimney sweep ('Smutty Tom') discovers a secret passage from the wealthy estate into the newly impoverished home of the widowed Mrs. Hargrave and her 18-year-old daughter, Edith, and he steals a locket containing a daguerreotype image of Edith. Walter De Lacy, the women's handsome and wealthy proprietor neighbor, is immediately taken with the young girl's image when Smutty Tom presents the locket to him. De Lacy wonders: "is it possible that I am fool enough to have fallen in love with a picture!"[45] Meanwhile, upon discovering the absence of her locket, Edith is unnerved by its inexplicable disappearance and suspects evil is afoot: "[M]ystery is always terrible, and this circumstance, however trifling it may seem, troubles me more than I dare confess."[46] Edith and her mother become anxious at the possibility that, unbeknownst to them, their home has been intruded upon by some interloper. Moreover, they are suddenly fearful of the old house and what its walls might hold, afraid it might collapse on them.

The "queer state of affairs"[47] in the city is emphasized when the story's lecherous villain, Mr. Snarley, De Lacy's rent-collecting agent, peruses the newspaper and remarks upon the mild punishments for corrupt financiers:

> He who steals thousands of dollars is merely an honorable defaulter; he goes abroad and lives in royal magnificence, while his victims are reduced to poverty, and want; but the starving wretch who steals a dollar or a loaf of bread is sent to the penitentiary [...] but it is all right for us financiers.[48]

---

[44] George Thompson, *The Locket: A Romance of New York* (P.F. Harris, 1855), 5.
[45] Ibid., 11.
[46] Ibid., 18.
[47] Ibid., 22.
[48] Ibid.

380 The City Mysteries' Queer Urbanity

Mr. Snarley realizes that it is the recent default of one financial manager named Monk that will plunge Mrs. and Miss Hargrave into ruin. Finding Monk's office in disarray and their inheritance gone, Edith immediately informs her mother of the tragedy. That same night, Walter De Lacy decides to use the secret passageway to pay a visit to sleeping Edith, the "jewell" contained in the "rough casket"[49] of the decaying house. Struggling to keep his moral wits about him, he regards the sleeping beauty with extreme infatuation, remarking upon the exceptional looks and character of a girl so unlike the wanton women he is accustomed to. As the city mysteries do as well, Thompson exaggeratedly draws on the tropes of sentimental literature, describing De Lacy's infatuated reaction to the girl:

> [n]ever before had he beheld a face of such ravishing loveliness as hers; she was even far more beautiful than her portrait had led him to suppose. He gazed upon her like one entranced – her charms seemed to have cast about him a magic spell, which prevented his moving and rivetted him on the spot where he stood.[50]

Thompson concludes that he must woo her but vows to be careful in this pursuit. He leaves a locket with his own image at Edith's bedside, and she is likewise immediately taken by De Lacy's likeness without knowing that he is, in fact, her own wealthy landlord. De Lacy is, of course, seduced, not only by the young girl's beauty, but also by the unique spatial deviance provided by the secret passageway between houses and social classes – a connection that their class difference usually prevents on the outside: "She is poor and lives in an humble sphere, while I am rich, fashionable and gay; and therefore an intimate acquaintance between us would be obviously improper and compromise her reputation [...]."[51] Enraptured De Lacy likens the sooty chimney entrance to "the flower path of Cupid"[52] in order to justify his questionable midnight break-in. This "drudgery of love"[53] constitutes

---

[49] Ibid., 12
[50] Ibid., 26.
[51] Ibid., 12.
[52] Ibid., 13.
[53] Ibid., 24.

the wealthy man's uncomfortable descent into the unfamiliar sphere of the lower class:

> it was with considerable repugnance that he began to climb that rough, dark, and dusty place; the soot which still clung to the brick-work [...] nearly choked him, while his hands and knees, and other portions of his body were much bruised by the rough surface with which he was necessarily brought in contact.[54]

Uniquely, this queer passageway does not lead De Lacy into immorality and evil as do those of Monk Hall or the Dark Vaults, but rather enables him to enter a virtuous space – that of two women who, by no fault of their own, are losing their good standing in society. The "notorious gallant" who readily admits that he is a "devoted worshipper of pretty women"[55] and whose wealthy peers have repeatedly urged him to tear down the dilapidated tenement is given the opportunity to (im)prove his morals and act as virtuously as young Edith deserves. Had it not been for the passageway and Smutty Tom, De Lacy would have been ignorant to the struggles of the lower-class next door.

When Mr. Snarley goes to collect the rent from the now entirely destitute mother-daughter pair the following day, he senses an opportunity and proposes marriage, first to Mrs. Hargrave and, upon being rejected, to her young daughter. The situation escalates drastically, and after Snarley attempts to sexually assault Edith, she is forced to flee the room via its only escape route, the window. As she lowers herself down the outside wall, De Lacy is already waiting below to offer assistance. Their meeting is the poor women's salvation. De Lacy welcomes them into his home, leaving Snarley to believe that they have disappeared into a further degraded life on the street. De Lacy allows Snarley and his housekeeper to move into the Hargraves's house with his housekeeper. 'Muff,' the housekeeper, is a cruel old woman, reminiscent of the vile creatures that inhibit Thompson's Dark Vaults in *City Crimes* – she is a lowly, rat-eating henchwoman and is said to be a cannibal who devours neighborhood toddlers. In an act of revenge, 'Master Tom,' formerly known as Smutty Tom and now risen to De Lacy's confidante and personal assistant, uses the secret passageway

---

[54] Ibid.
[55] Ibid., 12.

382   The City Mysteries' Queer Urbanity

between the houses to appear in Snarley's bedroom fashioned as a 'ghostly' apparition. On his first visit, he introduces himself to Snarley as 'Remorse': "I shall never leave you, you can never shake me off."[56] On his last visit, he finds out that Snarley is already dead, having been poisoned by Muff, who then dies in shock upon seeing the 'ghost.' The passageway is used, lastly, to exact revenge upon one who preys on the less fortunate, concluding a moral lesson and underscoring the ever-present social critique of the genre. Contrary to Monk Hall and the Dark Vaults, the queer space in *The Locket* immediately enables social change, at least for its main characters. It is not a den of evil, nor does it serve those who do evil. Regardless, it fulfills the same two functions I have previously noted: it introduces an element of secrecy and sensationalist voyeurism to the story, engaging the reader; and it utilizes a distortion of urban space, and the transgressive behaviors this space enables, to reveal a precise social critique with regard to a growing urban society.

The Locket ends, as one may have expected, with the sentimentalist climax of marriage. Edith and De Lacy are wed and immediately embark upon their honeymoon, a tour of the United States. The "model couple,"[57] uniting social classes, seem to serve as a moral role model for the nation. "The beauty, amiability and unpretending, yet lady-like manners of the fair bride elicited unqualified admiration wherever she went; while the elegance, gentlemanly bearing and princely liberality of the handsome De Lacy, caused him to be a prodigious favorite."[58] Their marital bliss falls in line with sentimentalist tropes around the value of domesticity and the personal fulfillment that moral integrity awards. The reader learns that they leave the city for good and that only Master Tom remains, becoming a professional actor. In true serial fashion, the novel's ending is followed by the announcement that the *Locket's* sequel *Tom De Lacy* is now available for purchase for those who wish to find out how Master Tom fared in the city. The story, and with that, the 'moral of the story,' that of the value of philanthropy, remains, at least in part, without closure; social evil is defeated only for the installment

[56]   Ibid., 81.
[57]   Ibid., 88.
[58]   Ibid.

past, and more entertaining transgressions may lurk around the corner at the nearest newsstand.

Whereas Lippard's *Quaker City* and Thompson's *City Crimes* are lengthy, convoluted novels that seem to outbid one another in grotesque and violent imagery, *The Locket* is a brief vignette about the increasingly dire conditions of urban life. Although it includes none of the revolting subterranean labyrinths of the former two, its narrative is nonetheless enabled by spatial deviance. Mrs. Hargrave and Edith find themselves in danger of being displaced by a type of gentrification taking place in antebellum Manhattan. Their home is a remnant of the past, no longer acceptable in a neighborhood of new buildings exuding wealth and progress. Their position in society isolates them so gravely that they do not even know their wealthier neighbors, and forego socializing with anyone but each other. The class divide in the neighborhood is so severe that it is only by spatial and moral transgression that the worlds of De Lacy and the Hargraves collide. The discovery of the secret passageway opens a gateway not only into neighboring bedchambers, but, more importantly, into the lives of the poor. To De Lacy, Edith is the 'other,' and their union would have been impossible had it not been for the passageway between the houses that enabled his voyeuristic interest in the woman. Regarding the sleeping Edith, De Lacy is able to project onto her all of the virtues he desires in a woman and to regard her as a potential mate rather than part of the lowly poor. Because this secret space exists within the confines of the city, Edith and her mother are able to escape their ruin and, eventually, escape the city altogether. Rewriting city spaces makes possible not only escape, but the critique of a status quo as well.

If transgression is a "therapeutic interrogation of social codes, a process of constant critique"[59] which prevents systems from becoming completely totalitarian, as Anne-Marie Smith writes in response to Kristeva, the serial city mysteries continuously perform that labor of interrogation. They 1) skillfully parody sentimentalist literature while serving the same readership, 2) refer back to the America of the forefathers and their ideals of liberty and democracy while warning of a future that neglects those ideals and where transgression becomes the

---

[59] Anne-Marie Smith, "Transgression, Transubstantiation, Transference," *Paragraph* 20, no. 3 (1997): 271.

norm rather than the exception, and 3) provide 'space' and form with which to formulate critique that reaches a mass audience. In the city mysteries, the queer city overrules the normative city, establishing meaning in those spaces that aren't spaces.

Works Cited

Altschuler, Sari. "'Picture It All, Darley': Race Politics and the Media History of George Lippard's *The Quaker City*." *Nineteenth-Century Literature* 70, no. 1 (2015): 65–101.

Altschuler, Sari, and Aaron M. Tobiason. "Playbill for George Lippard's *The Quaker City*." *PMLA* 129 (2014): 267–273.

Bodenhamer, David J. "Criminal Punishment in Antebellum Indiana: The Limits of Reform." *Indiana Magazine of History* 82, no. 4 (1986): 358–375.

Foucault, Michel. "A Preface to Transgression." In *Language, Counter-Memory, Practice: Selected Essays and Interviews*, translated and edited by Donald F. Bouchard, 21–52. Ithaca: Cornell University Press, 1977.

Hahn, Alois. "Transgression und Innovation." In *Poetologische Umbrüche*, edited by Werner Helmich et al., 452–465. Paderborn: Fink, 2002.

Lippard, George. *The Quaker City or, the Monks of Monk Hall: A Romance of Philadelphia Life, Mystery, and Crime*. Edited by David S. Reynolds. Amherst: University of Massachusetts Press, 1995.

Looby, Christopher. "George Thompson's 'Romance of the Real': Transgression and Taboo in American Sensation Fiction." *American Literature* 65, no. 4 (1993): 651–672.

Presdee, Mike. *Cultural Criminology and the Carnival of Crime*. London: Routledge, 2001.

Reynolds, David. *Beneath the American Renaissance: The Subversive Imagination in the Age of Emerson and Melville*. Cambridge: Harvard University Press, 1988.

---. "Introduction." In *The Quaker City; or, The Monks of Monk Hall: A Romance of Philadelphia Life, Mystery, and Crime, by George Lippard*, edited by David S. Reynolds, vii–xliv. Amherst: University of Massachusetts Press, 1995.

Smith, Anne-Marie. "Transgression, Transubstantiation, Transference." *Paragraph* 20, no. 3 (1997): 270–280.

Stein, Daniel. "Serial Politics in Antebellum America: On the Cultural Work of the City-Mystery Genre." In *Media of Serial Narrative*, edited by Frank Kelleter, 53–73. Columbus: Ohio State University Press, 2017.

Stein, Daniel, and Lisanna Wiele. "Introducing Popular Culture – Serial Culture: Serial Narrative in Transnational Perspective, 1830s–1860s." In *Popular Culture – Serial Culture: Serial Narrative in Transnational Perspective, 1830s–1860s*, edited by Daniel Stein and Lisanna Wiele, 1–15. London: Palgrave Macmillan, 2019.

Stewart, David M. *Reading and Disorder in Antebellum America*. Columbus: Ohio State University Press, 2011.

Streeby, Shelley. "Haunted Houses: George Lippard, Nathaniel Hawthorne, and Middle-Class America." *Criticism* 38, no. 3 (1996): 443–472.

Surkis, Judith. "No Fun and Games Until Someone Loses an Eye: Transgression and Masculinity in Bataille and Foucault." *Diacritics* 26, no. 2 (1996): 18–30.

Thompson, George. *City Crimes; or, Life in New York and Boston*. Boston: Berry & Co., 1849.

---. *The Locket: A Romance of New York*. P.F. Harris, 1855.

Unger, Mary. "'Dens of Iniquity and Holes of Wickedness': George Lippard and the Queer City." *Journal of American Studies* 43, no. 2 (2009): 319–339.

Wiele, Lisanna. "Dead Man Walking: On the Physical and Geographical Manifestations of Sociopolitical Narratives in George *Thompson's City Crimes – or Life in New York and Boston*." In *Popular Culture – Serial Culture: Serial Narrative in Transnational Perspective, 1830s–1860s*, edited by Daniel Stein and Lisanna Wiele, 247–271. London: Palgrave Macmillan, 2019.

HARALD ZAPF

The Long Shadow of Romanticism: (Un-)Popular Theories of Lyric Poetry and the Popularity of the Lyric

The lyric usually does not tell us how to treat it. Audiences in Literary Studies, such as professors and poet critics, tend to treat lyric poems and lyric lyrics as fiction, whereas non-academic audiences tend to treat them as nonfiction – an example of this being teenage readers whose first book of poetry is Rupi Kaur's immensely popular volume *Milk and Honey*. I think that both audiences could sharpen their reading skills by paying more attention to each other's approaches.

In this article, I deal with popular as well as unpopular theoretical approaches to the lyric and with particular lyric(al) texts ranging from the nineteenth-century lyric of the Romantic movement – "in whose long shadow we live today,"[1] as Robert McCrum rightly wrote on the 27th of May, 2019 – to post-modern New York School poetry, contemporary Instagram poetry or social media verse, rap, and performance poetry. The most popular understanding of the lyric outside of Literary Studies and probably the most unpopular approach within this scholarly field is based on the notion that lyric poems are nonfictional and expressive in the Romantic sense of "individual self-expression," of "sincerity, spontaneity, and originality," of "the emotional directness of personal experience" and of "emotional intensity, often taken to extremes of rapture, nostalgia (for childhood or the past) [...] melancholy, or sentimentality."[2]

---

[1] Robert McCrum, "*The Making of Poetry* by Adam Nicolson: When Coleridge Met the Wordsworths," *The Guardian*, May 27, 2019.

[2] Chris Baldick, *The Oxford Dictionary of Literary Terms* (Oxford: Oxford University Press, 2015), 316.

388 The Long Shadow of Romanticism

Many of today's popular poets in the romantic spirit prove Alain de Botton right, who says in his introduction to The School of Life anthology *An Emotional Education* that "we are the troubled inheritors of what can be defined as a Romantic view of emotions."[3] Contemporary popular poems and poets often rely on and exploit what the School of Life calls "characteristics of Romantic [...] personalities" such as intuition, spontaneity, honesty, idealism, earnestness, purity, and the rare.[4] The popularity of romantic Instapoetry, for example, demonstrates the point that the School of Life makes:

> For a long time now, [...] Romantic attitudes have been dominant in the Western imagination. The prevailing approach to children, relationships, politics and culture has all been coloured more by a Romantic than by a Classical spirit.[5]

Taking the long-lasting dominance of the Romantic orientation as a given, sophisticates probably cannot avoid reading the following statement from Bridgett Devoue's 2018 book *Soft Thorns* as ironic: "romantics are the new rebels."[6] But the dominance of the Romantic orientation ensures that a trite remark like this, which signifies the old (or always new?) Romantic attitude belonging to Western mainstream culture, can be easily understood by the vast majority of readers without them having to be literature-literate. When Instapoet Devoue writes that "romantics are the new rebels," her readers do not have to be familiar with the 'Romantics' in the literary historical sense. For a smooth and correct understanding of the intended meaning of the twenty-first-century line "romantics are the new rebels," it might even help to know nothing at all about the late eighteenth- and early nineteenth-century Romantic Movement, about the "literary rebellion of Wordsworth in England and Victor Hugo in France."[7]

---

[3] Alain de Botton, *The School of Life: An Emotional Education* (London: Hamish Hamilton, 2019), 2.
[4] Ibid., 257–261.
[5] Ibid., 261–262.
[6] Bridgett Devoue, *Soft Thorns* (Kansas City: Andrews McMeel, 2018), 201.
[7] Baldick, *The Oxford Dictionary*, 317.

In the first half of the 19th century, Victor Hugo produced masterfully intense and self-expressive romantic art by exploiting the personal experience of losing a loved one. His poem "Quand nous habitions" ("When We Were Living") is a case in point. Hugo's lament is of interest here as a paradigm of the romantic poem and of the lyric: "a short poem in any meter or free verse, in which the expression of emotion, often by a voice in the first person, is given primacy over narration."[8] T. E. Hulme, who around 1911 or early 1912 objected "even to the best of the romantics," probably would have listed poems such as Hugo's emotional poem of loss under the rubric "moaning or whining about something or other."[9] There is no doubt that Hulme also would have subsumed contemporary poetry books with titles such as Madisen Kuhn's 2018 collection *Please Don't Go Before I Get Better* and much of contemporary romantic Instagram and YouTube lyric poetry under "whining about something:" Think of Orion Carloto's "Mixed Feelings," for example, "I couldn't tell you / what was worse. // When she went away / or when I realized / she wasn't coming back;"[10] or think of Bridgett Devoue's "it's so painful to talk to you / because I just remember / everything you turned out / not to be."[11] Even John Ashbery's post-modernist endorsement of nineteenth-century romanticism in the second half of the 20th century – "All my stuff is romantic poetry,"[12] Ashbery said in an interview in 1974 – could not obliterate Hulme's modernist dismissal from the beginning of the 20th century. Hugo, Ashbery, Carloto, or Devoue implicitly support Walter Pater's a-historical view of romanticism as "a spirit which shows itself at all times, in various degrees."[13] But France, Pater thought, was once the

---

[8] Margaret Ferguson et al., "A Glossary of Poetic Terms," in *The Norton Anthology of Poetry* (New York: Norton, 2018), A10.

[9] T. E. Hulme, "Romanticism and Classicism," in *Selected Writings*, ed. Patrick McGuinness (Manchester: Carcanet, 1998), 75.

[10] Orion Carloto, *Flux* (Kansas City: Andrews McMeel, 2017), 82.

[11] Devoue, *Soft Thorns*, 81.

[12] Qtd. in Helen Vendler, *The Music of What Happens: Poems, Poets, Critics* (Cambridge: Harvard University Press, 1988), 231.

[13] Walter Pater, "Postscript (Romanticism)," in *Selected Writings of Walter Pater*, ed. Harold Bloom (New York: Columbia University Press, 1974), 217.

390   The Long Shadow of Romanticism

epitome of the romantic spirit: "[N]either Germany, with its Goethe and Tieck, nor England, with its Byron and Scott, is nearly so representative of the romantic temper as France, with Murger, and Gautier, and Victor Hugo."[14]

"Some of" Hugo's "best poems," translator Brooks Haxton says in the introduction to his selection of the French poet's work, "were written in memory of his daughter Leopoldine, who, six months after she was married at the age of nineteen, drowned with her husband in a boating accident […]."[15] "When We Were Living," the mood poem mourning the author's deceased daughter, is unreliably dated "September 4, 1844."[16] The stylized date, which differs from the manuscript's date (October 16, 1846), is the first anniversary of Léopoldine's death on the Seine in Villequier. It therefore foregrounds the commemorative aspect and the ritualistic dimension of the poem, because, as Jonathan Culler says, "it captures first of all the principle of iterability – lyrics are constructed for repetition – along with a certain ceremoniousness."[17] Hugo's chosen date indicates that his poem is supposed to be re-uttered, not only each year on the anniversary but infinite times – now, for example. Here are some excerpts from the poem in Haxton's unrhymed translation, which reproduces the 13 quatrains of the original text. I am going to quote the first three stanzas, stanza five and six, and the last 13 words of the final quatrain:

> When we were living, all of us,
> under the hill where the river spoke,
> where the rosebush shook, and the house
> in innocence touched the woods,
>
> she was ten, and I was thirty.
> I was her world! and she was mine!
> How the scent of the grass grows

---

[14] Ibid., 213.
[15] Brooks Haxton, "Introduction," in *Victor Hugo: Selected Poems*, trans. and ed. Brooks Haxton (London: Penguin, 2002), xi–xii.
[16] Victor Hugo, "When We Were Living," in *Selected Poems*, trans. and ed. Brooks Haxton (London: Penguin, 2002), 33.
[17] Jonathan Culler, *Theory of the Lyric* (Cambridge: Harvard University Press, 2015), 123.

sweet under the dark green trees!

She made good luck of my life,
all of it swept up in the blue,
and when she said, Papa! I felt
God tremble in the word.

[...]

She would be the one to lead me
when I took her hand.
We looked everywhere for flowers,
meeting the poor at the wayside:

she gave gifts the way some steal,
in secret, for the thrill.
Oh! and that little frock
she wore, do you remember?

[...] now
everything she gave is gone.
The past is shadows in the wind.[18]

Strictly speaking, the poem itself does not tell us how to treat it. How to deal with it is less a matter of textual features than of different kinds of attention and critical options, which can be roughly classified into two major categories: fictional and nonfictional approaches; one can treat the poem, its speaker, or his utterances as nonfictional or fictional phenomena. It depends on your theoretical approach whether you hear a real poet (expressive criticism), a fictional character (New Criticism), fictional speech acts (Barbara Herrnstein Smith), or nonfictional but biographically indeterminable enunciation (Käte Hamburger, Jonathan Culler).

Hugo's personal poem can be read as a typical example of what Isaiah Berlin once described as the "doctrine of art as expression,"[19] of

---

[18] Hugo, "When We Were Living," 33–35.
[19] Isaiah Berlin, "The True Fathers of Romanticism," in *The Roots of Romanticism*, ed. Henry Hardy (London: Pimlico, 2000), 60.

392   The Long Shadow of Romanticism

"the romantic/expressive model of lyric"[20]: "lyric as the intense expression of the poet," as "expression of the feelings of the poet."[21] It is a poem that encourages what has been very unpopular in Literary Studies for a long time, namely expressive criticism: Hugo's poem rewards readers for judging the literary work "by its sincerity," for treating it "primarily in relation to its author," "as an expression, or overflow, or utterance of feelings or as the product of the poet's imagination operating on his or her perceptions, thoughts, and feelings."[22] As fruitful as this approach may be when it comes to Hugo's poem, it is not an unproblematic one. First, expressive criticism has an image problem: it will always appear to be the obvious choice for readers who are more interested in people than in works of art. This problem aside, expressive criticism, as an essentially biographical and nonfictional approach, often yields unsatisfactory and irrelevant results. For example, could the addressee in Hugo's "When We Were Living" be identified beyond a shadow of a doubt, and if so, what would have been gained by that? The delightful vagueness, inscrutability, and universality of poetry would have been lost.

The approach of expressive criticism was anathema to the New Critics. According to them, poems are never spoken by historical subjects but always by fictional personae. In his *Sound and Sense: An Introduction to Poetry*, Laurence Perrine maintains that

> even when the poet does speak directly and express his own thoughts and emotions, he does so ordinarily as a representative human being rather than as an individual who lives at a particular address, dislikes dill pickles, and favors blue neckties. We must always be cautious about identifying anything in a poem with the biography of the poet. [...] We may well think of every poem [...] as being to some degree *dramatic*, that is, the utterance of a fictional character rather than of the poet himself.[23]

---

[20]   Culler, *Theory of the Lyric*, 31.
[21]   Berlin, "The True Fathers," 84.
[22]   M. H. Abrams and Geoffrey Galt Harpham, *A Glossary of Literary Terms* (Boston: Cengage, 2015), 72.
[23]   Laurence Perrine, *Sound and Sense: An Introduction to Poetry* (San Diego: Harcourt, Brace and Company, 1956), 21.

HARALD ZAPF 393

Though the New Criticism has gone out of fashion, this attitude persists and arguably continues to be very popular in Literary Studies today. The New Critical caricature of expressive and biographical criticism has badly and lastingly damaged this approach's status. But expressive and biographical critics should not let themselves be blown off course too quickly by the biting wind still whipping from the New Critics. It is a fundamental flaw in the New Critics' strictly aromantic and decidedly anti-expressive approach to dealing with verse that they dismiss, to the greatest degree possible, the authorial dimension of poems and therefore can no longer see the difference between real lyric and genuine dramatic poems such as Hugo's "When We Were Living" and, for example, John Ashbery's "The Young Prince and the Young Princess." Here is stanza one and most of stanza six, the last quatrain of Ashbery's dramatic poem, which intertextually refers to – among other sources – Hugo's lyric poem:

> The grass cuts our feet as we wend our way
> Across the meadow – you, a child of thirteen
> In a man's business suit far too big for you
> A symbol of how long we have been together.

> [...] Some day
> We will wake up, having fallen in the night
> From a high cliff into the white, precious sky.
> You will say, 'That is how we lived, you and I.'[24]

If "[w]e may well think of every poem [...] as being to some degree *dramatic*, that is, the utterance of a fictional character rather than of the poet himself," as Perrine said,[25] how are we supposed to differentiate between a lyric voice that *may* be the author's voice, as in Hugo's case, and a dramatic voice, such as Ashbery's, that *cannot* be the author's voice? This lack of discriminatory precision results from the popular New Critical fictionality bias which led them and other professional

---

[24] John Ashbery, "The Young Prince and the Young Princess," in *Contemporary American Poetry*, ed. Donald Hall (New York: Penguin, 1972), 192.

[25] Perrine, *Sound and Sense*, 21.

394 The Long Shadow of Romanticism

readers to forget only too often that some poems can also be "to some degree" nondramatic.

The conceptualization of poetic utterance as fictional only and the concomitant inability to distinguish between lyric and dramatic voices is also a weakness of Barbara Herrnstein Smith's theory. "[W]hat is central to the concept of the poem as fictive utterance," Smith writes, "is not that the 'character' or 'persona' is distinct from the poet, or that the audience purportedly addressed, the emotions expressed, and the event alluded to are fictional, but that the *speaking, addressing, expressing*, and *alluding* are themselves fictive verbal acts."[26] "This theory," Jonathan Culler comments, "now very widespread even though Smith is seldom recognized as its theoretician, urges students to treat every poem as a dramatic monologue, a fictional act of speech by a speaker whose situation and motives must be reconstructed."[27]

Countering the popular fictionality bias dominant in the 20th century and avoiding its rigid either/or-structure, Käte Hamburger wisely positioned herself in an in-between space by reading neither fictionally nor biographically, which is a fairly good compromise between nineteenth-century author- and twentieth-century text-centered voice criticism. In Hamburger's view, "there is no exact criterion, neither logical nor aesthetic, neither intrinsic nor extrinsic, that would tell us whether we could identify the statement-subject of a lyric poem with the poet or not."[28] In his twenty-first-century *Theory of the Lyric*, Culler subscribes to Hamburger's views about nonfictionality and states that there is a "need for a broader conception of lyric, one not centered on a fictional speaker."[29]

In my view, Alessandro Barchiesi's conception of lyric, which is capable of including a broad range of theoretical perspectives by linking voice to reading options, is the most comprehensive, balanced, nuanced, and adaptable contemporary theory of lyric. It is also the most appropriate theoretical approach for a reading of Hugo's poem hovering between biographical reality and fiction. In an essay on Horace, Barchiesi writes,

---

[26] Qtd. in Culler, *Theory of the Lyric*, 110–111.
[27] Ibid., 111.
[28] Qtd. in ibid., 106–107.
[29] Ibid., 115.

[l]yric can be tentatively (transhistorically) defined as *a first-person utterance whose performative conditions are reconstructed by a 're-performing' reader*, who typically positions herself somewhere in a continuum whose extremes are a generic voice and some individual idea of the author. Extreme positions are of course possible: one can certainly prefer a *very* author-centered reading. [...] In less clear-cut cases, readers will opt for a very generic reading [...]. Most re-performances of lyric will happen somewhere in the intermediate spectrum between those extremes [...].[30]

Adding to Barchiesi's argument, I would point out that there is no need to adopt a particular position with reference to the poem as a whole. The position of the person analyzing a poetic text may change from one aspect or textual element to the other. In poetry analyses it is good to be flexible and ready to switch between the extremes and from approach to approach. As far as "When We Were Living" is concerned, I would opt for a more author-centered reading of the pronouns "she" and "her;" in other cases, for example with reference to the whereabouts of "we," I would prefer a less author-centered reading and position myself so I could hear a more generic voice. Generally, the text of "When We Were Living" and the immediate context of its biographically relevant date allow for a more author-centered reading, but not for a simplistically nonfictional one.

The aesthetic effect of the textual feature of a 'real' auto-expressive voice is the construction of nearness, the artifice of proximity. What is supposed to be experienced as a mode of sincere speech is, in fact, at least to a certain extent, artifice, a performance of sincerity or – in other words – role-playing. In Ashbery's "The Young Prince and the Young Princess," role-playing goes a step further without being as complex as in Hugo's lyric poem: Whereas Hugo was hiding the dramatic dimension of his lyric poem behind a personally expressive biographical date, Ashbery is foregrounding it in his fairytale romance-like text. But by foregrounding its dramatic status and by trumpeting its theatricality, Ashbery's poem gives up the quality of being the performance of

[30] Alessandro Barchiesi, "Carmina: Odes and Carmen Saeculare," in *The Cambridge Companion to Horace*, ed. Stephen Harrison (Cambridge: Cambridge University Press, 2007), 150–151.

396 The Long Shadow of Romanticism

sincerity that Hugo's text is and thereby also reduces its potential for popularity. Much of contemporary popular poetry features unabashedly phonocentric voices that purport to be un-haunted by previous voices. But with Ashbery we can see "the rich texture of intertextual relations that relates" poems "to other poems rather than to worldly events,"[31] or popular human-interest events such as the death of a daughter, one could add with reference to Hugo's poem.

Instagram poems deal less with particular human-interest events than with universal human-interest topics. Their speakers seem to know everything they talk about from personal experience, but what they say is often utterly devoid of personal qualities and does not give us personal information about them – neither are there paratextual personal dates, as in Hugo's case, for example. The popularity-producing effect of super-relatability can only be achieved with poems that are as non-personal as possible while appearing to be completely personal and deeply expressive. Trying to be both popular and profound, Instagram poems often celebrate seemingly nonfictional, romantic emotive expression in short prose and Free Verse forms. They fit into our Twitter Age and the contemporary culture of mindfulness where human-interest poems are supposed to function as therapeutic instruments – for "Healing the Heart," as goes the subtitle of Courtney Peppernell's second volume of *Pillow Thoughts*, a contemporary Twitterer's and Instagrammer's "collection of inspirational and comforting poems for anyone who is mending from a broken heart."[32] This description on the back cover of Peppernell's 2018 book is very much in the fashion of Rupi Kaur, who self-advertised her bestselling book *Milk and Honey* with the following lines: "this is the journey of / surviving through poetry / this is the blood sweat tears / of twenty-one years / this is my heart / in your hands / this is / the hurting / the loving / the breaking / the healing."[33] Atticus, who is advertised as "Instagram's most mysterious poet" on the back cover of his volume *Love Her Wild*, offers his readers a similar, albeit more positive, poetics of expression: "Poetry / to me / is

---

[31] Culler, *Theory of the Lyric*, 119.

[32] Courtney Peppernell, *Pillow Thoughts II: Healing the Heart* (Kansas City: Andrews McMeel, 2018).

[33] Rupi Kaur, *Milk and Honey* (Kansas City: Andrews McMeel, 2015).

stumbling in the dark / searching for / the right words / to describe / the feeling / I get / when she smiles / while she sleeps."[34]

The writers and readers of the popular contemporary Instalyric effectively use and ardently follow what Jonathan Culler, in his seminal book *Structuralist Poetics*, "called the rule of significance: read the poem as expressing a significant attitude to some problem concerning man and/or his relation to the universe."[35] The Instalyric is based on the widespread assumptions that sentences "broken into" verse "suddenly take on greater resonance," and that poems deal with important aspects of the human condition: love, life, death, for example.[36] As far as this rule of significance is concerned, let me compare "Personal Poem #2," a relatively unpopular lyric poem by the New York School's Ted Berrigan, with a personal or pseudo-personal lyric text from the second collection of Instagram's Atticus. Whereas Berrigan subversively plays with the rule of significance, Atticus seriously obeys it. Here is Berrigan:

> I wake up 11:30 back aching from soft bed Pat
> gone to work Ron to class (I never heard a sound)
> it's my birthday. 27. I put on birthday
> pants birthday shirt go to ADAM's buy a Pepsi for
> breakfast come home drink it take a pill
> I'm high!
>
> I do three Greek lessons to make
> up for cutting class. [...] I wonder if
> I'm too old. I wonder if I'm fooling myself
> about pills. I wonder what's in the icebox.
> I wonder if Ron or Pat bought any toilet paper
> this morning.[37]

---

[34] Atticus, *Love Her Wild* (London: Headline, 2017), 24.

[35] Jonathan Culler, *Structuralist Poetics: Structuralism, Linguistics and the Study of Literature* (Ithaca: Cornell University Press, 1976), 115.

[36] Lois Tyson, *Critical Theory Today: A User-Friendly Guide* (London: Routledge, 2006), 231.

[37] Ted Berrigan, "Personal Poem #2," in *The Collected Poems of Ted Berrigan*, ed. Alice Notley et al. (Berkeley: University of California Press, 2007), 116.

398 The Long Shadow of Romanticism

Compared to Berrigan's amusingly unromantic speaker, who babbles on about insignificant, common matters and everyday things such as "toilet paper," Atticus's conventionally romantic speaker intones a remembrance of rare, beautiful things and significant, personal events:

In the mornings
she taught me French
and after breakfast she would paint
and I would write
and as the spring rain fell on the skylight
and the tea steamed from its mugs
my heart hummed
to the music
of the dream
we'd found.[38]

Here, as in Hugo's "When We Were Living," a wonderful phase in someone's life has come to an end, which is a difficult situation the individual speaker has to cope with. This is a speaker seriously expressing intense emotions such as nostalgia, a speaker with whom many a reader may feel a strong identification. Buyers of Rupi Kaur and Company possibly see in popular Instagram Poetry something comparable to what Joyce Carol Oates saw in poetry by Robert Frost: "This is a distinctly American poetry, accessible to anyone. It isn't the subjects we write about but the seriousness and subtlety of our expression that determines the worth of our effort."[39]

An important reason why popular lyric poems and popular lyric lyrics are – in the common denotative sense of the word *popular* – "liked by a lot of people," by "ordinary" readers and listeners, is that these texts not only invite them to read and listen to but also to re-express 'serious' and 'beautiful' words, thoughts, emotions, and values that are supposed to be and sometimes deserve to be spoken and "shared by all or most people in the general public."[40] Let me illustrate my point

---

[38] Atticus, *The Dark Between Stars* (London: Headline, 2018), 11.
[39] Joyce Carol Oates, *The Faith of a Writer: Life, Craft, Art* (New York: Ecco, 2004), 20.
[40] "Popular, *adj.*," in *Longman Advanced American Dictionary* (New York: Pearson, 2013), 1315–1316.

with "The Hill We Climb," Amanda Gorman's immensely popular inaugural poem, which is in the American romantic tradition of Emersonian-Whitmanian verse and of rap and performance poetry. Metaphorically speaking, through a line from Emerson's poem commemorating the first battle of the American Revolution, one could say that Gorman's poem was "the shot heard round the world" on January 20, 2021.[41] Sure, the popularity of Gorman's text is heavily context- and event-related. It is very dependent on the poem's performer in a particular place and time: *this* young, African-American female poet with *that* specific appearance and stage presence *there* and *then*, at the inauguration of President Joe Biden after Donald Trump's unsuccessful re-election campaign and the January 6 Capitol riot. I think one can safely assume that a lot of people around the world simply liked hearing and seeing her at that special moment. But historical, political, cultural, social, and individual circumstances – extrinsic factors – do not provide sufficient reasons for an explanation of the popularity of Gorman's poem, for popularity is already potentially intrinsic to it, almost an inherent part, a formal element of the text itself. "The Hill We Climb" is an address to everyone on our planet: "Mr. President and Dr. Biden, / Madam Vice President and Mr. Emhoff, / Americans, and the World."[42] Though it is a poem expressing, "[i]n the modern sense" of the word *lyric*, "the personal mood, feeling," and "meditation of a single speaker,"[43] it is not a private but a public poem with a collective voice characterized by an all-embracing Whitmanian inclusiveness. The poem's emotional beginning immediately tries to draw everyone into the text: "When day comes, we ask ourselves: / Where can we find light / In this never-ending shade? / The loss we carry, a sea we must wade."[44] With its use of the first-person plural, its inviting grammatical form, the poem gives everyone a warm welcome and makes you want to speak it.

---

[41] Ralph Waldo Emerson, "Concord Hymn," in *Ralph Waldo Emerson: The Major Poetry*, ed. Albert J. von Frank (Cambridge: The Belknap Press of Harvard University Press, 2015), 130.

[42] Amanda Gorman, *The Hill We Climb: An Inaugural Poem for the Country* (New York: Viking, 2021), 9.

[43] Chris Baldick, *The Oxford Dictionary of Literary Terms* (Oxford: Oxford University Press, 2015), 206.

[44] Gorman, *The Hill We Climb*, 11.

400   The Long Shadow of Romanticism

Maybe you are inclined to accept this with caution at first, because with its different meanings and implications, the pronoun *we* seems to make you both come near and remain in respectful distance. When you proceed from one *we* to the next, you might ask yourself: Am I or do I want to be part of this? Is this also about me or us? But the welcoming *we* keeps enticing you into the poem and to join the speaker. The text's Whitmanian anaphoric structure, the rhythmical repetition and continuous recurrence of the attractive pronoun, does not want you to refuse its invitation and to stay outside but to drop your reserve and be involved in it. Everyone is supposed to become a part of the poem's celebratory communality and speak with its alluring voice.

What the poetic texts and most of the theoretical approaches I have dealt with here have in common is that they are centered around a speaker. The speaker is also the most important popularizing feature of lyrics and the lyric. It is hard to imagine truly popular forms of poetry that do not feature continuous, identifiable, or recognizable speakers speaking their mind, talking to someone about something (important), or expressing ideas, thoughts, opinions, feelings, etc. And only the lyric gives us the special opportunity to feel a really strong identification with the speaker. Readers often feel a strong identification with the narrators or characters of narrative or dramatic texts, too, of course, but this identification is – for structural and formal reasons – not as strong as it is with lyric texts. The lyric's genre-specific potential for identification and (therefore also) for popularity is based on what Roland Greene calls "its ritual mode:" In his book on *Post-Petrarchism*, Greene writes that "lyric is utterance uniquely disposed to be re-uttered."[45] This is exemplified clearly in the lyric, non-narrative lyrics of rap, one of the most popular forms of American poetry today and the most popular genre of contemporary American music. Just think of the so-called Golden Age of rap, of NWA and Rakim, for example! We just quote the voices of the narrator and the characters of NWA's narrative text "Dopeman" when we recite the lines "It was once said by a man who couldn't quit / 'Dopeman, please can I have another hit?' / The Dopeman said, 'Cluck,

---

[45]   Roland Greene, *Post-Petrarchism: Origins and Innovations of the Western Lyric Sequence* (Princeton: Princeton University Press, 1991), 5.

I don't give a shit / If your girl kneel down and suck my [...],'"[46] but we become the voice and are the speaker of Rakim's lyric text "My Melody" when we re-utter the words "My unusual style will confuse you a while / If I was water, I'd flow in the Nile."[47] Only the words of the lyric can seemingly become and actually feel like ours whenever we read them – silently or aloud. The structural and formal difference of the lyric matters.

But form is seldom everything to readers and writers of (contemporary popular) poetry. The formally aware poet Cathy Park Hong is a case in point. In *Minor Feelings*, she expresses annoyance, disappointment, and frustration about her time at the University of Iowa Writers' Workshop: "Back when I was a graduate student, [...] there was a piety about poetic form that was stifling. Any autobiographical reveal, especially if it was racial or sexual, was a sign of weakness."[48] Certainly, times have changed since Cathy Park Hong's student days. The making known or foregrounding of autobiographical pieces of information, "especially if" they are "racial or sexual," is increasing in popularity. As a paradigm of the (re)new(ed) interest in "auto-biographical reveal," these lines from "The Hill We Climb" spring immediately to mind: "[...] a skinny Black girl, / Descended from slaves and raised by a single mother, / Can dream of becoming president, / Only to find herself reciting for one."[49] The Gorman phenomenon is a remarkable instance of the renaissance of the author, who has never been completely dead in popular culture and literature. But there are also clear signs that author-centered attitudes are returning to power and popularity again in the professional realm of the social system of literature. There seems to be a growing tendency for people in Literary Studies to reinstate the author as the principal authority figure in the institution of literature, which often becomes most noticeable when an

---

[46] NWA, "Dopeman (Remix)," in *The Anthology of Rap*, ed. Adam Bradley and Andrew DuBois (New Haven: Yale University Press, 2010), 233.

[47] Eric B. & Rakim, "My Melody," in *The Anthology of Rap*, ed. Adam Bradley and Andrew DuBois (New Haven: Yale University Press, 2010), 173.

[48] Cathy Park Hong, *Minor Feelings: A Reckoning on Race and the Asian Condition* (London: Profile, 2021), 17.

[49] Gorman, *The Hill We Climb*, 14.

402 The Long Shadow of Romanticism

individual author's authority is challenged or questioned. Biographical and expressive criticism are gaining in popularity and seem to be making a comeback in the wake of approaches based on identity politics: context-oriented methodologies such as Postcolonial and Critical Race Theory; Gender, Queer, and Disability Studies; Social Justice and Activist Scholarship. Identity politics even has the potential to bridge the chasm between academic and non-academic audiences of the lyric.

Eventually, writers, translators, critics, publishers, professors, and 'ordinary' readers of poetry may overcome their differences by way of common causes. Maybe romantics from different fields will fall into line and make the paradigm of the author really popular again, even beyond verse cultures of popular lyric poetry.

Works Cited

Abrams, M. H., and Geoffrey Galt Harpham. *A Glossary of Literary Terms*. Boston: Cengage, 2015

Ashbery, John. "The Young Prince and the Young Princess." In *Contemporary American Poetry*, edited by Donald Hall, 192. New York: Penguin, 1972.

Atticus. *Love Her Wild*. London: Headline, 2017.

---. *The Dark Between Stars*. London: Headline, 2018.

Baldick, Chris. *The Oxford Dictionary of Literary Terms*. Oxford: Oxford University Press, 2015.

Barchiesi, Alessandro. "*Carmina: Odes and Carmen Saeculare.*" In *The Cambridge Companion to Horace*, edited by Stephen Harrison, 150–151. Cambridge: Cambridge University Press, 2007.

Berlin, Isaiah. "The True Fathers of Romanticism." In *The Roots of Romanticism*, edited by Henry Hardy, 60. London: Pimlico, 2000.

Berrigan, Ted. "Personal Poem #2." In *The Collected Poems of Ted Berrigan*, edited by Alice Notley et al., 116. Berkeley: University of California Press, 2007.

Carloto, Orion. *Flux*. Kansas City: Andrews McMeel, 2017.

Culler, Jonathan. *Structuralist Poetics: Structuralism, Linguistics and the Study of Literature*. Ithaca: Cornell University Press, 1976.

---. *Theory of the Lyric*. Cambridge: Harvard University Press, 2015.

de Botton, Alain. *The School of Life: An Emotional Education*. London: Hamish Hamilton, 2019.

Devoue, Bridgett. *Soft Thorns*. Kansas City: Andrews McMeel, 2018.

Emerson, Ralph Waldo. "Concord Hymn." In *Ralph Waldo Emerson: The Major Poetry*, edited by Albert J. von Frank, 130. Cambridge: The Belknap Press of Harvard University Press, 2015.

Eric B. & Rakim. "My Melody." In *The Anthology of Rap*, edited by Adam Bradley and Andrew DuBois, 173. New Haven: Yale University Press, 2010.

Ferguson, Margaret, et al., eds. *The Norton Anthology of Poetry*. New York: Norton, 2018.

Gorman, Amanda. *The Hill We Climb: An Inaugural Poem for the Country*. New York: Viking, 2021.

404 The Long Shadow of Romanticism

Greene, Roland. *Post-Petrarchism: Origins and Innovations of the Western Lyric Sequence*. Princeton: Princeton University Press, 1991.

Haxton, Brooks. "Introduction." In *Victor Hugo: Selected Poems*, translated and edited by Brooks Haxton, xi–xii. London: Penguin, 2002.

Hong, Cathy Park. *Minor Feelings: A Reckoning on Race and the Asian Condition*. London: Profile, 2021.

Hugo, Victor. "When We Were Living." In *Selected Poems*, translated and edited by Brooks Haxton, 33. London: Penguin, 2002.

Hulme, T. E. "Romanticism and Classicism." In *Selected Writings*, edited by Patrick McGuinness, 75. Manchester: Carcanet, 1998.

Kaur, Rupi. *Milk and Honey*. Kansas City: Andrews McMeel, 2015.

McCrum, Robert. "*The Making of Poetry* by Adam Nicolson: When Coleridge Met the Wordsworths." *The Guardian*, May 27, 2019.

NWA. "Dopeman (Remix)." In *The Anthology of Rap*, edited by Adam Bradley and Andrew DuBois, 233. New Haven: Yale University Press, 2010.

Oates, Joyce Carol. *The Faith of a Writer: Life, Craft, Art*. New York: Ecco, 2004.

Pater, Walter. "Postscript (Romanticism)." In *Selected Writings of Walter Pater*, edited by Harold Bloom, 217. New York: Columbia University Press, 1974.

Peppernell, Courtney. *Pillow Thoughts II: Healing the Heart*. Kansas City: Andrews McMeel, 2018.

Perrine, Laurence. *Sound and Sense: An Introduction to Poetry*. San Diego: Harcourt, Brace and Company, 1956.

"Popular, *adj*." In *Longman Advanced American Dictionary*, 1315–1316. New York: Pearson, 2013.

Tyson, Lois. *Critical Theory Today: A User-Friendly Guide*. London: Routledge, 2006.

Vendler, Helen. *The Music of What Happens: Poems, Poets, Critics*. Cambridge: Harvard University Press, 1988.

Section III: Other Media and Art Forms

JULIANE BOROSCH

Changing the Metonymy: Michigan Central Station and the Face of Detroit

A city can be defined as "a space of mental images, superimposed on physical space."[1] But who shapes these images, who puts them into action, and (how) do they become universally pervasive? Such questions of the connections between agency and imagery are standard in the study of popular culture, which Kelleter defines as "a set of social and aesthetic practices that first surfaced in the mid-nineteenth century, closely tangled up with the logic of industrial reproduction and the affordances of new mass media."[2] The visual and verbal language of popular culture and the landmarks of industrial production are blended in the idea of the city. It is only through the cooperation of the two that we can experience the city as a whole, according to Lindner;[3] and, as the German word 'Wahrzeichen' suggests, these landmarks represent ways of characterizing and preserving cities for posterity. However, there is a stark difference between internal and external descriptions of cities, and nowhere is this more apparent than in so-called cities in crisis, namely western cities that have lost their function as the heart of industrial production. The 'Wahrzeichen' of these is often said to be Detroit.

---

[1] Rolf Lindner, "The Imaginary of the City," in *Toward a New Metropolitanism: Reconstituting Public Culture, Urban Citizenship, and the Multicultural Imaginary in New York and Berlin*, ed. Günter H. Lenz et al. (Heidelberg: Universitätsverlag Winter, 2006), 210.

[2] Frank Kelleter, "Five Ways of Looking at Popular Seriality," in *Media of Serial Narrative*, ed. Frank Kelleter (Columbus: Ohio State University Press, 2017), 9.

[3] Lindner, "The Imaginary of the City," 211.

408 Changing the Metonymy

Detroit has been labelled "America's most iconographic city"[4] and is thereby posited as a metonymy for America.[5] Cognitive linguists Lakoff and Johnson define a metonymy as a type of trope in which one entity is used to stand for another.[6] A metonymy only makes sense because it is determined by language, but it is grounded in experience, attitudes, and actions.[7] Regarding Detroit, such anchoring factors would include racial divisions, capitalist democracy, and an urban frontier spirit. Detroit, with its iconic abandoned architecture, has become a stand-in for post-industrial cities in media portrayals and public perception. These depictions zoom in on a specific condition of industrial decline and urban bankruptcy.

In the case of Detroit, ruins have come to stand for the city. And more precisely, Michigan Central Station (MCS) has come to represent all ruins. The station functions as a stand-in for all of Detroit and as a *projection screen* for people watching the city from the outside as well as from within. Therefore, I argue that different groups of city insiders are now using the building itself as a popular medium (a channel and material of mass communication) in order to reclaim control over their city's future script rather than have the building be used by outside media to portray present shortcomings.[8] This paper thus traces how

[4] Kate Wells, "Detroit was Always Made of Wheels: Confronting Ruin Porn in its Hometown," in *Ruin Porn and the Obsession with Decay*, ed. Siobhan Lyons (London: Palgrave Macmillan, 2018), 15.

[5] Benedict Feldges explains that "[in] order for such a collective [...] vocabulary of visual terms to be generated and cultivated, two conditions need to be met: Pictures must be disseminated to a large [...] audience, and they must repeatedly feature a number of icons, emblems, and other generic symbols, so that audiences can recognize and share in the process of developing their significance." Benedict Feldges, *National Icons: The Genesis of a National Visual Language* (Taylor and Francis e-Library, 2007), 3.

[6] See George Lakoff and Mark Johnson, *Metaphors We Live By* (Chicago: University of Chicago Press, 1980), 39.

[7] Ibid.

[8] How scripts as de-, re-, and prescriptive (micro) narratives are used to influence and design the future of cities is the subject of the University Alliance Ruhr research group "Scripts for Postindustrial Urban Futures: American Models, Transatlantic Interventions." For conceptualizations of this see Barbara Buchenau and Jens Gurr, "'Scripts' in Urban Development:

MCS has come to reflect the face of Detroit, how it was used to establish the city's ruinous image, and how Detroiters are inverting this representation on screen by using the station itself as a projection screen. The trope of the face of Detroit is rooted in both the practice of personification and the tradition of portrait making. As Lakoff and Johnson explain, "we look at a person's face [...] to get our basic information about what that person is like."[9] Detroit, however, has shown a series of both faces and façades: After rising to fame as the Motor City in the early twentieth century and becoming the arsenal of democracy during WW2, it was then turned into a symbol of industrial decline. Once the façade of industrial wealth deteriorated, the consequences of decline dominated portraits of Detroit. In public life, this meant civil unrest in the form of street violence as a symptom of larger social problems, and, most recently and pervasively, the city in ruins. Since 2013, when Detroit declared bankruptcy, the return of downtown as the hip and hungry Comeback City has gained traction as a media image. Still, depictions of urban wastelands and ruination seem ubiquitous.

These images become universally pervasive in the popular aesthetic genre of ruin porn. The term, a less neutral version of ruin photography, is attributed to Detroit-based photographer James D. Griffioen, who coined it in 2009 to describe non-Detroit photographers' desire to be shown the "best ruins in town" so they could all take the same, supposedly soul-baring shots of the city. Kate Wells sees this as problematic because

---

Procedural Knowledge, Self-Description and Persuasive Blueprint for the Future," *Charting Literary Urban Studies: Texts as Models of and for the City*, ed. Jens Gurr (London: Routledge, 2021), 141–163; Buchenau and Gurr, "On the Textuality of American Cities and their Others: A Disputation," *Projecting American Studies: Essays on Theory, Method and Practice*, ed. Frank Kelleter and Alexander Starre (Heidelberg: Universitätsverlag Winter, 2018), 135–152; Buchenau and Gurr, "Urban American Studies and the Conjunction of Textual Strategies and Spatial Processes," *Spaces – Communities – Representations: Urban Transformations in the USA*, ed. Julia Sattler (Bielefeld: transcript, 2016), 395–420.

[9] Lakoff and Johnsons, *Metaphors We Live By*, 37.

410   Changing the Metonymy

[t]he images may be cropped to cut out aspects that would take away from their tragedy or morose qualities, such as functioning buildings, or the existence of people. The images are also manipulated in terms of tone and palette or by dint of HDR photographic technology.[10]

One could argue that ruin photography serves the purpose of historical documentation and has the potential to express constructive resistance and a warning regarding the current situation.[11] However, the manipulation of images to create a perceived emptiness in a city "speak[s] to a pointed aim to portray vulnerability without considering the actual space of the city and those populations that are truly vulnerable."[12] This rings especially true for Detroit, the "'hometown' of ruin porn."[13] In various media, the city has become synonymous with a small, almost standardized repertoire of images of urban (often specifically architectural) decay. Mass media "restrict the field of vision,"[14] which seems necessary regarding the stark discrepancy in scale and movement between increasingly smaller screens and increasingly sprawling expanding, complexifying cities. This strategic guidance of vision is used to "intensify expression."[15] Rolf Lindner explains how this type of abstraction and illusion of "untouched space"[16] is created by what Bourdieu describes as "deliberately disregarding everything that derives from the fact that it is an inhabited and appropriated space."[17]

---

[10]   Wells, "Detroit Was Always Made of Wheels," 14.

[11]   Cf. Dora Apel, *Beautiful Terrible Ruins: Detroit and the Anxiety of Decline* (New Brunswick: Rutgers University Press, 2015), 20.

[12]   Wells, "Detroit Was Always Made of Wheels," 13.

[13]   Siobhan Lyons, "Introduction: Ruin Porn, Capitalism, and the Anthropocene," in *Ruin Porn and the Obsession with Decay*, ed. Siobhan Lyons (London: Palgrave Macmillan, 2018), 6.

[14]   Aragon qtd. in Patrick Keiller, "Architectural Cinematography," in *This is not Architecture: Media Constructions*, ed. Kester Rattenbury (Taylor and Francis e-Library, 2005), 38.

[15]   Ibid.

[16]   Lindner, "The Imaginary of the City," 210.

[17]   Pierre Bourdieu, "Physischer, sozialer und angeeigneter physischer Raum," in *Stadt-Räume*, ed. Martin Wentz (Frankfurt, Main/New York: Campus, 1991), 28. Translated by Rolf Lindner in "The Imaginary of the City," in *Toward a New Metropolitanism: Reconstituting Public Culture, Urban*

Fig. 1: Apocalyptic framing of MCS.

Critics like Richard B. Woodward have further pointed to a detached escapism and the fascination of watching large-scale catastrophes "from a safe distance [...] through someone else's lens."[18] Ruin porn trivializes and hides the deeper roots of ruination. This abstracted depiction inhibits further action which might address the cause of Detroit's ruins. Instead, it provides a voyeuristic form of pleasure.[19]

The sheer size of MCS seems to maximize this fascination. The Beaux-Arts style building opened in 1913 – the same year Henry Ford implemented the first assembly line – and functioned as an office building and a train station. It was designed in the context of the City Beautiful Movement, which at the turn of the twentieth century "sought to attenuate the miserable conditions of the urban labor force and to address the environmental crisis in the cities" in North America and called for "grand public buildings at the end of dramatic vistas."[20] The

---

Citizenship, and the Multicultural Imaginary in New York and Berlin, ed. Günter H. Lenz et al. (Heidelberg: Universitätsverlag Winter, 2006), 210.

[18] Richard B. Woodward, "Disaster Photography: When Is Documentary Exploitation?" *ARTnews*, February 6, 2013.

[19] See Wells, "Detroit Was Always Made of Wheels," 21.

[20] Boris Vormann, "Infrastructures of the Global: Adding a Third Dimension to Urban Sustainability Discourses," *European Journal of American Studies*

plans for MCS therefore included a public park in front of its main entrance, adding to its monumental, unified look: "[C]ity elites and planners drew from classical symbols 'encoded in the terms of capitalism and political triumph.'"[21] MCS then was meant to "evoke empire"[22] and "provide a grand entrance to a new and superior city."[23] From its conception, MCS was thereby envisioned as the face that Detroit would show to the world. In line with the City Beautiful ideology, it was "intended to invoke a civic commitment to unity and pride" in Detroiters – which explains the prominence of the station in and for the city.[24]

Fig. 2: Postcard of MCS with parts of Roosevelt Park.

10, no. 3 (2015); Dan Austin, "Michigan Central Station," *Historic Detroit*, accessed May 9, 2021, historicdetroit.org/buildings/michigan-central-station. Notably, the City Beautiful Movement's origins lay in the Progressive Era and a rising fear of social and racial upheaval, a fear sometimes rooted in and acting on xenophobic prejudices.

[21] Wells, "Detroit Was Always Made of Wheels," 15.
[22] Ibid., 16.
[23] Ibid., 15.
[24] Ibid., 16.

However, due to the increase of car ownership and air travel after World War II, as well as the downswing of the automobile industry post-1950s, the station's importance dwindled until it finally closed in 1988. MCS was privately sold off in sections and was fully owned by the Moroun family from 1995 until 2018. They were widely criticized for not investing in the property and for leaving it vulnerable to decay and vandalism. Only "under pressure from the city, the Moroun enterprise installed more than 1,000 windows to the station's tower, restored a working elevator and cleaned up the interior"[25] in the early 2010s. Yet, owing to its former grandeur and prominent placement, the station has since been turned into the supposedly prototypical Detroit ruin. From its construction to its ruination, MCS can thus be posited as a symbol of the city it represents.

This type of framing is continuously employed by various mass media. Rebecca Kinney – drawing on Steve Macek's work on *Urban Nightmares* – finds that popular culture and news media in the 1980s and 1990s

> were essential in establishing the cultural resonance of fear of postindustrial urban space. Social policy and media representations worked together to produce a 'moral panic' about the U.S. city, resulting in a 'culturally authoritative discourse on the urban crisis' that produced Detroit and other postindustrial cities as 'landscapes of fear'.[26]

With the focus on ruins, such "landscapes of fear," which still included urban actors, have since been replaced by the "drama of landscape."[27] These urban scripts still produce haunting and sensationalist reports, but human actors have disappeared. Instead, a hollowed-out MCS represents *the city*. Rattenbury et al. argue that "[s]ometimes a photo [...] frames a specific architectural interpretation so successfully that it becomes the

---

[25] JC Reindl and John Gallagher, "It's Official: Morouns Sell Detroit Train Station to Ford," *Detroit Free Press*, June 11, 2018, eu.freep.com/story/money/cars/ford/2018/06/11/moroun-detroit-train-station-ford/689841002/.

[26] Rebecca Kinney, *Beautiful Wasteland: The Rise of Detroit as America's Postindustrial Frontier* (Minneapolis: University of Minnesota Press, 2016), xix.

[27] Wells, "Detroit Was Always Made of Wheels," 23.

414   Changing the Metonymy

quintessential image: the 'real' or 'authentic' version of it."[28] While such photos can draw attention to problems, this opportunity is often neglected on magazine covers and in popular coffee table books that turn ruin porn into high art. Such aestheticizations effectively

> mystify into 'poetic' inconsequence and remoteness the past that is represented by Detroit, and along with it the conclusions we might draw as a result. The otherwise troubling conclusions, and the actions that might follow from them – actions undertaken in the name of shared responsibility – are now translated into matters of taste and technique.[29]

Yet MCS frequently functions as the background for news reports and press conferences about some form of urban decay or economic decline. The problem, however, as former *Vice* editor Thomas Morton points out, is that "aside from looking the part, [the station] doesn't have too much to do with any of the issues it usually gets plastered above." The outside view of MCS is so pervasive, however, that the station has become a "happening spot," an over-mediated tourist attraction that has been "completely shot to death."[30] Morton's comments once again underline the screen's impact on perceptions of the city and its ability to produce its own version of a city. Jeff Rice, evoking Marc Augé's concept of non-places, argues that "[t]he 'spectators' of Detroit – the popular press, the nightly news, the daily conversations we hear and speak, and ourselves as we pity the city or look upon it in disgust – tend to totalize Detroit and make it a non-place".[31] It is therefore difficult not to be

---

[28] Kester Rattenbury et al., "Iconic Pictures," in *This is not Architecture: Media Constructions*, ed. Kester Rattenbury (Taylor and Francis e-Library, 2005), 40.

[29] Jerry Herron, "The Forgetting Machine: Notes Toward a History of Detroit," *Places Journal*, January 2012, placesjournal.org/article/the-forgetting-machine-notes-toward-a-history-of-detroit/?cn-reloaded=1.

[30] Ibid.

[31] Jeff Rice, *Digital Detroit. Rhetoric and Space in the Age of the Network* (Carbondale and Edwardsville: Southern Illinois University Press, 2012), 9. According to Augé, "a space which cannot be defined as relational, historical, or concerned with identity will be a non-place." Marc Augé, *Non-Places: Introduction to an Anthropology of Supermodernity*, trans. John Howe (London: Verso, 2000), 77–78.

seduced by these powerful narratives or tricked into the same metonymic practices, despite an awareness of such mechanisms.

Fig. 3: Windowless MCS and drive-up in June 2012.

For years, thousands of people came to Detroit to tour a perceived wasteland, an almost theme park-like artificial environment that decontextualizes the ruins from their causes and present surroundings. In response, Wells has perceived a "resistance within the collective unconscious of the city."[32] Factoring into this is the fact that the "materiality of the city is not simply a manifestation of years of urban decline and municipal disinvestment, but it is a present space, which both reflects and reproduces conditions of insecurity and uncertainty."[33] The

---

[32] Wells, "Detroit Was Always Made of Wheels," 14; See also Thomas Morton, "Something, Something, Something Detroit," *VICE*, August 1, 2009, vice.com/en_us/article/ppzb9z/something-something-something-detroit-994-v16n8.

[33] Eve Avdoulos, "Re-reading the ruins: Exploring conditions of insecurity and uncertainty in Detroit," *Architecture Magazine* 36 (2019): 20.

416 Changing the Metonymy

resistance of inhabitants specifically addresses two problems that Detroiters face in their personal perception and in the way the city is perceived.

On the one hand, this resistance addresses a "bizarre dichotomy of ruin and prosperity"[34] that in recent years has entered public perception as the concept of the Comeback City. This urban script is fostered by major downtown developments in real estate and infrastructure. Often feared to only attract affluent outsiders, it is rooted in what one may even infer to be a white and wealthy frontier myth.[35] In this controversial nostalgic rewriting, wealthy whites are re-conquering a city they left behind during the so-called white flight now that downtown Detroit is profitable again. Due to the previous exodus of the white middle class to the suburbs and greater metropolitan area during the deindustrialization crisis, Detroit's population has consistently been over 80% Black and suffered from economic and infrastructural neglect. Yet media coverage of the Comeback City effectively portrays an "erasure of blackness from a potentially profitable Detroit."[36] Without regard for existing city structures, private entrepreneurs have invested in the downtown area to shape the place to their liking. This has fostered an influx of people from outside Detroit and municipal investment in an area of just 18.6 square kilometers. While there are still many vacancies in the city, the influx of people into downtown and midtown set in motion displacement mechanisms frequently described as gentrification. All the while, the rest of the city (around 359.2 square kilometers) remains lacking in necessary investment.

On the other hand, Detroiters have started to address the continuous coverage of their lives in a supposed wasteland, an experience that Christopher T. Gullen describes as the "cyclical consciousness of trauma."[37] For residents of a city taught to identify with and emotionally invest in the built infrastructure of Detroit, the stories of its rise and

---

[34] Christopher T. Gullen, "Gods and Monsters: A Solastalgic Examination of Detroit's Ruins and Representation," in *Ruin Porn and the Obsession with Decay*, ed. Siobhan Lyons (London: Palgrave Macmillan, 2018), 34.

[35] See Wells, "Detroit Was Always Made of Wheels," 22; see also Rebecca Kinney, *Beautiful Wasteland*.

[36] Wells, "Detroit Was Always Made of Wheels," 22.

[37] Gullen, "Gods and Monsters," 34.

collapse are a part of the "family history."[38] It is therefore no surprise that Detroiters were the first to realize the importance of narratives for their city's identity, and that the mayor's office hired the nation's first official chief storyteller as part of city government in 2017.

Along the same lines, groups of Detroiters have started to invert the media's practice of depicting ruins by turning Detroit's most popular ruin into a medium itself. To loosely reference Marshall McLuhan: "*The medium* [in this case] *is* [in fact] *the message*." Thus, the (sur)face of MCS has frequently been turned into a projection screen to reflect and change the image of the city. Media façades as "the representation of a dynamic text, graphic or image"[39] are contextualized in media architecture, which situates the building and its installation within the city as Haeusler argues. Media architecture differs from static light architecture that uses daylight or artificial light and possibly colors to highlight certain parts or characteristics of a building.

Projections must usually be carried out in darkness, leading Tom Gunning to address their "dual role of cancelling out and conjuring up space."[40] This description works especially well for projections carried out in open urban space and cast upon buildings, as they not only create a new space but temporarily transform an existing one: While projections can simply be thought of as a "play of light," they can also create a "space of illusion."[41] Spectators are invited to immerse themselves in an – at least spatially – transformative performance.[42] Contrary

---

[38] Kinney, *Beautiful Wasteland*, xix.

[39] M. Hank Haeusler, *Media Facades: History, Technology, Content* (Stuttgart: Avedition, 2009), 13.

[40] Tom Gunning, "The Long and the Short of It: Centuries of Projecting Shadows, From Natural Magic to the Avant-Garde," in *Art of Projection*, ed. Stan Douglas and Christopher Eamon (Berlin: Hatje Cantz, 2009), 24.

[41] Ibid., 23.

[42] In this context, the "conjoined technological and psychoanalytic resonances of the term 'projection'" may also be considered. Thomas McDonough, "Production/Projection: Notes on the Capitalist Fairytale," in *Art of Projection*, ed. Stan Douglas and Christopher Eamon (Berlin: Hatje Cantz, 2009), 124. In the context of MCS and its role as a stand-in for the city in its glory or decline, psychological projection may refer to the extreme problems and opinions that (media) portrayals tie to the station, as well as to the constant reminder of trauma that this connection holds for the affected

418 Changing the Metonymy

to mass media and ruin porn photography, this projection places images in the city (albeit in darkness) without physically cutting out the surroundings. This allows for a contextualization of the pictures in their landscape, puts the projection into perspective, and somewhat dissolves the stasis of the portrayed ruin.

After the station's abandonment, the first true acts of projecting visions onto MCS from within Detroit came in the form of graffiti. Graffiti artists used MCS more as a canvas than a media screen, but they still approached the landmark as a medium to reclaim the ruin. Spraying and tagging a space is a political act, a physical and artistic means of claiming urban space from a marginalized position in order to inscribe one's existence onto it. This resonates with French sociologist Henri Lefebvre's conceptualization of space as the result of human production in a hegemonic struggle for people's Right to the City. Graffiti designates a location's importance for a particular purpose or community and makes a semi-permanent claim to it. However, this graphic form of expression by sub- and counter-cultural groups is also a form of producing art. Following Wells, one can even speak of "dialogic art"[43] that either proclaims a message to an audience or artistically encourages and engages. While some forms of graffiti are regarded as vandalism, they have also become highly popular in other contexts depending on how they are interpreted. Similar to the aesthetic fetish embodied by ruin porn, street art has been absorbed into commercialized popular culture and the high-end art scene, possibly jeopardizing the ability of street art to function as a medium of bottom-up protest – a dilemma that also applies to MCS.

Continuing the commercialization of residential protest and art, a sequence of two individual projections in 2017 brought about the current trend of using MCS as a medium for change. In 2017, a collective of influential Detroit entrepreneurs including the owner of the station held a Detroit Homecoming event to generate new investment in the city. A running light projection ran across the façade of MCS in the style of a news ticker. By means of a rear projection technique and window cladding, the words "Detroit Homecoming," "Reimagine" and "Re-

---

people. Literal, technological projections onto the building may then be able to untie these connections and create new visions.

[43] Wells, "Detroit Was Always Made of Wheels," 25.

invest" were projected onto the station in running capital letters. This ensured high visibility within the city and signaled the entrepreneurs' awareness of the importance of the building. It also showed the intended homecoming of financial power and engagement in the city. Then, in December 2017, local hip-hop icon Eminem announced his new album by projecting a static image of the cover art for *Revival* onto the building's façade via drone. This promotional projection entwined the artist's biography with that of Detroit and sought to evoke a similar homecoming message: a proclamation of the city coming back to life.

Both projections seem to have restored faith in the station's potential within Detroit. In June 2018, the Ford Motor Company announced a big reinvestment in the city by purchasing the area around MCS, including the iconic station itself. After decades of decay, the building – as part of Ford's new mobility campus – would be restored with near historical accuracy. Ironically, one of the companies that made Detroit the Motor City and contributed to the rise of individual transport and, thus, to the decline of MCS is now in charge of the station. Still, instead of letting it decay any further, Ford is using the legacy of this iconic building as part of the future of transport and the future of Detroit.

To announce the purchase of this emblematic building, the company commissioned an installation: For a week leading up to the big announcement, a quote related either to Detroit, the station's history, or its future was projected onto the building's façade each night. Each projection was photographed and posted on Ford's Twitter account for the public to see on a different type of screen. This type of publication can be criticized for taking away from the temporary transformation of space for the Detroiters who were present on site and, like the Eminem installation, for using the building as a multi-media advertising column. Yet it also did what Detroiters had been missing for years: It addressed insiders and outsiders at the same time while also juggling the two versions of the building in order to reconcile them.

To further promote their purchase of MCS, Ford organized a reception inside the entrance hall of the station. The design company Red Paper Heart, which notably is not from Detroit but New York City, created projections for the interior arches and domes of the station. They used "scaffolding-based design language to signify the excitement of the

420 Changing the Metonymy

beginning of a construction project"[44] but, in contrast to how it is used in regular construction, the scaffolding did *not* hide the building; rather, the architecture and actual surfaces of the walls were again used as a screen. The interactive installation allowed visitors to enter their own messages and wishes for MCS and the future of Detroit – and to broadcast them. Red Paper Heart proclaimed the installation "a platform that lifts the hopes and goals of Detroit's current residents for what their city's future will be. Because ultimately this is a story best told by the people of Detroit." Despite its choreographed, corporate design, this conceptualization provided an opportunity for Detroiters to get involved in shaping their city's story or at least provided a temporary platform for them to publish their visions for Detroit's future.

Following the overwhelmingly positive reception of Ford's purchase of MCS, the company continued to keep the renovation project in the headlines while also ensuring good will in Detroit. In January 2019, they organized a public winter festival outside the station which included a 3D projection onto MCS. The projection was far more elaborate than previous ones: It was a 10-minute immersive audio-visual narrative of MCS and its representative role for the city that temporarily treated the façade of the building, its screen, as a palimpsest.[45] The projection also positioned Ford as the second face of the city and entwined their respective histories. Starting with the station's historic roots, the installation covered the journey from the glory years of the station,

---

[44] Red Paper Heart, "For Detroit," accessed January 17, 2020, redpaperheart.com/work/fordetroit.

[45] The palimpsest is an increasingly popular metaphor to describe layered urban spaces. It worked particularly well in this case, as the actual architectural surface of MCS was layered onto the station and peeled off or painted on through light projections. Still, there is criticism that the traditional notion of the palimpsest lacks the presence of an observer who can decipher a place's layers, and that palimpsests are not only spatial, but temporal (meaning historical) phenomena (Gurr). Palimpsests can furthermore be temporary appearances, such as the experiences had while walking the city as described by Michel de Certeau in *The Practice of Everyday Life* (Berkeley: University of California Press, 1984). Correspondingly, the interdisciplinary work on site-specific performances and urban pop-ups which layer a place for a limited time only seems important.

showcasing Ford as a good employer in Detroit, to the station falling into misuse and its status as a ruin that Detroiters claim through graffiti.[46] The struggles and failures of the car industry were notably not portrayed. Instead, Ford's future vision for the station and its continued importance for Detroit were revealed: This vision posited mobility, mobility industries, and thus Ford at the center of Detroit's future. MCS as the face of Detroit merged with Ford in the grand finale of the projection, when a giant hand signed the company logo on the front of the building.

Fig. 4: Projection of a hand signing the Ford logo onto the façade of MCS.

This not only highlighted the advertising character of the installation, but once again problematically blended the company's fate with that of

[46] Jerry Herron describes this phenomenon concerning the ruins of MCS, among others: "what people remember is not exactly historical reality; instead, the memory [...] has become a kind of screen upon which we can replay an idealized past." Jerry Herron, "The Forgetting Machine."

422 Changing the Metonymy

the city. Branding a symbol of civic pride with a commercial company's logo would seem to warrant an outcry of protest, yet, from what can be deduced from official responses and (social) media, responses to Ford laying claim to the building have been surprisingly positive.[47] This can be seen in the context of a larger trend that Conrad Kickert has described as a "movement from spaces of transaction to spaces of experience," in which historic downtown buildings stand as "3D advertisements" because "big companies want you to know that their brand is somehow spiritually connected to Downtown Detroit."[48] Ford's purchase of MCS, with its size and prestige, may have significantly boosted this strategy while also writing a hopeful narrative for the future of Detroit's "most famous ruin."[49]

This essay has argued that the metonymic relationship between Michigan Central Station and postindustrial cities in general reflects the fact that the immense media presence of MCS in popular culture had already begun with the conception and construction of the building. MCS was intended to be the first thing outsiders saw when arriving in Detroit. Simultaneously, the architectural grandeur and symbolism of the station were meant to instill pride in Detroiters and Americans at large. This contextualization, however, is rarely thematized in portrayals of the city in ruins. In fact, MCS has often been used for dehumanized projections of fear and distancing from the outside. In turn, groups of Detroiters now project popular American claims and visions for the city onto it: While grassroots activists tag the station to reclaim it, impactful messages of restoring Detroit's pride through MCS are often based on or tied to a commercial or corporate adaption of this tagging process. This holds true for Eminem's cover reveal and the Ford campaigns. But elites and planners have been imposing city pride onto citizens since the City Beautiful Movement. Is it possible to change preconceptions of a place

---

[47] There are no representative surveys and statistics in this case, but media publications can indicate public opinion and social media posts can portray the opinions and reactions of individuals.

[48] Staes, Jer (Host/Producer), "Downtown Detroit's Development Paradoxes with Retail & Urban Design Expert Conrad Kickert," *Daily Detroit Podcast*, January 24, 2020, podbay.fm/podcast/1220563942/e/1579903479.

[49] Peter Valdes-Dapena, "Ford to remake Detroit's most famous ruin," *CNN Business*, June 18, 2018, money.cnn.com/2018/06/17/news/ companies/ford-michigan-central-station/index.html.

that have been propagated by mass media? Ford's elaborate projections seek to change the ruinous metonymy of MCS, and the reactions to this media form of urban redevelopment have been overwhelmingly positive. However, these reactions have largely come from within the city. It remains to be seen whether global popular culture will reflect the face of Detroit differently. Corporate activism in the shape of popular culture feeds into Detroiters' long-standing dependency on industry for city pride. The cultural value of the contemporary MCS has renewed the connection between Ford and the city's claim to fame – popularizing a twenty-first century version of Fordism and the industrial age. These metonymic endeavors feed into a vicious circle in which corporate investments in the city propel extreme dynamics of rise and fall. The spiral now seems directed upward, with Detroit's restoration moving along and Ford on track to finish the historically accurate restoration and repurposing of MCS in 2023. In the meantime, Ford has continued to use the station as a medium during public and corporate events such as a drive-through haunted house and light projection shows during the Covid-19 pandemic, working to reconcile Detroiters to the repurposed MCS. Media portrayals of the station from both outside and within the city are now turning the page and focusing on a spirit of optimism and transformation, which can also be witnessed in portrayals of Detroit in general. This media presence and the continued metonymic character of MCS alongside a former industrial magnate is a testament to popular culture's anchorage in American industrial reproduction.

424   Changing the Metonymy

Works Cited

Apel, Dora. *Beautiful Terrible Ruins: Detroit and the Anxiety of Decline.* New Brunswick: Rutgers University Press, 2015.

Augé, Marc. *Non-Places: Introduction to an Anthropology of Supermodernity.* Translated by John Howe. London: Verso, 2000.

Austin, Dan. "Michigan Central Station." *Historic Detroit,* accessed 9 May 2021. historicdetroit.org/buildings/michigan-central-station.

Avdoulos, Eve. "Re-reading the Ruins: Exploring Conditions of Insecurity and Uncertainty in Detroit." *Architecture Magazine* 36 (2019): 18–20.

Berger, John. *Ways of Seeing.* London: Penguin, 1972.

Bourdieu, Pierre. "Physischer, sozialer und angeeigneter physischer Raum." In *Stadt-Räume,* edited by Martin Wentz, 25–34. Frankfurt am Main: Campus, 1991.

Buchenau, Barbara, and Jens Gurr. "Scripts' in Urban Development: Procedural Knowledge, Self-Description and Persuasive Blueprint for the Future." In *Charting Literary Urban Studies: Texts as Models of and for the City,* edited by Jens Gurr, 141–163. London: Routledge, 2021.

---. "On the Textuality of American Cities and their Others: A Disputation." In *Projecting American Studies: Essays on Theory, Method and Practice,* edited by Frank Kelleter and Alexander Starre, 135–152. Heidelberg: Universitätsverlag Winter, 2018.

---. "Urban American Studies and the Conjunction of Textual Strategies and Spatial Processes." In *Spaces – Communities – Representations: Urban Transformations in the USA,* edited by Julia Sattler, 395–420. Bielefeld: transcript, 2016.

de Certeau, Michel. *The Practice of Everyday Life.* Berkeley: University of California Press, 1984.

DJANDYW.COM. "Save the Depot." *Flickr,* August 4, 2011. flickr.com/photos/100494965@N07/31328400802.

Feldges, Benedict. *National Icons: The Genesis of a National Visual Language.* Taylor and Francis e-Library, 2007.

Gonzales, Martin. "Train Spotting In Detroit." *Flickr,* June 10, 2012. flickr.com/photos/25165196@N08/7550055908/.

Gullen, Christopher T. "Gods and Monsters: A Solastalgic Examination of Detroit's Ruins and Representation." In *Ruin Porn and the Obsession with Decay*, edited by Siobhan Lyons, 31–44. London: Palgrave Macmillan, 2018.

Gunning, Tom. "The Long and the Short of It: Centuries of Projecting Shadows, From Natural Magic to the Avant-Garde." In *Art of Projection*, edited by Stan Douglas and Christopher Eamon, 23–35. Berlin: Hatje Cantz, 2009.

Gurr, Jens Martin. "Palimpsests? – Spatialized Urban Memory and Postindustrial Cities." Schichtungen des Urbanen, November 7, 2019. Keynote Address.

Haeusler, M. Hank. *Media Facades: History, Technology, Content*. Stuttgart: Avedition, 2009.

Herron, Jerry. "The Forgetting Machine: Notes Toward a History of Detroit." *Places Journal*, January 2012. placesjournal.org/article/the-forgetting-machine-notes-toward-a-history-of-detroit/?cn-reloaded=1.

Keiller, Patrick. "Architectural Cinematography." In *This is not Architecture: Media Constructions*, edited by Kester Rattenbury, 37–44. Taylor and Francis e-Library, 2005.

Kelleter, Frank. "Five Ways of Looking at Popular Seriality." In *Media of Serial Narrative*, edited by Frank Kelleter, 7–36. Columbus: Ohio State University Press, 2017.

Kickert, Conrad. "Downtown Detroit's Development Paradoxes." *Daily Detroit Podcast,* January 24 2020. podbay.fm/podcast/1220563942/e/1579903479.

Kinney, Rebecca. *Beautiful Wasteland: The Rise of Detroit as America's Postindustrial Frontier*. Minneapolis: University of Minnesota Press, 2016.

Lakoff, George, and Mark Johnson. *Metaphors We Live By*. Chicago: University of Chicago Press, 1980.

Lefebvre, Henri. *Le Droit à la Ville*. Sankt Augustin: Anthropos, 1968.

Lindner, Rolf. "The Imaginary of the City." In *Toward a New Metropolitanism: Reconstituting Public Culture, Urban Citizenship, and the Multicultural Imaginary in New York and Berlin*, edited by Günter H. Lenz et al., 209–215. Heidelberg: Universitätsverlag Winter, 2006.

426 Changing the Metonymy

Lyons, Siobhan. "Introduction: Ruin Porn, Capitalism, and the Anthropocene." In *Ruin Porn and the Obsession with Decay*, edited by Siobhan Lyons, 1–11. London: Palgrave Macmillan, 2018.

Macek, Steve. *Urban Nightmares. The Media, the Right, and the Moral Panic over the City*. Minneapolis: University of Minnesota Press, 2006.

McDonough, Thomas. "Production/Projection: Notes on the Capitalist Fairytale." In *Art of Projection*, edited by Stan Douglas and Christopher Eamon, 124–140. Berlin: Hatje Cantz, 2009.

McLuhan, Marshall. *Understanding Media: The Extensions of Man*. London: Routledge & Kegan Paul, 1964.

Morton, Thomas. "Something, Something, Something Detroit." *VICE*, August 1, 2009. vice.com/en_us/article/ppzb9z/something-something-something-detroit-994-v16n8.

Rattenbury, Kester, et al. "Iconic Pictures." In *This is not Architecture: Media Constructions*, edited by Kester Rattenbury, 37–44. Taylor and Francis e-Library, 2005.

Red Paper Heart. "For Detroit." Accessed January 17, 2020. redpaper-heart.com/work/fordetroit.

Reindl, JC, and John Gallagher. "It's Official: Morouns Sell Detroit Train Station to Ford." *Detroit Free Press*, June 11, 2018. eu.freep.com/story/money/cars/ford/2018/06/11/moroun-detroit-train-station-ford/689841002/.

Rice, Jeff. *Digital Detroit: Rhetoric and Space in the Age of the Network*, Carbondale and Edwardsville: Southern Illinois University Press, 2012.

Staes, Jer (Host/Producer). "Downtown Detroit's Development Paradoxes with Retail & Urban Design Expert Conrad Kickert." *Daily Detroit Podcast*, January 24, 2020. www.dailydetroit.com/2020/01/24/downtown-detroits-development-paradoxes-with-retail-urban-design-expert-conrad-kickert/.

"The Michigan Central Station Winter Festival by Ford." YouTube.com, January 19, 2019. youtube.com/watch?v=yf6N9JwApeo.

Valdes-Dapena, Peter. "Ford to remake Detroit's most famous ruin." *CNN Business*, June 18, 2018. money.cnn.com/2018/06/17/news/companies/ford-michigan-central-station/index.html.

Vormann, Boris. "Infrastructures of the Global: Adding a Third Dimension to Urban Sustainability Discourses." *European Journal of American Studies* 10, no. 3 (2015).

Wells, Kate. "Detroit was Always Made of Wheels: Confronting Ruin Porn in its Hometown." In *Ruin Porn and the Obsession with Decay*, edited by Siobhan Lyons, 13–29. London: Palgrave Macmillan, 2018.

Woodhead, Jason. "PHOSTINT." *Flickr*, June 18, 2011. flickr.com/photos/woodhead/5846971724/in/album-72157623397995563/.

Woodward, Richard B. "Disaster Photography: When Is Documentary Exploitation?" *ARTnews.com*, February 6, 2013. www.artnews.com/2013/02/06/the-debate-over-ruin-porn/.

Illustrations

Fig. 1: Apocalyptic framing of MCS. Credit: DJANDYW.COM/ CC BY-SA 2.0

Fig. 2: Postcard of MCS with parts of Roosevelt Park. Credit: Jason Woodhead/ CC BY 2.0

Fig. 3: Windowless MCS and drive-up in June 2012 Credit: martin gonzales/ CC BY 2.0

Fig. 4: Projection of a hand signing the Ford logo onto the façade of MCS. Screenshot from www.youtube.com/watch?v=yf6N9JwApeo.

DUSTIN BREITENWISCHER

#ART: Westside Gunn's "Aestheticism"

Hip Hop, Art, and #ART

The relationship between hip hop culture and art is as old as hip hop itself. Charlie Ahearn's early hip hop movie *Wild Style* (1982), for instance, tells the story of the fictional graffiti artist "RAY" (played by graffiti legend Lee "LEE" Quiñones) and the cultural dilemma "RAY" faces when his illegal street art attracts the attention of the highbrow New York gallery scene. A year after the movie's premiere, painter wunderkind Jean-Michel Basquiat (and hip hop musicians Rammellzee and K-Rob) produced, in Warhol-Factory-Velvet-Underground-like fashion, the track "Beat Bob" in an attempt to introduce Basquiat's avant-garde aesthetic to the pop-cultural sphere of hip hop.[1] And in their analyses of the poetics of rap lyrics and the aesthetics of hip hop culture, scholars such as Adam Bradley, Michael Eric Dyson, Tricia Rose, and Richard Shusterman have valorized the culture of hip hop (and particularly rap music) as art for decades.[2]

---

[1] After his death, Basquiat steadily became the patron saint of hip hop musicians. The list of hip hop tracks alone that contain his name in their title is indicative of this transcultural homage. See, for example, Apollo Brown & Skyzoo, "Basquiat on the Draw"; Bun B & Statik Selektah, "Basquiat"; Yasiin Bey (a.k.a. Mos Def), "Basquiat Ghostwriter"; or, for that matter, the discussed Westside Gunn & Conway the Machine (as Hall & Nash), "Brains on the Basquiat."

[2] Cf. Adam Bradley, *Book of Rhymes: The Poetics of Hip Hop* (New York: Civitas, 2017); Michael Eric Dyson, *Know What I Mean? Reflections on Hip Hop* (New York: Civitas, 2007); Tricia Rose, *Black Noise: Rap Music and Black Culture in Contemporary America* (Middletown: University Press of New England, 1994); Richard Shusterman, "The Fine Art of Rap," *New Literary History* 22, no. 3 (1991): 613–632.

430 Westside Gunn's "Aestheticism"

In the early 2000s, when hip hop became a cultural powerhouse and some of its most established musicians ascended the ladder from millionaire rappers to multi-millionaire executives, the economic and symbolic relationship between hip hop and art materialized even more substantially. Fully immersed in the lifestyle of the *nouveau riche*, musicians like Rick Ross and Drake began to tour leading art exhibitions in order to start and expand their collections, while the Wu-Tang Clan auctioned off their album "Once Upon a Time in Shaolin" (2015) as a single vinyl copy. Beyoncé and Jay Z rented the Louvre in Paris to shoot the video for their song "Apeshit" (2018) in front of Da Vinci's *Mona Lisa*, and Jay Z used his single "Picasso Baby" (2015) for an Abramović-inspired six-hour performance of the song at the Pace Gallery in New York. The performance was subsequently released as a ten-minute "Performance Art Film" featuring, among others, Marina Abramović herself, conceptual artist Lawrence Weiner, art dealer Sandra Gering, and hip hop pioneer Fab 5 Freddy (who, to come full circle, played the role of Quiñones's friend Phade, who introduces the graffiti artist to the gallery scene in *Wild Style*).[3] Even though the social ascendency of a rapper like Jay Z was as unlikely as it is impressive, and despite his claim in the video that he and all other artists are "cousins" – which makes one wonder about an ever-growing cultural aristocracy in which assumed 'family ties' often trump the politics of an egalitarian cultural dehierarchization – Jay Z's 'family membership' and his ability to host a 'family meeting' at Pace Gallery depend largely on his established socio-economic elitism and the ensuing willingness to accept and appropriate certain hegemonic standards and institutions. What may appear as a subversive dynamic of levelling ultimately unfolds as the socially reproductive dynamic of distinction (about which I will say more below). "Picasso Baby" is arguably very entertaining as a highly aestheticized spectacle of bourgeois taste, cultural elitism, and economic privilege. And so, the performance of a hip hop track about art in a closed-off art gallery does not epitomize the potentially resistant quality of popular music but a dominant strain in the current relationship

---

[3] "Apeshit," YouTube, June 16, 2018, youtube.com/watch?v=kbMqWXnp XcA; "Picasso Baby (A Performance Art Film)," Universal Music Group, accessed January 6, 2022, universal-music.de/jayz/videos/picasso-baby-a-performance-art-film-326307.

between hip hop and art. It takes hip hop away from the street, the underground club scene, and the popular media and reinforces the almost hermetic embourgeoisement of the musician.

Against this backdrop, I want to turn to a very recent phenomenon in U.S. hip hop culture that complicates this relationship: the work of Buffalo-based rapper, gallery owner, and record and fashion label executive Alvin Lamar Worthy, a.k.a. Westside Gunn. Since the mid-2010s, Westside Gunn has been one of the leading figures in alternative U.S. hip hop, in which 'alternative' must not be understood as an ideological rejection of market success in the popular mainstream, but as an intrageneric differentiation. The 'alternative' is a particular aesthetic that highlights deviance and dissonance in sound, style, and lyrics toward the pleasurable and easily consumable music of that so-called mainstream. A number of alternative hip hop acts seek to produce music and cater to an idea of creative subjectivity that is indicative of an artistically inclined disposition. Accordingly, Westside Gunn's records (and those produced by his record label Griselda Records) are marked by a curious aesthetic audacity with regard to both their music and their visual appearance. In his collaborations with producers such as Daringer, The Alchemist, or Madlib, whose works may be described as artfully minimalistic, and with artists and designers such as Isaac Pelayo or Virgil Abloh, Westside Gunn explores a niche in hip hop that experimentally deviates from the mainstream without lacking the proper professionalism. Aside from producing and promoting his music, which increasingly plays a side role in his career, Westside Gunn, I argue, uses this niche (a) to explore the limits of his creative subjectivity, and (b) to unfold, and intricately so, a visual aesthetic that is shaped as much by his label's provocative cover art as by his self-representation as 'artist,' meticulously choreographed in images for his Instagram profile.

Fig. 1: Westside Gunn, Instagram Account

Fig. 2: Westside Gunn, Instagram Post

Westside Gunn fuses these two concerns in his ever-growing visual archive and in his recurrent and strategic use of the hashtag "ART," which may initially pass unnoticed or, at best, be seen as a gimmicky part of a given Instagram post's paratext. However, this essay will focus on Westside Gunn's use of #ART and its cultural implications, as it seeks to analyze a moment when the self-understanding of the hip hop musician as artist becomes exhilaratingly unstable and demands from the artist to undertake attempts at formal, stylistic, and imaginative reconsideration and reintegration. I want to look at a dynamic that sets in at the cultural threshold between art and popular culture and in which, as we will see, the latter seeks to excel in an exaggerated performance of "art" (I will explain the quotation marks below). This essay is thus neither interested in the normative distinction between art and popular culture nor in the subversive dissolution of that distinction – i.e., the debate between Critical Theory and Birmingham School cultural studies – but in a moment of cultural communication that shapes a niche in contemporary hip hop culture and may prove to be informative beyond

434 Westside Gunn's "Aestheticism"

that division. I will discuss the use and the effects of #ART both in Westside Gunn's Instagram account and as a concretion of his larger aesthetic objectives. By looking at a series of #ART's interrelated effects and implications, I argue that Westside Gunn takes up a liminal position on the very threshold between experimental popular culture and the art scene, and that his #ART offers a different calibration of economic and symbolic capital in hip hop in order to strategically stress the stylization and aestheticization of his liminal creative subjectivity as modes of cultural distinction.

#ART as a Punchline

The introduction of the hashtag in social media has shaped much of our contemporary communication, both within and beyond the realm of the digital. Hashtags are decidedly not narrational, but evocative. As a way to hyperlink a potentially infinite number of statements, comments, and images (especially on social media platforms such as Twitter or Instagram), hashtags open real and imaginary spaces by way of reference, allusion, insinuation, exclamation, or provocation. Hashtags are as much a marketing tool as they are an instrument of political resistance.[4] A hashtag might serve as the beginning, the middle, or the end of a conversation; it might introduce, frame, or summarize a given discourse. It is as much a radically condensed amalgamation of a more extensive discourse as it is a punchline. Particularly in that latter sense, the hashtag has shaped the way we speak and tell stories online.

In 2010, musician and entrepreneur Kanye West introduced the term "hashtag rap" to the poetics of hip hop in order to describe lyrics in which the punchline is served up in a single word, separated by a pause from the previous preparatory, cascading verses. Even though this style of rap can be traced back well into the 1990s, contemporary appropriations of hashtag rap decidedly reflect upon the socio-cultural

---

[4] See, for example, Sarah Florini, *Beyond Hashtags. Racial Politics and Black Digital Networks* (New York: New York University Press, 2019); Alissa V. Richardson, *Bearing Witness While Black: African Americans, Smartphones, and the New Protest #Journalism* (New York: Oxford University Press, 2020).

phenomenon of the social media-based, punchline-seeking, and polarizing ways we communicate (in text and image) with each other and the world.

Westside Gunn's rap style certainly relates to the poetics of hashtag rap, but it differs significantly in that it is not driven by the apex of a punchline. Rather, his rap excels as a never-ending list of brief and often unrelated images, a collage of sentiments, assumptions, and the insertion of onomatopoetical gun sounds *"dodododododo,"* *"brrrrrrr,"* *"boomboomboom"* reminiscent of Dada aesthetic as well as Amiri Baraka's "Black Art" (1966).[5] Instead of turning his rap into a series of hashtag-like punchlines, Westside Gunn uses his Instagram account to introduce #ART as both the source and the telos of his creative exploration of music and visuality. He does not mimic the style of the hashtag, but rather stylizes the hashtag in his desire to excel in art.

#ART and Aesthetic Hedonism

As of June 2021, more than 800 million Instagram posts were hyperlinked with #ART. From the ever-same images of sunsets to discussions about misogyny in the cultural scene, everything that is, in the minds of the users, somewhat related to art or a semblance thereof is being tagged and shared accordingly. Hashtags forge connections between users as 'artist communities', and they seek to distinguish the aesthetic and artistic value of images. Accordingly, Westside Gunn's conceptualization of #ART is built on the instable and increasingly indeterminate threshold between popular culture and art; a threshold, that is, which stills owes its persistence to Adorno's distinction between autonomous art and the products of the culture industry. By this logic, #ART simultaneously highlights and distances itself from a cultural subjectivity that Adorno identifies as "aesthetic hedonism," which "banishes art's negativity to the instinctual conflicts of its genesis and suppresses any negativity in the finished work" and, in the case of the culture industry, thus promises a seamless distancing from the world in

---

[5] Amiri Baraka, "Black Art," in *Selected Poetry of Amiri Baraka/LeRoi Jones* (New York: William Morrow & Co, 1979), 106.

an experience "in which profit is hidden."[6] While I am not interested in yet another contribution that discusses the forces of the culture industry in our understanding of popular culture, I want to further explore Adorno's rarely referenced idea of "aesthetic hedonism." But instead of using Westside Gunn as a phenomenon that may or may not contradict Adorno's notion of hedonistic aesthetic autonomy which favors pleasure over critique, I argue that Westside Gunn's aesthetic hedonism may best be understood as a hedonistic aestheticism that seeks to align art and the popular.

Fig. 3: Westside Gunn in front of the cover art of Armani Caesar's *The Liz* by Isaac Pelayo

The traditional subject of hedonistic aestheticism is, of course, the turn-of-the-century avant-gardist who "emphatically aspires the artificial, the

---

[6] Theodor W. Adorno, *Aesthetic Theory* (London: Continuum, 2002), 12; 57.

triumph over ordinary naturalness," as Andreas Reckwitz notes.[7] I argue that, under the completely different social and economic conditions of late capitalism, the inherent aestheticism of Westside Gunn's investment in #ART as an expression of creative subjectivity delineates art in its confrontation with artifice in a curiously similar vein, and it toys with the idea, but ultimately stops short of suggesting a consequential avant-gardist dissolution of art and life for the sake of artifice and the fake.[8] In turn, I do not encroach on the vicinity of what Peter Bürger refers to as the historical avant-garde's "revolutionizing of art," which aspires to the "total abolition of the institution that is art."[9] Rather, there is an underlying aestheticism looming in #ART which surfaces as a celebration of hedonistic decadence over revolutionary subversion. In the exploration of his creative subjectivity, Westside Gunn uses the role of the aesthete as a catalyst through which deviance becomes a pleasurable performance. On the surface of gesture, style, and rhetoric, this clearly relates to the historical avant-gardes – to the fluidity and the self-irony of Dada and to the spontaneity and affectivity of Expressionism – yet its desire for newness is not invested in a break with cultural commodification but with the production and nurturing of a differently and more excessively stylized and aesthetically dis-tinguished consumer desire.[10] I will return to this below. But first, I want to further discuss Westside Gunn's visual aesthetics and his exploration of the creative self as aesthete, i.e. his Camp aesthetics.

---

[7] Andreas Reckwitz, *Das hybride Subjekt. Eine Theorie der Subjektkulturen von der bürgerlichen Moderne zur Postmoderne* (Berlin: Suhrkamp, 2020), 306. My translation.

[8] Cf. Jacob Copeman and Giovanni da Col, eds., *Fake: Anthropological Keywords* (Chicago: HAU, 2018); Heinz Drügh, "Fake – Drei Aspekte einer Ästhetik des Konsums/Fake – Three Aspects of an Aesthetic of Consumption," in *After Facts: Pudding Explosion Rearticulated* (Frankfurt am Main: Universität Frankfurt Kunstgeschichtliches Institut, 2018), 122–143.

[9] Peter Bürger, *Theory of the Avant-Garde* (Minneapolis: University of Minnesota Press, 1984), 72; 63.

[10] Cf. ibid.; Reckwitz, *Das hybride Subjekt*, esp. chapter 3.

438   Westside Gunn's "Aestheticism"

#ART and Camp

In her 1958 "Notes on 'Camp,'" Susan Sontag famously discusses a
"particular fugitive sensibility," "a certain mode of aestheticism," a
"love of the exaggerated," and "the spirit of extravagance" which is
"wholly aesthetic" – in short: Camp.[11] "Camp is a woman walking
around in a dress made of three million feathers."[12] Upon closer
examination, Westside Gunn's Camp aestheticism is a not entirely new
yet nonetheless surprising appropriation of the Camp aesthetic in the
context of hip hop. Clearly inspired by the 'queer' aesthetics of Sly
Stone, Prince, and Blaxploitation cinema, his Instagram pictures show
him in fur coats, skinny jeans, various kinds of hats, diamond-rimmed
glasses, flashy colors, and an excessive amount of jewelry as well as
luxurious and extravagantly customized automobiles. As I have mentioned above, this particular sense of 'queerness' (which transcends by
far the spectacle of a deviant hip hop expressivity) is determined by the
aesthetic exploration of the self as artist. By embracing Camp as a
celebration of consumer aesthetics and as a mode of aesthetic self-
creation, Westside Gunn, in his fashion and design choices, embodies
#ART as the indistinguishability "between the unique object and the
mass-produced product."[13]
    Contrary to Sontag's claims that "Camp is art that proposes itself
seriously, but cannot be taken altogether seriously because it is 'too
much'" and that "[t]he whole point of Camp is to dethrone the
serious,"[14] I argue that due to Westside Gunn's specific (dis)position as
a creative subject and his use of Camp as an exploration of that
subjectivity, there is a particular sense of 'seriousness' in the 'too much'
of Gunn's Camp aesthetics – a seriousness, that is, which does not
(only) relate the popular to bourgeois art but which aesthetically reflects
upon what Uri McMillan notes in his analysis of the Camp sensibility of
hip hop artist Nicki Minaj, namely Camp's "recurring reduction to white
gayness [that] is especially pronounced when racial difference,

---

[11]   Susan Sontag, "Notes on 'Camp,'" in *Against Interpretation and Other
       Essays* (New York: Farrar, Straus and Giroux, 1966), 277; 279; 283; 287.
[12]   Ibid., 283.
[13]   Ibid.
[14]   Ibid., 284; 288.

particularly in the form of blackness, enters the fray."[15] Camp, McMillan writes, is instead very much a tool "in subaltern identity formation," a "[method] of resolving self-contempt and reclaiming pride in denigrated identities."[16] There is a need to see "blackness and camp as interlocutors, rather than antinomies."[17] The dynamic that is produced by this aesthetic interlocution in the Camp aestheticism of Westside Gunn is excessively transgressive, not least with regard to the explicit exploration of his creative subjectivity and the implicit scrutiny of race and racism. In that regard, he certainly involves his Camp, as Sontag notes, in "a new, more complex relation to 'the serious.'"[18] More precisely, in the implementation of #ART, Westside Gunn inadvertently relates to what Juliane Rebentisch refers to as "serious camp," i.e., works that do not aim "to stabilize identity but to instill a totally different relation between subjects."[19] In an extraordinary combination of evocations and representations of high-end designer fashion, professional wrestling, Warhol-like Pop Art, Basquiat's painting, and a highly ironic decoding and recoding of religious and fascist iconography and idolatry of the historical figures of Mary, Jesus, and, above all, Hitler, Westside Gunn evokes such a 'different relatability.'

Westside Gunn's Camp aesthetic is curiously imbued with images of Hitler and the use of fracture font (*Frakturschrift*) often associated with

[15] Uri McMillan, "Nicki-Aesthetics: The Camp Performance of Nicki Minaj," in *Women & Performance: A Journal of Feminist Theory* 24, no. 1 (2014): 3. Juliane Rebentisch makes a similar argument when she urges her readers to "understand Jack Smith's oeuvre as camp, but as camp that takes itself deadly serious" and that one needs to overcome the established opposition in Camp theory of "aesthetic space and moral space." See Juliane Rebentisch, "Camp Materialism," in *Criticism* 56, no. 2 (2014): 236; 247. And even though my essay on Westside Gunn has a different trajectory and seeks to unfold a different aesthetic phenomenon, I agree with Rebentisch in that new takes on Camp may need to acknowledge and overcome the limitations of Susan Sontag's "Notes," both with regard to nature and history (as in the case of Rebentisch) or subjectivity (as in the case of my discussion of Gunn).

[16] Ibid., 4.
[17] Ibid., 3.
[18] Sontag, "Notes on 'Camp,'" 288.
[19] Juliane Rebentisch, "Camp Materialism," 242.

Nazi Germany. Since 2012, Westside Gunn has released a series of eight mixtapes entitled *Hitler Wears Hermes*.[20] Even though the series lacks a consistent conceptual logic, the rapper is fascinated with a particular iconography, and the cover art is striking: Hitler as a Pop Art icon, Hitler as a messianic figure, Hitler on a vandalized portrait, Hitler as a three-eyed cyclops, Hitler smiling and hugging Jesse Owens at the 1936 Olympics, Hitler as a Dada-like distorted collage, Hitler painted in oil colors, Hitler as a photomontage, Hitler as a glued-together paper figure. If the devil wears Prada, Gunn seems to suggest, let Hitler wear Hermès.

Fig. 4: Westside Gunn, cover art *Hitler Wears Hermes*

---

[20] Westside Gunn misspells "Hermès" on all album covers, using a regular "e" instead of a grave accent. On Westside Gunn's appropriation of political iconography, see Dustin Breitenwischer, "*Hitler Wears Hermes*: Pop, Paratext und Politische Ikonographie," *Kritische Berichte* 50, no. 3 (2022): 17–27.

The Camp aesthetics of this visual archive allow the Black creative subject to imagine a counter-historical execution of a revenge plot, the mounting of Hitler's head onto the body of a posing Arnold Schwarzenegger – *Hitler on Steroids*. In fact, Westside Gunn's Camp aestheticization of fascist terror might also be understood as an extensive commentary on the possibilities (and seriousness) of Black grotesquerie, as Aliyyah Abdur-Rahman defines it: "Marked by structural ambiguity and excess, black grotesquerie undermines normative perception and action, renders contingent the presumed fixity of meaning, and ruptures the given world." It is "a practice and poetic of formal disintegration."[21] The exaggerative visual appropriation and aesthetic deconstruction of Nazi iconography wreak vengeance on the terror against 'degenerate art' and mark the point on the liminal threshold where #ART is not only deadly serious but a locus of creative self-empowerment – where #ART becomes "art."

#ART as "art"

In her "Notes," Sontag claims, "Camp sees everything in quotation marks. It's not a lamp, but a 'lamp'; not a woman, but a 'woman'. To perceive Camp in objects and persons is to understand Being-as-Playing-a-Role."[22] Camp is thus not only a matter of appearance but of perception, it is a way to see the world and not merely a performance that determines how the world perceives oneself. Which brings us back to an idea I have developed above. I argued that Westside Gunn embodies #ART in a performance of the indistinguishability "between the unique object and the mass-produced product."[23] As such, #ART, for Gunn, is as much a tool to direct and redirect the audience's attention and interpretation as it is a mode of perception, an expression of how to perceive and ultimately construct the aestheticization of one's world and of the construction itself. #ART is, as Sontag would phrase it, art in

[21] Aliyyah I. Abdur-Rahman, "Black Grotesquerie," *American Literary History* 29, no. 4 (2017): 700.
[22] Sontag, "Notes on 'Camp,'" 280.
[23] Ibid., 289.

quotation marks. #ART is "art." It is simultaneously the appearance of art as an idea, a fiction, a potentiality, and the declamation of the aesthete who is decidedly not interested in art as art, but in everything in its relation to "art." (Which is, for that matter, the most obvious difference between Jay Z's above-mentioned gallery performance and Westside Gunn's Camp aestheticism. In the logic of his music, his visual archive, and his meticulously performed self-representation in social media, Westside Gunn's notion of #ART as "art" is, in a way, a play on Jay Z's 'serious' performance as artistic self.)

#ART refers to "art" predominantly as a source of creative playfulness. When following this logic of #ART – as it repeats itself in Westside Gunn's Instagram feed and as it relates to his larger archive of aesthetic expressivity – it thus exposes an intrinsic desire for perpetual mirroring, of confronting not the world directly but the self in ever-new creative interventions in the world. Interventions, in other words, which refuse to distinguish between pleasure and critique, aesthetic hedonism and negativity. As such, Westside Gunn's aestheticism cannot, as the concept might suggest, be reduced to an end in itself. In Westside Gunn's logic of #ART, aestheticism consequentially appears as "aestheticism," as aestheticism, that is, that always already acknowledges an ironic distance to the sociopolitical consequences of aestheticism proper. Returning briefly to the image of the critical and, as such, questionable threshold that shifts and changes dynamically between the spheres of popular culture and art, Westside Gunn's "aestheticism" is a performative act of measuring, of delineating the difference between mere aesthetic excess – which is indeed self-serving – and a substantial cultural transgression. #ART poses two questions: "What can be art?" and "Who can be an artist?" And the hashtag confidently appears as if it is, in fact, the answer itself.

Part of the excessive pleasure and the pleasurable excess of #ART is that it constantly touches upon a feedback loop of self-fetishization which, in turn, throws the spotlight on the underbelly of Westside Gunn's exploration of creative subjectivity. #ART does not simply lure its audience (i.e., consumers) into the auratic sphere of the autonomous work of art, but it bewitches its consumers with forces it ultimately does not possess. #ART cloaks the fiction of an intrinsically valorized commodity with the modernist idea of the intrinsically valorized work of art, and it thus reinforces performatively its own fetishization. Or, to put it differently, #ART signifies an idea of art as "art" that is, by definition, unable or at least unfit to separate culture and economy, aesthetics and commodification, creativity and consumption. And it can do so because it is both its own point of departure and its logical end; it is both the entrance of the rabbit hole in which it becomes indistinguishable from its semblances – as I mentioned, #ART hyperlinks to more than 800 million images on Instagram – and a punchline.

#ART is a performative act, but it is not solely a performance of "art" as a product of Camp exaggeration, artifice, and self-empowered aestheticization. It is also the performative implementation of what Pierre Bourdieu has famously referred to as "distinction," which, in short, depends upon the acquisition of cultural and symbolic capital – in Bourdieu's study: education, titles, taste, etc. – that cement class difference and perpetuate cultural hegemony.[24] In our case, #ART evokes somewhat of a micro-distinction between its connoisseurs and the common consumer of mainstream hip hop. #ART demands that its audience plays by its rules, willing into existence the implied cultural hierarchization that distinguishes the knowledgeable few, i.e., the fellow aesthetes (or "aesthetes"), from the ignorant many.

In many of Westside Gunn's Instagram posts, #ART becomes #BUYART, which, in yet another spin, turns the connoisseur into a collector (not 'merely' consumer), and the distinction-based self-fetishization of #ART culminates in a performance of the market.[25] Due to the allegedly small amount of goods that contribute to the compensation of the artist, the distribution of sought-after limited editions of vinyl records, fashion items, and merchandise is cultivated as a resistant calibration of economic and symbolic capital as compared to the consumer logic of mainstream popular music.

[24] Cf. Pierre Bourdieu, *Distinction: A Social Critique of the Judgement of Taste* (Cambridge: Harvard University Press, 1996).

[25] For an insightful discussion of the relation between art and the world of commodification, see Maria Slowinska, *Art/Commerce. The Convergence of Art and Marketing in Contemporary Culture* (Bielefeld: transcript, 2014). Particularly insightful and informative for this essay is Slowinska's notion that "the convergence of 'art' and 'commerce' should be understood not as a simple instrumentalization of a formerly autonomous aesthetic sphere, but rather as a development that is closely linked with the strategies of avantgarde art itself" (ibid., 14).

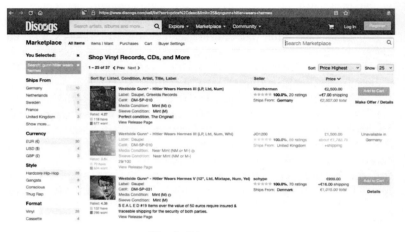

Fig. 5: Discogs

But regardless of the fact that Westside Gunn is, of course, compensated sufficiently by ticket sales, label contracts, streaming platforms, etc., the idea(lism) of an economic and symbolic recalibration fuels the cultural status of #ART as the epitome of his excessive "aestheticism."

While #ART is undoubtedly an expression of popular culture's inherent commercialization, or, rather, its aestheticized commercialization, it suggests a cultural communication that is more complicated than the common charge against popular culture as 'selling out'. #ART is driven by the desire to provide its audience (i.e., its users) with ever-new shapes, forms, and narratives. The collector's need to regularly check the websites on which #ART, by extension, sells its products and lets the most basic dynamic of a consumer market appear as a distinguishing aesthetic education. To buy and collect is a perpetuation of #ART's "aestheticism" and a performance of its inherent distinction. The collector becomes a creative actor who not only reproduces #ART, but co-produces "art" as the performativity of the market. In the end, this correlation between reception and (co-)production, experience and creative action, which surpasses even Umberto Eco's idea of the "open work," is indicative of our present, as it caters to late capitalism's dominant logic of the so-called creative industries and of what Andreas Reckwitz (following Foucault) refers to as the *creativity dispositif*.[26] In *The Invention of Creativity*, Reckwitz notes that "[m]odern society has become geared to the constant production and reception of the culturally new. This applies to the economy, the arts, lifestyle, the self, the media, and urban development. We are witnessing the crystallization of what I have called a *creativity dispositif*," which "intensifies an aestheticization process focused on the production and uptake of *new* aesthetic events" and "reorients the aesthetic towards the new while at the same time orienting the regime of the new towards the aesthetic."[27] "The creativity dispositif thus constitutes an intersection between a process of aestheticization and a social regime of novelty."[28] It has, as Johannes Voelz argues, "flourished, in the last three decades, into a full-fledged 'aesthetic capitalism.'"[29] What follows is a pluralization of creativity and a concomitant growing and calculated indistinguishability of the difference between art and commerce, aesthetic critique and aestheticized consumption, or between art and "art" – which is strikingly, and quite ironically, typified in Westside Gunn's recently opened Buffalo Kids Gallery in the Walden Galleria shopping mall.

---

[26] Cf. Umberto Eco, *The Open Work* (Cambridge: Harvard University Press, 1989). On reception as production, see Rieke Jordan, *Work in Progress. Curatorial Labor in Twenty-First-Century American Fiction* (London: Bloomsbury, 2019).

[27] Andreas Reckwitz, *The Invention of Creativity: Modern Society and the Culture of the New* (Cambridge: Polity, 2017), vi; 9. Original emphasis.

[28] Ibid., 21.

[29] Johannes Voelz, "Looking Hip on the Square: Jazz, Cover Art, and the Rise of Creativity," *European Journal of American Studies* 12, no. 4 (2017).

Fig. 6: Walden Galleria, Buffalo Kids

#ART fantasizes "art" not as the dissolution of art and life but of art and recipient, of artist and collector. The priceless distinction of the self as "aesthete" (and of #ART as "art") can thus not be directly monetized, but it forces its agents into a recurring state of need for recognition and self-actualization because distinction itself appears as #ART's object of consumption.

Beyond #ART

In Westside Gunn's visual archive, #ART is the epicenter of perpetually erupting renegotiations of creative subjectivity. Aestheticist, bourgeois, expressive, exaggerative, and artificial are varieties of #ART's exploration of late capitalist "aestheticism" and "art." #ART is a social media phenomenon and the logical consequence of a culture still clinging to the distinction between popular culture and art, culture industry and artistic autonomy, pleasure and critique. I would thus like to end this discussion of the phenomenon of #ART with a consideration of what Sianne Ngai refers to as "our aesthetic categories."[30] In her research, Ngai insists that the established aesthetic categories of the beautiful and the sublime – the Burkean categories that would shape much of modern European philosophy – can no longer do justice to our late-capitalist aesthetics, whether in philosophy, art, or consumption. Our judgment of aesthetic value needs to adapt to a time in which that judgement is passed, hence her introduction of the alternative categories of the zany, the cute, and the interesting. Accordingly, #ART desires an integration of "art" in the praxis of life, for "art" as an exaggeration, artifice, and the product of aesthetic hedonism might not run the risk of immediate devaluation. It is, in the words of Heinz Drügh, a "fleeting effect" with "no eternal values."[31] #ART's recurring appearance in a constantly evolving timeline lacks the substance of a stable presence and the promise of completion, and it suggests a relation in which consumption and reception become indistinguishable. As such, #ART raises questions about our investment in "stereotyping the inflationary aestheticization of society" and its logic of market principles.[32] This is not to say that Westside Gunn's #ART is a critique of the dynamics it relies on. In its desired proximity to the pleasures and capitalization of its self-commodification, though, it performatively disregards established cultural hierarchies by expressing and exaggerating new ones.

[30] Cf. Sianne Ngai, *Our Aesthetic Categories: Zany, Cute, Interesting* (Cambridge: Harvard University Press, 2012).

[31] Drügh, "Fake – Drei Aspekte einer Ästhetik des Konsums," 140.

[32] Ibid., 143.

Works Cited

Abdur-Rahman, Aliyyah I. "Black Grotesquerie." *American Literary History* 29, no. 4 (2017): 682–703.

Adorno, Theodor W. *Aesthetic Theory*. Translated by Robert Hullot-Kentor. London: Continuum, 2002.

Baraka, Amiri. "Black Art." In *Selected Poetry of Amiri Baraka/LeRoi Jones*, 106. New York: William Morrow & Co, 1979.

Bourdieu, Pierre. *Distinction: A Social Critique of the Judgement of Taste*. Translated by Richard Nice. Cambridge: Harvard University Press, 1996.

Bradley, Adam. *Book of Rhymes: The Poetics of Hip Hop*. New York: Civitas, 2017.

Breitenwischer, Dustin. "*Hitler Wears Hermes*: Pop, Paratext und Politische Ikonographie." *Kritische Berichte* 50, no. 3 (2022): 17–27.

Bürger, Peter. *Theory of the Avant-Garde*. Translated by Michael Shaw. Minneapolis: University of Minnesota Press, 1984.

Carters, The. "Apeshit." YouTube, June 16, 2018. youtube.com/watch?v=kbMqWXnpXcA.

Copeman, Jacob and Giovanni da Col, eds. *Fake: Anthropological Keywords*. Chicago: HAU, 2018.

Drügh, Heinz. "Fake – Drei Aspekte einer Ästhetik des Konsums/Fake – Three Aspects of an Aesthetic of Consumption." In *After Facts: Pudding Explosion Rearticulated*, edited by Stefanie Hereaus et al., 122-143. Frankfurt am Main: Universität Frankfurt Kunstgeschichtliches Institut, 2018.

Dyson, Michael Eric. *Know What I Mean? Reflections on Hip Hop*. New York: Civitas, 2007.

Eco, Umberto. *The Open Work*. Translated by Anna Cancogni. Cambridge: Harvard University Press, 1989.

Florini, Sarah. *Beyond Hashtags: Racial Politics and Black Digital Networks*. New York: New York University Press, 2019.

Jay Z. "Picasso Baby (A Performance Art Film)." Universal Music Group, accessed January 6, 2022. universal-music.de/jayz/videos/picasso-baby-a-performance-art-film-326307.

Jordan, Rieke. *Work in Progress: Curatorial Labor in Twenty-First-Century American Fiction*. London: Bloomsbury, 2019.

McMillan, Uri. "Nicki-Aesthetics: The Camp Performance of Nicki Minaj." *Women & Performance: A Journal of Feminist Theory* 24, no. 1 (2014): 1–9.

Ngai, Sianne. *Our Aesthetic Categories: Zany, Cute, Interesting.* Cambridge: Harvard University Press, 2012.

Rebentisch, Juliane. "Camp Materialism." *Criticism* 56, no. 2 (2014): 235–248.

Reckwitz, Andreas. *Das hybride Subjekt: Eine Theorie der Subjektkulturen von der bürgerlichen Moderne zur Postmoderne.* Berlin: Suhrkamp, 2020.

---. *The Invention of Creativity: Modern Society and the Culture of the New.* Translated by Steven Black. Cambridge: Polity, 2017.

Richardson, Alissa V. *Bearing Witness While Black: African Americans, Smartphones, and the New Protest #Journalism.* New York: Oxford University Press, 2020.

Rose, Tricia. *Black Noise: Rap Music and Black Culture in Contemporary America.* Middletown: University Press of New England, 1994.

Shusterman, Richard. "The Fine Art of Rap." *New Literary History* 22, no. 3 (1991): 613–632.

Slowinska, Maria. *Art/Commerce: The Convergence of Art and Marketing in Contemporary Culture.* Bielefeld: transcript, 2014.

Sontag, Susan. "Notes on 'Camp.'" In *Against Interpretation and Other Essays*, 275–292. New York: Farrar, Straus and Giroux, 1966.

Voelz, Johannes. "Looking Hip on the Square: Jazz, Cover Art, and the Rise of Creativity." *European Journal of American Studies* 12, no. 4 (2017).

Illustrations

Fig. 1: Screenshot of Westside Gunn's Instagram Account, Westside Gunn, Instagram (@westsidegunn), March 7, 2022, original in color.

Fig. 2: Instagram Post, Westside Gunn, Instagram (@westsidegunn), February 22, 2022.

Fig. 3: Westside Gunn in front of the cover art of Armani Caesar, *The Liz*, by Isaac Pelayo, Griselda Records, 2020. https://www.businessinsider.com/rapper-westside-gunn-contemporary-art-collection-toys-griselda-records-2020-11.

Fig. 4: Westside Gunn, *Hitler Wears Hermes* series, cover art, originals in color, Griselda Records, 2012–2019. https://daupe.bandcamp.com/merch.

Fig. 5: https://www.discogs.com/sell/list?sort=price%2Cdesc&limit=25 &q=gunn+hitler+wears+hermes.

Fig. 6: Walden Galleria, Buffalo Kids. Accessed June 21, 2021. https://www.waldengalleria.com/tenants/buffalo-kids/.

NAGHMEH ESMAEILPOUR

Transmedial Historiography and the Representation of Iran and Iranians in Video Games

Introduction

Having worked for more than three years as a translator and editorial assistant for an Iranian video games magazine, I have been influenced by how games, particularly those based on real events, introduce their users into a new kind of reality by employing transmedial historiography. But what are the goals of the games? Do games only serve to induce a sense of amazement and being entertained in the players, or do they follow more serious incentives, aiming to introduce a new reality or promote popular culture? In what ways do games employ historical or social events in their storylines?

This article investigates transmedial historiography in the video games *Blacklist* and *Black Friday*. Although they belong to different genres, *Blacklist* is an action-adventure stealth game, and *Black Friday* is an adventure-interactive drama, they follow a similar transmedial narrative in order to convey historical facts that occurred in Iran or are related to Iran. To show this similarity, I bring together various ideas about transmediality (from Ryan and Jenkins, among others) and read transmediality in relation to the historical narrative. I ground my hypothesis on an eclectic approach, and I examine the transmedial historiography by focusing on the presence of different media in creating the storyworlds. Moreover, I study the representation of Iran and its political events across media. Tracing narrative transmedial historiography in *Blacklist* and *Black Friday* will provide insight into the future study of transmediality and offer a key to reading games from a new angle.

452   Transmedial Historiography in Video Games

Transmedial Historiography: A New Reading

Transmediality, as Marie-Laure Ryan defines it, refers to "the creation of a storyworld through multiple documents belonging to various media," which are related to "the three fundamental characteristics of transfictionality – expansion, modification, and transposition."[1] In her description, video games are among the media which spread "culture-defining stories across media" in the form of a "time-honored phenomenon," transmitting "all semiotic types of information. [...] The ability to create a world, or more precisely, to inspire the mental representation of a world."[2] Because of this ability, games have not just a story, but a storyworld.

In another interpretation, Jan-Noël Thon focuses on the mediality of texts, such as films and video games. He makes the application of "a cultural point of view" to Ryan's definition of the medium the center of his study and emphasizes the "cultural mediality" of different media.[3] In Thon's readings of new media, such as video games, transmediality is not only used for the purpose of storyworld-creation/storytelling across various media. Instead, like Ryan, Thon points to transmediality's narrational functions. Henry Jenkins, in comparison, argues that

> transmedia storytelling represents a process where integral elements of a fiction get *dispersed systematically across multiple delivery channels* for the purpose of creating *a unified and coordinated entertainment experience.*[4]

---

[1]   Marie-Laure Ryan, "Transmedial Storytelling and Transfictionality," *Poetics Today* 34, no. 3 (2013): 361.

[2]   Ibid., 363.

[3]   Jan-Noël Thon, "Toward a Transmedial Narratology: On Narrators in Contemporary Graphic Novels, Feature Films, and Computer Games," in *Storyworlds across Media: Toward a Media-Conscious Narratology*, ed. Marie-Laure Ryan and Jan-Noël Thon (Lincoln: University of Nebraska Press, 2014), 25.

[4]   Henry Jenkins, "Transmedia Storytelling 101," March 21, 2007, henryjenkins.org/blog/2007/03/transmedia_storytelling_101.html. Emphasis in original.

NAGHMEH ESMAEILPOUR

Each medium, in Jenkins's ideal form of transmedia storytelling,

> does what it does best – so that a story might be introduced in a film, expanded through television, novels, and comics; its world might be explored through gameplay or experienced as an amusement park attraction.[5]

In this sense, a good transmedia platform is the one which "attract[s] multiple constituencies by pitching the content somewhat differently in the different media" and "dictates the flow of content across media."[6]

All the scholars mentioned above emphasize the transfer/representation/narration of a story across various media – which, from Ryan's perspective, leads to the creation of the storyworld. In this respect, storyworlds can be conceived of as "mental representations built during the reading (viewing, playing, among others) of a narrative text," and they are "dynamic models of evolving situations."[7] Thus, the primary question is how the storyworld is connected to the media in each form. Storyworlds, in Ryan's interpretation, can bear three different types of relations to texts or the narrative of the media:

> A one-text/one-world relation. Here the text projects a determinate storyworld. [...] A one-text/many-worlds relation. This relation is found when the text is so indeterminate that it can be related to many different stories. [..] Another example of the one-to-many relation is the case of digital texts, such as hypertexts or video games, where the user's choices determine one of many possible sequences of events. [...] A one-world/many-texts relation. This relation is typical of the oral tradition.[8]

Ryan's definition of the storyworld connects narrativity (fictional text) to practicality (the representation of that fictional text across media). For Ryan, video games constitute a one text/multi-world relation in transmediality.

---

[5]   Henry Jenkins, *Convergence Culture: Where Old and New Media Collide* (New York: New York University Press, 2006), 96.

[6]   Ibid.

[7]   Ryan, "Transmedial Storytelling and Transfictionality," 364.

[8]   Ibid., 365.

454 Transmedial Historiography in Video Games

By comparison, Jenkins points out that "transmedia represents a structure based on the further development of the storyworld through each new medium."[9] From his perspective, the critical elements in a transmedial storyworld and transmediality are "extensions." Jenkins argues that extension is a crucial factor in the transmedia storyworld because it provides "insight into the characters and their motivations," fleshes out "aspects of the fictional world," bridges gaps "between events depicted in a series of sequels," or even adds "a greater sense of realism to the fiction as a whole."[10] Video games, according to Jenkins's analysis, employ extension as their main feature of transmediality.

Regardless of this, how is transmediality related to historiography? In defining transmedial historiography, I start from Ryan's position that video games are a form of transmedial storytelling which create "one-text/many-worlds" relations. In my opinion, transmedial historiography relates to transmedia narrativity and storyworlds. It constitutes a kind of multiple narrativity through "experiential or augmentary" narrative by employing various media to produce multi-storyworlds, which borrow their fictionality from real events.[11] In other words, the storyworld "covers both factual and fictional stories, meaning stories told as true of the real world and stories that create their own imaginary world, respectively."[12] The storyworld is a tool used by video games to change realistic events into popular culture products. In this form of mediality, a local incident becomes global by being broadcasted to international audiences. Accordingly, the local events are transformed by trans-mediality into (popular) cultural-interactive narratives that aim to create a media-defined reality – or even hyperreality.

[9] Henry Jenkins, "Transmedia 202: Further Reflections," July 31, 2011, henryjenkins.org/blog/2011/08/defining_transmedia_further_re.html.

[10] Jenkins, "Transmedia Storytelling 101."

[11] Celia Pearce proposes six forms of narrative which operates in games: Experiential, Performative, Augmentary, Descriptive, Metastory, and Story System. Celia Pearce, "Towards a Game Theory of Game," in *In First-person: New Media as Story, Performance, and Game*, ed. Noah Wardrip-Fruin and Pat Harrigan (Cambridge: MIT Press, 2004), 145.

[12] Marie-Laure Ryan, "Story/Worlds/Media Tuning the Instruments of a Media-Conscious Narratology," in *Storyworlds across Media: Toward a Media-Conscious Narratology*, ed. Marie-Laure Ryan and Jan-Noël Thon (Lincoln: University of Nebraska Press, 2014), 35.

In this respect, transmedial historiography means that a shared (cultural, political, social, or even economic) narrative world is created based on real (historical) events. Transmedial historiography in video games refers to how a specific narrative (or the creation of popular narratives) of a historical incident becomes believable and is accepted by a large audience (through the targeting of popular culture). The reason behind this new creation lies in the connection between popular culture and social/historical reality. In the end, the product – in this case, video games – acts as a cultural franchise to broadcast a specific kind of media-related reality, some of it factual and some fictional.

From Hayden White's perspective, the ability to change fact into fiction is similar to the work of the historian, whose oeuvre is the "translation of facts into fiction" or "a list of facts [which] is transformed into a story."[13] Transmedial historiography in video games, which I have developed as an extension of Jenkins's and Ryan's conceptions, thus refers to the transmission of a specific historical narrative to the users, with the intention of initiating those narratives into a new reality. This act of transmission occurs through the blending of various media such as television news, newspapers, photographs, and graphic novels within one genre: the video game. Video games, in this regard, can integrate multiple texts to make a shared narrative, which then becomes the common vehicle for promoting its perspective in various nations and cultures. It functions as a cultural practice which induces the users (players) to accept a particular form of reality. The central *gestalt* in video game transmedial historiography, with reference to Ryan, is "the collective values that define a culture, such as belief in free speech in Western societies, or latent stereotypes and prejudices, such as narratives of race, class, and gender."[14]

In the following, I examine how, in the second form of storyworld relations and transmedial historiography, the abovementioned games employ other forms of media to connect to other worlds and create a new reality. I study these games on two levels. First, I explore how the presence of various media narrates a new story or creates a new

---

[13] Qtd. in Marie-Laure Ryan, *Avatars of Story* (Minneapolis: University of Minnesota Press, 2006), 49–50.

[14] Marie-Laure Ryan, "Defining Media from the Perspective of Narratology," (unpublished manuscript, 2019), 1–14.

456   Transmedial Historiography in Video Games

storyworld from one text or event. Second, I examine how Iranians' or Iran's role in the world is represented using popular culture's norms and models.

Tom Clancy's Splinter Cell: Blacklist

In *Tom Clancy's Splinter Cell: Blacklist*, "splinter cell" is the code name for a super-secret training program at the U.S. National Security Agency (NSA) that involves special international missions related to U.S. security. The main character, Sam Fisher, a commander, is the first person nominated to be part of the NSA program and trained to complete missions around the world. Tom Clancy (1947–2013) was a novelist known for espionage-and military-related storylines about U.S. and Russian military interventions and their consequences on a global level. Because of his talent for writing detailed military-and-political-themed novels, Clancy was highly sought after in the film and game industry. For this reason, Ubisoft bought the rights to some of Clancy's books and created the *Tom Clancy's Splinter Cell* series. *Tom Clancy's Splinter Cell: Blacklist* is the sixth installment in the series and the sequel to *Splinter Cell: Conviction*.

Blacklist starts with Sam Fisher, the hero of the series' games, leaving a U.S. military camp referred to in the game as Guam. Upon his departure with a friend named Vic, they are attacked by a group calling themselves "The Engineers." The action begins when the apparent leader of the terrorist group announces, "The Blacklist is live now." The story then shifts to show the news of the same incidents being reported in the American media under the title Breaking News (figure 1). Media outlets re-narrate what has happened in Guam and add new stories about what has happened, as well.

Fig. 1

The attackers then broadcast a message on the internet, indicating what the Blacklist is and how they are pursuing their goals:

> America. This is the Blacklist. One new attack every seven days. You have soldiers in 153 countries. Bring your troops home. Now. Or every week we will attack you. We will not negotiate. You will not stop the Blacklist. You have seven days until the next attack. The choice is yours. We are the Engineers.[15]

The Blacklist is comprised of the following issues or places: American military power (in Guam, their first target), American Consumption, American Freedom, American Fuel, American Blood, and American Dust. The targets are going to be attacked in seven-days intervals: 00, 07, 14, 21, and 28. What "the Engineers" want is for America to bring back all its soldiers stationed abroad in 153 countries within the period indicated; otherwise, they will continue to attack until they reach their goal. The repetition of "The Blacklist" across media (figure 2) echoes the targets' importance and reinforces a sense of immediate terror not on the part of the players, but the world, as if the events were real.

---

[15] *Tom Clancy's Splinter Cell: Blacklist*, Windows PC version, Ubisoft Toronto, 2013, Introduction Demo.

Fig. 2

In this way, *Blacklist* creates the representation of a world which the players receive as one story, but not only as linear storytelling or in one medium. Rather, the story is re-narrated through three different media simultaneously: television news, the internet, and CIA secret information services. In this respect, transmediality is not limited to the transposition of one story (Clancy's novels) to other media (the *Splinter Cells*' games series). Rather, it refers to how, in a medium such as video games, and in my case the *Splinter Cells*' series, one story is re-narrated through the representation of other media forms (such as television news) in order to build many-folded storyworlds and narrations of one story. This constitutes an expansion of the concept of transmediality.

The most obvious example of transmedial historiography occurs as Sam embarks on the missions. When Sam enters the operational locations, he faces various scenes and people. In a very attractive, add-on storyworld, Sam connects to the base for more information and, suddenly, his surroundings transfrom into a virtual image screen showing the history of the person or place through references to other sources (figures 3–4).

Fig. 3–4

The presence of other media in the middle of the operations is used to relate the original world (text) to the transmedial world in three ways: "overlap, inclusion, and same world, just growing bigger."[16]

The second level of my analysis relates to the representation of Iran and Iranians in the game. In attempting to warn the world about the impending war targeting America, *Blacklist* focuses on re-narrating the familiar U.S.-Middle Eastern policies. Again, it seems that *Blacklist* wants to present Iran as being behind most of the Middle East crisis, and as the country that harbors the most hostility toward America – a popular trend among most American politicians and government officials as well.

---

[16] Ryan, "Transmedial Storytelling and Transfictionality," 367.

460 Transmedial Historiography in Video Games

Moreover, from the beginning of the game, the Blacklist topics, all focus on American characteristics and motives which have mostly been criticized by one country: Iran. This argument is proven by mentions here and there of how the U.S. suspects Iran's involvement in the Blacklist:

> NSA suspects Nouri has ties to Iran. (Mexico Operation)
> DC suspects Iran may have a hand in the Blacklist. Nouri could be one of their operators [. . .] The situation with Iran is too volatile.[17]

> Sam: We've got files from Iran. Looks like Qods Force.
> Grim: Might explain why they had eyes on Nouri.
> Sam: Scan it now.
> Grim: If we wanted evidence Iran was behind the Blacklist. We just found it.[18]

The role of Iran is narrated through cut-scenes and dialogues between Sam and his colleagues in the game. On the one hand, Sam and his group attempt very seriously to dig up proof of Iran's involvement in the Blacklist by following the intel from NSA and CIA. On the other hand, they are afraid of bringing about a "wrong war" with Iran because of released but unproven documents that lead the U.S. media to echo the old aim of attacking Iran and finally getting revenge for the 1980 hostage crisis, among others:

> Grim: We found documents. We didn't prove Iran was involved with the Blacklist.
> Charlie: Well, they [the media] don't seem to be concerned with the details…
> Sam: Bogus documents or not, Congress wants blood, and all they can see is Iran.[19]

After Sam sends the documents to HQ, the U.S. president broadcasts them in the media. At this point, a new layer of the story is developed through media. Once again, it is television news, newspapers, and the internet, which become the source materials for introducing a new layer

---

[17] Ibid.
[18] Abandoned Mill Operation.
[19] Special Mission, Tehran.

of the storyworld to the game. The new story is about the imminent, inevitable war with Iran being propagated and advertised through the TV news and social media (figure 5).

Fig. 5

At this point, Sam and his team are presented as rescuers and defenders of the peace who attempt to find evidence proving that Iran has nothing to do with the Blacklist in "a hell ambitious op."[20] It is worth noting that the reason behind the mission[21] is to avoid the war being advertised in the U.S. media: "we can't be the reason the country gets into the wrong war."[22]

The mission is to enter the former U.S. Embassy, which is now the headquarters of the Qods Force, talk to General Rohani, and find evidence to disprove Iran's involvement in the Blacklist by penetrating its database. When Sam enters, he begins to talk with Rohani about his mission and how Sam is there to help Iran not become involved in a wrong war. While it first appears that Rohani accepts to cope with Sam sneaking into the main building, he then ambushes him by leading him to a location surrounded by Iranian special forces. In this moment of feeling superior to Sam (an American, ironically), Rohani lectures Sam

---

[20] Ibid.
[21] Special Mission HQ, Tehran, Iran.
[22] Ibid.

462   Transmedial Historiography in Video Games

about Americans and Iranians and how they confront the terrorists: "Rohani: Americans. You think you invented the bravery. [...] Racing around, pointing your guns, threatening innocent people. You have no idea how to stop the Blacklist, do you? I will teach you how to deal with the terrorist."[23] Rohani's statement about teaching Sam how to fight the terrorists and stop the Blacklist stands in opposition to the stories narrated throughout the game of Iran being a supporter of terrorists, not a fighter against them. The Tehran operation, in my interpretation, shows the players how to "use signs of various kinds and speak to various senses,"[24] to find the data which "clears Iran of any involvement with the Blacklist."[25]

In a review on the website Gamespot, Kevin VanOrd says that *Blacklist* is more about the plot and story rather than the characters and killing. He even calls it a "political potboiler" because the game indicates that "information is power, and technology are the assets" in politics.[26] In another review, Adam Sessler states that the game offers users the ability of "different narrative," meaning that it gives the gamers the chance to use an ability they obtain in the other parts of the game to define a new storyworld.[27] In short, the focus in *Blacklist* is not merely on Sam, as previous versions have been, but rather on the narrative and the story which Sam follows. Sam becomes a silent killer who rushes the enemies and ambushes them. The theme is a campaign against *others*, meaning there is us – Americans – and there are others – Middle Easterners, who are equated with terrorists and have anti-American/Western motives.

---

[23] Special Mission, Tehran.
[24] Ryan, "Story/Worlds/Media," 30.
[25] Special Mission, Tehran.
[26] Kevin VanOrd, "Tom Clancy's Splinter Cell: Blacklist Review," *Gamespot*, October 8, 2013, gamespot.com/reviews/tom-clancys-splinter-cell-blacklist-review/1900-6412806/.
[27] Adam Sessler, "Splinter Cell Blacklist Review! Adam Sessler Reviews," YouTube, August 14, 2013, youtube.com/watch?annotation_id=annotation_3253031439&feature=iv&list=PL221B2F579F5E074F&src_vid=OEjQ7_zP SOk&v=z2DyCDMozfU.

1979 Revolution: Black Friday

Black Friday is an adventure-interactive drama game whose primary aim is to depict Iran at the pivotal moment of regime change – from a monarchy to an Islamic Republic. In fact, Black Friday (*Jomeh Siah* in Persian) refers to a turning point in contemporary Iranian history that led to the Revolution in 1979. It is named for the day (8 September 1978) on which a vast number of people demonstrated in Jaleh Square in Tehran against the Shah for his responsibility in the death of nearly 400 people in the Cinema Rex fire in Abadan. The demonstration ended with a brutal clash between the Shah's military forces and the demonstrators; nearly 88 people were shot dead in the street – an act that put an end to any reconciliation between the Shah and the opposition.

Black Friday is produced by iNK Studios, founded by Navid Khansari, who is also the director of the game. An Iranian who grew up in Canada, Khansari is well-known in the games industry for his works on projects such as *Grand Theft Auto III* (and the sequent series) and *Max Payne*. *Black Friday* was his first attempt at creating an independent game and working in a new genre.

Simon Parkin describes the game as "eschewing the first-person-shooter template for a more interactive adventure-game format," which "lets players explore Tehran and complete mini-games, their choices shaping the story as it progresses."[28] Khansari himself argues that "narrative is at the heart of the experience" of playing *Black Friday*.[29] What makes *Black Friday* different from other games, in Khansari's opinion, is that the "game is set in a real place and time – accountable to history."[30] Transmediality in *Black Friday*, unlike in *Blacklist*, which is based on a series of Clancy's novels, revolves around a historical event, and the many narratives approach this event from various angles and through different media forms. In other words, employing various media forms and narration techniques such as the use of graphic-novel-style-sequential illustration,[31] historical photography, and stock footage, *Black*

---

[28] Simon Parkin, "A Truly Revolutionary Video Game," *The New Yorker*, December 11, 2013.

[29] Qtd. in ibid.

[30] Ibid.

[31] By graphic-novel-style-sequential illustration, I refer to the technique of story-narration which is similar to those of graphic novels, through which

464   Transmedial Historiography in Video Games

Friday starts by acknowledging to the players that it is a game based on a historical event. However, players have the chance to reshape the course of this event through their selection of the path upon which they embark:

> During the summer of 1978, thousands of the Iranians flooded the streets and fought for change despites their class, religious beliefs, and political allegiance.
> The protest erupted into a bloody uprising against Iran's self-appointed king – the Shah.
> What you are about to experience is based on real stories, real events and real people.
> The choice you make will shape your experience in this revolution, and the fates of those around you.[32]

From its very first moment, *Black Friday* informs players that it is based on historical events that actually occurred in Iran. Moreover, it warns them that their choices shape the story. The game, like *Blacklist*, begins by using photos and a cassette recording as media for transferring its storyworld. Reza Shirazi is a photojournalist who narrates the story:

> With the U.S. hostage situation, it's become unsafe to get anything out of Iran. You must get these to the press immediately. Many people's lives depend on it – including my own. If anything should happen to me, you must trust Bibi. I'm worried that our darkest days are still ahead of us.

Referring to the hostage crisis means that the revolution has happened, and that Khomeini has become the leader of the country. Moreover, it refers to the hostility between the U.S. and Iran because of America's support of the Shah and spying on Iran for its own benefit. These actions

> images, cartoons, and illustrations are employed in the game to narrate its story. There is also an intertextuality with Marjane Satrapi's *Persepolis* (2000, 2004), which is an autobiographical graphic novel about the childhood, adulthood and the immigrant experience of a girl during and after Islamic Revolution. The novel is a mixture of cartoons and paragraphs which narrate the story – *Black Friday* employs a similar technique as well, and for this reason I connect it to the graphic novel genre.

[32]   *1979 Revolution: Black Friday*. Windows PC version, iNK Stories, 2016.

led to the demonstrators' famous slogans, which have remained prevalent to this day: "Death to America" or "No West, No East, Only Islamic Republic."

In this regard, *Black Friday* narrates two stories by blending fact and fiction. One story takes place in 1980, when Reza is captured by the Revolutionary Guard and is now in Evin prison, being interrogated by Asadulah Lajvardi (Hajj Agha in the game). The second story is revealed through Reza's flashbacks to the summer of 1978, when he is confronted upon his return from Germany with constant, massive demonstrations in the street and decides to document them as a journalist working for international news agencies. The storyworlds in *Black Friday* oscillate between these two narratives by employing various media. Transmediality begins when Reza records a message (see monologue above) to be sent outside Iran, and with the zooming in and out on pictures taken by Reza for Western news agencies (figure 6).

Fig. 6

The players then have four main options (or, rather, narratives) for following the storyworld of the game, and they are (again) alerted to the fact that their choice affects the outcome of the story. Moreover, players must always decide on one out of four different choices throughout the game, both when Reza is in Evin prison or on the street with his friends. The rest of the story is narrated based on this decision, and the game moves on. For example, in figure 7, Reza has four options for every question Hajj Agha asks him in Evin. Reza (i.e. the players) can choose one of the four options, and Hajj Agha reacts according to Reza's choice. It needs to be mentioned here that the three dots in the option fields mean players remain silent and do not answer the questions. This method of choosing, to cite Henry Blumenthal's argument, combines "the roles of reader, viewer, participant, performer, and author."[33] In other words, this method of storytelling in *Black Friday* "tell[s] through language what is currently happening," which, "besides oral storytelling, story-generating programs, and hypertext novels also produce variable outputs."[34]

Fig. 7

Additionally, as the game progresses, the players receive extra information, through various media, as they do in *Blacklist*, as well. The

---

[33] Henry Blumenthal, "Storyscape, a New Medium of Media" (PhD diss., Georgia Institute of Technology, 2016), 3.
[34] Ryan, *Avatar of Stories*, 185–188.

story is re-narrated by a documentary film of the Shah giving speeches, the U.S. president talking, and other background stories, which again blurs what has (or would have) happened.

Overall, the story moves from the present to the past, from Reza's interrogation at Evin during the Islamic Republic era to Reza at the national demonstrations in 1978. Throughout this trajectory, the players are confronted with social and moral choices by facing various types of people. As a result, there are three main subplots that go along with the movement between the present and the past.

Through these stories we become familiar with different political groups that existed at that time in Iran, namely, Mojahedin-e Khalq (MEK), the Tudeh Party, and Islamist supporters of Khomeini. These groups, and their zeal for the demonstrations, are introduced to the readers through photos. The photos, which are taken by Reza, serve as a tool for documenting the events. Accordingly, through cut-scenes and these photos, a new layer of the storyworld is revealed in the game. The players see comparisons of the photos they have taken with real photos taken by Michel Setboun[35] plus a detailed memo of the events (figures 8–10.). This technique, as Julie Muncy states, makes *Black Friday* "an attempt at bringing documentary filmmaking to game design, a blueprint for what Khansari describes as a new genre he calls 'verité games.'"[36]

---

[35] A French photojournalist who documented both sides of the revolution in Iran. As Reza, players can take photographs in the game and compare their images with the ones taken by Setboun – blurring fact and fiction.

[36] Julie Muncy, "*1979 Revolution: Black Friday*: Gripping Adventure Game Puts You in the Iranian Revolution," June 17, 2016.

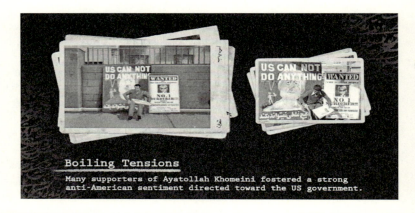

Fig. 8–9

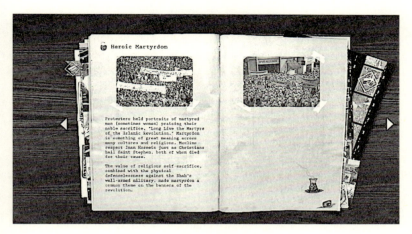

Fig. 10

The transmediality becomes evident as Reza walks through the streets and passes by people. The story of the demonstrations is narrated across media: Reza's pictures are compared to Setboun's in the form of a documentary film (figures 8–10), and then radio broadcasting (VOA/BBC) can be heard as he moves through the streets. This method of re-narrating one story is "to attract multiple constituencies by pitching the content somewhat differently in the different media."[37] In other words, referring to Jenkins' argument about transmediality, *Black Friday* creates "the active participation of knowledge communities," as "the art of world making," that leads to the creation of the transmedial story-world.[38] In short, the game creates two worlds for the player to deal with both fact (based on historical events) and fiction (based on Reza's [the players'] experience as a photojournalist).

Another example of transmediality in the game are the films posters in a closed cinema. Revolutionaries are hiding in the Radio City cinema, which has been shut down following the Cinema Rex fire. Accordingly, there are two narratives or roles for cinema in the course of the revolution. First, cinema is commonly considered to be Western (namely

---

[37] Jenkins, *Convergence Culture*, 96.
[38] Ibid., 21.

470 Transmedial Historiography in Video Games

Hollywood) culture and lifestyle propaganda. A cinema is an unsafe place that threatens Islamic doctrines and which should be burnt down and closed, as happened in the case of Cinema Rex.[39] The second narrative depicts the cinema as a secure place where the revolutionaries can gather and exchange their ideas for planning the revolution, and which reflects the intellectuals' perspective that films and cinema educate society. Moreover, in this safehouse, Reza passes various posters of films and singers, each of which conveys a specific message. In other words, *Black Friday* initiates a degree of narrativity which "can be understood in two ways, one pertaining to story and the other to discourse."[40] It is an attempt to make an "open order" of narratives for the story through "the free-floating events" in its storyworld.[41] As a result, it creates "multimodal-born narratives that use images and text as separate but ontologically equal modes of access to the storyworld and language-born narratives that use illustrations as a kind of paratext."[42]

Despite *Black Friday*'s success outside Iran, it was not received positively within the country. Khansari indicates that his aim in creating the game was to lead the players to not only "experience the historical highlights of the revolution but actually engage with the dynamics of the different factions that existed in Iran."[43] *Black Friday*, in his view, is "a historical story. A historical story that's unique to Iran, but the trajectory of revolutions is universal."[44] In this regard, Nina Roberts states that *Black Friday* is "a form of interactive storytelling that combines ad-

---

[39] In 1978, people were trapped in the cinema while watching the popular movie, *Gavaznha* [*The Deer*] and burned alive. At that time, it was not clear who set the Rex Cinema on fire. The Shah accused the Islamic Marxists and the people accused SAVAK. The event is still debated among Iranian historians.

[40] Ryan, *Avatar of Stories*, 232.

[41] Ibid., 186.

[42] Ryan, "Story/Worlds/Media," 40.

[43] Navid Khansari, "Interview with Navid & Vassiliki Khonsari," MIT *Open Documentary Lab*.

[44] Ibid.

vanced video game technology with elements from a documentary film and a flexible fictionalized narrative."[45]

Conclusion

In summary, even though Iran and its history are reduced to only one mission in *Blacklist*, it is depicted as a country that everyone in the U.S. media thinks is behind every crime or terrorist attack in the Western world – a propagation of popular trends. Iranians, furthermore, are depicted as thinking they are more powerful than Americans, which according to *Backlist* is not valid. As in most of the popular U.S. propaganda, Iranian officials in *Blacklist* are presented as not caring about their families, instead considering nationalism and Islamic doctrine to be the most important thing. This historical perception is presented across various media in the game through the one text/many worlds relation.

In comparison, *Black Friday* depicts Iranians who are seeking democracy, freedom, well-being, and social equality. It describes how different political groups such as the Tudeh party, the MEK, clergies, and nationalists gather to overthrow the Shah dictatorship – the U.S. puppet regime. In the end, however, they separate and reject any commitment to, or trust for one another. Even though historical narratives (/history) hinge on interpretation and are frequently shaped by those in power, *Black Friday* attempts to remain neutral toward all of the Iranian groups regarding their roles and powers in shaping the Iranian Revolution. Nevertheless, it echoes some popular trends regarding U.S.-Iran relations. From the transmedial perspective in this article, it is through Reza's photo documentation, fact-checking films, and news broadcasting that the story of Iran's revolution and Iranian life is narrated.

Therefore, in terms of their storyworlds, both games have one grand narrative, related to many marginal stories that the players must fulfill in order to finish the game. Moreover, while *Blacklist* makes excessive use of other media forms like television news, newspapers, and the internet

---

[45] Nina Roberts, "Haunted by the past: the man behind 1979 Revolution," November 9, 2014.

to narrate its storyworld, in *Black Friday,* the story is narrated through photos and by employing graphic novels, cinematic, and documentary cut-scenes. In addition, whereas *Blacklist* discusses matters related to Iran, attempts to depict Iranians as weak soldiers in confrontation with the West and presents America as its rescuer from war and destruction, in *Black Friday*, Iran is portrayed as a country moving toward democracy and as being home to enthusiastic people who want to establish a free country.

As a result, both games are categorized as adventure games, albeit presenting different styles. However, what they have in common is that in both games, "players become characters with distinctive identities, and their fate and actions carry an exemplary value."[46] Unlike in computer games that do not create a narrative, players of *Blacklist* and *Black Friday* fabricate stories and narratives through their actions and choices. To summarize, in both games, the interactions between players, characters, and storyworlds produce a fictional world based on a factual one, which leads to a new (media)(hyper) reality or a new perspective on reality.

[46] Ryan, *Avatar of Stories*, 87.

NAGHMEH ESMAEILPOUR 473

Works Cited

1979 Revolution: Black Friday. Windows PC version. iNK Stories, 2016.

Blumenthal, Henry. *Storyscape, a New Medium of Media*. PhD diss., Georgia Institute of Technology, 2016.

Jenkins, Henry. "Transmedia 202: Further Reflections," July 31, 2011. henryjenkins.org/blog/2011/08/defining_transmedia_further_re.html.

---. "Transmedia Storytelling 101," March 21, 2007. henryjenkins.org/blog/2007/03/transmedia_storytelling_101.html.

---. *Convergence Culture: Where Old and New Media Collide*. New York: New York University Press, 2006.

Khansari, Navid. "Interview with Navid & Vassiliki Khonsari." MIT *Open Documentary Lab*. docubase.mit.edu/lab/interviews/interview-with-navid-vassiliki-khonsari/.

Mashreghnews. "1979 انقلاب بازی به نگاهی" [A Review of *1979 Revolution*]," January 2015. mashreghnews.ir/news/385767/%D9% 86%DA%AF%D8%A7%D9%87%DB%8C-%D8%A8%D9%87-%D8%A8%D8%A7%D8%B2%DB%8C-%D8%A7%D9%86%D9%82%D9%84%D8%A7%D8%A8-1979-%D8%B9%DA%A9%D8%B3-%D9%88-%D9%81%DB%8C%D9%84%D9%85.

Muncy, Julie. "*1979 Revolution: Black Friday*: Gripping Adventure Game Puts You in the Iranian Revolution." *Wired*, June 17, 2016. wired.com/2016/06/1979-revolution-black-Friday/.

Parkin, Simon. "A Truly Revolutionary Video Game." *The New Yorker*, December 11, 2013. newyorker.com/tech/elements/ a-truly-revolutionary-video-game

Pearce, Celia. "Towards a Game Theory of Game." In *In First-person: New Media as Story, Performance, and Game*, edited by Noah Wardrip-Fruin and Pat Harrigan, 143–153. Cambridge: MIT Press, 2004.

Roberts, Nina. "Haunted by the past: the man behind 1979 Revolution." *The Guardian*, November 9, 2014. theguardian.com/business/ 2014/ nov/09/1979-revolution-video-game-documentary-launch.

474 Transmedial Historiography in Video Games

Ryan, Marie-Laure. "Story/Worlds/Media Tuning the Instruments of a Media-Conscious Narratology." In *Storyworlds across Media: Toward a Media-Conscious Narratology*, edited by Marie-Laure Ryan and Jan-Noël Thon, 25–49. Lincoln, NE: University of Nebraska Press, 2014.

---. "Transmedial Storytelling and Transfictionality." *Poetics Today* 34, no. 3 (2013): 361–388.

---. "Defining Media from the Perspective of Narratology." Unpublished manuscript, 2019.

---. *Avatars of Story*. Minneapolis: University of Minnesota Press, 2006.

Sabounchi, Ali. "تاریخ تحریف برای ای پروژه 1979 انقلاب بازی" [1979 Revolution: A Project to Falsify History]," April 2016. tnews.ir/site/0e5861327554.html.

Sessler, Adam. "Splinter Cell Blacklist Review! Adam Sessler Reviews." YouTube, August 14, 2013. www.youtube.com/watch? annotation_id=annotation_3253031439&feature=iv&list=PL221B2F 579F5E074F&src_vid=OEjQ7_zPSOk&v=z2DyCDMozfU.

Thon, Jan-Noël. "Toward a Transmedial Narratology: On Narrators in Contemporary Graphic Novels, Feature Films, and Computer Games." In *Storyworlds across Media: Toward a Media-Conscious Narratology*, edited by Marie-Laure Ryan and Jan-Noël Thon, 67–102. Lincoln: University of Nebraska Press, 2014.

Tom Clancy's Splinter Cell: Blacklist. Windows PC version. Ubisoft Toronto, 2013.

VanOrd, Kevin. "Tom Clancy's Splinter Cell: Blacklist Review." *Gamespot*, October 8, 2013. gamespot.com/reviews/tom-clancys-splinter-cell-blacklist-review/1900-6412806/.

Zakeri-nasab, Mostafa, and Hamed Shateri. "'1979' ایرانی ضد بازی" [Anti-Iranian Game, 1979]," April 2016. farsnews.com/tag/%D8% A8%D8%A7%D8%B2%DB%8C%D8%A7%D9%86%D9%82%D9 %84%D8%A7%D8%A8-1979.

MARLON LIEBER

Money Form and Master Painting, or, When Warhol Wanted to Paint the Universal Equivalent Form

> "I hate just objects, they have no interest for me at all, so when I paint I just make more and more of these objects, without any feeling for them."[1]

In his recollections of the 1960s, Andy Warhol, a master of the eminently quotable anecdote if ever there was one, admits to having frequently asked others for recommendations on what he should paint[2] and recounts a specific instance: "It was on one of those evenings when I'd asked around ten or fifteen people for suggestions that finally one lady friend of mine asked me the right question: 'Well, what do you love most?' That's how I started painting money."[3] This is almost certainly a reference to works like *200 One Dollar Bills* (1962), a silkscreen print depicting the eponymous banknotes arranged in a 20-by-10 grid. To be sure, the easiest way to paint money is to paint money, that is to say, to produce a figurative painting in which money becomes the subject – an iconic representation of actual, existing money. Two decades later, Warhol went on to paint dollar signs for a 1981 show in Leo Castelli's gallery, selling, ironically, "not one painting."[4] While a greater degree of abstraction is involved here – the dollar sign metonymically represents

---

[1] Gretchen Berg, "Nothing to Lose: An Interview with Andy Warhol," *Cahiers du Cinéma in English* 10 (1967): 39.

[2] Andy Warhol and Pat Hackett, *POPism: The Warhol Sixties* (New York: Penguin, 2007), 20.

[3] Ibid., 22.

[4] Arthur C. Danto, *Andy Warhol* (New Haven: Yale University Press, 2009), 130.

476 Money Form and Master Painting

all bills and coins that could be used as "means of circulation"[5] – something like the concept of money, or of the currency of the U.S., remains the subject of the work.

In what follows, I want to propose a reading of some of Warhol's statements that uncovers yet another understanding of what it might mean to paint money. My reading, however, refers not so much to any actual works produced by Warhol, but instead to the ambition – expressed repeatedly and in varying ways – to simply "do the same painting whether it looks different or not."[6] The point is not to produce the representation of a particular object, but instead to treat the work of art as a form capable of subsuming every conceivable type of content. I will argue that, as such, what Warhol calls the "master painting" is structurally analogous to the "money form" as conceptualized in Karl Marx's *Capital*; that is, Warhol is not the painter of commodity fetishism, often falsely understood to express the subjective experiences of shoppers, but of the money fetish, which is a function of money's role as being directly exchangeable for every conceivable type of commodity.

My discussion will draw on passages from *The Philosophy of Andy Warhol*, originally published in 1975, where the artist at length discusses art and money. I am, however, not interested in art historical and art sociological questions about Warhol's position-taking in the field of art[7] or his claims about the artist's role more generally[8] nor even in a

[5]   Karl Marx, *Capital: A Critique of Political Economy*, vol. 1., trans. Ben Fowkes (London: Penguin, 1990), 211–212.

[6]   Warhol qtd. in Benjamin H. D. Buchloh, "Andy Warhol's One-Dimensional Art," in *Neo-Avantgarde and Culture Industry: Essays on European and American Art From 1955 to 1975* (Cambridge: The MIT Press, 2003), 490; cf. Donna De Salvo, "Andy Warhol: I Work Seven Days a Week," in *Andy Warhol: From A to B and Back Again*, ed. Donna De Salvo (New Haven: Yale University Press, 2018), 17.

[7]   See Nina Tessa Zahner, *Die neuen Regeln der Kunst: Andy Warhol und der Umbau des Kunstbetriebs im 20. Jahrhundert* (Frankfurt am Main: Campus, 2006).

[8]   See Thierry de Duve, *Sewn in the Sweatshops of Marx: Beuys, Warhol, Klein, Duchamp* (Chicago: University of Chicago Press, 2012), 17–35.

discussion of the intermingling of art and money on the art market.[9] These issues are clearly important for any account of Warhol; yet, they are also well-researched, and I will use the available space to pursue a different line of inquiry. That is, I will read Warhol's statements as comments on the ontology of the work of art – or its "social ontology," if you will[10] – to tease out a possible analogy between art and money which Warhol seems to aim to articulate. I will begin by reading selected passages from *The Philosophy* to show how Warhol conceives of money and art.[11] To clarify why I believe that his projected "master painting" would share properties with the money form, I will then turn to Marxian value-form theory to provide an account of what the social function of money is in the context of capitalist production and exchange relations. In conclusion, I will return to Warhol in order to demonstrate why his "master painting" projects an analogy between aesthetic and social form.

It is customary to discuss Warhol's art in terms of its subject matter, and there are good reasons for doing so. His silkscreened canvases of

[9] See Isabelle Graw, *High Price: Art Between the Market and Celebrity Culture* (London: Sternberg Press, 2010); Dave Beech, *Art and Value: Art's Economic Exceptionalism in Classical, Neoclassical and Marxist Economics* (Chicago: Haymarket, 2016).

[10] Nicholas Brown, *Autonomy: The Social Ontology of Art Under Capitalism* (Durham: Duke University Press, 2019), 27.

[11] This discussion could be complicated by paying attention to the heavy use of irony in Warhol's text which should caution the reader not to take some of Warhol's provocative statements at face value. See Frank Kelleter, "Warhol, Andy: Das Prosawerk," in *Kindlers Literatur Lexikon*, ed. Heinz Ludwig Arnold (Stuttgart: J.B. Metzler, 2020). On the other hand, I find that Paul Mattick offers an intriguing argument that the desire to discover in Warhol a demystifying impulse may indicate a "left-modernist" sensibility which believes that "art embodies, or ought to embody, a critique of the alienation and oppressiveness of capitalist society" and, consequently, tries to salvage it for this critical project. See Paul Mattick, *Art In Its Time: Theories and Practices of Modern Aesthetics*, (London: Routledge, 2003), 151. In this essay, I will not inquire into whether Warhol's claims about money and art perform a demystification of consumer culture or received notions of the artist's originality (which they very well might). Instead, I will proceed as if Warhol is entirely serious when he expresses his love for money and for all the things it makes possible.

478   Money Form and Master Painting

commodities, celebrities, advertisements and other objects many Americans in the 1950s and 60s regularly encountered in their everyday lives are striking, at first glance, not so much because of a specific painterly technique, but due to the apparent universality of their content. Benjamin Buchloh argues that Warhol was engaged in one-upping Jasper Johns's practice of producing "neutral and universal [...] icons" by going for the "*real* common denominators of collective perceptual experience" insofar as he drew on the "mass cultural iconography of consumption."[12] Leaving unaddressed the question of whether one of Johns's American flags is truly a "neutral" sign (Anne Wagner would beg to differ[13]), there is much to be said for the claim that Warhol relied on the iconography of mid-twentieth-century consumer society. David Joselit, for instance, suggests that Warhol was interested in the "special ideological force" exerted by bottles of Coke or cans of Campbell's soup and goes on to call Coca-Cola an "icon of America."[14] What he has in mind is not the Peircean type of sign characterized by its resemblance to the referent, but something closer to the paintings of saints in the Christian tradition (which may have influenced Warhol via his "very devout" mother Julia[15]). Joselit elaborates:

> The term 'icon' refers to a venerated symbol representing fundamental religious or cultural beliefs. In his choice of subject matter, Warhol [...] recognized that commodities and their human counterparts – celebrities – function as the icons of consumer society. [...]. The power of the contemporary icon thus lies not in its *uniqueness* – it is patently reproducible – but rather in its capacity to constitute a community through recognition and identification.[16]

By appropriating these well-known subjects, Joselit argues, the works reflect and reiterate the community-constituting power of these iconic commodities.

---

[12]   Buchloh, Andy Warhol's One-Dimensional Art," 499; original emphasis.

[13]   See Anne Middleton Wagner, *A House Divided: American Art Since 1955* (Berkeley: University of California Press, 2012), 11–13.

[14]   David Joselit, *American Art Since 1945* (London: Thames & Hudson, 2003), 77.

[15]   See Blake Stimson, *Citizen Warhol* (London: Reaktion Books, 2014), 45–68.

[16]   Joselit, *American Art*, 77; original emphasis.

Arguing that these objects possess a "special emotional charge,"[17] Joselit focuses less on the commodities themselves but rather on the effect they exert on consumers. To be properly constitutive of a community, these objects need to be not just universally recognizable but universally appreciated as well. This would seem to be the point of Warhol's famous remark that "all the Cokes are good," an assertion he claimed is acknowledged by everyone, whether rich or poor, which is what he thinks is what makes the U.S. "great."[18] Coca-Cola, then, acts as a synecdoche for what has been called the "Democracy of Goods."[19] In the context of Cold War geopolitics, this focus on the availability of consumer goods was used as a "powerful marker of difference" meant to reinforce American identity by way of distinguishing the U.S. from the Soviet Union which was allegedly lacking the "freedom of consumer choice" and consequently offered no genuine "Democracy."[20] This articulation of "democratic equality" with "commodity consumption" was actively pursued in advertising in the 1920s already:

> [A] Chase and Sanborn's Coffee tableau, with an elegant butler serving a family in a dining room with a sixteen-foot ceiling, reminded Chicago families that although "compared with the riches of the more fortunate, your way of life may seem modest indeed," yet no one – "king, prince, statesman, or capitalist" – could enjoy better coffee.[21]

Warhol, who had begun his career as a commercial illustrator in the 1950s and was particularly renowned for shoe advertisements[22] was familiar with this rhetoric. In the passage alluded to above, he, too, presents a litany of social characters signifying different positions in

---

[17] Ibid.

[18] Andy Warhol, *The Philosophy of Andy Warhol (From A to B and Back Again)* (New York: Penguin, 2007), 101.

[19] Roland Marchand, *Advertising the American Dream: Making Way for Modernity, 1920-1940* (Berkeley: University of California Press, 1985), 217; qtd. in Susan Buck-Morss, *Dreamworld and Catastrophe: The Passing of Mass Utopia in East and West* (Cambridge: The MIT Press, 2000), 203.

[20] Buck-Morss, *Dreamworld and Catastrophe*, 204.

[21] Marchand, *Advertising the American Dream*, 218.

[22] Morgan Falconer, *Painting Beyond Pollock* (New York: Phaidon, 2015), 225.

social space – "Liz Taylor […], the President […], the bum […], and you" – and claims that none of them enjoys a "better Coke" than anyone else.[23] At first, it may seem as if Warhol, too, discovered the ground for the peculiarity of the community of American citizen-consumers in the availability of universally appreciated commodities, which he then painted: those "icons of consumer society."

But what if not all the Cokes are good? Warhol could produce a list of even more individuals who can purchase a bottle of Coke, allowing for even finer distinctions on the basis of race, sex, gender, age, religion and so on, suggesting that everyone believes Coke to be good. Yet, however well-founded this assumption may be, it remains mere conjecture. In other words, it may be reasonable to suggest that a majority of Americans feel this way about Coke; it remains impossible to argue that this is necessarily so. Assessments of specific commodities might always diverge, since they are made by individuals who are sensual beings with particular preferences.[24] All of this simply means that properly universal community cannot be a function of the paintings' subject matter. In fact, Warhol himself goes on to clarify the origin of universality in societies in which the reproduction of individuals is mediated by the commodity form. No one, he writes, could "get a better hot dog" by virtue of being rich or famous. In fact, the Queen herself "could get one for twenty cents and so could anybody else."[25] The formal equality of "anybody" is, thus, constituted not through having access to the same commodities, but by using the same medium – money – in order to access them, and, as such, it follows a universalizing logic, if only in theory, as "anybody" could have the twenty cents to buy the same commodities as "anybody else." That is, while there are vast material differences between individuals – having more money means you can get more hot dogs, Cokes and many other things – they are formally equal as money-owners.

---

[23] Warhol, *The Philosophy*, 101.

[24] See Marlon Lieber, "Art and Economic Objecthood: Preliminary Remarks on 'Sensuous Supra-Sensuous' Things," in "The Return of the Aesthetic in American Studies," ed. Winfried Fluck, Rieke Jordan, and Johannes Voelz, special Issue, *REAL – Yearbook of Research in English and American Literature* 35 (2019): 62–63.

[25] Warhol, *The Philosophy*, 101.

But *The Philosophy of Andy Warhol* is not merely invested in the formal egalitarianism of American – that is to say, capitalist – society. More pertinently, money does not only allow *everyone* to buy any commodity; it also allows anyone to buy *every* commodity. Throughout his book, Warhol celebrates money's power to mediate acts of exchange. Lacking "[c]ash," he is "not happy." But the reason for this is not that Warhol wants to hoard money, nor is it that he appreciates money as a means to the end of attaining useful products. "The minute I have it I have to spend it," he admits, but adds that it matters little which articles he purchases. "I just buy STUPID THINGS,"[26] he writes, including food when he is not hungry, "just because I have money."[27] Warhol also claims that he never shoplifts[28] as a consequence. Stealing would amount to a practice that provides direct access to products which he could subsequently use. Money would then be rendered obsolete, however. In short, Warhol is neither interested in money as a physical object nor in its role as a vanishing mediator that makes possible the sensual pleasures of consumption. What he loves about money is merely its power to purchase every commodity, regardless of that commodity's specific qualities.

It thus becomes possible to imagine another idea of what it might mean for Warhol to paint money as the thing he loved most. In fact, in *The Philosophy of Andy Warhol*, the discourses on art and money begin to blend into one another. Claiming to "like money on the wall,"[29] Warhol suggests that, instead of hanging a "$200,000 painting," people might simply attach the same amount of money to their walls.[30] But apart from the idea to literally replace art with money, Warhol returns to the idea of a "good" object in a passage that establishes a "parallel" between the "democratic-egalitarian aspect of the commodity form" and Warhol's "own work," as Sebastian Egenhofer points out.[31] In this passage, Warhol reflects on what it takes to create "good" paintings:

[26] Ibid., 130; original capitalization.
[27] Ibid., 131.
[28] Ibid., 238.
[29] Ibid., 133.
[30] Ibid., 134.
[31] Sebastian Egenhofer, "Geld und Bild bei Andy Warhol," in *Einwegbilder*, ed. Inge Hinterwaldner et al. (Paderborn: Wilhelm Fink Verlag, 2016), 119; my translations.

482   Money Form and Master Painting

> I always wanted to do nothing but the same-size picture [...]. You see, I think every painting should be the same size and the same color so they're all interchangeable and nobody thinks they have a better painting or a worse painting. *And if the one 'master painting' is good, they're all good. Besides, even when the subject is different, people always paint the same painting.*[32]

Here, the fact of being good is derived not from the painting's subject matter but precisely in abstraction from it. A painting is good not because it depicts a Coke bottle or another icon of consumer society. As long as the beholders' assessment of it was contingent on its subject matter, the painting's good-ness could not be guaranteed. If the paintings depict objects, these might be "just objects" which Warhol reproduces without "feeling."[33] The mere "feeling" that an object is good could, after all, not claim to compel general "conviction," as Michael Fried[34] might put it. Instead, Warhol expresses the ambition to create a type of painting that is able to subsume and is entirely indifferent to all conceivable content, which would always already be good prior to its representations of any object. It is in this respect, I argue, analogous to the money form. Thus, it is precisely the idea of the "master painting" that would serve as the realization of Warhol's desire to paint what he loved most: money. And it is to the latter, as it is conceptualized in Marx's critique of political economy, that I will turn now in order to substantiate my claim.

It is, however, only by way of a discussion of Marx's notion of the fetish-like character of the commodity that I will arrive at his theory of money. As I have suggested above, there remains an influential tendency to read Warhol's work for its content, viz. icons of consumer society, as in Joselit's survey of *American Art Since 1945*. Similarly, Marx's account of fetishism is often believed to focus on how individuals fetishize consumer goods akin to the way members of so-

---

[32] Warhol, *The Philosophy*, 149; emphasis added.
[33] Warhol in Berg, "Nothing to Lose," 39.
[34] Michael Fried, "Art and Objecthood," in *Art and Objecthood: Essays and Reviews* (Chicago: The University of Chicago Press, 1998), 151.

MARLON LIEBER

called 'primitive' cultures worshipped inanimate object.[35] Consequently, commodity fetishism would describe practices of venerating objects qua objects. A passage from a 2015 piece for *Artforum* by Andrew Cole, which contains an exuberantly imaginative summoning of the commodity's soulful spirit, serves well to illustrate what it means to understand commodity fetishism as a form of idol worship:

> Marx knew a thing or two about human nature as well – especially our tendency to personify objects. In his great work *Capital*, he speaks about commodities and, in a memorable passage, talks about that table you just have to have, especially now that it's on sale and would look so good in the front room. (Who cares if we never have guests over for dinner. I need this table!) The table has a certain allure, Marx tells us, thanks to its 'metaphysical subtleties' and complex of 'properties.' We don't know how those properties satisfy our needs and wants – what is it about the wood? or the shape? Likewise, we can't fathom what those properties tell us about how the table was made – by whom and under what labor conditions. But the table has meaning for us nonetheless and becomes ensouled under our gaze. We so admire the table as a commodity that it magically 'changes into a thing' like no other. [...] This is what Marx calls the 'mystical character of the commodity' – mystical because we can only think the object's inner properties by personifying it in a focus so narrow that we ignore the larger drama, the greater historical process that makes a commodity a commodity, an object an object, and capitalism capitalism.[36]

Remarkably, pretty much every single proposition is a mischaracterization of Marx's argument in the final section of *Capital*'s first chapter

---

[35] Marx, indeed, drew on the description of fetishism in Charles de Brosses' 1760 book *Du culte des dieux fétiches*. I find Samuel Chambers contention that this does not imply that Marx used the concept in the same way convincing. Samuel A. Chambers, *There's No Such Thing as "The Economy": Essays on Capitalist Value* (Santa Barbara: Punctum Books, 2018), 116.

[36] Andrew Cole, "Those Obscure Objects of Desire: The Uses and Abuses of Object-Oriented Ontology and Speculative Realism," *Artforum* 53, no. 10 (2015).

484 Money Form and Master Painting

(and elsewhere).[37] The entire issue of mystified social forms is dissolved here into a case of subjectively flawed perception. Worse still, this "tendency" is assumed to be a function of "human nature" and would, as such, characterize not just capitalism but every conceivable social formation. Ironically, the "memorable passage" in which Marx enters the mind of the prospective buyer of a table which is "on sale" and serves as the vessel for all sorts of desires cannot be found in the pages of *Capital*. Indeed, Cole projects a meaning onto Marx's text in the same manner that "we" allegedly attribute supernatural qualities to the table "ensouled under our gaze." And yet, for all its flaws, this passage succinctly expresses the common understanding of commodity fetishism as a process wherein consumers falsely perceive the objects they can purchase to be the bearers of almost magical qualities, turning the objects into the venerated icons of consumer society. The "mystical character of the commodity," appears here as the fetishization of particular content conjured up in the imagination of the interested party – this table has a "certain allure."

And it might well – it is not exactly my point to suggest that people do not attribute all sorts of things to the commodities they want to buy. Still, this has little to do with Marx's notion of the fetish. In what follows, I will offer a reading of Marx that is committed to a greater fidelity to the text. For reasons of space, however, I will confine myself to the analysis of the "fetish-like character of the commodity and its secret" in the first volume of *Capital*, ignoring the various fetish forms that make their appearance only in later chapters and volumes. It is possible to claim that Marx, like Warhol, is not particularly interested in "just objects," but instead in social forms. The commodity fetish, especially in its developed form as money fetish, is not about individual "feelings" for particular commodities. Instead, it is about the "seemingly transcendental power of money"[38] to express the value of every conceivable commodity regardless of the latter's concrete properties – just

[37] There is a discussion of the fetish in Hegel and Marx that pays closer attention to Marx's actual writings in Andrew Cole, *The Birth of Theory* (Chicago: The University of Chicago Press, 2014), 86–103, which does not get to what I believe to be at the center of the theory, either, as it fails to discuss the equivalent form of value and its peculiarities.

[38] Karl Marx, *Grundrisse: Foundations of the Critique of Political Economy (Rough Draft)*, trans. Martin Nicolaus (London: Penguin, 1993), 146.

like Warhol's "master painting" was meant to be "good" regardless of its subject matter.

I agree with the Soviet economist Isaak Illich Rubin, who claimed in a pathbreaking 1924 essay that the "theory of fetishism is, *per se*, the basis of Marx's economic system, and in particular his theory of value."[39] Thus, to grasp the former it is necessary to understand the latter. Yet, discussions of Marx's value theory are often marred by misunderstanding. There is a "substantialist" reading of Marx's theory of value[40] which argues that the magnitude of a commodity's value is quantitatively determined by the amount of human labor "congealed" in it,[41] thus paving the way for the later analysis of exploitation and providing something like a moral foundation for the claim that workers are cheated out of some of the wealth that they produce. This is not entirely false, but it does not quite get to the heart of the matter, either. Indeed, Marx grants that classical political economists like Adam Smith or David Ricardo have "analysed value and its magnitude, however incompletely," even "unconver[ing] the content concealed" therein,[42] but argues that they fail to ask "why this content has assumed that particular form, that is to say, why labour is expressed in value."[43] By failing to properly historicize value as a social form, the discipline of political economy naturalizes capitalist social relations.

Marx, on the other hand, attempts in his critique of political economy to analyze the historical specificity of the capitalist mode of production. Marx posits that all societies must work and, moreover, distribute total social labor "in specific proportions" to meet social needs, but the form this assumes depends on how social production is organized.[44] In the capitalist mode of production, there are formally independent private producers, who only enter into social relations in the

---

[39] I. I. Rubin, *Essays on Marx's Theory of Value*, trans. Miloš Samardźija and Fredy Perlman (Delhi: Aakar Books, 2008), 6.

[40] See Frederick Harry Pitts, *Value* (Cambridge: Polity Press, 2021), 18–28 for a critical discussion.

[41] Marx, *Capital*, 128.

[42] Ibid., 173.

[43] Ibid., 174.

[44] Karl Marx, "Letter to Ludwig Kugelmann, 11 July 1868," in *Karl Marx and Friedrich Engels: Collected Works*, vol. 43 (London: Lawrence & Wishart, 1988), 68.

486 Money Form and Master Painting

marketplace. There is "no conscious social regulation of production,"[45] no plan that determines in advance how much of a given product is socially needed. Instead, the private labor expended by producers is validated retrospectively as social labor if – and only if – it is successfully exchanged, that is to say, its products are bought and sold. The mystery to be solved, then, or what Marx's theory of value means to explain, is how the universal exchange of products of labor as commodities is possible in the first place.

Capital famously begins with a consideration of the commodity as the form in which capitalist wealth first appears. Its usefulness or "use-value" does not concern Marx at this point, as he is interested in its specifically capitalist form determinations. The amount of a commodity that can be exchanged for another is its "exchange-value."[46] Since a commodity can be exchanged for many other commodities, it has a multitude of exchange-values and Marx, therefore, reasons that these must be the "form of appearance" of a shared "content"[47] that makes them exchangeable in determinate quantities – value. In the third section of the first chapter, Marx returns to the form in which value can appear and, thus, exist in a practical sense. This section has often been ignored, as readers of Marx have mistaken it for a mere repetition of earlier arguments which, moreover, did little but needlessly complicate matters further.[48] However, this reading fails to recognize that a shift in perspective has occurred. In the first section, Marx looks at the "exchange relation" in order to argue that commodities need to share the property of value in order to be exchangeable. Now, however, he turns to the "value-relation" that presupposes this exchangeability[49] and

---

[45] Ibid., 69.

[46] Marx, *Capital*, 126.

[47] Ibid., 127.

[48] Louis Althusser goes so far as to recommend readers to "put THE WHOLE OF PART ONE [of *Capital*, volume one, including the entire section on "Commodities and Money"] ASIDE FOR THE TIME BEING and BEGIN YOUR READING WITH PART TWO." Louis Althusser, "Preface to Capital Volume One (March 1969)," in *Lenin and Philosophy and Other Essays*, trans. Ben Brewster (New York: Monthly Review Press, 1971), 81; original capitalization.

[49] Marx, *Capital*, 139; see also Michael Heinrich, *Die Wissenschaft vom Wert: Die Marxsche Kritik der politischen Ökonomie zwischen wissenschaftlicher*

anticipates that it is only the "dazzling money-form" that will enable commodities to relate to one another as values. In this section, in other words, Marx solves the "mystery of money"[50] as the form of immediate exchangeability or the expression of the value of all commodities, which amounts to the same thing.

In the simplest conceivable scenario, a given commodity expresses its value as the determinate amount of another, or, x commodity A = y commodity B. This "simple form of value"[51] is not to be mistaken for a description of a historical stage of exchange that once existed, but simply the most abstract way in which the value-relation can be conceived in thought. Here, the two commodities assume distinct roles. Commodity A, whose value is expressed, is in the "relative form of value"; commodity B is in the "equivalent form" and its "physical body" serves as a "bearer of value," providing a material in and through which value can appear. This, in short, is how a commodity "acquires a value-form different from its natural form."[52] If it is being equated with another commodity in exchange the commodity in the equivalent form "counts as"[53] an object that possesses value "just as it is in its everyday life [*wie es geht und steht*]." A property that is the result of a social relationship between things is treated like a substance that naturally inhered in the object.: "The character which is constituted for it out of its *relationship* with the linen thus does not appear as the result of *its own relating*, but as present without any additional activity of its own."[54] Marx thereby anticipates more recent claims for a "relational ontology

---

Revolution und klassischer Tradition (Münster: Westfälisches Dampfboot, 2014), 224.

[50] Marx, *Capital*, 139.

[51] Ibid., 151.

[52] Ibid., 143.

[53] Ibid.

[54] Karl Marx, "The Commodity," in *Value: Studies by Karl Marx*, trans. and ed. Albert Dragstedt (London: New Park Publications, 1976), 23–24; original emphases.

488 Money Form and Master Painting

that rejects the metaphysics of relata,"[55] but does so in the process of coming to terms with a historically specific "social ontology."[56]

The "mystery of the form of value" has, thus, essentially been solved. Grasping the fetish-like character of the commodity and its secret requires little more than an understanding of what Marx calls the equivalent form – and, paradoxically, this can be grasped before the section of Chapter 1 on the fetish has even begun. However, Marx has not provided for a description of a practice that characterizes actually existing capitalist exchange relations. In their social intercourse, in other words, commodity-owners do not exchange individual commodities – one coat for 20 yards of linen, say. Capitalist exchange, unlike barter, does not rest on the direct exchange of products. Instead, individuals use money to purchase any commodity they want. The point of the Marxian dialectic of the value-form is to show that, in order for universal commodity exchange to be possible in the first place, all products of labor must express their value in and through a commodity that stands in the "universal equivalent form," thus obtaining "the form of immediate and universal exchangeability."[57] Instead of a commodity in the relative form expressing its value in sometimes this equivalent and sometimes that one, the entirety of commodities is only "really brought into relation with each other as values"[58] once one commodity is excluded, thus assuming the role of universal equivalent. This commodity – gold, historically – becomes the "money commodity"[59] and, in practice, the universal equivalent form is nothing but the money form.[60]

If, however, the fetish-like character of the commodity is, in essence, based on the peculiarities of the equivalent form,[61] and if the equivalent form only becomes practically valid as the universal equivalent or money form, one might conclude that the commodity fetish only appears

---

[55] Karen Barad, "Posthumanist Performativity: Toward an Understanding of How Matter Comes to Matter," *Signs: Journal of Women in Culture and Society* 28, no. 3 (2003): 812.

[56] Beverley Best, "Distilling a Value Theory of Ideology from Volume Three of *Capital*," *Historical Materialism* 23, no. 3 (2015): 117.

[57] Marx, *Capital*, 162; translation modified.

[58] Ibid., 158.

[59] Ibid., 162; translation revised.

[60] Ibid., 163.

[61] Ibid., 148–151.

in practice as the money fetish. Put polemically, one could argue that commodity fetishism as such does not exist. While commentators have, for decades, read it as a sort of phenomenology of lived experience under capitalism – a "lived ideology of capitalist society"[62] –, wherein individuals venerate individual commodities by granting them supernatural powers – Cole's account of the prospective buyer of "that table you just have to have" or Joselit's "icons of consumer society" – it would be more precise (and less polemical) to call it a *"non-empirical"* category.[63] This is why Marx can claim that the "riddle of the money form is therefore the riddle of the commodity fetish, now become visible and dazzling to our eyes."[64] In practice, only money possesses the *"social virtue"*[65] of expressing the value of each and every possible product of labor and can thus be used to purchase everything. Finally, if the commodity fetish only becomes actualized as the money fetish it becomes easier to see that it has nothing to do with the veneration of specific content such as a table, a shoe or a bottle of Coca-Cola. Instead, this power belongs to the money form qua form as that which makes possible the expression of the value of all commodities, regardless of their differences as material objects.

This, finally, makes my claim for an analogy between the Marxian money form and Warhol's "master painting" comprehensible. To wit, the latter was meant to render all potential paintings "interchangeable" by providing a form that was "good" regardless of its "subject." If Warhol's "master painting" should perform this function in the realm of art, the money form is the social form that, according to Marx, makes universal commodity exchange possible in the first place, by offering a medium in which each and every conceivable product of labor can express its value. Warhol envisioned that "if the one 'master painting' is good, they're all good. Besides, even when the subject is different, people always paint the same painting." This can now be rephrased in a Marxian idiom: If the money form expresses value, the commodities are

---

[62] Jean Baudrillard, *For a Critique of the Political Economy of the Sign* (Brooklyn: Verso, 2019), 75.

[63] Heinrich, *Die Wissenschaft vom Wert*, 157; original emphasis, my translation.

[64] Marx, *Capital*, 187.

[65] Rubin, *Essays on Marx's Theory of Value*, 21; original emphasis.

all bearers of value. After all, even when the commodities in the relative form are different, people always use the same universal equivalent form.

Works Cited

Althusser, Louis. "Preface to Capital Volume One (March 1969)." In *Lenin and Philosophy and Other Essays*, translated by Ben Brewster, 71–101. New York: Monthly Review Press, 1971.

Barad, Karen. "Posthumanist Performativity: Toward an Understanding of How Matter Comes to Matter." *Signs: Journal of Women in Culture and Society* 28, no. 3 (2003): 802–831.

Baudrillard, Jean. *For a Critique of the Political Economy of the Sign*. Brooklyn: Verso, 2019.

Beech, Dave. *Art and Value: Art's Economic Exceptionalism in Classical, Neoclassical and Marxist Economics*. Chicago: Haymarket, 2016.

Berg, Gretchen. "Nothing to Lose: An Interview with Andy Warhol." *Cahiers du Cinéma in English* 10 (1967): 38–43.

Best, Beverley. "Distilling a Value Theory of Ideology from Volume Three of *Capital*." *Historical Materialism* 23, no. 3 (2015): 101–141.

Brown, Nicholas. *Autonomy: The Social Ontology of Art Under Capitalism*. Durham: Duke University Press, 2019.

Buchloh, Benjamin H. D. "Andy Warhol's One-Dimensional Art." In *Neo-Avantgarde and Culture Industry: Essays on European and American Art From 1955 to 1975*, 461–529. Cambridge: The MIT Press, 2003.

Buck-Morss, Susan. *Dreamworld and Catastrophe: The Passing of Mass Utopia in East and West*. Cambridge: The MIT Press, 2000.

Chambers, Samuel A. *There's No Such Thing as "The Economy": Essays on Capitalist Value*. Santa Barbara: Punctum Books, 2018.

Cole, Andrew. *The Birth of Theory*. Chicago: The University of Chicago Press, 2014.

---. "Those Obscure Objects of Desire: The Uses and Abuses of Object-Oriented Ontology and Speculative Realism." *Artforum* 53, no. 10 (2015).

Danto, Arthur C. *Andy Warhol*. New Haven: Yale University Press, 2009.

de Duve, Thierry. *Sewn in the Sweatshops of Marx: Beuys, Warhol, Klein, Duchamp*. Chicago: University of Chicago Press, 2012.

De Salvo, Donna. "Andy Warhol: I Work Seven Days a Week." In *Andy Warhol: From A to B and Back Again*, edited by Donna De Salvo, 16–33. New Haven: Yale University Press, 2018.

Egenhofer, Sebastian. "Geld und Bild bei Andy Warhol." In *Einwegbilder*, edited by Inge Hinterwaldner et al., 109–125. Paderborn: Wilhelm Fink Verlag, 2016.

Falconer, Morgan. *Painting Beyond Pollock*. New York: Phaidon, 2015.

Fried, Michael. "Art and Objecthood." In *Art and Objecthood: Essays and Reviews*, 148–172. Chicago: The University of Chicago Press, 1998.

Graw, Isabelle. *High Price: Art Between the Market and Celebrity Culture*. London: Sternberg Press, 2010.

Heinrich, Michael. *Die Wissenschaft vom Wert: Die Marxsche Kritik der politischen Ökonomie zwischen wissenschaftlicher Revolution und klassischer Tradition*. Münster: Westfälisches Dampfboot, 2014.

Joselit, David. *American Art Since 1945*. London: Thames & Hudson, 2003.

Kelleter, Frank. "Warhol, Andy: Das Prosawerk." In *Kindlers Literatur Lexikon*, edited by Heinz Ludwig Arnold. Stuttgart: J.B. Metzler, 2020.

Lieber, Marlon. "Art and Economic Objecthood: Preliminary Remarks on 'Sensuous Supra-Sensuous' Things." In "The Return of the Aesthetic in American Studies," edited by Winfried Fluck, Rieke Jordan, and Johannes Voelz. *REAL – Yearbook of Research in English and American Literature* 35 (2019): 61–80.

Marchand, Roland. *Advertising the American Dream: Making Way for Modernity, 1920-1940*. Berkeley: University of California Press, 1985.

Marx, Karl. *Capital: A Critique of Political Economy*, vol. 1. Translated by Ben Fowkes. London: Penguin, 1990.

---. "The Commodity." In *Value: Studies by Karl Marx*, translated and edited by Albert Dragstedt, 1–40. London: New Park Publications, 1976.

---. *Grundrisse: Foundations of the Critique of Political Economy (Rough Draft)*. Translated by Martin Nicolaus. London: Penguin, 1993.

MARLON LIEBER

---. "Letter to Ludwig Kugelmann, 11 July 1868." In *Karl Marx and Friedrich Engels: Collected Works*, vol. 43, 67–70. London: Lawrence & Wishart, 1988.

Mattick, Paul. *Art In Its Time: Theories and Practices of Modern Aesthetics*. London: Routledge, 2003.

Pitts, Frederick Harry. *Value*. Cambridge: Polity Press, 2021.

Rubin, I. I. *Essays on Marx's Theory of Value*. Translated by Miloš Samardžija and Fredy Perlman. Delhi: Aakar Books, 2008.

Stimson, Blake. *Citizen Warhol*. London: Reaktion Books, 2014.

Wagner, Anne Middleton. *A House Divided: American Art Since 1955*. Berkeley: University of California Press, 2012.

Warhol, Andy. *The Philosophy of Andy Warhol (From A to B and Back Again)*. New York: Penguin, 2007.

Warhol, Andy, and Pat Hackett. *POPism: The Warhol Sixties*. New York: Penguin, 2007.

Zahner, Nina Tessa. *Die neuen Regeln der Kunst: Andy Warhol und der Umbau des Kunstbetriebs im 20. Jahrhundert*. Frankfurt am Main: Campus, 2006.

FRANK MEHRING

"You Can't Always Get What You Want!" Sonic State Fantasies and the Political Use of Popular Music under Barack Obama and Donald Trump

Barack Obama has been labeled a "jazz president"[1] due to his love and use of music as a cultural glue at political rallies, celebrations, and commemorative performances. The musicscapes of the Trump administration and the alt-right are part of a different political agenda. Both former presidents made popular music an integral part of their political strategies and campaigns. Music fulfilled a number of functions, including sending messages, exciting voters, branding group identities, forging affective bonds among citizens, and connecting people's emotions to a political program or a political personality. In this article, I will critically analyze the use of popular music in the Obama and Trump administrations and will follow a three-part structure. First, I will problematize the potential of music to underscore what I call sonic state fantasies. Second, I will analyze the ways Obama embraced music as an integral tool in domestic politics. Third, I will compare my findings regarding the political use of popular music during the Obama administration to that of Trump, asking: What has the function of music been in recent presidential rallies and at other political events? How is the American and transatlantic archive of popular music re-mediated and appropriated for specific political purposes? In order to answer these questions, I will turn to the intersection of politics and music as a space

---

[1] John Dickerson, "Presidential Anger Management: Why Obama, Like His Predecessors, Can't Get Angry in Public," *SLATE*, February 2, 2020, slate.com/news-and-politics/2010/06/why-obama-like-his-predecessors-can-t-get-angry-in-public.html.

496   The Political Use of Popular Music

in which state fantasies are communicated, branded, and – in an often subliminal fashion – internalized by the audience.

Sonic State Fantasies

The modern nation state is shaped not only by politicians, laws, and political institutions but also, as Jacqueline Rose has argued, by a category which most political theorists have neglected so far: "fantasy."[2] When singer-songwriter Bob Dylan was awarded the Nobel Prize for literature in 2016, the jury recognized American popular music as a medium that reflects upon social issues and moments of crisis as well as narratives of protest and transcendence. Joan Baez's and Bob Dylan's presence at the 1963 March on Washington for Jobs and Freedom, at which Baez sang "We Shall Overcome," is but one reminder of the powerful – yet oft-neglected – influence music can exert during socio-political and historical moments of change. Without a doubt, music underpins social and political movements and can strengthen a sense of community among voters. It has the power to both reveal and camouflage beliefs, convey implicit knowledge, and activate social or political commitments. Depending on the media framing, musicians can become truth bearers of political causes and agendas. As Justin Patch argues,[3] politicians recruit musicians as proxies in order to utilize music for their campaign purposes.

Popular music has always been able to transcend its entanglement as a mass culture commodity. It has functioned as a means of negation, protest, and dissent. Access to audio-visual content on social media not only leads to a furthering of the "process of democratization in the sphere of culture production and distribution"[4] but also increases the power of music to frame cultural events as political performances. Music can also frame political events such as rallies and presidential

---

[2]   Jacqueline Rose, *States of Fantasy* (Oxford: Clarendon Press, 1996).

[3]   Justin Patch, *Discordant Democracy: Noise, Affect, Populism, and the Presidential Campaign* (New York: Routledge, 2019), 5.

[4]   Olaf Kaltmeier and Wilfried Raussert, *Sonic Politic: Music and Social Movements in the Americas* (London: Routledge, 2019), 7; Mark Mattern, *Acting in Concert: Music, Community, and Political Action* (New Brunswick: Rutgers University Press, 1988), 15.

inaugural concerts, turning them into cultural performances. I am interested in the shared affective and discursive space in which popular music and politics merge. If popular culture is, as Stuart Hall claims, an arena of consent and resistance in the struggle over cultural meanings, a ground of contestation where ideologies are worked out,[5] then political rallies involving popular music become part of such an arena. This opens up new research venues with regard to how the sonic experience of politics affects our responses to political agendas. I call this affective nexus of politics and music the sonic state fantasy.

In addressing the connections between music and the cultural imaginary of a nation, I find Don Pease's definition of "state fantasies" compelling. Pease does not refer to a kind of mystification of the nation but rather uses "state fantasy" to describe "the dominant structure of desire out of which U.S. citizens imagined their national identity."[6] The state needs to offer scenarios in which citizens (and voters during election campaigns) are invited to internalize rules, norms, agendas, and political brands. I argue that music plays a constitutive role in the creation of state fantasies such as George H. W. Bush's "New World Order," William J. Clinton's "New Covenant with America," George W. Bush's "Homeland Security State," Barack Obama's "Change We Can Believe In," or Donald Trump's "Make America Great Again." In order to understand the complex ways in which music unfolds its power, we have to understand the socio-cultural frame in which music is used. In the case of the Obama and Trump administrations, I will analyze political events for which specific songs and artists were selected and explore how these songs and artists have become complicit in presidential state fantasies.

As George Lipsitz reminds us, popular music can function as a "vital repository for collective memory."[7] Hence, musicians become agents in

---

[5] Stuart Hall, "Culture, the Media and the Ideological Effect," in *Mass Communications and Society*, eds. J. Curran et al. (London: Edward Arnold, 1977), 315–418; Stuart Hall, "Gramsci's Relevance for the Study of Race and Ethnicity," *Journal of Communication Inquiry* 10, no. 2 (1986): 5–27.

[6] Donald E. Pease, *The New American Exceptionalism* (Minneapolis: University of Minnesota Press, 2009), 1.

[7] George Lipsitz, *Footsteps in the Dark: The Hidden Histories of Popular Music* (Minneapolis: University of Minnesota Press, 2007), vii.

498　　　　　　The Political Use of Popular Music

generating "alternative archives of history" in the minds of listeners and fans. In the twentieth century, American presidents have exploited the potential of popular music to create an affective bond between the emotions evoked by pop songs and politics or political leaders themselves.

On a surface level, campaign songs connect the image of a presidential candidate with happiness, optimism, and an exceptionalist rhetoric of progress for a better tomorrow. Upon close scrutiny, however, the songs are more complex than the titles and sing-along choruses imply. As a matter of fact, they are likely to run counter to the message the political candidate wants to exploit. For example, it is well known that Reagan mistook Bruce Springsteen's song "Born in the U.S.A." for a patriotic celebration of American values and the contributions of U.S. veterans to the American cause of freedom.[8] The song actually offers a double-edged commentary on the shortcomings of the American dream, the post-traumatic stress symptoms of soldiers returning home, and the challenge of making ends meet in a struggling American economy.

These inherent tensions and contradictions, however, are considered less important for the purposes of branding during a campaign or in a political commercial. What matters is the sound of the songs.[9] The repetition of the 'hook' – a line that is catchy and easily remembered – acquires a larger presence in the consciousness of the audience[10] than the work of decoding the narrative expressed in the verses. In this con-

---

[8]　Holly George-Warren et al., *The Rolling Stone Encyclopedia of Rock & Roll* (New York: Fireside, 2001), 942; Anthony DeCurtis et al., *The Rolling Stone Illustrated History of Rock & Roll: The Definitive History of the Most Important Artists and Their Music* (New York: Random House, 1992), 622; Benjamin S. Schoening and Eric T. Kasper, *Don't Stop Thinking About the Music: The Politics of Songs and Musicians in Presidential Campaigns* (Lanham: Lexington Books, 2012), 155.

[9]　See Frank Mehring et al., *Soundtrack Van De Bevrijding: Swingen, Zingen En Dansen Op Weg Naar Vrijheid* (Nijmegen: Uitgeverij Vantilt, 2015), 64.

[10]　See Chaïm Perelman and Lucie Olbrechts-Tyteca, *The New Rhetoric: A Treatise on Argumentation* (Notre Dame: University of Notre Dame Press, 1969), 116; Schoening and Kasper, *Don't Stop Thinking*, 247.

FRANK MEHRING

text, it is important to understand that music is, above all, symbolic.[11] Communication studies has shown that meanings are constructed by people interacting with each other in specific socio-political contexts. Symbols thereby acquire "different meanings for different audiences."[12] In my analysis, I will show how popular music has become complicit with various political state fantasies.

Sounding the Obama Era and the Post-Racial Fantasy

Throughout his time in office, former President Barack Obama frequently turned to music to add an affective frame to his political agenda. He promoted the sonic state fantasy on three different levels. The first concerns the use of music during his election campaign and at events related to his inauguration. A rare moment of aligning half a century of American popular music with politics can be observed in We Are One: The Obama Inaugural Celebration, which was held at the Lincoln Memorial. This public event, which was held on January 18, 2009 to celebrate the upcoming inauguration of Barack Obama as the 44th president of the United States, featured performances by renowned artists such as Beyoncé, Bruce Springsteen, and Stevie Wonder. At the Washington Mall in the presence of famous musicians performing African American, Latin American, and European-American music, Obama embraced this sonic performance to allude to a new nation in which racism would be replaced by a shared sense of unity:

> And yet, as I stand here tonight, what gives me the greatest hope of all is not the stone and marble that surrounds us today, but what fills the spaces in between. It is you – Americans of every race and region and

---

[11] See Kenneth Burke and Joseph R. Gusfield, *On Symbols and Society* (Chicago: University of Chicago Press, 1989), 59; Dorothy Miell et al., *Musical Communication* (Oxford: Oxford University Press, 2005), 1.

[12] David R. Dewberry and Jonathan H. Millen, "Music as Rhetoric: Popular Music in Presidential Campaigns," *Atlantic Journal of Communication* 22, no. 2 (2014): 85.

500 The Political Use of Popular Music

station – who came here because you believe in what this country can be and because you want to help us get there.[13]

Two days later, on January 20, African American superstar Beyoncé performed "At Last"[14] at the Neighborhood Inaugural Ball, where Obama and First Lady Michelle performed the opening dance. The song, best known in the R&B version by soul singer Etta James, has become a staple of 1960s-era music and is intrinsically linked with the civil rights movement. In 2009, the lyrics acquired a double meaning: on the one hand, they highlighted the romantic moment of two lovers being united; on the other hand, they seemed to celebrate the election of the first African American president who – at last – embodied the breakthrough of the kind of post-racial dream that Martin Luther King Jr. and others had envisioned for so long. Baudrillard might have said that we and the global television audience saw and heard "utopia achieved."[15] Music and politics aligned in the promise of finally heralding the end of what I have called, in a different context, the "democratic gap," or the discrepancy between democratic principles and racist practices.[16]

The second level of sonic state fantasy involves the support and attendance of musical events. On a number of occasions, Obama connected the aura associated with being the first African American

---

[13] Qtd. in Steve Hendrix and Jonathan Mummolo, "Jamming on the Mall for Obama," *The Washington Post*, January 19, 2009, www.washingtonpost. com/wpdyn/content/article/2009/01/18/AR2009011800917.html?hpid=topne ws&sid =ST2009011802825&s_pos=.

[14] "At Last," Mack Gordon and Harry Warren (RCA, 1942), Etta James version (Argo Records, 1961), Beyoncé version (Columbia Records, 2008).

[15] Jean Baudrillard, *America* (Brooklyn: Verso, 1988), 77. Jaap Kooijman has convincingly argued that the performances of Beyoncé and Obama seem to reaffirm "the belief that the boundaries of race can and will be overcome." Jaap Kooijman, *Fabricating the Absolute Fake: America in Contemporary Pop Culture* (Amsterdam: Amsterdam University Press, 2008), 148.

[16] Frank Mehring, *The Democratic Gap: Transcultural Confrontations of German Immigrants and the Promise of American Democracy* (Heidelberg: Universitätsverlag Winter, 2014), 2. The performance becomes part of what Baudrillard describes as a hyperreality: a dance between an African American president and his attractive wife is a cinema-like event that had been foreshadowed and enacted in fiction, film, and music many times before.

president with the power of music to unite people. Music offered the sonic glue to transcend geographical, racial, and gender boundaries. The fifth International Jazz Day All-Star Global Concert, held at the White House in 2016, marked a crucial event in the history of jazz. In his opening remarks, President Obama characterized jazz music as being "driven by an unmistakably American spirit." By hosting this event, he made all of the high-profile musical talent from both America and overseas, such as Aretha Franklin, Herbie Hancock, Buddy Guy, Al Jarreau, Diana Krall, and Till Brönner, complicit with his political agenda. Obama added: "It is, in so many ways, the story of our nation's progress: Born out of the struggle of African-Americans yearning for freedom. Forged in a crucible of cultures – a product of the diversity that would forever define our nation's greatness."[17]

The compositions presented at the jazz gala transcended the frameworks of the specific times in North American, South American and European history from which they respectively emerged. "'Jazz is a good barometer of freedom,' Duke Ellington once said. No wonder it has such an outsized imprint on the DNA of global music. It has spread like wildfire across the world, from Africa to Asia. And jazz blended with the bossa nova of Brazil or the tango of Argentina."[18] In the context of the gala, Obama acknowledged that the performance of some of the best-known compositions by world-famous artists rendered jazz as a kind of "truth telling music." This "truth" is part of the U.S. and, by implication, related to all human beings. In the presence of the American president, the connection between jazz and the African American freedom struggle became part of a sonic state fantasy, namely the narrative of American progress and the post-racial promise of the Obama presidency. Obama's efforts to surround his presidency with events at which many famous legends of American blues, jazz, and rock

[17] Barack Obama, "Remarks at the White House International Jazz Day Concert," *American Presidency Project*, April 29, 2016. Obama functioned as the host. In a joking way, he mentioned Dizzy Gillespie who ran for president in 1964. Obama promised to turn the White House into a "Blues House," turning the musicians, in a way, into what Percy Bysshe Shelley in another context called "the unacknowledged legislators of the world." Percy Bysshe Shelley, *Complete Works of Percy Bysshe Shelley*, vol. 7, eds. Roger Ingpen and Walter Edwin Peck (New York: Gordian Press, 1965), 109.

[18] Obama, "Remarks."

502   The Political Use of Popular Music

performed allowed him to create a sonic state fantasy of collective alliances embodied via popular music. Simon Frith has framed this potential in a different context as a key element of pop songs:

> Pop songs and pop stars mean more to us emotionally than other media event or performers [...] The experience of pop music is an experience of placing: in responding to a song, we are drawn, haphazardly, into affective and emotional alliances with the performers and with the performers' other fans.[19]

Obama used this experience of alliance to not only connect with U.S. citizens, but also to express his vision of a post-racial society in which music functions as a vital glue.

On a third level of sonic state fantasy, Obama turned to singing on different occasions to celebrate, mourn, and heal. Instead of turning to "presentational music," a term I am borrowing from Thomas Turino,[20] Obama used participatory music. Here, the difference between artist and audience is transcended through the shared experience of singing. Among the songs Obama intoned (at least partly) include, for example, "Let's Stay Together"[21] during a speech at a 2012 fundraising event at Harlem's Apollo Theater which was attended by the singer and soul legend Al Green; Dionne Warwick's "Walk On By"[22] during a New Jersey democratic rally in 2009; and Aretha Franklin's "Chain Of Fools"[23] during a Detroit campaign rally on September 1st, 2009, during which Obama paid tribute to the Franklin (who was in the audience) as the "queen of soul."

Among Obama's several powerful singing performances, one stands out as particularly remarkable. The incident occurred during the memorial service for Clementa Pinckney, one of the victims of the 2015 Charleston church shootings. After giving forty-minute speech in front

---

[19]   Simon Frith, "Towards an Aesthetic of Popular Music: Music and Society," in *Taking Popular Music Seriously: Selected Essays*, ed. Simon Frith (London and New York: Routledge, 2007), 263.

[20]   Thomas Turino, *Music as Social Life. The Politics of Participation* (Chicago: University of Chicago Press, 2008), 2.

[21]   "Let's Stay Together," Al Green, Willie Mitchell and Al Jackson Jr., 1972.

[22]   "Walk On By," Burt Bacharach and Hal David, 1963.

[23]   "Chain of Fools," Don Covay, 1967.

of a crowd of approximately 6,000 people, Obama repeated the expression "Amazing grace" before introducing a long pause for reflection. During the thirteen seconds of silence, Obama appears to be looking for the right words with which to continue. He glances to the right, then down at his script. To the surprise of the priests behind him, he then begins to sing the spiritual. The unusual performance releases positive emotions and energizes both the priests and the audience. Spontaneous laughter, clapping and cheers can be heard. On the words "a wretch like me," the organ joins in, transforming the president into a quasi-religious leader. Appropriately, Obama raises his voice to pronounce the individual names of the nine victims, saying that they found "*that* grace." The audience participates with a cheerful "yes" amplified by a chord played on the organ in a call-and-response pattern. It is exceptional to have a president indicate through song that there are certain times when language alone cannot properly express one's feelings. The *New York Times* called this event "one of his presidency's most impassioned reflections on race," in which he asked the nation "to emulate the grace that he displayed in his work and that the people of South Carolina demonstrated after the massacre of nine worshipers at Emanuel African Methodist Episcopal Church."[24] Obama activates an American myth along the same lines as Don Pease, who argues that "traumatic events precipitate states of emergency that become the inaugural moments in a different symbolic order and take place on a scale that exceeds the grasp of the available representations from the national mythology."[25] While Pease was referring to the traumatic events of 9/11, the situation in Charleston offers a revealing perspective on how Obama turned to the power of music and singing in order to offer a state fantasy in moments of crisis.

To sum up: During his election campaigns, at the inauguration, and throughout his presidency, Obama turned to popular music to evoke a sonic state fantasy. In the moments described above, the difference between artist and audience, between president and nation, seemed to be

---

[24] Kevin Sack and Gardiner Harris, "President Obama Eulogizes Charleston Pastor as One Who Understood Grace," *The New York Times*, June 26, 2015, nytimes.com/2015/06/27/us/thousands-gather-for-funeral-of-clementa-pinckney-in-charleston.html.

[25] Pease, *The New American Exceptionalism*, 5.

504 The Political Use of Popular Music

erased. Sonically, the foundation of the democratic principle of the U.S. – of the people, by the people, for the people – became tangible.

While Democrats celebrated these events and European newspapers reported on them in an emphatic fashion, these performances also show the manipulative power of the participatory mode of music that has the potential to be exploited for non-democratic agendas, as examples from fascist or communist regimes reveal. It comes as no surprise that similar songs, musicians, and bands have been employed by the Republican Party to sonically frame different and often opposing political agendas.

Sounding the Trump State Fantasy

The band The Rolling Stones were instrumentalized by the Obama administration to support the post-racial state fantasy. Their music, however, also played an important role during the Trump campaign rallies. While the Obama era has largely been defined by widespread support among mainstream artists from the blues, jazz, rock, pop, and rap genres, the situation under Trump was different. During the transitional period from presidential candidate to President of the United States, Trump and his team encountered a number of difficulties in securing top-tier talent for the inauguration. Artists such as Elton John, David Foster, U.K. superstars Charlotte Church and Rebecca Ferguson, Moby, 2 Chainz, The Beach Boys, and Ice-T made it clear in public statements that they had declined to perform in the honor of Donald Trump's presidency. Others such as Celine Dion, Andrea Bocelli, and Kiss were asked, but they decided to refrain without offering an explicit explanation.[26] The dissent of artists who did not want their work to become complicit with the Trump administration reveals the blurred lines between music, protest, and the use of popular music in political contexts.

Like Hillary Clinton, his democratic opponent in the 2016 election campaign, Donald Trump turned to popular music during campaign

[26] See Hugh McIntyre, "Here Are All The Musicians Performing At Donald Trump's Inauguration," *Forbes*, January 17, 2017, forbes.com/sites/hughmcintyre/2017/01/17/here-are-all-the-celebrities-performing-at-donald-trumps-inauguration/#34ea9720184c.

rallies to get his audience in the right mood and dramatically frame his entrance. "We're Not Gonna Take It,"[27] from the glam-rock band Twisted Sister, or the blatantly heroic theme from the Hollywood blockbuster *Air Force One* (1997)[28] sonically framed Trump's arrival by helicopter to great cinematic effect. The Trump playlist included rock and pop hits of the last fifty years, from songs by the Beatles and the Rolling Stones to Neil Young and R.E.M; the famous Puccini aria "Nessun Dorma" from *Turandot* performed by the star tenor Luciano Pavarotti set an overtly dramatic tone. While it is unlikely that the majority of the audience members understood the Italian lyrics, the well-known melody and grandiosity of the singer's performance spoke to the audience on a purely affective level. As Simon Frith has described such performances in another context, the most powerful part of songs is often related to the tone of voice, which is "more important in this context than the actual articulation of the lyrics."[29]

One of the songs that Trump repeatedly used during the 2016 Republican primaries and the presidential election was a song by The Rolling Stones: "You Can't Always Get What You Want"[30] from the 1969 album *Let it Bleed*.[31] Turning to a band John Covach has described as "one of most critically and commercially successful acts in rock music history,"[32] the Trump administration did not intend to activate memories of the so-called "British invasion" – the storming of U.S. charts by British pop bands. Rather, The Rolling Stones had, in a sense, already become "Americanized" when they were inducted to the Rock and Roll Hall of Fame at the end of the Reagan presidency. "You Can't Always Get What You Want" has been a staple in the Stones's live set list ever since and was named the 100th greatest song of all time by *Rolling Stone* magazine in 2004. The song's multi-generational appeal

---

[27] "We're Not Gonna Take It," Dee Snider, 1984.

[28] *Air Force One*, directed by Wolfgang Petersen (Sony Pictures, 1997).

[29] Frith, "Towards an Aesthetic of Popular Music," 120.

[30] "You Can't Always Get What You Want, Mick," Jagger and Keith Richards (Decca, 1969).

[31] The Rolling Stones management unsuccessfully tried to stop Trump using the song.

[32] John Covach, "The Rolling Stones: Albums and Singles, 1963–1974," in *The Cambridge Companion to the Rolling Stones*, eds. Victor Coelho and John Rudolph Covach (Cambridge: Cambridge University Press, 2019), 3.

506 The Political Use of Popular Music

constitutes an asset that can be used to subliminally engage audiences before the appearance of a presidential candidate. In addition, the song features a catchy sing-along chorus. It can thus unfold its potential to encourage audiences to actively participate in a fantasy of unity on a sonic level. While the song has been described by the band's lead singer Mick Jagger as referring to the drug-infused Chelsea scene of the late 1960s, the inclusion of "You Can't Always Get What You Want" is designed to activate a different response during the political campaign rally.

While the lyrics of the first part of the chorus claim that "you can't always get what you want," the final conclusion, which comes after the parental-sounding warning has been invoked three times, is more self-assertive: "But if you try sometimes well you might find / You get what you need." Beyond the participatory effect of the composition, the affirmative rhetoric implies to the campaign rally audience that Trump will ultimately "get what he needs" to realize his campaign slogan of "Make America Great Again" – including "building a wall and making the Mexicans pay for it," creating jobs in an unprecedented fashion, and reversing political decrees of the Obama administration.

Music, therefore, may embody political values and experiences. It helps us to organize our response to society as political thought and action, both as a vehicle for political expression and as that expression,[33] depending on the ideological framing. Hence, music's relation to politics can, to a certain degree, be complicit and function as a free-floating signifier as well. If Lipsitz and Street are right to argue that style is often more important than content – that, indeed, the content is in the style – music used at the Trump rallies should be analyzed beyond the lyrical level. "You Can't Always Get What You Want" opens with a children's choir, suggesting a return to the simpler time of childhood. Rather than presenting the song as the offspring of African American blues and the gospel tradition, however, The Rolling Stones added a sense of irony[34]: The London Bach Choir was chosen over the more obvious choice of the African American Baptist choir. "I'd [...] had this idea," Jagger

---

[33] John Street, *Music and Politics* (Cambridge: Polity Press, 2012), 4.
[34] See Bill Janovitz, "Guitar Slingers and Hired Guns: Musicians of the Stones," in *The Cambridge Companion to the Rolling Stones*, eds. Victor Coelho and John Rudolph Covach (Cambridge: Cambridge University Press, 34).

explains, "of having a choir, probably a gospel choir, on the track, but there wasn't one around at that point. Jack Nitzsche, or somebody, said that we could get the London Bach Choir, and we said, that will be a laugh."[35] Rather than emphasizing the African American roots of many Stones compositions, the choir offers a racial counterpoint which subliminally served Trump's target group of white Republican voters. In the words of Keith Richards, the Stones decided to include a "straight chorus. In other words, let's try to reach the people up there as well. It was a dare, kind of [...] And then, what if we got one of the best choirs in England, all these white, lovely singers, and do it that way? [...] It was a beautiful juxtaposition."[36] This seven-and-a-half-minute finale to *Let It Bleed* has been described as a sonic stage that offers a binary juxtaposition of the present and the past, England versus America, African American versus "white" music productions, and the "black" versus the "white" church.[37]

While the use of popular music during Donald Trump's campaign rallies is suggestive of a certain political stance, the musical preferences of the alt-right movement are more clearly defined. While the alt-right has been referred to as a movement or ideology, J.M. Berger suggests that it is more useful to describe the group as "a political bloc that seeks to unify the activities of several different extremist movements or ideology."[38] Richard Spencer, a white nationalist, neo-Nazi, and staunch supporter of the alt-right, coined the term. The alt-right has strong racist and anti-Semitic undercurrents with ties to neo-Nazi or Nazi nostalgia, while other members are part of the Ku Klux Klan. Because of its opposition to Muslims and immigration, the alt-right bloc is unified in its support for Trump and his nationalist political agenda. Trump considers the alt-right an integral part of his "base," and he described alt-right members who attended a 2017 white supremacist and neo-Nazi

---

[35] Qtd. in Keith Richards and James Fox, *Life* (Boston: Little, Brown and Co., 2010), 201.

[36] Richards, *Life*, 268.

[37] Victor Coelho, "Exile, America, and the Theater of the Stones, 1968-1972," in *The Cambridge Companion to the Rolling Stones*, eds. Victor Coelho and John Rudolph Covach (Cambridge: Cambridge University Press, 2019), 67.

[38] J. M. Berger, "Trump Is the Glue That Binds the Far Right," *The Atlantic*, October 29, 2019, theatlantic.com/ideas/archive/2018/10/trump-alt-right-twitter/ 574219/.

508   The Political Use of Popular Music

rally in Charlottesville, Virginia as "very fine people."[39] On websites and social media platforms, the alt-right bloc presents a state fantasy that is closely tied to the sonics of the 1980s and the 'Reaganomics' era. The then-new sounds of a decade associated with electronic effects and synthesizers have been embraced by alt-right followers and compiled in playlists entitled synthwave, vaporwave, or fashwave (a clear verbal reference to fascism). In an interesting twist, the alt-right sonic state fantasy, with its embeddedness in 1980s sonic aesthetics, is in line with a white nationalist, hyperpatriotic agenda in which fake news and post-truth politics have become more important than the fact checking done by investigative journalists.

Conclusion

I have shown that music offers a framework for affective com-munication that is used to mediate and brand political agendas. A comparison of the use and function of music during the Obama era and the Trump administration has revealed decisive differences. Obama repeatedly turned to music and performance culture to add a sonic glue to political debates. Music helped express the agenda of "change and hope we can believe in" in order to overcome societal polarization. Obama opened up the White House to international musicians to perform a sonic state fantasy. The various stages on which Obama cele-brated blues and jazz in transnational contexts established the first Black president as a leader in chief in whose presence national, racial, and political differences were transcended through popular music. The performances thereby suggested a post-racial fantasy in which the salience of race was diminished to near negligibility.

In contrast, during the Trump administration, racial classifications took center stage. Music became a tool with which to enhance, as Schraub writes, "the salience of race by treating it differently."[40] Music

---

[39]   Rosie Gray, "Trump Defends White-Nationalist Protesters: 'Some Very Fine People on Both Sides,'" *The Atlantic*, August 15, 2017, theatlantic.com/politics/archive/2017/08/trump-defends-white-nationalist-protesters-some-very-fine-people-on-both-sides/537012/.

[40]   David Schraub, "Post-Racialism and the End of Strict Scrutiny," *Indiana Law Journal* 92, no. 2 (2017): 599.

was used as an agent to highlight racial and political differences for the sake of a nationalist, white supremacist, hyperpatriotic state fantasy. The alt-right's musical DNA of 1980s sounds and aesthetics created a sonic state fantasy mired in Reagan-era nostalgia, which took that "me"-era's sense of the enforced simplicity of the 1950s and reframed it for the Trump era within the digital arena of his presidency. The comparison of the uses of popular music reveals that it can be the glue between culture and politics. My analysis has shown that popular music can be molded to do ideological work via its immediate affective potential to produce state fantasies, whether they are post-racial or white supremacist. As the Rolling Stones would have it in their song "You Can't Always Get What You Want": through music, you get what you need.

510 The Political Use of Popular Music

Works Cited

Bak, Hans, et al. *Politics and Cultures of Liberation: Media, Memory, and Projections of Democracy*. Leiden: Brill, 2018.

Baudrillard, Jean. *America*. Brooklyn: Verso, 1988.

Berger, J. M. "Trump Is the Glue That Binds the Far Right." *The Atlantic*, October 29, 2019. theatlantic.com/ideas/archive/2018/10/trump-alt-right-twitter/574219/.

Bolter, J. David, and Richard A. Grusin. *Remediation: Understanding New Media*. Cambridge: MIT Press, 1999.

Burke, Kenneth, and Joseph R. Gusfield. *On Symbols and Society*. Chicago: University of Chicago Press, 1989.

Coelho, Victor. "Exile, America, and the Theater of the Stones, 1968-1972." In *The Cambridge Companion to the Rolling Stones*, edited by Victor Coelho and John Rudolph Covach, 57–74. Cambridge: Cambridge University Press, 2019.

Covach, John. "The Rolling Stones: Albums and Singles, 1963-1974." In *The Cambridge Companion to the Rolling Stones*, edited by Victor Coelho and John Rudolph Covach, 3–17. Cambridge: Cambridge University Press, 2019.

DeCurtis, Anthony, et al. *The Rolling Stone Illustrated History of Rock & Roll: The Definitive History of the Most Important Artists and Their Music*. New York: Random House, 1992.

Dewberry, David R., and Jonathan H. Millen. "Music as Rhetoric: Popular Music in Presidential Campaigns." *Atlantic Journal of Communication* 22, no. 2 (2014): 81–92.

Dickerson, John. "Presidential Anger Management: Why Obama, like his predecessors, can't get angry in public." *SLATE*, February 2, 2020. slate.com/news-and-politics/2010/06/why-obama-like-his-predecessors-can-t-get-angry-in-public.html.

Dudley, Shannon. *The World of Music* 51, no. 2 (2009): 157–159.

Dwyer, Michael D. *Back to the Fifties: Nostalgia, Hollywood Film, and Popular Music of the Seventies and Eighties*. Oxford: Oxford University Press, 2015.

Frith, Simon. Simon Frith, "Towards an Aesthetic of Popular Music: Music and Society." In *Taking Popular Music Seriously: Selected Essays*, edited by Simon Frith, 257–274. London and New York: Routledge, 2007.

George-Warren, Holly, et al. *The Rolling Stone Encyclopedia of Rock & Roll*. New York: Fireside, 2001.

Gray, Rosie. "Trump Defends White-Nationalist Protesters: 'Some Very Fine People on Both Sides.'" *The Atlantic*, August 15, 2017. theatlantic.com/politics/archive/2017/08/trump-defends-white-nationalist-protesters-some-very-fine-people-on-both-sides/537012/.

Hall, Stuart. "Culture, the Media and the Ideological Effect." In *Mass Communications and Society*, edited by J. Curran et al., 315–418. London: Edward Arnold, 1977.

---. "Encoding/Decoding." In *Media Studies: A Reader*, edited by Sue Thornham et al., 28–38. Edinburgh: Edinburgh University Press, 2009.

---. "Gramsci's Relevance for the Study of Race and Ethnicity." *Journal of Communication Inquiry* 10, no. 2 (1986): 5–27.

Hendrix, Steve and Jonathan Mummolo, "Jamming on the Mall for Obama." *The Washington Post*, January 19, 2009. www.washington post.com/wp-dyn/content/article/2009/01/18/AR2009011800917.html?hpid=topnews&sid=ST2009011802825&s_pos=.

Janovitz, Bill. "Guitar Slingers and Hired Guns: Musicians of the Stones." In *The Cambridge Companion to the Rolling Stones*, edited by Victor Coelho and John Rudolph Covach, 18–39. Cambridge: Cambridge University Press, 2019.

---. *Rocks Off: 50 Tracks That Tell the Story of the Rolling Stones*. New York: St. Martin's Press, 2013.

Kaltmeier, Olaf, and Wilfried Raussert. *Sonic Politic: Music and Social Movements in the Americas*. London: Routledge, 2019.

Kooijman, Jaap. *Fabricating the Absolute Fake: America in Contemporary Pop Culture*. Amsterdam: Amsterdam University Press, 2008.

Leppert, Richard D., and Susan McClary. *Music and Society: The Politics of Composition, Performance, and Reception*. Cambridge: Cambridge University Press, 2001.

512 The Political Use of Popular Music

Lipsitz, George, *Footsteps in the Dark: The Hidden Histories of Popular Music*. Minneapolis: University of Minnesota Press, 2007.

Loewenstein, Dora, and Philip Dodd. *According to the Rolling Stones*. San Francisco: Chronicle Books, 2003.

Lott, Eric. *Black Mirror: The Cultural Contradictions of American Racism*. Cambridge: The Belknap Press of Harvard University Press, 2017.

Margotin, Philippe, et al. *The Rolling Stones: All the Songs: The Story Behind Every Track*. Paris: Hachette Book Group, 2016.

Mattern, Mark. *Acting in Concert: Music, Community, and Political Action*. New Brunswick: Rutgers University Press, 1988.

McIntyre, Hugh. "Here Are All The Musicians Performing At Donald Trump's Inauguration." *Forbes*, January 17, 2017. forbes.com/sites/hughmcintyre/2017/01/17/here-are-all-the-celebrities-performing-at-donald-trumps-inauguration/ #34ea9720184c.

Mehring, Frank. "'Only a Pawn in their Game?' Civil Rights Sounding Signatures in the Summer of 1963." In *Sonic Politics: Music and Social Movements in the Americas*, edited by Olaf Kaltmeier and Wilfried Raussert, 51–72. London: Routledge, 2019.

---. *The Democratic Gap: Transcultural Confrontations of German Immigrants and the Promise of American Democracy*. Heidelberg: Universitätsverlag Winter, 2014.

Mehring, Frank, et al. *Soundtrack Van De Bevrijding: Swingen, Zingen En Dansen Op Weg Naar Vrijheid*. Nijmegen: Uitgeverij Vantilt, 2015.

Miell, Dorothy, et al. *Musical Communication*. Oxford: Oxford University Press, 2005.

Newman, Jason. "Depeche Mode Reject Alt-Right Leader's Band Praise." *Rolling Stone*, February 23, 2017. rollingstone.com/music/music-news/depeche-mode-reject-alt-right-leaders-band-praise-124411/.

Obama, Barack. "Remarks at the White House International Jazz Day Concert." *American Presidency Project*, April 29, 2016. presidency.ucsb.edu/documents/remarks-the-white-house-international-jazz-day-concert.

Patch, Justin. *Discordant Democracy: Noise, Affect, Populism, and the Presidential Campaign*. New York: Routledge, 2019.

Pease, Donald E. *The New American Exceptionalism*. Minneapolis: University of Minnesota Press, 2009.

Perelman, Chaïm, and Lucie Olbrechts-Tyteca. *The New Rhetoric: A Treatise on Argumentation*. Notre Dame: University of Notre Dame Press, 1969.

Priewe, Marc. "The Power of Conformity: Music, Sound, and Vision in Back to the Future." *European Journal of American Studies* 12, no. 4 (2017).

Reagan, Ronald. "Remarks Accepting the Presidential Nomination at the Republican National Convention in Dallas, Texas." August 23, 1984. presidency.ucsb.edu/documents/remarks-accepting-the-presidential-nomination-the-republican-national-convention-dallas.

Richards, Keith, and James Fox. *Life*. Boston: Little, Brown and Co., 2010.

Rogin, Michael Paul. *Blackface, White Noise: Jewish Immigrants in the Hollywood Melting Pot*. Berkeley: University of California Press, 1996.

Rose, Jacqueline. *States of Fantasy*. Oxford: Clarendon Press, 1996.

Sack, Kevin, and Gardiner Harris. "President Obama Eulogizes Charleston Pastor as One Who Understood Grace." *The New York Times*, June 26, 2015. nytimes.com/2015/06/27/us/thousands-gather-for-funeral-of-clementa-pinckney-in-charleston.html.

Schoening, Benjamin S., and Eric T. Kasper. *Don't Stop Thinking About the Music: The Politics of Songs and Musicians in Presidential Campaigns*. Lanham: Lexington Books, 2012.

Schraub, David. "Post-Racialism and the End of Strict Scrutiny." *Indiana Law Journal* 92, no. 2 (2017): 599–651.

Shelley, Percy Bysshe. *Complete Works of Percy Bysshe Shelley*. 10 vols. Edited by Roger Ingpen and Walter Edwin Peck. New York: Gordian Press, 1965.

Street, John. *Music and Politics*. Cambridge: Polity Press, 2012.

Turino, Thomas. *Music as Social Life: The Politics of Participation*. Chicago: University of Chicago Press, 2008.

Uschan, Michael V. *The History of the Blues*. San Diego: Lucent Books, 2013.

514   The Political Use of Popular Music

Songs:

"A Song For You." Leon Russell (Shelter Records, 1970).
"At Last." Mack Gordon and Harry Warren (RCA Victor, 1942). Etta
    James version (Argo Records, 1961). Beyoncé version (Columbia
    Records, 2008).
"Born in the U.S.A." Bruce Springsteen (ASCAP, 1984).
"Chain Of Fools." Don Covay (Atlantic, 1967).
"Don't Stop." Christine McVie (Universal Music, 1976).
"Let's Stay Together." Al Green, Willie Mitchell and Al Jackson Jr.,
    (Hi, 1972).
"Only in America." Randall Jay Rogers, Don Cook and Kic Brooks
    (Sony/ATV Music Publishing LLC and Peermusic III, Ltd., 2001).
"This Land is Your Land." Woody Guthrie (1945).
"Walk On By." Burt Bacharach and Hal David (Scepter, 1963).
"We're Not Gonna Take It." Dee Snider (Atlantic, 1984).
"You and I (Were Meant to Fly)." Aldo Caporuscio and Jacques Duval,
    (BMG Platinum Songs BMII), Aldo Nova, Inc (SOCAN), Songs of
    Peer Ltd (ASCAP) and Avenue Editorial (ASCAP), 2009).
"You Can't Always Get What You Want." Mick Jagger and Keith
    Richards (Decca, 1969).
"(You Make Me Feel Like) A Natural Woman." Carole King and Gerry
    Goffin (Atlantic, 1967).

Films:

Air Force One. Directed by Wolfgang Petersen (Sony Pictures, 1997).
Back to the Future. Directed by Robert Zemeckis (Universal Pictures,
    1985).
Chasing Rainbows. Directed by Charles Reisner (Metro-Goldwyn-
    Mayer, 1930).
Goodfellas. Directed by Martin Scorsese (Warner Brothers, 1990).
Rocky III. Directed by Sylvester Stallone (MGM/UA Entertainment Co.,
    1982).
Top Gun. Directed by Tony Scott (Paramount Pictures, 1986).

JOHANNES C. P. SCHMID

Internet Memes as Popular Cultural Practices

Internet memes and popular culture form a complex, reciprocal liaison. Memes feed off other media such as photographs, films or television scenes, transforming them into new digital artifacts. The semantic transfer is limited, though. Parts of the base materials are decontextualized, reframed and reduced to an essential meaning – one that is, axiomatically, unintended by the original author(s). The newly generated meme constitutes a schema that provides blanks for numerous users to fill in, creating their own exemplars through which to share their experiences, jokes or statements. Often, but not always,[1] internet memes propel minimal narratives based on a newly imagined agent with one central tenet or a simple constellation of characters. To this end, renderings of, sometimes well-known, persons or characters become signifiers for a distinct new meaning. The question of why a particular cultural artifact becomes a meme can often be explained by the fact that many source materials offer readily deducible meanings that can be isolated and are widely relatable. In this way, a still that shows Jean-Luc Picard from *Star Trek: The Next Generation* in an apparent state of aggravation becomes a means for users to express outrage at all kinds of situations by adding text blocks that specify a concrete scenario (see fig. 1).

---

[1] In a more general definition, internet memes may also be purely linguistic and based on phrases or poems, or they can be performative, such as, for instance, the Harlem Shake or "planking."

Fig. 1: "Annoyed Picard" (Literally Media Ltd.).

While internet memes stem from more obscure online niche cultures such as *4chan*, the medial phenomenon has diffused into mainstream popular culture. Some internet memes are now part of digital popular culture themselves, while other memes are particular to certain subcultures and online communities – whether they be fandoms, political movements, or professional, academic or localized communities. The concept of popular culture applies to internet memes in different ways: first, memes draw on familiar icons established by mass culture, transforming such symbols through digital practices to create new meanings. Second, internet memes are decidedly bottom-up in nature, as there is little direct commercial value in them. They even subvert conventional sales models by effectively pirating cultural commodities from commercial franchises, stock photography providers and even private websites. Memes, therefore, shape digital counter-publics, from the hacker group Anonymous to the alt-right and the masculinist Gamergate movement.[2] Third, since the success of a meme is tantamount to its

---

[2] Andrea Nagle, *Kill All Normies: Online Culture Wars from 4Chan and Tumblr to Trump and the Alt-Right* (Winchester: Zero Books, 2017), 3;

collective usage, internet memes, as uniquely participatory popular phenomena, are emblems of dominant digital mass culture as well, offering great potential for companies[3] and political actors to partake in trending popular discourses.

This contribution will outline the internet meme as a cultural phenomenon that oscillates between the different aspects of popular culture that define the mediality and usage of memes. To illustrate their form, function, and cultural impact, several examples and different types of memes will be discussed, including stock characters, character constellations, and the dialogical "American Chopper Argument." Moreover, this paper will outline the complex relationship between irony and racist, classist and sexist stereotypes in internet memes as well as the general, problematic lack of consent involved in the practice of using the likenesses of individuals and intellectual property in memes.

Internet Memes, Cultural Practices and Ideology

Similar to the concept of viral images or video clips, the notion of the meme projects a biological framework upon cultural artifacts and their distribution on the internet. The conceptualization of memes as self-replicating, quasi-biological entities draws on familiar semantic contexts to explain the rapidity with which ideas and artifacts are spread online. Coined by evolutionary biologist Richard Dawkins in 1976, the concept of the "meme" sought to describe how cultural ideas are reproduced by using genes as an analogy.[4] The concept was hampered, however, by its tendency to mask the human agency involved.[5] Although Dawkins's approach remained a niche phenomenon, with the advent of digital mass

---

Anastasia Denisova, *Internet Memes and Society: Social, Cultural, and Political Contexts* (New York: Routledge, 2019), 27.

[3] See Bradley E. Wiggins, *The Discursive Power of Memes in Digital Culture: Ideologies, Semiotics, and Intertextuality* (New York: Routledge, 2019), 85.

[4] Richard Dawkins, *The Selfish Gene* (Oxford: Oxford University Press, 2006), 192.

[5] Cf. Henry Jenkins et al., *Spreadable Media: Creating Value and Meaning in a Networked Culture* (New York: New York University Press, 2013), 19.

518   Internet Memes as 'Popular' Cultural Practices

culture, the idea of the meme was taken up by internet users to account for the rapid and global dissemination of digital artifacts.

Internet memes are best understood as an example of "spreadable media," which entails that "audiences play an active role in 'spreading' content rather than serving as passive carriers of viral media: their choices, investments, agendas, and actions determine what gets valued."[6] "Spreadability" delineates a participatory cultural environment shaped by both emergent digital practices of remixing and sharing as well as the economic and medial structures that restrict, enable or stimulate circulation.[7] In one of the first major studies on the subject, Limor Shifman defines internet memes as "(a) a *group of digital items sharing common characteristics* of content, form, and/or stance; (b) that were created *with awareness of each other*; and (c) were circulated, imitated, and/or transformed *via the Internet by many users*."[8] Although this definition encompasses many essential characteristics, I contend that an internet meme does not so much subsist in a "group of digital items" but rather as a socially shared frame in the sense of a schema or script, which enables users to materialize such groups of items by means of digital practices that involve remixing and online sharing. Using hardware and software to edit template images or videos, users enact and negotiate such frames by creating individual exemplars; hence, they productively adopt a fixed formula to create ever-new digital artifacts that perform and consolidate the underlying concept. While the individual artifact that is produced is commonly referred to as "a meme" as well, the essence of a meme is found in its processuality. Internet memes thus constitute concise, socially shared textual schemata that provide fixed elements and blanks to fill in, and on the basis of which users produce individual digital artifacts that they share online.[9]

---

[6]   Ibid., 21.

[7]   Ibid., 4.

[8]   Limor Shifman, *Memes in Digital Culture* (Cambridge: MIT Press, 2014), 7–8.

[9]   See also Florian Busch and Johannes C. P. Schmid, "Internet Memes as Digital Practices: Stock Characters Macros in Multimodal Structure, Function, and Metapragmatic Reflexivity," in *Language, Media and Technologies: Usages, Forms and Functions*, eds. Lozzi Martial Meutem Kamtchueng and Camilla Arundie Tabe (Munich: LINCOM, 2019), 186; Stefan Tetzlaff, "Memes und Frames. Zur Markiertheit als semiotischem

Internet memes commonly revolve around a basic notion, such as a stereotypical character trait or behavior, which is isolated from a medial artifact and then repurposed for parodies, critiques and other statements.[10] Due to their concentrated textuality, memes disallow complexity; rather, they posit a normative argument in basic binaries that often paint the represented events or behaviors as either categorically positive or negative. However, this normativity is frequently treated with a certain irony that acknowledges its oversimplification. Numerous memes draw on stereotypes of class, race and gender – in many cases, in a tongue-in-cheek manner, in other cases, less so.

While Anastasia Denisova argues that memes "are an empty versatile vehicle that people fill with their ideas and agenda; an attractive conduit that helps to affect discourses and minds,"[11] this assessment is misleading. Despite the degree of openness that is a structural requirement for memes, the structures that devise such blank spaces are clearly ideological. Hence, the process of spreading a meme must be understood as an ideologically charged practice of signification,[12] both in terms of the choice of the base material from which the meme is isolated as well as in the way a particular schema is applied. Which representations are selected from the sheer wealth of available medial artifacts and what aspects are isolated as familiar symbols reflects cultural values and norms. Internet memes harness the collective power of users to define which signifiers and concepts are most apt to designate a particular normative concept. Collective usage also determines whether a meme becomes successful, i.e., widely used at a certain point in time, indicating the prevalence of the underlying assumptions. Of course, not only the question of which signifier encodes a meme is relevant but also how the schema is applied: individual exemplars of a meme define ideas, situations or behaviors in terms of the respective schema and may be widely shared as single artifacts. Online com-

---

Verfahren," in *Praktiken medialer Transformationen: Übersetzungen in und aus dem digitalen Raum*, eds. Johannes C.P. Schmid et al. (Bielefeld: transcript, 2018), 180.

[10] Wiggins, *The Discursive Power of Memes*, 13.

[11] Denisova, *Internet Memes and Society*, 40.

[12] See Stuart Hall, "The Rediscovery of 'Ideology': Return of the Oppressed in Media Studies," in *Culture, Media and Society*, eds. Michael Gurevitch et al. (London: Routledge, 1990), 64.

520 Internet Memes as 'Popular' Cultural Practices

munities decide whether they agree with the 'correct' schematic evaluation of a given situation in terms of a certain meme by means of interactive digital practices, such as up- or downvoting, by either sharing or ignoring the meme, or by commenting – the latter being a major source of metapragmatic knowledge transfer.[13]

Memes and Popular Culture

As a new medial form, internet memes are born of the affordances of participatory digital culture and enabled by the fact that myriads of users have access to editing software that lets them create and spread their own exemplars, which in turn propagate and consolidate the meme itself as a schema.

The origins of internet memes are often attributed to the message board *4chan*, infamous for transgressions of all kinds of boundaries set by mainstream society. Two aspects of *4chan*, in particular, help explain the phenomenon. First, posts are not archived but deleted automatically after a certain amount of time. Therefore, memes must be reproduced in order to remain traceable, which explains the prevalence of schemata over particular artifacts. Second, it is not possible to register individual accounts, so all posts are made under the username "anonymous" and no limits are placed on what can be posted. As Andrea Nagle explains, "[t]his culture of anonymity fostered an environment where users went to air their darkest thoughts."[14] The *4chan* mentality can certainly still be felt in many memes: medial artifacts posted online in any context are generally considered 'fair game' by users, especially when they are decontextualized and subsequently reframed as meme templates on meme-generator websites, for instance. A lack of knowledge of internet culture or attempts to criticize, fight or censor certain content are often met with incredibly harsh abuse.[15] Authorship remains opaque not just on *4chan*, but for memes in general – a meme is partly defined by the fact that countless users propagate the schema – providing safety in

---

[13] See Busch and Schmid, "Internet Memes as Digital Practices," 201.

[14] Nagle, *Kill All Normies*, 14.

[15] Ibid., 15.

numbers. In this way, memes can both circumvent censorship[16] and enable mob mentalities.[17]

As spreadable media, internet memes "challenge the commonplace assertion that, in the era of Web 2.0, user-generated content has somehow displaced mass media in the cultural lives of everyday people."[18] Instead, memes draw heavily on mass media content for inspiration and are part of audience engagement processes that accompany and follow any major cultural event. Internet memes generally draw on three types of audiovisual source material: popular fiction, current events and entertainment, as well as digital materials of all kinds, including private photographs and videos. The relationship between different memes and their respective source materials is multi-faceted. In some cases, the connection is largely arbitrary, casting the continuation of the meme as an inside joke among certain communities. Often, however, the selection of source materials is motivated by the recognition of familiar cultural symbols that are nevertheless semantically flexible enough to apply to many different contexts. Moreover, a humorous dissonance with their original contexts informs many memes. Consider again, for instance, the "Annoyed Picard" meme[19]: the ostensibly displayed behavior is decidedly uncharacteristic for the generally mild-mannered and thoughtful character Jean-Luc Picard, and the routinely included expletives are even more so. In order to understand and use the meme, however, knowledge of this dissonance is dispensable: the gesture speaks for itself and is, thus, instantly relatable. Being familiar with *Star Trek: The Next Generation* helps add an ironic twist, however. The fact that the scene the meme is based on shows Picard reciting Shakespearian sonnets rather than ranting at anyone may similarly be considered all but non-essential yet humorous trivia, fostering the inside joke.

[16] Denisova, *Internet Memes and Society*, 40.
[17] Nagle, *Kill All Normies*, 16.
[18] Jenkins et al., *Spreadable Media*, 15.
[19] Literally Media Ltd., "Annoyed Picard," *Know Your Meme*, August 1, 2012, knowyourmeme.com/memes/annoyed-picard.

522 Internet Memes as 'Popular' Cultural Practices

Becoming a Meme: People and Stock Characters

"Annoyed Picard" is an early example of a stock character, a type of meme that is generally materialized through *image macros*, which include writing at the top and bottom. Stock characters identify the displayed human or nonhuman animal as a particular character, ascribing a central trait to it.[20] Frequently, such internet memes are based on private individuals and spread without their consent, elevating the people in them to the level of popular icons.

An illustrative example is Oklahoma citizen Kimberley "Sweet Brown" Wilkins. Following a fire in her apartment complex in 2012, Brown gave an interview to a local television station during which she uttered several memorable statements, including: "I got bronchitis. Ain't nobody got time for that."[21] The video clip of the interview went viral, making Wilkins an internet star overnight and causing the original interview to be remixed or single lines to be extracted from it as images or animated gifs. "Ain't Nobody Got Time for That" became a meme through which users communicated all the issues and problems that 'nobody got time for' – a sentiment that resonated with people around the globe (see fig. 2). Wilkins shares her sudden fame with other black eyewitness interviewees who have similarly gone viral for unwittingly performing a racist and classist stereotype that has been labeled "the hilarious black neighbor."[22] While criticizing Wilkins's exploitation in mainstream culture, though, black commentators have also lauded her authentic expression of vernacular in public since she defies the conventional expectation of code-switching when speaking to white audiences.[23] As this example demonstrates, spread among different

---

[20] Busch and Schmid, "Internet Memes as Digital Practices," 189.

[21] KFOR Oklahoma's News 4, "Sweet Brown on Apartment Fire: 'Ain't Nobody Got Time for That!,'" YouTube, April 11, 2012, www.youtube.com/watch?v=ydmPh4MXT3g.

[22] Aisha Harris, "The Troubling Viral Trend of the 'Hilarious' Black Neighbor," *SLATE*, May 7, 2013, slate.com/culture/2013/05/charles-ramsey-amanda-berry-rescuer-becomes-internet-meme-video.html.

[23] Charles E. William II, "I am Charles Ramsay and Sweet Brown: 'You Do What You Have To Do' and 'Ain't Nobody Got Time for Dat,'"*HuffPost*, October 5, 2013, huffpost.com/entry/i-am-charles-ramsey-and-s_b_ 3248502.

contexts of usage, popular memes may include aspects that are usually irreconcilable.

Fig. 2: "Ain't Nobody Got Time for That" (*Askideas*).

As a viral video, "Ain't Nobody Got Time for That" without question draws on and perpetuates a racist stereotype; as a meme, however, it ultimately becomes a marker for the widely relatable sentiment of not being willing to devote time to a particular nuisance. Here, Wilkins's reaction, in its perceived authenticity, is isolated as an ultimately human sentiment that transcends social groups. For Wilkins, the meme led to participation in traditional mass culture entertainment formats, such as a 2014 cameo on a *Jimmy Kimmel Live* sketch in which she was played by Queen Latifah. "Ain't Nobody Got Time for That" also inspired a segment of *The Daily Show* in which several minor news stories were combined. Wilkins started businesses, appeared in advertisements and was quoted by superstar Beyoncé in an interview following her 2013

524   Internet Memes as 'Popular' Cultural Practices

Super Bowl half-time show performance.[24] Beyoncé's performance, however, led to a meme of its own.

Following the half-time show, video stills from the singer's performance posted by the website *Buzzfeed*[25] showed Beyoncé scowling and flexing her muscles in a hulking bodily display. Interest in the pictures was only heightened when Beyoncé's manager allegedly requested that they be removed, as *Buzzfeed* reported in a piece titled "The 'Unflattering' Photos Beyoncé's Publicist Doesn't Want You To See."[26] The image thus sparked the "Unflattering Beyoncé" meme, and her photographic likeness was photoshopped to, for instance, appear as a green "She-Hulk" or replace Muhammed Ali in the iconic Sonny Liston knockout photograph.[27] It should be noted that the schematic practice is reversed in cases such as these, and the cropped figure of Beyoncé becomes a stable filler that is added to other pictorial environments. "Unflattering Beyoncé" became part of a postmodern digital pastiche culture that revels in the joy and excitement received from an unusual spectacle and its recontextualization into fitting scenarios, performing a joke by finding coherence among disparate elements.

This case clearly shows the ideological foundations of internet memes: generally, the unifying aspect required to motivate the multitude of users to create a meme involves the deviation of a cultural norm and/or its reduction to an essential sentiment that is readily relatable. In the case of "Unflattering Beyoncé," the meme both punishes the deviation from a normatively female bodily performance and illustrates the unspoken rule of the internet that free speech trumps everything else. Celebrity memes are also characterized by the fact that ordinary people embrace the collective power to destabilize a rich and famous person's

---

[24]   Greatviralvideo, "Beyoncé Quotes Miss Sweet Brown: 'Lord Jesus It's a Fire,'" YouTube, February 7, 2013, www.youtube.com/watch?v=TmFFa GdxTFg.

[25]   Lauren Yapalater, "The 33 Fiercest Moments from Beyoncé's Half-Time Show," *BuzzFeed*, February 4, 2013, buzzfeed.com/lyapalater/the-fiercest-moments-from-beyonces-halftime-show.

[26]   Buzzfeedceleb, "The 'Unflattering' Photos Beyoncé's Publicist Doesn't Want You to See," *BuzzFeed*, February 5, 2013, buzzfeed.com/buzzfeed celeb/the-unflattering-photos-beyonces-publicist-doesnt-want-you-t.

[27]   Literally Media Ltd., "Unflattering Beyonce," *Know Your Meme*, February 19, 2020, knowyourmeme.com/memes/unflattering-beyonce.

carefully curated public image. Assuming a mob mentality and thriving on *schadenfreude*, the online public employs the meme to publicly ridicule and achieve comeuppance against the celebrities they otherwise aggrandize – a tendency that is, of course, eagerly exploited by media outlets like *Buzzfeed*. However, sadly, but not surprisingly, such dynamics do not only involve celebrities but amount to cyberbullying of private citizens as well. Take the author and motivational speaker Lizzie Velasquez, for example, who suffers from a rare congenital disease and was subjected to sexist and ableist abuse after being labeled "the ugliest woman in the world."[28]

In political discourse especially, pundits, journalists and influencers routinely seek to turn actors from the opposing side, including private citizens, into memes. For instance, another deliberately unfavorable video still of an unnamed, agitated woman with short hair and glasses has been spread as "Triggered Feminist."[29] The still is taken from a clip showing a confrontation between Trump supporters and anti-Trump protestors that was originally posted on YouTube by far-right radio show host Alex Jones. Right-wing users employ the meme to ascribe behaviors and statements to a character they deem ridiculous or hypocritical, using concepts such as "being triggered" or the line "did you just assume my gender?" They project all of the worst qualities they ascribe to their political opponents onto a tangible character represented by the recording of an actual protestor, reducing an individual to a caricature. Turning a private citizen into a stock character serves to define and delegitimatize the opposition. At the same time, the fact that certain statements or actions are ascribed to a character represented by an actual person creates a sense of faux authenticity that hand-drawn caricatures, for instance, do not.

In the online culture wars of recent years,[30] politics and popular culture frequently refer back to each other. When Disney released *Captain Marvel*, the first female-led film to take place in the Marvel Cinematic Universe, in 2019, a misogynistic backlash followed – as is common with cultural products that stem from formerly male-centered

---

[28] Lizzie Velasquez (@Littlelizziev), Instagram, December 11, 2016, https://www.instagram.com/p/BN3pwsGh2Wj/.

[29] Literally Media Ltd., "Triggered Feminist," *Know Your Meme*, February 19, 2020, knowyourmeme.com/memes/triggered-feminist--2.

[30] For a more substantial discussion, see Nagle, *Kill All Normies*.

526   Internet Memes as 'Popular' Cultural Practices

geek cultures.[31] In March 2019, Donald Trump Jr. – son of the President of the United States, and a self-declared "General in the Meme Wars"[32] – posted an image to his Twitter account showing a mashup of the "Triggered Feminist" character's face photoshopped onto the body of Captain Marvel, a character played by Brie Larson, with the caption "Captain Triggered."[33] Of course, the movie and its surrounding discourses do not involve the concept of "being triggered" in any way. The meme, however, allows right-wing pundits to spin the conversation by forcing a schema they have established, quite literally, on top of it.

Although often presented as a harmless joke, as Trump Jr.'s comment "let's have some fun with pictures here" implies, the internet meme, in this case, serves as a tool for political spin. As was suggested earlier, internet memes constitute frames that can be applied to different scenarios; in doing so, said scenario is presented in terms of "a central organizing idea for making sense of relevant events and suggesting what is at issue,"[34] including and highlighting some aspects while excluding and obscuring others.[35] In this case, the film's feminist aspirations are presented as its defining issue, which is simultaneously ridiculed. Hence, the meme effectively reframes *Captain Marvel* as an exercise in what is implied to be "pointless feminist outrage." That such frames are subject to change, however, is exemplified by "Idiot Nerd Girl,"[36] a stock character initially used to ridicule girls as inauthentic non-

[31]   Nate Jones, "*Captain Marvel* Is a Groundbreaker for the MCU, and Also Not a Great Movie, Which Matters More?," *Vulture*, March 8, 2019, www.vulture.com/2019/03/captain-marvel-backlash.html; Nagle, *Kill All Normies*, 24.

[32]   Donald Trump Jr. (@donaldtrumpjr), Instagram, February 19, 2020, instagram.com/donaldjtrumpjr/.

[33]   Donald Trump Jr. (@donaldtrumpjr), Twitter, March 14, 2019, https://twitter.com/DonaldJTrumpJr/status/1106023332472713218.

[34]   William Gamson, "News as Framing," *American Behavioral Scientist* 33, no. 2 (1989): 157.

[35]   See, for instance, Robert Entman, "Framing: Toward Clarification of a Fractured Paradigm," *Journal of Communication* 43, no. 4 (1993).

[36]   Literally Media Ltd., "Idiot Nerd Girl," *Know Your Meme*, February 19, 2020, knowyourmeme.com/memes/idiot-nerd-girl.

members of geek cultures, but which was later re-appropriated to criticize precisely that dynamic.[37]

Character Constellations and Debates

A more recent development of stock characters involves memes that display not only one character, but several, and which derive their meaning from their displayed interactions. In a technique referred to as "object labeling,"[38] various displayed elements are assigned particular roles by either adding written labels or photoshopping other images on top of them. The relation between the displayed characters and objects is metaphorically transferred to those between other referenced entities. Memetic potential is thus realized in a default relation among these different elements, which is why I shall refer to them as character constellation memes. A prime example of this type can be found in the "Distracted Boyfriend" meme, which is based on a 2015 stock photograph by Spanish photographer Antonio Guillem titled "Disloyal man with his girlfriend looking at another girl."[39] The man in the photo purses his lips while turning his head toward a blurred woman walking by, while "his girlfriend" stares at him in apparent outrage. The meme, which emerged in 2017, presents the display as a conflict of interest between an element one ought to be interested in and a morally less-suitable option that distracts from it (see fig. 3). Examples include "me" looking at "solar eclipse" while "scientific evidence supporting the dangers of staring at the sun" stares in disbelief,[40] or Donald Trump's

---

[37] Esther Zuckerman, "Taking Back a Meme: Idiot Nerd Girl," *The Atlantic*, September 10, 2012, theatlantic.com/national/archive/2012/09/taking-back-meme-idiot-nerd-girl/323790/.

[38] Literally Media Ltd., "Object Labeling," *Know Your Meme*, February 19, 2020, knowyourmeme.com/memes/object-labeling.

[39] Antonio Guillem, "Disloyal Man with His Girlfriend Looking at Another Girl Stock Photo," iStockPhoto, November 2, 2015, shutterstock.com/de/image-photo/disloyal-man-walking-his-girlfriend-looking-297886754.

[40] Literally Media Ltd., "Distracted Boyfriend," *Know Your Meme*, February 19, 2020.

photoshopped head looking at "Twitter" while "Acting like a normal President" stares in disbelief.[41]

Fig. 3: "Distracted Boyfriend" (@penguinrandom).

Similar versions of this character constellation have circulated as well, albeit to a lesser extent. These include a woman looking at another man, or a man at a beach wedding looking at another man in a swimsuit emerging from the water.[42] Likewise, historic predecessors have been identified, such as a scene from the 1922 Charlie Chaplin movie *Pay Day* that features a similar display.[43] This all goes to show that internet memes draw on established pictorial conventions and traditions of how we visually conceptualize a conflict of interest. Likewise, it demonstrates that, to the majority of internet users, such heteronormatively gendered performance remains a highly familiar icon with which to signify a conflict of interest. Indeed, the meme has sparked a discussion

---

[41] Ibid.
[42] Ibid.
[43] Tom Gerken, "Charlie Chaplin: The Original Distracted Boyfriend," *BBC*, June 12, 2018, bbc.com/news/blogs-trending-44451519.

on whether it is discriminatory, and a Swedish advertisement watchdog deemed a recruitment ad based on the meme sexist.[44]

The question of whether the meme is sexist, however, is a complex one. On the one hand, the photo's portrayal of gender relations is so comically overdone that it appears intrinsically ironic instead of authentic, which may well be the reason why it is used for self-deprecating jokes. More importantly, the meme is not about the three displayed characters but about the schema referenced by their constellation. On the other hand, the fact remains that stereotypically gendered behavior provides the schema's conceptual backdrop. At the very least, "Distracted Boyfriend" perpetuates stereotypical gender roles, regardless of whether one reads the meme as ironic or not.

The concise format of internet memes allows for only very limited scope in terms of the information presented; a meme usually makes a single point, or it frames a single issue in terms of the presented scenario. A deviation from this norm that stretches the limits of complexity a meme can take on is the so-called "American Chopper Argument." [45] Based on a scene from a 2008 episode of the reality television series *American Chopper*, the meme, popularized in 2018, consists of a vertical sequence of five pictures that display the escalation of an argument in which the two main characters, Paul Teutul Sr. and his son Paul Teutul Jr., shout at each other. As in a photo comic, the first three images alternate between the two men, while the fourth picture shows Teutul Sr. throwing a chair at his son, and the fifth and final image shows Teutul Sr. standing in a doorway, shouting and pointing his finger (see fig. 4). As an argument meme, it follows a logic of "proposition, rebuttal, reaffirmation, second rebuttal, and a final statement," writes columnist Matthew Yglesias, lauding the meme as a modern incarnation of "Socratic dialogue."[46]

---

[44] Jon Henley, "Distracted Boyfriend Meme Is Sexist, Rules Swedish Ad Watchdog," *The Guardian*, September 26, 2018, theguardian.com/world/2018/sep/26/distracted-boyfriend-meme-sexist-swedish-advertising.

[45] Literally Media Ltd., "American Chopper Argument," *Know Your Meme*, February 19, 2020,
knowyourmeme.com/memes/american-chopper-argument.

[46] Matthew Yglesias, "The American Chopper Meme, Explained," *Vox*, April 10, 2018, vox.com/2018/4/10/17207588/american-chopper-meme.

530 Internet Memes as 'Popular' Cultural Practices

Fig. 4: "American Chopper Argument" (@besttrousers).

The base material for the meme is characterized by stereotypical male rage and working-class masculinity, which also informs the television show it is taken from. However, it is not so much *American Chopper* but a more general working-class male rage that is presented as the most recognizable marker of dispute. Moreover, "American Chopper Argument" is largely informed by irony: many particularly successful incarnations of the meme revolve around arguments not generally associated with shouting and chair-throwing, such as (fan-)culture debates concerning the morality of *Garfield*[47] or an alleged plot hole in *Lord of the Rings*,[48] but also more serious subjects as the gender pay gap (see fig. 4), and even academic debates.[49] The ethnography meme site Deathnography uses the meme to address fundamental problems of orientalism in foundational texts of anthropology and includes a Works Cited section in the accompanying Facebook post.[50]

Addressing questions of representation, Yglesias argues that the Teutuls, as "the perfect Trump-era Republicans – a couple of lowbrow regular guys who happen to be incredibly rich business owners," constitute an antithesis to the "young, debt-burdened recent college graduates" who delight in the meme.[51] Indeed, Paul Teutul Sr. endorsed Donald J. Trump during his presidential bid,[52] and reality television personas certainly deserve less consideration concerning the protection of their privacy – a writer for the website *Vice* even speculated about "a guerilla marketing scheme to revive awareness about *American*

---

[47] @garfieldfanart, Twitter, March 22, 2018, https://twitter.com/GarfieldFanArt/status/976884083933499398.

[48] "The 'American Chopper' Meme's Criticism of a 'Lord of the Rings' Plot Hole Is Perfect," *Relevant Magazine*, April 4, 2018, relevantmagazine.com/culture/american-chopper-memes-criticism-lord-rings-plot-hole-perfect/.

[49] Literally Media Ltd., "American Chopper Argument."

[50] Deathnography, Facebook, March 29, 2019, https://www.facebook.com/deathnography/photos/a.1450183618356657/1943632222345125/?type=3&theater.

[51] Yglesias, "The American Chopper Meme."

[52] Luke Barr, "'American Chopper' Star Endorses Trump," *The Hill*, February 22, 2016, thehill.com/blogs/in-the-know/in-the-know/270278-american-chopper-star-endorses-trump.

532 Internet Memes as 'Popular' Cultural Practices

Chopper."[53] However, one must not make the mistake of confusing the reality television stars of *American Chopper* with the stock characters of the "American Chopper Argument": knowledge of neither the series nor the Trump endorsement is required to laugh at the display of men who look like the Teutuls citing Edward Said.

In the same way that "Distracted Boyfriend" takes a familiar heterosexist cliché as the marker for the base formula of a relatable moral conflict, "American Chopper Argument" takes a classist cliché of male rage as the marker for a rhetorical "exchange of blows." The question of whether the Teutuls signify "uneducated but rich business-men" or simply "white trash" cannot be universally resolved. Indeed, as with many products of popular culture, the success of such memes must be ascribed to the fact that they allow for the coexistence of various, and especially ironic, readings and usages informed by disparate states of knowledge and emotional and political investments. The defining aspect of highly popular memes such as these is the fact that they co-opt widely shared cultural symbols and turn them into readily replicable formulas.

Conclusion

Internet memes remain an ambivalent phenomenon: they are exemplary of the internet's anarchic tendency to push back against the curated narratives circulated by corporate media outlets; however, they are also indicative of its inability and/or unwillingness to safeguard the rights of individuals. The very fact that formulaic repetition defines a meme is also the reason why they are relevant as instances of popular culture. They are symptomatic of ideas, ideologies and symbols that connect internet users worldwide. Therefore, they spark creative commentary or parodies of the medial events of the hour, but they also enable cyber-bullying and political spin under the guise of humor. While the participation of celebrities, influencers and other mass cultural actors with large online followings certainly propagates the spread of a meme to a higher degree, for better or worse, the number of participating users

---

[53] Peter Slattery, "This Angry 'American Chopper' Meme Is Our New Favorite Meme," *Vice*, March 28, 2018, vice.com/en/article/ywxwdy/this-angry-american-chopper-meme-is-our-new-favorite-meme.

remains the element most crucial for its spread. Popular taste is, therefore, the hallmark of an internet meme. As this discussion has exemplified, successful memes routinely trade in racist, sexist and classist stereotypes as cultural symbols. However, these symbols are often employed ironically, which provides the potential to subvert such stereotypes as well.

As John Fiske argued of pre-digital mass culture icons such as jeans,[54] internet memes are polysemous and contradictory and lend themselves to both the resistance to dominant ideologies as well as to their affirmation. Memes allow users to become part of social trends in order to define themselves against a perceived cultural mainstream, and yet they also allow for visibility in the dominant digital culture. The "semiotic richness of jeans means that they cannot have a single defined meaning, but they are a resource bank of potential meanings," writes Fiske.[55] As emblems of popular culture, internet memes take this quality even one step further: the semiotic richness of the base material becomes merely the entry point from which to formulate a schema that, in itself, enables the generation of all kinds of meaning based on a shared concept. Hence, internet memes are characterized by a balancing act between semantic flexibility – allowing for ironic usages in particular – and familiar cultural symbols as well as relatable, seemingly universal notions that strike a chord with popular audiences.

---

[54] John Fiske, *Understanding Popular Culture* (London: Routledge, 1994), 5.
[55] Ibid.

534 Internet Memes as 'Popular' Cultural Practices

Works Cited

@besttrousers. Twitter, April 4, 2018. twitter.com/besttrousers/status/981643328394612736?s=20&t=lYstc2NfSD6joGtTdj4ijg.

@garfieldfanart. Twitter, March 22, 2018. twitter.com/GarfieldFanArt/status/976884083933499398.

@penguinrandom. Twitter, August 29, 2017. twitter.com/penguinrandom/status/902624800442646528.

Barr, Luke. "'American Chopper' Star Endorses Trump." *The Hill*, February 22, 2016. thehill.com/blogs/in-the-know/in-the-know/270278-american-chopper-star-endorses-trump.

Busch, Florian, and Johannes C. P. Schmid. "Internet Memes as Digital Practices: Stock Characters Macros in Multimodal Structure, Function, and Metapragmatic Reflexivity." In *Language, Media and Technologies: Usages, Forms and Functions*, edited by Lozzi Martial Meutem Kamtchueng and Camilla Arundie Tabe, 186–206. Munich: LINCOM, 2019.

Buzzfeedceleb. "The 'Unflattering' Photos Beyoncé's Publicist Doesn't Want You to See." *BuzzFeed*, February 5, 2013. buzzfeed.com/buzzfeedceleb/the-unflattering-photos-beyonces-publicist-doesnt-want-you-t.

Dawkins, Richard. *The Selfish Gene*. Oxford: Oxford University Press, 2006.

Deathnography. Facebook, March 29, 2018. www.facebook.com/deathnography/photos/a.1450183618356657/1943632222345125/?type=3&theater.

Denisova, Anastasia. *Internet Memes and Society: Social, Cultural, and Political Contexts*. New York: Routledge, 2019.

Entman, Robert. "Framing: Toward Clarification of A Fractured Paradigm." *Journal of Communication* 43, no. 4 (1993): 51–58.

"Feeling Sick Ain't Nobody Got Time for That." *Askideas*, April 21, 2016, https://www.askideas.com/feeling-sick-aint-nobody-got-time-for-that-funny-memes-about-being-sick-picture/.

Fiske, John. *Understanding Popular Culture*. London: Routledge, 1994.

Gamson, William. "News as Framing." *American Behavioral Scientist* 33, no. 2 (1989): 157–161.

Gerken, Tom. "Charlie Chaplin: The Original Distracted Boyfriend." *BBC*, June 12, 2018. bbc.com/news/blogs-trending-44451519.

Greatviralvideo. "Beyoncé Quotes Miss Sweet Brown: 'Lord Jesus It's a Fire.'" YouTube, February 7, 2013. www.youtube.com/watch?v=TmFFaGdxTFg.

Guillem, Antonio. "Disloyal Man with His Girlfriend Looking at Another Girl Stock Photo." iStockPhoto, November 2, 2015. shutterstock.com/de/image-photo/disloyal-man-walking-his-girlfriend-looking-297886754.

KFOR Oklahoma's News 4. "Sweet Brown on Apartment Fire: 'Ain't Nobody Got Time for That!'" YouTube, April 11, 2012. www.youtube.com/watch?v=ydmPh4MXT3g.

Hall, Stuart. "The Rediscovery of 'Ideology': Return of the Oppressed in Media Studies." In *Culture, Media and Society*, edited by Michael Gurevitch et al., 52–86. London: Routledge, 1990.

Harris, Aisha. "The Troubling Viral Trend of the 'Hilarious' Black Neighbor." *SLATE*, May 7, 2013. slate.com/culture/2013/05/charles-ramsey-amanda-berry-rescuer-becomes-internet-meme-video.html.

Henley, Jon. "Distracted Boyfriend Meme Is Sexist, Rules Swedish Ad Watchdog." *The Guardian*, September 26, 2018. theguardian.com/world/2018/sep/26/distracted-boyfriend-meme-sexist-swedish-advertising.

Jenkins, Henry, et al. *Spreadable Media: Creating Value and Meaning in a Networked Culture*. New York: New York University Press, 2013.

Jones, Nate. "Captain Marvel Is a Groundbreaker for the MCU, and Also Not a Great Movie, Which Matters More?" *Vulture*, March 8, 2019. vulture.com/2019/03/captain-marvel-backlash.html.

Literally Media Ltd. "American Chopper Argument." *Know Your Meme*, March 28, 2018. knowyourmeme.com/memes/american-chopper-argument.

---. "Annoyed Picard." *Know Your Meme*, August 1, 2012. knowyourmeme.com/memes/annoyed-picard.

---. "Distracted Boyfriend." *Know Your Meme*, August 22, 2017. knowyourmeme.com/memes/distracted-boyfriend.

---. "Idiot Nerd Girl." *Know Your Meme*, June 9, 2010. knowyourmeme.com/memes/idiot-nerd-girl.

---. "Object Labeling." *Know Your Meme*, January 24, 2018. knowyourmeme.com/memes/object-labeling.

---. "Triggered Feminist." *Know Your Meme*, March 14, 2019. knowyourmeme.com/memes/triggered-feminist--2.

---. "Unflattering Beyonce." *Know Your Meme*, February 7, 2013. knowyourmeme.com/memes/unflattering-beyonce.

Nagle, Andrea. *Kill All Normies: Online Culture Wars from 4Chan and Tumblr to Trump and the Alt-Right*. Winchester: Zero Books, 2017.

Shifman, Limor. *Memes in Digital Culture*. Cambridge, MA: MIT Press, 2014.

Slattery, Peter. "This Angry 'American Chopper' Meme Is Our New Favorite Meme." *Vice.com*, 28 Mar. 2018, vice.com/en/article/ywxwdy/this-angry-american-chopper-meme-is-our-new-favorite-meme. Accessed 28 Jan. 2022.

Tetzlaff, Stefan. "Memes und Frames: Zur Markiertheit als semiotischem Verfahren." *Praktiken medialer Transformationen: Übersetzungen in und aus dem digitalen Raum*. eds. Johannes C.P. Schmid et al. Bielefeld: transcript, 2018.

"The 'American Chopper' Meme's Criticism of a 'Lord of the Rings' Plot Hole Is Perfect." *Relevant Magazine*, April 4, 2018. relevantmagazine.com/culture/american-chopper-memes-criticism-lord-rings-plot-hole-perfect/.

Trump, Donald, Jr. (@donaldjtrumpjr). Instagram, February 19, 2020. instagram.com/donaldjtrumpjr/.

---. Twitter, March 14, 2019. twitter.com/DonaldJTrumpJr/status/1106023332472713218.

Yapalater, Lauren. "The 33 Fiercest Moments from Beyoncé's Half-Time Show." *BuzzFeed*, February 4, 2013. buzzfeed.com/lyapalater/the-fiercest-moments-from-beyonces-halftime-show.

Yglesias, Matthew. "The American Chopper Meme, Explained." *Vox*, April 10, 2018. vox.com/2018/4/10/17207588/american-chopper-meme.

Velasquez, Lizzie (@Littlelizziev). Instagram, December 11, 2016. https://www.instagram.com/p/BN3pwsGh2Wj/.

Wiggins, Bradley E. *The Discursive Power of Memes in Digital Culture: Ideologies, Semiotics, and Intertextuality*. New York: Routledge, 2019.

William II, Charles E. "I am Charles Ramsay and Sweet Brown: 'You Do What You Have To Do' and 'Ain't Nobody Got Time for Dat.'" *HuffPost*, October 5, 2013. huffpost.com/entry/i-am-charles-ramsey-and-s_b_3248502.

Zuckerman, Esther. "Taking Back A Meme: Idiot Nerd Girl." *The Atlantic*, September 10, 2012.
theatlantic.com/national/archive/2012/09/taking-back-meme-idiot-nerd-girl/323790/.

GUNTER SÜß

In Praise of Short Forms: Teaching American Cultural Studies with Music Videos by African American Artists

Music videos as a genre have some advantages that make them ideal objects of study in the Cultural Studies classroom. First, their short duration means that they can be screened in class in five minutes, providing students with immediate input. Second, they are highly condensed with music, visuals, and lyrics compressed into a usually overdetermined text full of intertextual references to the history of (popular) culture. In analyzing music videos, students acquire knowledge of cinematography, editing, and sound-image relations. Third, music videos usually demonstrate an awareness of their own media history and their respective media ecology, which makes them self-reflexive and self-observing entities. Fourth, students often have prior knowledge of most contemporary music videos and actually like them, creating intrinsic motivation. Fifth, music videos 'have never been more dead,'[1] meaning that they have found a new place in the present media system on Vevo and YouTube. Music videos had been pronounced dead with the decline of the music channels MTV, VH1, and (in Germany) Viva, and the decline of the music industry at large.[2]

---

[1]   For a discussion of the supposed (non-)death of music videos see Kirsty Fairclough and Daniel Cookney, "The Music Video Is a Zombie," *The Conversation,* October 17, 2017, theconversation.com/the-music-video-is-a-zombie-it-may-look-dead-but-its-just-been-re-animated-85493.

[2]   Eckart Voigts lists twelve reasons why "pop music video continues to be a viable and even necessary element in syllabi." Eckart Voigts, "Pop Music, Video and Gender," in *Cultural Studies in the EFL Classroom*, eds. Werner Delanoy and Laurenz Volkmann (Heidelberg: Universitätsverlag Winter, 2006), 381–382.

540 In Praise of Short Forms

Yet in the last few years, some extraordinary music videos have been produced – most of them by African American artists. I want to argue that they are invaluable primary texts in the Cultural Studies classroom for the reasons above. Furthermore, they can serve as starting points for in-class discussions, group projects, or term papers about the media and cultural history of African Americans and their relationship to mainstream American culture. In this paper, I will analyze JAY-Z's videos for "The Story of O.J." and "Moonlight." In order to provide necessary context and contrasting material, I will also have a look at Beyoncé's visual album *Lemonade* (in particular, the singles "Formation" and "Sorry" from that album) and "Apeshit" by The Carters, which is the name JAY-Z and Beyoncé use when performing together.

I will argue that JAY-Z as well as Beyoncé provide powerful analyses of systemic racism in the United States. Their videos are aesthetically complex and full of intertextual references to the history of popular culture as well as the history of African Americans in the U.S. They also provide narratives of female empowerment and male redemption. These are, however, rooted in an individualized neoliberal ideology, which does not take into account systemic discrimination based on gender and class and ultimately forfeits any intersectional thinking and solidarity. Moreover, the narratives actively take part in the neoliberal project and in "postfeminism" as its "powerful legitimizing agent."[3]

Family Business

Individually, Beyoncé and JAY-Z are among the most popular and highest-grossing African American artists of our time. JAY-Z grew up as Shawn Corey Carter in rather poor circumstances in Brooklyn, New York. His father abandoned the family when he was young. As a teenager, he sold crack[4] before launching a career as a rapper and businessman. He was Chief Executive Officer of Def Jam Recordings, founded his own clothing line, Rocawear (sold in 2007), and his own

---

[3] Laura Martínez-Jiménez et al., "Neoliberalism Goes Pop and Purple: Postfeminist Empowerment from Beyoncé to Mad Max," *Journal of Popular Culture* 51 (2018): 405.

[4] JAY-Z, *Decoded* (New York: Random House, 2010), 15–16.

entertainment company, Roc Nation. Furthermore, he co-owns the streaming service Tidal, which brands itself as an artist-owned company, and several luxury firms (D'Ussé Cognac and Armand de Brignac Champagne) as well as an art collection worth about 70 million dollars.[5] According to Zack O'Malley Greenburg in *Forbes* magazine, JAY-Z is the first hip-hop artist to become a billionaire.[6]

Beyoncé (Beyoncé Giselle Knowles-Carter) grew up in Houston, Texas, and made her breakthrough as an artist with the R&B girl band Destiny's Child in the late 1990s. In 2002, Beyoncé started a solo career, and she has published seven studio albums so far, all of which went to number one in the Billboard 200 album charts.

In 2008, Beyoncé married JAY-Z, with whom she had already collaborated in 2003 on "03 Bonnie & Clyde." Beyoncé is often regarded as the more successful artist of the couple, a fact which is reflected in the usage of the expression "Beyoncé and her husband" when talking about the pair. They have been on the front pages of the yellow press and in the gossip columns for much of their marriage, especially after rumors of JAY-Z's infidelity surfaced. One incident that particularly fueled public interest was the night of the Met gala in 2014, when an elevator surveillance camera filmed what appeared to be Solange Knowles, Beyoncé's sister, attacking JAY-Z. While Solange can be seen kicking and screaming at JAY-Z, Beyoncé remained motionless for most of the video. JAY-Z didn't fight back.

While critics may oppose an incorporation of these 'private' issues in analyses of the music videos, I will show in the following that they are an integral and inseparable part of the discourses and practices that form the cultural 'formation' under discussion, and – especially in economic contexts – the respective brand images.

Lemonade and "Sorry"

On April 23, 2016, Beyoncé released her 'visual album' *Lemonade* on the streaming platform Tidal, which she co-owns. What made the album

---

[5] See Zack O'Malley Greenburg, "Artist, Icon, Billionaire: How Jay-Z Created His $1 Billion Fortune," *Forbes*, June 3, 2019, forbes.com/sites/zackomalleygreenburg/2019/06/03/jay-z-billionaire-worth/.

[6] Ibid.

542   In Praise of Short Forms

'visual' was the accompanying movie of the same title, which also premiered on April 23, 2016 on HBO and contains the music videos to individual songs, but also additional material such as poems by Warsan Shire and excerpts from Malcolm X's speech "Who Taught You to Hate Yourself." *Lemonade* is a multilayered and aesthetically rich multimodal work of art which can be used in the Cultural Studies classroom to address questions of gender and ethnicity alongside representations of the American South. It has been called "a visually stunning homage to Julie Dash's masterpiece, *Daughters of the Dust*,"[7] and a juxtaposition of these two texts will repay the didactic effort.

The first single on the album, "Formation," had already been released on February 6, 2016, with Beyoncé performing the day after in the Super Bowl 50 halftime show with Bruno Mars. The performance spawned a controversy as Beyoncé's dancers wore berets and afros reminiscent of the Black Panthers.[8] The song is an examination of Beyoncé's own black heritage and an affirmation of blackness as being self-empowering:

> My daddy Alabama, momma Louisiana
> You mix that negro with that Creole, make a Texas bama
> I like my baby heir with baby hair and afros
> I like my negro nose with Jackson Five nostrils[9]

Furthermore, Beyoncé asserts her autonomy in a sexual context as well by reversing traditional gender roles. When the man satisfies Bey's sexual appetite, she will buy him something nice and take him out to a seafood restaurant:

> When he fuck me good, I take his ass to Red Lobster, 'cause I slay
> When he fuck me good, I take his ass to Red Lobster, we gon slay
> If he hit it right, I might take him on a flight on my chopper, I slay

---

[7] Oneka Labennett, "'Beyoncé and Her Husband': Representing Infidelity and Kinship in a Black Marriage," *differences: A Journal of Feminist Cultural Studies* 29, no. 2 (2018): 166.

[8] In the week after, *Saturday Night Live* ran a three-and-a-half-minute clip taking on the controversy and claiming ironically, "It's the day white people never saw coming: when Beyoncé turned black." The video is available on YouTube: www.youtube.com/watch?v=ociMBfkDG1w

[9] Beyoncé, "Formation," track 12 on *Lemonade* (Columbia Records, 2016).

GUNTER SÜß 543

Drop him off at the mall, let him buy some J's, let him shop up, 'cause I slay[10]

These lines show the central conflicts and contradictions in much of Beyoncé's work. Sarah Olutola states:

[H]er claims that '[i]f he hit it right, I might take him on a flight on my chopper, 'cause I slay' sells a kind of black female power fantasy couched in the kind of materialism that most of her black female fans will never achieve even as they are taught by a continuing formative neoliberal culture to emotionally invest in the fantasy.[11]

Conversely, the economic and material hardships faced by most of her black female fans are intangible, even unimaginable, for "Queen Bey," the brand and artist. Moreover, in discourses like the one in "Formation" and other songs on *Lemonade*, Beyoncé shows and praises exactly the characteristics of what Martínez-Jiménez et al. call the "post-feminist individual – active, free to choose and capable of reinventing herself."[12]

The discussion as to whether Beyoncé can and should be called a feminist has become very heated indeed. While she herself has appropriated the term at least since her performance in front of a feminist sign at the MTV Music Video Awards in 2014 and through the incorporation of the work of Chimamanda Ngozi Adichie, black feminist activist bell hooks called her a "terrorist especially in terms of the impact on young girls"[13] in a New School discussion in 2014. *Lemonade* was no different in this regard. The editors of *The Lemonade Reader*, Kinitra Brooks and Kameeiah Martin, read hooks's criticism of *Lemonade*[14] "to be symptomatic of a second-wave feminism that is unable to account for those women that employ their sexuality as power,

---

[10] Ibid.
[11] Sarah Olutola, "I Ain't Sorry: Beyoncé, Serena, and Hegemonic Hierarchies in Lemonade," *Popular Music and Society* 42 (2019): 104.
[12] Martínez-Jiménez et al., "Neoliberalism Goes Pop and Purple," 405.
[13] Hillary Crosley Coker, "What bell hooks Really Means When She Calls Beyoncé a 'Terrorist,'" *Jezebel*, May 9, 2014, jezebel.com/what-bell-hooks-really-means-when-she-calls-beyonce-a-t-1573991834.
[14] bell hooks, "Moving Beyond Pain," bellhooksinstitute, May 9, 2016.

particularly in high femme performance."[15] I read *Lemonade* as an example of postfeminism, as it shares what Martínez-Jiménez et al. define as one of its key features: It "integrates and celebrates certain feminist claims while nonchalantly coexisting with all kinds of inequalities, including, above all, gender inequalities."[16] Systemic concerns (in Beyoncé's case especially with regard to class) make way for individual opportunities and free choices that, in a neo-liberal culture, not many can afford.

The second single on *Lemonade* was "Sorry," a very personal coming to terms with JAY-Z's infidelity and, more generally, a discussion of female-male relationships in the black community. The song begins with a musical clock and spoken words:

> So what are you going to say at my funeral now that you killed me?
> Here lies the body of the love of my life whose heart I broke
> Without a gun to my head
> Here lies the mother of my children, both living and dead [...][17]

A reckless, irresponsible male has metaphorically killed the protagonist of the lyrics, who is the mother of living and dead children (a reference to Beyoncé's miscarriages). When the song begins, Beyoncé exclaims that she is not sorry and some lines later: "Suck on my balls, pause, I had enough (Sorry, I ain't sorry), I ain't thinking 'bout you."

> Looking at my watch, he shoulda been home
> Today, I regret the night I put that ring on
> He always got them fucking excuses
> I pray to the Lord you reveal what his truth is[18]

In these and other lines, Beyoncé refers publicly to the infidelity that JAY-Z later conceded to. Furthermore, she sings: "He only want me when I'm not there, He better call Becky with the good hair," which can

---

[15] Kinitra D. Brooks and Kameeiah L. Martin, "Introduction: Beyoncé's Lemonade Lexicon: Black Feminism and Spirituality in Theory and Practice," in *The Lemonade Reader*, ed. Kinitra D. Brooks (New York: Routledge, 2019).

[16] Martínez-Jiménez et al., "Neoliberalism Goes Pop and Purple," 405.

[17] Beyoncé, "Sorry," track 4 on *Lemonade* (Columbia Records, 2016).

[18] Ibid.

be read as a reference to a white woman with whom JAY-Z enjoys himself. The video to the song is set in a Southern mansion and in an old bus that is headed to "Boy Bye." In the video, different black women, among them tennis star Serena Williams,[19] dance and sing "middle fingers up."

While the interest in the state of Beyoncé and JAY-Z's marriage might be understandable from a yellow press perspective, the discourses also reveal very much about "entrenched notions about the dysfunctionality of black marriage"[20] and the (ir-)responsibility of absent, incarcerated, or dead black fathers that can also be addressed in the Cultural Studies classroom.

4:44

On June 30, 2017, JAY-Z released his thirteenth album, entitled *4:44*. The album can at least partly be seen as a response to Beyoncé's as it features some lines from *Lemonade* and also deals openly with the couple's problems. In the title track of the album, JAY-Z apologizes to Beyoncé ("Look, I apologize, often womanize. Took for my child to be born, see through a woman's eyes.") and takes the responsibility "for all the stillborns 'cause I wasn't present."[21] In the opening track, he kills his alter ego Jay Z (without the hyphen), the hard and irresponsible male in favor of somebody "softer," the father of Blue Ivy: "But you gotta do better, boy, you owe it to Blue. You had no father, you had the armor. But you got a daughter, gotta get softer."[22] While these and other tracks present a mixture of personal confessions and reply to *Lemonade*, other songs discuss the history of slavery, Jim Crow, and racism in the context of today's culture. Two of them are especially helpful as starting points for discussions in the Cultural Studies classroom: "The Story of O.J." and "Moonlight."

---

[19] For a discussion of the significance of Serena Williams's dance performance see Olutola, "I Ain't Sorry, 109–112.
[20] Labennett, "'Beyonce and Her Husband,'" 166.
[21] JAY-Z, "4:44," track 5 on *4:44* (Roc Nation, 2017).
[22] JAY-Z, "Kill Jay Z," track 1 on *4:44* (Roc Nation, 2017).

546   In Praise of Short Forms

"The Story of O. J."

"The Story of O.J." opens with a sample from Nina Simone's "Four Women," first released in 1966, which characterizes four African American women who exemplify different aspects of suffering from racism and the repercussions of slavery. While "Aunt Sarah" has black skin and "wooly" hair and is "strong enough to take the pain, inflicted again and again," Saffronia's hair is yellow. Her "father was rich and white" and "he forced my mother late one night." "Sweet Thing," the third woman in the song, is a prostitute whose "hips invite you."[23] The fourth woman introduces herself like this:

> My skin is brown.
> My manner is tough.
> I'll kill the first mother I see.
> My life has been rough.
> I'm awfully bitter these days
> because my parents were slaves.
> What do they call me?
> My name is Peaches.[24]

JAY-Z begins rapping with what reveals itself as the chorus. In a similar fashion to Simone, but explicitly using the n-word, he opens up a tableau of African American types:

> Light nigga, dark nigga, faux nigga, real nigga
> Rich nigga, poor nigga, house nigga, field nigga
> Still nigga, still nigga.[25]

The terms "house nigga" and "field nigga" refer to Malcolm X's speech "Message to the Grass Roots," in which he differentiated between "house" and "field negroes" on the plantations during slavery.[26] While the "house negro" defended and protected the master, with whom he lived in the same house, the "field negro" lived in a hut or shack and

---

[23] Nina Simone, "Four Women," in *Wild is the Wind*, Philips, 1965.
[24] Ibid.
[25] JAY-Z, "The Story of O.J.," track 2 on *4:44* (Roc Nation, 2017).
[26] Malcolm X, "Message to Grassroots," speech originally delivered on November 10, 1963.

hated his master. Malcom X called himself a rebellious "field negro" in contrast to black civil rights leaders such as Martin Luther King who Malcolm X likened to "house negroes" or "modern Uncle Toms, twentieth-century Uncle Toms"[27] in this speech. JAY-Z puts himself in the tradition of the "field negro" and raps in the first verse that he "play[s] the corners where the hustlers be."[28]

While the use of the n-word and explicit lyrics may already be regarded as offensive,[29] the visuals add another layer. The video, directed by Mark Romanek and JAY-Z, is reminiscent of the racist cartoons of the 1930s and 1940s which portrayed African Americans as grotesque caricatures, lazy good-for-nothings with extremely large lips and big white eyes who eat watermelons all day or steal chickens.

Through the sample of "Four Women," the reference to Malcolm X, the self-stylizing as Jaybo[30] in the video, and the intertextual activation of the racist tropes of 1930s and 1940s cartoons, which themselves have a much longer history in the minstrel show and blackface, JAY-Z lists and describes a wide range of African Americans stereotypes and self-

---

[27] Ibid.

[28] JAY-Z, "The Story of O.J."

[29] In the last two decades of the twentieth century, rap musicians appropriated the "n word" (with an "a" as the last letter) as a slang term with a positive meaning. Tupac Shakur pointed out the differences in an interview with MTV: "Niggers was the ones on the rope hanging out on the field. Niggas is the ones with gold ropes hanging out at clubs." Qtd. in Mark Abley, *The Prodigal Tongue: Dispatches from the Future of English* (Boston: Mariner Books, 2008), 154.

[30] Jaybo is a reference to the racist "Sambo" stereotype, the happy, docile, lazy black male who was not capable of living on his own. The stereotype was used as a defense for slavery since Sambos were supposedly content with their position and unable to be independent of their masters. After the Civil War, the Sambo image was slowly replaced by the "Coon." The Coon also was a simple and unintelligent black male, but he was not content with his position. He was aggressive toward whites, or, as David Pilgrim puts it: "[B]y the 1900s, Sambo was identified with older, docile blacks who accepted Jim Crow laws and etiquette; whereas Coons were increasingly identified with young, urban blacks who disrespected whites. Stated differently, the Coon was a Sambo gone bad." David Pilgrim, "The Coon Caricature," *Jim Crow Museum*, October 2000, ferris.edu/HTMLS/news/jimcrow/coon/homepage.htm/.

stereotypes. This is contrasted by the plain and factual expression "still nigga" at the end of the chorus, highlighting that, in the end, race is the prime determining factor, the leading discourse. It is important that, in this reading, race tops class and that, according to JAY-Z, African Americans are "still niggaz" at the end of the day.

It is in this regard that the title of the song, "The Story of O.J.," comes into play. In the video, a stylized O. J. Simpson can be seen, who claims: "I'm not black, I'm O.J." JAY-Z's laconic reaction is a very dry "okay," which expresses his doubts in O.J.'s assertion.

O. J. Simpson is a former American football star, sports commentator, and advertising model. Although he had already attained stardom as an active professional athlete, his appearance in a commercial for Hertz car rental consolidated his celebrity status. Moreover, as Anthony Crupi notes, the ad for Hertz "marked a watershed moment for advertising, race and culture in the United States."[31] Sociologist Harry Edwards adds: "O.J. was the first to demonstrate that white folks would buy stuff based on a black endorsement" and "[t]he way they did that was to remove black people totally from any scene that O.J. was in. [...] They bought the notion that you could erase the black character, the culture. This is what made O.J. marketable."[32] O. J. Simpson himself bought this notion when he said to friends: "I'm not black. I'm O.J."[33]

However, the situation changed dramatically when his ex-wife Nicole Brown Simpson and her friend Ronald Goldman were murdered with a knife in June 1994 and O. J. Simpson was accused of being the murderer. Simpson had a record for beating and assaulting his wife. In 1989, he was sentenced to two years on probation and 120 hours of

---

[31] Anthony Crupi, "The Run of his Life: How Hertz and O.J. Simpson Changed Advertising," *AdAge*, June 14, 2016, adage.com/article/media/run/304487.

[32] Harry Edwards in *O.J. Made in America*, ESPN Films, 2016.

[33] This is also the title of the first episode of the above-mentioned ESPN documentary series *O.J.: Made in America*. In the episode, sociologist Harry Edwards recalls how he invited Simpson to take part in a group of black athletes fighting for civil rights. O.J. Simpson replied with the now iconic line: "I'm not black. I'm O.J."

community service for spousal abuse.[34] The couple had divorced in 1992.

The criminal case, which was dubbed the "trial of the century" by journalists, was marked by the strategy of the defense to "re-racialize" Simpson: "reinscribing a blackness onto a body that had largely been stripped of the stereotypical features once commonly associated with African American males."[35] Through this re-invention of O.J. as black, the defense[36] could make the case that their client had been framed and that evidence was planted by racist cops, and that the LAPD was plagued by institutionalized racism. African Americans could definitely relate to this narrative, especially after the beating of Rodney King by LAPD officers and the subsequent trial against the cops involved, which ended with their acquittal and led to the riots of 1992.

When O. J. Simpson was found not guilty by the jury, this verdict in the criminal case was seen as an absolute exception, almost 'magic.' Ta-Nehisi Coates writes in this regard,

> Simpson's great accomplishment was to be indicted for a crime and then receive the kind of treatment typically reserved for rich white guys. His acquittal, achieved as incarceration rates skyrocketed, represented something grand and inconceivable for blacks. He had defied the police who brutalized black people, the prosecutors who tried them, the prisons that held them. He had defied them all, and in the process, much like Houdini, he escaped.[37]

[34] Sara Rimer, "The Simpson Case: The Marriage; Handling of 1989 Wife-Beating Case Was a 'Terrible Joke,' Prosecutor Says," *The New York Times*, June 18, 1994, 10.

[35] Priscilla Walton and Jonathan Chau, "'I'm Not Black, I'm O.J.': Constructions, Productions, and Refractions of Blackness," *Canadian Review of American Studies* 48 (2018): 74.

[36] It was not only his defense team that re-racialized Simpson. Some mainstream media publications artificially darkened his face to underline his blackness, too. One case in point is the cover of *TIME* magazine from June 27, 1994. The cover is available on the *TIME* magazine website: content.time.com/time/covers/ 0,16641,19940627,00.html.

[37] Ta-Nehisi Coates, "What O. J. Simpson Means to Me," *The Atlantic*, September 12, 2016, theatlantic.com/magazine/archive/2016/10/what-o-j-simpson-means-to-me/497570/.

550 In Praise of Short Forms

However, Simpson was found guilty for the wrongful deaths of Brown and Goldman in a civil suit in 1997, which awarded the families of the victims millions in damages.[38] In 2008, he was sentenced to at least nine years in prison (or a maximum of thirty-three years) for an armed robbery in Las Vegas, which took place in September 2007.[39] Simpson was released from jail in October 2017.[40]

O. J. Simpson's case highlights the complexity and contradictions of race, class, and gender in American culture. He had oscillated between being black and being O.J. for a period of thirty-five years. While being black is race-related, being O. J. is primarily class-related. Simpson is O. J. when he's the celebrity, the star, and everything is fine. O.J. can even be an abusive and violent (ex-)husband. Simpson is black when he is wanted by the police. The fact that Simpson was an abusive and violent male almost gets lost in the interplay of class and race in the coverage of the case, and surely in JAY-Z's video.

The life and narrative of O. J. Simpson both contradicts and (eventually) reinforces JAY-Z's statement in the chorus of "The Story of O.J." that whatever happens, African Americans are "still niggaz" after all. In the acquittal of O.J. in the criminal case, class tops race; but in the aftermath, race tops class. The last statement is in accordance with the song and video.

In the remainder of the song, JAY-Z offers a solution to the gridlock experienced by the African American community: "financial freedom, my only hope." He advises drug dealers "not to die over the neighborhood that your mama is renting. Take your drug money and buy the neighborhood. That's how you rinse it." In the interlude, JAY-Z raps:

> You wanna know what's more important than throwin' away money at a strip club? Credit.

---

[38] B. Drummond Ayres Jr., "Civil Jury Finds Simpson Liable in Pair of Killings," *The New York Times*, February 5, 1997, 1.

[39] Delano Greenidge-Copprue, "Simpson, O. J. (1947–)," in *Encyclopedia of African American Popular Culture*, ed. Jessie Carney Smith (Santa Barbara: Greenwood, 2011), 1263.

[40] Paul Vercammen and Faith Karimi, "O.J. Simpson out of Nevada Prison after 9 Years, Plans to Stay in Vegas," *CNN*, October 2, 2017, edition.cnn.com/2017/10/01/us/oj-simpson-released-from-prison/index.html.

You ever wonder why Jewish people own all the property in America? This how they did it.[41]

These lines repeat an old anti-Semitic cliché and led the Anti-Defamation League to express their concern, but the ADL also said they know that JAY-Z is not an anti-Semite.[42] JAY-Z defended himself in an interview with the Rap Radar Podcast, emphasizing that he exaggerated every black image in the lyrics ("the guy eating watermelon") and also did so with the image of the Jewish property owner.[43] In this reading, the song addresses the black community with a recommendation to follow the example of the Jewish community and buy property instead of throwing away money in the strip club. In a rather twisted way and with the help of an anti-Semitic stereotype, the Jewish community is portrayed as a role model for the black community.

I bought some artwork for one million
Two years later, that shit worth two million
Few years later, that shit worth eight million
I can't wait to give this shit to my children
Y'all think it's bougie, I'm like, it's fine
But I'm tryin' to give you a million dollars' worth of game for $9.99.[44]

These lines feature JAY-Z the self-made man who gives advice ("a million dollars' worth of game") on how to become a successful businessman. The advice comes in the form of his back catalogue of records, which are available through his online streaming platform Tidal. The monthly fee for Tidal is $9.99.

As in the *Lemonade* videos, "The Story of O.J." paints a detailed and comprehensive picture of systemic racism in the United States, but when it comes to class, it neglects the systemic level and repeats the myth of individual self-empowerment. Furthermore, the song and video ignore the manifold connections and parallel histories of systemic classism and

---

[41] JAY-Z, "The Story of O.J."
[42] Jon Blistein, "ADL Questions Jay-Z Over Jewish Lyric in 'The Story of O.J.,'" *Rolling Stone*, July 6, 2017, rollingstone.com/music/music-news/adl-questions-jay-z-over-jewish-lyric-in-the-story-of-o-j-204517/.
[43] "Interview with Jay-Z," *Rap Radar Podcast*, September 7, 2017.
[44] JAY-Z, "The Story of O.J."

552   In Praise of Short Forms

systemic racism, and as such also fall short of debunking some classist justifications of racist stereotypes (e.g. the lazy Sambo).

"Moonlight"

The video of JAY-Z's "Moonlight" starts with a frame-by-frame remake of the beginning of the *Friends* episode "The One Where No One's Ready," but with an all-black cast. In a break on the set, Ross (here played by Jerrod Carmichael) welcomes comedian Hannibal Buress and asks him what he thinks about this black version of *Friends*:

> Buress: "It was terrible, man. It was wack as shit. It was just *Seinfeld* episodes with black people. Who asked for that?"
> Carmichael: "When they asked me to do it, I was like, 'Okay, this is something that's subversive, something that'll turn culture on its head.'"
> Buress: "You did a good job of subverting good comedy. You gonna do black *Full House* next? *Family Ties*?"
> Carmichael: "Ahm, ahm. Huh. What are you doing?"
> Buress: "I just booked this role on *Pirates of the Caribbean: Cruise Line*. I play a parrot with a bad attitude, but he has a heart of gold. It's terrible, but it's way better than this shit."

This dialogue points to the limited availability of good and commercially successful roles for African American actors in the entertainment industry. For Buress, even the absurd role of a parrot in the imaginary sequel *Pirates of the Caribbean: Cruise Line* is better than this black version of *Friends*. Moreover, a remake of *Friends* with an all-black cast can be seen as a sarcastic nod towards the production history of *Friends*, which has been seen as an (unacknowledged) white remake of *Living Single*, a sitcom about the lives of six black friends living in the same Brooklyn brownstone. The all-black remake is an act of subversion, but as Buress's reaction shows, there is a fine line between subversion and kitsch.

    The interlude with Carmichael and Buress is followed by another scene from black *Friends* before Carmichael is led off the sound stage by Issa Rae. The picture gets blurry and the music of "Moonlight" starts with the chorus:

GUNTER SÜß

We stuck in *La La Land*
Even when we win, we gon' lose
We got the same fuckin' flows
I don't know who is who
We got the same fuckin' watch
She don't got time to choose
We stuck in La La Land
We got the same fuckin' moves[45]

The chorus presents two layers of meaning. On the one hand, the line "we stuck in *La La Land*" refers to the Academy Awards ceremony in 2017, when Faye Dunaway mistakenly announced that the Oscar for "Best Picture" had gone to *La La Land*, a predominantly white musical, instead of *Moonlight*, an LGBT[46] drama with an all-black cast. After a few minutes, the mistake was corrected. JAY-Z uses this situation to claim that even when the black community wins, it loses. On the other hand, "we stuck in La La Land" can also refer to the poor and uninspired state of rap music ("We got the same fuckin' flows, I don't know who is who").

This continues in the first verse when JAY-Z talks about the outward appearance of rappers posing with (imitations of) assault rifles ("Fake Dracos all in the videos. We show 'em, we shoot 'em in my city though"[47]) In the second verse, the topic shifts to the relationship between musicians and their record companies or publishers:

Y'all niggas still signin' deals? Still?
After all they done stole, for real?
After what they done to our Lauryn Hill?[48]

This refers to Lauryn Hill's disputes and fights with Columbia Records, as well as with some of the musicians who allegedly wrote parts of her 1998 album *The Miseducation of Lauryn Hill*. More generally, these lines can refer to the unfair and sometimes fraudulent treatment of

---

[45]   JAY-Z, "Moonlight," track 8 on *4:44* (Roc Nation, 2017).
[46]   The (traditional) hip hop scene is known for its homophobia and anti-gay lyrics. JAY-Z sets an example here and in the song "Smile," track 3 on *4:44*, in which his mother Gloria Carter came out publicly.
[47]   JAY-Z, "Moonlight."
[48]   Ibid.

554 In Praise of Short Forms

African American artists by their record labels, the most well-known example probably being Prince and Warner Brothers. In 2015, JAY-Z's streaming service Tidal acquired the streaming rights to Prince's back catalogue. It is ironic that after Prince's death, his estate sued JAY-Z's management firm Roc Nation over these streaming rights.[49]

In the classroom, the analysis of "Moonlight" could lead to a discussion of the media and cultural history of black artists in the United States. It is a history of *Love and Theft*,[50] as Eric Lott puts it in his eponymously titled book about blackface minstrelsy: a history of ridicule and admiration, of appropriation and libidinous investment, of racism and capitalism. It ranges from "Jump Jim Crow" and minstrelsy to Bert Williams, to Billie Holliday and Josephine Baker, to John Lee Hooker and all the white blues rock bands, to Elvis Presley and his impersonation of African American artists, to Elvis impersonators themselves,[51] to Run-DMC and Aerosmith, to Public Enemy and Eminem.

"Apeshit," Notions of Beauty, and the Apotheosis of the Neoliberal Individual

The last video I want to discuss is "Apeshit" by The Carters, which is the name of JAY-Z and Beyoncé's musical duo. "Apeshit" was released on the album *Everything Is Love* in June 2018. For the video shoot, the couple rented the Louvre.

On a formal level, the video works as a juxtaposition of stunning images of The Carters and their crew dancing in the Louvre in front of

[49] "Prince's Estate Sues Jay Z's Tidal over Streaming Rights to the Pop Star's Music," *The Guardian*, November 17, 2016, theguardian.com/music/2016/nov/16/prince-estate-sues-tidal-music-access-jay-z. In his song "Caught their Eyes," which is also on the 4:44 album, Jay-Z raps directed at the lawyer of Prince's estate: "I sat down with Prince, eye to eye. He told me his wishes before he died. Now, Londell McMillan, he must be color blind. They only see green from them purple eyes."

[50] Eric Lott, *Love and Theft: Blackface Minstrelsy and the American Working Class* (New York: Oxford University Press, 1993).

[51] Eric Lott, *Black Mirror: The Cultural Contradictions of American Racism* (Cambridge: Harvard University Press, 2017).

well-known paintings and sculptures with gritty images of black youth that could be found in the *banlieues* of the bigger French cities or in the housing projects of American cities. It consists, for instance, of visual parallels between contemporary black lovers and lovers in the painting *Francesca da Rimini and Paolo Malatesta Appraised by Dante and Virgil* by the Dutch-French painter Ary Scheffer. In one scene, Jay-Z raps:

> I said no to the Super Bowl.
> You need me, I don't need you.
> Every night we in the endzone,
> tell the NFL we in stadiums, too.[52]

According to these lines, JAY-Z turned down an offer to perform in the Super Bowl halftime show, which is considered the most prestigious event for performers. When JAY-Z raps this, the video shows young black people "taking a knee," a symbolic gesture of protest against police brutality first introduced by NFL player Colin Kaepernick. The parallelism of lyrics and images suggest that JAY-Z turned down the NFL's offer for political reasons. However, in August 2019, a partnership between JAY-Z's Roc Nation and the NFL was announced. Roc Nation signed on as an advisor for the NFL and their Inspire Change initiative.[53]

If we look at the visual level of the video, it discusses notions of art and beauty. What is considered art and what isn't? It discusses the racism and colonialism inscribed and perpetuated in museums like the Louvre, but it also critiques notions of beauty found in everyday life. Through their dance performance and their rapping, The Carters overwrite white, colonial art with black urban art. Like the different layers in a palimpsest, they add black bodies to the white ones already found in The Louvre.[54]

---

[52] The Carters, "Apeshit," track 2 on *Everything Is Love* (Roc Nation, 2018).

[53] Evan Simko-Bednarski et al., "Jay-Z on Social Justice Partnership with NFL," *CNN*, August 14, 2019, edition.cnn.com/2019/08/13/sport/jay-z-roc-nation-nfl-partnership/index.html.

[54] The most well-known black person represented in the Louvre is *Portrait of a Negress* (1800) by Marie-Guilhelmine Benoist.

556 In Praise of Short Forms

Furthermore, the video addresses notions of beauty. What has been regarded as beautiful, especially in connection with race and ethnicity? How have notions of beauty changed over time and across cultures? In the Cultural Studies classroom, "Apeshit" can be brought into dialogue with other texts, for instance with Malcolm X's speech "Who taught you to hate yourself." In this speech, he discusses how African Americans have internalized white ideals of beauty such as light skin tones, straightened hair, small lips and nostrils. Another possible text is Kiri Davis's documentary *A Girl Like Me*, which recreated the famous doll experiments that African American psychologists Kenneth and Mamie Clark conducted in the 1930s and 1940s.

Performances by Beyoncé can also be seen as examples of changing beauty ideals. In 2001, Destiny's Child released the song "Bootylicious." The word is a combination of "booty" (bottom) and "delicious," praising women with larger hips and thighs, such as Beyoncé, Jennifer Lopez, and Kim Kardashian. "Bootylicious" re-evaluates and celebrates bodily features that were not considered beautiful both traditionally and in white mainstream society, and that are frequently associated with African American or Latina women.

On the level of the lyrics, Adam Rothbart sees "the most boring aspect of the album [...]: the couple's obsession with their wealth."[55] This is also true for "Apeshit":

> Bought him a jet
> (Yeah, yeah, yeah, yeah, yeah, yeah)
> Shut down Colette
> (Yeah, yeah, yeah, yeah, yeah, yeah)
> Phillippe Patek [...]
>
> Stack my money fast and go (Fast, fast, go)
> Fast like my Lambo (Skrrt, skrrt, skrrt)
> Jumpin' off the stage, ho (Jumpin', jumpin', hey, hey)
> Crowd better save her (Crowd goin' ape, hey)
> I can't believe we made it (This is what we made, made)
> This is what we're thankful for (This is what we thank, thank)

---

[55] Adam Rothbart, "Review of The Carters Everything Is Love," *Tiny Mix Tapes*, February 7, 2020,
tinymixtapes.com/music-review/carters-everything-love.

I can't believe we made it (This a different angle)
Have you ever seen the crowd goin' apeshit? (Offset!)[56]

On the one hand, the lyrics consist of endless lists of luxury goods, such as the jet plane that Beyoncé bought JAY-Z for Father's Day, Givenchy dresses, Patek watches, and Lamborghinis. On the other hand, The Carters stress the unlikeliness of their success and the importance of them standing together as a family. Antonia Baum writes that The Carters try to establish a new narrative for black Americans: wealth should be accumulated, but this can only be achieved through self-respect, hard work, and cohesion within the family – and the prerequisite for this is respect for black women.[57]

While the Carters may represent the old myth of rags-to-riches, they do so in a slightly updated, neoliberal version of the American dream. While the songs on *4:44* and *Lemonade* offer an elaborate visual and lyrical critique of systemic racism in the United States, the video for "Apeshit" remains one of the few remarkable, culturally complex, and visually outstanding moments of *Everything Is Love*.

Considered in their entirety, the videos discussed here are, nonetheless, invaluable materials in the Cultural Studies classroom and can help to build inroads into the discussion of such diverse topics as African American (self-)stereotypes, the history of the entertainment industry, the history of notions like beauty and art, media, and television history or the history of the Civil Rights movement. Furthermore, these videos facilitate understanding of how myths like the American Dream and the free, unregulated, creative individual have been updated under the conditions of neoliberalism and postfeminism.

[56] The Carters, "Apeshit."
[57] Antonia Baum, "Beyoncé und Jay-Z: Eine ganz unwahrscheinliche Geschichte," *Zeit Online*, June 20, 2018, zeit.de/2018/26/beyonce-jay-z-everything-is-love-ehepaar.

Works Cited

Abley, Mark. *The Prodigal Tongue: Dispatches from the Future of English*. Boston: Mariner Books, 2008.

Baum, Antonia. "Beyoncé und Jay-Z: Eine ganz unwahrscheinliche Geschichte." *Zeit Online*, June 20, 2018. zeit.de/2018/26/beyonce-jay-z-everything-is-love-ehepaar.

Beyoncé. "Formation." Track 12 on *Lemonade*. Columbia Records, 2016.

---. "Sorry." Track 4 on *Lemonade*. Columbia Records, 2016.

Blistein, Jon. "ADL Questions Jay-Z Over Jewish Lyric in 'The Story of O.J.'" *Rolling Stone*, July 6, 2017. rollingstone.com/music/music-news/adl-questions-jay-z-over-jewish-lyric-in-the-story-of-o-j-204517/.

Brooks, Kinitra D. and Kameeiah L. Martin. "Introduction: Beyoncé's Lemonade Lexicon: Black Feminism and Spirituality in Theory and Practice." *The Lemonade Reader*, edited by Kinitra D. Brooks, 1–4. New York: Routledge, 2019.

Coates, Ta-Nehisi. "What O. J. Simpson Means to Me." *The Atlantic*, September 12, 2016. theatlantic.com/magazine/archive/2016/10/what-o-j-simpson-means-to-me/497570/.

Coker, Hillary Crosley. "What bell hooks Really Means When She Calls Beyoncé a 'Terrorist.'" *Jezebel*, May 9, 2014. jezebel.com/what-bell-hooks-really-means-when-she-calls-beyonce-a-t-1573991834.

Crupi, Anthony. "The Run of his Life: How Hertz and O.J. Simpson Changed Advertising." *AdAge*, June 14, 2016. adage.com/article/media/run/304487.

Drummond Ayres Jr., B. "Civil Jury Finds Simpson Liable in Pair of Killings." *The New York Times*, 5 Feb. 1997.

Fairclough, Kirsty and Daniel Cookney. "The Music Video Is a Zombie." *The Conversation,* October 17, 2017. theconversation.com/the-music-video-is-a-zombie-it-may-look-dead-but-its-just-been-re-animated-85493.

Greenidge-Copprue, Delano. "Simpson, O. J. (1947–)." In *Encyclopedia of African American Popular Culture*, edited by Jessie Carney Smith, 1281–1283. Santa Barbara: Greenwood, 2011.

hooks, bell. "Moving Beyond Pain." *bellhooksinstitute*, May 9, 2016.

"Interview with Jay-Z." *Rap Radar Podcast*, September 7, 2017.

JAY-Z. "4:44." Track 5 on *4:44*. Roc Nation, 2017.

---. "Caught their Eyes." Track 4 on *4:44*. Roc Nation, 2017.

---. *Decoded*. New York: Random House, 2010.

---. "Kill Jay Z." Track 1 on *4:44*. Roc Nation, 2017.

---. "Moonlight." Track 8 on *4:44*. Roc Nation, 2017.

---. "Smile." Track 3 on *4:44*. Roc Nation, 2017.

---. "The Story of O.J." Track 2 on *4:44*. Roc Nation, 2017.

Labennett, Oneka. "'Beyoncé and Her Husband': Representing Infidelity and Kinship in a Black Marriage." *differences: A Journal of Feminist Cultural Studies* 29, no. 2 (2018): 154–188.

Lott, Eric. *Black Mirror: The Cultural Contradictions of American Racism*. Cambridge: Harvard University Press, 2017.

---. *Love and Theft: Blackface Minstrelsy and the American Working Class*. New York: Oxford University Press, 1993.

Malcolm X. "Message to Grassroots." Northern Negro Grass Roots Leadership Conference, 10 Nov. 1963. King Solomon Baptist Church, Detroit, MI, teachingamericanhistory.org/library/document/message-to-grassroots/.

Martínez-Jiménez, Laura, et al. "Neoliberalism Goes Pop and Purple: Postfeminist Empowerment from Beyoncé to Mad Max." *Journal of Popular Culture* 51, no. 2 (2018): 399–420.

O.J. Made in America. ESPN Films, 2016.

O'Malley Greenburg, Zack. "Artist, Icon, Billionaire: How Jay-Z Created His $1 Billion Fortune." *Forbes*, June 3, 2019. forbes.com/sites/zackomalleygreenburg/2019/06/03/jay-z-billionaire-worth/.

Olutola, Sarah. "I Ain't Sorry: Beyoncé, Serena, and Hegemonic Hierarchies in Lemonade." *Popular Music and Society* 42, no. 1 (2019): 99–117.

Pilgrim, David. "The Coon Caricature." *Jim Crow Museum*, October 2000. ferris.edu/HTMLS/news/jimcrow/coon/homepage.htm/.

"Prince's Estate Sues Jay Z's Tidal over Streaming Rights to the Pop Star's Music." *The Guardian*, November 17, 2016. theguardian.com/music/2016/nov/16/prince-estate-sues-tidal-music-access-jay-z.

Rimer, Sara. "The Simpson Case: The Marriage; Handling of 1989 Wife-Beating Case Was a 'Terrible Joke,' Prosecutor Says." *The New York Times*, June 18, 1994.

Rothbart, Adam. "Review of The Carters Everything Is Love." *Tiny Mix Tapes*, June 19, 2018. tinymixtapes.com/music-review/carters-everything-love.

Simko-Bednarski, Evan, et al. "Jay-Z on Social Justice Partnership with NFL." *CNN*, August 14, 2019. edition.cnn.com/2019/08/13/sport/jay-z-roc-nation-nfl-partnership/index.html.

Simone, Nina. "Four Women." *Wild is the Wind*. Philips, 1965.

The Carters. "Apeshit." Track 2 on *Everything Is Love*. Roc Nation, 2018.

Vercammen, Paul and Faith Karimi. "O.J. Simpson out of Nevada Prison after 9 Years, Plans to Stay in Vegas." *CNN*, October 2, 2017. edition.cnn.com/2017/10/01/us/oj-simpson-released-from-prison/index.html.

Voigts, Eckart. "Pop Music, Video and Gender." In *Cultural Studies in the EFL Classroom*, edited by Werner Delanoy and Laurenz Volkmann, 381–391. Heidelberg: Universitätsverlag Winter, 2006.

Walton, Priscilla, and Jonathan Chau. "'I'm Not Black, I'm O.J.': Constructions, Productions, and Refractions of Blackness." *Canadian Review of American Studies* 48, no. 1 (2018): 61–76.

List of Contributors

MAXI ALBRECHT is a postdoctoral researcher in the DFG project "Serial Circulation: The German-American Mystery Novel and the Beginnings of Transatlantic Modernity (1850–1855)" at Siegen University.

LAURA BIEGER is chair of American Studies at Ruhr University Bochum.

ASTRID BÖGER is professor of American Studies at the University of Hamburg.

JULIANE BOROSCH is a member of the research group "Scripts for Postindustrial Urban Futures: American Models, Transatlantic Interventions" (funded by the Volkswagen Foundation) of the University Alliance Ruhr. She is a doctoral candidate in American Studies at the University of Duisburg-Essen.

DUSTIN BREITENWISCHER is associate professor of American Studies at the University of Hamburg.

NAGHMEH ESMAEILPOUR is an independent scholar who received her doctoral degree in General and Comparative Literature from Humboldt-Universität zu Berlin.

ABIGAIL FAGAN is a postdoctoral researcher in American Studies at the Leibniz University of Hannover.

RUTH GEHRMANN is a postdoctoral researcher at the Collaborative Research Center on Human Differentiation at Johannes Gutenberg University Mainz.

BRIGITTE GEORGI-FINDLAY is chair of North American Studies at the TU Dresden.

ALEXANDRA HARTMANN is a postdoctoral researcher in American Studies at Paderborn University.

ZOHRA HASSAN-PIEPER is a doctoral candidate in North American Literary and Cultural Studies at the University of Duisburg-Essen.

MARIUS HENDERSON is a postdoctoral researcher in American Studies at Friedrich-Alexander-Universität Erlangen-Nürnberg (FAU).

LINDA M. HESS is Akademische Rätin in American Studies at the University of Augsburg.

CARSTEN JUNKER is chair of American Studies with a focus on Diversity Studies at the TU Dresden.

KATJA KANZLER is the chair of American Literature at Leipzig University.

MARLON LIEBER is assistant professor of North American Literature at the Goethe University Frankfurt.

FRANK MEHRING is professor of American Studies at Radboud University Nijmegen.

MICHAEL LOUIS MOSER is a joint doctoral candidate in North American Studies at the TU Dresden and Cultural Studies at the KU Leuven.

MARIAN OFORI-AMOAFO is a doctoral candidate in American Studies at the University of Bayreuth. She is a research associate at the University of Passau's BMBF-funded project "'Welfare Queens' and 'Losers': a Critical Race and Intersectional Perspective on the U.S. American Welfare State."

CLARA PETINO works in academic publishing at the FOM University of Applied Sciences. She also teaches American literature at the VHS Ratingen and the VHS Neuss.

JOHANNES C.P. SCHMID is a postdoctoral researcher in American Studies at Europa-Universität Flensburg.

FLORIAN SEDLMEIER is guest professor of American Studies at Ruhr University Bochum.

HEIKE STEINHOFF is junior professor of American Studies at Ruhr University Bochum.

JOHN STREET is professor of Politics in the School of Politics, Philosophy, Language and Communication Studies, University of East Anglia.

MARITA STURKEN is professor of Media, Culture and Communication at New York University.

GUNTER SÜß is assistant professor at the IKKS, Mittweida University of Applied Sciences.

JENNIFER VOLKMER is a doctoral candidate in American Studies at LMU Munich.

LISANNA WIELE is an independent scholar.

HARALD ZAPF is Akademischer Oberrat in American Studies at Friedrich-Alexander-Universität Erlangen-Nürnberg (FAU).